STOCKHOLM TEXT

ALEXANDER BARD / JAN SÖDERQVIST
THE FUTURICA TRILOGY

!
For more books of this kind,
have a look at stockholmtext.com

Stockholm Text
www.stockholmtext.com
stockholm@stockholmtext.com

© 2012 Alexander Bard and Jan Söderqvist
Translation: Neil Smith
Editing: Starfalk Produktion
Photo: Mikolai Berg
Art Direction: Allen Grubesic
Grooming: Therese Svenbo
Cover: Dorian Mabb
ISBN e-book: 978-91-87173-03-5
ISBN print book: 978-91-87173-24-0

Content

INTRODUCTION 7

THE NETOCRATS—THE FUTURICA TRILOGY PART 1

1. TECHNOLOGY AS THE DRIVING FORCE OF HISTORY 13
2. FEUDALISM, CAPITALISM AND INFORMATIONALISM 30
3. PLURARCHAL SOCIETY – THE DEATH OF ETATISM AND THE CRISIS OF DEMOCRACY 50
4. INFORMATION, PROPAGANDA AND ENTERTAINMENT 67
5. CURATORS, NEXIALISTS AND ETERNALISTS – THE NETOCRATS AND THEIR WORLDVIEW 81
6. GLOBALISATION, THE DEATH OF MASS MEDIA AND THE GROWTH OF THE CONSUMTARIAT 101
7. THE NEW BIOLOGY AND NETOCRATIC ETHICS 120
8. THE CONVULSIONS OF COLLECTIVITY, THE DEATH OF MAN AND THE VIRTUAL SUBJECT 139
9. NETWORK PYRAMIDS – ATTENTIONALISTIC POWER HIERARCHIES 157
10. SEX AND TRIBALISM, VIRTUAL EDUCATION AND THE INEQUALITY OF THE BRAIN 173
11. BEHIND THE FIREWALLS – NETOCRATIC CIVIL WAR AND VIRTUAL REVOLUTIONARIES 194

THE GLOBAL EMPIRE—THE FUTURICA TRILOGY PART 2

1. THE ROAD TO THE WORLD STATE AND HISTORY AS A PROCESS OF DOMESTICATION 207
2. EMPIRE, PLURARCHY AND THE VIRTUAL NOMADIC TRIBE 232

3. THE GENEALOGY OF NETOCRATIC ETHICS 257
4. THE RENAISSANCE OF IDEOLOGY 279
5. THE DIALECTIC BETWEEN ETERNALISM AND MOBILISM 300
6. THE PARADOX OF METAPHYSICS AND THE METAPHYSICS OF PARADOXISM .. 320
7. THE METEOROLOGY OF KNOWLEDGE AND THE PARADOXICAL SUBJECT 334
8. ETERNALISM'S RADICAL PRAGMATISM 357
9. NEO-DARWINISM AND HORIZONTAL BIOLOGY 375
10. THE WAR BETWEEN THE REPLICATORS – THE MEMES' VICTORY OVER THE GENES 392
11. PERFORATED BODIES AND CHEMICAL LIBERATION 407
12. SOCIOANALYTICAL ETHICS AND THE COLLAPSE OF THE CAPITALIST LEFT .. 426
13. THE ECSTASY OF THE EVENT AND THE FADING GAZE OF NATURE 447
14. NAZISM AS A SOCIOTECHNOLOGICAL PHENOMENON 469
15. SEX, POWER AND NETWORK DYNAMICS – THE NECESSARY METAMORPHOSIS OF FEMINISM 483
16. THE INFRASTRUCTURE OF THE EMPIRE AND ETERNALISM'S MORAL IMPERATIVE 501

THE BODY MACHINES—THE FUTURICA TRILOGY PART 3

1. THE RISE AND FALL OF THE SOUL 515
2. A BRIEF HISTORY OF THE BRAIN 534
3. THE PROBLEM WITH SUBJECTIVITY 555
4. THE MYTH OF THE EGO 573
5. THE MYTH OF FREE WILL 588
6. THE MECHANISMS OF THOUGHT 605
7. A SHORT HISTORY OF LANGUAGE 622
8. THE RISE AND FALL OF MORALITY 642
9. THE CURSE OF CULTURAL RELATIVISM 659
10. THE ETHICS OF INTERACTIVITY 677
11. THE THEORY OF SCHIZOANALYSIS 697
12. THE PRACTICE OF SCHIZOANALYSIS 713
+1. (A SORT OF AFTERWORD) 729
FUTURICA GLOSSARY 733

INTRODUCTION

THIS IS QUITE AN OCCASION for us, actually: the international publication of the Stockholm Text digital edition of The Futurica Trilogy. And for many reasons.

Early on, when we were busy with the very first draft of the synopsis for The Netocrats (originally published in Swedish in 2000), we were convinced about three things. First of all, just one book would not be enough, it would eventually have to be a trilogy, and the whole pattern would emerge only upon reading the entire work. This explains why it is so satisfying finally to see the three books – The Netocrats, The Global Empire, and The Body Machines – published in Neil Smith's excellent translations as a unity, one big text in three separate but closely related movements.

Second, the project needed a whole new literary category. What was needed to tackle the issue at hand was a combination of philosophy (the creation of brand new concepts, precisely what the art of philosophy does), sociology (the right questions asked as much as the right answers found) and futurology (the establishment of the level of relevance to human activity of all emerging individual technologies). Which is precisely what futurica is: a brand new literary genre to study and describe forthcoming dramatic changes of the human condition with the support of both philosophical creativity and empirical vigor.

Finally, it was obvious to us even at the very start of this project that we were authors of text, not of books in the old sense. We have nothing against old-school paper books as such, it is just that digital distribution of texts makes brilliant sense in the age of Informationalism, the world that we are writing about. So finally: here they are, all three of them, packaged as a trilogy, as they were always meant to be, and in their proper, digital element.

A lot of time has passed since the conception and writing of this trilogy, and it is perfectly reasonable to ask if these texts are still relevant — if they ever were, that is. Well, let us just say this: When people in Russia started gathering in large number to protest against the blatant rigging of the parliamentary elections a few months ago, an event that surprised a whole world, Russian friends and readers got in touch with us, saying that this was, without question, "A Netocracy Moment". And now that it certainly looks like political reforms are on the cards, this is absolutely necessary if the governing party wants to retain at least a shred of legitimacy.

The same goes for the events called the Arab Spring in Western media. Social Media will quickly change politics beyond recognition and undermine the old elites. We have been saying this for more than a decade now, and we have explained why in minute detail. Forming groups of people with common interests and coordinating action is not only possible, it comes completely natural for people young enough to have been growing up with the Internet as part of their social environment. They will demand accountability from those in power. If they don't get it, they will take their anger to the streets. These days, if you lie to people, it will be exposed on a global scale within minutes. If you let your army open fire on unarmed demonstrators, everyone will know. All it takes is one person with a smart phone, and the avalanche starts.

And we told you so. Before the dot.com crash we said that people investing heavily in IT didn't have a clue about the dynamics of the Internet and didn't know what they were paying millions of dollars for. Well before 9/11 we warned about the new terrorist networks using the latest digital tools. The good guys aren't the only ones using the Net, and the Net certainly doesn't mean the solution to all of society's problems. It will provide the solution to some old problems, but it will create numerous new ones.

Our rallying cry rings truer with every passing day: the Internet is a hydra! There is no better metaphor to describe this profound phenomenon. We have naively unleashed the monster and now there is no going back. What has been done can not be undone. The Internet is one of the biggest - if not the biggest - technological and social revolutions in human history. Such an occasion is certainly cause for both humility and the undertaking of a creative and intense social critique: we have no idea what this hydra is going to do to us and our children. Nobody knows. All we can do, and must do, is to keep on guessing. And the quality of that guesswork will make all the difference in the world.

Frankly speaking, this is a matter of Darwinian survival. We need to know as much as we possibly can, to prepare as best we can for the turmoil and waves of change sweeping through human society. And it will take intelligence, creativity and scientific stringency to get it right. Because the situation is identical with previous revolutions in human history: it is precisely those who understand what is going on, who make sure to be in the right place at the right time, who are going to adapt quicker than others and truly reap the benefits of the revolution. The rest will be left behind in shock. Ignore the message at your own peril.

Stockholm, February, 2012
Alexander Bard & Jan Söderqvist

1.

TECHNOLOGY AS THE DRIVING FORCE OF HISTORY

THERE IS A POPULAR STORY that tells how a Japanese soldier was found several decades after the end of the war in an inaccessible part of the Asian jungle, where he had single-handedly carried on fighting the Second World War. As a result of a combination of circumstances he had been left there alone. Perhaps he had been ordered to remain at his isolated post, and had been exercising his duties to the fatherland with exemplary loyalty for all those years, or perhaps he had simply been too frightened to venture into populated areas. But time had passed and no-one had told him that peace had been declared. So the Second World War was still raging inside his head.

We have no reason to laugh at this confused soldier. He may have been wrong, but then so have we, countless times. The soldier was not particularly well-informed, but then neither are we always. We all suffer to some extent from confused perceptions of what is going on outside the small part of our immediate world that we can get a direct impression of. This does not prevent us from forming, and being forced to form, opinions about one thing after the other, even in complicated matters where our knowledge is limited to say the least. Most of what we believe that we know is precisely that: what we believe ourselves to know. Other people's actions are comprehensible to us only in so far as we actually know what they in turn believe themselves to know. Which is something we seldom know. The constant inadequacy of this information means that we have to swim through an ocean of misunderstanding on a daily basis, an activity which is both demanding and costly.

Like the Japanese soldier we form our lives inside our heads. We have to, because the world is far too large and complicated for us to open ourselves to its every aspect without protecting ourselves with a multi-layered mental filter. For this reason we create fictions for ourselves, simplified models of how we believe the world works, or how we think it ought to work. These fictions have to fill the immense vacuums between our limited areas of knowledge. It is within this world of private fictions that we think and feel, but it is outside in the collective reality that our actions have their consequences. The more complicated a situation, the higher the degree of guesswork and the greater the contribution of fiction to our perception of reality.

This dependence upon fictions often has dramatic consequences, not just for us personally but for society as a whole. Like the Japanese soldier we are fumbling blindly through dark forests. We react to signals that we can only partially understand, the consequences of which are only partially visible to us. Important political decisions are based upon shaky foundations and often have completely different results than were foreseen; great weight is placed on diffuse expressions of opinion, most often in the form of general elections, which are in turn the result of minimal knowledge, a problem which has been discussed, amongst others, by the author and journalist Walter Lippman in a couple of perceptive and intelligent books. This increasing lack of an overview explains for instance why the today's voters find it easier to understand the credit card fiascos and alcohol consumption of individual politicians than serious political issues. Symbolism becomes attractive when real problems are perceived as being far too complicated. The business world is constantly forced to redefine its prognoses and adjust its decisions retrospectively in order to conceal the fact that they were based upon fictional rather than factual conceptions, as a result of the perpetual and chronic lack of information.

Becoming informed is an attempt to synchronise your own head with the reality outside. There are good reasons to make the effort: it is easier to interact with your surroundings when you have a relatively correct understanding of its mechanisms. Someone who has educated themselves in the psychology of the stock market has better prospects of succeeding in the markets; someone who has educated themselves in their own and other people's inner needs has better prospects of succeeding in relationships, and so on. Every failure reveals that we were not as well-informed as we thought or had hoped. The discrepancy between our own and other people's perception of reality, and between our own fictions and actual reality, was far too great. We learn from our mistakes; we take account of our earlier failures in the future and adjust our behaviour accordingly. To put it another way, we make use of information.

Fictions can be more or less truthful, more or less applicable. They come in all possible forms, from private hallucinations to scientific theories. We are constantly testing them. Our culture consists of a perpetual evaluation and combination of both seemingly promising fictions and already proven fictions. The relationship between the fictions in our heads and unaccommodating realities is a recurrent theme in literature. Don Quixote, Othello, Raskolnikov and Emma Bovary are all victims of their own feverish ignorance. They are all relatives of the Japanese soldier. In attempting to study and gain an impression of the world around us we have to learn to differentiate between our prejudices – simplified models that we make use of not because they reflect empirical evidence but because they appeal to our own personal interests – and factual analyses and prognoses – necessary and intelligent simplified models of reality which make it comprehensible to us, even if the results do not appeal to us or fit in with our cherished fictions.

Our thoughts are directed by access to information. The story of the Japanese soldier is an illustration of this: without access to news from the outside world he lived out an imaginary war for several decades. The same thing applies to whole societies and civilisations. Available information dictates which thoughts and actions are possible. It was not a lack of raw materials that prevented the Vikings from using water-skis or the Romans from videotaping their orgies – it was a lack of relevant information. Civilisation, in essence, is a matter of information. This means that any technological development which dramatically alters the preconditions for actions and the dissemination of information also implies a thorough re-evaluation of old and ingrained patterns of thought. The consequences of such a technological revolution are defined as a new historical paradigm.

The advent of language was one such revolution. The apes, our closest relatives, are intelligent animals with fantastic learning capabilities. But we cannot teach them to speak. From a physiological perspective we can say that their upper airways cannot function as vocal organs. But apes cannot use sign-language in any real sense either. Chimpanzees can learn to combine signs in order to communicate on the level of a small child; they can indicate that they want something or that they want someone else to do something, but they never exchange experiences, never speculate about the great mysteries of life. They lack the capacity to communicate their thoughts and experiences with linguistic symbols, which seriously hampers the exchange of information. Man's path diverged from that of the apes about five million tears ago, but language took longer to develop. To begin with we had elementary problems with our vocal organs, and evolution is a slow process. It is difficult to specify an exact time for the advent of spoken language, but current research suggests that it occurred as recently as 150,000-200,000 years ago. Only when the development of both the brain and our anatomy was sufficiently advanced was spoken language possible.

Language differentiates man from other animals. The creation of technology requires abstract thought, which in turn arises from a linguistic system of symbols. Language made it possible for man to develop socially and to gather and maintain collectives, which opened up a new world of interwoven relationships between individuals. Social life developed entirely new and rich nuances as communication became more advanced. Language offered the possibility of innovative thought, with all its countless possibilities of expression, and stimulated creativity and intelligence. It also made possible the dissemination of information to everyone who was connected to a community. The basic facts of life for a hunter-gatherer society – which plants are edible, which poisonous plants are edible after various treatments, which animals leave which tracks, and so on – became possible to communicate throughout a large group, and between generations. Other people could gain knowledge of both successes and failures, and could go on to develop further the combined experience of the collective. Mankind developed memory. Knowledge could develop, but only to a certain point. Spoken language does not permit, at least not without a tape-recorder, the reliable and comprehensive storage of information.

The mathematician Douglas S. Robertson has calculated the combined amount of information that a group or tribe of linguistically capable but illiterate people can access. He takes the poem The Iliad as his basis, a work comprising approximately five million bits (one bit indicates a choice between two alternatives: yes or no, black or white, one or zero), and which we know it is possible for one person to memorise. If the amount of information that a human brain can store is h, then h would appear to be somewhere between one and two Iliads, or, in other words, somewhere between five and ten million bits. If we multiply h by the size of a prehistoric tribe, a number between 50 and 1000, we get the maximum amount of information available within a society that was not capable of writing. We ought to bear in mind that there is a sizeable amount of redundant information here. Large amounts of the total store of information – how to hunt, how to fish, and so on – can reasonably be assumed to have been shared by most members of the community, which means that the total amount of information must be adjusted downwards accordingly. The numbers themselves must, of course, be taken with a pinch of salt, but Robertson's calculations provide an excellent illustration of the impact of written language when it was developed during the third millennium BC, and of the explosion in the amount of available information this represented.

Four of the so-called cradles of civilisation – Egypt, Mesopotamia, the Indus Valley and China – developed at roughly the same time, and what united them, and simultaneously differentiated them from the surrounding societies in which trade and metallurgy were also practised, was the invention of written language. To begin with clay tablets were used to write on. The earliest 'book' consisted of several of these tablets, stored in a leather bag or case. Certain texts, laws for instance, where inscribed on large surfaces so that everyone could see them. In this way the fundamental ideas and norms of the society were transformed from something mystical and ancient which had been communicated orally by shamans, into a visible and limited number of clauses and decrees that were available to everyone. Primitive, closed societies assumed a more open and more complex character. At the same time it became clear that knowledge gave power. Early forms of writing were initially an instrument of power. The Sumerian kings and priests used scribes to work out how many sheep different people ought to pay in tax. Another use of writing was propaganda: the ruler reminded his people of who was in charge and of the glittering victories he had won for them.

It was never intended that the written word would come into the hands of every Tom, Dick and Harry. The purpose of the first writings was, in the words of the French anthropologist Claude Lévi-Strauss, 'to facilitate the enslavement of other people'. But revolutions have their own velocity, impossible to control for any length of time, and this is particularly true of information technology. Things that occurred either long ago or far away assumed a completely different accessibility and visibility when communicated via written text. The amount of available information exploded thanks to the ingenious invention of a visual code for communication. Intellectual life became far more vital. Thanks to the phonetic alphabet – where each sign represents a sound instead of a word or concept – the ancient Greeks were able to develop philosophy and sciences that had a far more firm structure, a grammar. The replacement of the ear by the eye as the main sense of linguistic reception brought with it a radical change in mankind's way of understanding the world.

Written language looked like magic: it was entirely logical that the Egyptian god Thoth, who gave the gift of writing to mankind, was also the god of magic. Reading and writing transformed both knowledge and the world. Empires could be established and held together only when written communication had developed; only then was it possible for detailed information such as orders to be communicated across large distances. This led to the dissolution of city states. The decline in papyrus production during the reign of the last emperors is held up by many historians as one important reason for the decline and ultimate collapse of the Roman Empire. Even hand-written information had its limits.

Johann Gutenberg's invention of the printing press in the middle of the fifteenth century was the start of the next epoch-making revolution in information management. The printing press was also a basic precondition of what became modern science, and of the great discoveries and technical advances that led to industrialisation. Printed books were the source material of the astronomer Nicholas Copernicus, and without the printing process his manuscript may well have gathered dust on the shelves of a monastery library. Instead his De Revolutionibus, the thesis proposing for the first time that the Earth moved in orbit around the sun, spread quickly across the world of learning, where nothing was ever the same again.

Once the ball had started rolling, nothing could stop it. To put it bluntly, the printing press provided gifted and innovative people with the necessary information and inspiration to a previously undreamed of extent. Christopher Columbus read Marco Polo, large numbers of manuals and other technical literature circulated in Europe, and the whole of this tidal wave of new information prompted the development of new techniques and new thinking on the management of information, methods which paved the way for the gradual development of the sciences. Among the many innovations which followed in the wake of the printing press, after a certain incubation period, and which thoroughly and comprehensively altered mankind's way of looking at himself and the world, can be counted the clock, gunpowder, the compass and the telescope.

One illustrative example of the power of developed information management, provided by the physiologist Jared Diamond, is the historically decisive meeting between literate Europe and essentially illiterate America in 1532. In the city of Cajamarca in the Peruvian highlands Francisco Pizarro, with 168 men, captured the Inca leader Atahualpa, who had at his command more than 80,000 troops. The event only becomes comprehensible in light of the fact that the Inca leader knew nothing about his uninvited visitors whereas the Spaniards were well-informed about their opponent. Atahualpa was completely unaware that these visitors were in the process of conquering the whole of that part of the world, and that the great Indian civilisations of Central America had already fallen to them. He was entirely dependent upon defective oral information.

Atahualpa did not take the invaders seriously, and when his troops saw troops on horseback for the first time in their lives they panicked. Pizarro himself may not have been able to read, but he was a participant in a culture of writing and printing, and therefore had access to a wealth of detailed information about foreign civilisations. He was also aware of every phase of the Spanish conquest, and based his campaign upon the tactics of Hernando Cortés when he had defeated the Aztec leader Montezuma. Pizarro's success soon became known in Europe. In 1534 a book was published describing the events of Cajamarca, written by one of his company, which was translated into several other languages and became a bestseller. There was a great demand for information, and its benefits were self-evident.

Today's electronic and digital media comprise the most comprehensive information revolution of all. For a long time we believed that the central purpose of the computer was to think, to produce an artificial intelligence that would far exceed our own. Many people claimed that this goal was within sight when a computer named Big Blue beat the world master Garry Kasparov at chess. Today we can see that technology was heading in a different direction, towards communication via networks. Increasingly powerful and fast computers are making possible infinitely complicated and time-consuming calculations and simulations which were previously impossible to perform, which is of incalculable benefit to mathematicians and other researchers. Our collective knowledge is growing exponentially. But it is the global, digital network which is the most interesting aspect of this development. A new, dominant media technology means that a new world is evolving.

The Internet is something completely new: a medium in which virtually anyone, after a relatively small investment in technical equipment, and with a few simple actions, can become both a producer and consumer of text, images and sound. In this sense it is hard to think of anything more democratic; on the Net we are all authors, publishers and producers, our freedom of expression is as good as total, and our potential audience limitless. There are oceans of every conceivable sort of information available at the touch of a button. The growth of this new medium has been unparalleled.

The foundations of the Internet were laid as early as the 1960s with the decision of the American defence organisations to use computerised networks to decentralise their resources via a series of distant but connected terminals. The purpose of this was to protect against and limit the effects of any nuclear war with the Soviet Union. Eventually American and foreign universities were connected to the system after it had proved stunningly effective in the organisation of joint research projects. This development explains why the World Wide Web, the system which later became the standard for homepages on the Internet, was developed not in the USA but by researchers at CERN, the European institute for research into particle physics in Switzerland.

It was not until the end on the 1980s, as a direct result of the breakthrough of the personal computer and the launch of telecommunications modems, that the Internet was transformed from a tool for the military and the scientific communities into public property. Even in the early 1990s there were relatively few people who had heard of the Internet. It was only in December 1995 that Bill Gates woke up and announced that Microsoft would be changing direction and concentrating on Net traffic. Since then the growth of the Internet has been phenomenal. It is practically meaningless to give any figures regarding the number of computers linked to the Net because its development is so dizzyingly fast. Figures that were accurate when this was written will be hopelessly out of date by the time it is read.

There are various responses to this development. Critics suggest that all this talk of IT-revolutions and new economies is preposterous, or at the very least seriously exaggerated. These sceptics often point to the fact that even if IT- related shares are soaring on trend-sensitive stock markets the world over, most of these companies are posting continual losses, and that this cannot continue in the long run. The only people who have become rich from computers and IT are the various consultants and the producers of the computers and the software that make the Internet possible, while consumers have invested heavily for little or no gain. Any reflected exponential growth in the economy as a whole has not materialised.

From the point of view of the sceptic, the world is essentially the same as it was. We still manufacture and sell hammers and nails, the banks continue to devote themselves to the lending and borrowing of money, a few office routines have changed, but the significance of all of this has been exaggerated. Most people now write their own business letters on a word-processor instead of using a dictaphone or a secretary, but the question is whether the state of things has been dramatically improved by this. What is known as e-commerce is just business as usual, even if we are using flashy new machines. According to this point of view, this is largely a case of following trends, that there is a certain cachet in being first with the latest innovations, no matter what concrete benefit these may actually bring. And it matters little what technology we use to communicate: it is still the content which is important. Old and tested truths will still be just that in the future.

The contrary point of view is ecstatic. Anyone who has seen the light on their screen claims that everything will automatically turn out for the best. The Internet is the solution to all our problems: the economy will blossom for everyone forever, ethnic and cultural conflicts will fade away and be replaced by a global, digital brotherhood. All the information that becomes available will make our duties as citizens more meaningful than ever, and the whole of the democratic system will be revitalised as a result. In the digital networks we shall find the social cohesion that we often lack today, and harmony will spread throughout society. Entertainment will become, thanks to the inexhaustible possibilities of this new technology, more interactive and hence more entertaining than ever.

Both the sceptic and the enthusiast are mistaken. Neither radical scepticism nor blind faith is a fruitful strategy for orientation in the accelerated process of change in which we find ourselves. Both of these points of view indicate in essence an unwillingness to think critically, an inability to see. They are not analyses or prognoses, but prejudices. A new, revolutionary technology for communication and information will undoubtedly change the preconditions of everything: society, economy, culture. But it will not solve all our problems. It would be naïve to believe that it could. Development means that we can approach certain problems in a dramatic way, but to balance this we will have to confront a whole raft of new problems. We can live longer and more healthily, perceive ourselves to be freer, and realise more of our dreams. But the fundamental conflicts between classes and groups of people are not going to go away, just develop into more intricate and impenetrable patterns and structures.

Change of this type is not instantaneous. The sceptic who triumphantly points out that most of the global economy is still based upon the production of physical objects like fridges, aeroplanes and garden furniture rather than digital services on the Net is partly a little impatient – we are still in many respects only in a preliminary phase – and partly incapable of grasping the extent of the change. There is no question of the fridge disappearing, but rather that the objects around us will take on new significance and new functions in an entirely new socio-ecological system. Marketing campaigns for fridges, for example, will no longer stress their capacity to keep milk cold, because we take that for granted, but rather their capacity to communicate intelligently in a network.

It is in the nature of things that it takes a certain amount of time for changes to be absorbed. Every revolutionary technology only reveals its true colours after an unavoidable period of incubation. As far as the printing press was concerned, it took more than three hundred years before it made its definitive breakthrough, the point at which it caused a dramatic shake-up of social structures and created a new paradigm: capitalism. It took time, quite simply, before literacy was sufficiently widespread for print to affect large social groups beneficially. It was not until the Enlightenment of the 1700s that thinking became sufficiently modern, the exchange of information sufficiently lively, and technical advances sufficiently explosive for there to be signs of nascent industrialism in the offing.

Literacy spread rapidly through northern Europe during the 1600s, but its growth only accelerated more noticeably during the following century, primarily as a result of Protestantism and the dissemination of Bible translations into the various national languages. The preconditions were created for a completely new sort of critical public life, whose platform was primarily the first newspapers of recognisably modern form. New publications, such as The Spectator in England, were aimed at (and therefore also helped to shape) an educated and cosmopolitan middle-class. The aim of the newspapers was to inform about and debate the latest ideas. In France the world of the salon arose, where the aristocracy and middle-classes came into contact with one another and together examined the signs of the times. This form of gathering quickly became popular and spread throughout Europe.

But even if literacy and the development of information technologies lay the basis for the changes that occurred in society, they cannot explain them fully. A whole mass of factors have to coincide and co-operate if any epoch-changing process of change is to be set in train. The French sociologist Jacques Ellul, whose interest is primarily with the internal logic of technology and its radical effects upon our lives and environment, has pointed out a number of key phenomena. The first and possibly most self-evident precondition is that the necessary apparatus must be in place already, which in turn presupposes a longer historical process. Every innovation has its roots in a previous era. Novelty consists of what can be termed a technical complex; in other words, a series of inventions of various sorts which together form a powerful combination which is stronger than their individual parts. Innumerable innovations saw the light of day between 1000 and 1750, many of them remarkable in themselves, but they played to different tunes, they did not communicate with one another. It was only after 1750 that innovations began to work together and thereby facilitate large-scale industrialisation.

Another important precondition, according to Ellul, is population growth. An increase in population means increased demands which cannot be satisfied without growth. Necessity is the mother of invention. From another, even more crass, point of view, an increase in population means greater preconditions for research and technical and economic development partly in the form of an increase in the size of the market, and partly by providing a human basis for various experiments with different types of product. A third effect is that two specific and at least partially contradictory demands are placed upon the economic environment, which has to be both stable but also in some form of dissolution. On the one hand, a stable base is required for scientific experimentation which is necessary but unprofitable in the short term, but on the other there must be a capacity for widespread and fast change, a willingness to stimulate and absorb new thought-processes. The fourth precondition concerns the social climate itself, and is, according to Ellul, probably the most important of them all. There has to be a loosening of various religious or ideological taboos, and liberation from any form of social determinism. For the development of industrialism, for instance, it was vitally important that a whole raft of traditional ideas about what was 'natural' were thoroughly revised. No longer were either nature itself or hierarchical social orders perceived as sacred and inviolable.

Perceptions of man and his place in the world underwent radical change. The individual gained a new position, and human freedoms and rights were spoken about, which undermined preconceptions of natural groupings and classes. Suddenly unimagined opportunities opened up, offering social advancement and an improvement in living standards. The liberation of the individual and increases in technological efficiency co-operated. An historical resonance arose, where various factors dramatically strengthened one another in an accelerating spiral. The middle-classes were rewarded for their willingness to adapt and made the most of this opportunity. Hence the middle-class became the dominant class of the paradigm of capitalism.

The Industrial Revolution meant that that mankind's physical power was multiplied may times over through the use of machines. The Digital Revolution means that the human brain will be expanded to an incomprehensible degree through its integration with electronic networks. But we are not there yet, the necessary preconditions are not yet in place. Technology may be accelerating with breathtaking speed, but we humans are slow. Once again we are hampered by all kinds of religious and ideological taboos. Once again we are on the brink of a period of necessary creative destruction. This development cannot be controlled to any great extent. History shows that every new technology worth the name has, for better or worse, 'done its own thing', completely independently of what its originators had imagined. In the words of the communications expert Neil Postman, technology 'plays its own hand'.

Take the clock, for example, an apparently neutral and innocent artefact, but actually an infernal little machine that creates seconds and minutes, which has retrospectively given a whole new meaning to our perception of time. When the first prototypes were developed by Benedictine monks during the 12th and 13th centuries their purpose was to establish a certain stability and regularity to the routines of the monastery, principally with regard to the prescribed seven hours of prayer each day. The mechanical clock brought precision to piety. But the clock was not satisfied with this. It soon spread beyond the walls of the monasteries. It may well have kept order over the monks' prayers, but above all else the clock became an instrument which synchronised and watched over the daily lives of ordinary people. It was thanks to the clock that it became possible to imagine something like regular production during a regulated working day. It became, in other words, one of the cornerstones of capitalism. This invention, dedicated to God, 'did its own thing' and became one of Mammon's most faithful servants.

The same thing happened to the printing press. The devout Catholic Gutenberg could scarcely have imagined that his invention would be used to deliver a fatal blow to the authority of the Papacy and promote Protestant heresies by making the word of God accessible to everyone, which in turn made everyone his own interpreter of the Bible. When information became generally available, the natural but no less unforeseen consequence was that various accepted 'truths' were put into question. From the 1700s, modern rationalism developed alongside the notion of the educated citizen, and it was the printed word that was to do the job. The goal was the extinction of every form of superstition, principal amongst them religion and the monarchy. According to the French

Enlightenment thinker, Denis Diderot, 'Man will not be free before the last king has been strangled with the entrails of the last priest'.

As long as information was an exclusive rarity, confined to the privileged few, it was unthinkable that ideas like that could be widely disseminated. Instead it became, after an incubation period of two hundred years, a mass movement. Technology played out its hand. And in the process, everything was changed. When the true agenda of the printing press began to appear, there was no longer any question of the old Europe plus a nice new invention, but of a completely new Europe which thought and acted in new ways. The progression had been uncovered, the historical process began to become clearer, and common-sense and science would lift mankind out of the darkness of ignorance and progressively improve standards of living. A new world view, and a new view of man, had been born.

A new, dominant information technology changes everything, not least language. This is partly because of new terminology, new words for new toys, but the most interesting and, to an extent, most problematic aspect of this is that old words assume new meanings. As language changes, so does our thinking. New technology redefines basic concepts such as knowledge and truth; it re-programmes society's perceptions of what is important and unimportant, what is possible and impossible, and, above all else, what is real. Reality assumes new expressions. This is what Neil Postman means when he talks of society going through an 'ecological' change. Technology shakes up the kaleidoscope of our intellectual environment and world of ideas and shows new, unforeseen patterns. We are entering a new social, cultural and economic paradigm.

The paradigm defines which thoughts can be thought, quite literally. The paradigm is simply the set of preconceptions and values which unite the members of a specific society. To take one example: when 'everyone' at a certain point in time is convinced that the world is flat, it is pointless to try to work out a way of sailing round the world. When Copernicus claimed that the Earth actually moved around the sun many people thought him mad. This is no surprise. Ridiculing his critics with the benefit of hindsight merely proves that one does not understand how a paradigm works. It is not possible to say categorically that his critics were wrong, because what they meant by the term 'Earth' was precisely a fixed point in space.

The terms still carried their former meanings, the paradigm shift had not yet taken place, people were still thinking along ingrained lines. The same thing occurred with the transition from Newton's physics to Einstein's. Many people dismissed Einstein's general theory of relativity for the simple reason that it presupposed that the concept 'space' stood for something which could be 'bent', when the old paradigm dictated that space was constant and homogenous. This was wholly necessary – if space had not possessed just these qualities, Newtonian physics could not have functioned. And since Newtonian physics had apparently functioned well for such a long time, they could not be abandoned easily. Hence a situation arose in which two paradigms competed with one another.

But two paradigms cannot exist for one person at the same time. It is either/or. The Earth cannot be both mobile and immobile at the same time, space cannot simultaneously be both flat and curved. For this reason individual transitions from one paradigm to another must be instantaneous and complete. It is like the Japanese soldier leaving the jungle and suddenly realising that he has been living an illusion for years: peace, not war, is the status quo, and Japan has become the driving force of the Asian economic miracle. We are speaking here qualitatively rather than quantitatively. To move from an old paradigm to a new is not merely a question of becoming informed in the sense of adding new facts to old ones with which we are already familiar, but rather in the sense that new facts, and old facts in a new light, change our world view entirely. And once we have perceived that our old world view is exactly that, old, and is no longer capable of explaining difficult phenomena, which it is in turn no longer possible to ignore or deny, then it is necessary to abandon large amounts of irrelevant knowledge. This is one of the sacrifices demanded by a paradigm shift.

From a narrower perspective this is an acute situation for someone trying to orientate themselves in the world which is being formed around us within and by the electronic networks. The problem is no longer a lack of information, but an incalculable excess of it. What appears to be new information and new ideas might actually be yesterday's news, or in the worst cases abject nonsense, which will direct us into time- and resource-wasting cul-de-sacs. Old recipes for success become outdated fast. It is only human to become more attached to old strategies if they have proved successful in the past, and it is therefore all the more difficult to abandon them. Someone who has built up a successful business, or who has merely managed to make his life tolerably comfortable, seldom recognises the necessity of dropping everything and starting again from scratch.

It is here that we find the true novelty in what is happening now. Previously the point of a paradigm was that it provided us with firm ground beneath our feet after a longer or shorter period of tremors. We need to get accustomed to losing that luxury and recognise that change itself is the only thing that is permanent. Everything is fluid. The social and economic stability that has been the ideal and the norm is becoming more and more the exception and a sign of stagnation. It is not enough to think, or to think in new ways; it is now necessary to rethink constantly, and to think away old thoughts. Creative destruction never rests.

Within the world of scientific theories, where the concept of paradigms was first established, there is talk of anomalies and crises. Anomalies are phenomena which are in part unforeseen, and in part difficult to adapt to fit the current paradigm. We can see them all around us these days: in society, within our cultural life and media, and in the economy. The preconditions which underlie politics are altering at a dizzying pace. Yesterday's ideological maps have nothing to do with the reality of today. Whole branches and great empires within the media are collapsing before our eyes. Working life is undergoing a dramatic revolutionary process which is effectively destroying all our old preconceptions of secure employment, automatic promotion and hierarchical organisation. Youngsters still wet behind the ears and wearing strange clothes are becoming multi-millionaires in a few short months, in businesses which few of their share-holders have any real grasp of.

When a large number of anomalies appear there are two possibilities. The first is to try to squeeze the new phenomena into the old system of explanations. This is what people have always done within science: patched up and repaired old theories, like for example the old Ptolemaic system of astronomy with the Earth in the centre and all the other heavenly bodies circling around it. It holds for a while, bearably, but with time it becomes gradually more apparent that the conditions produced by the old theory are no longer of any use. And then we are confronted unavoidably with option number two: to admit that the old system has had its day, even if there is no new system ready to take its place. This precipitates a crisis. The importance of this crisis is that it signals a need for new thinking. And this is where we are at the moment, in the middle of the crisis which has arisen from the old capitalist paradigm showing that it is incapable, but before any new system has won over enough adherents to be able to function as a generally accepted explanatory model. A lot of people are still patching up and repairing the old system, and there is a noticeable lack of new thinking. Sullen scepticism as to whether the new is actually anything genuinely new, and blind faith in the new which maintains that everything is now on its way to ordering itself automatically for the best, do not count as new thinking.

Writing about the future is obviously incredibly problematic because is does not yet exist. The best we can do is to produce more or less qualified guesswork. Someone who understands how dominant information technologies have played out their hands throughout history, and who understands how the dynamism within and between digital networks functions, has the best possible preconceptions for grasping the essential points of the current revolution. As an introductory note we claim two things. The first is that a new social, cultural and economic paradigm is taking shape. The main reason is the ongoing revolution within the management of information: digitalisation, and the astonishingly fast development of electronic networks. One immediate consequence of this is that our mental ecology is drastically changing, which in turn forces a whole sequence of necessary adjustments. And secondly we suggest that the form that the new paradigm is in the process of assuming will not be concrete, but fluid. It is not merely that we are developing new social norms; it is a matter of a completely new sort of norm.

The Japanese soldier in the jungle was ill-informed, and was fighting his own private world war within his own head, but then his circumstances were hardly optimal. We, on the other hand, cannot blame anything other than laziness or stupidity if we do not manage to garner a relatively clear picture of what is going on around us and if we cannot draw the relevant conclusions from this picture. Because one thing we can say without any doubt is that it will not be the meek who inherit the earth.

2.

FEUDALISM, CAPITALISM AND INFORMATIONALISM

OF COURSE, THE MEEK HAVE never inherited much of anything. In every age, the power and the glory have belonged to those who are receptive and industrious, those who are sensitive to changes in the prevailing climate, who look out for their own interests and those of their particular group, and who have the great good fortune to be blessed by historical developments moving in their particular direction. Every new paradigm creates its own winners and losers. Altered preconditions for development and adjusted measurements of social status benefit new, up-and-coming social classes to the detriment of others. In order to understand the consequences of the current shift from capitalism to informationalism it would be helpful to take a look at the most recent historical paradigm shift, from feudalism to capitalism, and then compare the realignment of power distribution that occurred then with what is happening to us now. As we shall discover, there are so many parallels, on so many different levels, that we have little choice but to define what is happening in our time as a genuine paradigm shift of similar magnitude.

We can use cartography as a way of illustrating these recurrent patterns in historical developments. The most applicable concept in this instance is the mobilistic diagram. With inspiration from the work of philosophers like the nineteenth century's Friedrich Nietzsche and Charles Darwin and the late twentieth century's power-theoreticians Gilles Deleuze and Michel Foucault, we can take as our starting point the idea that existence is a continual conflict between a multitude of different forces that are in permanent opposition to one another, yet which presuppose and define each other precisely as a result of this opposition. The main point here is not the forces themselves, but the tension in their relations to each other, how positions of strength are maintained or displaced, and the eternal struggle between them. Interaction, confrontation and communication are key terms here. By illustrating these complex relationships we can make them easier to identify and understand.

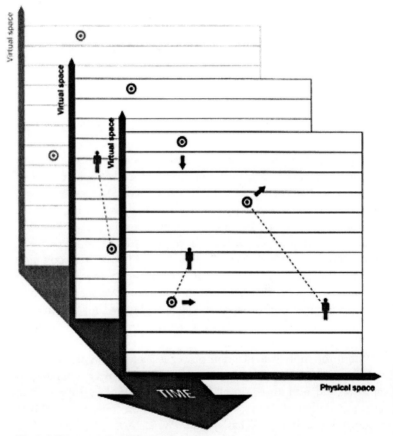

Fig.2.1 Diagram of mobilistic power

Within the mobilistic diagram we can complement the Nietzschean-Darwinian two-dimensional plan of the existential conflict with a third dimension, a temporal axis which makes it possible to identify at any given point in time the specific value around which the conflict revolves. In other words, we are talking about an assumed point which we can allow ourselves to identify precisely because we are aware that we, the observers, are in a position of constant flux ourselves (the fact being that we in our role as viewers are just as much a force in this as those on the two-dimensional plan). This conflict is about power. The closer the interaction between any two complementary and/or opposing forces gets to the assumed point in this extra dimension of the mobilistic plan, the more power is at stake.

It is important to remember that this assumed point is not the only value that is the subject of conflict, but rather the central value in society, the defining feature of the paradigm in question. We might call this value "the religion of the time", or, more relevant to us, "the axiom of the time"; in other words, the basic suppositions in any given age about the structure of existence, the world view that is generally accepted and which is therefore socially functional. This assumed point makes it possible for us to orientate ourselves and focus upon what is going on. Because vested interests, not least the ruling classes of any given age, have expended a great deal of resources in the presentation of this assumed point as being not assumed, but real, in other words as being an eternal truth, then the fact that it is assumed becomes a highly sensitive area. When its assumed nature is revealed, the mat is pulled from under our feet, which can lead to a certain amount of giddiness. The common phrase "I don't know much, but there's one thing I know for certain…" is a good illustration of this problem. We are prepared to acknowledge that our knowledge is limited, but we imagine that we need to know at least something for certain in order to orientate ourselves in life.

Within the mobilistic diagram power is a moveable phenomenon with no inherent value, a neutral concept. Power migrates, is captured and recaptured, in all directions. Identities arise purely in relation to other identities. Definitions must be constantly tested as circumstances change. What's what? Which force is which? Can they be kept apart despite the fact that they're drifting into one another? We are on the sidelines watching a feverish struggle for status; a struggle about who creates what, who can gain control over whom, who defines what and why, with the ever-present supplementary questions: at what price and at the cost of whom?

The relations between forces, their interaction, are the crux of the matter. The master cannot exist independently of the slave, just as little as the slave can exist independently of the master. Each is conditional upon the other. It is the slavery of the slave which makes the master a master, and both are engaged in the eternal struggle for recognition which, according to G W F Hegel, another of the nineteenth century's great philosophers, is the motor which drives the entire historical process. According to Hegel, it was the desire for recognition by other people that set off the struggle for prestige in the earliest social groupings which lay the foundations for later divisions of humanity into different classes. These struggles have continued to rage, keeping society in a constant state of flux, so long as different groups perceive that they have too little recognition and consequently believe that they deserve greater influence and higher status.

A paradigm shift occurs when the assumed constant is moved and undergoes a qualitative redefinition. It is no exaggeration to compare this shift in underlying values to an historical earthquake. Every other factor in the arena of conflict is fundamentally affected by the fact that its point of origin, the instance around which a society revolves, is suddenly in motion. The consequence of this is that the actors no longer believe that they know anything for certain. Everything is in flux. Some of the older actors remain frozen in their historical roles, marginalised at the point in the arena where the central value used to be. New forces, new actors step into the arena and immediately instigate a new struggle around the point towards which the assumed value is moving. When the shock has subsided the old actors have to find new, less impressive roles for themselves.

This sudden movement of the assumed point is countered at once by strong resistance from those who regard their position as being under threat. When people and social classes become conscious of the fact that the constant around which the whole of their lives has revolved, and which has formed the basis for their identity, is in motion, they generally react at first with strong denials – "this can't be happening!". After a while, when the changes can no longer be denied, their reaction becomes one of either resignation or aggressive opposition – "this mustn't happen!". This is strengthened by the fact that the old authorities upon which everyone has relied have a highly confused understanding of what is actually happening. A good example of this sort of process is the destructive conflicts experienced by the western world since the transition from feudalism to capitalism about the concept of God, and the inevitable death of God. For every new mental barrier in our world-view that scientists have demolished, for every new boundary that has been transgressed, God has been pushed one step further into the unknown by his large but gradually diminishing crowd of supporters. To begin with God lived above the firmament, then beyond the sun and the planets, then beyond the stars, before finally being despatched beyond time and space. But he had to survive at all costs. Axioms connected to decrepit paradigms are often remarkably tenacious of life, not least among marginalised groups and classes.

Many people simply have difficulty understanding that the concept of God arose in a different paradigm to their own, with a purpose specific to that era: to the advantage of certain then current interests at the expense of others. In feudal society God was, in mobilistic terms, an assumed constant whose existence was unquestionable. (Merely trying to scratch the surface of this constant was punishable by death). With the transition to capitalism the fixed structures which supported the concept of God collapsed. When the central value began to move, the foundations which had earlier seemed unshakeable suddenly collapsed. God's majesty became relative, and it was now possible to question his very existence. Christianity fell into an abyss of doubt about its own legitimacy from which has never managed to recover. What we regard today as phantoms and demons once had a very real impact on people's realities. This is not a matter of theology, or of the weakness of evidence supporting the existence of God, but a matter of power. The authority of both monarchy and church rested ultimately upon the existence of something called God; God was the assumed constant and could therefore never be called into question under any circumstances. If doubts were allowed to spread, the whole power structure would have been in danger of imploding.

As a result of obstinate denials of any movement in the assumed constant, and unwillingness to surrender the claims of religion, atheism was elevated to the status of a new axiom, and became an oppositional and effective tool for the acquisition of power by the developing bourgeoisie. This is illustrated most clearly in the most spectacular social experiment of the capitalist paradigm: the communist project. Communism was an inverted form of Christianity, an expression of the age-old dream of heaven on earth that was entirely typical of its time. The communist faith was inspired by the idea of social improvement through human rather than divine agency. The new State was to be the tool; new Man – thoroughly rational and reasonable – was the utopian goal. This dream lay waste to entire nations and continents, and led to between 85 and 100 million people (for obvious reasons it is difficult to be precise) being slaughtered in peacetime for the greater good of the cause.

The existence of people who still defend the communist project is explained by the fact that this is a matter of religious faith, whose irrationality is a blind spot in the otherwise perpetual invocation of logic. The power of this faith was precisely a reflection of its original opposing force, organised religion, which refused to the last – in Russia, China and Latin America – to let go of power. It is quite conceivable that had the last Russian Tsar publicly declared his belief in atheism, he would have denied communism much of its appeal and thereby prevented the Russian Revolution. The demon of the assumed constant is so strong that even its antidote - and hence its equivalent in the following paradigm -inherits and exerts an almost magical influence on our thinking.

During the current transition from capitalism to informationalism we can see several parallels to the displacements that occurred during the last paradigm shift. What has been characteristic of capitalism, its blind spot, its assumed constant, has been the Human Project. To begin with, it is interesting to note that the Human Project in its most naked form, the Project of the Individual, has been elevated to the point where it is the last remaining life-raft for humanists and others with faith in humanity to cling to in a sea full of the wreckage left when the more glorious parts of the Project, such as communism, capsized one after the other.

This explains why all the political ideologies of capitalism during this final phase of the paradigm proudly proclaim in the introductions of their manifestos their fundamental faith in "the individual". Under external pressure capitalism has returned to its infancy and taken refuge in its philosophical origins, to pre-industrial thinkers like René Descartes and Francis Bacon. What we see are desperate attempts to re-establish the project, even as it is being relentlessly dismantled, in the form of hyper-individualism. By shouting loudly enough they imagine that they can breathe life into the corpse again. This ideological Frankenstein's monster goes by the name of libertarianism.

Just as the Protestant revivalist movements, which appeared in conjunction with the breakthrough of the Enlightenment, can be described as a supernova phenomenon, a sudden flaring-up of obsession with the old assumed constant, we are now experiencing similar supernovas in the paradigm shift from capitalism to informationalism. Today's hyper-egoism, hyper-capitalism and hyper-nationalism are all examples of this sort of supernova phenomenon. This development has arisen because the entire Human Project, the elevation of the individual alongside the state and capital, its pole star, and all its allied progeny – academic, artistic, scientific and commercial projects – have made up the fundamental axiom of the capitalist paradigm. They have been assumed to be eternal, a guarantee of stability, but they are now in motion. The great struggle has only just begun, and the death of the Human Project, like God's funeral, will carry on for a long time yet, and be accompanied by convulsive spasms. It is enough to remember the amount of interest and resources that are invested in this project to realise the degree of social trauma inherent in the developments which have just begun. This can't be happening, this mustn't happen! Nevertheless, collapse is inevitable, for the simple reason that this project is indissolubly linked with a paradigm that has passed its expiry date.

Of course it is difficult to try to localise the assumed constant of the new paradigm at this point, or to identify the forces that will struggle for power. A contemporary analysis from our position in the midst of the tornado of the paradigm shift can never be anything other than a construction of qualified guesses. As long as the assumed constant is in motion (and it will be for a long time yet) the variables are incalculably large, which makes the task similar to a meteorologist trying to forecast the weather several years in advance. This does not mean that any analysis is uninteresting or unnecessary. On the contrary. A critical examination of existing power structures is never more important than when a new class-society is developing. That is the only time when an observer can play an active role in the struggle surrounding the assumed constant. Analysis itself has a chance to become a constructive part of the historical process which is under analysis, and can become one of the many factors which influence the events under discussion.

Even before the assumed constant has settled upon a new fixed point, one force, the seeds of a new dominant class, begins to form around it. But is it really possible to talk of a new dominant class simply because the assumed constant has moved? Even if this constant has changed its character, why should this mean that the dominant force in society must change? Ought we not to assume that when the dominant class of the old paradigm realises that the constant around which it built its position is in the process of moving, it would seek out, ascertain and occupy this new position? The old dominant class would thereby become the new dominant class, albeit in a new guise. But there are several reasons why this is not the case.

To begin with, man is essentially a conservative creature. In situations like these there is a psychological term for a phenomenon known as cognitive dissonance which, put simply, states that we have a marked tendency to cling to old beliefs despite the fact that they are at odds with known facts. The reason for this is simply that the old beliefs are just that, old and familiar, and that we are therefore fond of them; they are part of what makes us mentally comfortable. This leads to intellectual sluggishness: we are prepared to make greater efforts to preserve the status quo in our heads than we are to learn new things. At the moment when we learn anything new we have to change our lives, albeit very slightly. For this reason our capacity to move across the historical map is in practice minimal.

One conclusion, therefore, that we can draw from analysing the mobilistic diagram is that our surroundings move and alter a good deal faster than we do. Our movement under these circumstances is primarily forced, a reluctant reaction to the maelstrom of social forces and information that make up our surroundings. It is a lack of satisfaction of our complicated and limitless desires, or to put it more correctly: the idea of this lack, the desire for desire, which compels us to consume. It is intolerance or narrow-mindedness in any given society that compels us to migrate. It is society, the system itself, which is constantly in motion, and individuals and groups are drawn against their will into the vortex and are forced to give up old and secure positions.

Because we are the sole observers of history, it is tempting to exaggerate our power over our surroundings and to see ourselves as the agents of free will, as the takers of initiative on the historical stage. But this is merely to give in to delusions of grandeur. Our scope for independent action is severely restricted. Those of our actions which are most visible on the historical map are generally easier to interpret as reactive rather than proactive. That people were attracted to communism and other grand utopian ideas is, amongst other things, the result of our constant need for adjustment to constant change. The lure of utopian dreams lies in their promise of rest, and there is a strong and widely-felt desire to put a stop to the movement that has been forced upon us. But if we are to put a stop to our own movement, then the historical process itself must stop, otherwise it will roll over us, and the historical process is by definition a process, something in motion. The end of the historical process would be the same as the end of society's, and therefore also our own demise.

This has been proven time after time throughout history. Every attempt to realise a utopia – communism is the most obvious example – and thereby put a stop to this constant motion, has led inexorably to the death of that society. Death is the only real alternative to constant turbulence. Buddha realised this over 2,500 years ago. We have to choose between nirvana, a state of permanent calm, or accept that everything around us is in constant motion and change, which brings with it an inescapable need for constant adaptation. The fact that our room for manoeuvre is so limited from a philosophical point of view makes us in practice slaves to the historical process. The Russian Tsar could not have been a committed atheist because he would thereby have been forced to recognise the illegitimacy of his position. He could scarcely deny the God upon whom his authority was based. And things went the way that they did.

During a paradigm shift change is so dramatic that the old dominant class is shown to be incapable of controlling the assumed constant which defines the new paradigm. A new dominant class develops at the point on the map where the advantaged group happens to find itself as a result of historical coincidence. The transition of a society from an old paradigm to a new is a protracted affair, which means that for a long while there is a considerable, albeit secondary and diminishing, residual value at the point where the old paradigm was focused. This acts as an incitement to the old dominant class to cling on to the old assumed constant. Even at the end there are doubters – this can't be happening, this mustn't happen! There is no need to learn anything new if there is any reason to avoid doing so.

It is therefore not the case that everything old becomes instantly worthless in a societal paradigm shift. Even if the central value, to take one example, moved from the ownership of land to capital in the transition from feudalism to capitalism, there was still an undeniable value in land-ownership. But the nature of its value changed. Land became a prized commodity. It is important to remember that it was the new dominant class that determined the value of land-ownership, which came to be expressed in monetary terms. The bourgeoisie bought and renovated old estates, transforming them into private playhouses and resorts for country pursuits, thereby signalling that the bourgeoisie were not only the lords of the burgeoning working classes, but also of the dominant class of the old paradigm, the aristocracy. It was the bourgeoisie who decided the new rules of the game.

Before this, country estates were not for sale. Their value lay in their heraldic shields and their proximity to the king's residence. Within the new paradigm these estates assumed a value according to new principles, the principles of the open market. They were given a price-tag. Their new value was decided by a whole range of new variables: the size and quality of their forests and farmland, as well as the new dominant class's desire to associate and play with the old dominant class, and to appropriate and display its traditional symbols. It did not take long before the old, traditional, feudal symbols of power lost their connection to power and were reduced to the state of faded and majestic curiosities whose value was purely nostalgic. The new dominant class had a right royal time (pardon the pun) with the old attributes and cast-offs of the aristocracy: the monarchy, the court, ancestral names and etiquette. The paradigm shift had completely stripped these of their metaphysical associations, and the bourgeoisie showed that everything had a price by buying and selling and marrying their way to the noblest titles. The aristocracy had little choice but to join in and swallow its humiliation; it was necessary to earn money, the overpowering value within the new paradigm.

The astonishingly crass business arrangements that were the result of the aristocracy's acute need of money and the bourgeoisie's desire for luxuries are a recurrent theme of nineteenth-century literature. The most cynical and entertaining observer of these transactions was Balzac, who was himself not above inserting a "de" before his surname to make it look more aristocratic. The old trappings of majesty were preserved, but their function was altered, and ceremonial costume became fancy dress. The same patterns are reflected today as the netocracy, the new dominant class of the information age, disrespectfully plays with the sacred cows of the bourgeoisie: individual identity, social responsibility, representative democracy, the legislative process, the banking system, the stock markets, and so on.

One of history's ironies is that the bourgeoisie's obsession with mass production – it was the printing press which instigated this stage of industrial history and which was of central importance in the capitalist revolution – undermined the market for heavily symbolic aristocratic treasures by flooding the market with cheap imitations. An artefact which had been unique was now merely the original, admittedly more valuable than all the copies, but whose aura nevertheless lost much of its attraction as a result of everyone surrounding themselves with exact replicas. Their value as status symbols was soon devalued.

Because it was the new dominant class which decided the rules of the game and decided the amounts on the price-tags of the old estates, the aristocracy became helplessly marginalised in the capitalist economy. As long as it had property to sell it could live on in style in the country, relatively less wealthy and, above all, ever more distanced from the centre of power and of society. Country estates were overshadowed by banks; family names and heraldry were replaced by financial empires and academic titles; the court and its jesters were replaced by parliament and political journalists. The stage was captured by new actors. Many of the new roles were similar to the old ones, but the script was newly written and the plot of the drama itself underwent drastic modernisation.

The assumed constants of the old and the new paradigm are so radically different from one another that any aspirant to a leading role in the new drama will need to learn an entirely different culture and a whole new set of values. The fact is that it is often easier for the old underclass to adapt to the cultural demands imposed by the dominant class of the new age than it is for the former dominant class. The stage is set for a major realignment. The old underclass has less to defend and lose, and finds it easier to learn new tricks and allow itself to be changed. In line with the thesis of continual historical movement we can say that acceleration comes easier to someone already in motion than it does to someone who is standing still. It often takes a while to realise that all the old recipes for success have lost their validity, and that realisation itself is difficult to handle – this can't happen, this mustn't happen! One example of this today is that it is often easier for the young immigrants to adapt to the new age's demand for cosmopolitan openness and cultural plurarchism than for their contemporaries from the homogenous and native bourgeoisie.

The members of the new dominant class have made no specific attempt to end up near the new assumed constant. They have simply had the good fortune to have been at the right place at the right time. Just as in nature, which is also in a state of constant flux, social evolution occurs arbitrarily: certain mutations turn out to be advantageous under current circumstances. It is not so much a matter of survival of the fittest as of survival of the best adapted. And what the best adaptation is changes with the circumstances. According to the principle of mankind's intellectual sluggishness, the new dominant class is made up of individuals and groups who by sheer coincidence happen to be close to the point where the new assumed constant ends up.

The bourgeoisie became the new dominant class in capitalist society. And where were these capitalist entrepreneurs recruited if not from the cities where they happened to be? They were also brought up under a Protestantism distinguished by a strong work ethic. The bourgeoisie did not seek power, did not seize power – it landed in its lap. The bourgeoisie was given power. If we take a closer look at this new dominant class there is further evidence that those who are already in motion are favoured above those standing still. New recruits to the bourgeoisie generally came from the surplus of peasants, the lowest of the low in the old power structure, rather that the heirs to aristocratic titles and estates.

The sociological equivalents to biology's genes are known as memes, ideas or interconnected systems of ideas, and a comparison of the origins and spread of genes and memes shows similar patterns. Just as biology has Darwinian development, sociology has its own memetic Darwinism. By studying genetic Darwinism we can draw interesting parallels to show how memetic Darwinism functions. The history of biology is a tough, eternal struggle for survival and reproduction among a wealth of haphazardly occurring species in a constantly changing environment. Coincidence determines which species will flourish at the expense of others; external circumstances determine which are best suited to current conditions, and the others are sifted out. The various species compete for a limited supply of resources with similar species, and, moreover, with related varieties of the same species.

Nature never rests, which is why the criteria for which mutations are best suited for survival are constantly changing. Human interference in nature also influences the conditions of the eternal struggle for survival, benefiting some and harming others. One famous example is the moths which during the nineteenth century became considerably darker in colour in industrialised parts of England. As a result of the environment becoming more polluted, the darker moths were better able to escape predators as they sat on dirty tree-trunks and walls. The birch trees were no longer particularly white, so it was the darker moths who reproduced and spread most successfully, with the result that within a few generations the appearance of the entire species had altered.

The same level of coincidence affects memetic Darwinism in sociology. In the dense jungle of complex and often contradictory information that surrounds us, the memes which can most easily survive and reproduce under the prevailing circumstances are the ones which eventually appear to be the strongest, while the memes which cannot find a firm footing gradually fade away and come to be regarded as weak. But the difference between strength and weakness in this case is seldom visible in advance, at least not if you are staring yourself blind at the memes themselves and forget the environment of information technology and its development. The task of futurists is to map out the ecological system in which the various memes are fighting, and, taking that as their basis, to make a prognosis of the various memes' chances of survival.

The values and cultural baggage of every individual or group is made up of a number of memes. Which of these proves to be either "strong" or "weak" in the Darwinian sense in conjunction with a paradigm shift can only be determined in retrospect. In the same way that various genes have no influence on natural changes during a genetic Darwinian revolution, all memes are impotent in the face of the immense social powers which are set in motion by a paradigm shift. The carriers of both memes and genes can merely hope that they will be fortunate. As far as the basic, theoretical preconditions are concerned, there is little real difference between biological and sociological Darwinism.

In order to understand the memetic Darwinian process it is useful, once again, to use cartography as a tool, this time with human beings and memes rather than social forces as the variables. We can see existence as a three-dimensional space once again, with the present as a two-dimensional plane with two axes. In studying the variables of human beings and memes, the axes become physical and virtual space. The third dimension is time, which we can ignore for the time being. By freezing a moment in time, like a photograph, we get a two-dimensional diagram which makes it much easier to examine the internal relationships of any given society. We can choose to fix either people or memes on the diagram, which makes it possible for us to study the relations between them.

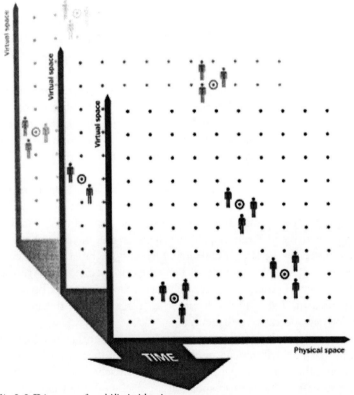

Fig.2.2 *Diagram of mobilistic identity*

In our current example we can fix the memes, spreading them evenly across the diagram. What we discover when we study the concentrations of people is that these actors, the citizens of the society in question, are only attracted to a limited number of the available memes, and gather around these in noticeable clusters. They build their social identity on their relation to these clusters. The members of one cluster are "us", the members of the other clusters are "the others". It is important to remember that the actors do not choose their relations to the various clusters freely; their positions in respect to both the physical and virtual axis reflect a fact, not an ambition or aspiration.

At every frozen moment in time we can see that the largest cluster on the diagram is gathered around the meme which makes up the kernel of what we have called the assumed value of the governing paradigm. Under feudalism the court is one such central cluster, with the monarchy as its focal meme. Another strong feudal cluster is the church, grouped around the religious meme. Under capitalism trade is the most powerful cluster, with the banks and stock markets as focal memes. Other capitalist clusters of note are the apparatus of the state, grouped around the meme of representative democracy, and the academic sphere around the meme of science. In informational society the most important forum will be the Nexus, the portal of power, the linking node in the all-encompassing net. Gathered around this function will be the most important cluster of the informational paradigm: the netocratic network.

When we add the third dimension, time, we get a hologram. The first thing to notice is the rapid succession of memes: comprehensive production of them, and an almost similarly comprehensive destruction. Naturally it is the memes which are surrounded by the largest clusters which survive most easily. People vote with their feet. Out of all the religious memes that struggled for survival in Ancient Rome, only two are left today: Christianity and Judaism. The others fell victim to forgetfulness, the historical equivalent of creative destruction.

But the fact that certain memes prove to be attractive does not mean that they will remain unchanged through the centuries: on the contrary, they have to adapt and modify themselves continuously, to such an extent that we can speak of a ceaseless flow of new memes which have their basis in old ones. Most memes die and disappear, leaving space for new ones. At the same time, the memes which do survive have to adapt constantly, recreating themselves, in order to survive. The closer a new meme finds itself to an important cluster, or, in other words, the better suited a new meme happens to be to fulfil the needs and desires of the cluster, the stronger its chances of surviving in the ongoing struggle. Let us take one example: Bill Gates, a person who happens to be the world's richest man, was born in Seattle, a city which both physically, virtually and historically is situated close to the fast-growing technological industries of California. If Bill Gates had been born as a peasant woman in sixteenth-century Madagascar, we would obviously never have heard a peep about the Microsoft meme, which in turn would have altered the historical plane on which we find ourselves at the moment.

History shows time after time that people are far too conservative and sluggish to be able to move sufficiently quickly in any meaningful quantity to gain any advantage from the changes caused by a paradigm shift. Being aware of the fact that the assumed value is in motion, or that this motion will affect other important memes and clusters, is not enough to facilitate sufficiently rapid movement in the right direction. The fact that a Madagascan peasant is aware of events in Silicon Valley does not mean that he can go ahead and set up an internet company there. When it comes to the positions of individuals on the plan we are forced to recognise that coincidence – or fate, if you prefer – is decisive.

While capitalism was making its breakthrough, the aristocracy were busy with their country estates, far from the banks and marketplaces of the cities. Members of the aristocracy were bred to regard both trade and financial management with distaste. The old dominant class was fully occupied protecting its inherited rights to its family names and estates, in spite of the fact that the value of heraldic names in wider society was sinking rapidly. The aristocracy busied itself with polishing its heraldry and compiling glorious tales of the golden age that had passed. It had missed the boat, quite simply, abandoned by the passage of time. With the development of pietism, European Christians were encouraged to handle money and were allowed to charge interest on loans. Until then, this had been the preserve of the Jewish proto-bourgeoisie. The aristocracy did not stand a chance in the struggle for power in capitalist society compared to the bourgeoisie who happened to be at the right place at the right time, a vibrant mutation with its origins in the old peasant class, well-suited from a memetic Darwinian point of view to become the dominant class of the capitalist paradigm.

An interesting and noticeable phenomenon of every paradigm shift is the establishment of a secret pact, an unholy alliance, between the old and the new dominant classes. As soon as the transfer of power is an indisputable fact, there is a peaceful and discrete handover of power which is to the benefit of both parties. This secret pact is entered into with the intention of protecting both the common and distinct interests of both groups. The instigation of the pact is often followed by a time-consuming and noisy display of various pseudo-conflicts about meaningless symbols, all with the intention of hiding the existence and purpose of the pact.

The most important function of this secret pact is to secure the monopolies on public space of both dominant classes during the paradigm shift. It is in the interests of both parties to create the greatest possible confusion, the maximum amount of fuss, so that the transfer of power can take place as quietly and efficiently as possible, without the disruptive involvement of the underclass or internal critics. A classic example of such a pact between dominant classes was the eighteenth century's marriages between the sons of the aristocracy, with their inherited titles, and the daughters of the bourgeoisie, with their inherited capital. But this process needed to be complemented with a constructed pseudo-conflict to disguise the existence of the pact. It was of vital importance that neither party appeared to be part of a conspiracy.

This was the background to the still rumbling artificial pseudo-conflict surrounding the to-be-or-not-to-be dilemma of European and Asian monarchies. The aristocracy was permitted to retain its castrated royal families and its state-subsidised opera houses in exchange for its co-operation in managing and maintaining the capitalist nation state's various historically romanticised propaganda projects. It agreed to take on the role of "disarmed oppressor". The aristocracy was permitted to run museums and similar institutions where history was revised to make the existing social structure look "natural". When members of the aristocracy had sold all their family treasures and could no longer finance life on the family estate, and the daughters of the bourgeoisie had begun to prefer rich young men from their own class to titled poverty, they were permitted to remain on their estates under the condition that these were opened to the public at weekends. They were transformed into state-subsidised historical museums, slightly run-down, picturesque destinations for bourgeois family outings and Sunday walks. The aristocratic past was presented as a charming, tragic theatre-set, against which capitalist society and its bourgeoisie could bask in their self-proclaimed perfection.

By effectively fitting muzzles to both the aristocracy and the church, the members of the bourgeoisie could set about rewriting history, as if their own class and its nation state had always existed. The social constructions of the new paradigm were presented as eternal and "natural" truths. Man became God, science his gospel, the nation his paradise, and capital his holy instrument of power. This was the means of defence for the bourgeoisie's monopoly on power, history, language and even thought itself. The eternal truths of capitalism could not, would not and, indeed, never needed to be questioned. Behind this traffic in symbolism is hidden the important role of the secret pact in the development of the power structures of the new paradigm. As a result of the new dominant class arriving first at, or rather happening to find itself in proximity to the new central value, it was able to make maximum use of this advantage. This it did by accumulating vast wealth, generated by the assumed constant of the new paradigm, and all with the blessing of the old dominant class. The new dominant class achieved this coup de grâce by establishing a monopoly on public space, and then using this position first to deny the very existence of the new underclass, and later to deny its members any possible rights.

As soon as it became clear that land could be protected with the help of laws and a monopoly on power in the hands of the nobility, the fundamental basis for feudalism, the aristocracy took control of all available land. Not even the most remote woodland castle was left out, because it could then have been used as a future base for the peasants' demands for land-ownership. In much the same way the bourgeoisie, with the blessing of the aristocracy, were able to spend the first decades of industrialism plundering the countryside, and various colonies, of raw materials and labour, and running factories operated by slaves at an enormous profit. There is little reason to believe that the new dominant class of informationalism, the netocracy, will behave any differently to previous dominant classes. The increasingly marginalised bourgeoisie will come to be willing participants in this perpetually recurring historical drama, this time under the direction of the netocracy: a drama which has at its heart the denial of the existence of the new underclass.

In the same way that the aristocracy instigated the most important legal preconditions for the expansion of capitalism, state protection of private fortunes, the increasingly marginalised bourgeoisie will use its control of parliamentary legislation and the police to legitimise and protect the most important components in the construction of netocratic power: patents and copyrights. The principal precondition for the success of the new dominant class is therefore, ironically, a gift from the old dominant class. The morality of the new age is created around this handover of the historical baton. Just as the aristocracy and the bourgeoisie once enshrined the inviolability of private property in old laws, so the bourgeoisie and the netocracy are today united in their call for copyright as an essential defence of civilisation. Immense amounts of "science" are produced with the aim of proving its blessing for humanity as a whole. Within this strategy it is clear that any form of power which will not be helped by copyright is "immoral", which the legal monopoly of the bourgeoisie will immediately interpret as "criminal".

But, sooner or later, the secret pact of the dominant classes will be put to the test by the merciless demands of mobilistic analysis that any force can only be defined by an opposing force. We cannot talk about a new dominant class without at the same time defining a new underclass. The dominant class will use every available means to assert its right to total control over the assumed constant. But because this constant only attains its value by being recognised by the new class which is subordinate to the new dominant class, there is conflict about its value. The dominant class's relation to the assumed constant is based upon its desire to possess the constant, and to ensure its control over it. The underclass, on the other hand, is made up of those whose activities, in the form of production or consumption, or whose coincidental position on the historical map gives the assumed constant its value. The new dominant class's monopoly on public space ceases to exist when the new underclass becomes aware of itself, organises itself, makes demands and challenges the existing order. The master/slave relationship becomes tense and uncertain. Thus a new conflict commences, full of constantly recurring trials of strength, interrupted by temporary truces, only to explode into activity once again. It is from this conflict, this fight for power among the classes, that society and history gain their momentum.

When the aristocracy passed on the baton of real power to the bourgeoisie, there was a contemporaneous and ongoing formal transfer of power from absolute monarchy to directly elected parliament. There is never any comparable historical meeting between the underclasses of two different paradigms. The reason for this is partly that the old underclass is the main recruiting ground for the new dominant class, and partly that the two underclasses have no point of contact, which, ironically, is precisely because they are not in conflict with one another. Everything points to the same thing happening in conjunction with the breakthrough of informationalism. The new underclass, rendered practically invisible by the new dominant class, will long remain an unknown force, even to itself. In a society which is in every other respect overflowing with information, there is a telling lack of information on this subject. It is, once again, a matter of control over the production of ideology.

3.

PLURARCHAL SOCIETY – THE DEATH OF ETATISM AND THE CRISIS OF DEMOCRACY

ACCORDING TO THE CLASSICAL Marxist view of history, the rulers of any given society exert power over their subordinates by their control of the means of production. Power is the act of owning and directing the apparatus of production. The principal and overriding task of culture, seen from the Marxist perspective, is to justify the existing power structure by presenting it as "natural". The main occupation of feudal society was the production and distribution of agricultural products. Power was intrinsically linked to the control of land and its produce, and the dominant class of the feudal era, the aristocracy, was continually concerned with this: the control and legitimisation of its control of the land. Culture was put to good use keeping the underclass of peasants in its place. The existing order of things, the structure of social hierarchy and the aristocracy's limitless right to do whatever it wanted with the land were constantly presented as "natural" and eternally valid. This view of the world did not tolerate any alternatives.

The aristocracy's mandate to exercise unlimited power over the means of production was of divine origin, and was derived from a religion that was tailor-made for that purpose: defending the right to ownership of land. In feudal Europe, this part was played by Christianity. Stained glass windows in churches related improving stories in which obedience to one's masters was rewarded, while independence and/or self-interest were punished. Religion performed an absorbing function at every level; it sucked up, diluted and suppressed all forms of social unrest and innovative thinking. By attracting the most incisive critics of the system from the underclass and awarding them prestigious positions within its organisation, the Church maintained a flexible buffer between ruler and subject.

Intellectual life in the feudal period was diverted to the monasteries, where monks and nuns with literary talents were occupied with eternal discussion of insoluble theological dilemmas, and with the manual reproduction of biblical texts which were then stored in aristocratic libraries where they gathered dust; all with the ultimate goal of negating the critical edge of their intellect and directing it instead towards the maintenance of the existing power structure. If any monk showed himself to be interested in power and glory for his own sake, there was always the colourful cardinal's garb with which to placate him. Potential leaders of unrest were dressed in cowls or cassocks from an early age, thereby reinforcing the relentless suppression of the underclass.

All that was right emanated from an almighty God, and below him a holy hierarchy was constructed. God's appointed representative on earth was the monarch, whose religious and worldly authority alike were formalised in the laws that he himself caused to be produced and promulgated. The monarch, in turn, gave guarantees to the aristocracy regarding its privileges, by granting this dominant class a monopoly on the use of force. This monopoly encompassed both a right and a duty to God and the monarch to exert force to crush any attempt at armed revolt from the underclass. In exchange for this monopoly on force, which was also a concrete guarantee of control over the means of production, the sons of the aristocracy swore an oath of allegiance to the crown and assumed the role of officers when the monarch ended up in conflict with other monarchs and chose to go to war.

Feudal society was upheld by this alliance between monarch and aristocracy, anchored by the Church and embodied by the army. This led to the establishment of what every dominant class in every age has sought: social stability. The status quo was the principal and common interest of monarch and aristocracy. Every threat to the existing structure had to be smothered at birth. So an almost hermetically sealed system of society was created, where there were no opportunities to establish alternative centres of power from which the ruling structure could be attacked or even questioned. Consequently, there were no threats within the system itself; only a revolutionary alteration of the basic technological premises of feudalism could achieve noticeable movement and upheaval within the hierarchy, which in turn would eventually, and inevitably, lead to an entirely new society. In order for this to take place, there had to be a genuine paradigm shift.

The high status of religion during the feudal period did not rest upon any particularly widespread interest in existential matters among the population as a whole, but was the result of the aristocracy's intensive production of ideology, the purpose of which was to sanction the dominant class's unlimited right to own and preside over land. The religious message was the same everywhere: that every single piece of land had been given in perpetuity by God to one specially chosen family, whose inalienable right (and duty) it was to pass that land from generation to generation. The conservative religion of the Church, the laws put in place by the monarch, and the aristocracy's monopoly on force acted in concert to deny the peasants any effective means of questioning or opposing the feudal hierarchy and the forces in power. Land and inheritance were all-important to the aristocracy. The fact that property, rather than capital or knowledge, was passed down in inheritance within the family was the single most important prop of the dominant class. Property and the family name were consequently intimately connected; they were inherited as a package, and combined to form the most important symbol of feudalism: the family coat of arms, which was therefore imbued with exceptionally high status-value.

The question of whether or not there is a god is very much a modern one. The dominant classes have always been aware of the fact that God's invisibility is a problem. God's absence from the Earth creates a vacuum which must be filled by a representative to combat unease in society. There has always been a need for an ultimate arbiter whose advice could be sought in moral and existential questions. So whether or not God exists does not matter, as long as there is someone who can take his place. The most important thing for the aristocracy was clearly that this representative came from the right circles and served its own interests. Hence the appearance of the monarch in history. The monarch has always had divine qualities attributed to him, ever since the expressed divine lineage of the Egyptian pharaohs – which led to their having to marry their sisters. The status of the monarch should not be, and could not be questioned, because, like the right to inherit property, it was one of the corner-stones of religion. In this way, the monarchy and aristocracy co-existed in a balanced climate of religious and legal terror. No movement was possible; neither party could seriously question the authority or rights of the other without simultaneously calling into doubt its own privileges.

This balance of terror acted to suppress open confrontation, but created at the same time a perpetual cold war. As long as external threats seemed to be under control, there was a continual, low-level conflict between monarch and aristocracy. The monarch did his best to divide the many-headed aristocracy in order to be able to control it, whilst being fully aware that an aristocracy that was too weak would threaten his own position, because the peasants would be able to rebel under such circumstances. The aristocracy, on the other hand, sought internal unity in order to be able to control, as best it could, the isolated figure of the monarch, who was relatively weak in resources. Despite the fact that the combined power of the aristocracy was immense, its relation to the monarchy was problematical. It had to accept that it could not depose and appoint new monarchs at will, because that would undermine respect for the divine right to inheritance of land, and thereby weaken the position of the aristocracy itself. Therefore the aristocracy was forced to accept that inheritance of the throne was also sanctioned by God, which in turn strengthened the position of the monarch in the conflict between them. This explains the gradual increase in strength of the European monarchs from the late middle ages, relative to that of their aristocratic subjects, in line with the fact that their thrones, like the Egyptian pharaohs' and Roman Emperors' before them, came to be inherited.

The fundamental requirement for the belief system that emerged victorious from the Darwinian meme-war for religious power during the feudal period was that it must rest upon an all-encompassing, strictly authoritarian hierarchy of power. This meant that the monarch was able to stand above the aristocracy, and the aristocracy, in turn, above the peasants. God had to stand above the Church, and the Church above its congregation. The monarch's unlimited power over the judicial system gave him a weapon with which he could keep the aristocracy in its place. If ever he was in a tight corner, all he had to do was repeal the aristocracy's monopoly on force by making it legal for peasants to bear arms. At a stroke, this would have enabled the peasantry to depose the aristocracy and, if their rebellion succeeded, be rewarded by the monarch with aristocratic privileges, including the right to own land. This was the real-politik of feudalism. We can conclude that history, once all the palace revolutions and peasant revolts were over, always returned to a hierarchy where the monarch stood above the aristocracy, which in turn stood above the peasantry – so long as the central value in society was tied to agriculture. The power exerted by the peasants was restricted, in reality, to the few small corners of life which were so insignificant and peripheral that they were of no interest to the aristocracy. This can be compared to the way in which the impoverished masses of the capitalist era have been forced to pick at the scraps left over by the dominant class.

Just as the aristocracy once needed a monarch at the apex of the hierarchy of power, in his capacity as God's representative on earth, so the bourgeoisie, the dominant class of capitalist society, needed a representative for Man, the god of the new age. And this zenith of the capitalist hierarchy, this bearer of ultimate responsibility for making Man both obedient and worthy of the role of God's successor, was the State. In the same way as the idea of God had died and been replaced by the idea of Man, so had the idea of monarchy died or been down-graded to a purely decorative function, and its place taken by the State.

Like the aristocracy before it, the bourgeoisie was highly conscious of the vacuum presented by the physical absence of the gods. This new god, Man, had no tangible shape either, but was more an abstraction, a representation of an idea, a phantom – which is why it was of vital importance to find a more or less credible representative which was reliable and could watch over the interests of the new dominant class. This new representative was the State in general, and parliament in particular; this was the voice of the people. A massive historical castling manoeuvre led to the displacement of the monarch: a law-making individual representing a fictional collective, by parliament: a law-making collective representing a fictional individual. Feudalism was replaced by and subordinated to capitalism, and the paradigm shift was a fact.

Christianity was the religion that was best suited as a guiding instrument for the aristocracy, and which therefore succeeded in the Darwinian meme-war between various different belief systems that was conducted during the introductory phase of feudalism. In the same way, a winner gradually crystallised out of the memetic Darwinian war between a mass of possible ideological mutations during the transition from feudalism to capitalism. The new paradigm demanded a new myth, and at its service it had humanism, ready to replace one fictional figure, God, with another, Man. Humanism was perfectly suited to the new circumstances, and became the perfect guiding instrument for the bourgeoisie, which now had to try to hold down the new underclass of capitalist society: the workers.

Like Christianity before it, humanism was a faith that presented itself as "the truth of the new age". Because God was no longer current, or, at least, not as unquestioned as before, Man was now at the apex of the value hierarchy, as holy as God had once been. Language, the capacity of the human species to think and express itself verbally, now magically accessible in mass-produced publications, was the starting point for a new, fictional structure where Man, as a result of this ability, was raised above and was of higher value than Beasts. But man was not born Man – because that would mean that humanism was an extremely poor instrument of power – but had to be educated and shaped over a long period, involving a great deal of effort, in order to reach the goal. For safety's sake, this was made a lifelong project. The State was appointed as a strict overseer, and the Market as the immutable yardstick.

This is the explanation for the creation of such phenomena as hospitals, prisons and educational establishments, as well as various political and academic institutions; their purpose was to define Man, and to correct undesirable deviations from the ideal "natural" state within the population. Capitalism has shown a sensational capacity for innovation in its constant production of new sicknesses, crimes and other defects among the citizens of its society, all of which require care and attention. The system has been so practically instituted that each new innovation creates a new market for therapists in white coats, and other experts, thereby granting them increased power. The perfect citizen has been one who has motivated him or herself to strive to imitate the ever more diffuse and unattainable ideal of Man; one who has been obsessed by the notion of living correctly, in accordance with the advice of the experts. All this to create a maximally effective producer during working hours and an insatiable consumer during leisure time; a citizen who gratefully spends every waking hour of the day on the constantly spinning hamster's wheel of capitalism.

Just as independently-minded individuals from the underclass were rendered harmless during the feudal era by being occupied with eternal theological questions in monasteries, the gifted children of the working class were placed behind school-desks, where their future was staked out by and within the social sciences. The entire project reached its culmination during the late capitalist period of the twentieth century, with the newly hatched idea of necessary "self-realisation", which led humanism into its final extreme phase, where every individual citizen was encouraged to become his or her own all-seeing moral policeman. With this, the supreme ideology of capitalism reached its climax. This explains why the bourgeoisie have defended holy humanism with such frenetic fervour against all attacks, real and imagined, and why it has been raised up as an eternal axiom, a religion. Almost every political party, from the Republicans in the USA to the East German Communist Party, has identified itself as humanist. It's the same old story: getting the ideology that legitimises power to appear "natural". It's simply a question of the bourgeoisie's own position as the dominant class of capitalist society, and how this is connected to humanism's position as the supreme ideology. In this light, capitalist society does not look like democracy in any real sense, but a humanist dictatorship.

The bourgeoisie sought what every dominant elite seeks: social stability, the undisturbed exercising of power, a social climate which is downright hostile to any imaginable alternative centre of power. In the same way as the aristocracy long before had sought to maintain the status quo, the new dominant class tried to create a closed social system; and, just as feudalism managed to absorb its own inherent contradictions, the immense tensions within capitalist society never posed any real threat to the hierarchy of power. It was only when the fundamental technological preconditions of capitalism underwent dramatic change that anything seriously affected it. It was time for another paradigm shift.

Because the capitalist system could not function without at least a semblance of a connection to the working masses, the entire legitimacy of the state rested upon the will of the people as it was assumed to be represented and expressed in parliament. The franchise was extended to avoid revolution. The idea that parliament represented the true will of the people was elevated to an axiom which could therefore never be questioned. A balance of terror was established between Ruler and Slave, and in order to consolidate its power the bourgeoisie made sure to create a mutual dependency between its own class and parliament.

Once the State had become an actor amongst all the others in the capitalist market, its existence dependent upon the tax exacted from labour and capital, parliament became subordinate to the capitalist system, and was incapable of questioning the fundamental basis of this without risking its own activities. Co-operation was paid for with money and privilege. Only advocates of a strong State were elected to parliament, because anything else was impossible by definition. The elected representatives may have defined themselves as right- or left-wing, but this was relatively unimportant; what mattered was that parliamentary debates never questioned the fundamental political idea of the bourgeoisie: Etatism. Governments may have changed colour from one season to the next, but the governing elite maintained its secure grip on power.

The political ideologies that have characterised bourgeois parliamentarism are really only different nuances of the same supreme ideology: Etatism, expressing a fundamental belief in Project Man, and in the historical task of the State to carry out this project. In order for them to exert power in peace and quiet, it has been in the Statists' interests to give the impression that every conceivable political force is contained beneath the parliamentary umbrella. This was what the dominant class had done during the feudal era: attract potential trouble-makers with offers of attractive positions close to the trough. In order to simulate a plethora of ideas and genuine contradictions, every little rhetorical difference between the parties' programmes was blown up to grotesque proportions. It was all a matter of making as much noise as possible in order to maintain the Statists' actual monopoly on the public arena.

Like every other collective, parliaments are based upon a common programme, at the same time as their activity is intended to conceal this basic fact. The strong State stamps everything that isn't Etatism or praise of a strong State as extremism, because this is part of the game. Great contradictions within Etatism are suggested in order to conceal the fact that its many different groupings are all co-operating to suppress the appearance of alternative oppositional forces. In actual fact all of them – conservatives, liberals and socialists, in both their democratic and totalitarian forms – subscribe to the same basic idea: that a strong State is necessary for the survival of a good, "natural" society. For many years the political parties were successful in their common manoeuvre for control of public opinion. But with the breakthrough of informationalism in the 1970s the situation was dramatically altered.

The most characteristic sign of a society on the brink of transition from capitalism to informationalism is a general medialisation. Before the breakthrough of interactive media in the 1990s, the media were characterised by a late-capitalist industrial structure. The leading media of this era, radio and, above all, television, were perfect instruments for the institutions of the bourgeoisie to transmit its message to the masses unchallenged – in the USA in the form of an oligopoly in which the largest industrial companies owned television stations, and in Europe principally in the form of state-run television monopolies. But with the pluralisation of the media – mainly as a result of the advertising industry's demands for a greater number of more specialised advertising markets – it was gradually released from the demand to play along with the ideological propaganda of Etatism. The media began to live their own life, forming the basis for a new power structure, and began instead to assume several of the characteristics of the informationalist paradigm's new dominant class: the netocracy.

As the medialisation of society has accelerated, representatives of the rapidly growing entertainment and media have become more willing to attack the interest groups that they perceive as blocking the path towards their own independence and growing power. Since the media are increasingly managing to exist independently of elected politicians, it is hardly surprising that politicians have been the main targets for sharp-shooting journalists. The media's strategy in their battle with the State is constructed around a fiction: the myth of the electorate's contempt for politicians. The core of this myth is the idea that the general population of late-capitalist society regards elected politicians as a group of corrupt crooks who are feathering their own nests at the expense of voters/tax-payers, and who consciously fail to carry out the tasks they have been elected to perform. Every nation has its own cultural variation of this myth; the politicians of every country are perceived as breaking the most sacred values of their particular culture. So American politicians are continually unfaithful to their wives, whereas their European counterparts engage in credit-card fraud, vote-rigging and tax evasion. So the citizens are turning their backs on politics in disgust – if the media are to be believed.

The problem is that this is a self-fulfilling prophecy: By constantly talking about this supposed contempt for politicians, the media have created a media phenomenon which, through its very existence, fuels demand for shocking reports. The concrete substance of all these reports is restricted to the fact that voter turn-out in elections in most western democracies has gradually fallen since the 1960s. Contempt for politicians has been elevated to an axiom, an irrefutable truth. Every politician or media-player who questions its existence is regarded as a heretic, an opponent who must be subdued, because he or she is standing in the way of the overriding ambitions of the media. It is not hard to see how public opinion and laws alike are constructed and shaped by the media. Politicians are producers, the voters consumers, and the media have appropriated the increasingly important role of curators of the political arena, and have therefore been able to exercise, according to netocratic principles, total control over the political process within informational society.

Everything to do with politics now takes place on the conditions of the media. The standard-bearers of representative democracy are in this respect completely powerless and can do nothing but adapt to the orders of their new masters. A political event which does not attract media attention is by definition a non-event. This means, naturally, that any last remnants of serious politics are confined to the shadows of media-driven dramaturgy, an apparatus whose main attraction is contempt for politicians. The fact that this is never questioned does not mean that it actually exists, merely that it is a "truth" which is popular within the circles whose purposes it serves: the netocratic media that have taken command of the public arena.

Let's suppose that contempt for politicians in its accepted form actually does exist. It ought to disappear or, at the very least, subside noticeably whenever a supposedly corrupt politician has been exposed and replaced. It would be a simple question of electing the right person to the right position. But this is not the case. There is no great difference in voter turn-out in elections whether the candidates are new and unsullied by scandal, or the same old faces. So this supposed contempt is not directed at any particular politician, hence it cannot be contempt for politicians that is the cause for the steady decline in voter turn-out. The explanation must be sought elsewhere. We can conclude that contempt for politicians is a myth, and that the people who created this myth probably have a vested interest in seeing it survive and appear to be "natural". This leads to a considerably more interesting question than the extent to which voters hold their politicians in contempt, which is the question of how this myth arose, and whose interests are served by its spread?

It is a question of power. If we compare the level of voter turn-out in different elections for different forms of political body, a clear pattern emerges. There is a direct link between power and turn-out: the more power is up for grabs, or, to put it another way, the more power is connected to the position or body to which people are being elected, then the greater the level of voter interest. This means that the crisis of democracy has nothing to do with a loss of faith in active politicians per se, but is mainly to do with a growing concern about the increasing impotence of politicians. The silent protest of a growing number of couch-potatoes is not directed towards politicians' abuse of power, but towards their loss of power.

This fact is, unfortunately, not particularly sexy, and does not fit in with media dramaturgy; it does not provide any attention-grabbing headlines, and it does not provide ammunition for a bout of populist mud-slinging. And, above all, it does not serve the interests of the media. So, instead, we are supplied with a constant stream of propaganda telling us about the righteous contempt that the people feel for the corrupt political class, which only serves to weaken the position of politicians still further, which in turn leads to a new round of gauntlet-running in the media. This process continues in a vicious circle, the inevitable culmination of which is the death of representative democracy, the complete impotence of politicians, and a hyper-real media dictatorship. This process is strengthened by feedback. Through the use of opinion polls, whose questions are obviously phrased by the media to serve their own purposes, the population is told what it thinks, and what it is "natural" to think. Then the media go on to show how adaptable politicians are adapting to this norm, or are allowing themselves to be adapted, and so the process goes on and on, ad infinitum. The investigations of the mass-media are, on their most profound level, investigations into the mass-media themselves. Statistics which purport to represent public opinion are actually the tools used by the media to manufacture opinion.

The sheer absurdity of this whole performance becomes obvious when the media start to judge candidates to all political positions according to purely media-driven criteria. The candidates' qualifications and competence to occupy the position in question are quite subordinate; the principal concern is that the candidates "give good media". The main consideration is whether or not they appear to be useful from a dramaturgical point of view, or, in other words, whether or not they can be exploited by the media in their constant search for new lambs to the slaughter, new sensations and scandals to fuel the headlines. The fact that attention is paid to this – the extent to which politicians are "media-friendly" – during the initial selection process illustrates the fact that the media are not content merely to reflect and cover the political process, but are actively directing and writing the script for it.

Political journalists are not concerned with politics as such, but with medial dramaturgy. Political questions are often far too complicated to come across well in the media, which is why anything that looks at all complicated is side-lined to provide space for artificial oppositions, symbolic questions and the private lives of politicians. Politicians willingly submit to get on intimate terms with the media's consumers – what else are they to do? To refuse would be tantamount to writing themselves out of the script of the political soap-opera. The boundary between politics and gossip is increasingly being erased. The politicians of the new age are like cabaret artists whose speciality is what the American sociologist Richard Sennett has called "psychic striptease". In other words, they make political capital out of their private lives. Intimacy attracts headlines which attract attention. The consequence of this growing phenomenon is that the feelings of public figures on this and that end up in the media spotlight while serious issues that demand time and thought are sidelined. But this increased intimacy also brings an increased risk for a media backlash. Being able to master the difficult art of personal exposure has become one of the most important keys for political success.

The process we are discussing is therefore created, controlled, reflected and "examined" by one and the same group – the media – and this system tolerates no scrutiny, analysis or criticism from the outside. Under the circumstances it is easy to believe that the goal of the entire apparatus is to serve the interests of the media. It is worth remembering here that those in positions of power within the media are not appointed by the people (whose interests are continually invoked), as politicians are – at least on a purely formal level. They are selected from within their own circles, hand-picked from internal networks, and given the task of serving the closed lodges and guilds of the netocrats. This is at the heart of the true crisis of democracy: the netocracy's assumption of power by stealth.

But because we are in a transitional phase there is still life in the old myths. The bourgeoisie is still cultivating the notion that representative democracy is immortal, and seems to have got grist to that particular mill from the collapse of the communist dictatorships of eastern Europe. The American social theoretician Francis Fukuyama has investigated the possibility that the historical process has come to a halt at the station of liberal democracy, but, at the same time, he has been unable to resist sowing the seeds of Nietzschean doubt: don't the equality and stability that crop up in every after-dinner speech actually imply an untenable stagnation?

Within the myth of representative democracy there is the idea of the excellence of civil society, whose dark-side is the fact that political apathy is a taboo subject. This cannot be discussed; silence shrouds the fact that those who possess the electoral franchise that so many earlier advocates of democracy fought and died for are declining to make their way to polling stations in ever increasing numbers, for the simple reason that politicians are increasingly impotent and powerless at the side of the arena in which the battle between well-organised interest groups is taking place. Obviously the media cannot be blamed – and cannot assume blame – for this flagrant lack of interest in politics: how could the media be in the wrong when it is they that are judge and jury in the case? Nor can the clients, the media's consumers, the people who must be entertained, be blamed, if audience figures are to be maintained. No, the ones who end up taking the blame are the naïve and defenceless elected politicians. Everything is the fault of politicians, but politics itself is supposed to be in great shape. This is the consciously constructed paradox that the netocracy is using to help it carry out its informationalist coup against the mortally wounded State.

The old myths of liberalism about the immortality of representative democracy and the excellence of civil society are based on the false assumption that these institutions are, once and for all, the best possible structures, which can therefore never be shaken or questioned. Nothing could be more wrong. The bizarre and tragic fact is that these same myths are managing to maintain their hold on a society that is undergoing a tornado of change. In actual fact the advance of informationalism has radically altered the conditions for the maintenance of society and democracy. Since the French social theoretician Alexis de Tocqueville enthusiastically reported home to Europe during the 1840s about how American democracy rested securely upon a network of interest groups, civil society has stood as the ideal and the precondition for a functional democracy. But the keyword here is network. When we enter a new historical phase, where social networks no longer have a complementary function, but instead dominate political development, the preconditions are dramatically altered. Tocqueville's civil society, the network of interest groups, has realised its potential thanks to informationalism, and has been transformed into an insatiable young cuckoo, a parasite on society, a reckless multi-headed monster, the jailer and overlord of representative democracy.

In the USA this network of interest groups, the lobby groups, have at least had the good taste to finance their activities themselves. In Europe, on the other hand, they are funded, via taxation, by the institution that they are fighting against, the State. If you examine this system from an informationalist perspective, you see how the new underclass is, in effect, financing the new dominant class's political lobby-groups through the tax system. As a result, representative democracy is effectively under attack from several directions at once. The rapid development of technology has resulted in the networks of interest groups becoming far more powerful, and their ability to exert political pressure has reached the extent where they have practically taken over and are actually in control of the political process. Forget the idea of one man, one vote. What matters now is being initiated into the right networks in order to be able to influence important decisions in any way that is not purely symbolic. The principal has become more like: one member of a network, one vote.

The new muscle of the lobby groups and advisory NGOs becomes even more powerful because of the fact that the working methods of these groups are perfectly suited to the general medialisation of society, which has created an unholy alliance between the interest groups and the mighty media. As soon as anyone from the marginalised political class tries to direct a specific issue in a particular direction, the affected lobby groups and advisory NGOs conjure up a speedy and pertinent expression of opinion, or, in other words: an artificial and well-directed rabble which, if necessary, goes on the attack both physically and virtually against the political project in question. From Greenpeace to legitimised white coats, from lawyers' associations to various netocratic mailing lists, concern and outrage can be arranged and produced to order. Time and again, the political process is paralysed, until in the end it subordinates itself entirely to the control of interest groups. These are in a position to dictate proposals themselves, in return for the poor politicians avoiding abuse from the media.

The only lingering function of the politician will be purely ceremonial; acting out a Punch and Judy show in the media, stamping documents which he has neither written nor understood on any level other than that of catchy slogans. In capitalist society the downgraded monarch had to be content with cutting blue ribbons to open shopping centres. In the same way, the power wielded by politicians under the netocrats will be limited to the use of their names to confirm and formalise decisions that have in practice been taken by other people whom the politicians have no real chance of influencing. But does this transition to an informationalist political structure necessarily mean that the principal of democracy is dead?

The explosive expansion of the internet has led many people to hope for a renaissance of democracy. Thanks to the fact that the technological preconditions exist for the citizens – at home, in the workplace, in libraries, etc – to express instantly their opinion on all manner of political issues, the net, according to this idea, could function as a sort of virtual parliament on both a local and national level. The net would do away with the need for representative middle-men and, therefore, not only function as the saviour of democracy in the face of media tyranny, but would also embody the fulfilment of definitive democracy, a liberal utopia. It's a fine thought. The problem is that the net does not make allowances for and does not recognise physical geography and its limitations. The identities around which people gathered and made decisions under capitalism were based upon preconditions that were directly connected to the old paradigm and which are now completely irrelevant. This means that the fundamental condition for a net democracy – that the group of people discussing and eventually taking decisions also has an interest in participating in the political process within a limited geographic area, a country, for instance – no longer exists. Why should people on the net engage in national political issues when the idea of the nation itself has collapsed?

The nation state is a fundamental part of the capitalist paradigm, and therefore has no credibility in informational society, where communication is built upon tribal identities and subcultures that are constructed according to completely different principals. This explains why wars between nations have ceased during the transition to informationalism, and have been replaced by conflicts between interest groups such as companies and pressure groups. People are simply no longer prepared to sacrifice their lives for a nation, just as the people of capitalism were no longer prepared to sacrifice their lives for feudal ideas like God or the monarch. The dream of a clinical war with no casualties, which has been nurtured during the latter days of capitalism (the Gulf War, the conflict in Kosovo, etc), must therefore be regarded as a direct result of the political opinion that defence of the nation or democracy is no longer worth any form of sacrifice. The difference between Hollywood's action films and postmodern war is negligible. War is only acceptable if it is reduced to a video-game with a predetermined victory for the "good guys". The nation has been reduced to a stage-set.

In the virtual world, virtual identities are important, which means that a new system for participation in the political process will have to be constructed, one which takes account of this fact. Parliamentary elections could certainly be conducted over the net, whereby everyone with the franchise could type in their personal code instead of going to the ballot box, but the democratic basis of democracy – broad debate in which all interested parties within a certain geographic area air their opinions on a specific issue – has now vanished. On the net everyone seeks out people of like mind, and constructs a new virtual space with them, free of the conflicts in and about physical space. No-one seeks out a group with which they have nothing in common. Ironically, the possibility offered by the net to find like-minded people, and to avoid people with whom we want no contact, also makes the net useless as a means of defending democracy.

The political structure which is developing on the net is fundamentally different from capitalist democracy. The netocrats' ever-present ability to leave the environment in which they find themselves, to move on if the current situation does not suit them, creates the preconditions for the growth of an entirely new and extremely complex political system: a plurarchy. The definition of a plurarchy in its purest form is a system in which every individual player decides over him or herself, but lacks the ability and opportunity to decide over any of the other players. The fundamental notion of democracy, whereby the majority decides over the minority when differences of opinion occur, is therefore impossible to maintain. On the net everyone is master of him or herself, for better or worse. This means that all collective interests, not least the maintenance of law and order, will come under intense pressure. A pure plurarchy means that it is impossible to formulate the conditions for a judicial state. The difference between legality and criminality ceases to exist.

This creates a society which it is almost impossible to get an overview of, in which all significant political decisions are taken within exclusive, closed groups, with no access to anyone outside them. Already during the late-capitalist period, the judicial system and the national banks of Europe and North America have left the democratic arena and become expert-led institutions, subordinate to the lords of the new order: judiciocrats within the field of law, and national-economic prophets. Political decisions are no longer taken through elections, in parliament or even in referenda on the net, but within closed networks whose members, like the members of medieval guilds, are selected from within their own ranks. Netocratic principals are replacing statist ones. Measurements of strength are replacing ideologies. The new ruling class that we are witnessing the birth of is not interested in democracy other than as a nostalgic curiosity. The ideological apparatus of the netocracy is now concerned with making this entire process appear "natural".

4.

INFORMATION, PROPAGANDA AND ENTERTAINMENT

IN THE BEGINNING WAS not the word. That came later. And for a long time it had quite different meanings to those we use today. The Latin word "information" has two lexical definitions: firstly "representation", "depiction"; secondly "explanation", "interpretation". So the term relates to the intellect and our conceptual apparatus. When Cicero uses the verb "informare", he uses it to describe a sophisticated mental activity: to give something a form, to bring matter to life with a sort of active vision, ennobling it in the process. Form and matter were perceived as being in dialectic opposition to each other, and could be united, according to this way of looking at things, in a synthesis which has the character of an act of creation. Matter + form = life, according to the Aristotelian formula. This was of great interest to the thinkers of the age, but it was not possible to discern any direct link to the economy or to society in general. This sort of abstract reasoning was not something that greatly concerned the man in the street. The English noun "information" appeared during the Middle Ages, but did not attract much attention for many centuries.

A shift in meaning gradually occurred, unnoticed, but without the term thereby acquiring any greater status or particularly useful function in the eyes of the general populace; rather the opposite, in fact. During the first half of the twentieth century, when capitalism was in full bloom, information was something you looked up in a reference book or stored in files and archives: facts, details about one thing or another, either more or less interesting. It might be a matter of numbers, names, addresses, dates and so on. Information was handled by lowly civil servants, or in the less glamorous departments of larger businesses. There was no mention of "information theory" or "information technology", and a career in the management of information was scarcely anything to boast about.

Since then, there has been a swift and thorough shift in meaning, and the status of the term has risen dramatically. Information, formerly regarded as a dull but necessary lubricant in the production of goods and services, is now generally thought to be the hottest product of the entire economy. But that's not all: information theory has established itself as an overwhelming, intellectual metastructure, the fundamental ideas of which have penetrated deep into a whole list of other important sciences, and which, to a large extent, determines the world-view which is taking shape within the new social and cultural paradigm. Technological information is today regarded as the very essence of the body of society, in the same way that genetic information is the key to biology. The economy revolves around information – indeed, life itself is a gigantic, endlessly complex and refined process of verification where information is stored and transported within and between us fragile individuals.

The shift in definition of the word "information" began in the USA during the 1950s, in conjunction with the evolutionary leap that occurred with the development of the earliest computers. The mathematician Norbert Wiener predicted a second industrial revolution driven by "thinking" machines which had the capacity to learn from the past and their own previous experiences. The central idea of this was feedback: that the machine used its own results as new data and made the necessary adjustments itself. Wiener regarded this feedback, and the "intelligent" handling of information, as the fundamental core of life itself. These ideas, with the help of the much-vaunted achievements of these remarkable computers, had considerable impact, first within the scientific community, and later in the general populace. They were the basis for the introduction of a whole new field of research at the intersection of mathematics, linguistics, electronics and philosophy, known as AI: artificial intelligence.

The mathematic theory of information completes the transformation of the term, which now denotes a purely quantitative measurement of communicative exchange. Prior to this, the word information may not have been a guarantee of quality – the information in question may have been extremely trivial and/or irrelevant – but now the word no longer assumes any position as to whether or not it denotes nonsense and/or sheer fabrications. Information is anything that can be transformed into digital code and communicated from a transmitter to a receiver through a communications medium, that's all. From an information-theoretical perspective, there is basically no difference between a scientific formula, a nursery rhyme, or a stream of clearly false election promises from a politician under pressure.

There is nothing new in science ascribing special meanings to commonly used words; this happens, for instance, in physics, just as it does in psychology, but this usually has no significance at all for general language usage, the contexts in which the words are used are far too exclusively scientific. But this instance is different, because it is connected to the paradigm shift and the generally increasing interest in information as a marketable product. The fact that information theory has been so successful, and has formed the basis of a succession of spectacular and profitable applications, has meant that the scientific usage of the word information has leaked into journalism and all sorts of popular- and sub-cultures. Information theory and economics alike are primarily interested in information in large quantities. The larger the better.

This means that the technology itself, the capacity for storing and communicating information, has become the focus of attention, while the actual content of the information is paid relatively little attention. This is in the nature of the beast:: anyone involved in information theory is primarily concerned with the process of communication taking place in front of him, and therefore lacks any incentive to reflect upon the quality of its content, which is in any case extremely difficult to measure and build theories upon. What happens when this perspective comes to dominate the surrounding culture is that technological advances are generally seen as having the potential to solve all the social and cultural conflicts of our age. The solution is to throw information at the problem. This is the reasoning of those with blind faith, the ecstatically enthusiastic cheerleaders of the new dominant class.

This fixation with technology, the medium itself, is in its way perfectly understandable. The medium is the message, as Marshall McLuhan stated. Changes within information management and the development of communications technology are the main causes of social and cultural advancement. Without this particular insight, the development of society becomes completely incomprehensible. But information is not the same as knowledge, and as information is becoming the great staple product of the new economy, and the world is drowning in an ocean of unsorted media impulses, relevant and exclusive knowledge is becoming increasingly valuable. The advancing netocracy has realised this, in contrast to capitalism's clueless cheerleaders.

Any new, dominant technology as significant as the networking computer creates a new constellation of winners and losers. The winners consist of what Harold Innis, the great pioneer of modern communication studies, and McLuhan's mentor, calls a monopoly of knowledge. Those who control the new technology and its applications quickly accumulate considerable power, which inevitably and immediately leads to consolidation of the newly formed group, and a strong impulse to protect the interests of that group. For obvious reasons, it is impossible to expect that there would be much desire to make this exclusive knowledge accessible to a wider circle, which would devalue both the power and the privileges. One way for the winners to manipulate opinion is to claim that there are no winners, and that the blessings of the new technology will be spread evenly and fairly across society. This is when the cheerleaders, the great bulk of whom ironically consist of misled losers, come in useful.

Norbert Wiener's idea that the management of information is the greatest secret of life received the most prestigious confirmation imaginable when the biologists James Watson and Francis Crick cracked the genetic "code" in 1953, and learned how to "read" the spiralling text of the DNA molecule. The new biology has completely adopted the model and terminology of information theory, and it is practically impossible to imagine it existing without the shift to the new IT paradigm. We now realise that protein synthesis is an unusually refined example of information transference And the DNA molecule itself is nothing less than a perfect miniature computer.

The collaboration of the two disciplines had a positive impact on both their own authority within the scientific community and their status in the general consciousness. The benefits were mutual. Biology, now marching towards a brighter future, repaid its debt to information theory with interest by investing it with a sort of unfathomable, almost holy aura, a reflection of the mystique that came from the most hidden secrets of life. As a result, the metaphysics of the new paradigm began to take on clearer contours: the old mechanical world revealed by Newton, created and more or less regularly serviced by a creative god, was now replaced by a world of digital information, created by a virtual programmer.

Thanks to this, information in its new theoretical meaning also assumed a substance with almost magical powers in the world of pop-cultural perception. This has, of course, both benefited and been enthusiastically reinforced by the winners of the new paradigm and the new economy. But the transformation of information has been going on for a long time. The earliest electronic media, such as the telegraph, meant that information began to assume the form of a commodity, appearing as a mass of small "packages" that could be "sent" across great distances without any significant time-delay. The ability to receive information over great distances without delay often had economic and/or military benefits. This made new technology seem extremely attractive. But we must still bear in mind McLuhan's thesis: the medium is the message.

Speed and the abolishment of distance hastened the materialisation of information. The telegraph revolutionised the transport of information over long distances, and, as a consequence, a great deal of contemporary attention was paid to transportation and speed, while other aspects – such as interpretation, context and comprehension – were neglected. A piece of quickly transported information came to be regarded as something valuable in itself, quite regardless of what it meant or could be used for.

But the fact that technology solves one problem does not mean that all related problems disappear or become less pressing. Working out how to transport information over great distances does not mean that people know how to interpret and understand the information in a relevant context. What happens is simply that some things are left in the shade when the sun rises over a new paradigm. For every problem solved by a technology, at least one new problem usually appears. We have become used to thinking of motion as progress, but motion always has its price. Electronic information appears to be an isolated phenomenon, as individual cries, lacking resonance, in an increasingly fragmented world.

The most interesting thing, justifiably so, was the revolutionary fact that people could communicate back and forth from one end of the country to the other, whilst it was seldom questioned whether or not people actually had anything to say to the recipient. The materialising, atomising tendency is strengthened further when the information is, over the passage of time, increasingly sent in the form of images. Words still require a modicum of grammatical context if they are to mean anything at all, but images are assumed to speak for themselves. A photograph says all that need be said about the frozen moment; in the world of the photograph, everything is open to view. The present emerges in the light of a flashbulb, the past retreats into the shadows, and context dissolves into a thin haze. The value of information is high, but the knowledge content is decidedly uncertain.

When a trend-setting science such as information theory prescribes a quantitative definition of the concept of information, and when an increasing proportion of the economy is based upon large quantities of information, there is fertile soil for an almost religious information cult. The netocracy is in charge of appointing the priesthood. Technology defines all problem-solving as a question of the production and distribution of the largest possible amounts of information. Information is thrown at problems. The mechanical manipulation of information is believed to guarantee objectivity and untainted judgement – just like the camera and the photograph before it. Subjectivity is synonymous with ambiguity, unnecessary complexity and arbitrariness. It marks a deviation from the straight line, and is therefore the heretical antithesis of technology. According to the gospel of the information cult, the guarantee of freedom in our age, creativity and eternal happiness is the unrelenting, ecstatic flow of information.

But information can hardly be said to be a rare commodity today. It is difficult to suggest seriously that a significant number of the pressing problems of our age – social, political or personal – have their roots in a lack of information. The free flow of ever-increasing amounts of information, as Neil Postman and others have pointed out, is the solution to a nineteenth century problem that has already been solved. What we lack today is not information, but overview and context. The unrelenting and ecstatic flow of information is unsorted and unstructured: it must be sifted, organised and interpreted against the background of a coherent worldview if it is to be a source of knowledge and not confusion.

Multiplicity and pluralism are the highest honours of the new paradigm, obvious lodestars for the information cult. But mass and pluralism are in themselves highly problematical. How are we to choose? How do we discern useful information from nonsense and deceitful propaganda? In a dictatorship the apparatus of power strangles the flow of information with the help of censorship, thus making itself unreachable. But by flooding every channel with a torrent of incoherent information, the elite in power within a democracy – the best-organised lobby groups, the most influential media conglomerates – can effectively achieve the same result. Against any given collection of "facts", another instantly appears; against the report of any given piece of alarming scientific research, another more reassuring one appears. And so on. And afterwards everything gets back to business as usual. It looks like a vital democracy, but it is merely a spectacle for the masses. This torrent of information is thus no unforeseen phenomenon, and certainly in no way a fortuitous lottery jackpot for the citizens and consumers, but is actually a conscious strategy for maintaining social control. Powerful interest groups send out murky clouds of distracting information in order to maintain the secrecy of certain essential knowledge.

The overload of information and the lack of context are intimately linked, two aspects of the same subject. Together with other contributing factors – rapid urbanisation, the collapse of the nuclear family, the decline of traditional authorities – this state of permanent insecurity creates a value-vacuum, which is readily filled by all sorts of more or less reliable experts, all fully armed with even more information. Marriage, raising children, work-skills: everything today is in a state of great doubt. There are constant new decrees from the experts. The only sure thing, the only thing the experts have to support them, is modern science, and what that has taught us is that all knowledge is provisional – that all truths about the world sooner or later come to be revised. We know today that Newton, to take one example, was wrong about most things, but his model functioned, and that was what mattered. There is always something new on the way. Instead of The Truth, we have to make do with The Latest.

It was not only for Karl Marx that science took over religion's task to provide a meaning for history and existence. The only real articles of faith for bourgeois democracy are economic growth and scientific rationality. This means that all our political and social institutions ultimately rest upon a programmatically insecure set of values. Everything is in motion. Rationality not only has to act rationally, but must increasingly fulfil the functions of irrationality as well. This is generally the case for the whole of the parliamentary über-ideology, from right to left and covering every alternative in between: everyone sets their faith in rationality. Even the romantically inclined environmental movement refers to scientific rationality when it attacks science and its applications. Ecologism is, as the British journalist and author Bryan Appleyard has pointed out, "a way of turning science against itself". We believe in science, but what is it exactly that we believe in, when we know that something new is always on the way?

Experts are the new priesthood, our guides in spiritual and moral questions, mediating and commenting upon the very latest information. Statistics are the language of the new oracle, information presented as science. But what does it really matter when it turns out that the relation between the number of twins born and the number of female detectives has shown a noticeable change? What does it really matter that an immigrant from one continent seems more intelligent than an immigrant from another? And what does it mean to be intelligent? The masses, poor in knowledge yet over-informed, at the bottom of all low-status networks, are completely at the mercy of The Latest in its vulgar and trivialised form. The frequent showers of contradictory information have one single coherent message: don't trust your experiences and perceptions, listen to The Latest instead. But The Latest is quickly succeeded by The Very Latest, and it is practically impossible to imagine any information, any combination of new facts, that could affect the status quo to any noticeable degree: partly for practical reasons, because facts are so fickle and their rate of replacement so high, partly purely theoretically, because there is an absence of any context that is valid for the whole of the social collective, from which the implications of these facts could be determined.

The public, consisting of engaged citizens with a common interest in and responsibility for the general good, the classic precondition of democracy, never materialised in reality. Instead, the ever more vocal mass of the population and the ever more ambitious middle-class, which had so terrified the privileged elite of the nineteenth century, is being transformed under the relentlessly increasing pressure of information into a divided and ruler-friendly multitude of antagonistic special-interest groups. This means that all these statistical investigations, all this quasi-scientific social research, all of this torrent of new information which is so readily available to us in our efforts to make the world a little more comprehensible, is actually, to borrow Karl Kraus's aphoristic summation of psychoanalysis, "precisely the mental disorder for which it believes it is the cure". Or, in the words of David Bowie: "It's like putting out fire with gasoline".

The noble thought, which has its basis in Enlightenment philosophy, was however that facts spoke for themselves and that intellect would inevitably triumph. All privileges would be abolished and justice would prevail on earth. Thomas Jefferson was one of those who expressly spoke about the "diffusion of information" as one of the corner-stones of his political beliefs. The free press became the very embodiment of the virtues of liberty. A greatly increased spread of information via all the newly-established newspapers would not only provide sustenance to diverse progressive ideas, but also create the public platform where man could exercise the capacity for rational reasoning that was his innate gift, and the social participation that was his natural right.

This was largely how it worked. To begin with, at least. Information in general, and newspapers in particular, were an effective and justly feared weapon in the hands of the bourgeoisie which was seizing control from the old, temporally displaced regime. But once power had been seized and consolidated, there was naturally no burning desire within the newly established elite to carry on with the experiment. Freedom quickly became problematical once again, and all those people with their innate gifts and natural rights no longer appeared so regularly in the columns of the newspapers. If the eighteenth century's newspapers and pamphlets had reflected a genuine, revolutionary opinion that was critical of power, then the press during the nineteenth century was considerably more of an instrument of power with which the public was consciously manipulated and a general opinion manufactured. This means that it is still correct to regard the press, and information, as a weapon. But also that it is important to keep an eye on whose finger is on the trigger, and which interests this person represents.

The capitalist elite, like every other, sought to maintain the status quo. The primary task of its propaganda was to protect social, economic and political privileges in an age when privileges were no longer the fashion, and when increasing welfare and improved education were leading to demands for more rapid equality. Those in power sought, quite consciously, with the help of the PR-experts who were beginning to sharpen their tools by the turn of the last century, to turn the increase in welfare and the improvements in education to their own advantage and persuade the ambitious middle-class of the advantages of entering into a tacit but nonetheless effective pact.

The trick was to present the alternative, i.e. political change, as something extremely unpleasant. The message was that the newspaper-reading middle-class risked losing its hard-won gilt-edged life if the existing order was disturbed: that chaos and mob-rule threatened if the winds of change were set free. The trick worked. It was possible, it turned out, to manufacture opinion. PR-methods were built on science – what else? The PR-men regarded themselves as scientists. One of their trend-setting predecessors was the Frenchman Gustave Le Bon, who with great trepidation warned of what the easily-led masses might do, and how little they cared about laws and every other social institution; another was Gabriel Tarde, who, more cautiously, preferred to talk about the general public instead of the mass, and who had greater hope in what might be achieved with the help of the developing mass-media.

Tarde took up the Enlightenment idea of the debating public, "the grandiose unification of the common mind". But he also recognised the power and possibilities that lay within reach of the artful opinion-manufacturer. In modern society, the carefully-wrought message not only reached those who read newspapers, but everyone who spoke to all the people who read newspapers, i.e. pretty much everyone. According to Tarde, newspapers had created the conditions for a co-ordinated, public conversation where it was possible to pre-programme the right opinions: "One pen suffices to set off a million tongues".

The electronic mass-media offered even better opportunities to set people's tongues in motion. The printed word still requires a certain level of education in order to be understood, whereas radio, for instance, requires nothing but the flick of a switch and adequate hearing. This gave propagandists of all descriptions an opportunity to get inside people's homes in a way that was historically unique. Film, and eventually television, offered the opportunity to communicate directly through images. For someone looking at images, either moving or frozen, their perspective and the act of seeing are determined by the originator of the image. This opens what the critic and philosopher Walter Benjamin calls "the optics of the unconscious": a shortcut for the camera to bypass the intellectual censorship which comes into effect when we have to adopt a position towards a message on the abstract level of words; a direct channel into the individual's private dream-factory where unexpressed desires and fears roam about. Anyone who can manage to stay awake will experience a stimulating massage of his or her irrational inner self.

The theatrical presentation of democracy demanded steady direction if it was not to go off the rails: this was the main creed and business idea of the developing PR industry. Historical factors – welfare and education – made it necessary for the ruling and – naturally – responsible elite to develop a well-stocked toolbox of power so as to be prepared for all eventualities. General opinion was in constant need of tending and pruning, no undesirable weeds could be permitted to grow too tall. The masses could easily start to think a mass of foolish ideas. The medicine for this was information, but it must be administered by experts within the mass-media and the world of social-psychology. With the help of precise science it would be possible, in theory at least, to fine-tune the intellectual and emotional life of the masses. This was known as the art of the Engineering of Consent.

When the bourgeoisie seized power from the aristocracy in conjunction with the previous great paradigm shift, information was, as we have seen, a valuable weapon, and when the bourgeoisie later sought to protect its position and privileges, information was an effective instrument of control. But now, when the netocrats are moving from their positions in the current transitional phase, information is a form of perpetual existential static-interference, making the figures in the image difficult to determine. It is no longer possible to achieve anything creative with information; the only result of a continued and unchecked torrent is an increase of mental pollution in society. The most characteristic quality of information in such great quantities are the great quantities themselves, and it is under all these layers of muffling and insulating padding that everything important that is going on is actually going on.

The PR-experts realised this at an early stage. These qualified forces are not engaged, therefore, with anything so simple as hawking information or opinions; they are re-creating reality itself. Today we live in a world where practically every moment of every individual's attention is exposed to the tender attentions of the PR-experts. All of life is packaged, stylised. Instead of doling out opinions about whatever happens to be the day's news, PR-experts set in play the very events that are the news. They do not provide a slant on reporting, but make sure that reality itself is pre-slanted for reporting so that general opinion is tinted in the desirable colour and nuance. Of course, lazy journalists can get ready-written articles from the PR-company to which they can put their name, but it is the performance of the event itself which is important.

This activity is carried out to an extent unimagined by the general population. One tangible example, taken from the sociologist Stuart Ewen, is how American opinion was programmed fundamentally and in good time for an eventual military offensive against Iraq in the early 1990s. One congressional enquiry that gained a great deal of media attention involved a fifteen-year-old girl from Kuwait, a hospital volunteer who testified that she had witnessed with her own eyes how, after the invasion of Kuwait, Iraqi troops had entered the hospital in Kuwait City, dragged premature babies out of their incubators and left them to die on cold corridor floors. This grim act of barbarism outraged the USA. No-one paid any heed to the fact that the girl in question remained anonymous, for the stated reason that her own safety was at risk. Only in retrospect, when the war was long over, did it emerge that the girl was actually Nayirah al-Sabah, daughter of the Kuwaiti ambassador to the USA, and that she could not possibly have seen the things she testified to having seen. It also became apparent that her appearance before the enquiry had been arranged by one Gary Hymel, vice-MD of Hill and Knowlton, one of the largest PR companies in the world, which counted the Kuwaiti royal family among its wealthy clients. Nayirah's testimony was part of a conscious and successful strategy, and was one of a great number of manufactured media events, all designed to direct American fury at Baghdad.

Sick and weak babies, dragged from their incubators and left to die on the floor: you need strong effects to attract attention and mobilise outraged emotions. Or any emotions at all. When access to information exceeds demand, the relationship is, for obvious reasons, quite the reverse where attention is concerned. Attention, pricked ears and focused eyed, is what there is a real shortage of in what is known as the new economy. This has to do with welfare and education. Sociologists from several countries have shown that there is a clear link between increased welfare and a higher level of education on the one hand, and a general sense of a lack of time on the other. Naturally, we have no less time than previous generations, or than exists in other less blessed regions of the planet: once again, it is multiplicity that is at issue here; the range of activities and leisure pursuits on offer is so much greater than before. There is so much that we would like to have the time to do within the time available.

Our patience with slowness is on the wane. We associate everything old with slowness, and we avoid everything old like the plague. Children and teenagers instinctively avoid black and white films when they happen to pop up during their channel-hopping, because they, not without reason, associate black and white with slowness. Anything that requires waiting is regarded as "dead time". The unspoken aim for anyone in tune with the age is to squeeze as much experience as possible into every single moment. Strong effects give the impression of a lot of experience, and entertainment is the cream that makes the sludge edible, and that separates it from other sludge-experiences. The one thing that we believe ourselves to know for certain is that life is short, and that our task in life is to fill it with as many different experiences as possible, as many kicks as possible. The winner is no longer the person who is closest to the king's arse (as under feudalism), or who has most money when he dies (as under capitalism), but the person who has experienced the largest number and the most extreme kicks.

Entertainment today is actually what information purports to be: a greater attention-magnet than any other, and therefore the economy's most significant driving-force. Development is approaching the point where every branch of the economy is coming to resemble entertainment, in great and eager strides. The shopping experience itself is being enriched with the addition of entertainment, a rich array of entertainment products is sold at petrol stations, and loaned out at libraries. Entertainment raises the consumer's sense of complete and appropriate consumption, and is therefore a decisive ingredient in the establishment of brand-names; it is, above all, "the e-factor", the entertainment factor, that makes one product appear more attractive than its competitors, and fuels turnover of goods on the shelves and on web-shopping pages.

Things have to be fun at all times. If people are bored, they go somewhere else at once, and consume something else. Las Vegas is not only the part of the world demonstrating the greatest growth, but is also trend-setting in terms of its intellectual climate. Academic stars invite their audiences to grand shows. And the need to be entertaining in the media has become one of the most important tasks for both politicians and businessmen. Everything suggests that we are now at the introductory stage of a phase in which information, paradoxically, is beginning to lose its prestige in the general consciousness. It is so easily accessible that it has become a logistical problem and an environmental hazard. If you conduct a search on the net and get four million hits, what are you supposed to do with all the information? There will come a day when the enthusiastic cheerleaders realise that they have been fooled. What is desirable is what is difficult to attain: an overview, context, knowledge. That is where power lies.

5.

Curators, Nexialists and Eternalists – The Netocrats and Their Worldview

AS A RESULT OF THE ongoing paradigm shift and the transition from capitalism to informationalism, power is leaving the salons of the bourgeoisie and moving into the virtual world, where a new elite, the netocracy, is ready to take over. So who are these netocrats, and in what ways do they differ from their predecessors, the bourgeoisie? Where can we find them, and what are their distinguishing characteristics? What are their ambitions and strategies, their interests and values? How do they regard themselves and their social identity? And how is this new elite structured, what are the netocrats' internal distinctions and hierarchy? In order to approach this complex of questions seriously, we first have to understand the thinking and the circumstances that form the foundations for the progress of this new dominant class. We have to place it and its values in a historical context.

Ever since the earliest philosophy, western thought has been split into two main paths. We have chosen here to call these the totalistic and the mobilistic traditions, whilst remaining fully conscious of the objections that could be made against this division. The philosophy of the mobilist Heraclitus, for instance, inspired Plato, the totalistic disciple of the equally totalistic Socrates, and his fundamental concept of the world of ideas. But nonetheless, for pedagogical reasons, we have chosen here to focus on the differences between these two paths, instead of studying the overlap between them.

The totalistic tradition is characterised by the construction of the great system: a desire to find a single theory to encompass and explain the whole of existence and history. Within Chinese thought we find an equivalent to this ambition in Confucianism. Socrates, Plato and Aristotle are the three central figures within this tradition

81

who have dominated western thought: their ideas have been nurtured and developed by great system-builders from Descartes and Kant to Hegel and the utopian Marx. But even Christianity and its theology, along with all of the political ideologies of the capitalist era, form part of the totalistic grouping. Both the church and the state as they have developed in our civilisation are to be regarded as totalistic institutions.

Totalistic thought is based upon the indivisible subject. The rules of philosophy are axiomatic, and are assumed as given from the outset. The ego is the basic building-block of this system, which means that the whole of existence is in orbit around this ego, like the moon orbits the earth. Thinking is situated within itself, and seeks to illuminate and regard existence from this assumed fundamental point. So observation is aimed from the ego, outwards at the world. Totalistic philosophy is interested in the relationship between the soul and the body (= ego and world). This is therefore basically dualistic. This way of thinking both presupposes and reflects upon its own productivity, and is fond of pondering moral and political questions. The ambition is to create a system which explains and provides a practical guide to life and the world. The fundamental questions revolve around man's identity: who is he, and what is his place in the world?

The totalistic question is a question in search of an answer. The question is the path, the answer is the truth, the truth is the goal, and a world in which all questions are answered is a perfect world, a translucent totality (hence the name totalism), a utopia made manifest. Plato claimed that this utopia already exists, that it is actually more real than the reality we believe that we perceive, which is merely a pale imitation of his hyper-real world of ideas. These ideas are the originals, out of our reach; the things that we perceive are of necessity only fallible copies. Christianity attached itself to this idea of the utopia that already exists, but in this case the connection to actual reality is more problematic. Utopia exists, but not here, and not now. The Christian utopia is in part a lost paradise, but also a coming state of heavenly joy; the world before the Fall, and the world after the Day of Judgement. In this way, when Christianity looks to the future, it is also looking to the past; its ambition is to reinstate what once existed.

For the totalists of later ages, in particular political ideologues, utopia is not a given fact but more a possible and desirable project.

It is man himself who is gradually making this utopia a reality, first in thought, in the form of a vision, then in reality, through concentrated political activity. Since God is out of the picture, man himself must transform himself into God and become master of his own fate if he is to realise his utopia. The task of totalistic philosophy is then to stake out the path showing how this can happen. What unites all totalists is the idea of some sort of utopia which either has been, can be, or, at the very least, ought to be realised. This idea is connected to the idea of objective truth, an absolute, against which the state of things can be evaluated. The question is not whether life has a predetermined purpose, but what this purpose is.

One consequence of this is that totalistic thought is concerned with moral distinctions such as good and evil, black and white, high and low, right and wrong, useful and useless, etc. The goal is to place human thoughts and actions on different scales where these values constitute the poles. The task of philosophy is to determine these values once and for all, directing them from an imagined ideal state, from the absolute, or to create them with mankind's eternal requirements in mind. The intention is to lay a firm foundation for categorical judgements; every time we are asked what we really think about something or other, we are being asked to act as good totalists. Two and a half millennia of totalistic thought have created an almost incomprehensible spider's web of laws, rules, prejudices and collective obsessions.

One common aspect of all forms of totalistic philosophy is that thought itself has no value. The task of philosophy is ultimately purely instrumental: to render itself superfluous. When utopia has been achieved, totalistic thought will no longer be required, in the same way that a ladder has served its purpose for someone who has climbed out of a dark well. Until then, philosophy is a working tool, one productive discipline among many, providing man with something both useful and enjoyable. What differentiates the various totalistic threads from one another are the different absolutes from which their philosophy stems, which are, in turn, dependent upon what the desired utopia looks like.

This means that totalists are deeply divided on various central points: within this great arena there is plenty of room for religious and ideological wars and conflicts, of which history can provide many sorry examples. The enormous wealth of variety of content beneath the totalistic umbrella can easily deceive the observer into thinking that thought itself must be totalistically structured, and that there simply cannot be any other way of thinking. Both Kant and Hegel were aware of this and struggled with this question. This impression is reinforced by the fact that totalistic thought has dominated western culture to such an extent and for so long. Language itself has been occupied by the totalistic tradition, which has made the possibility of thinking in alternate ways more difficult.

Totalistic philosophy is almost obsessed by man's capacity to think abstractly, and, above all, it is fascinated by his ability to comprehend the fourth dimension, time, and to use this to view the world from both a backward- and a forward-looking perspective. For a totalist, it is natural to stress this awareness of time, so unique to man, and to remark constantly upon his consequently unique position in nature. For instance, man shares 98% of his genes with chimpanzees, but it is still this difference from his surroundings which is important. Life is a process of motion which has a decided direction, a clear beginning and a foreseeable ending. This means that the present is something secondary: it is the starting point in the past and, above all, the final destination in the future which are of most interest.

There is a central totalistic value in this. In this anthropocentric world-view everything is related to man and his needs: what is interesting about an object or an event or another creature is its similarities or usefulness to man, who is thus the measure of all things. The meaning of life is man himself, his wishes, and/or his individual salvation. The greater the similarity and/or usefulness to him, the greater the value. Taking Descartes, the first modern philosopher, as our lead, we can formulate the creed of humanism as follows: I think, therefore I am; and because it is I who think, it is also I who decide; and because it is I who decide, I shall force reality to bend to my will.

Totalistic thought is in all its forms strictly hierarchical. The definition of a man is a being who refuses to be an animal, and who is therefore of higher standing than an animal. When man is the measure of all things, the inevitable consequence is that man has an objectively true unique status. He is characterised by his ability to think and formulate abstract ideas, and this is what gives him a higher value. As long as man is alone in this, he possesses the highest value in creation, and everything around him is of a subordinate nature. This reasoning is clearly circular. Man is at the top of the hierarchy because he possesses the supreme qualities that make him man.

This is the crux of the great and insoluble dilemma of totalistic thought: how can a philosophy which refers to a pre-ordained hierarchy in which man stands higher than all other species avoid advocating an internal hierarchy within different species, and ultimately also between different human beings? How can it question an individual's claim to be allowed to rule over the rest of mankind? Perhaps he possesses these supreme qualities in especially large quantities? Plato claimed, famously, that the ideal would be to hand power to philosophers. Many other totalists have had the same idea. Some people are simply better suited than others to rule over the dull masses. And once the principle of hierarchy has been recognised and established, there is no end to the number of levels it can have. The less suitable may very well end up a long way from the top.

The fact that totalistic thought has dominated western culture to the extent that it has depends less upon the idea that it is intellectually superior, than that it has been, from the perspective of pure power, fantastically useful as a platform for social construction. During both feudalism and capitalism, every significant social force and myth took up position beneath a totalistic structure. Anyone with a utopian or eschatological vision has been able to call upon this structure, and in doing so has strengthened the legitimacy of the structure in return.

The dynamism in totalistic thought has made it useful both for supporting existing power structures and for criticising and toppling them. With reference to the totalistic ideal, God, the monarch, the state, democracy and other symbols of the elite in power have all been defended, just as revolutions and other projects for social upheaval have been legitimised. But now there is a spanner in the works. What is happening with the breakthrough of the informationalist paradigm is that this carefully constructed, universally recognised philosophical platform is under devastating attack from several directions at once. The bolts are straining, the joints are cracking. The grandiose totalistic model, the fundamental basis for the western social system, is imploding.

The transition from feudalism to capitalism was connected to paradigm shifts within both science and technology. It was astronomers and scientists like Copernicus, Kepler, Galileo and Newton who built the foundations for the new world-view. What the thinkers of early capitalism, the so-called Enlightenment philosophers, were concerned with was not so much genuinely new thought as patching and repairing the old, adapting traditional thinking to the new sciences and their revolutionary revelations about the nature of reality. The desire to ascertain an independent, objective truth and a centre of existence was still pressing, however. There was no ideological room to draw the philosophical consequences of this new world-view and its lack of a centre. This would have necessitated the abandonment of the totalistic platform, and it still had important tasks to fulfil.

The bourgeoisie had no problems coming to terms with the new perception of reality in which the earth was no longer the centre of the universe. In actual fact this indisputable fact, reinforced by the empirical evidence that could now be demonstrated, was an extremely useful weapon in the struggle against the old feudal power-structure. When it turned out that the earth revolved around the sun instead of vice versa, this meant that the whole authority of the old order was undermined and began to teeter. The whole of the old construction with God, the church, the monarch and the aristocracy had acted out its role, the players could be moved to the wings. But, on the other hand, it was impossible for the bourgeoisie to take this reasoning one step further and recognise that the new world-view also meant that man himself had been downgraded, and could no longer be the measure of all things and the central starting-point for philosophy. Such a conclusion was unacceptable, because it constituted a threat to the vital interests of the bourgeoisie. Man was God's appointed representative, and for this reason it was necessary, philosophically, to consolidate his unique position at the top of the hierarchy. For safety's sake, philosophy was fettered and marginalised by being designated a subordinate position as an eccentric deviant among the new humanist sciences. The capitalist era became a humanist dictatorship.

Three far-sighted and ground-breaking philosophers broke against the rules of adaptation, but their innovative thinking also had a high price. The Dutchman Baruch Spinoza was, quite simply, frozen out by his contemporaries, including his own Jewish community. His monism constituted a radical break with totalistic dualism. The Scot David Hume was forced to retreat and moderate his most radical ideas; and the first in a line of great German thinkers, G W Leibniz, found it necessary to camouflage the truly ground-breaking elements of his thinking – that the innermost essence of existence was motion rather than substance – amongst diverse advances within totalist thought that were more easily comprehensible and palatable to his contemporaries. In totalistic history books, Leibniz is more often regarded as a brilliant mathematician, "the last great Renaissance man", than a precursor of the Baroque within philosophy.

The breakthrough of the new world-view was incredibly powerful. For the capitalist power machinery, the empiricism of the natural sciences, i.e. the precision of mathematics applied to real experience instead of airy speculation about how reality ought to be arranged, appeared to be an extremely attractive attribute. The possibility of politics being associated with science and borrowing some of its credibility was regarded as potentially valuable. This would grant solidly-founded legitimacy to political power. In the long run politics could become a science in its own right. This project was accomplished in the 1800s when national economics, sociology and political science were established as academic disciplines. Hence an unholy alliance between politicians and academics was established, with the academics being left alone to manufacture truths that suited the ambitions of the bourgeoisie. But the advantages of this alliance were considerable even for science, which was guaranteed abundant resources and a wealth of attractive new tasks. The academic world gradually replaced old, outdated institutions like the court and the church as the recruiting ground for the political leadership-caste. Academic titles complemented a healthy bank-balance as the main attribute of the bourgeoisie.

Up to the end of the 1700s science was free, in so far as researchers could devote themselves, quite untroubled, to whatever they chose: to translate the Bible into the new national languages, to classify plants and languages, to study the heavens through telescopes. But thereafter political and commercial direction of the academic world was initiated, as a result of science being given great and prestigious tasks under capitalism: to provide protection for man's unique position in nature and install him in God's place at the top of the hierarchy. This is why the so-called humanist sciences were invented. The academic world was thus woven into, and became an indivisible part of the capitalist power-structure. The new, grand Project Man had been launched.

Since the capitalist system defined itself as thoroughly rational, there was no longer, ironically enough, any need for a philosophy that pointed out what was intellectually and morally correct, or what was irrationally and morally reprehensible. Questions like this were believed to be perfectly well handled by science, the market and representative democracy. Totalistic philosophy had, in other words, made itself redundant. Because totalistic thought was intimately connected to the abolished Aristotelian/Ptolemaic world-view, a fact which its practitioners refused to see, it could be reduced to a sort of therapeutic museum activity. To acknowledge the need of a new world-view would undermine the whole of their activity, and not many thinkers were willing to pay that price. Particularly not in a society where social exclusion meant rapid transportation to the proudest invention of the humanist sciences: the mental hospital.

At the same time, the bourgeoisie was not prepared to tolerate any philosophical alternative to totalistic tradition, since that was the basis of the humanist über-ideology that was sacred and above question. The tragic consequence of this deadlock was that philosophy under capitalism was controlled by a totalistic priesthood, a collective Gorbacheverie, that was doomed to wither away slowly and impotently, but which neither wanted to nor was permitted to abdicate. This, in turn, meant that the philosophical paradigm shift never happened: humanism meant, to all intents and purposes, a continuation of the old, the traditional; a secularised Christianity nailed up between St Paul and Aristotle. An all-encompassing revolution within philosophy would have to wait.

Only now, with the worldwide net taking shape and capitalist power-structures beginning to crumble, is the time right for totalism to be broadly questioned. The netocratic world-view is based upon thought which is certainly not new, and which itself can be traced back to Ancient Greece, but which has not hitherto been able to form a powerful alternative to the totalistic thought that has dominated philosophy up to now. We have called this alternative which characterises the thinking and perceptual world of the informationalist elite, the mobilistic tradition. It has its origins with the Greek philosopher Heraclitus, and has developed in near-obscurity throughout history, glowing faintly in the dark shadow cast by the dominant, totalistic tradition.

The mobilistic tradition is characterised first and foremost by a desire for universal openness. There is a desire in the subject to submit to the actual conditions of existence; to come to terms with existing circumstances, in order to use this position as the basis for attempting to improve the conditions imposed by fate. In other words, it concerns an attitude which is the complete opposite of totalistic philosophy: thought is here positioned out in existence, and looks at man from the outside. The ego is not taken for granted. Philosophy works from the world, towards the subject, an attitude which in eastern thought is found in Taoism and Mahayana Buddhism. The mobilistic question does not require an answer. It is instead a question which is constantly seeking the question which is concealed behind the question at hand. What the question expresses is a passionate desire for free and uncompromising thought, intellectual integrity; the answer can therefore never be anything but a cul-de-sac of thought, a comfort-blanket as a solace for philosophical cowards, a red herring detracting attention from the actions of underlying forces. The present is what exists, actuality is what is real.

Utopia, in its various forms, the dream of a controlling totality, is the main target of mobilists. Utopia is regarded solely as an instrument of power, demanding man's total submission and stopping him from thinking freely and living completely and fully in the present. Man is promised a reward in a more or less distant future, in return for giving up his freedom. He exchanges freedom for progress and the hope of participation in the coming utopia.

□

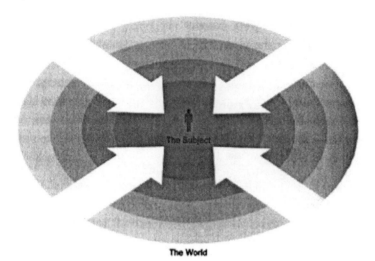

Fig. 5.1 *Totalism and mobilism*

The path is lined with all the "objective truths" of totalistic philosophy, the axioms that the mobilist calls into question and identifies as the most cherished deceits of power: the ego, existence, dualism, hierarchy, laws, guilt, sacrifice, angst, memory, revenge, sympathy, progress, and so on. All these "truths" come together at the point where the reward is located, a reward for the self-assumed slavery that man is fooled, or allows himself to be fooled, or wants himself to be fooled, into suffering. One concrete example of this difference is when capitalists proudly renounce the present and postpone satisfaction of their needs to an uncertain future where this very postponement of life, this capitalisation, has a positive value.

Mobilistic philosophy rejects all of this and offers instead, as the only reward, the intoxication of freedom and the limited but real possibilities of the present. The primary task of mobilistic philosophy is that of a janitor: to clear the ensnaring intrigues of power away from thought. To uncover every attempt to objectify the hierarchies we are subjectively forced to construct in order to make existence comprehensible. This requires philosophers to formulate their criticism of power so that it stands above attitudes about "constructivity", because the demand for "constructivity" is power's demand that philosophy itself be made useful to power. A constructive critic of power is really an integrated part of the ideological power-system, because criticism of that sort is domesticated and harmless even at the moment it is formulated. It patches and mends. The task of the critic is reduced to protecting power by pointing out its failings, strengthening it against coming attacks, defending its position.

In the mobilistic tradition, thought has a value in itself. Mobilistic criticism therefore does not develop any dialogue with power, does not enter into horse-trading, but reveals the given "truths", "progress" and "rewards" as illusions and obsessions. It is, thus, "out of time". The demand for freedom also applies to the philosopher's relation to his own philosophy: thought must be entirely free. The very moment a philosopher proclaims ownership of his ideas, he is allying himself to the power that he is criticising. This is naturally problematic, because it means the mobilistic thinker can never be held responsible for the actual and practical consequences of his thoughts. There is a colossal risk in this, but also the enormous possibilities that are always part of mobilistic philosophy. You can never determine in advance where you are going to end up.

Ironically, mobilistic thinkers have always been able to count on the admiration of their totalistic colleagues, which has often taken the form of avarice. One example is how Machiavelli's revelatory reflections upon which strategies were effective in power-games at the highest level were appreciated and used as an instruction book by both politicians in Renaissance Europe and the leaders of late-capitalist businesses. Another example is how Nietzsche's fundamentally anti-fascist philosophy was turned inside out and used as an attack-weapon by the Nazis in 1930s' Germany. In this way, the mobilists' greatest admirers are often their worst enemies. Imitation is, famously, the sincerest form of flattery, but the imitator often misses or does not understand the very essence of what he is imitating. A totalist looks for benefits, not least to himself, and insists on logical strictness. Thought must be kept within the boundaries of language. This is why the acceptance in mobilistic philosophy of paradoxes, disinterested thought that is enough in itself, appears incomprehensible to him.

Even if mobilistic thought can be used by a cynic, mobilistic thinkers themselves often appear unfathomable and even ridiculous. This is the price of their refusal to join in the dance around totalistic truths. But with the arrival of informational society, the preconditions for thought are changing dramatically. This must not be understood as meaning that the informationalist paradigm is in any way "superior" or "more advanced" than its predecessors; reasoning in those terms means that we are still stuck in totalistic values which have been declared redundant by circumstances. On the contrary, informational society will, in many important respects, demand greater honesty of its participants. It will be more intellectually brutal than previous eras. This honesty and brutalisation are central to an understanding of the netocracy and its values. Mobilism already offers these qualities, and is therefore rejecting – in meme-Darwinian fashion – totalism, which is collapsing under the weight of its discredited axioms. Mobilism can therefore, ironically, be said to be closer to the innate "truth" that it so firmly denies the existence of.

During the transition from capitalism to informationalism, a radical re-evaluation of man's self-image and world-view is being forced upon him. The altered circumstances demand new thought, but this new thought is actually not new, but something previously ignored, marginalised and misrepresented which is now in focus. Looking at developments from a biological/evolutionary perspective, socio-economic changes are favouring a mutation of thought which previously led an enfeebled existence. Voices from the periphery are beginning to be heard stronger and stronger. Ever since Christianity triumphed over Mithraism in the struggle over which belief system would replace ancient mythology as the state religion of the Roman Empire, mobilistic tradition has been confined to a secluded place on the edge of western thought. Freethinkers like Lucretius, Machiavelli, Spinoza and Hume all recognised the limitations of the totalistic tradition, and attacked it to the extent that they thought advisable. But it was first in the 1800s, with Friedrich Nietzsche, that the mobilistic tradition seriously staked a claim within the philosophical arena. Immanuel Kant threw the door open, but it was Nietzsche who took the step into the new world-view.

Nietzsche rejected traditional totalistic questions about the meaning of everything, and the morals from the philosophical canon, and went instead straight to more demanding mobilistic questions about who it was who was saying what was being said, and why. With his "amor fati", love of fate, he ripped holes in the understanding that had governed philosophy since Descartes' time.

He exposed the great totalistic project: the ambition for a totality of existence within philosophy, politics, science and art, a truth that was eternal and universally valid, to devastating criticism. Nietzsche rejected all talk about existence having an innermost core or objective purpose. There is, he claimed, merely an endless mass of conflicting forces that are constantly jousting with each other. It is basically pointless to speak of a fixed state of being; it is a question of a constant state of becoming. Existence is not something, it is becoming something, in the constantly shifting interplay of conflicting forces.

According to Nietzsche, all talk of morals was really about giving those in power an instrument with which to hold the masses in check, and above all, for the masses to hold the individual in check. He therefore called into question the entire totalistic Enlightenment project. Nietzsche claimed that it was not at all a question of creating a more open and better world for everyone, but rather the opposite: enclosing people within a sealed system where normality was the chosen lodestar and where bitterness and conformity were the predominant characteristics. The two main targets for his attack were Pauline Christianity and what he perceived as being its latter-day successor: humanism. Nietzsche regarded these forces as reactive and therefore reprehensible. He advocated instead his own ideal, the superman, whose actions are active and positive. He placed life and its immense wealth of variety above everything else. Free, uninhibited creativity was expressed by Nietzsche as what he termed the desire for power.

The single event that left the deepest impression on twentieth century philosophy was the student revolt in Paris in 1968. Students and organised communists met on the barricades in a unified revolt against bourgeois society. The large post-war generation that had taken over within French universities was driven, like flower power and the peace movement in the USA of the Vietnam War era, by the conviction that the capitalist system was bankrupt and was in need of a well-aimed shot to put it out of its misery. This diverse movement was led and inspired by a selection of charismatic figures, including the Marxist and existential philosopher Jean-Paul Sartre, who was strongly inspired by Mao.

But the student revolt failed. Fantasy never came to power. After a few months order was restored. This defeat led to a comprehensive re-evaluation of the accepted truths that had been cherished by the French intelligentsia. The working masses had not shown themselves at all interested in armed conflict, as the Maoist students and academics had imagined and hoped. The utopia had not been sufficiently attractive. During several hectic years the intellectual scene was radically transformed. At the beginning of the 1970s there was a general breakthrough for a new philosophy, with two Nietzscheans, Gilles Deleuze and Michel Foucault, in the vanguard. Mobilistic tradition thereby achieved a foothold in the academic world and began to exert an influence that kept on growing. Nietzsche conquered France and quickly expanded his empire.

Deleuze, Foucault and their many followers have been called, mainly by their philosophical opponents, post-modernists. This controversial title is based upon the idea that their criticism is mainly directed at the great project of latter-day totalism: modernism. As a counterweight to the dominant totalistic thinkers, Deleuze championed instead the pioneers of the mobilistic tradition – from Heraclitus, via Spinoza and Hume, to Nietzsche – but he also developed his own thought, which, according to many observers, Foucault among them, will go down in history as the most significant contribution to philosophy during the twentieth century. By unifying Spinoza's monism with Nietzsche's ultra-materialism, Deleuzianism makes a frontal attack on totalism's perception of the ego as a stable phenomenon, and on its dualism and dialectics.

Like Nietzsche, Deleuze sees existence as a constant conflict between forces moving in different directions; the balance of power between them is in a constant state of flux. The difference between the various forces is what interests him, and, from the point where the difference occurs, the point that Deleuze identifies as the singularity, it continues to expand unchecked at the same time as it constantly gives rise to new differences. This is thus a matter of a world-view in which existence cannot possibly be contained within human consciousness, since it is changing and expanding in all directions and at varying speeds, and in patterns whose complexity exceeds our capacity to comprehend. Consequently the totalistic ambition to gain a complete overview of existence appears completely absurd. Deleuze is completely uninterested in totalism's linear thought: of introductions, conclusions and totalities. His philosophy is instead concentrated on the centre of the mobilistic temporal axis, on the event, the feedback loop at the centre of things.

It is not the ego that produces thought but rather thought that produces the ego. When thought changes, so does the ego. There is no such thing as the fixed ego, the basic premise of totalism. So it is impossible to say that man in his capacity as sovereign subject can discover "the truth" by examining his surroundings. Instead we are forced to conclude that he largely constructs the truth that fits his purpose and circumstances. No truth survives outside the circumstances in which is created and where it fulfils a function. Totalism's search for "the universal truth" is therefore absurd. According to Deleuze, the task of philosophy is considerably more modest: it is to create functional concepts that help people to orientate themselves in existence, encouraging them to make their lives works of art. A new paradigm demands new concepts.

Deleuze, like Nietzsche, praises art. He sees philosophy as an artform, connected to painting and music. He is concerned with the history of ideas, fascinated by how ideas gather in clusters in specific historical periods, only to disperse gradually afterwards. These ideas, like bodies, are in perpetual motion. He therefore called his thinking nomadic philosophy. Deleuze's ideal is what he calls "a body without organs", a complex structure which can be compared to an egg, where a mass of different factors are permitted to interact without the existence of any hierarchies between them, in order to create a whole which is greater than the sum of its parts. Deleuze is therefore usually counted as part of the mobilistic movement known as natural mobilistic philosophy.

The Deleuzian concept of a body without organs constitutes a passable parallel to Darwinism's genes and memes. In the meeting between Nietzsche, Darwin and Deleuze, the preconditions are in place for the first of three central figures in the netocratic system: the thinker whom we call the eternalist (after the Nietzschean concept of an eternal state of becoming). In the eternalist worldview, all existences, genes as well as memes, and the Deleuzian clusters, have a starting point, a singularity. From this singularity the phenomenon expands into eternity, giving rise, time after time, to new singularities, new complex patterns.

In the final trembling minutes of the capitalist paradigm the universe itself, through the consolidation of physics behind the Big Bang theory, has been transformed into a single, vast eternalistic phenomenon. The Big Bang theory is based upon the idea that the universe was created from a singularity from which it then expands for all eternity. In the eternalistic world-view this can be applied to all forces. And when a series of such forces work together as a Deleuzian historical cluster, a body without organs, then what eternalists would call a resonance-phenomenon or a feedback loop occurs. These temporarily blossoming clusters and resonances make up the nodes of civilisation. In the eternalistic world-view every single individual, the subject, is therefore a resonance-phenomenon rather than a fixed ego.

When singularities which have sprung from each other end up in a confined space, they are bound to meet sooner or later. The patterns which are then conjured up are an exact parallel to the system of contacts that arises in the development of a network. This is where the eternalistic world-view meets reality in netocratic society. The world is perceived as a single organic network, the all-encompassing net, where the clusters of genes and memes that arise are the nodes of the network. If eternalists are the interpreters of this reality, then the actors who appear at the nodes, the entrepreneurs, are another category of netocrats: the nexialists (after Latin "nexus"). The path to these nexialists, or the connection between them is managed by the third and most powerful of the netocratic categories: the curators. It is the curators who point the way for the nexialists, while their mutual world-view is constructed by the philosophers of netocratic society, the analytical eternalists. In the interaction between these three roles, netocratic society is created. If we make a general comparison with capitalism's power hierarchies, we could say that the curator replaces the politician, the nexialist replaces the entrepreneur, and the eternalist replaces the academic in netocratic society.

If Deleuze has become the supreme mobilistic philosopher, Foucault has become the great mobilistic historian, or rather its archaeologist of knowledge, as he himself preferred to be called. To Foucault, nothing in society is "natural": the word itself is an expression of the totalitarian ambitions of those in power, a desire to do away with everything undesirable by declaring it "unnatural". The central aim in social conflicts is to conquer the power of definition. Foucault works from the marginalised groups of capitalist society, the outcasts and their desires and needs, the excluded, as he defined himself. According to Foucault, the task of the philosopher is to silence power, to free man from the enslavement of utopias. The goal is for the weak man to be able to express himself.

Instead of a democracy, where the majority constantly overrides the minority, Foucault advocated a plurocracy, a society where everyone could make decisions for himself, but is not allowed to decide over anyone other than himself. What Foucault did not foresee was that this plurocracy would largely be realised by informational society's technologically driven transfer from democracy to plurarchy (plurocracy is an imagined political model, whereas plurarchy is a social state). Deleuze and Foucault were both fascinated by the electronic media, and showed an almost intuitive understanding of the changes and new possibilities that would follow in the footsteps of technological development. Their thinking has many aspects in common with our own analysis of the informationalist paradigm, and is highly applicable for anyone hoping to understand how both the new elite, the netocracy, and the new underclass, the consumtariat (CONSUMer proleTARIAT), see themselves and the world.

One example of a typical netocratic dilemma is the recurrent choice between exploitation and imploitation. Suppose two netocrats meet on a far-off island with picturesque ruins and beautiful beaches, but with no tourist industry at all. This is a typical netocratic destination, a perfect place for someone who practises tourism in the form of imploitative consumption. When the two netocrats are sitting on their sun-loungers, sipping cold drinks at sunset, they are faced with the question of whether they should keep the island a secret and only tell their closest friends of its existence, or build hotels and an airport and then market the island as a destination for all the tourists of the world: put simply, should they improve it and then sell it to the highest bidder.

If they choose to keep the island secret, they will be following an imploitative strategy; if they choose to make a profit from their discovery, they will be following the opposite, exploitative strategy. The difference between netocrats and classical capitalists is that the netocrats have these two options. Knowledge of the island has such a high value to the netocrats, and profit such a relatively low one, that exclusivity could well weigh heavier than economic profit. For the capitalist there is no choice. For him the accumulation of capital is the central project in life, a project compared to which everything else is subordinate. But the netocrat does not share this view. Conscious of the fact that his new-found paradise would lose its unique aura if it was exploited, the netocrat can choose, thanks to his independence from and lack of interest in capital, to imploit the island instead: to keep it secret and reserve it for the pleasure of himself and his netocratic colleagues.

Characteristic of exploitative consumption is that payment is made with capital. This is different to imploitative consumption, where money is largely uninteresting, and where it is a matter of knowledge and contacts instead, belonging to the chosen few who possess exclusive information. Entry into this circle cannot be bought with money, in the way that the nouveaux riches used to buy status with the profits of their businesses, but can only be achieved if you yourself have knowledge, contacts and exclusive information to offer in return. This means that for the old dominant class, the bourgeoisie, and the new underclass, the consumtariat, exploitative consumption is all that is on offer. Imploitative consumption is reserved for the netocracy.

The same dynamic forms the very basis for the power structures of informational society. A common misconception among the information theorists of late-capitalism is that the network's transparency will result in a more open society with full democratic visibility on all levels and where all participants have the same possibility to influence and the same access to information. But this reasoning should be regarded as palliative netocratic propaganda. This democratic utopia is an sign of rationalistic wishful-thinking and is based upon the misunderstanding that the internal dynamic of networks, on the micro-level, is automatically transferable to society at large. It is not that simple. What is valid within a network is only valid there, and says nothing about the dynamic that pertains on the macro-level, between the different networks, or, in other words, for virtual society as a whole.

Informational society is highly dominated by power hierarchies. These, however, are not constructed in the traditional way – with individuals, companies or organisations – but with membership of networks. At the bottom of this power-pyramid we find, once again, the consumtariat, trapped in a network of exploitative consumption where anyone can become a member. This base network is characterised by the fact that its main activity, directed consumption, is regulated from above. The system prompts desire with the help of adverts and then provides sufficient payment to maintain consumption on a level deemed suitable by the netocracy. This is hyper-capitalism sublimated to the level of sedative: the main concern is not to maximise profit but to prevent riots and virtual violence directed at the netocracy. Above this broad basal network, constantly-renewed and smaller networks are constructed, all competing with one another. These function according to capitalist principles (the traditional golf-club is a suitable model). Only those who can afford it can gain access here. But at the top of the hierarchy, only those who possess attentional value gain entry, in other words: those who have contacts and knowledge that are in themselves valuable to the network. It is here, at the top of the hierarchy, that we find the dominant netocratic class.

In this calculated way a merciless power structure of networks is constructed, where the most exclusive network, to which only the uppermost netocratic elite has access, is at the top. Family names mean nothing here, as they did under feudalism. Wealth means nothing here, as it did under capitalism. The decisive factor governing where in the hierarchy an individual ends up is instead his or her attentionality: their access to and capacity to absorb, sort, overview, generate the necessary attention for, and share valuable information. Power will be more difficult than ever to localise, not to mention how difficult it will be to watch over and influence. Social climbing will become even more complicated than it was under capitalism, the unwritten rules even more complex and inaccessible.

The interest of the netocratic powers in exclusivity and secrecy, combined with the increasingly rapid pace of change within society, means that the rules of netocratic society will be impossible to formalise. As a result of the fact that netiquette is a matter of what is unspoken rather than written down, of the intuitive rather than the rational, it will be the only possible set of rules for social relations in a society characterised by discretion and mobility. Laws and regulations of the traditional western variety have essentially played out their role. The ironic thing in these circumstances is that the netocracy is achieving its advantage over both capitalists and the consumtariat by making use of the virtues of mobilistic philosophy. In high-status networks there is no room for boasting and self-assertion. Instead, openness and generosity are what is most prized there.

It is, paradoxically, the netocrat's ability to think beyond his own ego, to build his identity on membership of a group instead of individualism, on electronic tribalism instead of mass-medial self-assertion, that lead to him understanding and being in control of the new world that is developing. Anxious tinkering with one's own ego, overplayed individualism, is instead characteristic of the new underclass. It is this very inability to see beyond their own ego and its desires that means that the underclass will remain an underclass. Much-vaunted self-realisation is becoming a form of therapy which is keeping the old bourgeoisie and the new consumtariat occupied with private problems instead of interesting them in questioning the new order. Anyone who "believes in himself" is by definition a hopeless loser in the society dominated by the netocracy. In important networks, no-one has the time or inclination to listen to a self-obsessed ego. Networking itself, the feedback loop and social intelligence are at the very heart of the netocracy.

6.

GLOBALISATION, THE DEATH OF MASS MEDIA AND THE GROWTH OF THE CONSUMTARIAT

ACCORDING TO MOBILISTIC philosophy every force has an opposite; every movement meets a resistant movement which offers a greater or lesser amount of opposition. In speaking of a new dominant class, the netocracy, we are presupposing the existence of its antithetical shadow, a new underclass which adopts the position and role occupied by the working class in the capitalist paradigm. The question is: which qualities are going to characterise and therefore define the new mass of people who will be the subjects of the netocracy? The defining characteristic of both peasants and industrial labourers was that they provided their masters with physical strength. Technological developments towards ever more refined and automated production processes have drastically reduced the significance of the human factor within the manufacturing industries; the physical labourer has either migrated to the service industries or become specialised in the supervision of sensitive and complicated apparatus; a labour mannequin, to borrow one of the philosopher Jean Baudrillard's phrases.

In other words, the underclass no longer consists of labourers in the accepted sense of the word. The defining characteristic of the new underclass is not its function either as raw material or as an expense for the enterprises of the dominant class, but rather as consumers of these enterprises. The main point here is not what the underclass produces, or even whether it produces anything at all, but, above all, what it consumes, and, even more importantly, the fact that it consumes at all. The proletariat of informationalism will first and foremost be a proletariat of consumption, or, as we have chosen to call it, a consumtariat. The defining characteristic of this class is not that it plays a subordinate role in production, but that it consumes on the orders of those above it.

In the capitalist paradigm paid labour was the basis of the entire economic system. This means that paid labour has been of vital ideological significance. To be productive was the very definition of being a successful human being. Talent was defined as the ability – and a quantifiable ability – to produce goods and services which could be sold in the marketplace. The combined economic value that the market placed on all waged labour – regardless of the extent to which this ended up in the workers' pockets as wages, in the investors' pockets as profits, or in the Treasury's pockets as taxes – has been the measure by which entire national production has been calculated. This is the only aspect of human activity which has seriously interested the bourgeoisie.

The overriding concern of every individual capitalist has been to maximise profits, which has often resulted in a hunt for unnecessary costs and the redundancies that are a natural consequence of this. But capitalism itself, both in practice and as an ideology central to society, has sought instead to maximise the number of paid workers, and involve as many people as possible in the apparatus of production. The state and the markets have therefore often been mistakenly regarded as opposites, particularly during the Cold War, but have actually comprised two separate but nevertheless mutually dependent pillars of the organic structure of capitalism, regardless of what the political system may have been called. The demands of the state for increased production and the demands of individual capitalists for increased profits have coalesced into one single aim, into a marriage between the state and the labour market which even its participants were unable or unwilling to hinder, a symbiosis that was impervious to other forces. This unholy alliance, this forced alignment of collective and individual wills has been both driven forward and defended by the overwhelming goal of capitalist ideology: to achieve maximum growth in the economy for the sake of growth itself. Different political ideologies have actually only disagreed on the best way of reaching this common goal.

Behind this overriding ambition is concealed the philosophical utopia of rationalism: all human needs, which are assumed to be constant, will be fulfilled by steady, continual growth. Once this point is reached the rationalist utopia will have been realised. With a common and abstract goal for the entire body of society, comprising all political ideologies and commercial forces, no-one need think for themselves any more. The supposed conflicts of the late capitalist era between individualism and communitarianism are best regarded as political theatre, because there have never been any fundamental differences between the various political programmes. Libertarian individualism has never, for instance, been a matter of freeing the individual from an enforced collective identity, but has been interested in the individual entrepreneur's demands for lower taxes ("tax is theft"), and higher productivity within the state apparatus ("the night-watchman state"). On the other hand, however, the fact that capitalism has forced individuals to set aside generalities within their own identity in favour of a specialism demanded by the system has never been called into question.

The dominant role of the state during the late capitalist era has manifested itself in two ways: one of them European, where the state is one of the leading players in the market, and the other American, where big business exerts strict control over politics by using the carrot and the stick approach. In both instances the result has been that the political and economic sectors have practically merged: politics has become economised, the market has become politicised. Political economy and economic politics have become one and the same thing: the rhetorical ritual of rationalist religion. Neither State nor Market has been able to accept any form of human activity outside their collective construction of civilisation. Measuring economic growth has been capitalism's means of quantifying the extent of civilisation itself. In the end the bourgeoisie imagined that it had reached its goal: a universal coalition behind the idea of the social body as a self-perpetuating, well-oiled, self-improving production machine. The problem is that capitalism has not really been victorious but has played out its historical role. The bourgeoisie has a new problem now: a new and developing dominant class with completely different ideas than those encouraged by the lords of the capitalist paradigm.

One consequence of this development is that what we call globalisation is actually two entirely separate phenomena. The capitalist globalisation process is a purely economic phenomenon and is directed towards continued specialisation and diversification. Increased competition is not visible so much in the form of direct confrontations as it is in the division of every market into several smaller, ever more specialised sub-departments. Every player, both individuals and entire cultures, is forced to distil those qualities which are in demand by the particular niche of the market holding sway at that moment, to the detriment of every other speciality and overview. This leads to the development of an increasingly tightly connected, finely-meshed network of mutual dependency. We are talking about a mercantile balancing act, an enforced act of co-operation in the shadow of the threat of the collapse of global trade. This aspect of globalisation is directly connected to the old paradigm, and it is necessary to distinguish this phenomenon from the parallel globalisation project which is part of the new paradigm.

The capitalist globalisation project implies a link-up between the most effective, and therefore most profitable, production apparatus with the wealthiest, and therefore most willing to pay, consumption apparatus. This arrangement is aimed exclusively at facilitating the traffic of goods, services and capital across old national boundaries. Interest in the freedom of movement of individuals is limited to their capacity as labour. It does not automatically follow that there is any general interest in individuals and/or their ideas. Ideas are only interesting in their capacity as products protected by copyright laws, or, in other words, as tradable commodities.

This project is a consequence of new technology: the extreme mobility it offers, its speed and diffuse locality, all qualities which in combination mean that the market is freeing itself entirely from traditional laws, rules and limitations. The basic idea of the project is to confront the politicians of the world with a fait accompli, and drive through a global market free from all tariffs, regulations and, as far as possible, taxes. The purpose of this is, of course, to maximise profits. Because the potential of new technology is so well-suited to capital, the already well-advanced globalisation is forcing the political establishment to retreat. This is expressed in various ways: either as a resigned and ultimately unsustainable isolationism, or, more usually, as an entirely new note in the rhetorical repertoire. Suddenly all the democratic socialists of the world are converting on the gallows and uttering uncompromising paeans of praise to free trade and classical liberalism. This sort of political volte-face should be regarded as a last desperate attempt by the professional political class of capitalism to cling to the last illusory remnants of power. At the same time it makes politics look important and relevant, so that it can "give good media".

The netocratic globalisation project is something altogether different, more of a social phenomenon, based upon the inherent possibilities of the new technologies for communication and contact across great distances and between different cultures. If the great goal of the capitalist is to maximise profit in order to eventually retire and nurture his individual identity, then the netocrat's great aim is to improve and facilitate communications between himself and all the strange experiences and lifestyles which new technology brings within reach. The netocrat seeks out the universal in the global arena, he wants to come up with a universal language, through the use of which he can experience all the exotic impulses he is longing for.

We do not mean to imply that one project is better than the other: it is simply a question of two different forces with different aims within two different systems. In both cases it is a matter of electronic colonialism; economic in the case of the bourgeoisie, cultural for the netocracy. What is interesting from our point of view is the possibility that these forces might not run parallel in the future. When the capitalist project develops in a direction contrary to the structures of the network, which are controlled by the inherent characteristics of technology, it becomes more difficult to control, particularly for the capitalists themselves, who slowly but surely will lose their power to the netocrats. The netocratic globalisation project, on the other hand, cannot possibly fail, and will reward its participants, the netocrats themselves, with increased power.

The late capitalist age is suffering from schizophrenia. It survives, and has always survived, through adaptation, but is obsessed with control, totality and zero risk gambles. If capitalism surrenders the nation state, for instance, this would not be evidence of any new thinking in principle, but merely recognition of the fact that the highest instance of control must be transferred to a supra-national, federal level. Totality expands but the controlling and guiding ambition remains the same. The agreement between capitalism and the netocracy is not merely concerned with differences in background, lifestyle and attitude. The paradigm shift is about a fundamentally altered world-view. History is losing its predetermined direction, utopia is disappearing. The only way forward is no longer the only way; from every point of departure there is an infinite number of possibilities in the form of untrodden paths. Totality, rationalism and orchestrated collectivism are collapsing under the pressure of the virtual world's diversity. The netocracy is replacing the bourgeoisie, dragging the consumtariat along behind it.

The capitalist world is by definition economic, and the choices we are confronted with each day are primarily economic in character. It highlights only those activities which can be registered and measured in economic terms. Consequently capitalism has made money from every possible market and has turned every conceivable resource into a commodity. This enforced economic exploitation of everything it can find is called by the Australian philosopher and social-theorist Brian Massumi "the additivity of capitalism". The state and the market are united in their hostility towards activities which take place outside the economic sector – housework, various forms of unpaid voluntary work, etc. This hostility explains the comprehensive transformation of such activities into controllable and taxable paid work. Instead of parents helping one another with the supervision of children, this activity has become a profession practised by educated experts in return for monetary payment. Professionalism expands, and no activity is too simple to escape the attentions of experts. It is not the task itself which carries status, but the career.

When parents look after one another's children instead of their own, their work can be taxed and included in the state's statistics. In this way there is growth; the parents are included in the production apparatus, they can be registered and become the objects of state legislation governing the care of minors, and everyone is happy. This combined redefinition and redirection of various types of work is a typical example of how growth can be manufactured with a few simple manipulations in the late stages of capitalist society. This also shows that it is not only profit-maximising companies but also, to a similar extent, the welfare state which is showing acute signs of accelerating additivity. Here we are talking about an "economism" whose claims on hegemony have never seriously been challenged.

Capitalism has simply been overwhelmingly successful; it has functioned, which has led to its ideology appearing to be self-evident, elevated above all criticism and therefore almost invisible. Capitalism's appearances under various names have camouflaged its actual monopoly on power by continuously airing political disputes between party-lines which all co-exist nicely under the same meta-ideological umbrella. But there is a reason why capitalism has succeeded so well, and that is that it has been so well-suited to the existing technological and social preconditions. Now that these are undergoing drastic change, everything is suddenly in question. With the breakthrough of informationalism, the previously unassailable position occupied by capitalism is under attack from several directions at once.

The task of the working class was to work at low cost. It has been in the interests of both the bourgeoisie and the state to keep wages as low as possible, but also to avoid violent clashes and if possible to maintain peace in the labour market. Strikes are the central issue here. By giving the workers the right to strike – that is to say, to protest peacefully against low wages – the bourgeoisie was able to guard its monopoly on power. The working classes were effectively disarmed by this, and at the same time it became possible to ascertain exactly, and under relatively orderly conditions, the point at which low wages and bad working conditions threatened to boil over in discontent. Businesses could maximise profits if wages were fixed just above this critical level, and all parties were expected to be satisfied with this. Revolution was postponed once more, and at the lowest possible price. This ritual was repeated each year with a good deal of commotion.

This entire procedure, and the whole of classical capitalist mythology, was permeated by and largely based upon a vague but nonetheless grand promise: the bourgeoisie's undertaking to use material improvements to raise the working class to its own level and thus peacefully achieve the Marxist utopia of a classless society. There was no need for an immoral and violent revolution, the working class just had to grit its teeth and apply itself, and it would be richly rewarded. In this way, with the help of a semblance of common interests, the elite could build alliances with the spokespeople of the working class. The elevation of the working class was a great project of cultural revisionism, and fulfilled its task perfectly: pacifying the individual worker and channelling his energy into an individual project to raise standards, rather than into collective manifestations of displeasure. It killed two birds with one stone: revolution was postponed, and the working class, with its dreams of social elevation, made itself useful through the industrious development of its abilities.

The most interesting difference between the West-European and North American bourgeoisie on the one hand and the Russian bourgeoisie, which had attempted to introduce large-scale industrialisation of the Tsarist empire in the middle of the 19th century, on the other was that the European and American industrialists had the sense to use correctly the available tools and yardsticks and fix wages at a suitable level, whereas in Russia these tools were wholly absent, since there had only ever been minimal contact between the different classes. It was only in the polarised social atmosphere of Russia – where the dominant class was entirely isolated from and dismissive of (at least in terms of recognition) the demands of the working class – that it was possible to conduct a revolution.

The further an industrial society developed from feudal structures, the more flexible and developed its brand of capitalism became, and the smaller the risk for a workers' revolution. It was no coincidence that only the most feudal and agrarian societies in the developed world, Russia and China, suffered turbulent revolutions when industrialism began to accelerate. The difference between revisionist and revolutionary political development within the capitalist paradigm was directly related to the dominant class's access to information about the demands and wishes of the underclass. Violent revolution was to be avoided at all costs; the march of democratic socialism towards power was directly connected to the sophisticated mechanisms of capitalist society in this respect. Nominal power over the state became the basis for the compromise between the demands of the working class and the interests of the elite. Socialist revisionism is the ideology behind this ingenious compromise. When the majority is in charge of the state, how could a revolution be called for in the name of the people?

The terror of political correctness today is an act of bitter revenge by the minority against this worship of the majority. So-called weak groups gather in noisy alliances and demand rights in the form of quotas and special privileges. Pressure is exerted primarily through the media, and minorities with greater media power than others succeed better in this symbolic struggle for control of definitions. The result is the total impoverishment of political culture: the political arena is gradually stripped of substance and becomes the theatre for a frenzied battle between special interest groups. Opinion-based representation – the system upon which western democracy is based and according to which a spokesman represents his voters through the power of his opinions and not on the basis of gender or any other characteristic – is being replaced with a bizarre accounting exercise: every other one must be female, every fifth a pensioner, every tenth an immigrant, etc., etc. in absurdum. This spectacle is comprehensible in late capitalist society where perceptions of political power and the key roll of the mass-media still exist as a form of special-interest wishful-thinking. But in an informationalist paradigm it all looks like very poor theatre, and, if the consumtariat of the future is to have any pretensions to power against the wishes of the netocracy, it will have to find completely new ways of doing so.

On a purely material level, everything suggests that the underclass can continue to expect certain improvements; the social elevation of the underclass which began with capitalism will continue and assume new forms. But because the new underclass is characterised by its patterns of consumption and not by its relatively high living-standards, it is not possible to speak of any genuine reduction in the distance between the classes. A member of the consumtariat will not become a netocrat simply because he gets a larger apartment or a bigger car; he will be just as powerless as before, it is just that the price for his co-operation will have been corrected upwards.

When the supply of workers with a specific skill decreases, wages rise in the sector in question. If this increase in wages is not accompanied by a corresponding rise in productivity, the inevitable result is rising inflation. This is not in the interest of any of the parties within the market, which is why inflation is fiercely combated. The traditional method of raising production without ending up in an inflationary spiral is to promote population growth. A constantly growing population has always satisfied the constant demands of industry for a larger workforce. This sort of development cannot continue for ever; the levels of education which were necessary to increase competence, and the improvements in welfare which were necessary to maintain social stability generally lead to lower birth-rates. When birth-rates in the western world began to decline in the post-war period, there was a need for an alternative method of population growth to make up for the missing infants: large-scale immigration.

A temporary slump in the global economy during the oil crisis of the 1970s led to slower rates of growth and increasing unemployment in Western Europe and North America. Increased competition in the labour market meant that the previously popular immigrants became noticeably less popular, and the importation of labour was drastically reduced. But the dramatic increases in productivity which took place in the early 1990s with the beginnings of the IT-revolution have necessitated a more lenient attitude towards immigration. This is for the simple reason that the western economies are no longer self-sufficient in terms of labour. All over the industrialised world demographic development is following the same trend: there are more old people, and fewer young people.

The number of native workers is decreasing at the same time as the economy is in a period of rapid growth. The demand for external labour is increasing dramatically, which is why the western world is not only able to open its borders, but is actually forced to do so. As a result, there will be a lot of grand rhetoric from officials about multi-cultural society; the elite will combat isolationism and romanticised nationalism as hard as it can. Tolerance towards and curiosity about everything unknown will become an increasingly prominent characteristic of this overheated rhetoric. Naturally, this does not mean that purely ethnic and cultural conflicts, or more generally class-motivated conflicts will disappear. On the contrary, everything points towards heightened polarisation within western culture: the fear of widespread disturbances will become more justified.

It must be admitted that the new dominant class is genuinely cosmopolitan in outlook. The netocratic globalisation project is creating an electronic global culture. What this means in practice, however, is that netocrats in every country will unite on the basis of close contact and common interests, but without any tangible solidarity towards the immigrants who are mowing their lawns and driving underground trains. The netocrats will be defined by the fact that they manipulate information faster than they manage property or produce goods; their activity is thus linked to global networks, which means that their loyalties are virtually rather than regionally based. For them, multi-culturalism at home is partly a question of getting simple tasks performed, and partly a touch of exotic spice to life: an exciting variety of restaurants, clothes and entertainment. The netocrats will pay whatever is necessary to get their lawns cut and to buy tandoori chicken, but will not assume any additional obligations.

The new elite, in contrast to the old, does not perceive itself to have much to do with society in general. Thanks to new technology, it has the best possible means of avoiding troublesome taxation, but in return does not burden the welfare state to any great extent. Private insurance takes care of any private medical care that may be needed, private schools educate their children, privately employed guards will keep thieves and vandals away from their private property. The political establishment will become increasingly powerless, and the common sphere of society will diminish. In conjunction with this, both duties and rights will disappear.

The ideology which makes this state of things appear to be "natural" is meritocracy, once it has been fully implemented: nothing is determined in advance, neither provenance nor money will determine your fate, only your talent and industry. The same old underclass dream of a glittering social ascent, in other words, but the difference this time is that the possibilities of climbing up through the hierarchy are to a large extent real. Whether or not this is perceived as a good thing depends on the perspective you adopt. If by increased equality you mean an individual's improved possibilities to affect his or her own success, then equality will improve. But at the same time individual responsibility will increase, along with individual liability; personal failure will become much more personal. From a class-perspective meritocracy means, as the historian Christopher Lasch has pointed out, that the underclass is continually drained of talent and therefore also of prospective leaders. The elite, on the other hand, is strengthened by this constant circulation and the addition of new talent. Privilege becomes easier to legitimise if it is based on merit, because it is earned, at least to an extent, rather than inherited.

The new immigrants will largely be take their place in the subordinate underclass of the western world. On the other hand, their circumstances will be more or less bearable because their labour is genuinely needed and because growth sectors in their native countries will provide competitive alternatives. But differences in power, status and living standards will still be unavoidable. There are no signs that the specific religious and cultural identities of the various groups of immigrants will dissolve and melt together as a result of globalisation and migration; on the contrary, people without power and status build up their identities around their defining characteristics. Inverted racism is one possible scenario: violence will no longer be the preserve of badly-off natives and directed against welfare-sponging immigrants, but of badly-off immigrants against relatively well-off natives, or against other immigrant groups who are perceived as being more successful.

The growth of informational society will bring with it comprehensive migration. As far as the underclass is concerned, this will be a case, naturally enough, of moving from places with low rates of growth and relatively high birth-rates to areas where the reverse is the case. In North America this will lead to large-scale migration from south to north, and in Europe from east to west. But it will be the netocracy who will lead developments and decide their direction. The new elite is highly mobile, and will move for mainly cultural reasons to those places which are most attractive. This is principally a question of netocratic lifestyle migration. It will not matter how beneficial economic circumstances are: The cities and regions in question will lose out if they cannot offer a sufficiently enticing lifestyle and a sufficiently stimulating cultural environment. The consumtariat will have good reasons to adapt and migrate. It will be better to mow lawns, prepare tandoori chicken and collect their wages as citizens in areas of high demand and strong purchasing power.

In Europe it is already possible to see how the evolving netocracy is migrating towards a belt of large cities stretching from London in the north-west to Milan in the south-east. For the rest of the continent this means an growing and increasingly serious problem of depopulation, a so-called "brain drain" of the same sort as the migration from the European countryside to the cities during the 1900s, when talent and initiative were concentrated in economically dynamic urban areas. This urbanisation under capitalism is now being followed by nodalisation: extensive migration across national borders, from places on the cultural periphery to the cultural centres of the new paradigm, its geographical nodes or junctions. Only a few oases in the depopulated areas will have the foresight to exploit this development to their advantage, by recognising the implications of nodalisation in good time and drawing the correct conclusions as far as their own situation is concerned. The important thing is to create the preconditions for lifestyles which the netocracy finds attractive, of preparing fertile ground for stimulating cultural development. This process demands an unfailing understanding of what the netocracy finds desirable, which in turn will create a thriving market for a post-capitalist meta-netocracy, the lords' overlords.

One fundamental factor for success in this resuscitated system of medieval city states is that political responsibility will be delegated from the nation state to the cities themselves, and that regions rather than nations will be the primary unit of political structures. With globalisation the state will become a burden rather than an advantage; once matters of defence, foreign policy and monetary politics have been elevated to a supra-national level there will be no important matters left for national parliaments to discuss, while at the same time the globalisation project of the elite and the ghettoisation of the underclass will help to dissolve national identity. Dynamic cities which manage to escape enforced subsidisation of the countryside will be well positioned in this struggle. Like the medieval cities of the Hanseatic League before them, they will enter alliances with other cities when this is to their advantage, as it often will be.

It is all a matter of charming the netocracy, of playing upon its desires. The winner in this case really will take it all: wherever the netocracy goes, its servants will follow, and with a well-developed service sector the city in question will become even more attractive. Size is definitely not everything, because quantity is primarily a capitalist valuation. Even at the time of writing it is possible to see how the netocracy in the USA is finding its way to medium-sized cities like Seattle, Miami, Austin and San Francisco rather than to the mega-metropolises of New York and Los Angeles. The same thing is likely to happen in Europe and Asia. A careful balance of a wealth of different factors will matter more than size alone. This is a matter, naturally, of housing, infrastructure, communications, but these things alone are not enough. The netocrats are pack-animals, they seek out their like, and places where the range of lifestyles on offer is most varied. They will move wherever there is greatest cultural dynamism.

It is difficult to distinguish between cause and effect, because there is a constant interplay where the different levels mutually affect one another. Cultural climate affects migration and demographics, at the same time as these naturally affect the cultural climate. The fact that the population is gradually ageing means that guaranteed pensions will diminish in value, which in turn will mean that the age of retirement will begin to vary and will gradually creep upwards. The trend of the late 20th century towards youth culture – a sort of cultural puberty lasting well into adulthood – will become exacerbated by this, but even this development will not be unambiguous. The most striking pattern will be quite different: an increasingly wide gap between the culture of the netocratic elite and that of the passive consumtariat. In order to understand how this dynamic will function, it is necessary to look at how the media industry is developing.

The 20th century was a golden age for the mass-media. Technology made it possible first via radio, then via television, to reach out with the same message to an entire nation at the same time, then, via satellite, to the whole world. The ether-based media were the best propaganda instruments the world had ever seen. It is impossible to overestimate the importance of radio to the maintenance of national unity in Britain and the USA during the Second World War. Television played the leading role during the latter half of the century, and television's domination of mass culture has given considerable support to the slowly dying nation-state. It does not matter whether television was commercial, as in North America, or state-controlled, as in Europe. The central message was always the same: the nation is a "natural" entity, and beyond discussion, because nation and television audiences were one and the same thing. People watching the same programmes formed a connected and "naturally" segregated group. All of us television viewers must join together and behave like good citizens and consumers so that the wheels of the production apparatus turn smoothly.

Ironically it is the further development of the technology which has artificially kept the nation state and capitalism alive which is now burying the old paradigm. When the sitcom Cosby, in which all the central roles were played by black actors, became the most popular television programme in the USA during the 1980s, this was held up as a promising sign of the growing tolerance of the television media and its beneficial influence on its audience and on society as a whole. In actual fact this development was confirmation of a phenomenon that was already well-known within sociology: the fragmentation of the television audience and the gradual decline of the mass-media. The number of available channels increased but viewing figures fell. The decrease in television consumption (decreased consumption of each distributed unit) was a clear indication of the marginalisation of the media. "Broadcasting" was becoming more a matter of "narrowcasting"; instead of trying to capture large audiences, television channels were forced to concentrate on strictly limited segments of the audience.

The fact that Cosby topped the charts of viewing figures for a while was not primarily an indication of a new interest in racial issues and/or social justice within American television, but simply that unemployed, single black women had become the largest identifiable target group for television advertisers. This indicates not only a fragmentation of the audience and the media, but also an alarming brain drain. Nappies and washing powder are examples of products which are still worth advertising on television, whereas advertising trendy clothes or advanced electronics on television would be a waste of time and money. The new elite itself has little interest in consuming television, it is far too busy building networks with the help of new, interactive media. This has not prevented the netocrats from taking control of the medium of television and learning rapidly to use it to divert and anaesthetise the heterogeneous underclass which is united only in terms of its lowly status and increasing powerlessness.

At a stroke everything has become entertainment: the weather, the news, not to mention political journalism and election reports – all specially produced for an underclass of passive consumers, couch-potatoes with remote-controls sitting in the flickering light of the post-modern campfire, prepared to let themselves be entertained to sleep, with the chance of a win on some televised lottery as the highpoint of the week. For those who happen to wake up from their dormancy, television offers a studied and cynical level of pretended interaction. Ring and vote for the best player in the match or the best song in the programme, let us know what the subject for this evening's populist orchestrated debate should be! Naturally, all of this quasi-activity from the viewers is monitored in detail to help fine-tune the targeting of different groups.

The bourgeoisie has always had the greatest respect for television, and registers anxious delight at its infernal effectiveness as an instrument of propaganda, regarding it both as a wet-dream and as a terrible threat if, God forbid, it should ever get into the wrong hands. For the bourgeoisie television is the sexiest thing going, while the netocracy has a considerably more cynical view of it. Televisual entertainment still functions tolerably as opium for the masses, but its future is anything but glamorous. Television's fate, like all old media that technology has left behind, will be to provide content for the new interactive media, in the same way that the novel provided content for film, and film in turn provided content for television. This explains the netocracy's nonchalance towards television. The ceremonial pomp that once surrounded television is gone, the fortified studio bunkers and glittering office palaces are gone, grand, prestigious programming is a thing of the past, as is its continually increasing budget. Netocratic television is minimalist and functional, fluid and flexible, and has been out-sourced to a range of independent production companies. But all of this does not mean that television is not consciously stupid and stupefying; the netocracy will not channel its creativity into a medium whose future is behind it and whose audience it wants to control but not be part of.

In the final days of the capitalist paradigm it is still possible to regard television advertising as a necessary evil, an antidote to the unpalatable fact that someone has to pay for production, hopefully with something left over. In the world of netocratic television there will no longer be any real difference between adverts and programmes. Every detail will be product placement. The actors are products, selling themselves as products, when they are not occupied in selling actual products during commercial breaks. The products in turn are actors selling both themselves and the actors who appear in the adverts. The result is adverts for adverts for adverts, and, for the consumtariat who lack both the possibility and the capacity to participate actively, passive acceptance of the ordained rules of the game will be the only possible practical option. You pay for your entertainment with the minimum of attention, and exercise your participation the next time you choose between different brands of washing-powder. This is how you are told to realise yourself within the consumtariat and establish an individual lifestyle: by choosing washing-powder X or washing-powder Y for your dirty towels and underwear. Are you an environmentally-friendly user of X or a domestically economical user of Y? Choose your identity and win a free packet, here's the web-address!

Ever since informational society began to take shape in the 1970s philosophers and sociologists have questioned traditional concepts and distinctions such as work/leisure and production/consumption. To what extent have these conceptual pairs functioned as instruments of control under capitalism? How can we reasonably define different human activities in a social construct dictated by informationalism? Once again, we can see how old and tested concepts assume new meanings when their ecological context, and technology, changes. Consumption rather than production will be the activity which defines the underclass, where roughly equal amounts of resources will be expended whether one is employed or unemployed; the consumption of goods and services ought therefore, according to thinkers such as Baudrillard and Deleuze, to be regarded as an alternative form of production, one which is maintaining the machinery of society.

This revision of the definitions "consumption" and "production" is actually central to any understanding of the informationalist paradigm. According to capitalism an unemployed person, or anyone who stays at home from work during the day, has not achieved anything that day. Admittedly the day may have been filled with various practical tasks and social contacts, as well as a certain level of consumption, but none of this counts for anything in a paradigm where the only thing that counts is the production of goods and services, along with the surplus value this is expected to generate.

Production is productive and is therefore by definition something positive for a capitalist, whereas consumption is regarded as a negative, a diminution of a constructed value, a form of impious indulgence that one might grant oneself if one has been particularly productive. From a mobilistic point of view this division, the whole of this mechanistic chain of cause and effect, is purely illusory. In actual fact each activity presupposes the other; one is not possible without the other, they are two aspects of one and the same process. The consumer's desire for all the products and services that he or she cannot actually be said to need in any real sense is the decisive factor in the whole construction, and this desire has to be nurtured. The process is complicated, but the formula is simple: adverts + consumtariat = desire. The whole thing is an informationalist cycle, analogous to photosynthesis. Adverts are the sunlight, the consumtariat the diverse vegetation which transforms light into the energy which is the precondition of biology. This is the role of the consumtariat in the whole process: subordinate, but at the same time indispensable. What line of work the individual consumer is occupied with, if he or she works at all, is actually fairly irrelevant in this context.

We cannot determine if it is desire which produces goods and services, or if it is the goods and services which produce desire. The truth is that they produce and are produced by each other. It is pointless to try to distinguish one from the other when consumers are increasingly being paid to receive and react to adverts, and when consumers are increasingly using their attention as payment instead of money. Who is performing the real work, and who is paying whom for what? What seems at first to be trivial wordplay is actually the decisive factor in the struggle for power. In the capitalist paradigm the superior position of the bourgeoisie was based upon its power to define the work of the working class; under the new paradigm the new dominant class governs the new underclass by manipulating what could be called the consumption tasks of the consumtariat – more simply called desire. The fundamental difference between the netocracy and the consumtariat is thus that the former controls its own production of desire, whereas the latter obeys the orders of the former. Hence there is a vital symbolic value for netocracy in continually signifying in one's choice of lifestyle that one is independent of the consumptive production of manipulated desire, and thereby indicating one's social distance from the vulgar masses.

A netocratic lifestyle demands unique abilities and a particular overview. Because the moment that a product, a service or an idea becomes part of the advertised message, it is profaned, and destined for shabby mass-consumption.

What differentiates the netocracy is instead "imploitative" consumption: knowingly exclusive and minimalist, utterly free from directives. Netocrats travel to places without a tourist industry, listen to music that is not available from any record company, get their entertainment from subscription channels or net-sites which neither carry adverts nor advertise their own existence, consume goods and services that are never mentioned in the media and which are therefore unknown to the masses. This lifestyle can never be fixed, it will always be in a process of constant change. When the netocrats tire of one desire and the experience has lost its value, they can always throw it to the masses, recreating it for the consumtariat with the help of adverts, which also has its economic advantages. But whatever is reserved for the time being for the netocracy will always be unknown, incomprehensible and out of reach for the consumtariat. In an age where automated factories or workers in low-cost regions of distant continents are increasingly responsible for the production of goods and services, work itself can no longer be the organising principle of society. The tiresome discussions of "the new economy" have to a lamentably large extent concentrated on glamorised slogans, capitalist-tinted descriptions of the future of the Internet, which suggest that this is a medium primarily intended for electronic mail-order sales. This suggests that nothing has fundamentally changed, as if new technology was merely a collection of trendy appliances with which we can happily go on mending and patching up old systems. The interesting thing about everything new is recognised all too seldom: that old definitions and concepts are being turned upside down, like for instance the production/consumption constellation, which forces us to revise all the associations we have regarding these concepts. A new paradigm implies new rules and new impulses in the struggle between the dominant class and the working class. Both capitalists and labourers worked, but it was the capitalists who dictated the terms. Both netocrats and the consumtariat consume, but once again it is the elite which is dictating the terms.

7.

THE NEW BIOLOGY AND NETOCRATIC ETHICS

ONE IMPORTANT REASON WHY "the new economy" seems so mysterious is that people generally, and economists in particular, have had such vague notions about how "the old economy" worked. Political ideologies and the social sciences that developed when the universities were granted a central position close to power in the capitalist paradigm obstinately followed the totalistic path, as we have already seen. National economists created sophisticated models that were impressive from every respect apart from the decisive fact that they gave a misrepresentative and useless image of economic reality. Their very starting-point was erroneous. Whether they represented the right or left of the political spectrum, the overriding goal was always the same: to build an all-encompassing theory that reduced the economy to an admittedly complicated, but coherent and manageable zero-sum game. Someone wins and someone loses, one presupposes the other, and all that was needed to avoid unnecessary friction and/or social injustice was distribution and regulation. Wishful-thinking about balance and order was mistakenly applied to a system whose normal state is characterised by constant change and a sizeable measure of destruction and annihilation.

Under feudalism the economy, or even the handling of money, were not things that serious people participated in. The production of goods and trade were consequently not regarded as sufficiently elevated or interesting to warrant philosophical analysis. Peasants grew crops and nurtured livestock, tradesmen engaged in bartering and aristocrats exacted tax in the form of goods and services. But when industrialisation, mechanisation and the transition from exchange of goods to coins and notes had reached a critical level, they brought with them dramatic social changes that gave rise to an entirely new set of questions. For instance, should the rapidly growing population be fed with the help of imported agricultural goods, or was it better to be self-sufficient in foodstuffs? Was it wise to protect your own country's peasants with the help of import tariffs? The rate of change was unparalleled, and the whole of the old rulebook was quickly outdated. So the first economic theory, the creed of wealth, was born, with the task of returning society to the harmonious social order which was supposed to have been lost.

The pattern for thought within the social sciences during the late 1700s and early 1800s was provided by the natural sciences in general, and physics in particular. The prestige of Newtonian physics was enormous, its achievements grandiose: uncovering the regulated mechanisms that governed the mysterious movements of the celestial bodies. What was required was an economic Newton, a philosopher who could 'discover' a law of gravity for economics, and uncover the eternal principles governing the divine order that was assumed to exist behind the apparent chaos. This was an impossible task, as economist Michael Rothschild and others have noted, for the simple reason that Newtonian physics was an unusable model, since it lacked a historical dimension. Time, or, to put it another way, a direction for physical processes, did not make its appearance in the natural sciences until the advent of thermodynamics later in the 1800s. For Newton, the universe is an unchanging perpetual motion machine, a sort of cosmic clock whose regulated movements never vary. This eternal, mechanical repetition was the whole point with Newton. His theory does not allow for qualitative change, and every economic model constructed with Newton as its pattern is consequently concerned with finding excuses for changes instead of understanding them. The goal was to achieve balance in the system, using suitable means, which is why the change that lies in the nature of things was regarded as unpleasant disruption.

Science finds what it seeks. The Scottish professor of philosophy Adam Smith, the central figure of classical national economics, consequently found an economic law of gravity: self-interest. When every individual is concerned with his own self-interest, the result, paradoxically, is the optimal state for social economics, according to Smith. Different people obviously have different talents and abilities, and it is when they have complete freedom to develop their talents and offer their services that the economy is maximised, to the good of everyone. Therefore regulations and import tariffs were bad, because the system was self-regulating. Expanding markets meant increased productivity, ran the optimistic gospel of laissez-faire liberalism. But even Smith did not accommodate change within the equation. His theory describes an imagined state of equilibrium, a liberal utopia, rather than the turbulence of reality. The system would automatically achieve balance and manage all possible disturbances internally if only it was left alone. But the idea that the system itself might undergo any decisive changes formed no part of Smith's calculations. That was a thought that could not be contemplated unless the illustrious Newtonian structure was abandoned, which it itself was unthinkable.

Smith's view of the economy as a well-oiled machine attracted many eager disciples. But not his optimism. David Ricardo worked from the theory that the amount of resources and goods in circulation on the market was finite. When the population is expanding and the number of consumers increases, increased demand leads to higher prices, especially of food. Hence equilibrium is disturbed in favour of wealthy land-owners; their profit corresponds to the consumers' and employees' loss in a desperate zero-sum game. There is no alternative way of keeping profits up other than keeping wages down, so strong social tension was to be expected. Fascination for the new economic science, thanks to Ricardo's theses, grew so large that national economics was believed to be capable of explaining everything. To a large extent it replaced philosophy, which was in a state of paralysis, as the meta-science, the explanatory model for everything.

Ricardo's system was the theory used and incorporated by Karl Marx in his historical philosophy: economic and social oppositions, with their basis in the fact that the masses were being relentlessly sucked dry by the ruling class, escalate to the critical point where it becomes necessary at all costs to carry out a radical transformation of society, followed by a planned economy. For Marx, the economy was also a machine, but not well-oiled and self-generating as it was for Adam Smith, but a machine in real need of constant supervision and ideological direction. The political goal was a static economy, a regularly ticking clock. This is also in all essential respects the view of national economics that has been dominant during its two-hundred-year history, which has left concrete evidence in the form of various political programmes for regulation of the markets and for distribution. Buttons and levers have been pushed and pulled in the vain hope of achieving permanent stability in the system.

The various political camps have only differed from each other in emphasis. For liberals and conservatives, the right to private ownership has been sacred. The right's alternative to the monopoly scare of the left has been competition, but the fundamental problematics have remained the same: limited resources and an expanding population. Of course it is possible to increase productivity in, for instance, agriculture, but not in proportion to the increased manpower required, according to the law of diminishing returns which John Stuart Mill, one of the central figures of liberalism, formulated at about the same time as Marx and Engels were writing The Communist Manifesto. Increased welfare would never increase enough to satisfy the growing population. The best that could be hoped for was that a socio-economic status quo would be achieved, by appealing to the people's better nature and keeping the birth-rate down that way.

These ideas of the economy as a zero-sum game, and the curse of population growth came mostly from the cleric, economist and historian Thomas Malthus, whose influence on thought during the 1800s and early 1900s can scarcely be exaggerated. It was the fear of the terrible consequences of over-population that Malthus managed to inspire in his contemporaries which eventually led to birth-control measures being made available for a larger market, even if Malthus himself preached abstinence, and marriage later in life. His theory was based upon the necessary balance between the number of individuals and the amount of resources. According to Malthus's merciless principle, the population increases at a dramatically higher rate ("geometrically" or "exponentially") than the production of food does ("arithmetically"). This imbalance is unsustainable in the long run, and the excess must be removed one way or another. In nature this was regulated by famine and other catastrophes, and for human beings war was another option. Suffering and misery are inevitable anyway, and progress is a chimera. Helping the poor with handouts only makes things worse, because it will only lead to even more mouths to feed.

One of the greatest ironies in the history of ideas is that Malthus, the gloomy godfather of zero-sum philosophy, was also the great facilitator of evolution – in other words: the theory of change, development and process. The cul-de-sac which Malthus manoeuvred into made a whole new way of thinking possible. What Charles Darwin did was to apply history to history. He showed that change is not a deviation from any divine order, or a disturbance of any equilibrium in nature, but that constant change is itself the natural state. The species which had hitherto been regarded as eternal and constant, like perfect geometric figures, are actually historical products of other, extinct species. They are developed and adapt themselves according to circumstances. The problem for Darwin was that for a long time he lacked a driving-force in the process, an idea of the reasons for and mechanisms of change. He was clear about the idea of evolution, which was itself revolutionary, but did not understand how evolution itself actually functioned. Every peasant already knew that it was possible to evolve, to "improve" livestock and crops. It was a question of using specimens with the necessary characteristics for breeding and cultivation. But who was in charge of breeding and cultivation in nature? Who was responsible for the selection, and how did it take place? This was the big question.

To begin with, Darwin imagined that the same laws applied to species as to individuals; that they are born, mature, and die of biological necessity. After spending a year and several months getting lost in hopeless dead-ends, almost by chance he happened to read Malthus's theory of population. "For entertainment", he wrote in his diary. Suddenly everything fell into place. It was nature itself that oversaw selection. If more individuals are born into a population than the available food can sustain, the consequence is that many of these individuals die prematurely, without having had time to breed. Those who survive anyway, and, in the next step, go on to breed, are those individuals who are best suited to circumstances. The same process repeats itself for generation after generation. The cumulative result of this process is, eventually, the evolution of the species: natural selection rewards only very few of all possible variants. At the same time, the surrounding environment is continually changing, partly as a result of geological and climatic factors, partly as a result of its own internal dynamic. The altered species influence their own and others' circumstances, which in turn fuels further changes within the various species. There is no natural balance. The process never ends.

The ironic thing is that Darwin completely misunderstood Malthus. Or, if you want to take a more generous view of the matter: he made a breath-takingly original and ingenious interpretation of Malthus's utterly pessimistic reasoning, so that it fitted in better with his own thoughts. The struggle for survival which, for Malthus, was the root of all the world's ills, was for Darwin the mechanism which gave evolution a power and a direction towards increasingly sophisticated organisms. Thus biology took a decisive influence from economic philosophy, while economic thinking rejected biology and its historical perspective in favour of Newtonian physics and its static world-view. The same thing applied generally to sociology and the other new social sciences; Newton's cosmic perpetual motion machine formed the basic pattern for the creation of models under capitalism. The study of society took as its starting point a fictitious system in an artificial state of rest, and change was regarded as a disruptive anomaly. Thought was trapped within fixed, totalistic structures.

When Newton presented his theory he was hailed as the leading light of his age. When Darwin presented his theory he was practically treated as a criminal, and the theory of evolution has remained, outside the world of the natural sciences, extremely controversial for a remarkable length of time. Resistance to the theory of evolution was emotional rather than intellectual. The eternal and predictable, with its roots in Judeo-Christian religion and totalistic philosophy, always appealed to self-indulgent western dreams of Man's control and omnipotence. So change and coincidence were regarded with terror. This is why classical Newtonian physics has remained the model for natural sciences and continued to provide the model for the general world-view during the whole of the capitalist paradigm, even after physics itself had moved on from Newton, incorporated a historical dimension (with the formulation of the laws of thermodynamics), and become programmatically unpredictable, virtual, and generally exotic (thanks to quantum mechanics). We can therefore draw the conclusion that the old economics, like the old sociology and everything else scientifically "old", has been old for a very long time.

To a large degree, Darwin turned everything regarded as sacred on its head. The beautiful tableau of nature is not complete, but a permanent work in progress, and the question is whether it is actually particularly beautiful. The species alive now are neither original nor constant, and merely constitute a phase of the long development from simple to more complex organisms. The infinite wealth of variety and complexity in nature presupposes no divine creator, or any hidden intelligence of any kind, not even a plan; all that is needed are oceans of time. Evolution is a sort of algorithm, a numerical operation of immense scale applied to real life. Or a computer programme, if you like. Its function is to sift out the losers.

The American philosopher Daniel C Dennett has compared this process to a tennis tournament: two players meet, one survives and goes on to the next round, while the other is lost to oblivion. All knockout championships produce one winner, who has the qualities most favoured by the rules. If we are talking about tennis, then skill is largely decisive, but coin-tossing is purely about luck, or, to put it another way, the ability to avoid bad luck. It is obviously extremely unlikely that anyone would win at coin-tossing twenty times in a row, but if we organise a coin-tossing tournament with 1,048,575 participants, then there will certainly be someone who manages this. This sort of algorithm also does what it is supposed to: they unfailingly pick out a winner irrespective of how large the number of participants. Evolution is a form of knockout tournament whose rules are not only extremely complicated and full of previously unpredicted elements of chance; they are also changing the whole time. One round of coin-tossing, the next round a backwards, blindfolded, slalom sack-race. There will always be someone who wins and many, many losers. We are all winners: we who are writing this, you who are reading it, your friends and pets and houseplants, the trees in the woods and the worms in the soil, everything that is alive here and now. The losers are all the others. 99.99 per cent of all the species that have ever existed are now extinct. They were, quite simply, knocked out of the tournament.

We use a parallel logic when we pose classic hypothetical questions about how our lives would have looked if one event or other had never taken place, or if we had taken important decisions differently. What is this but a meme-Darwinian equivalent to Dennett's gene-Darwinian analysis? The other selves that we imagine we might have become instead of our current self, if the course of events had been different, could be said to be examples of inferior meme-Darwinian mutations, compared to the "I" who "survived", and who therefore enjoys the advantage of posing the

126

hypothetical reasoning at the cost of "the extinct selves". This is the basis of the Foucauldian process of subjectification which is replacing individualism in netocratic society, and we shall return to this in the next chapter.

Nature is no picnic. Ruthless pruning promotes what is functional under the existing circumstances. Even our aesthetic comprehension of the existence which has survived with us, nature itself, is based upon the ingrained survival strategy of our genes. The beauty that we believe that we see in the colours of an orchid or the gaudy feathers of a peacock, and the fascination we feel at the giraffe's long neck, only become "beauty" and "fascination" to us because they confirm and underline evolutionary adaptability in our own great brain. Aesthetics are also a built-in genetic warning lamp. We appreciate a small child's attempts to walk and speak, or a dog's loyalty towards his master or mistress; the child and the dog are both useful and pleasurable to us, the usefulness and pleasure are mutual, the child and the dog appear to be aesthetically attractive, and we seem the same to them. At the same time we retreat from poisonous rattlesnakes and dustbins reeking of bacteria, because these phenomena are a threat to our own survival and have therefore been programmed into our genes as aesthetically repulsive.

Darwin's theory was far from watertight. One significant gap was the absence of a satisfactory explanation of how the winning characteristics were inherited from one generation to the next. A child generally shows a clear resemblance to its parents, but even children are not an even mixture of their parents' characteristics. One white and one black cat do not get a uniformly grey litter of kittens. If the parents' disposition to certain characteristics was completely mixed, the result would be an smoothing-out of all spectacular distinctive features, an even and uniform mass of bio-matter. But instead nature exhibits a constantly increasing level of complexity, variation and specialisation. How can this multiplicity and colourful display be explained?

The answer was given in a series of ground-breaking scientific discoveries in the latter half of the 1900s. In 1953 the researchers Francis Crick and James Watson described the unique structure of the DNA-molecule for the first time. By the beginning of the 1960s it was possible to read individual words written in genetic code, and by the middle of the same decade the whole of the code had been cracked, and now, at the beginning of the twenty-first century, the whole of the human genome has been mapped. The whole of our biological past, all the genetic preconditions for our future will be an open book. Quite literally. All the words in the book are written with the four chemical letters: A, C, G and T (adenine, cytosine, guanine and thiamine) in various combinations. Every living organism that has ever existed is created according to similar, now easily-read, instructions, all of them written in the same language.

The new genetics is one of the greatest intellectual revolutions ever. Suddenly biology is entirely digital. Life itself, the reproduction of cells and their creation of ordered systems of varying complexity, is a process which basically stems from information management. Life is fundamentally a question of the dispersal of information. Our genetic constitution is a collection of recipes, or programmes, for the production of proteins, which in turn regulate the body's chemistry. The body is the vessel of tissue which biological information has chosen to use. Thanks to pre-programmed information, the cells of the body know where they are and what they are supposed to do. No-one has to teach the egg how to become a chicken, the egg already knows. So the ancient information theorists were right in principle. It is information that breathes life into matter. One of the Nobel Prize-winners for medicine in 1969, Max Delbruck, suggested, possibly as a joke, that Aristotle ought to be awarded the same prize posthumously for the discovery of DNA. The old philosopher was right in that the form of the hen is already innate within the egg.

But genetic information does not merely constitute a recipe for anatomy, but also for behaviour. Classical humanists do not want to believe this, and insist that man has a soul, and that this soul and all spiritual phenomena are in some way independent of both the body and biology. Only soulless animals have instincts, we humans are above such things. Committed behaviourists are also sceptical, they claim that reflexes and behaviour are learned. Nature, and society, are regarded as one vast educational establishment, a sophisticated system of punishment and reward which forms the individual by encouraging certain behaviours and suppressing others. Man is, according to this view, an unwritten page. But the new genetics has smashed this way of seeing things. We can never learn things which we cannot learn. We will never be able to learn things that we lack the genetic predisposition for, however much we are rewarded or punished.

The brain is pre-programmed to be able to handle certain determined types of problem with the help of certain determined processes. The acquisition of language is one obvious example: our ability to understand and use grammar is innate, and research has localised one of the genes that is central in this context in chromosome number seven. A deviant "spelling" of this gene, what you might call a spelling mistake, means markedly lower linguistic capabilities (SLI, Specific Language Impairment) in otherwise entirely normally intelligent people: they lack the capacity to internalise grammatical structures. This means that every new word they encounter really is new to them; for every verb, for instance, they must learn each conjugated form separately, along with every plural form of each new noun, and so on. Quite simply, the pattern is not instinctively clear to them.

This means it is not possible to replace instincts with learning. Of course, someone with SLI can learn to communicate with the outside world, albeit with certain difficulties in understanding and making him- or herself understood, but he or she can never learn to think grammatically. That we humans, in contrast to our close relatives among the apes, have learned to use grammatically constructed language is not because we have been more industrious and have tried harder than they have, but that, thanks to genetic changes, we have developed new, species-specific instincts. Language – which in its spoken and, later, written forms has been the dominant means of cultural transfer and development – has, without any doubt, its roots in biology. We have learned what we have been able to learn. On a fundamental level, it is the information in our genes that determines "who we are".

The consequence of this is that there really is a "human nature", and that this influences to a high degree not just our capacity for language acquisition, but our behaviour and our culture generally. A new-born child is not a blank page, but the carrier of a programme that admittedly allows for an enormous amount of development, learning and interactivity with the surrounding world, but which, in spite of this, has its special structures and its special limitations which are ultimately determined by biological history. The brain is a product of evolution, and from this follows a whole succession of collective, fundamental thought-patterns. Genes keep culture on a leash, as Edward O Wilson suggested.

But the idea that there is a connection between biology and society is still met with bitter opposition from many directions. The same ideas are often summed up, in a semantically dubious way, as "reductionism" or "determinism". This opposition is largely politically motivated: one basic thesis in Marxism is that society entirely shapes the citizen's consciousness, and that a new society would mean the creation of a completely new person. If it turns out that biology is the ultimate determinant, then the Marxist left will have to think again. But even within the social and human sciences, the accepted stand-point of the entire twentieth century was that biological evolution and cultural development are two separate phenomena with no points of contact. What has been of interest for research has consequently been questions about how the social environment has shaped human behaviour, rather than how man's social instincts have shaped society.

Even this point of view has its ideological causes, mainly the fact that coarse misinterpretations of the theory of evolution, together with other quasi-sciences, have been used by a long succession of charlatans to legitimise various racist and other suspect ideologies. "Lower standing cultures" have been "explained" with reference to a supposed innate refinement, and so on. The desire to dissociate from such "vulgar biologisms" is in itself quite understandable, but any consequent attitude of "guilt by association" constitutes just as destructive an act of intellectually blinkered thinking in the other direction. Blinkers are always blinkers, no matter how noble the reason for wearing them.

The fundamental idea of the theory of evolution, that it is chance which is decisive, is the complete opposite of the starting-point of vulgar biologisms. All talk of different races and their varying genetic disposition for highly developed culture is complete nonsense. The fact that people in the fertile crescent of the Middle East abandoned life as hunter-gatherers at an early stage and built the first agricultural society was purely the result of the fact that circumstances there were right. The climate was favourable, and, above all, there were plants which were suited to domestication and cultivation on a large scale. One led to the other in an increasingly advanced feedback loop. Increased access to food and fixed dwellings led to population growth, which in turn created dramatically improved conditions for increased specialisation and a more advanced social structure. Which in turn generated even more economic growth, and, later on, cathedrals, sonnets and string quartets.

But the right conditions alone are not sufficient as an explanation. Any friend of order might ask: the conditions for what? It is not possible to avoid biology and social instincts any more. The humanist bourgeoisie were passionate about the refinement of culture that they saw as characteristic of Man, and which raised him above beasts and the law of the jungle. Like a fundamentalist sect, humanism insisted on Man's unique position, sort of floating just above the rest of nature. That culture had its roots in biology, and was an indivisible part of it, was unthinkable. But what possible alternative is there? If the construction of society and culture do not have an evolutionary basis, what sort of origin might it have? The answer can be found among the absolutes of religion and myth: culture as miraculous creation, a gift to humanity from God knows who. For the netocracy which is now assuming power, these metaphysical bolt-holes lack intellectual credibility. So the wall between nature and culture is being torn down and humanism is going to its grave.

When we compare cultural evolution with biological, this is not only a matter of a spectacular metaphor. It is a question of a scientific and socio-philosophical earthquake. The Newtonian/static/mechanical view of society, culture and the economy is finally relinquishing is cast-iron grip on thought now that the capitalist paradigm is drawing to its close. Physics, in particular Newtonian physics, is no longer the model science. The twenty-first century belongs to biology. An entirely new world-view is taking shape before our eyes. We are talking about a world beyond humanism, trans-humanism.

Genetics has one important characteristic which makes it irresistibly interesting: it works. Advances within plant and animal production have been spectacular in recent years. It is no longer possible to question seriously either the methods or the theoretical basis. At the same time, our knowledge about the human species is increasing at a dizzying rate. The mapping of the human genome means the identification of the circa 100,000 genes which, spread over 23 chromosomes, make up the chemical formula for a human being. The whole of this incomprehensibly long text – about a billion words, which is the equivalent of 800 Bibles – will be readable, which will give us detailed information about both our past and our future. Moreover, the text can be edited.

With knowledge of his genetic predispositions, man can, for the first time in his history, plan his life from genuinely fundamental information: he can choose an education and a career that suits him, create children with a partner who possesses a complementary set of genes, choose not to eat harmful foodstuffs, and so on. Employers and authorities will have access to aptitude tests worth the name. The meritocracy, as Swedish biologist Thorbjörn Fagerström has pointed out, will materialise in the entirely new form of a "genocracy". This development will naturally be met with protests, not least from classical humanists who take offence at the fact that people's inherited aptitudes are compared and ranked. But it will be difficult to claim that the process is not "natural". Nothing could be more natural than comparisons and ranking, that is what natural selection is all about, and what principal of selection could be more "natural" than the genetic? This development will be unstoppable, for the simple reason that its application actually works, and that the principle of "right man, right job" is so valuable for the interested parties. It will be claimed that certain job categories are so important that for that particular case the end justifies the means. And that is where the dam will burst. When a taboo has been transgressed in one specific area, it is impossible to maintain this taboo for society in general. Particularly in a plurarchic society.

The connection between sexuality and reproduction is disappearing. Sex is becoming more of a hobby, an expression of identity, with neither desired nor undesired consequences. Instead, reproduction will be managed under orderly conditions in laboratories. Who is the parent of whom will be a complicated question when sex-cells, which in principle could come from anywhere, are installed in artificial wombs. "Pregnancies" will be carefully monitored. When it is time for the "birth", the chance of surprises will be drastically reduced. As a result of gene-manipulation cancer, Alzheimer's, allergies and a whole list of other illnesses will be preventable at the embryo stage. It will be possible, to a large extent, to shape, or rather programme, your "offspring". And even to add qualities that we hardly used to think of as "human".

This development is being hastened by the demise of the belief in a perfect "natural order" regulating how reproduction should happen. Means of reproduction have actually varied a lot during the evolutionary process. Our original forbears practised cell-budding. Later on they laid eggs and determined the sex of their offspring by regulating the temperature around the eggs. The reason why gender-determining genes got the upper-hand was that every individual, even at an early stage, needed to prepare for the gender-determined tasks that awaited after birth. So the only evolutionary "natural" is change itself. One humanistic argument against placing an artificially inseminated egg in an artificial womb is that this would be a typical example of interference in and assault on nature. The problem with this sort of reasoning is that it assumes that culture and nature are two essentially different phenomena in opposition to each other. But this schematic way of seeing things is completely outdated in the informationalist paradigm. Culture is a new version of nature: Nature 2.0.

The increasingly marginalised humanist institutions of power from capitalism will raise demands for restrictive laws governing genetic technology. They will demand observation and strict control by the state and academic experts of all research which comes into contact with the old taboos of the bourgeoisie. In many cases these demands will get a response from politicians, and in certain cases more or less extensive regulation of genetic experimentation has already come into force. But this is of little importance. The constantly weakening position of the nation-state in comparison to new, growing forces – such as the adventurous netocracy and the expansive multinational biotechnology companies – will impose insurmountable obstacles for these political efforts. The most advanced genetic research is already carried out in closed laboratories and under great secrecy on privately owned domains, which makes it extremely difficult to control. Besides, the West's strongly Judeo-Christian-coloured attitudes about the sanctity of the unique individual is anything but universal. In other parts of the world, in Asia for instance, there is a far less sentimental view of the matter, and research carries on unhindered.

We can count on a shaky and conflict-filled process of acclimatisation. Radical biomedicinal advances have traditionally aroused feverish debate and met resistance from groups which believe their moral authority to be threatened. Corneal transplants are an instructive example. When it became medically possible to save people's sight with the help of fresh corneas from the recently deceased, this met with strong resistance and the method was banned in Great Britain, amongst other countries. The method was classified as unethical on the basis of its use of body-parts from the deceased. Their dead bodies were regarded, ironically, both as sacred and impure at the same time. But today this method is a routine procedure. Saving the sight of the living became, as information about the procedure spread and superseded old moralisations, more important than maintaining the sanctity of the corpse.

In a society without a central moral authority, even without a parliament, it will be this silent battle for power between these interest groups which will determine what is regarded as acceptable and, above all, what is practised. Something which is unethical today might well be totally accepted tomorrow. In spite of everything, people will willingly accept the new medicines offered by applied genetic technology. They might suddenly be able to accept the specially created organs of manipulated pigs for transplantation, if they or someone close to them is in dire need of them. And when they have the chance to choose, people would like to have well-formed children, without a known predisposition to cancer, for instance. Pragmatism directs medical ethics, not vice versa. Netocratic ethics are therefore a hyper-biological pragmatism.

It is hard to imagine that people would choose to do without the very possibility of choosing. From a historical point of view, the choice of forbidding choice is only applicable within extremely hard-line religious sects (like for instance the Amish people's rejection of electricity). It is simply not in our genes, as the history of science clearly demonstrates. We are curious by nature, and extremely adaptable. On the basis of all available information, within the near-future it will be possible to create trans-genetic clones of ourselves, completely identical except in the aspects we choose to modify: not near-sighted, not bald, whatever we want. These lightly retouched copies could even be used as living stores of reserve parts; perhaps we will need, for instance, a fresh new liver to replace the old one that we sacrificed to drink?

The loss of any central political power makes this development entirely possible, even if a majority of citizens might be negative towards cloning, for instance. In informational society it is not the voter but the prosperous consumer who is in charge, a thought which has been proposed by the zoologist Matt Ridley. This was what happened with test-tube fertilisation. A sufficient number of childless couples showed themselves sufficiently keen and sufficiently wealthy, and the possibility was there. Today test-tube fertilisation is a routine procedure. Within the near future we will see numerous examples of this sort of "netocratic decision-making"; beyond the classical political model, and beyond the influence of the majority.

What is fundamental for all these rapid changes is that the concept of "natural" is completely losing its value-content. The more we learn about our biological history, and the more we learn about the history of culture and the construction of human society, the clearer it becomes that the oppositional relationship between these two phenomena, which has been held to be self-evident, is the only thing in this context which is genuinely artificial. Nature and culture are both fundamentally immensely complicated systems for the management of information. They both follow exactly the same law: natural selection. They both demonstrate the same inherent logic: a movement away from the simple and particular towards ever more sophisticated interaction on an increasingly large scale. In the new world-view which is rapidly taking shape – and here we are not talking about objective truths, it is the new paradigm which will ultimately determine what can be thought – nature and culture are two complementary sides of one and the same thing: evolution.

In the beginning the earth was an energy-filled soup where the simplest cells imaginable, the forefathers of our cells, drifted about and multiplied. The first step towards cathedrals and string quartets was taken when a number of these original cells bumped into what you might call a parasite, a bacterium, the forefather of our mitochondria (the organelle which manages the cells' metabolism). The meeting was not friendly: either the cell tried to swallow the parasite but failed to digest it, or the parasite tried to invade the cell but failed to kill it. Either way, the result was a collaboration which benefited both parties: a new type of cell where different elements managed different tasks. This cell, which practised internal division of labour, was the precondition for an even more developed biological collaboration in the form of multi-celled organisms where different cells were given different roles. Since then natural selection has, incredibly slowly, created ever more complicated forms of collaboration between cells by deselecting competitors that were less prepared to collaborate. The genes which have been suitable for advanced integration have been favoured.

Increased specialisation and co-ordination made considerable advances in productivity possible. Together, the cells became "intelligent". They constructed what the biologist Richard Dawkins has called "survival machines": gradually more refined animal bodies which were instructed to do intelligent things in certain situations, for instance to seek out warmer places when there was a threat of frost. But size is not everything, as every businessman knows. A large amount of co-ordination also entailed costs in the form of increased use of energy. Natural selection weighed one against the other. For this reason, bigger and bigger organisms were not the obvious solution to all problems in the harsh environment of the genes, which explains why co-operation between cells has assumed other, even more ingenious forms, with collaboration between individuals, schools, flocks and societies. A society which looks after its members' interests benefits the genes involved to the highest extent, increasing their possibility of surviving and reproducing.

The pattern in history is the same: one plus one equals more than two, co-operation benefits all parties involved. Natural selection prefers people and societies that learn to play non-zero-sum games (in contrast to zero-sum games) together. What happens when nomadic hunter/gatherer tribes settle down and begin to work the earth is that the conditions for a successful non-zero-sum game are radically improved. Over time a constructive spiral develops: technological and economic progress gives rise to population growth, which in turn means better conditions for further technological and economic progress. The towns which eventually develop are sufficiently tightly populated to support functioning markets, and economic growth gains still more speed. Contact between the different towns leads to the organisation of a more comprehensive system of co-operation. Thanks to ground-breaking technological breakthroughs, man is able to cross difficult thresholds and develop ever more advanced forms of non-zero-sum game.

But every force has a counter-force. History demonstrates an intricate dynamic between zero-sum games and non-zero-sum games. All the wars which have laid waste empires and cost countless human lives are excellent examples of explicit zero-sum games, or even minus-sum games. What someone wins is lost by someone else, at the same time as enormous resources go to waste. This does not stop the final number from actually being a positive. The threat of war unites a society and leads to the establishment of alliances with other societies, such as when the Greek city-states united to combat the Persians. The journalist Robert Wright, who wrote Non Zero, one of the books in which the biologically-influenced world view appears most clearly, suggested that war has a sort of coagulating effect by forcing people into organic solidarity; war provides an external threat which necessitates various forms of close co-operation. This is a thesis which can be seen as a parallel to the mobilistics idea that man's knowledge of his ultimate death (war against illness and ageing) has a central function in the creation of his individual identity.

The actual situation, at the transition between an old and a new paradigm, is ambiguous. On the one hand we can see in the collapse of the nation state a tribalisation: how larger entities are broken up into smaller ones where identity and loyalty are bound to different subcultures. On the other hand the declining nation state is being replaced by supra-state institutions, in politics, economics and culture. On the one hand fragmentation, on the other integration. Wright calls this phenomenon "fragmegration". But the new information technology which is driving development has its own programme, it offers co-operation and non-zero-sum games. The struggling indigenous population, fighting for increased rights and varying degrees of self-determination, co-operates with other groups in the same situation in world-wide electronic networks. Isolation is not a strategy with a future; the tension between local and global is only apparent in the virtual world. For Wright and others, the current situation is bringing to the fore the old question of a global state, a matter we will address in more detail in our next book.

Of course, what is relevant for the evolutionary development of society and culture is also valid for the economy, as Michael Rothschild insists. The market economy is "natural": an unplanned but still highly structured ecological system in a state of constant change. There is no equilibrium, no lasting state of repose. Even here the laws of natural selection apply, favouring the actors who are skilful non-zero-sum players with the capacity to build strategic alliances. Poorly organised companies that cannot learn new methods and therefore cannot cope with competition under the rules which apply within their particular niche of the market are sifted out, which gives more space for new players. Even conspicuous consumption of luxuries has its evolutionary logic: the sexiest people attract a partner most successfully, and sexiness in nature is often synonymous with big horns or colourful tail-feathers – an extravagant waste of resources, in other words. Just as rationality is not always most rational, so effectivity is not always most effective, either in nature or culture. The netocrats' imploitative consumption expresses the same thing, but in another way: consumption as a mark of status or seductive artistry. We are talking about an intuitively guided, trans-rational economy which plays upon the exhibition of exaggerated resources, an economy which would drive classically educated accountants and stock exchange analysts mad with its playfulness and transgressions against the laws of rationalism.

This means that the mythical concept "the new economy", like "globalisation", is actually two completely different things. To begin with, it is the old economy appearing in an entirely new light, as a result of old models and thought-processes being replaced for new ones as a consequence of the current paradigm shift. The new models which are constructed on the basis of these new insights are likely to be considerably more clarifying than the old ones, as far as both new and old are concerned. And secondly, the new information technology gives willing learners the chance to play entirely new non-zero-sum games with each other. Co-operation is seeking out unexpected paths, completely new categories of information are becoming valuable, strategic alliances are becoming increasingly extensive and transgressive of boundaries. Producers, suppliers, distributors and consumers are being bound ever tighter into digital networks. A genuine understanding of the former will dispel much of the confusion surrounding the latter. And power in informational society will end up with those who understand, and manage to dispel the confusion.

8.

THE CONVULSIONS OF COLLECTIVITY, THE DEATH OF MAN AND THE VIRTUAL SUBJECT

ONE CONSEQUENCE OF THE revolutionary advances within genetics, and biology's increasingly dominant position within our thought, is a total relativisation of the concept "individual". If by individual we mean the ultimate instance of control, literally indivisible, then the individual is looking more and more like a sheer illusion. An analysis of the interaction between body, brain and genes in different situations reveals that there is no instance of control. The genes release different chemical reactions which influence the body, but the genes, in turn, are activated by the brain, whose decisions are themselves instinctive reactions to external stimuli, via the body. We could say that it is the situation that decides, but since we ourselves are part of the situation, we would inevitably end up in a feedback loop without beginning or end. No-one decides. What we find in place of the individual that we thought existed, is a sort of turbulent market economy in micro-format, where a wealth of factors contribute; a constantly changing tension between different forces and counter-forces. The subject's undecided nature and mutability is leaving the philosophical sphere in netocratic society and becoming instead the acute and tangible stuff of the everyday for the common man.

One basic precondition for the possession of power is access to and control over information. In feudal society the flow of information was strictly controlled by those in power. The average individual's entire social interface with the outside world throughout their life was strictly limited, and was restricted in total to roughly as many people as could fit into the local church or would turn up to village dances. Trade was limited, communications with other regions negligible, news from outside limited and strictly regulated.

The representatives of the church and the aristocracy had power over a relatively comprehensive flow of information, which they passed on to the underclass in small and carefully weighed-out portions in the form of sermons and decrees, naturally adapted to serve the interests of the elite. The news that reached the village through legitimate channels therefore first passed through a strict control apparatus with branches in the monasteries and manor-houses. Everything possible was done to silence unauthorised sources of news and brand them as criminal; the many itinerant travellers who existed in spite of everything were regarded as bandits, a lawless rabble, and they retained that label in the history books of the capitalist paradigm. The enemy was by definition strange, and strangers were by definition the enemy.

The individual traveller was supposed to offer simple handicrafts and entertainment; he might make decorations, or perhaps music at village fairs. But he was not a trusted member of the village community. The wanderer had no rights, in principle, and was subordinate to the whims of the local aristocratic and religious leadership. Having a fixed abode was one absolute minimum requirement for anyone wanting to get married, the ritual by which society sanctioned reproduction. People outside the village community were worthless. For a soldier who was ordered into battle, the punishment for refusal to defend the local community against the evil barbarians was ex-communication, not just from the social community (the aristocracy's threat) but also from heavenly paradise (the church's threat).

Feudal structures began to give way when the flow of information could no longer be monitored effectively as a result of an increase in organised trade. The first tendencies towards capitalism emerged when communication between towns intensified, which meant that each individual's social interface expanded enormously. Tradesmen in towns around the Baltic Sea formed the Hanseatic League to protect their common interests and to encourage trade in any way possible, and this confederation became strong enough to set itself against the Danish king and keep trade routes free from piracy. The Italian city-states came together in the Lega Lombarda in order to form a united front against the Germano-Roman emperor's demands for obeisance. Co-operation was worthwhile. A new power structure was growing stronger.

Villages grew into towns. Urbanisation and the increasing power of the young bourgeoisie meant that information flourished and was distributed to a completely different extent to before, and it became necessary to adapt the use of power to these new circumstances. Feudal towns had been completely surrounded by walls and moats, partly because they needed physical protection from the outside world, but partly because this facilitated the operation of effective tollgates and thus a considerable income for the town. Capitalist towns, on the other hand, grew so quickly that this sort of enclosure and demarcation became unsustainable. It is actually questionable whether we can talk of towns in their real sense before early capitalism; even imperial Rome consisted largely of a loosely-connected community of villages compared to the town-development that arose with capitalism.

As a result of these changes, the town rulers could no longer exercise unlimited power over a clearly demarcated area. The arrival of capitalism is clearly visible geographically, when town walls stopped functioning as a barrier between town and country.

The aspirations to power of capitalist cities therefore extended far beyond the boundaries of the city itself, reaching out into the surrounding countryside and not stopping until it came up against a natural barrier in the form of mountains, seas or large rivers. The reason for this expansion was not merely that the populations of the cities was growing, but that this population was in need of regular deliveries of food and that the new factories needed regular supplies of raw materials in considerably greater quantities than the main occupations under previous conditions, concentrated on the market-square, had done. The city therefore colonised the surrounding area and within this naturally defined area a common identity developed, based upon appearance, language, mythology, articles of faith and customs. Thus was the modern nation created.

Thanks to improved communications and rapidly growing urban populations who lacked any restrictive regional loyalty, the new social identity could spread to cover a considerably larger area and many times more people than before. Expansion was a necessity, but must be kept within reasonable limits. Like all biological organisms, it was necessary for the nation to establish strict boundaries with the outside world. Self-protection requires the establishment of fixed boundaries, so that it is clear what is actually being defended, and so that limited resources are not wasted in feeding the rest of the world. Therefore it was in the nation's interest to mark clearly who "we" were, in contrast to "the others"; consequently power over information was used to this end. Censuses, registration and cataloguing of all settled inhabitants who could claim national identity and belonging were organised. The state accumulated more and more tasks, which necessitated increases in taxation since the growing administrative apparatus was swallowing ever more resources. As a result, the power of the state grew.

The increasingly powerful bourgeoisie of the rapidly growing cities laid claim to the surrounding countryside in order to secure their supplies and protect their power. This happened by the bourgeoisie using its new-found position of strength to compel or out-manoeuvre and marginalise the rulers of the countryside, the aristocracy. Regardless of the formal constitution, in reality the state assumed the right of the monarch and the aristocracy to levy tax by shifting the right to impose toll-charges from town-walls to national boundaries. The nation replaced the old town as the geographic basis of citizenship, which was confirmed by the supreme instance of capitalist identity: the passport.

In the new geographical entity, power was organised in a centralised system, which meant that all power came from, and all information was directed towards, a clearly defined centre: the capital. This organisation and the image of a centre surrounded by increasingly peripheral outposts left its mark on contemporary thinking about society and the world. The model was still the Christian heaven with God and his angels. The word "capitalism" has its origin, like the English word "capital" (city), in the Latin "caput" (head). The capital was thus the nation's head: the giver of orders and information centre, as well as the symbol of the values around which the nation was gathered.

This new age required a new individual, a new ideal of humanity adapted to the needs of the state and the market; the feudal peasant patiently ploughing his fields and waiting for the return of Christ was far too passive and intellectually sluggish, and therefore not sufficiently receptive to the sophisticated propaganda of the new age. In rapid succession a clutch of new concepts appeared, forming the basis for the definition of the new individual: the nation, race, citizenship, income tax, education, mental illness, criminality, the foreigner. Around all of this was formed the "common ground" which was the cohesive cement of the nation state. The bourgeoisie was protecting its newly-won monopoly on information as best it could.

According to this model, the citizen should not need to be threatened in order to make him protect his country. Instead, the sense of national belonging and the values it contained should be seen as so valuable that no-one would hesitate to take up arms whenever the nation's sovereignty was threatened from ill-intentioned neighbouring peoples. Consequently considerable energy was expended on the production of a nationalistic culture, through the mythologisation of the nation's origins and a romanticisation of its history. Poets conjured forth an heroic past. The traditions of the nation were supposed to be linked to its geographic area in a sacred symbiosis. Hence the myth of the origin of the nation arose.

But at the same time this required the demonisation of the outside world. The feelings towards other nationalities that were propagated were a mixture of fear and loathing. The very essence of nationalism is based upon establishing distance from, and a disdain for anything foreign and unknown. Confused race-biology was one completely logical consequence of this development, a frenetic desire for empirical support for feelings of superiority, the feeling that gilded nationalism and raised national citizenship to something elevated and sacred. Aside from this, racism had another attractive function. Nationalism alone could only summon forth suitable demons in time of war and conflict with neighbouring countries. But thanks to racism, demons could be produced even in peacetime in the form of internal minorities with deviant physical characteristics and cultural traditions, like for instance Jews or gypsies, and oppression of these groups could thus be legitimised. The nation state was thereby assured that there would always be demons to hand, and scapegoats on which to blame all shortcomings.

The fateful consequences of these centralised mechanisms of nationalism kick-started the accelerating decline of nationalism and the inevitable collapse that is evident in late-capitalist society. The eternal human search for a basic sense of belonging has, first through the appearance of popular culture in the mass media in the post-war period, then, above all, through the establishment of electronic tribes on the Internet, found credible alternatives to floundering nationalism. In informational society virtual subcultures are replacing feudalism's village communities and capitalism's national communities as the basis for man's social identity. In a society like this, obviously no-one is prepared to die for his country. National boundaries and their physical guards, military organisations, are imploding. New boundaries between social groups are being established with great seriousness in the virtual world.

It is therefore interesting to note that the most stiff-necked extreme nationalists – neo-Nazi groups in western Europe, fascists fighting for regional self-determination in eastern Europe, isolationist and historically romanticising fundamentalists in North America, east Asia and the Middle East – i.e.: the nationalists who for the sake of consistency are still clutching the banner of racism – are the only groups who have succeeded in building functional electronic networks which are based entirely upon national identity. This is a fragmegrational phenomenon (see previous chapter); strictly disciplined and organised subcultures promoting their interests by constructing strategic alliances with like-minded people on the net. All "milder" forms of nationalism – flags, traditions, pride – have, in contrast, never gained a foothold in the virtual world and therefore have no future in informational society. The boundaries of the nation state are today as irrelevant as moats were at the breakthrough of capitalism. Besides, the disintegration of the nation state is strengthened and accelerated when its institutions stand helpless in the face of the task of controlling and, above all, taxing "the new economy".

One problem which is becoming acute as a consequence of this development is the constant undermining of the authority of the nation state's institutions. When laws in key areas can no longer be maintained, this drastically reduces the citizens' respect for the legislative collective and the judicial apparatus; this is particularly the case among the groups who are being favoured economically and in terms of status by technological development. Those who are clinging most tightly to the wreckage of the nation state are in part members of the old, obsolete dominant class who can see their position and their privileges sinking to the bottom, and in part members of the new underclass who consciously or unconsciously realise that no changes in the current direction will do them any good.

For the netocrats, on the other hand, the nation state and its barriers appear mostly as an irrational, but passing, cause of irritation impeding the flow of traffic in the global village. The remnants of nationalism are, in the eyes of the netocrats, a shameful sickness that ought to have been eradicated by now, a sort of mental handicap which is maintaining the old dominant class in a state of impotence and decadence, and is suppressing the degraded underclass in a permanent state of inferiority. In short: an epidemic and a delusion which it is a humanitarian act of charity to combat. For the netocracy, the raising of the national flag is the most offensive example of vulgarity and bad taste. This of course does not prevent the new dominant class from exploiting every opportunity to project the symbols and trademarks that represent their own electronic sects. Symbols which, ironically enough, are often superannuated old national flags. The domain address of the Soviet Union, .su, was for instance one of the most popular Internet addresses among netocrats after the collapse of the Soviet Union.

The police and the judicial system are increasingly powerless in the face of growing electronic crime, a sort of global networking mafia where the motivation for criminal activity is more the creation of identity and increased status within their own group than economic profit. This is leading to shrill political cries for increased resources for the police and public prosecutors. But just as national tax authorities find themselves in a hopelessly inferior position compared to the mobile netocracy which is in charge of the boundary-busting virtual economy, so national criminal justice authorities are coming off badly against a "criminality" that has no specific geographical location.

At the same time the bourgeois family is rapidly being undermined: when industrial production falls dramatically, to the benefit of information management and an expanding service sector, the conditions of the labour market are altered. Poorly educated men are becoming superfluous whereas a wealth of new opportunities is opening up for women, which is in turn undermining the already highly-pressured nuclear family. The instance of divorce has risen constantly in the west since the beginning of the 1960s. These factors are working together to form a serious, destabilising crisis in informational society. Great amounts of uncontrolled energy are released when the social institutions of the old paradigm collapse and the very basis for the social identity of the majority of people disappears.

In parallel with the development of capital cities during early capitalism, another completely different type of city culture developed: what the American philosopher and historian Manuel De Landa calls a metropolis, a form of city that first became possible in capitalist society. The metropolis did not form the centre of the nation, either politically, culturally or geographically, unlike the capital; instead it was positioned on the coast, in connection with the increasingly well-trafficked and important intercontinental sea lanes, and was therefore in several important respects isolated from the rest of the nation. While the capital imported its workforce and raw materials from the surrounding countryside, the metropolis built its expansion mainly on international trade. The imported raw materials and tradable commodities came from foreign countries and, not least, from other metropolises. These independent seaports became junctions for vital transport routes, through which passed an enormous traffic of people, base products and luxury goods desired by the capital cities and their nations. The metropolises' power was not based upon control of territory, but on control of financial flow.

The capital and the metropolis had entirely different functions in capitalist society. While the capital embodied the structure of power itself, the metropolis was largely free of the restrictive laws and regulations that applied to the nation state. Therefore the metropolis became a base for various activities and phenomena which were regarded, for various reasons, by nationalism's propagandists and the rulers of the state as morally dubious and dangerous to society. It might be prostitution or the slave-trade, or the loaning of money at interest, something which was regarded as fundamentally suspicious during the late Middle Ages. For this reason the metropolis became an arena for all sorts of experimentation in both lifestyles and thinking, because it provided a level of freedom that was unthinkable within the nation state itself. In the metropolis the feared and hated nomad could find a haven. People came and went, this was not only accepted but entirely in line with the idea of the metropolis; less attention was paid to control, and nomadic lifestyles developed over time to the point where they were almost the stylistic ideal of the metropolis.

In the metropolis, mobility was far too great for it to be possible to establish majority rule based upon a unified group identity. Mobility and the multitude of identities forced a flexible political structure, characterised by temporary alliances between different interest groups. Politics was more about finding functional compromises than achieving consensus around an ideology. Certain trade-orientated and pluralistic nation states that developed early on, for example Switzerland and the Netherlands, developed relatively passive and pragmatic political institutions of a metropolitan rather than centralistic character. It is worth noting that neither of these states, nor any of the obvious metropolises, was affected by the revolutionary mass-movements which periodically brought about violent social convulsions in the centralistic nation states. This supports our thesis that the idea of political revolution is an integrated part of the overriding capitalist ideology, a symbiotic parasite on etatism and its nationalism, rather than an anomaly or an ominous portent.

Thanks to the fact that the capital took as its task the creation and management of the nation state with its bureaucratic and military apparatus, the metropolis was able to concentrate on trade, shipping and the colonisation of foreign territory. This co-operation and division of labour benefited both parties. The metropolises were responsible for international contacts, they received, developed and passed on impulses from outside, and, thanks to their banking systems, could be sure of stimulating the movement of capital that was necessary for the expansion of capitalism. The capital sent on extra labour and provided basic necessities, and the metropolis in return could offer luxury goods such as fabrics and spices. Besides this, the metropolis established colonial territories in distant continents in the name of the nation state. The monopolistic trading companies which several European countries established in eastern Asia are a typical example of this. In exchange for the metropolitan trading companies raising the nation state's flag on foreign land – which often happened in connection with the creation of brand new metropolises: Hong Kong, Macau, Singapore and Goa – they were permitted to exploit unchecked the new-found wealth of raw materials and virgin markets.

Because this co-operation benefited both parties, collaboration as a non-zero-sum game, a form of symbiosis soon developed between the capital and the metropolis. Intense traffic moved between the two types of city, a rapid exchange not only of goods and services but also of people and ideas. The capital stood for the exercise of political and military power: registration, cataloguing, legislation, as well as the production of ideology and collective identity; the metropolis contributed entrepreneurial skills, finance, trade, art, culture and individualism. It is important to bear in mind that right up to the end of the 1800s, it was the countryside which answered for almost all of the growth in population. Within the towns there were viruses and bacteria which weeded out any excess population. The epidemics which periodically swept across the world affected towns, mainly because of their population density and lack of hygiene, far worse than the countryside. This fact means that the countryside not only had to supply the towns with raw materials, but above all that it contributed a continual new supply of much-needed workforce.

The capital had a cohesive, stabilising function, whereas the metropolis stood for openness, new thinking and an experimental frame of mind which at times could be downright reckless. Apart from the concrete economic benefit these cities gained from each other, there was always a more subtle and mutual exploitation: they contributed to each other's identity and cohesion by acting as mutually demonised threats. The nationalistic ideologues and moralists could use the metropolis as the very embodiment of immorality and corruption. In a corresponding manner the leading tradesmen of the metropolis could ensure that the population remained in its place within the hierarchy, working hard to maintain the city's economic and political independence, by presenting the culture of the capital as intolerant and repressive. There was no real reason for these two types of city to work seriously against each other. The conflict that was encouraged was more of a symbolic and theatrical character, and actually had as its main purpose the reinforcement of those in power on both sides.

We have described types of city as purely theoretical opposites. It ought therefore to be pointed out that the great global cities which developed during the early stages of capitalism naturally showed characteristics of both capital and metropolis. But even where both variants collaborated within one and the same finite area, where settlements flowed together, if we look at the internal flow within the city there is a difference between capital and metropolis. The central square, with its parliament or council building, and the factory district on the outskirts, represent the capital. The harbour district, with its more or less sinful entertainment and artistic districts, thus represents the metropolis. In these melting-pot cities the boundaries between the two structures were both physical and mental, and often difficult to breach. Examples of this sort of hybrid city are London, St Petersburg. New York and Buenos Aires. Other cities belong, from an historical point of view, more clearly to one category or the other. Classical capitals include Paris, Madrid, Berlin, Moscow and Beijing. The metropolises include Venice, Amsterdam, San Francisco, Shanghai and Hong Kong.

If all of this development is linked to how the social interface of the average citizen during his lifetime grew from the church in the peasant village to comprise the flood of people in city squares, we can draw certain conclusions about how power structures and control mechanisms will be influenced in the transition from capitalism to informationalism, since the social interface of the individual citizen is now expanding enormously to correspond to the traffic on the global electronic net.

One example of how the "natural" connection between town and country in the nation state is disintegrating with the breakthrough of informationalism is the increasingly irreconcilable demand of the city that the countryside stand on its own two feet after centuries of subsidy. The nation, which was previously an invaluable asset to the capital, is now merely a handicap, an unjustified expense. In informational society seas and mountains are no longer required as "natural" boundaries and defences against the outside world, but as locations for recreation. The value of the raw materials that the countryside can offer in the form of wood and ore has collapsed, because the proportion of any product constituting the cost of raw materials has sunk dramatically while the value of the immaterial: ideas and design, have rocketed.

Population growth now takes place within the big cities while the countryside, in spite of ambitious regional political programmes, has been steadily and relentlessly depopulated. The war for market share between the different cities is no longer fought with weapons on land or at sea, but with information management as a weapon in virtual space. Under these new circumstances, a dislocation is taking place in the relationship between the capital and the metropolis: the capital is falling behind, while the metropolis, with its well-nourished banks of knowledge, its flexibility and its superior ability to build up boundary-breaking networks, is emerging as the urban ideal of the new age. The capital city's envy of the metropolis's freedom, mobility and independence is hastening the collapse of the nation state.

It is no coincidence that the most entrenched defenders of the nation state are the rural population which has most to lose when the strong nation is weakened and can no longer uphold its lofty promises. In the absence of any realistic negotiating position, pleas are being made for sympathy from the rest of the world, and for compensation for centuries of exploitation. Consequently the necessary but painful reduction of the gigantic subsidies which most industrialised countries pay to the countryside for the maintenance of their livelihoods is the great stumbling block during international negotiations on increased free trade. But the capital has little choice; the merciless competition between all the world's expansive metropolises which is the consequence of nodalisation has made it necessary for the capital, in a desperate attempt to transform itself into a metropolis, to dispose of its ever more burdensome responsibility for an entire nation.

The result is the denationalisation of informationalism, an increasingly rapid deconstruction of the nation state, a sort of global perestroika for nationalism. This development is reinforced by the fact that decisions within the capitalist system are made through elections, and that a majority of voters lives in cities, while, at the same time, informational society is controlled by networking, something the metropolitan part of the urban population has conscientiously practised for centuries. Squeezed between the power structures of both paradigms, the countryside does not stand a chance. Not even democracy can save rural subsidies in the long term, because the rural electorate is a minority, a group of opinion which is steadily shrinking and becoming easier to ignore. With a radically dwindling income from taxes for the state as a result of the expansion of the virtual economy, the urban population will use its majority position to vote down any further support for the countryside, which is therefore being decolonised and left to its fate.

Even the military is retreating from the countryside during the last phase of capitalism, which can only be explained by the fact that there is no longer any territory left to defend, still less any desire to defend anything. Territory is reduced to an area for environmental politics. Carbon dioxide levels are measured, the acid content of bathing lakes is neutralised, and there are discussions about whether the countryside should be open (as under capitalism) or covered with forest (as under feudalism), and about who should pay for it all. The question of which flag happens to fly in the wind in some distant end of the country is not something which keeps urban inhabitants awake at night. During informationalism the leading capital cities will no longer compete for how much territory they control. On the contrary, they would sooner be rid of the responsibility for as much territory as they can, in order to make the grade and join the leading metropolises of the world. This development is most noticeable in Europe and east Asia, because there it has been reinforced by a declining birth-rate.

In the aftermath of these collective convulsions, it is inescapable that the self-image of every individual is going to undergo a radical change. The breakthrough of informationalism means that the Enlightenment idea of the perfect Man as a replacement for God, and therefore the idea of the need to realise one's "true self", will finally be laid to rest. Instead, there is a vision of the body's liberation from predetermination, the possibility of switching between different identities, rather like changing clothes according to situation and context. The subject will find him or herself in a state of permanent becoming, always receptive to new impulses, a continual system of evaluation without a clearly defined goal. The ambition will not be to achieve something finished, thanks to effort and discipline, but rather to keep alive as many opportunities as possible. We are talking here, to borrow a phrase from Deleuze, about a dividual rather than an individual. This dividual does not have one identity, but many, and is constantly divisible. This is consistent with the biological fact that it is impossible to localise the ultimate instance of control within the self. Man is recognised as a meeting place for a mass of contradictory desires and powers, with no centre.

Technological development is forcing a new mobilistic identity onto man, by pulling the carpet from beneath the totalistic ideal. On the net the individual's identity will arise in the context that is actual at the time, only to perform a breath-taking transformation the next moment. Out goes the intact individual, chained to his identity as to a heavy rucksack, and in comes the free-flowing dividual. In a first phase the dividual will stop trying to be Man, then in the second phase it will become impossible for him to return to being Man, however much he may want to. This new freedom both attracts and frightens, but it cannot be avoided. What we are describing is the virtual subject of the plurarchical, and hence post-democratic, society; where everyone decides over him or herself, where no-one can decide over anyone else in the name of a superior majority.

It would be a big mistake to confuse this plurarchy with anything resembling anarchy. Plurarchy is not the same as the abolition of rules, where everyone can do as he or she pleases. In plurarchical society there are actually more rather than fewer laws and rules than in a democracy, more complicated, abstract, and, to a greater degree, elevated out of sight and beyond discussion. The plurarchical rules of the game are, however, not determined by political or judicial institutions of the nation-state variety: the courts and parliament will quickly see their status and power dramatically devalued. Instead, the rules of the game on the net will be meme-Darwinian, the intricate system known as netiquette, and it will be this that characterises the strict ethics of informationalism, and which will increasingly replace the laws and regulations of the capitalist paradigm.

These rules cannot be permanent in their nature. Like everything else in informational society, they must be constantly updated because their complicated context is in permanent flux. Netiquette ought therefore to be understood as a living document without given limits, a sort of quasi-judicial organism in perpetual motion, a net within the net which both forms and at the same time reflects cultural values and ideology. Crimes against netiquette will not be punished like crimes against laws in the old paradigm, with prison sentences and forced internment in other institutions, nor with fines or economic punishments: treatment like this is not sufficiently recognisable as punishment in a society where life is mainly lived on the net.

Anyone transgressing netiquette will instead have to look forward to virtual displacement: expulsion from essential networks. Like anyone breaking the norms of the nomads of the savannah or the villages of feudalism, anyone breaking the norms of the electronic tribe will be punished with exclusion from the community of the group, which will lead to a dramatic loss of social identity. In milder cases it might be sufficient with network harassment for a determined length of time, but more serious or repeated crimes against netiquette will lead to virtual isolation. A parallel to this system of punishment is the trauma caused by enforced unemployment in capitalist society. Add to this an inability for the unemployed to find any imaginable alternative occupation, and the extent of the effects of network exclusion becomes clear.

It is the curator, the overseer of the network, who will shoulder the role of legal administrator in informational society, and who imposes and enacts punishment. Within the curators' own network, informational society's equivalent of Interpol, there will be a constant flow of information about which net-citizens are undesirable within attractive networks for the time being. Only in so far as it is possible to maintain vital competition between different curators and their different networks can the plurarchy function; otherwise the whole of virtual society is threatened by an oligopoly of the curatoriat, a virtual form of minority rule with a strong concentration of power and with great scope for corruption and arbitrary behaviour.

But at the same time, the citizens of the net will keep control over themselves to a remarkably large extent, because flexibility and adaptability will pay in the informational system of punishment and reward. If you study the historical development of modern society, one of the very earliest noticeable trends, as identified by the German-Jewish sociologist Norbert Elias and others, is a constantly increasing degree of internalisation. This means a process by which the prohibitions which previously had to be expressed, written in law and maintained with the help of severe punishment, come to be regarded more and more as self-evident: repression has moved from external social institutions to within the consciousness of the citizen. Novelists like William Burroughs and philosophers like Foucault and Deleuze have been interested in how the maintenance of social morality during late-capitalism has moved from being a question of state-organised discipline to one of internalised control. One consequence of this development has been that commands and directly expressed threats have been increasingly replaced by pedagogically expressed propaganda, whose purpose has been precisely to educate the citizen to put in overtime as his own moral policeman. The control society has replaced the disciplinary society, treatment has replaced punishment, and observation has been delegated to the person under observation. It is much cheaper that way.

One condition for this control society has been that the myth of Man has been kept alive, that each individual citizen has recognised this ideal and has constantly been reminded of the fact that he has not been able to live up to the demands that have been made, and that he therefore has every reason to continually improve himself in every possible respect. To become Man has been a lifelong project which no normal person has ever managed to accomplish. The myth of Man has proved to be extremely tenuous of life, which explains why the elite corps of capitalism has, despite everything, succeeded in keeping power over a society which has rapidly developed towards a plurarchy, and where the ideological legitimacy of power has largely been eroded. Kidnap victims often display irrational connections to their guards – the so-called Stockholm Syndrome – and the same symptoms have been observed among the consumers of late capitalism: a mysterious inability to let go of the dated and deforming myth of self-realisation and "the true me".

During the final period of capitalism, state organisations and various research institutes have laid out a formidable minefield of alarming reports where the increasingly deficient morals of the citizens are illustrated with tables and diagrams. Everything from obesity and lazy dietary habits to TV-viewing and a lack of empathy have been depicted in strident tones, which have then echoed even louder through the megaphones of the mass media. The immorality that is perceived as being spread by the Internet has been particularly problematic, for obvious reasons. Each problem has been worse than the other, and they all require powerful initiatives in the form of information campaigns from state organisations and various research institutes, which are consequently in great need of the allocation of massive resources. Little man, as all studies obviously show, has not proved mature enough to fulfil the sacred task of realising his true self. He therefore needs masses of tender loving care and direction. The result has been a bizarre campaign of slander where the dying capitalist institutions: the political classes, psychologists, socionomists, the mass media, school and family, are all accusing each other of a lack of responsibility for the education of the people: Why will no-one take responsibility and try to stop people taking responsibility for themselves?

This intimate collaboration between politics, research and the media has been so intricately wrought that every hint of a criticism has been organised out of existence. It has certainly not been in the interests of the headline-hungry media to subject any of these alarming reports to close scrutiny. And the commercial powers have been able to watch the entire spectacle as a single huge advertising campaign for all manner of ego-boosting products and services. A citizen who is dissatisfied with himself is generally a high-achieving consumer. Perfection is an impossibility, but there will always be new products and services to try out, proclaim the mass media through their one-way communication, and to try to improve oneself at the very least is one's duty as a citizen. No-one is thin or beautiful or well-dressed enough to be left in peace from the constantly repeated incitements to improvement. The perpetually piled-on self-loathing is the very basis for the therapeutic hyper-consumption which is keeping the late-capitalist wheels turning at such a rate. Advertising is the carrot and the shock reports the stick. State and capital are sitting lashed together in the same boat.

In informational networks, where communication is interactive, capitalism's old truths about the individual will be subjected to hard critical evaluation. The myth of self-realisation will be seen through, and the whole idea of a unified self to nurture will appear antiquated. As a result the political, academic and commercial forces behind this propaganda production will gradually lose their influence over the collective consciousness. But this certainly does not mean that the terror of overheated commands is a closed chapter, it just means that new "truths" will be packaged differently. The netocracy and its higher functionaries, the curators, step into the arena and lay out the new, constantly changing text of the law, constantly new little netiquettes for the new dividual. Even if plurarchical structure makes it possible for every single player to question the single curator's current set of rules, there is no alternative other than to submit to the rules of another curator, and the differences between them might well be negligible because the curators in turn have organised themselves into a meta-network to defend their power as a group.

The rules will change, but the constant underlying message of the curators to their net-citizens will be simple and unambiguous: you can never network well enough, you can never be good enough at communicating, you can never let yourself rest, you must constantly be ready to jump, constantly ready to learn new things. Thus a new set of masters will seize power and the language of power with which to control informational society. The definitive difference between a capitalist strategy and an informationalist strategy for power is that the curators understand the consequences of interactivity and how this is indissolubly linked to power. So the curator will not speak to his subordinates, he will converse with them. The netocrats in power are listening rather than commanding, they communicate discretely and subtly instead of brutally giving orders. Netocratic power is not the power to take decisions as such, because in plurarchic society decisions will be taken by the individual concerned, but control over the understanding of the consequences of alternative decisions.

In informational society the function of the individual net-citizen as his own moral policeman is no longer prompted by an arrogant and effectivity-maximising nation state's guardian-bureaucrats, but instead inspired by constantly changing netocratic trends which determine what it is that makes someone "hip", and how to show that you've got "it". Ethics will become more and more a question of aesthetics. "Poor style" will become synonymous with social suicide. Every single player in a network will always be assumed to be fully aware of netiquette, the unwritten laws for how members ought to behave towards one another. Because net-competency is the key to success in the informational society, there will be a rich blossoming of all sorts of communication therapies and courses to teach hopeful networkers what is "good netiquette".

The problem is just that because we are talking of dynamics, new knowledge will soon be old. The truly terrible thing about these rules is actually that the more widespread they become, and the more people learn to live according to them, then the sooner they will lose their value. The most acute threat of inflation in informational society will not affect currencies or securities, but the value of each single player's actions. The single net-citizen's social interface is global, his access to information practically unlimited. His social identity is an open question, and his position of power is ultimately a question of style.

9.

NETWORK PYRAMIDS – ATTENTIONALISTIC POWER HIERARCHIES

ONE OF THE FUNDAMENTAL concepts in the discussion of informational networks is transparency: the network as a translucent, pellucid, and therefore equal and democratic system. The principle of transparency is that all the members of the network have access to all relevant information, and that at any time they wish they can make their own contribution to the internal debate. All cards are on the table, everyone can form their own opinion and make comments, everyone can participate in the decision-making process. If transparency is the dominant principle in informational society, this will entail a revolution in the labour market. When a traditional business is transformed into a transparent network, the employer can no longer treat his employees according to feudal principles governing the exercise of power. Everyone's eyes are on him. A Machiavellian cannot act in a Machiavellian way when he is constantly under the gaze of his subordinates from every direction.

This is the background to late-capitalism's sudden blaze of interest in ethics, which should be regarded as a textbook example of gallows conversion. What is to be done? When despotism and capricious behaviour no longer work, new strategies must be found for leadership and the exercise of power. Technological development is driving society and is giving, in this particular instance, the individual employee previously unimagined influence over his work situation. The networks' internal transparency and the workplace democratisation connected to it has led management theorists to proclaim triumphantly that "Marx was right": development of the conditions for production has made old production practices obsolete and untenable, the workers are assuming power. But there is one snag in this rose-tinted scenario.

The problem is that informational society is considerably more complicated than that, businesses are becoming virtual networks to an increasing extent, with fewer stable structures and rigid employment practices. The dynamic of the network is a phenomenon with considerably more aspects than mere transparency, and of greater importance as well.

For the network to live up to the harsh demands of effectivity that exist in the curators' market, everyone who is not regarded as contributing anything valuable, or who is simply perceived as a threat to the network members' common interests, must be unconditionally placed or kept on the outside. Every network with the slightest ambition to be attractive and successful must thoroughly sift prospective members, otherwise it will soon collapse under the torrent of irrelevant information that will flood in and fill up the limited amount of space. Development like that will inevitably lead to the key members losing interest and allowing themselves to be enticed to join other networks where the policy is more restrictive, whereupon the network they leave behind them will be transformed into an empty shell doomed to become extinction, full of impotent actors who, in confusion, are producing irrelevant nonsense.

The open networks that have been made possible by the rapid expansion of the Internet will either be transformed into closed networks, or will fall into disrepair and become gathering points for worthless garbage-information. In closed networks, the members are hand-picked by the human curators, the doormen of the virtual world. Tall, thick firewalls will be constructed around the networks, to protect against unauthorised observation and undesired entry. The more attractive a network is, the more people will want to become members, and the higher up the power hierarchy the network wants to get, the tougher the entry requirements will be, and the more insurmountable its firewall will need to be.

☐

Fig.9.1 Network pyramid
The direct consequence of this dynamic is that virtual society is forming itself into a long series of network pyramids, a power hierarchy where consumtarians are directed towards the least attractive networks full of garbage-information, while the netocrats lay claim to and themselves define the highest networks where power and status are concentrated. This society is by definition post-capitalist, because the requirements needed to achieve status under capitalism – money, fame, titles, and so on – no longer have any value for entrance applications to any of the higher and more powerful networks. The netocratic status which is now in demand requires entirely different characteristics: knowledge, contacts, overview, vision. In other words: qualities which contribute to increasing the network's status and making it even more powerful.

Capitalism's perception of power-structures, that all valuable human activity stems from and is controlled from a central core, has also become obsolete. There is, quite simply, no centre in the virtual world. The netocratic network pyramid is not primarily constructed with the aim of exercising power, it is actually not constructed at all in any usual sense, but should be seen as the structure that technology itself has promoted according to Darwinian principles of natural selection, and which renders impossible the control necessary for protection of certain specific interests. The principle of the network pyramid is more decentralisation than any centralised concentration of power. It will never achieve equilibrium, its power relationships are constantly changing, which means that the power that is exercised stems from temporary, nebulous, unstable, mobile alliances rather than from any particular geographic point or any particular constitutional entity. Power will thus become incredibly difficult to localise at all, and therefore naturally even more difficult to criticise or combat. But the fact that power becomes more abstract and invisible does not mean that it vanishes or is even weakened, but rather the exact opposite.

The social status of the networks is determined by how well their professional doormen, the human curators, who are just as much arbiters of taste and supervisors of netiquette, perform their difficult task. Because the curators in turn are competing within the market of the networks, they will constantly need to advertise their own network and convince other people of its excellence, partly to entice attractive new members, and partly to be able to enter into influential alliances. Each successful decision one way or another might lead to spectacular gains, while each unsuccessful decision about access or exclusion might have devastating consequences for the curator's, and therefore the network's, reputation and credibility. It is reputation, or capital of trust, which is the network's most important asset; with the help of reputation, attention is attracted to the networks, and there is a great shortage of attention, rather than money, on the net. Money will follow attention, and not vice versa. Attention is the only hard currency in the virtual world. The strategy and logic of the netocracy are therefore attentionalist rather than capitalist.

The individual curator's existence is turbulent and uncertain, but the group of curators need hardly worry. Their collective position of power is unthreatened, a circumstance not unconnected to the fact that the curators' activity cannot, for the foreseeable future, be carried out by machines, and is not regulated by any standardising rules. There is no accumulated wisdom, no ideological tradition, no precedent to call upon, no education or exams to fall back on. There are, quite simply, no formal criteria to refer to. This means that none of the old public institutions from the old paradigm has in the long term any prospect at all of successfully competing in a developed network market, where fingertip sensitivity, intuition and stylistic consciousness, excellent social skills, will be more in demand than anything else.

One consequence of this development is that the most sought-after and therefore most valuable information of all on the net is that which concerns networking itself: how to construct and administer your network in the most intelligent way. This means in turn that the most powerful network of all is the meta-network where the curators cement contacts with, learn from and enter into alliances with each other. The global meta-curatoriat, the highest network in the curators' own network pyramid, is the most powerful institution of netocratic society, informational society's equivalent to a global government. But the fact is that the whole system is fluid, which means that its constitution will constantly shift, making an empirical analysis of power more difficult.

Informational society presents an entirely new topography. Under capitalism, despite the slower and generally more limited communications, there was still a considerable degree of clarity, as a result of the fact that circumstances and the overriding logic were largely the same throughout the system. In this way capitalist society can be said to resemble an open field where people can see each other, admittedly at a distance, and communicate with each other, even if it is not always easy to hear. We call this common area of interests "the public arena". The topography of informationalism, paradoxically, is more like a labyrinth. The arena is crooked, and events are unpredictable. Round every corner there is a complete surprise. What was relevant yesterday will seldom have any relevance today. It might well be necessary to abandon a successful strategy without any warning at all. The transparency is essentially a chimera, a netocratic propaganda myth, existing only within extremely narrow, horizontal sections. We can see and hear everything more clearly over short distances, but the cost of this is that our far-sight, and with it the public arena itself, has disappeared.

When an excess of information is produced, attention is at a premium. In the netocratic network information itself is of limited value. In contrast, there is a value in being able to avoid unnecessary information, in order to free up valuable time and facilitate concentration. The information which is sought-after must be relevant and reliable, and preferably also exclusive, and this particularly valuable information can only be found within the highest networks. And it is only in the highest networks that there is the knowledge and overview necessary to use information in an optimal way. Meta-information, about how different types of information can be connected in the most effective way, is in itself the most valuable form of information.

The sale of first-hand information to the highest-bidder at some sort of public auction will in time become an increasingly unlikely scenario, for several reasons. Exclusivity declines if the business transaction is public, and the risk for costly leakage from the highest-bidding network so great, since attention and not money is the strongest currency, that information will eventually find its way to the highest ranking network in any case. For the netocrats, who you communicate with is simply more important than how much you get paid for the information you have to offer. In the higher networks a capitalist strategy will only work in the extreme short-term, because the social costs of further sale of valuable information will, in the long term, be unsustainably high. Survival among the netocrats demands that you acquire long-term, attentionalist thinking based precisely upon the insight that attention has a higher value than money. Capitalists will become an underclass which has to content itself with haggling over old, second-hand information from the scrapheap, while the netocracy – the networking elite – carries off the prize of power and status, as well as experiences and kicks. The netocrats will, of course, also eventually carry off the financial profits, in spite of the fact that these are of only secondary interest; they control the knowledge, after all, and can create the attention that is more valuable than anything else. Only when the netocrat has used the most important information for his own advantage will he sell it, with the blessing of his network, to the highest-bidding capitalist. So the capitalists will be forced to adapt and subordinate themselves to attentionalist conditions and play a game whose rules they have not decided themselves, and which they in many cases do not understand at all. Already during latter-day capitalism this pattern was becoming apparent when the capitalist with the best network behind him beat the capitalist with the most capital in the struggle over who was going be allowed to invest in the new economy. As a result, the capitalist economy had already been subjected to attentionalist principles.

During the initial period it is possible that certain human curators will try to sell their power for money. But this short-term action will soon turn out to be self-destructive, because this sort of transaction will rapidly undermine the curators' own credibility, which means that they will soon have nothing left to sell when the standard and status of their networks has plummeted. As a result they will inevitably lose the power they once had, and be knocked out of the extreme competition that exists within the curators' market. It is clear that the netocratic power that can be bought for money is not worth it, since it will run through your fingers like sand the moment anyone tries to capitalise on their purchase. Thus money has an indisputably inferior value in the power-hierarchies of informational society.

The dynamic that already exists both within and between the different networks is forcing an entirely new prioritization in the game for status and power: careful care of one's own trademark. The players simply cannot afford to be seen in any sleazy old context, because then they would lose all credibility. At the same time, it is invaluable to be seen in the right context, to belong to the truly interesting alliances, something which can no longer be bought with money, because money is no longer interesting enough. Therefore it is no exaggeration to say that the paradigm shift is bringing about the death of capitalism, simply because capital is being forced to court attention, instead of vice versa.

Attention, which there is such a shortage of, is what every player wants. According to fundamental national economic principles of supply and demand, it is no longer financial profit which drives development and motivates people. Old values are being badly devalued. This is the case with both money and titles; it does not matter whether these titles are connected to family, politics, business, or education: their value is sinking. Attention is superior to everything else; society is attentionalist rather than capitalist. If the word informationalism were not already established within sociology as a collective term for the new paradigm, the word attentionalism would possibly be even better for capturing its most characteristic feature. It is thus of crucial importance to be clear about what attentionalism means, and what the unavoidable consequences of its inherent dynamics are.

The Internet differs from latter-day capitalism's mass media on one conclusive point. The daily press, radio and television are all examples of one-way communication. The consumer consumed, while the transmitter sent out his message in peace and quiet. A closed system without dialogue, without a forum for criticism or questioning, apart from the strictly managed contents of the letters page. The net, on the other hand, is about communication in at least two, and often even more directions. Before, the medium was the message, but now it is the user. By acting on the net, the user is creating content: the boundary between production and consumption is dissolving. This means that those in power under capitalism, the possessors of the much-vaunted hegemony of public space – politicians, propagandists, preachers – are no longer serious players in the media arena. They are now being deposed by finely-tuned network consumers, who are constructing increasingly sophisticated feedback loops of information. These are then thrown back into the system and undergo a long series of manipulations in the hands of the many participants. It is a matter of spectacularly complicated processes with infinite variables and often astonishing results.

The fact that the new network citizen is not particularly interested in old, worn-out rituals from the capitalist paradigm, like for instance political elections, is therefore not particularly surprising. The audience has simply got up out of its chairs and left the theatre. The old capitalist is left alone on the stage asking himself more and more indignantly why no-one is listening to his words of wisdom. From the foyer there is an increasing noise: the audience has started to communicate amongst itself. Someone is offering drinks, and from the loud-speakers in the corners dance music is playing. In this half-lit night-club world it is the host of this improvised party, the curator, the virtuoso networker, who is the big new star. Power in informational society does not belong to the person who dictates, nor to the person who believes that the centre is in the spotlight, but to the person who sets the social game going with discrete effectiveness. What is decisive is not what is communicated, but how it is communicated, and who is communicating with whom. The aim is not so much an aim as a direction; to create, maintain and strengthen a process in motion. The ambition is not to shout louder than the media hubbub, but to use the wind-machine as a musical instrument on which the netocrat can play a seductive melody.

The displaced balance of power that is the result of this development is reflected in the growing medialisation of politics. Politics is being forced to adapt to media dramaturgy and become TV-friendly and entertaining in order to attract any attention at all. In the long run this will lead to politicians losing all real power; they will become a new category of low-paid TV-entertainers, harmless enactors of other people's scripts, mercilessly reviewed the whole time, and mocked by their journalistic overseers. There is no alternative. Anyone trying to resist developments and persist with political agitation in the old way would not survive in the society ruled by the netocracy. He or she would look like a despicable information-tyrant. The new conditions of the informational media landscape mean that the plurarchic public is turning its back on the old political stage.

The players' own ambitions, what or who he or she has decided to be, are no longer of consequence. No-one "makes their own fortune" any more. The whole of the perceptual world reflected in this phrase has passed away. What matters instead is the player's capacity for instant conversion the moment the requirements and desires of his or her surroundings shift. The incredibly complex and constantly changing system of rules for virtual behaviour which is now being developed and endlessly updated is shaping and expressing the netocratic ideal. The only useful key to impenetrable netiquette is maximal flexibility and highly developed social intelligence. Nothing can ever be taken for granted; all our prejudices, all the fictions that we use to orientate ourselves in life must be constantly re-evaluated. Every new situation requires a new judgment, as well as the courage to act without hesitation according to this judgment, and to behave accordingly. Only those who are prepared to allow themselves to constantly change can survive socially in a world which has realised its own constant mutability.

This has a number of interesting consequences. The netocrats' therapy sessions, to take one example, will no longer be based upon prevailing psychological or psychoanalytical models of a more or less integrated, unified ego. Freud and all his followers, interpreters, successors and adversaries within the therapeutic genre have played out their roles. Instead the situation- and interaction-based ideas about social intelligence and controlled exploitation of personality-division of progressive communication theorists and schizo-analysts will come to dominate the field. In informational society more people will seek treatment for the many problems connected to an excessively unified personality than for any difficulties connected with schizophrenic tendencies. It is almost the case that a manageable form of schizophrenia is a netocratic ideal.

The netocrats are not interested in realizing themselves or establishing contact with their true selves. This sort of concept is, in their eyes, old nonsense, superstition. They neither believe nor want to believe in what they perceive as the social constructions of a bygone age. Instead they strive to nurture and refine their capacity for simultaneity and the art of constantly developing a multiplicity of parallel identities. Personal development is the realization of all one's possibilities as a dividual, a pragmatic alliance of essentially different temperaments and personality traits. The old individual will look like a feeble, one-dimensional wretch rather than the ideal. Schizophrenic, kaleidoscopic identity is in contrast exemplary in the sense that it is functional. Schizo-analysis will contribute to strengthening the capacity for constant change according to constantly changing circumstances.

Communication in informational society can only take place within systems that allow feedback. Old, one-way communications will become curiosities in museums. The very concept of communication presupposes not only a recipient but even a more or less qualified reaction which returns to the original transmitter and functions as incoming data in the revolving process of the feedback loop. It is in this rapid interplay of interactive information management that the many facets of the dividual glint and glimmer. All the various dividuals illuminate, determine and confirm each other, in restless motion yet extremely co-ordinated, like fish in a shoal. The affirmation of the dividual rests in the reaction of its counterpart, or counterparts. He or she will regard him or herself as a network dependent upon other networks in order to use a constant flow of information to continually update his or her keenly desirable virtual identity.

The netocratic dividual will seek rest on a platform, only to discover at once that the platform in question is in motion. He will then step onto another platform on another level, once again in search of firm ground under his feet, only to discover once again that that platform is in motion. So the process goes on, motion in different directions on different levels. But the receptive dividual will soon turn stepping from one platform to another into an art-form, and continue his search for firm ground despite knowing that the project is illusory, yet fascinated by his virtuoso abilities. The floating state which arises in an environment of consciously constructed and constantly revised fictions will replace belief in firm ground. Consciousness of the fragility of fictions will lead to a disillusioned clarity and loss of meaning, but also to a creative intoxication of freedom and limitless possibilities. When fictions are created in interaction with other dividuals the possibility for communication arises, and then anything can happen. This is the floating point of departure for mobilistic thought which is the only perceptible path through informational society.

One distinguishing characteristic of informationalism is the escalating medialisation of society, which is propelling all previous reasoning about credibility to its limit. A pedagogical way of explaining this process is to use a classic mass-medium, for instance a weekly or monthly magazine, to illustrate what this general medialisation entails. When we buy a monthly magazine, we do so to get a certain amount of relevant, substantial, engaging or at least entertaining information, what the netocracy calls content. But the magazine also contains a large amount of information that we do not want, but which we have to accept, at least fleetingly, in exchange for getting the desired information at a lower and manageable price, in other words: the magazine contains adverts. And the adverts bother us. A monthly magazine with too many adverts in relation to content cannot hope to retain very many readers. Besides this, a magazine that does not differentiate properly between adverts and content loses credibility and therefore readers. A magazine with no adverts at all is the one with the highest credibility, if not necessarily the most readers. At least if this is the result of a conscious policy and not merely a failed attempt to attract advertisers.

In a completely medialised society it will become necessary to apply this thinking not only to media consumption in its classic form, but also to all social activities in general. In the virtual community on the net the difference between content and adverts, in the sense of purchased information, must be constantly maintained; the battle for attention never lets up, but cannot merely be described with capitalist logic. Competition between the new people in power, the distributors of information, the curators, is so cut-throat that any curator who has the wherewithal and the integrity to limit the purchased information to an absolute minimum will be the one who accumulates greatest credibility for his network and therefore the one who emerges victorious. Purchased information, the only information that capitalism is interested in or even has the capacity to understand, has a mainly negative value to the netocracy. It is only asked for by the consumtariat who are looking around in confusion for instructions for consumer behaviour. In this way the capitalist renders himself impossible in netocratic circles, his activities disqualify him from membership.

In the attentionalist culture which is taking over from capitalism it is thus access to relevant and exclusive information, much more that access to money, which is decisive in the distribution of status and power. Innumerable investors will gather around every informationally wealthy person or organization, hunting for information, begging and pleading to be allowed to invest their financial capital in the activity which he does not himself understand, and they will be forced to adapt to the various wishes and whims of the netocrat. The Fortune 500 will be reduced to a sort of kitsch entertainment literature, rather like Debrett's under capitalism; as a piquant diversion, one can study how a bygone era ranked its citizens according to long-lost principles. Other measurements apply under informationalism. It is now network-membership that determines a person's social status, and this is constantly changing, both with time and depending on context. A list of the aristocracy of the new paradigm could never be a printed book, because it would be immediately outdated, and because anyone would be able to read it. Netocratic relationships are mapped out online instead, constantly updated and hidden behind codes and virtual keys, for use by selected party-organisers and other curators.

Invaluable contacts are literally invaluable: they cannot be purchased for money. Contacts only become accessible through the transfer of other contacts of equivalent total value. Attentionalism will therefore create a sort of sophisticated bartering system. Contacts will be established when a player has valuable information to pass on, and, above all, when the person concerned exhibits an exceptional capacity to manage and present the information in question in an appealing way that arouses interest. Here yet another distinguishing feature of attentionalism becomes apparent: it is possible both to have your cake and eat it, you keep the information yourself, and its value, at the same time as sharing it with a select few. The fact is that value is accrued in connection with the transaction: communication creates attentional value for the person offering the information, and that value remains so long as the information in question is of interest. The value will also persist for as long as there is any reason to expect more of the same product from the information source.

The information you choose to keep to yourself obviously has no attentional value at all, and the information you sell for money has an extremely short-lived and limited value, whereas valuable information that is beneficial to the network increases the attentional status of the informer enormously. This is the principle of the internal life of the network, a micro-medialisation on the level of the transparent network. It is within this process that the individual player can climb socially, it is within this process that the network ensures a regular supply of valuable information. It is from the players who play this game to its conclusion that the highest networks recruit the occupants of their formal positions. The consumtariat, on the other hand, is directed to scratch its living on the virtual market of temporary occupation; they are project-nomads who are constantly hunting between the employment-offering homepages.

The faith in progress that was a characteristic of the capitalist paradigm and which was expressed once again in the clueless technological optimism of latter-day capitalism – everything will be alright, the Internet is a vitamin injection for democracy and everyone will share in the benefits of the new economy – appears to the netocracy to be a vulgar substitute for religion. This does not stop it from being an important element of netocratic propaganda; religious needs are constant and the consumtariat needs to be tranquillised with a substitute for traditional expressions of faith when secularization increases. The consumtariat must therefore be kept in a good mood with constant new varieties of spectacular entertainment, which is synonymous with success on the consumtariat's level. But within the netocracy the idea of progress will be replaced with extreme mobilism and relativism.

Networks will blossom with lightning speed, capture power and status rapidly, only to disappear just as quickly. Nothing is permanent, no value lasts, all platforms are in motion in different directions. Admittedly, from the perspective of evolutionary sociology it is possible to discern a historical trend; the broad sweeps are all pointing unambiguously in the same direction: growing globalization, ever more sophisticated non-zero-sum games, increasingly complicated networks of mutual dependency. But this is not the same as progress; new technological and social circumstances may well create new winners, but also new losers. Some social problems become less acute, while others more so and new ones appear.

Rapidly blossoming networks should equally be seen as a so-called "event", as an organization with a enduring temporal presence. Intensive activity in temporarily constructed feedback loops will create social energies that are difficult to harness. The resonance is multiplied many times over through feedback; the pressure waves spread quickly through the whole body of society and therefore the meme-Darwinian preconditions for other networks and their players are altered. In the same way that an organism's surroundings in nature essentially consist of other organisms, so a network's surroundings are basically other networks. There is a perpetually ongoing race – one predator gets stronger, its prey have to counter with ingenuity or speed, and its competitors among the predators have to come up with a counter-reaction; network X goes on the offensive, whereupon networks Y and Z have to come up with counter-offensives. Every change has consequences that are infinitely difficult to foresee (the variables are infinite), but nevertheless fully logical. Nothing is more important to an understanding of informational society than knowledge of these mechanisms. Therefore analysis of network dynamics will be the social science which attracts the greatest interest in the informational paradigm.

In this way, the Network will replace Man as the great social project. The network of curators will replace the State as the visionaries, managers and ultimate power of the great project. Netiquette will replace law and order as fundamental human activities increasingly move into the virtual world, at the same time as the authority and power of the state diminish as its income through tax shrinks and national boundaries dissolve. The curator will assume the state's function as moral guardian and will punish all transgressions against netiquette by expelling the delinquent from attractive networks. Exclusion, restricted access to information and other forms of rescinded membership privileges are the netocracy's methods for deterring and controlling dissidents. Severe limitations of virtual mobility will be the informational equivalent to internment.

In order to protect their common interests and make the administration of the networks more effective, the curators will establish their powerful meta-networks for policy questions about net-policing. Note that the curator acts as policeman as well as prosecutor and judge, and that no formal legal rights can be created in the changeable system of networks. The deliberations that take place within the highest networks will be protected against every intimation of observation, and need not stem from any democratically reached decision or any generally embraced traditions. The entire principle of public life and the public's right to observe generally will become extremely difficult to maintain; in spite of all optimistic hopes to the contrary, the public arena will disappear and be replaced by the labyrinthine topography of informationalism. A general perspective of overview will be impossible.

But informational society is still not totalitarian. It will not, admittedly, be possible to appeal against the curator's decisions in the usual sense, and the chances of getting justice for wrongly meted-out punishments will not be great. But the extreme mobility and multiplicity within the system will ensure that there are always alternative networks to join, so long as you really do have something which is attractive to the market. If you have, the other networks will not be able to afford to decline and refuse membership, nor will they have any reason to. And this complex topography will affect every player. Even the most powerful of the curators will lack a complete overview of informational society and will therefore already be exposed to a limitation of his potential power.

What we know today as capitalism will not vanish, just as feudal structures were not destroyed with the advent of capitalism; they simply carried on in a weaker state, subordinate to the victorious paradigm and its logic. The same thing applies now: a capitalist pattern will form an important component of a superior, informational system. Capital will become, to a very great extent, something sought by the consumtariat, and money will be the language used to describe and measure traditional consumption of goods and services. But the fact that money has been digitalised, that the movements of financial capital are instantaneous and impossible for politicians and bureaucrats to regulate, will disadvantage to a greater extent than before an underclass without access to relevant information, at the same time as it benefits a well-informed netocracy with its finger on the pulse of the flow of capital.

The fact that speed is increasing and the markets' complexity is growing means that the information abyss between the initiated and the excluded is becoming wider and wider, at an increasing rate. When the information that was once attractive has filtered down to the lowest-ranking networks – after a few minutes or several weeks, in so far as it filters down at all – it will be so old that it is worthless. The possibility for action, for instance to make gains from moving money from European bonds to some obscure growth market in deepest Asia, has long since vanished. Information will only have been interesting, and only had any real value, so long as only a chosen few knew about it.

Of course, the netocracy has ensured that it has the services of leading experts, indentured underlings providing discrete and effective protection of the new power's interests. But in spite of this, for the netocracy power and status are still a matter of something completely different, namely exclusive information that cannot be bought with money, the sort of information that would be exchanged for blank cheques if you were in the mood, and if cheques were still around. What is important is the capacity to create attention within the circles that matter. Having something to say which gets the noise of information to fall silent. Welcome to attentionalism!

10.

SEX AND TRIBALISM, VIRTUAL EDUCATION AND THE INEQUALITY OF THE BRAIN

□

TRENDS HAVE A DISTINCT MESSAGE for us. The fact that information and communication technology is breaking through a high threshold and entering a new historical phase means that everything is changing. We are being forced to see ourselves and our surroundings with new eyes. The paradigm shift will have wide-reaching and very real consequences when our old "truths" lose their validity. The institutions which supported the old society, and which seemed under the circumstances of the time to be eternal and "natural", are now suffering extreme crises and being revealed as products of a society and an ideology that were intrinsically tied to the circumstances of their period. Their rapidly approaching demise under the crushing weight of change therefore appears inevitable. This trend is inescapable. The institutions most affected by this are the nation state, parliamentary democracy, the nuclear family and the education system.

The concept of a "trend" ought not to be understood as synonymous with fashion or anything like that; it has nothing to do with the world of glossy magazines. We are using the words trend and countertrend in analogy with Friedrich Nietzsche's conceptual pairing of action and reaction. For Nietzsche, action was connected to the desire for power; it is, in a philosophical sense, an original impulse, independent of other impulses. Reaction, on the other hand, is a secondary impulse, and only arises as a response to action. It is quite literally reactionary in the sense that its main aim is to support and preferably strengthen existing power structures against which the action is a threat. The reaction, therefore, is a mobilization of defence, an act of life-support for a power whose position is disputed as a result of the emergence of a rival power; a prime example of this is when the dominant class of a dying paradigm defends itself against a new elite which has the winds of history in its sails. If we transfer this conceptual pairing to sociology we get trend and countertrend. A trend in this sense is a movement in time which is connected to the struggles of a certain group to achieve and manifest a social identity. A trend is an original impulse in the sense that it is not principally a response to another movement; it encounters resistance only when it collides with other interests, which it always does sooner or later.

A trend can be recognised by two distinguishing characteristics: partly that it has everything to gain from increased dissemination of information, and partly that it is intimately connected to and benefited by the territorial gains made by new technology. This means that the development of the Internet itself, as well as the social developments which presuppose or are benefited by the existence of the Internet, such as globalization and the bourgeoisie's loss of power and status to the netocracy, can be identified as genuine trends. A countertrend, on the other hand, can be defined as a reaction against such a trend. It does not stand for anything other than the defence of the status quo, or a return to a past which has been highly sentimentalised. A countertrend is therefore principally concerned with combating and disarming a trend. Current examples of countertrends are the hypernationalism and isolationism which are being nurtured in various places in the western world, or so-called Muslim fundamentalism in the Arab world. These are both reactions against the dominant trend which is moving towards globalization, secularization and increased plurarchisation in society. A countertrend is always secondary in that it is always dependent upon a trend for its existence.

If we look at developments over a longer period, the pattern becomes considerably more complicated. Often one and the same social movement contains elements of both trend and countertrend. A good example is the environmental movement, which contains a "trendy" faction, which regards technological advances and open debate positively, and which claims that the only way to create an environmentally aware society in the long term is to use information and discussion to stimulate new research directed towards a new, green form of advanced technology. But the environmental movement also contains a "countertrendy" faction which is opposed to economic growth and wants to suppress information by forbidding research, and which more or less wants to enforce the relocation of city-dwellers to the countryside, thereby returning to its romanticised image of the past.

Another example is the international movement against free trade, which has thrived as a result of a comprehensive network constructed with the help of the Internet, and which must therefore be regarded, at least formally, as a trend. But in essence this movement is driven by the ambition to protect well-organised vested interests in wealthy countries against competition from cheaper imported goods, effectively shutting out poor countries from all profitable markets; this desire to limit information is clearly an example of a countertrend. For obvious reasons this sort of hybrid movement is extremely unstable. Their similarity to rapidly decaying chemical elements with large atomic cores has led us to define them as quantum-sociological phenomena.

Without making any qualitative comparison between trends and countertrends – Nietzsche for his part always favoured action – we can confirm that history tends to favour trends, and that countertrends are generally doomed to fail in the end. This is in the nature of things: a countertrend implies a limitation of access to information, a strategy which in the long run can never be anything but unsustainable wishful thinking. Countertrends play on people's fears and apprehensions about trends, but can ultimately only delay the historical process, never change it. Once information has begun to seep out into society the countertrend loses its potency, and the trend breaks through on all levels. However we must not forget that today's countertrend is often yesterday's radical and innovative trend; in tune with the times when times were different.

Nationalism and democracy were originally fine examples of social and political trends, completely in tune with the technology of the age and supported by an increase in information. But the forces which are struggling to maintain old institutions today are the countertrends of our time. In spite of the occasional success, these forces are doomed to failure in a broader spectrum. The Internet is a fact. Mass-communications are rapidly becoming interactive. On a purely national level there is little that is of any real political interest. This means that globalization, secularization and pluralisation are ultimately unstoppable.

At a generous estimation, bourgeois democracy is little more than 200 years old, but in that time an impressively tenacious myth has developed around it, and has convincingly maintained that its structure and ideology are eternally valid. This myth has been supported by the fact that bourgeois democracy, seen as a trend, was spectacularly successful in its heyday, and has contributed to an unparalleled increase in general welfare. In the mild delirium of the end of the capitalist era, bourgeois democracy has been seen, particularly after the pathetic collapse of communism in eastern Europe, as not merely a precondition but almost a guarantee of economic growth, despite the fact that it is easy to refute this rather unsophisticated thesis. If we turn our critical gaze towards Asia, for example, we can see that it is hardly thanks to democratic virtue that Singapore, a shamelessly repressive one-party state, has been able to demonstrate an incomparably strong economy for several decades, and that democracy has not paved the way for an economic miracle in Bangladesh. But in spite of this the myth lives on.

The American political scientist Francis Fukuyama has proposed the idea that bourgeois democracy represents "the end of history" in a Hegelian sense, a completion of the political process. History should be seen as process of development common to all people, a lengthy struggle between different social systems and philosophies, a conflict that will rage until all available possibilities have been tried and all unsatisfactory solutions discarded. Fukuyama is suggesting that all possible alternatives to bourgeois democracy have been swept aside. The decisive factors in favour of democracy are that it was best suited to cope with all the contradictory interests which arise in an advanced, global market-economy, and also that democracy, with its theoretical equality, was the best able of all imaginable alternatives to satisfy its citizens' need for recognition and respect. Fukuyama is both right and wrong about this. Bourgeois democracy is admittedly the most suitable social system in most respects, but only within the framework of the capitalist paradigm. When circumstances change, history is in motion once more.

So much ideological capital has been invested in the idea of bourgeois democracy that every attempt to examine its propaganda critically, and every discussion of possible faults in the democratic theory, have been rejected with distaste and labelled as heresy by the immense forces guarding this myth. A cult has been constructed around democracy and its rituals, a cult with strikingly irrational elements, a mass movement whose cohesive idea is the notion that the magical power of the correct political procedure can solve, or at least ameliorate, all serious social problems. The forms of democracy themselves are believed to conjure up sound political content. The correct method of taking decisions always results in wise decisions, according to this most potent of democracy's dogmas. The self-appointed representatives of political goodness have persuaded themselves, and anyone who has cared to listen, that there is no difference between one and the other, and whenever someone has the bad manners to point out that the Nazis, to take one striking example, came to power as a result of democracy and parliamentary elections, the response is always a series of diffuse explanations about the German population's "democratic immaturity", and the existence of that specific situation at that particular time, but seldom or never a recognition that democracy itself is no guarantee for good and wise decision-making.

Every exception is turned around so that it confirms the general rule: as soon as the democratic maturity of the population has reached a certain acceptable level, democracy will automatically produce wise decisions like a well-oiled political machine. This faith in the process of democratic maturity of the population is as unshakeable as it is unfounded. It is a matter of religious faith rather than empirical knowledge. According to the axiom, voters cannot vote wrongly, and if the people should nonetheless do so– like the Austrian people did when a populist right-wing party was elevated to government in the dying weeks of the 20th century, a result which the rest of the European Union strongly opposed – then it is simply a matter of pronouncing loudly that a mistake has been made and bringing about a correction through suitable actions.

This is all about the bourgeoisie parading democracy as if it in itself were something holy, yet being unable to accept democracy when it conflicts with the bourgeoisie's own interests. There is a considerable amount of hypocrisy in the ceremonial rhetoric of democracy. What is at best a problematic and fragile compromise between conflicting political forces, and at worst a method of legitimizing the decisions that the elite wants to force through, is elevated as something good, eternal, and beyond doubt, something in accordance with the laws of nature. Feudalism maintained that people could believe what they wanted to so long as they believed in

God; capitalist tolerance stretches to the point that people can vote for whomsoever they want to so long as they vote for the bourgeois democratic state in one of its sanctioned variations.

As is the case with all the obvious contradictions in a governing paradigm, this one is a sign that the old paradigm has played out its role. Just one decade after the discussion of bourgeois democracy as the culmination of history there is now, ironically, a growing consciousness of a crisis of democracy. Apathy towards utopia is accelerating, and democracy is being gradually stripped of both internal and external components. At the same time as technological development is promoting an entirely new ecology for humanity, the value of the democratic "recognition" upon which Fukuyama based large parts of his argument is being devalued. Fukuyama himself was the first to address the problems in his own cheerily optimistic theory with a dose of good old Nietzschean doubt. What is the point, he wondered, of universal recognition in the end? Who will be satisfied with something which is available to everyone? Invoking Nietzsche, Fukuyama pointed out the connection between the tolerance on offer and a dissolution of values that would be fatal for society. What genuine sense of self-respect can allow itself to be detached from every form of achievement? And is universal recognition actually possible? Can we ever hope to get away from a system of values and a hierarchy of various achievements?

An entirely equal person is incapable of contemplating social and moral issues, because to do so presupposes a basic difference between good and bad, which is at odds with the extreme tolerance which is the hallmark of "political correctness", the last desperate attempt by an imploding democracy to flirt with everyone at the same time. Creative momentum is lost when society values everything as equal and has as its aim the equal distribution of resources. Stagnation accompanies stability, which leads to a gradual corrosion of democracy, both in its inert and active states. But stability ought in this context to be the least of our problems; it is a chimera, a socio-scientific abstraction. Stability does not exist in complex systems; Fukuyama's great mistake was to confuse the model with the reality.

Democracy has become a great worry: it demands attention in the form of education and nurture, which is why all sorts of authorities and research institutes are insisting on comprehensive budget increases. The warning implied by this is that we can no longer take democracy for granted. Democracy must at all costs be strengthened, runs the message from those whose power is entirely dependent upon democracy, and who for obvious reasons have no interest in any form of plurarchy. Propaganda declares that the only alternative to bourgeois democracy is a nightmarish dictatorship which, as history has illustrated, is all too easily attainable through exemplary democratic means, while plurarchy is suppressed as best it can be. There is an impression that it does not exist, that it is not even conceivable. This is why it is highly ironic that the Internet is being promoted as the tool which will facilitate the ultimate triumph of democracy. In actual fact the Internet is responsible for the new media-technological ecology in which plurarchy is thriving on natural selection and in which democracy is therefore doomed to failure. The crisis in democracy is here to stay. From now on democracy will be synonymous with the crisis affecting both itself and the whole of the declining paradigm. As a result of the paradigm shift the unthinkable has become thinkable.

Informationalism will force the development of new political structures. One concrete political problem is that in areas where politicians want to make decisions there is no longer anything to decide about. The market and the economy have moved. In this situation growing federalism will be the final straw for democracy, because developments are moving ever more rapidly towards a global state. The introduction of such a project is probable, not least because the survival of the political class is at stake. A world trade organization will be followed by a world tax organization, and so on. But all efforts in this direction will be in vain, not because any attempt to mobilise enthusiasm for the project amongst all the world's voters would take immense effort, but because plurarchy will already be an accomplished fact before a detailed plan for a global state has even been sketched out. In the virtual world, politics will become powerless.

But even the virtual world will spontaneously establish certain global state structures. The electronic elite will establish a new lingua franca, a Net-Latin based upon English, already the global language of communication for the netocracy. This highly modified form of English, in which subcultural dialects will come to the fore, where standard phrases will be drastically shortened, where innovative neologisms will be encouraged and sub-clauses abandoned, will be the universal language of the global networks.

The overwhelming Anglo-Saxon domination of the international music and entertainment industries indicates the central role played by a common language in the current medialisation of the world. We can already see how the English-speaking countries of various continents have established a lead over their neighbours in the race towards informational society. This is obviously the case with Great Britain and Ireland, Canada, Australia and South Africa, all of whom are playing leading roles in spreading the Anglo-Saxon-dominated Internet culture to every corner of the world; this without even mentioning the role of the USA. But even Hong Kong, Singapore and India are doing the same in Asia. Or the Netherlands and the Scandinavian countries in Europe, where proficiency in English has become so advanced that it has practically become a second native language. The convergence of global communication is leading to an increasing demand for some form of uniform, common language, which will further benefit the Anglo-Saxon media industries which were already well-developed before informationalism, and which are now the main suppliers of content to the Internet.

It is entirely logical that it has been easier for small countries with highly restricted domestic markets to think and act globally than for countries with large domestic markets. The relative uselessness of their native languages has forced them to adapt and gradually switch to the English-based Net-Latin. Those countries which have had ambitions of competing with English as the global lingua franca of the Internet – primarily those countries in which French, Spanish, German, Arabic, Japanese and Chinese are spoken – are experiencing, on the other hand, comparatively large and intractable problems in connecting their national network structures to the global net. For this reason there will be initially a limited number of people from these linguistic areas taking part in the international networks. While we are still waiting for comprehensive translation software, language is still a barrier.

Local and regional languages and dialects are maintaining their strong position within large populations, but are gradually assuming an recognizably inferior position. Native languages will live on among the consumtariat, while the netocracy will regard them as a kind of amusing hobby with sentimental connections to the past, one of many sources of entertainment and amusement based upon identity. In much the same way as the middle-class tourists of former times spouted sentences culled from phrase-books during their holidays abroad, the netocrats will amuse themselves during their summer holidays in their digitally wired country houses by practicing the characteristic traits of the local language, all with a high degree of ironic distance. Within the porous framework of Net-Latin there will of course be a number of different dialects, but these will not be geographically anchored but instead linked to different virtual subcultures, and will function mainly as identification markers to distinguish their speakers from the members of other electronic tribes.

On important reason why the USA has found it so easy to adapt to virtual culture is the pre-pluralistic attitude to geographical space which has always suffused the American mentality since the time of the first settlers. Majority decision-making has never had the same strong roots in the collective consciousness of North America as it did in Europe, thanks to the concept of the "frontier", the continual exploration of the boundary of the unknown. When an American did not see eye to eye with his neighbour, there was always the possibility of upping sticks, moving further west and breaking new ground. There was a lot of spare land, and colonization took a long time. When the settlers had reached the Pacific, they continued to Hawaii and Alaska. Connections to secure territory have never been particularly strong in American culture. There has always been an emotive and irresistible desire for the unknown, a permanent preparedness to move on, a romanticisation of the nomadic. We need to bear this in mind when we look at the great space projects of the 1960s and 70s; once the earth had been mapped and colonised there was only space left. Space became "The Final Frontier".

But only as long as our thinking was confined to physical space. The truly revolutionary adventure was waiting within the digital universe of satellite-linkups and fibre-optic cables. During the 1980s the Internet was made available to everyone, a completely new "frontier", and the first people who began to explore this virtual world were precisely the outsiders of American society, lone wolves or members of diverse subcultures who were ill at ease in the dominant cultural climate. They felt out of place, so they upped sticks, turned their back on mainstream culture and moved on, breaking new ground in a new world. This virtual mass migration, described by the American social theoretician Mark Pesce as "the

Gnostic Frontier", marked the beginning of colonization of a new world which was quite literally infinite. A continuous stream of new and unexplored virtual territories awaits the nomadic Americans. The journey need never end. The pre-pluralist tradition has prepared the way for a smooth transition from democracy to plurarchy, and the shift will be experienced as relatively mundane. What will be harder for Americans to accept will be the devaluation of money and the death of capitalism.

Another sacred social institution which is undergoing a fatal and intensely debated crisis at the onset of the informational paradigm is the nuclear family. There is a good deal of confusion in this discussion, in which conservative elements are arguing for a return to "tradition". What we need to be clear about is that what is usually called the "traditional family", where the man goes out into the world to earn money while the woman stays at home and looks after the house, is anything but traditional. In actual fact, the "traditional family" was a child of the 1950s, a result of increased welfare and the dream of fully-fledged suburban bliss free from social obligations. The middle-classes moved out to the suburbs to get away from an urban community that felt altogether too stifling and oppressive. The suburbs, with their lush vegetation, were attractive because they appealed to our tribal instincts.

The real traditional family is something entirely different: an economic union and socialization project which links various generations together. The nuclear family – which is, interestingly enough, the same age as another post-war phenomenon, nuclear weapons – ought therefore to be regarded as an integral part of latter-day capitalism's obsession with individualism: total freedom at the cost of total isolation, consumption instead of communication. There is a simple and obvious logic to this. It is in the interests of the state, as well as of capital, (once again in the same boat) that people develop into "independent individuals" rather than as members of wide-ranging networks of social communities. Quite simply, it makes it easier to exercise central control, and at the same time people develop a sense of individual responsibility for their own self-realization, which is expressed in intense and often therapeutic consumption.

The nuclear family arose because it was the smallest, most individualised social entity that was feasible once the necessary requirements of reproduction had been taken into consideration.

But as far as the state, and capital, are concerned, it does not need to be stable at all. A single parent is more dependent upon subsidies than a couple, and is therefore more submissive and more easily controlled, and a marked increase in the number of single-occupancy homes also means, naturally, that consumption increases dramatically. The ideal would be for everyone to live alone in their own home, with their own car, so that optimal demand for houses, cars, sofas, cookers, etc, could be achieved. The path of the isolated, independent individual towards self-realization always passes through increased consumption.

For these reasons the great wave of divorces that has swept the western world since the mid-1960s does not actually constitute a violation of capitalist values; on the contrary, it is a logical continuation of increasing individualization on all levels, and of the escalating development of social structures under the capitalist paradigm: from village communities and the tribal family which consisted of several generations, to the single urban citizen, who himself constitutes the ultimate capitalist family unit. This will not prevent a number of noticeable elements of the introductory phase of informationalism from strengthening some of these tendencies. The clearest example is when industrial production decreases to the benefit of information management and an expanding service sector. This means that a large number of poorly educated men will be rendered superfluous in the labour market. At the same time, an increasing number of career opportunities for women are opening up, suggesting a further increase in divorce-rates and the number of single people.

Sexuality is another matter: the Pill meant that sex could be differentiated from familial responsibility. Francis Fukuyama has suggested that the Pill not only granted women the freedom to live out their desires without consequences, but that, primarily, it released men from any sense of responsibility for the children that were born anyway. Maternal care for infants is highly biologically programmed, whereas paternal care is more of a cultural product, and therefore more sensitive to disruption. Added to this is the fact that reproduction is gradually becoming separated from sexuality generally, with both fertilization and pregnancy being increasingly taken over by biotechnical laboratories. This is hardly going to strengthen family bonds.

The freedom from censorship offered by the Internet also means that sexuality is becoming less dramatic, and is just one pastime amongst others: the link between sex and cohabitation is being weakened, which means partly that sexuality is being distanced from relationships generally, and partly that a wealth of cohabitation forms is appearing in which sex plays no part. You no longer need to live with your sexual partner, just as little as you need to live with your tennis partner: You do not need to have sex with the person you are living with, as little as you need to have sex with your boss or your therapist. Conventional forms of personal relations are dissolving and disappearing. Circumstances will determine the form of a relationship, and not vice versa.

The lack of a normative majority on the Internet means that every conceivable sexual preference is becoming socially acceptable; every taste has its own more or less global network. Homosexuality, sadomasochism, different forms of asexuality: everything is going on alongside more generally inclusive activities, which is providing inspiration for the most disparate lifestyles and forms of relationship. The Internet has already stimulated unparalleled experimentation in areas of sexuality and relationships, a development which is now exploding. The keyword in this context is queer. Queer culture implies the liberation of heterosexual society from the compulsion to be normal and normative, and is growing rapidly through imitation of the successful networking of gay society. Sexuality is no longer a subject for control and regulation, is not made to perform a socially cohesive role within the State or the Market, but is now the basis for the creation of new, more or less temporary, tribal identities on the Net. Queer culture is thus a genuine trend. Sex and cohabitation are being replaced by sex and tribal identity.

It is the search for tribal identity within the practically limitless framework of virtual nomadic society which is forming new, fluid family structures. This tribalization of culture, this virtual return to nomadic existence made possible by electronic networks, means that permanent homes are no longer regarded as the fixed point in life, which itself stimulates further unconditional experimentation with lifestyles. The rapid increase in mobility and speed in society is leading, for better or worse, to a growing sense of rootlessness. The new sense of homelessness is simultaneously imposed and desired, a burden and a possibility. The new nomadic life implies a permanent migration between different cities, different workplaces, different identities.

The mobility of the netocracy, first virtual, but increasingly physical, is leaving deep traces on society and culture. The idea of a home and a place of residence is changing beyond recognition. The higher your status, the greater your degree of mobility. The consumtariat, securely settled in fixed dwellings, is easily accessible to the homogenizing effects of the mass-media, and the remaining political powers and their ever more desperate tax authorities. The netocracy is abandoning the traditional suburban fortress established by and for nuclear families. Now hotels, monasteries and meditation centres are the major influences on the new elite's way of life. The function of the secure home to act as an identifying factor is disappearing and being transferred to the Net, to the virtual equivalent of the home: the homepage. A homepage is what a genuine Netocrat can accept as his fixed point in existence. As long as it can be regularly updated!

Another institution in deep crisis is public education, one of the fruits of large-scale population growth in Europe and North America during the 1800s, which in turn, like the explosive population growth of the Third World during the 1900s, was a consequence of the habitual delay between technological changes and cultural behaviour patterns. As we have earlier asserted in our analysis of mobilistic diagrams, history moves far faster than people can possibly react. Changes which affect material circumstances often achieve their cultural impact only after a delay of several generations. Populations grew in Europe and North America because infant mortality dropped and the general preconditions of life improved radically, at the same time as the birth rate remained at its earlier high level. A noticeable decline in the birth rate did not occur for several decades, which meant that for a long time there were colossal numbers of children. The working-class families of the countryside and the city slums were turned into veritable production-lines for the making of children.

This development forced wide-reaching political activity: the growing mass of children needed to be cared for and protected in a satisfactory way, to be civilised and brought up as useful members of society, as diligent workers and insatiable consumers. These ambitions were co-ordinated in the middle of the 1800s in a new institution: the state school. Apart from their practical function, schools also had an ideological role. During the early years of industrialization the hoards of children had been put to hard work in factories at an early age. But the middle- and upper-classes eventually forced through legislation regulating child labour, and in time also introduced compulsory education. Partly inspired by the romantic cult of the child, and its imagined closeness to some original state of innocence and purity, they wanted to protect and nurture the young, sheltering them from the more brutal sides of life and carefully introducing them to the secrets of adult life.

It is important to remember that childhood is a cultural product, created during the Renaissance. During the age of feudalism children were not regarded as belonging to a special category, and were not assumed to have any special needs, and their entry into adulthood was not a question of nurture and education. Children were purely and simply small people, far too weak to be of any real use. The word "child" did not describe an age, but a relationship; you were the child of so-and-so, and always would be, which underlines the obsession of feudal society with family names.

The advent of childhood during the Renaissance is, as Neil Postman has pointed out, closely connected to the printing press. This new information technology brought with it a new perception of what it meant to be an adult, the ability to read; consequently the definition of a child was the opposite: a person who had not learnt to read. One did not automatically become an adult with time, but through education. Education is in some respects a revolt against nature: a small child is made to sit still and fret over the alphabet and other studies when play and other physical activities are much more appealing. In this way education coincides with the need for the child to control its impulses. Childhood thus became one of the basic discoveries of capitalism, and as such became the subject of endless ideological conflicts.

Universal education meant that the process of becoming an adult and a member of society became industrialised, and encompassed even the children of the working-class. What was grandly described as a human right was at the same time a social duty. Someone who did not go to school could not become an adult, nor, therefore, a fully-fledged citizen. Society's values were instilled, and the necessary capabilities to ensure that society's needs were fulfilled were taught. Education itself was a visible example of progress, and the idea of progress suffused the whole enterprise. Everyone had reason to greet universal education warmly: for the working-class it was necessary if its children were to have even a theoretical chance of climbing socially, and for the bourgeoisie it offered the chance to recruit new talent to the administration of the state apparatus, and to form the remainder of the working-class into an effective workforce for the factories.

Nothing was left to chance. The whole enterprise was rigorously planned according to the most advanced pedagogical programs of the time, and the model for the organisation was taken from related institutions such as the military, and mental hospitals. Schools became the instruments of selection for the capitalist meritocracy, and functioned satisfactorily so long as the labour market demanded clearly defined competencies for a more or less stable list of standardised careers: in other words, as long as there was a direct link between education and working life. But with the breakthrough of informationalism the entire capitalist notion of the "career" is crumbling. A crisis within our schools is inevitable.

The informational labour market has an entirely new structure. Employment is no longer a lifelong contract, and length of service is no longer of prime importance. Business organisations are becoming less rigid and are concentrating on temporary projects, for which people with specific competencies are employed. Temporary constellations are created only to be dissolved when a project is completed. Education is never a completed chapter but must be constantly updated. Every new task involves a new situation, which generally requires new knowledge. The unavoidable consequence of this is that all diplomas, titles and certificates are practically worthless the day after the exam. This, in turn, means that schools are really losing every other role except for those of a holding-pen and a place for social training; children can learn more sitting in front of their computers at home than at their desks at school. In an increasingly fragmented and changing society, the whole idea of centralised, homogenised schooling linked to the nation state seems outdated.

Already, increasing demand for further education and the development of skills both inside and outside of business has led to many old academic institutions sensing that change is in the air. Politicians fight to be able to inaugurate new subsidised business parks aimed at growth industries like information technology and bio-technology, connected to universities and colleges. Increasingly costly educational packages are being tailor-made for companies in a seemingly limitless spirit of generosity. But it would be a mistake to take this as a sign that traditional educational institutions will play a leading role in informational society. Business parks are not a trend but a countertrend, an increasingly desperate attempt to protect old hierarchical structures under new circumstances, and are therefore doomed to fail. These actors from the old paradigm are far too closely tied to their old historical positions to be able to move easily and quickly enough to survive in the virtual ecosystem.

The feudal roots of academic culture are evident in its hidebound fascination for titles and old qualifications. Its closed frame of reference, its rigid hierarchy, its incapacity to assimilate criticism as something constructive: all of this is creating a problem of credibility. The academic world appears, in the eyes of the netocracy (whose scepticism towards self-proclaimed experts in every field is practically constitutional), to be obsolete and corrupt. This opposition between the netocracy and the academic world is to a certain extent superficial. But beneath the surface there is a more fundamental difference in attitude which is becoming more apparent as the universities desperately seek to protect their increasingly exposed position in informational society.

To put it simply, it is a question of opposition between two completely different temperaments. For the netocracy speed and an overview are the primary requirements, whereas traditional research prioritises thoroughness and depth, which explains the persistent studies of a stability that is purely fictional: purely theoretical constructions with little connection to reality, which dominated social science during the 1900s. The netocracy is interested in change, whereas academics are concerned with static models. Or, to put it another way: the netocracy is interested in bodies in motion, while academics prefer to perform autopsies on old corpses. There will be not so much an encounter as a brutal cultural clash between these two participants, a clash which can only end badly for academics, whose obsessively neurotic attachment to scientific scrupulousness, references, footnotes, etc., make them incapable of attaining the speed and overview which appeal to the netocracy.

What the netocracy is seeking and needs is something quite different to what the universities are offering: the ability to absorb and assimilate large amounts of information, combined with an intuitive understanding of what is relevant in each specific situation;

quick associations and irrational playfulness rather than conscientious analysis of sources. The netocracy's attitude to knowledge is at the same time instrumental and aesthetic. When the netocrats do not find what they want in either universities or business parks, they will turn their backs on the academic world and construct their own primarily virtual institutes and think-tanks, free from outsized administration, intellectual snobbery and a tyranny of detail.

Education will in the future be characterised by an interactive and constantly adapting pragmatism. It will be offered and developed on the Net in the form of small, precisely adapted modules, specially designed for the task at hand. It will be the student who decides the rules, not the institution. There will be stiff competition between these sophisticated and flexible systems, and in this market there will not be room for capitalism's inflexible and resource-hungry monster universities. There will no longer be any need to sit isolated in some regional college, divorced from the labour market, adapting to obsolete conventions in the hope of getting a diploma which, like the Soviet Order of Lenin today, only has kitsch and curiosity value. The future of collective education is behind it.

This development is being hastened by the academic institutions' inability to create functional networks. The mailing-lists and web-archives that have been launched so far by the leading universities in Europe and North America are based upon the entirely mistaken belief that creativity and problem-solving can be stimulated with the help of eternally rumbling debates, open to everyone. This attitude seems unforgivably naïve to a netocratic observer. Within the netocracy there is an acute awareness that qualified networks can only function if they are created as time-saving arenas for contact between selected participants, and as contact points for the exchange of exclusive information. This requires strict and sensitive curators; it requires the ruthless manipulation of information, presentation and accessibility. This means, in effect, that practically any teenager is capable of managing his own private network more effectively and, above all, more purposefully, than naïve and clumsy universities with their feeble presence on the Net, in spite of all their enormous subsidies.

It is ironic in this respect that the Internet was originally created for, and partially by academic institutions that did not understand how to use the new medium with whose management they were entrusted. Recent developments have left them behind. We can see once again how creativity rather than financial resources or politically directed regulations is decisive in the allocation of power in informational society. It follows from this that there is no reason for the netocracy to boast of academic titles; on the contrary, it will be more prestigious to highlight a lack of formal qualifications. In the eyes of the netocracy, completed educational programmes and doctoral titles are not signs of merit, but an indication of an inexcusable lack of judgement. Universities will come to be regarded as protected workshops for intellectual therapy, and anyone who has spent his time there will be treated with an increasing amount of suspicion. At the same time, academic institutions represent a powerful interest which cannot be disregarded; they will be perceived as a potential source of countertrends which might harm the netocracy. For this reason it is unlikely that the netocracy will be content merely to ignore the academic world, but will actively oppose it, if only by excluding its representatives from attractive networks.

Trends are encountering countertrends on every social and cultural level in the transition between capitalism and informationalism. One far-reaching trend, related to welfare and education, which is showing signs of getting stronger, is the diminishing birth-rate of western countries. Giving birth is simply not fashionable any more. In a majority of western nations women are giving birth to less than two children on average, and the consequences of this are not hard to work out: the population is declining at an increasing rate. The politicians of the 21st century have no hoards of children to take care of; one of the truly large problems will be the exact opposite – how to manage the decrease in population numbers. A shrinking number of young people is expected to provide for an increasing number of old, and steadily older, people. In a democratic society the elderly would be able to force through a gerontocracy by using their majority position to outvote the smaller number of young people. But, as we have already seen, in a pluralist society there is no connection between positions of power and purely numerical superiority, as little as there is any direct connection between power and money. On the contrary, it is probable that a minority of young people will have power thanks to their relevant abilities and their greater manoeuvrability on the Net.

While the netocrats are experimenting with identities and lifestyles in their heavily guarded networks, the consumtariat is held in place thanks to the Disneyfication of the whole of the popular cultural landscape. Entertainment, consumption and leisure time are melting together into a single, enormous industrial sector. Large holiday resorts with adjacent entertainment factories are being built near airports, where the consumtariat are carried to be entertained to sleep. The very latest and most expensive entertainment technology is offered by so-called "multi-media theme-parks": collective experiences for alienated keyboard-slaves. On the innumerable recreation sites on the Net there are interactive soap-operas and every conceivable variety of bingo, lotto, betting, and every possible sort of game. Each form of game will have its own television channel and a host of homepages. This theatre performs all day, every day, always.

It will become considerably more difficult than before to use mass media for propaganda purposes, as we have already discussed in an earlier chapter. It will not be possible to use the same clumsy strategies as during the days of centralised one-way communication. Simultaneously, increasingly medialised, virtual reality will become sensitive to media manipulation. Any attempt to use the media will increasingly be an invasion of reality itself. The boundary between one and the other will become steadily less distinct, and will eventually prove more or less impossible to maintain. As a result, propaganda will become invisible, no longer discernible even to an expert; it will become its own reality, in its own right, the ever more subtle manifestation of the power of the elite in the form of pleasant and soothing mental massage for the masses.

Both art and philosophy are trying to find new tasks and new means of expression. The ambition to create an all-encompassing synthesis, total art, a universal explanatory model, has gone now. Virtual daily life will make that sort of thing seem as thoughtless as it is pointless. The linguistic philosophy of the 20th century has left us with an awareness of the limitations of our conceptual apparatus. The big problem is that the amount of information on offer is increasing exponentially, while our perception and our capacity to deal with incoming impulses is developing with the studied slowness of biological evolution; in other words, scarcely noticeably at all. The virtual world is rushing away from us, that is the tragic realisation of mobilism, which presents us with the task of making what in reality is an unmanageable world somehow manageable. This necessarily artificial level of comprehension contains an increasing amount of incomprehension; we are becoming increasingly dependent upon our ability to create functional models in order to orientate ourselves.

The new rationalism is therefore becoming transrationalistic, and contains a fundamental understanding of the unavoidable limitations of rational thought; it denies every form of transcendentalism and metaphysics at the same time as humbly acknowledging the shortcomings of rationalism. A mobilistic credo would be able to take as its starting point Nietzsche's exhortation to capitulate willingly to infinity, to be filled with "the joy of tragedy". Or Spinoza's exhortation to love this unfathomable world despite the fact that we can only expect frosty indifference in return. We must, according to the mobilists, abandon our infantile need for response and affirmation. Quite simply, we have no choice, life cannot be anything other than what it is.

The vacuum which remains when rationalism has given up, the "trans-" in transrationalism, can only be filled with painting, literature, music and all the new hybrid forms of art which are being opened up by new technology. Creative possibilities are practically limitless. The flip-side of the coin is that art, more than ever before, will become the exclusive province of specific electronic tribes. Art will probably not reach other groups to any noticeable extent, partly because of the extremely targeted output of media on the Net, and partly because of other groups' lack of a frame of reference. The whole apparatus which makes slightly more demanding culture comprehensible exists only under highly fragile circumstances on the Net. This is why culture will become yet another dividing barrier separating different groups from one another in the electronic class society, and a cohesive and identity-supporting factor only within narrowly-defined groups.

Informational society is anything but equal. And the inequality it offers seems more "natural" than was the case in earlier times because its meritocratic element is so large, because power is so difficult to localise, and because its representative mechanisms are so discrete. The netocracy is fairly untouchable; it has not taken anything from anyone, and its position of strength and status is built upon its undeniable suitability to thrive in the new ecosystem created by information technology. Nor does the new underclass share the same exciting, sexy attributes and the justified pathos which the underclass of the capitalist paradigm could demonstrate, and which aroused a certain level of sympathy. The consumtariat is the underclass because of its own lack of social intelligence, according to the norms of intelligence established by informational society.

No doors have been closed to anyone; the problem is that it requires a special talent to understand how to grasp the handle and get in, a talent lacking in the masses. Is this inequality necessarily unfair? And if it is, according to whose criteria? And, if so, what can be done about it? Ought we to hold back those who have the ability to make the most of the opportunities on offer? Ought we to carry on giving new chances to people who have failed so many times before? How can we solve the problem of increasing inequality in a society where inequality cannot be rectified by redistribution? We have not yet worked out how to swap brains with one another.

11.

BEHIND THE FIREWALLS – NETOCRATIC CIVIL WAR AND VIRTUAL REVOLUTIONARIES

☐

AS THE CENTRAL CAPITALIST institutions collapse, an echoing vacuum is appearing. As long as they retained any authority, these institutions fulfilled a stabilising function; what is coming instead will be a state of institutionalised turbulence whose dynamic is extremely difficult to predict. Certain trends are abundantly clear, but when so many trends and countertrends interact, there are so many parameters and the level of abstraction is so high that even the most sophisticated guesses become a sort of intellectual meteorology: reliable only at very short range. Despite this, there is every reason to gather such qualified prognoses as are possible, most appropriately by trying to identify and analyse the social tensions that will characterise informational society.

Political and cultural debate within informational society will take place against a background of entirely new circumstances. The debate about equality that took place under capitalism will appear hopelessly tied to a bygone age, where status and power were primarily distributed according to an arbitrary system. Neither family background, wealth, gender nor skin-colour will have any decisive significance in informational society, where individual status and power will instead depend upon the individual's capacity to acquire and manage information, upon social intelligence, receptivity and flexibility. The liberal ideal of equality: equal opportunities for everyone to realise their life's project, has therefore already been realised in practice (while the socialist ideal of equality: equal rewards for all regardless of context, must be regarded as discredited and consigned to history with the collapse of the communist utopia).

But at the very moment this realisation takes hold, it will be clear that informational society is in several respects more unequal and static than any other. What we call "the new sociology" is devoted to describing these conditions. The system is characterised by great permeability on all social levels, and consequently great mobility for the individual, but these porous structures are, in return, much stronger. The mechanisms of meritocratic classification will become increasingly refined, each and everyone with enough talent and initiative to constitute a threat will automatically be promoted to a privileged position within the network hierarchy and incorporated into the elite. And it is difficult to imagine any political activism aimed at the inequality of the brain, or the fact that talent is rewarded. It is, after all, only "natural"!

The new patterns of this class division under informationalism will contribute, together with network society's increasing opaqueness and the collapse of traditional left-wing ideology, to creating a seedbed for a dramatic increase of violence in society. The consumtarian protest movement will suffer a chronic lack of leaders – because potential talents are constantly absorbed into the netocracy – and will have little ideological sophistication. Its thinking will be contradictory, its actions erratically sporadic and impulsive. Social discontent will be blind. Consumtarian rebels will lack the old workers' movement's education and discipline, and will have no long-term objective. They will have no ambition to unite the consumtariat around a common cause, either within or outside the system, and no-one will believe in either organised revolution or revisionism: a sort of gradual netocratisation of the consumtariat through political struggle and hard work. What remains will be a sort of revolutionary aesthetic, a romanticisation of resistance as such, an intoxication of spontaneous, confused, collective destructiveness. But that will be all.

In this context it is important to remember that the consumtariat, in contrast to the old working class, lacks any solid conviction of a brighter future. A consumtarian rebel could never enflame his colleagues by claiming that the future belongs to the underclass; there is thus no notion that violent expressions of discontent would be progressive in any sense whatever. Instead, the consumtarian rebel is more likely to flaunt his regressivity and his hatred of both present and future. The consumtariat's revolutionaries will therefore have no ideological connection to either the old workers' and trade union organisations, or the peasant revolts of feudalism. They will take from these precursors at most only their rhetoric. Consumtarian rebels will instead take their ideological inspiration from the closed guilds of the Middle Ages and the puritan revivalist movement of the Enlightenment; a desire for isolation from their surroundings in expectation of the end of time and the collapse of the universe.

Early precursors to these consumtarian protest movements are already emerging in the transition between capitalism and informationalism, in the form of various headline-grabbing doomsday sects. These sects recruit their members from and are most attractive to the underclass of mass-medial society, which incorporates both the last remnants of the traditional working class and the expanding consumtariat. Doomsday sects are not a geographically localised phenomenon, and are appearing in disparate parts of the world – some that have attracted attention have been based in the USA, Switzerland, Japan, Russia and Uganda – which means that their appearance cannot be explained with reference to specific national cultures. They are, instead, a global phenomenon, an early example of consumtarian counter-culture. While the ambition of the netocracy is to conquer the world, these groups are turning their backs on hostile surroundings and are willing to cause damage before it is time to meet the group's own, self-chosen, physical destruction.

This distanced attitude towards their surroundings, this construction of a parallel reality is something which seems quite natural to the citizens of an increasingly medialised society, where the boundaries between the "reality" that was so carefully protected under capitalism and the fantasy promulgated by the media are increasingly difficult to discern, and progressively less interesting to maintain. The news is entertainment, directed and presented according to the aesthetic of entertainment; politics has, in the words of talk-show host Jay Leno, become "show business for ugly people", a sort of drama-drama about sensationalised social problems. Supply is usurping demand thanks to increased welfare and refined advertising; trademarks give a product an admittedly fictitious but no less powerful personality in an economy where entertainment is a central value; lifestyle is replacing life. This development is being strengthened by the fact that the netocracy is consciously turning its back on "reality" and taking refuge in its electronic tribes.

The arrival of informationalism and the breakthrough of the interactive media constitute yet another great step towards what Jean Baudrillard has called "hyper-reality". There is every reason for a lot of people within both the netocracy and the consumtariat to prefer fiction to reality, because the former allows far greater choice when it comes to the construction of a social identity. There is a gradually increasing Disneyfication of our entire environment; old ruined castles are renovated and turned into places for stressed city-dwellers to go on outings, unprofitable farms are becoming theme-parks with an agricultural theme (so-called "agritainment"); cruise ships, hotels and entire destinations are being planned for longer or shorter stays in carefully realised fantasies, and so on. People are, to a great extent, becoming actors in their own lives, playing the "role" of themselves more or less convincingly. Reality is becoming an ever more subordinate part of hyper-reality, just as nature is becoming an ever more subordinate part of culture. There is no longer any actual reality, just virtual arenas in which performances are staged. The virtual environment is therefore becoming entirely synonymous with "the environment".

By the end of the 1990s, the Internet had reached distant villages in India and Latin America where there was still no running water. The netocracy has grand colonial ambitions, which is why the consumtariat need not worry about not getting access to exciting new technology and all it offers – quite the reverse! The underclass's only real chance to express discontent with its subordinate position will be to refuse to take part in the role-play of informational society. The aesthetic of passive resistance will then become a self-selected act of exclusion, while the strategy of active resistance will be violent demonstrations, inspired by the Luddites of early industrialisation who smashed the machinery that was undermining the value of their manual skills and destroying the preconditions for their traditional way of life. The threat of violence is the only thing that will make the dominant class listen.

Consumtarian rebels will therefore establish reactionary cells for the production of countertrends in an effort to achieve both technological and social exclusion. They will be following the path of the revivalist movement rather than the workers' demonstrations of 1st May, trying to break out rather than reform from within. Their answer to technology and sedative entertainment will be violent resistance. The effects will be dramatic, but this is not to say that the drama will be effective, since the consumtarian rebels will be far too lacking in resources. A genuine informationalist class-war will only be possible when consumtarian rebels get support from outside their own ranks, which will only happen when the only partially apparent unity within the netocracy splits at the seams. As a result, powerful, anti-netocratic networks will spring up for the first time: an unholy alliance of the consumtariat's revolutionary desperados and netocratic class-traitors, and it will be between these alternative, power-hungry hierarchies and the genuine netocracy that the informationalist class-struggle will be acted out in the form of irregular, explosive and potentially violent confrontations.

One inescapable precondition for this struggle is, then, internal netocratic conflict which is fundamentally ideological in form. This conflict is inherent right from the start, and concerns the infernally thorny question of immaterial rights. Just as the aristocracy once accepted its historical fate and co-operated with the bourgeoisie that was taking its power, so the bourgeoisie is now smoothing the way for the netocracy by helping to legalise the ownership of ideas. In order to understand the background to this virtual issue of ownership, it is necessary first to be familiar with four key concepts in this context: copyright, patents, encryption and firewalls. These four functions form the basis for what is called "the new economy", and therefore also the basis of the netocracy's appearance and assumption of power.

Copyright means the exclusive right to exploit, or control the exploitation of every form of immaterial right. A patent is the exclusive right, or control over the right, to exploit a certain invention over a certain limited period. Copyright and patents were fundamental functions even within the late-capitalist economy. With the breakthrough of informationalism, these rights apply, to an increasing extent, to digitally produced, stored and distributed information. The first digital products to be protected with the help of copyright and patents were software for computers and music stored on CDs, but with the growth of the informational economy, the value of digital information has grown phenomenally. This development means that the sale of ideas and design constitute a steadily growing proportion of the value of the economy as a whole.

This in turn means that the question of the copyright and patenting of digital products is becoming ever more central in informational society. It is a survival issue of the highest priority: the growth of an informational economy will be hampered and delayed if there is a lack of laws and rules in this area that are in tune with the times, and a judicial apparatus which is capable of implementing them. Enormous resources all over the world are therefore being expended on strengthening the legal protection of the right to exploit ideas. Legislation and police activities in different countries are being co-ordinated and standardised. One leads to the other: the fact that the informational proportion of the economy as a whole is constantly growing leads to an acceleration of these processes within business law, which in turn leads to increased informational growth. The growing netocracy and its allies, such as venture capitalists and specific political interest groups, have good reason to unite to protect their immaterial rights: their own survival is directly connected to the success of the project.

In countries like Russia, China, India and Argentina, there was no initial inclination to respect copyright and/or patents, because these judicial constructions only seemed to favour the already highly developed economies of western Europe, North America and Japan. Instead, these countries developed a strategy of imitating ideas and digital products which had originally been developed elsewhere. Without compensating the owners of the copyrights and patents, they mass-produced and sold cheap pirate copies of computer programmes, music and drugs, for example.

But a combination of heavy pressure from European, American and Japanese interests on the one hand, and the development of the countries in question in the direction of an informational economy on the other, has led to a radical U-turn on the issue. Globalisation has thus led to the political establishment all over the world uniting around the matter of protecting immaterial rights. The price exacted from anyone who chooses to remain outside this consensus is far too high, namely exclusion from the informational economy. For this reason, local authorities in China, Russia, and other places are cracking down on pirate-copying with considerably greater energy than before, at the same time as they are developing their own systems of copyright and patenting. Netocratic entrepreneurs and their capitalist investors can start to breathe easily again.

But within business and politics there is still not a complete understanding of what the Internet and technological development will mean. Culture on the net has its own dynamics, its own driving-forces, which are often at odds with late-capitalism's interest in the ownership of ideas. This means that the whole global system for copyright and patent agreements is starting to be eroded from beneath. On the Internet people all over the world can set out digital information on their homepages; this might be text, images, music, film, programmes, and so on. They can exchange this information between themselves as they choose, without any intermediaries or regulation, and without having to take into account any legal limitations or someone else's claims to copyright or patent. The people eagerly encouraging and carrying out this activity are netocratic class-traitors. The traffic in pirated information increased phenomenally during the 1990s. Neither national nor supra-national police organisations have any real chance of controlling or, still less, prosecuting this sort of activity, because it takes place in virtual space and therefore lacks any geographical basis.

The defenders of immaterial rights are also fighting in an increasing ideological headwind. A prohibition against copying physically tangible products – tables, cars, boats – is easy for almost everyone to accept. Someone who has constructed and manufactured a product also owns the right to control both product and construction, this is hardly controversial. But in contrast, it is not at all obvious to the new net-citizens that a comparatively small group of software-producers should earn large sums of money by selling expensive digital information which is incredibly easy and cheap to copy and distribute.

The special conditions that pertain within the informational economy mean that the production costs, storage and distribution of digital products are practically negligible, a fact which would benefit the whole of the net community if the right of ownership of information was dismantled. An unavoidable analogy is how the workers in the factories of early capitalism accepted the feudal right to ownership of land as being natural, but gradually began to question the fact that capitalism's means of production, the factories and their inventories, should belong to the bourgeoisie. We are all too aware of what violent and bloody conflicts this struggle for the means of production led to. There is no reason whatever to believe that the informational class-struggle will be any calmer or more peaceful.

The problem for anyone protecting restrictive copyright-legislation is that the increasingly dominant mobilistic ways of thinking are negative to the very idea that a certain combination of ones and zeros could belong to any particular person or organisation, which means that this ownership will in time come to seem more and more "unnatural". All this legislation and all attempts to implement it will be regarded as the protection of illegitimate special interests, which will in turn lead to the fragile alliance between netocratic entrepreneurs and capitalist investors coming under severe pressure. Those protecting the right to immaterial ownership will be forced to fall back on a collapsing political structure: the nation state, which will have no economic or even practical capacity to call out the police whenever immaterial rights of ownership are transgressed.

How could any police force or group of politicians set about closing web-sites that operate from some isolated island off Africa or in the Pacific, or even from a nation without control of its virtual domains (the Soviet Union's domain name .su was, for instance, quickly snapped up by opportunistic hackers after the collapse of the Soviet Union)? Besides, there is every reason to question what moral right the informational economy, which is increasingly avoiding national taxation, might have to demand any protection from the state. As a result of this development, netocratic entrepreneurs will be forced to construct new systems to protect their desirable information. They will encrypt the ones and zeros before distribution; they will build increasingly sophisticated firewalls, virtual walls, around their activities to protect against eventual break-ins. The netocrats will educate their own guards and create their own networks carrying constantly updated information about electronic pirates and traffickers in stolen goods. In this way they will make themselves independent of the state and will accelerate, ironically enough, their own acquisition of power.

The conflicts of the informationalist era will therefore not take place between nation states fighting over tracts of land of questionable value. Instead we can see how ideological and economic conflict between different netocratic groups, in more or less loose alliances with consumtarian rebel movements, is developing. The dividing-line runs between the netocracy which is protecting what it regards as its rightful ownership of the information that forms the basis of the group's power and status, and netocratic class-traitors who regard every form of hindrance to the spread of information as immoral, and instead see the maximal expansion of the organisational non-zero-sum game as the core-value of the new age. One clear example of this sort of internal netocratic conflict was the frenetic struggle to be the first to present a complete map of the human genome. The two sides consisted of an international consortium of academic research institutes, HGP, which claimed to be working for the general good and without profit-motivation, and a purely commercial company, Celera, whose business plan is to restrict and make money from specific patents in the genetic arena.

But because the central value of the informational economy does not lie in information itself, but in the sorting and combination of information, the most powerful netocrats need not concern themselves with ownership of copyrights and patents. Nor do they need to invest time and effort in the construction of encryption programmes or firewalls. The ability to network and get an overview of large amounts of information which is sought after by everyone cannot be copied or stolen; the owner is threatened by nothing but the possibility that someone else will prove themselves more talented. And this will form the basis for the growth of an alternative netocracy, an elite which will base its power and status upon entirely different factors than copyright and patents (and therefore ownership of the means of production).

This new group, the eternalists, will sympathise and collaborate with the industrious members of the same class, the nexialists, only when it is in the interests of the group itself. In other cases, when opposition splits the netocracy, it might well betray its own class and make common cause with the consumtariat, rather like academics with leftwing sympathies in late-capitalist society at least on occasion tried to make common cause with the working class against the class in power, to which they themselves de facto belonged. The academic left will have a successor in the eternalistic netocracy which regards certain of the ruling elite's actions as immoral and offensive. This is an attitude it can afford to adopt even when the situation in question does nothing to enhance its own interests.

All of this, together with the new view of the relationship between production and consumption, gives a clearer picture of how the class-conflicts of informational society will manifest themselves. The most fundamental form of consumtarian resistance will be to refuse to produce desire, by boycotting both adverts and technology, and by withdrawing from the informational economy as far as possible. The activist form of resistance will be to attack the key functions of the netocratic entrepreneurs, the nexialists: copyright and patents. Revolutionary resistance will find expression in both virtual and physical violence. Every form of protective wall around highly valued information will become a target.

What the struggle is ultimately about is no longer control of production, but control of consumption. One characteristic of the netocrat is that he controls his own desires and exerts strong influence on others', while the consumtariat's production of desire is directed from above. The consumtariat will become resistant to the power of the netocracy at the moment it no longer accepts this state of things. The cheerleaders of "the new economy" believe, or pretend to believe, in the emergence of a collective, joyous realm where social tensions will be dispelled by the winds of change and everything will be resolved to the good thanks to large amounts of information. This is far too naïve an attitude, probably often a simulated one. On the contrary, tensions will increase in the electronic class society which is developing under informationalism. History is not dead, it is being resurrected in the present in an entirely new guise. And in the same way as this resurrection of history demands new players, any credible observation of informational society demands new observers.

1.

THE ROAD TO THE WORLD STATE AND HISTORY AS A PROCESS OF DOMESTICATION

IN THE END, EVERYTHING depends on knowledge. The dynamism behind social development, the energy that enables us to crawl over decisive thresholds, arises from ideas and communication. How are we to play the cards we have been dealt? Of course the cards themselves are of crucial importance. Circumstances determine which aspects of knowledge are useful. A refined interplay is established: certain circumstances give rise to certain social structures, which in turn give rise to new circumstances, and so on. Out of what was originally a series of random events a pattern emerges which can be discerned from a distance. Developments point in a particular direction, making it possible to put together relatively credible hypotheses about the future.

One of the decisive thresholds in history was the fixed dwelling-place, and this revolutionary innovation was only made possible by a long sequence of random factors which happened to coincide. For a variety of reasons, there was a shortage of animals to hunt in many areas, which provided a strong impetus to crawl across the threshold and set about something entirely new: the production of food instead of hunting and gathering. But before this could happen, certain preconditions had to be satisfied: for instance, the soil had to be good enough to support crops, and the climate had to be favourable. But there also had to be a good supply of animal and plant species that were suitable for domestication. Besides this, a modicum of rudimentary knowledge about growing crops was essential, since the most fertile soil in the world is useless to people who do not know how to manage it. Consequently there had to be a transitional phase during which mankind could begin to produce food on a small scale, as a complement to the spoils of hunting and gathering. To start with, all of these circumstances coincided in one single place on earth, the region around the Euphrates and Tigris rivers known as the Fertile Crescent, approximately 11,000 years ago.

One thing led to another. Population growth took off, partly because of increased access to food, and partly because women could have children at closer intervals because they were no longer restricted by how much they could carry in their arms during their eternal migration. Increased welfare resulted in larger settlements, with a higher population density, which in turn created favourable preconditions for further economic and technological development, which in turn led to increased welfare. The population grew rapidly, and its internal solidarity of interests became stronger and stronger, and the network of mutual dependence became ever more finely meshed. Co-operation, trade, the exchange of services and favours became more and more important. Increasingly people began to play non-zero-sum games with each other, in other words: more and more opportunities for different forms of mutually beneficial social and economic interaction arose and were exploited. One person would exchange a surplus of grain for a load of ceramics, and both parties would be happy with the deal, thinking that they had profited by it.

A relative surplus of food, and better methods of storing food for future needs paved the way for a new type of economy and a completely new society, with a considerably more sophisticated division of labour than before, and a hierarchical social structure. Subordination and solidarity turned out to be an effective strategy in a society which was in more or less peaceful competition with other societies. The general good benefited by decision-making being concentrated in one or a few leaders, because this gave savings of efficiency and time. Mankind therefore allowed itself to be tamed in the service of maximised self-interest. 'The tamest tribes are the strongest', as the English nineteenth-century critic Walter Bagehot put it. The political élite which assumed power appropriated the right to levy taxes. Debts arose, and accumulated. The expanding and increasingly complex economy reached the critical point where a system of accounting was needed, and from this system written language arose in approximately 2000 BC. And with that we reach the next revolutionary innovation, which in turn necessitated a far more effective feedback loop, and the process of civilisation accelerated still further.

To begin with, written language was primarily a useful tool for the élite which was in power. With the help of the written word they could not only keep records of tax debts, but also disseminate propaganda and issue orders from a distance, with a reasonable expectation that these orders would be carried out to the letter. At the same time the amount of knowledge available to the reading and writing élite multiplied many times over, which only served to increase levels of social and intellectual complexity. The law showed itself to be much more than an instrument of repression; it also became a lubricant reducing levels of friction within society. Because contracts had to be obeyed, and the citizens were made aware that cheats ran the risk of being prosecuted under the law, so faith in social order increased, a faith which would prove an immensely valuable social capital. The tamed population began to tame everything in sight with the help of its dramatically increased knowledge. The intensity of intellectual exchange increased, and different cultures began to influence one another. New, hitherto unimagined possibilities to play non-zero-sum games opened up. Written language was imbued, not surprisingly, with a magical shimmer. The word was made holy.

With the arrival of written language, history and politics began to take serious shape. With the help of written language, people began to put down mythical roots in the soil and in their regions – rather than in the tribe and in nomadic existence, as had been the case under the preceding primitivism – and these were reflected in the power relationships that developed. Power was no longer a question of strength, speed and the other physical capabilities that marked out a successful hunter or gatherer, but was increasingly a matter of control of the land which was becoming the basic value within society. As society grew in size and became ever more close-knit, and as mankind allowed itself to be tamed, then the desire to protect personal property became more abstract and passed into a participation in a collective desire to protect territory instead. The transition from chieftancy to state became possible. A paradigm shift took place from the perspective of history as the history of information technology, and feudalism began to take shape. The idea of the state grew steadily stronger and the first empires were established in the river valleys of Asia and North Africa. History underwent an experimental phase in which different structures and ideologies were tried out. The increased mass of expanding state civilisations exerted ever greater gravitational pull on the surrounding remnants of hunter-gatherer society. A social order which rested heavily upon the written word was established and proved to be superior to its primitive predecessors.

A fundamental ideological assumption in this context is the idea that the process of domestication as such – the taming of raw materials, plants, animals, and, in extension, mankind itself – is the ultimate precondition for the unique status of mankind in the world. We have managed to raise ourselves above nature by subordinating it, and, in extension, also ourselves. The reading and writing human being is basically, for good or ill, 'unnatural'. Socrates, who had no intention of leaving any writings behind him, expresses through Plato the thought that writing is quite unnatural, that it replaces true wisdom with superficial wisdom because it encourages people to locate their memory outside of themselves, and therefore to neglect the function of their own memories.

But this is precisely the point. Socrates' ideas, ironically enough, have reached us precisely thanks to writing. With the help of intelligent technology, mankind has throughout the course of history managed to position itself in an increasingly intelligent environment, and has therefore dramatically increased the amount of knowledge available. Of course writing is in one way 'unnatural', but one could equally claim that the continual acquisition of the unnatural is part of mankind's particular nature, and that this, more than anything else, is what makes us human. Our history is ultimately the paradoxical story of how we have gradually become less natural, and, as a result, more cultural, by following our innate nature; how we have allowed ourselves to be tamed at the same time as taming everything around us. Philosophies, ideologies and religions both reflect and shape this process. Within eternalistic philosophy this all-encompassing metaphilosophical movement through history is known as civilisationism. No human activity, not even Socrates criticism of mankind's increasing unnaturalness, is outside of this process.

The paradigm shift from primitivism to feudalism made mankind the first ethical creature in history. We began to look further into the future, temporal perspective took on a whole new significance, and we had cause to reflect upon our actions and their consequences. When food production replaced hunting and gathering as the main occupation, it was essential to wait patiently for the postponed pay-off from the labour expended; the farmer had to wait months, even years, to harvest the fruits of his labours, a harvest whose size would hopefully compensate for the wait. In the same way, investment in learning to read and write only pays off after a long period of study, but this pay-off is, in return, greater in terms of acquisition of knowledge and associated social status. This long-term thinking is thus a winning strategy, both for the individual and for society. Patience becomes one of the foremost virtues. Utopianism becomes subordinate to pragmatism and finds expression in feudalism's shimmering dream of a paradisical existence as the just reward for the patient homo domesticus in another life.

The principal function of revolutions in information technology – each of which means that we crawl across yet another of civilisation's thresholds; from spoken language to written language, to print, to interactive media – is to drive the process of domestication one step further. We become caught up in ever more finely-meshed and comprehensive communities; we internalise more and more of the codes of behaviour which were previously imprinted in laws and books of etiquette; we distance ourselves, in other words, more and more from nature and the animals that we once were. Increasing complexity of social structures goes hand in hand with a higher level of abstract thought. The pious hope has always been that this narrative contains an in-built rationality: that the complete person, finally realised in the future, will have succeeded in freeing himself entirely from such atavistic bad habits as jealousy, competition, violence and so on. In the desire to attain this increasingly secularised utopia, this final accomplishment of society, the socially constructive properties of written (and later printed) language were put to good use.

Laws became part of history. With the help of the written word those in power could distribute decrees and encourage the standardisation of social morals. The problem was that worldly laws, as opposed to those that were believed to have been given by God, were not written in stone. As society grew and empires acquired colonies, it became absolutely necessary for the sake of credibility to make sure that the law was universally applicable. As a consequence, primitivism's old tribal myths were abandoned in favour of theological discourse: laws may be written on degradable material, but the Word itself, as an idea, came directly from God. And because there could only be one law, universally applicable, there could only be one god. Universalistic monotheism out-performed tribalistic polytheism not because of any intellectual superiority, but because it was a necessary condition for the marriage of empire and written language; it provided the increasingly powerful state and its growing armies with the indispensable universal legitimacy for wars of conquest. Whereas a tribal chieftain sought credibility by dint of being the descendant of the founding father, the monarch, leader of permanent settlements and military commander of armies in wars against competing societies, pronounced himself the representative of the only true god on earth.

The Iranian religious founder, Zarathustra, is in many ways pre-eminent among the early ideologists of the feudalistic paradigm. He realised the decisive role that permanent settlements would play in the historical process when he lay the foundations for Zoroastrianism, the first recorded monotheism in the world. In his philosophy Zarathustra focuses on the continual struggle which, after the invention of written language, has been raging between on the one hand mankind's desire to allow itself to be tamed – man as civilised being, fundamentally different from and of higher standing than animals – what he calls asha, and, on the other hand, the desire for liberation from this impulse – mankind as untamed lone wolf – which he calls druj. Because Zarathustra's ethical reasoning ends up favouring asha over druj, Zoroastrianism is therefore the first thought-out political philosophy which promotes the benefits of civilisation. Later philosophical and theological discourses have struggled endlessly with the same question, and oscillated between the two poles of asha and druj to varying degrees, according to the fashion of the age. All later philosophies which point in the same civilisationist direction, from the Egyptian monotheism of the pharaoh Akhenaton onwards, should therefore be seen as variations of Zoroastrianism, the original ideology of domestication.

The conflict between the desire to be tamed and the desire for freedom from this impulse is turned on its head with the transition from capitalism to informationalism. Once Friedrich Nietzsche had launched the concept of the eternal recurrence of the same, this destructive conflict in the collective consciousness seems to have become the fundamental precondition for human existence. Compliance and submission to the collective is transformed into the individual's desire for self-realisation in contrast to the collective, which is transformed into obedience and submission to the individual, which is transformed into the collective's desire for identity, which brings us back to the start. Mankind's ambitions and desires are enclosed within an eternal circle: the eternal recurrence of the same. The process of civilisation can be reduced philosophically to the dialectic tension between eternalism (in lay terms: structure and culture) and mobilism (chaos and nature). Out of this relationship, so paradoxical on all its levels, a steadily more complex social structure emerges.

The word empire has its roots in military Latin. The emperor is the man who has the right to express imperatives or commands; the emperor and the successful general are one and the same person. The empire is the conquered territory over which the emperor exerts his authority and in which he is obeyed. But the concept of empire also comprises the idea of a single state encompassing the whole world. Consequently the Roman Empire was thought to encompass the whole world, or rather, the only part of it that was thought to matter. Beyond the borders of the empire a few groups of uncivilised barbarians lived a meaningless existence in the depths of ignorance; they could just be left to get on with it. Eventually, of course, the Romans paid a high price for their pride. Similar ambitions and thoughts have existed within every people with an imperial view of themselves, such as the Persians, and within imperial China – in the same way as the Romans demonised the Germanic tribes, the Persians demonised the Turks and Arabs, and the Chinese demonised the Mongols – and all of them, sooner or later, suffered the same fate as the Romans. External circumstances changed, internal structures grew weaker, the empires imploded.

It is clear that the worldview of these feudal empires contained a problematic gap between ideology and reality: they must therefore be regarded as unrealised or false empires. The imperial identity rested upon the large-scale production of barbaric demonology, which demanded the aggressive denial of neighbouring people's humanity. In false empires the Other is still excluded and is denied human status on racial grounds. The Other has a value only as part of the demonology in question. Because of the threat and the terrifying example he provides, he is a cohesive factor. The boundaries of the empire are the boundaries of civilisation, and civilisation cannot expand unless the empire destroys barbarity with military means, after which any survivors among the enemy could be converted to the empire's monotheistic world-view through missionary work. But before this project is realised, the barbarians remain by definition inhuman. Captured barbarians are at best good enough to act as slaves within the empire. Consequently the 'discovery' of the New World can hardly be seen as a meeting of two civilisations, but as the starting-shot for a most brutal form of annexation.

The political philosophy of eternalism concentrates, for the first time in history, on preparing the way for an authentic empire as an alternative to false empires. In the authentic empire no-one can use force against the Other to create his own social identity, because the Other is already included in the empire before it even existed. Nationalism, racism and class struggle are all rejected, and society's production of identity comes instead from subcultural demonologies, which are created with the help of sophisticated sociometric instruments which act in the collective subconscious. This means that eternalism is strongly opposed to the demands of both liberalism and Marxism for a Hegelian dialectic as the basis for the production of all social identity. Thanks to the ideas of mobilistic philosophers such as Baruch Spinoza, Friedrich Nietzsche and Gilles Deleuze, Hegelian dialectics undergo a dramatic modification within eternalistic thought: the authentic empire is an open, not closed, social construction, whose only boundary is the entire collective existence of all humanity. For the first time in history there is nothing outside the entirety of society, and therefore no possibility to nurture any form of demonised Otherness, other than the almost playful demonologies constructed between subcultures within the boundaries of the empire.

Consequently it is almost unnecessary to point out that the global empire has never yet existed; it becomes historically imaginable and possible only with the advent of informationalism. But numerous indications point clearly in this direction: in one arena after the other, power is gradually being lifted from the national level to the supranational. The national dimension is becoming irrelevant in an increasing number of spheres. When China enters the WTO and Russia concludes co-operation pacts with NATO, there are no longer any alternative power-centres which can seriously compete with the emerging global conglomerate, either politically, economically or militarily. Because the main source of collective identity under capitalism – the nation state – is gradually being broken up and losing its significance, the idea of the authentic empire has arisen and is quickly developing to become the dominant vision of informationalism. As a result, the domestication process is entering an entirely new phase. New opportunities for non-zero-sum games are opening up.

The question is not so much whether a global political organisation will emerge, but when it will happen, and what shape it will assume. Many players are admittedly sceptical towards anything connected to globalisation, and suggest that it is a fiction, that the nation state is and will remain the metaphysical basis for politics; but they forget that even the system of nation states was once largely fictional, and that it could only be established at the price of blood-letting on an industrial scale. Well into the twentieth century, war was still the dominant organisational principle and source of the nation state's production of identity. What is controversial today will be banal tomorrow; within the informationalist paradigm globalism will become as given a basis for politics as étatism was under capitalism. Isolationism and anti-globalism have already been transformed into pointless attitudes; the debate will instead hinge upon which of the various competing globalisation alternatives is most desirable. Consequently the globalisation process is not a matter of the end of history in the sense that Francis Fukuyama meant, but about new conflicts taking place within a new arena.

The question which interests us most of all is the role of eternalism in this new globalism. What is possible, what should we hope for, and why? It is important to remember in this context that the eternalist idea of a global state cannot be seen as a classic utopia in any ideological sense, but should be seen as an unavoidable stage in a historical process whose progress towards ever greater and more structured complexity is clearly discernible. The global state is not the desired solution to any particular social problem; it ought instead to be regarded as the next stop of the domestication process, and is therefore the system within which a long series of new social problems will arise and even be solved. This means that the global system has no transcendental status within eternalism as it has in Hegelian and Marxist thinking. Instead, eternalistic thinking is about repeatedly applying the necessary radical pragmatism:

constantly questioning the many changing and shifting aspects of the world state.

Determinism in this context merely applies to the truly broad perspective, concerning the material/technological framework. The world state ultimately only reflects developments within, and is the necessary result of increasingly sophisticated information and communication technologies and the growth of mass-interactivity. Global communications are not only becoming more rapid, but also more intensive and therefore more constitutive. The medium is, more than ever before, also the message. Developments within the information-technological complex also mean that mankind's ecological circumstances are changing. Our genes do not have time to adapt – a process that takes an agonisingly long time – but our memes, on the other hand, do. New memes will be favoured by the new circumstances which arise in the ecological system. Consequently our social structures will have to change, and relatively quickly as well; this is unavoidable, and wishing for anything else is as pointless as it is misdirected. Human activity will in turn alter the ecosystem. The process is immensely complex, different alternatives bring with them advantages as well as disadvantages: it is necessary to continually evaluate and adopt a position to different trends and counter-trends, forces and counter-forces, one at a time. The only value that remains constant and universal in this society will be the significance of value-production itself. Eternalism's focus on the world state is therefore ultimately about something as pragmatic as the maximisation of value-production within a global political organisation.

Under the capitalist paradigm the nation state was the basic political institution and étatism the cohesive supreme ideology. This structure developed out of the revolution in information technology embodied by the printing press and the concrete products connected with it: the printed book, the newspaper, the banknote. Only when printed texts were accessible in mass editions were there the preconditions for the growth of literacy skills, which in turn created an audience for pure information, one which helped manufacture political opinion. When this gigantic snowball finally started to move, it swept aside the old feudal society. The increase in knowledge, improved communications, technical advances, increased welfare, the rise of salon-culture: all of these combined and strengthened one another in the productive feedback loop that was the capitalist ecosystem, and whose sovereign lubricant was the ever more refined monetary economy.

The underlying dynamic in this system was imperialist and colonialist. The rapidly expanding manufacturing industries needed both a constant supply of cheap raw materials as well as new markets to exploit. Predetermined economic laws forced capitalism into constant and increasing expansion. When this expansion had finally covered the whole world, there was nothing left for capitalism to consume other than capitalism itself. This critical, self-consuming state, hypercapitalism, came about at the end of the twentieth century once all possibilities for continued external expansion had been exhausted. There were no new markets left to discover, and the old ones were showing worrying signs of saturation. Appetites were of necessity forced inwards. What had once been individual markets had become integrated through this process into a single, global market; a process which had been supported and accelerated by the development and spread of interactive information technologies. These were in turn popularised and spread by the market, in a cultural development parallel to economic globalisation. What we see today is how the capitalist feedback loop is ebbing away and being replaced by an informationalist alternative, which is in turn generating a new ecosystem with a new set of rules.

This crisis is built into the internal logic of capitalism, which seems to pull the rug out from under itself. Businesses are continually pressed to improve their products and cut their costs in order to retain customers and attract new ones. Their margins shrink as competition gets tougher. This development is accelerated dramatically by interactive information technologies, which give consumers powerful new tools. It is suddenly possible to compare goods and services from a global array of suppliers. The boundaries between nation states are becoming irrelevant in this context; the international geography of capitalism is being replaced by informationalism's attentional topography.

Intensively networking and relentlessly disloyal consumers are forcing profit-driven businesses down on their knees. The customer is constantly ready to change supplier, businesses must be permanently ready to offer some unique form of added value – which their competitors copy at once – or must cut their margins still further. All the talk about 'meaner and leaner' becomes, to the horror of the share-holders, grim reality. It is the growth of this network-economy, rather than the rise and fall of any internet-adapted mail-order company, which is the genuinely new aspect in all this talk of a 'new economy' for the information age. In the long term this development will mean that traditional expansionist businesses will fall away and be replaced by businesses as events, the only credible model for business in an attentionalist economy.

The opponents of global thinking have often chosen to see the process in purely economic terms, and have been horrified at how transnational companies have been allowed to practice ruthless exploitation without any restraining legislation. This sort of reasoning, however, is based upon a serious misunderstanding; economic globalisation presupposes and is actually dependent upon an equivalent, albeit delayed, process of political and judicial globalisation. A lawless situation is to no-one's advantage, at least not long-term. The smallest production companies in poor developing countries and the largest supranational conglomerates of the western world share the same interest in being tied into a comprehensible structure, economic as well as political and judicial. Consequently it is not the state as administrator of power and jurisdiction which will become obsolete under informationalism, but the nation as the basis for the state. The state as an institution is being transferred from the national to the global level.

The American constitution is in this respect a good example because it is based upon a desire to create a community and a collective identity upon a willingness to submit to certain ideals, rather than the closed idea that the nation must be founded upon the common ethnic background of its inhabitants. In this instance identity is not something one is born with, but something one creates together with one's surroundings, a process which agrees with the strategies and interests of the netocracy. The word 'nation' certainly crops up frequently in official American rhetoric, but its meaning is entirely different to what it would be in Europe, for instance. This does not mean that American opinion will find it any easier to take to the global empire as an idea, or to accept the global state as supreme in a concrete politico-judicial sense. There are many more factors at play in the struggle between the new global-state level and the old organisation of nation-states than just attitudes to the production of identity. But as far as the central role of ethics is concerned – and the subordinate role of ethnicity – then the American constitution can be seen as practically identical to the multicultural model the global state must be built upon.

Naturally the establishment of a global politico-judicial order should be regarded as an élite programme. The netocracy, the upper-class of the global empire, will divide the key positions between their respective subordinate groupings: the curators who sort information, the entrepreneurial nexialists, and the ideology-producing eternalists. At the same time, paradoxically, the globalisation project is the only chance for the consumtariat, the global underclass, to achieve a functional distribution of resources. Dealing with the politics of distribution on a national level in informationalist society where economic resources move like lightning across old national boundaries is of little use. The complexity of the global economy, and the absence of self-evident areas of community, mean that the regulatory function of the state is more important now than ever before in history. And since the price of anarchy is so high for all interested parties, all available resources will be used to come up with a set of rules which are acceptable to as many people as possible, where attentionality, the credible maintenance of the rules, will be more central than ever.

One central aspect of this development is the growing need for a means of identity production which is adapted to informationalism: how new transnational and subcultural forces arise and how they relate to the growing global state. The issues which stand out as the most significant will produce a deficit of identity which will be filled by new ideological movements, partly as suggestions at solutions to these issues, and partly because they provide an attractive, subcultural identity both for the activists in the innermost network and to their more loosely-connected sympathisers. This process is taking place with the close collaboration of the media, and the result is an explosion of event-oriented, global movements based upon identity-producing, network-dynamic complexes. These are usually temporary – look at how quickly the glow faded and activity died within Attac – but often noisy and attention-generating movements are conquering more and more of the public arena from political parties. They have something which is not wholly irrelevant in this context – they are simply more entertaining.

The merciless competition for media attention is fostering a hard, Darwinian knock-out system between the virtual subcultures. Only those best-suited, most clearly meaningful and most relevantly defined in relation to the political and media realities will survive. Politics as ideology is changing more and more into politics as lifestyle; credibility is not to be found in any more or less realistic utopia, but in a successfully arranged Event. Movements develop, explode and disappear; identities are swapped and upgraded. The norm is not that the movement outlives the activist, but precisely the reverse, that the activist will only engage as long as the movement is vital – in other words: as long as the movement can be seen as an event – and will then move on. This is eternalism's radical pragmatism at grass-roots level. Radicalism is no longer connected, as it was under capitalism, with imaginative utopias, but with attention and concrete results. The achieved level of attention corresponds to the amount of awareness multiplied by credibility; both of these amounts have to be high if the level of attention is going to be of significant size. With this definition we can present the fundamental sociometric instrument for working out how attention can best be maximised under certain political and economic circumstances (see illustration).

One clear example of how the expanding netocracy is spontaneously adopting the radical pragmatics of eternalism is how the first generation of netocratic philanthropists is demonstratively breaking the rules set down by capitalist philanthropy. Capitalist fortunes tended to be bequeathed to the sons and daughters of the bourgeoisie. Only a small portion was left for philanthropic causes, usually in return for some sort of tax rebate, and often in a way which was designed to highlight the donor's generosity: hospital wings named after the deceased, donations to cultural institutions in exchange for prominently displayed notices of the donor's name. But the inherited fortune was always central, first as a material basis for the heirs' social identity, and secondly as concrete confirmation of the central, transcendental idea of the paradigm, that of Progress.

The netocracy has a completely different view of financial resources to that of the bourgeoisie. Money has no great transcendental value in itself, but is merely a tool. The fortune has lost its capitalist position as central cultural fetish. The new élite's view of progress is different as well: the economy they are living in is characterised not by continually growing businesses and fortunes, but by quickly blossoming and subsiding business events, which means that individual ownership is characterised by risk being spread more evenly. Business in the attentionalist economy is definitively separate from the individual, whose heavy investment in the company in question is limited to a matter of time and talent. As a result there is no company left to inherit, just a colourful portfolio of shares covering a wide range of interests.

This distanced attitude adopted by the netocracy characterises a new way of looking at financial resources. The dividual is replacing the individual as the human ideal, even within the business world. Businesses are primarily seen as events, whereas the financial resources which have been liberated from wholly-owned companies are instead attached to purely symbolic values. Assets have been given an attentional surface, which under current circumstances is the determining factor in their value, far more so than their nominal value on the stock exchange. For this reason the netocracy is not tempted by the thought of the unconditional transfer of financial resources, either to its offspring or through any form of philanthropic activity. Each transaction is instead closely bound by specific conditions, where the donor's own future gain from the transaction is reckoned into the bargain; not out of avarice, but because the transaction's attentionality in the eye of the recipient must be maintained at all costs if the transaction is to have the desired constructive effect.

The recipient must first and foremost, and for the good of all parties, see the positive result as being to his or her own advantage rather than that of the donor. Ironically, this means that the donor, right from the outset, must demand his own gain from the project if the project is to succeed. And this at the same time as the netocracy's actual reward for its realistic attitude to the timeless, psychological rules of the economic game is the self-respect justified by history: the netocrat is in his capacity of active and engaged banker a considerably more effective philanthropist than the sentimental and irresponsible capitalist donor. He would sooner burn his fortune than give it away, because donated money is always harmful to the accomplishment of the non-zero-sum games that matter more than anything else. The aim is always to move your money around in a way that will be constructive for all parties. Otherwise it would be better not to have any money.

To the netocrat, inherited fortunes increasingly appear as a vulgar, lower-class concept, which gives rise to entirely different strategies for money and resources. At the same time philanthropy is changing from being a demonstrative expression of the dominant class's goodwill, to being a radical pragmatic activism with a clearly stated goal; a political project which often starts as an aid to self-support, but which quickly develops into a creative network which benefits all involved parties. It is thus no longer a matter of successful people being more or less generous, but of being more or less smart and constructive. The netocratic philanthropist is not proud of his morals, but his intelligence. The Nietzschean Superman is taking on the role of financial manager.

The netocratic ideal is to create functional events, network-based situations which during their existence are characterised by creative interaction. The participants play non-zero-sum games with one another, with the aim that all participants should be able to leave the event as winners. The desire to allow oneself to be tamed also plays a central role here: the network and circumstances present a series of irrefutable demands to which participants must subject themselves if they are to benefit from the situation. These inherent demands are the basis for what is known within eternalist philosophy as socioanalytical ethics. At the same time, the desire for freedom from being tamed is an unavoidable ingredient. A thoroughly rational use of the network's resources can never be entirely exhaustive. Far too many variable parameters are in play at the same time; within the vital and productive power-centre there is a constant creative insecurity. Discipline and subordination must be complemented with improvisational abilities and well-developed social instincts.

Security is therefore a word which is assuming, at least in part, new meanings. Genuine security lies in the project lacking internal security, stability exists in the process being in perpetual change. As a result, the netocrat, in contrast to the old capitalist, has no interest in annihilating his competitors: quite the reverse. Instead the netocrat welcomes increased competition in order to increase the creative insecurity in his own project, safe in the knowledge that these interesting games are all non-zero-sum in character, and that another person's gain does not imply his or her own loss. It is just as much the competitors as collaborators who make it possible for the netocrat fully to realise his talents, which in practise means that the competitor is a highly valued partner. It is in this sort of break with rationalism, in the recognition of the necessary transrationalism of genuine interactivity, that eternalism diverges from the quasi-radical utopianism of the capitalist era. This is the most interesting ideological dimension of eternalism's radical pragmatism.

During the transition from capitalism to informationalism a range of political problems is arising on a global level, with the result that every realistic attempt at action must also be on a global level. The most obvious example is a question which is crying out for supranational politics, and which also engages people and groups of activists all over the world: the hotly debated problem of environmental destruction. It is in the nature of the beast that a subject of this sort necessitates a global strategy, and even today it is already the subject of global action. It is a question of a rapidly progressing power-play between on the one hand multinational economic interests, which often underestimate the extent of the damage in question, and, on the other, an array of multinational environmental organisations, which in turn tend to exaggerate the threat. The respective under- and over-estimates of business and the activists ought, however, not only be seen as negotiating tactics or a means of media pressure, but must also, under informationalism, be seen as contributions to the production of social identity. The whole thing is further complicated by the fact that politicians on the global arena often try to make national politics of the issue. What is most important from our point of view however is that the subjects of debate – air, water, animal life – cannot be discussed in terms of the nation state. Nature respects no national boundaries, which makes them meaningless in this context. Only a global state can deal seriously with this issue of vital significance for mankind.

The main driving force behind the global management of political problems is not, however, demands for altered, supranational legislation, but rather demands for a boundary-transgressing method of supervision as a guarantee that legislation already in place is being upheld. This is certainly the case with environmental crimes, where difficulties arise when different jurisdictions collide, and because there is no single relevant and comprehensive jurisdiction – as is the case with international waters, a political phenomenon which would actually disappear if the world-state came into being – but also because local authorities often develop far too close ties with local business, with the result that external pressure is needed, from a global police-force, for instance, with no attachments to particular interests. Where tax is concerned, it is a matter of plugging the loopholes and co-ordinating resources in the first instance in order to implement existing legislation. And as far as so-called crimes against humanity are concerned, international courts are already quickly being established, with the task of enforcing legislation which would otherwise be purely decorative.

Even individual economic participants have every reason to press for global legislation and functional global enforcement. With the transition from an economy based on manufacturing industries to one based primarily on ideas, the majority of both interest and profit opportunities is displaced onto digital products and services. This development in turn leads to an economy increasingly based on patents and copyright. Establishing and protecting copyright will be of decisive importance to the global economy. All of this is in turn based upon a global system of regulation and the global co-ordination of police activity. The result of this globalistic development is that legislation and implementation in one area after the other have to be raised to a supranational level. As a result of the increasingly comprehensive network of military treaties, even the right to use violence has been raised to the same level. All this has very little to do with traditional political ideology; it is instead a matter of sheer pragmatism. Nothing but the exercise of power on a global level and global domestication offers even a theoretical solution to the most pressing problems.

It might look as though this system can, indeed, ought to be questioned, and that there are no compulsive reasons for poor countries to submit to these supranational sets of rules which primarily protect the advantages of businesses based and taxed in rich countries. The nation states which position themselves outside more or less global agreements regarding the rules of copyright law, or which sign up formally but will not or cannot ensure that these rules are enforced within their boundaries will also see certain short-term benefits. Domestic industry can rake in profits by copying inventions and products and ignoring their legal protection: the music industries of China and Russia, and the Indian and Brazilian pharmaceutical industries at the turn of the millennium are all good examples of this. But in the long run these economies are harming themselves, firstly because the drawbacks are greater than the benefits of not being able to participate fully in supranational non-zero-sum games, and secondly because pirate copying will eventually force prices down to such a low level that it will not be possible to use resources to develop current products further, which will lead to the stagnation of the market. The problem here is that the price levels of a pirated market never reflect the actual costs of producing the product in question; someone else is always responsible for considerable additional costs. So a lawless situation arises where there is no account taken of the long-term need to be competitive in an ideas-based economy. The collapse of the market in question will become permanent because the most innovative companies in the area will stay away. Instead, they will seek out regions where copyright is protected, regions which in the long run will gain an advantage in terms of both knowledge and economic success, which in turn will increasingly attract leading-edge competence within an ever more mobile and global netocracy. A positive feedback loop becomes established, while the neglected lawless economies are sucked into a destructive spiral. Slowly but surely the benefits of the domestication process are becoming clearer: the global protection of copyright is in the longer term a necessity. It is to everyone's advantage. And because this is not merely a matter of producing rules, but primarily of seeing that existing rules are enforced, the system of global jurisdiction and supranational means of control which has been gradually established will secure widespread support. Once the nation's position as the organising principle for wielding power has been abandoned, there will be no going back. The global state will be the only credible solution when it comes to filling the power vacuum.

This vacuum will initially be an acute problem in two areas in particular: long-term investment, and social measures such as healthcare and education. The growing mobility of capital and workforce, and increased competition between different states and regions for the most attractive companies will lead to regional political bartering with tax rebates and other benefits, which will mean that the income of the nation state will shrink and its room for manoeuvre will become increasingly limited. Large investment packages in infrastructure will become more difficult to put together. All the promises of the old welfare state will become, not least for purely demographic reasons, impossible to honour; one after the other, different activities will be farmed out to the private sector, and the subsequent stress on cost-effectiveness will reduce the level of service. High quality education and healthcare will increasingly become a class issue, a privilege for those with most money and the best contacts, with the result that there will be widespread and growing discontent.

The instinctive reaction to this discontent is a nostalgic harking back to the good old days of the strong nation state, which in the short term will benefit isolationist and locally patriotic politicians who oppose developments towards globalisation. But this nostalgia fails when its anti-globalist proponents fail to produce the promised results with their historically romanticised, unrealistic solutions. Old strategies work badly in changed circumstances. In the absence of realistic alternatives, there will be a growing opinion that a global economy demands global politics. Even issues of taxation will become global. Only with the establishment of a world state will there be sufficient political power to get to grips with the so-called tax havens around the world, which will be essential in the long-term if economic policies are to have a minimum of credibility.

The world state tolerates no alternative jurisdictions, no sanctioned sanctuaries for special interest groups, no pockets of resistance where anti-globalisation movements can establish themselves; it also demands the necessary military means to maintain a legitimate system. A consensus is not always possible or even desirable, severe conflicts will arise, and the use of force in the name of unity is not impossible. It is important to remember that the capitalist system of nation states, which alternately co-operated with and fought with each other, was to a great extent the result of the brutal use of force. National unity also had a strong element of force to it. Religious minorities, ethnic identities, local dialects and subcultures – all of these struggled against the ideology on offer, and were often mercilessly subdued. The creation of the world state risks being at least as bloody; a large number of often powerful groups fear for good reason that their power and status are going to be destroyed by developments. And they will probably offer serious resistance.

The reason that we will eventually accept a certain level of force for the sake of global order is that the alternative looks even worse. The alternative to the global state is not a peaceful system of international co-existence built on mutual tolerance and understanding, but a state of global confusion and lawlessness which will benefit no-one but those in power locally: often oppressive regimes which would otherwise be dethroned. But all the while these local élites would be undermined by a continually expanding level of digital interactivity. Just as no nation in the long term can deny an internally democratic decision-making process – not least because of the breakthrough of mass-interactivity – so no nation can stand outside the jurisdiction of the world state, for the same reasons. The isolation and gulagisation of entire countries is unsustainable in the long term. Punishment in the form of withheld prosperity is too painful, and the temptation to participate in the global community will eventually become too strong.

The increasing pressure on the system of nation states is strengthened further by three growing problems which are becoming increasingly prominent in the political arena both on the national and transnational level: migration, epidemic illnesses and network-related crime. All of these problems are related to increased mobility and the collapse of national boundaries. This development is in turn irreversible, firstly because the advantages of increased mobility are perceived, for good reason, to outweigh the disadvantages, and secondly because the spread of mass-interactivity makes it impossible to limit information in such a way that traditional boundaries can be maintained. These problems are so serious, however, that they cannot be effectively countered unless power is exerted on a global level.

Global urbanisation has gradually eroded traditional ties to large, cohesive families and old tribal traditions. Existence has been 'atomised': identity has been changed into each individual's own project, a matter of lifestyle choice rather than of cultural belonging. At the same time, global access to the mass media is growing dramatically and thereby limiting the cultural differences between what was previously the centre and the margins. Young people feel an increasing sense of community with people of the same age no matter which country they are from, and feel increasingly unconnected with their fellow countrymen of other ages. Network-based subcultures are growing in their extent and importance. The remaining differences between regions, for example in welfare and career opportunities, are thus more apparent, which, when combined with an increased need for workforce immigration and the low birth-rates of the old industrialised nations, is placing the more developed regions under powerful migratory pressure. Someone has to care for the well-off but isolated elderly. Even the most precious national and ethnic characteristics will gradually be eroded.

Migrationary pressure means that the rich regions are competing for the most attractive workforce from poorer regions. Recruitment will therefore become the subject of intense business, which will create a whole new set of problems. One of the most significant of these is the brain drain from poorer, less developed regions; educated, imaginative young people are migrating en masse to wealthier but aged regions. Demography and migration will bring about radically altered political circumstances, where the earlier gulf between North and South moves into each separate region. Demands are growing for a functional, supranational political structure which will protect the legitimate interests of migrants and handle other problems connected with the rapid rise in global mobility.

Large-scale movement across borders and the growing overcrowding of big cities is increasing the risk that new viruses and bacteria previously unknown to the human immune system will arise and spread across the world. Behind the tabloid headlines about 'killer bacteria' there is a grim reality. There is scarcely any other threat to man – including environmental catastrophes and nuclear accidents – that would cause as much damage as a new influenza virus unlike the viruses we have previously been exposed to, which we would therefore be unable to counteract. Even if research did manage to identify the virus quickly, it would take weeks, maybe months, to produce and distribute a vaccine, whereas the virus would only take a few days to cover the planet.

This phenomenon is in no way a new one: the evolutionary theorists and historians Jared Diamond and Manuel De Landa have shown how, in the early stages of capitalism, urbanisation favoured viruses and bacteria at the expense of human beings. People died like flies in overcrowded squalor; the eventual advantages of city life had a high price. In this respect history could quite easily repeat itself, and the consequences would – thanks to rapid communication and increased mobility – be many times worse than previous epidemics. Influenza may not be the disaster scenario most favoured by the media or by different ideologies, but when the day comes and people start dying in a new epidemic, it will not be long before there are desperate cries for global action, with no regard for national sovereignty. A global strategy for minimising the risk of spreading dangerous viruses and bacteria is therefore of immense value. It would be enough for the threat of such an epidemic to be perceived as real for support for a world state to grow considerably.

The most acute problem propelling development towards a supranational political system at the beginning of the twenty-first century is, however, the rapid expansion of global criminal networks. Whether it be the threat from religious fundamentalist terrorist sects based in the margins of the geopolitical map, or the more conventional criminality of trafficking in drugs, people or weapons, time and time again the need is becoming apparent for a supranational police and judicial system which can at least keep pace with these organisations, whose effectiveness is largely dependent upon their use of new, interactive technologies.

This global clampdown on crime will bring with it a fundamental cultural shift in so far as the need for prioritisation will lead to a re-evaluation of what really can and ought to be defined as a crime. What in the eyes of the wider world could be regarded as the moralising prejudices of any single culture should not reckon on receiving much of the available resources, especially not when these values are measured against a general threat of violence against the world state itself. It is therefore unlikely, for instance, that any particular drug would be combated when it is permitted and accepted in other parts of the world. Border controls will no longer be relevant, just like city tolls under capitalism. In accordance with the radical pragmatism of eternalism, all organised dealings in goods and services will eventually be decriminalised, and will be regulated and taxed in the usual way.

Under capitalism the concept of sovereignty was central to the presentation of the state. Each nation was sovereign, in other words: supreme and self-determining within its own borders, which every other nation was expected to respect, at least in peacetime. In this way it was hoped that no-one else would get involved in the nation's own internal affairs. This national sovereignty was in practice, and often also in theory, identical to the sovereignty of the ruler, and it therefore reflected the patriarchal system. Just as the patriarch was the ultimate decision-making instance within the family, so the head of state's wishes were law within that particular state. The welfare of the nation was a question of the ruler's welfare. But as a consequence of increasing democratisation and the growth in trade between nations, views of sovereignty gradually changed, from having been primarily legal to being mostly economic in character: national sovereignty became largely a matter of controlling the national economy.

Now that the whole idea of national economy if collapsing, now that companies and investors have the whole world to move in, and now that the mutual dependence among the members of any particular nation are weakening, so the concept of national sovereignty is becoming problematical, as has already been seen in the arena of global politics. It is no longer easy to see what comprises a legitimate nation whose sovereignty must be respected, when outsiders keep getting mixed up in conflicts which would traditionally be seen as internal, and who do so with a professed humanitarian and definitively global purpose.

As a result, the very concept of the nation has ceased to be interesting in terms of realpolitik. Power is engaged in a upwards movement, and is migrating from the national to the global level. The domestication process is entering a new and revolutionary stage. We have been dealt a new hand of cards, and the big question is whether we are capable of playing them in a remotely intelligent way. The table is laid for the global banquet, there are no longer any significant objections in principal. That is not to say that events are predetermined in detail, or that the transition will proceed smoothly. But it is difficult to see how any other platform for the exercising of power could work once informationalism has broken through entirely.

To a great extent the globalisation project is a question of opinion-forming, and of active engagement both within what is called civil society and among the different players in the world's various markets. It is a matter of highlighting the advantages of non-zero-sum games. The American writer Robert Wright stresses this when he presents three reasons for the establishment of the world state: firstly, executive power has historically always tended to expand to the geographic extent that is necessary to solve social problems of non-zero-sum character which neither the market nor moral codes can deal with successfully. Secondly, the problems of non-zero-sum character which arise with informationalism are generally supranational. And thirdly, technological development is the driving force behind this whole process. As a result, pressure towards a world state will gradually increase with time. That is where we are today.

Ironically, the world state may yet prove to be the salvation of the nation state. Just as the nation state was once in a position to return a measure of political authority to the regions which subordinated themselves to national sovereignty, so there are good reasons to allow the nation to retain at least a ceremonial function in the global system. This could create a typical non-zero-sum game in which all participants win. The alternative scenario is global disintegration, an inferno of regional conflicts, antagonistic city states with their own armies, et cetera. Consequently there is a clearly defined task for and an acute need of eternalism's radical pragmatism. The great enemy is not so much the divided opposition's forces, but a lack of fantasy and engagement on our part. Informationalism signifies a renaissance of political activism, not least because interactive media-technologies offer the perfect instrument for people who want to be active and influence the passage of history.

2.

EMPIRE, PLURARCHY AND THE VIRTUAL NOMADIC TRIBE

☐

ALL STATES, PARTICULARLY EMPIRES, require a cohesive idea about a collective subject, a common history with a common fate, a sort of cultural root-system out of which the exercising of power could be said to grow organically. This relationship between the idea of the state and the immanence of the state becomes more important the more comprehensive and complex the state in question actually is. Consequently the world state most definitely presupposes an idea of a global community, where the things that unite people are prioritised over those that separate them. Within eternalistic philosophy this concept is called the global empire, in full awareness that this must precede the world state as an established political fact. By studying and mapping out the global empire in the collective unconscious, it is possible to predict and even influence political developments. As a result, there will be a stable, universal platform for the political philosophy of eternalism, and thereby also for the political activism of informationalism.

Naturally, cultures that cross boundaries are nothing new. We can, for instance, see how the world's great religions spread during the end of the first and the beginning of the second millennium, and how this had political consequences for the construction of empires. There is, however, one important difference between all the pre-informationalist, transnational movements, and current developments towards a virtual nomadic tribal culture: the explosion of interactivity on all levels of society, which will lead to the demise of the nation-state structure based upon parliamentary democracy (for more in-depth discussion of these mechanisms, see Netocracy). The nation state will no longer survive as a credible institution within the power arena, so all old notions of interstate co-operation will lose their credibility, and supranational structures will look more and more like the only realistic alternative.

Virtual nomadic tribes are spreading across the world thanks to interactive media technologies. The really interesting thing is, however, not the various networks' recruitment and expansion – even if they themselves often think it is – but how they are collaborating in the creation of a genuinely global culture which is in radical opposition to the old nation state. This conflict is brought to a head every time the interests of the virtual nomadic tribes collide with the laws and moral codes of the nation state – for instance, the advance of sexual and chemical liberation – and is intensified still further when a necessary and unavoidable awareness of their own leading role in the paradigm shift begins to dawn on the networks. In order to achieve their goals, the virtual nomadic tribes first have to oust the enfeebled leaders of the capitalist order, and this requires their otherwise pluralistic culture to nurture and gradually unite around a common political strategy. This process, undermining capitalist power structures, has already been underway for several decades. The global empire, as a gravitational focus in the netocracy's production of identity, is assuming ever clearer contours.

Feudalism produced social identity from monotheism's single god, with the Congregation as the transcendental projection screen for the collective libido. Capitalism did the same, taking the Ego as its starting point, with the Nation as the projection screen for the dreams of the people. Informationalism also has its own built-in metaphysics, reflecting the tantalising implications of the dominant information technology. Within informationalist metaphysics, the metaphysical basis is supplied by the Net, the all-encompassing metanetwork which connects all other networks; this time the World itself is the projection screen for the collective libido. This means that there is no image as important to informationalist metaphysics as the picture of the Earth photographed from space.

It is easy to forget that we only gained our definitive visual idea of the Earth when the first satellite photographs of the planet reached us in the middle of the twentieth century, as Martin Heidegger has pointed out. It is from this image of the world, acquired so improbably recently, that people will proceed under informationalism – and because it is a matter of an image, this also includes the billions of illiterates in the Third World – as they bravely try to construct and maintain some form of social identity. Nature's representative, the visible planet, also symbolises culture's representative, the invisible net. Together the Earth and the Net make up informationalism's metaphysical idea of the World: a planet entwined in threads of communication, oscillating and resonating, but invisible even from space. But how does this world differ from all other imaginable worlds? And who am I in relation to this mystical world I am observing? Or, more appropriately: who does this world turn me into? And how does this make me different to all other imaginable beings?

This is the single most important manoeuvre in the construction of eternalism's political philosophy: when we apply the cosmic basis of the informationalist world view, the Net, to the projection screen, the Earth, an entirely new historical phenomenon arises: the Global Empire (see illustration on page XX). After the completion of this manoeuvre, we discover that the virtual nomadic tribes, living and competing with one another in the memetic Darwinian topography of interactive media technologies, are all generating their vital social gravitation in relation to the global empire. The Other, or in this instance the Others, in the virtual nomadic tribe's process of identity production, are made up of the global empire minus the members of that particular tribe. Social identity emerges from the loaded and continually shifting, testing and redefining tension towards the Others; a relationship with the world as its arena and the global empire as its metaphysical frame of reference. This development forms, in turn, the new values associated with informationalism. Civilisationist ethics take an important new step: instead of fighting and trying to annihilate the Others, as has previously been the case throughout history, or at the very least trying to isolate oneself from and become independent of them, informationalism is characterised by a desire for a mutually beneficial dynamic, a desire to play non-zero-sum games with the surrounding world.

Because the Net is invisible on satellite photographs, it is naturally, just as much as the other metaphysical absolutes in history, ultimately a form of fiction. So it is even possible to imagine that sooner or later some form of sceptical 'anetism' might arise, analogous to capitalism's atheism. But it is far too early to speculate what expression such a movement might take, and what it might lead to. Informationalism's interactive media technologies have to play out their hand first, and the paradigm's dominant thinking needs to become securely established, before it is possible to say anything meaningful about the new conditions which might form the basis for post-informationalism. Memetic Darwinism has taught us that rationality always has a boundary at the limits of the collected knowledge of the age. Transrationalism realises and acknowledges that we can never think outside the paradigm or its rules of survival. Post-informationalism is, quite simply, beyond the horizon.

Because it is so difficult to get an overview of informationalist topography, orientation and outlook are of great importance. As a result, there is a constant exchange of information between the virtual nomadic tribe and those around it on every structural level. This in turn means that social identity within netocratic organisations cannot, as before, develop from the demonological exclusion of the Others. Such a strategy would be both risky and unproductive; risky because the credibility of such demonisation would be constantly questioned thanks to the intensive level of interactivity, and unproductive because it would hinder attractive non-zero-sum games. The social identity of the virtual nomadic tribe must instead be built upon the responsibility the group feels towards the Others, and the opportunities they believe themselves to have of influencing circumstances in a mutually beneficial way.

Netocrats are in this way neither 'better' nor 'worse' than earlier players throughout history. In fact, because they have seen through the insubstantial fog masking classical morality and have instead fostered eternalism's civilisationist ethics, they have become amoral. This could be expressed as netocrats being intuitively 'smarter' than their predecessors, because they make creative use of the exponentially increasing access to knowledge in a society where information is moving in every direction, literally at the speed of light. This even applies to the higher echelons within the netocracy, which have to be permanently open, firstly to important new impulses and recruits, and secondly to the possibility of co-operating constructively with other organisations. Curiosity and generosity, not suspicion and greed, are the keywords as informationalism replaces capitalism. The central value in informationalist society is not the possession of important information, but access to it at the right moment, and knowing what to do with it. The value of information is no longer constant, but is determined – as a consequence of the long-term effects of transparency – in relation to a temporal axis.

The production of identity within the virtual nomadic tribe is connected to its position in relation to other networks, and the level in the hierarchy it is aiming to reach. Consequently the virtual nomadic tribe shares 'its' information freely with others after first having made use of it, or it uses it as a tool in non-zero-sum games with other networks. So the tribe cannot really be seen as a culture in itself, but must instead be seen as a subculture within a global framework. Every dividing line is provisional, permanently open to negotiation and re-evaluation; exclusion mechanisms can be brutal, but there is always the right of appeal.

Demonology is no longer characterised by the same deadly seriousness with which it was treated under capitalism. Instead, antagonisms are more playful, when the dividual, the netocratic equivalent of capitalism's individual, takes the form of homo ludens: the playful human being. The process which was initiated when the tensions between nation states during the late capitalist era were transferred from the battlefield to the sporting arena is being completed. The Cold War did not culminate in an exchange of nuclear warheads, but in the two superpowers' boycotts of each other's Olympic Games, Moscow in 1980 and Los Angeles in 1984.

At this point it is important not to succumb to pacifistic naïvety. Violence is obviously still with us – informationalism will not transform us into angels, as evidenced by obsessive consumtariat behaviour in gaming arcades – but recurs in a sublimated form, internalised within the networking dividual. Without this internalised violence and the threat of violence, the gravity of the virtual nomadic tribe would be too weak to hold the single dividual within the group. Memetic Darwinian competition between networks is murderous, whilst both the start-up and maintenance costs of networks are low, which makes the entrance requirements to the network market negligible. In order to raise the stakes and facilitate the production of social identity, there has to be a constant impending threat of violence.

One of the basic functions of the capitalist power-structure is fulfilled by parliament, which is in turn supported by the much-lauded idea of democracy. In étatistic ideologies, democracy is the process with which ideological variety is protected and the political will of the people transformed into decisions on every conceivable subject. In the final stage of capitalism a sharp dividing line was drawn between, on the one hand, legitimate politics and the differences of opinion that could be tolerated within the given framework of democracy, and, on the other, grubby populism. Legitimate politicians presented their legitimate opinions in the media, particularly strongly when elections were looming, whereupon the populace, generally passive in all significant matters, was expected to vote for one of the legitimate parties. As a result the legitimacy of both the politics in question and the political process was strengthened, at the same time as permitting the citizens to participate to a degree deemed acceptable by those in power. Opinions which were not represented by the parliamentary parties were axiomatically undemocratic, and therefore had nothing to do with the process.

Despite this, colourful representatives for these supposedly undemocratic opinions could count on making a great impact in the media, because they offered a bit of welcome drama. These players were characterised as populists, and were said to fawn on the electorate, appealing to their baser instincts, such as fear and envy, in contrast to the genuinely democratic politicians who were assumed to exercise leadership through training and education in all the noblest virtues. In this way populism played its role perfectly as the diabolical demon in the demonology of étatism, and this in an age when democracy had already begun to implode under the pressure of the medialisation that was transforming the process into a cynical play to the gallery, a gallery which happened to be quite empty. By focussing so heavily upon populism, a real pseudo-issue, the exponents of the étatistic establishment for a long time managed to avert attention from the real problem. The more stress was placed on the threat from populism, the more holy and elevated beyond all critical discussion transcendentalised democracy seemed to be, while voters intuitively turned their backs on the whole process and switched over to something else instead.

So populism was never the threat to democracy that it was made out to be, but was more a means of artificial respiration in that it made democracy seem attractive and urgent. Because unity was more important than anything else in the struggle against a demonologically constructed enemy, conspicuous problems could be swept under the carpet. In actual fact the difference between the forces of democracy and what was denounced as populism was, from a political point of view, never more than rhetorical. Both parties benefited, in accordance with the laws of demonology, from blowing up this absurd pseudo-conflict between them to grotesque proportions: they made each other seem important. The result was that the étatistic supraideology emerged strengthened from the media frenzy.

In practice, late-capitalist politics was actually about two different forms of populism, two different types of fawning on the large electoral groups in the political centre. Constant opinion polls merely served as a means of producing opinion: the polls became normative thanks to adaptable politicians' constant adaptation of their message to match the measured opinion, upon which another opinion poll was taken and the whole process was repeated. No-one either could or would play the part of genuine political strategist and ideologue; politicians were gradually reduced to playing the part of an increasingly helpless nodding doll, trapped in the firm grip of the opinion polls, headline-writers and heavily funded lobby groups. Populism emerged victorious under a false flag. Democracy imploded and was replaced by purely executive representation for powerful special interest groups.

Classical democracy was never intended to be applied to populations that were too large for every inhabitant to have a real possibility of participating in the process. Nor did the immense one-way communication media-machine of the capitalist era figure in the original design. Through the advent of first the nation state, then the mass media, democracy was transformed into something quite different from what the political philosophers of early capitalism had intended. The element of active government by the citizens was gradually diluted to the point where it disappeared entirely. The politicians ceased to be the representatives of the voters and were instead transformed into their own class. Their rhetoric was full of fine promises, but unlike priests – whose promises generally lasted a lifetime, thanks to the ingenious construction of the religious utopia – they were subjected time and time again to humiliating debates about their failure to deliver.

Politics never quite managed to replace religion as the kernel of the collective subject's metaphysics; the voters' dissatisfaction was well-motivated. The acute crisis arose when late-capitalist politicians used the mass media to plead for the engagement of the people in order to secure their own legitimacy, all in order to conceal the fact that they had neither the power that would ensure their relevance, nor even the entertainment value that would make them interesting. As a media product, politics was becoming just one more docusoap among countless others. The population turned away en masse. It was becoming clear that democracy could no longer live up to its own billing, and that it had therefore lost its credibility. Democracy was simply not democratic enough. The politicians' mistake was to believe that their rivals for attention were other politicians. In actual fact politics had been transformed into little more than one branch of the entertainment industry among all the others – competing with cinema, music, sport and television – and, as such, was found to be one of the most naïve, worst acted and therefore also least attractive. Political theatre was interesting and persuading fewer and fewer people.

All of this changed with the arrival of plurarchy. When politics becomes global rather than national, the system is exposed to a veritable onslaught of quite overwhelming amounts of information at each and every moment. The structure with a clearly defined communications centre is replaced by a sophisticated interaction between a range of diverse and intimately linked nodal-points, meaning that the whole system is fundamentally transformed. The globalist politician, the networking plurarch, is not a demagogue but a curator; in other words, he is a sorter of information rather than a producer of information, a mediator rather than a spokesman for a particular interest group. The overriding priority is always the global empire, which means that every attempt by different lobby-groups to promote themselves over others must be quashed, both for attentionalist reasons – horse trading and corruption are made visible by the transparency of network society – and in order to combat unnecessary bureaucratic sluggishness.

Selfish special interests are the mortal enemies of the global empire. Consequently the globalistic project cannot be accomplished without the abandonment of what has hitherto been known as the democratic process, with all the fawning and toadying involved in fishing for votes. Plurarchy produces instead a completely new type of political leadership, at the same time more discrete and more robust than that of national parliamentarism, and, above all else, it is highly goal-oriented. The continued aggressive promotion of special interests will be seen as more and more counter-productive and unattractive, because it is precisely this sort of short-sighted group-egotism which hinders informationalism's advanced non-zero-sum games.

An interesting taste of post-democratic politics is offered by the supranational appointment of the leaders who have governed, with unusual effectiveness, in the territories which arose after the multinational military action which was carried out in the collapsing Yugoslav Federation in the 1990s. Their actual effectiveness is a direct result of this new type of leadership being liberated from the antagonistic special interests which characterise the nation state, which is supposed to be made up of a common ethnicity. The fact that these non-political administrators look likely to go down in history as the precursors of the developing world state's leaders ought to be regarded as an irony of history, and an excellent example of a general winning himself to death.

After the end of the Cold War and the disintegration of the Communist block, it suddenly became possible to do away with the territorial sovereignty of the nation state. A pre-globalistic 'world community' started to think in global terms, resulting in direct interventions in various conflict zones around the world. These multinational military actions were superficially concerned with the attempts of nation states to use often complicated co-operation across international boundaries to satisfy the growing international opinion in favour of perceived universal human rights. Geopolitical and other strategic concerns still played an important role, but were subordinated to a policy that was steered by media opinion.

According to the traditional interpretation, these multinational military activities were extremely dubious, as was vocally claimed by a legalistically reactionary minority among opinion-formers. On top of this, these actions were more reminiscent of police activities within a global state than any form of traditional, interstate conflict. As a result, a large and in principal extremely important step had been taken on the path to a world state. George Bush senior was more correct than he himself knew when, at the beginning of the 1990s, he spoke of 'the new world order'. After the abandonment of the nation state's territorial sovereignty, there were no principal impediments to the foundation of the world state. No nation, not even the USA, stands outside the moral authority which the global empire exerts over all nation states. It is ironic in the circumstances that it was those most nationalist and isolationist of all politicians, the American presidents at the turn of the millennium, who managed to throw the door open for the sovereignty of the global empire.

The keyword in this context in farsightedness. Under informationalism, the ground rule will be that people who keep the whole picture in mind, rather than wanting to appease the noisiest current opinion, will be rewarded in the long term with considerably greater attentionality. And certain knowledge makes certain types of foolishness impossible. After the anthropological sciences have deconstructed the idea of ethnicity – until only a collection of proto-racist stories remain – it will no longer be possible in enlightened circumstances to extract any sustainable form of social identity from nationalism. And because social gravity is therefore shifting from nationalism to the fast-growing and global virtual nomadic tribes, it will no longer be possible to demand that ethnic composition, or even a notional geographic homeland, be reflected in political representation. As a result, the very foundations of the national state will have been completely destroyed.

Democracy was, in theory, representative of opinion: what mattered was that a voter voted for and was represented by someone who presented his or her opinions in important matters. But in the late-capitalist, heterogeneous state, this system was in practice impossible to maintain. Each interest group demanded representation commensurate to its size, preferably larger, because it was possible to gain points in the media by pointing to the weakness of the group and institutionalised oppression. Globalistic politicians represent instead an entirely new ideal: the socioanalyst, the collectivist equivalent to Lacan's psychoanalyst, a plurarch who practices and embodies the radical pragmatism of eternalism. The socioanalyst is an cool, neutral wall upon which both the dividual's and the virtual nomadic tribe's exaggerated hopes of favouritism and privileges are first projected in order to be deconstructed, without the socioanalyst's status or formal position being threatened in any way as a result. The insatiable hunger of specific dividuals and networks for recognition, status and various sorts of favour are always met with constructive criticism, a consequent and well-formulated aid to self-help, and with encouragement for continued attempts to create favourable conditions for increasingly profitable non-zero-sum games. The plurarch, the globalistic leader who best manages to realise the socioanalytical ideal, will be the one who keeps hold of power.

This political paradigm shift is connected with the fact that the all-encompassing interactivity of informationalist politics is completely changing the relationship between governors and governed. While the democratic populist is being replaced by the socioanalyst, the capitalist voter is being replaced by the socioanalysand, or, to put it another way: the specific dividual's profit from his or her dealings with the socioanalyst will be directly dependent on the effort he or she puts in. It will no longer be possible to demand favours in return for votes; the socioanalyst simply cannot afford to give in to that sort of blackmail without losing his vital attentionality. The communication loop between the analyst and analysand presupposes that mutual demands are made and met. As a result the hypocrisy and the element of theatre that have dominated the democratic process will disappear, and ingratiation will be replaced by plain talking. The radical pragmatism of eternalism will break through on every level of the political process; socioanalysts will replace opinion-poll populism.

Note that we keep referring to the global empire and the world state as a global state, not as an international empire or some sort of international political organisation. It would be quite wrong to think of the world state in federalist terms, as some sort of United Nations with an expanded mandate. Even the most advanced examples of international co-operation are based upon the nation as their constituent part. The global empire, on the other hand, is based upon the idea of power itself being exercised on a global level. Even if information management is dispersed to a multitude of different nodal networks, some central decision-making functions – such as the use of force – will need to be concentrated in the hands of a very limited number of socioanalysts. The critical moment will be when the growing netocracy has drained all power from the nation state in all important spheres, because that will force the powerless democratic elite to vote for its own abolition. Farsighted leadership candidates have had a long time to position themselves and present themselves as credible socioanalysts in the eyes of the socioanalysands.

Since one important dimension of the world state is centralistic – which is necessary to balance the plurarchic fragmentation which characterises developments in every other area – the overriding question about the global power-structure is made yet more complicated. This gives us a reason to return to one of the most important components of eternalist writing of information-technological history: the so-called tripolarity theory. According to this theory, political power in every historical paradigm tends to be divided between three separate poles. A form of functional balance of terror is set up between the poles, which, when established, forms a basis for the relative social stability that arises, so long as a certain complex of information and communication technology sets its particular mark on proceedings. Before the era of permanent settlements, in hunter-gatherer society, the poles of the power triangle were made up of the chieftain, the hunter and the shaman; under feudalism by the monarch, the aristocracy and the church; and under capitalism by the nation state, the bourgeoisie and science. The equivalent fundamental tripolarity in the informationalist power structure is made up of the curator, the nexialist and the eternalist (for more complete definitions and explanations, see Netocracy).

As a principle, tripolarity has proved to be functional at many levels. The French Enlightenment philosopher Montesquieu applied the formula to the division of power within the state, differentiating between the legislature, the executive and the judiciary. The balance and stability that arise from tripolarity are the key, and Montesquieu's ideas had immense influence, not least on the American Constitution, where Congress, the Presidency and the Constitutional Court all co-operate with and counteract each other in such a way that none of them can exercise power alone. Other countries' uni- and bipolar constitutions have proved to be comparatively unmanageable and considerably more vulnerable to abuse and the effects of corruption.

As a result of the aestheticisation of political culture under informationalism, tripolarity will be most clearly visible as an internal phenomenon within the virtual nomadic tribes. The global empire will ally itself with the curators, and will thereby become the very centre of the curators' own arena. The curator who manages to create most attentionality and the highest status will de facto become the leader of the global state. The rankings within the various elite networks will determine who occupies other leading positions, and recruitment will only take place on strictly meritocratic grounds (see Netocracy). No other principles are possible, because interactivity will have become so intensive; in the slightly longer term, transparency within each horizontal section of the structure will become almost total.

The fundamental driving force behind developments leading to the paradigm shift is technological innovation; firstly through the new knowledge it brings, and secondly because of the new non-zero-sum games it facilitates. Our surroundings are becoming more intelligent thanks to technology, and are therefore demanding a higher degree of competence. At the same time, we are becoming more domesticated, more tightly bound to greater and more complex mutual dependence, which means that the ground beneath the collective elite is shifting. Planning and farsightedness are becoming steadily more important, and the horizons of expectation and consequentiality are constantly moving further away The revolution is made visible when the previously dominant enmity between the different competing collective subjects is replaced by the considerably more ambiguous and nuanced rivalries of the virtual nomadic tribes. The fact that we are learning to make use of our competitors instead of fighting them, and that competition now seems more 'civilised', does not make us morally superior to our predecessors, it is purely a consequence of circumstances favouring new forms of behaviour.

Homo ludens is becoming established as the netocratic ideal, not because any particular dividuals or powerful networks have actively chosen him, but because the built-in rules of interactivity (and therefore informationalism) favour him at the expense of other players. The decisive difference in this context between the tribal rivalries of informationalism and the international conflicts of capitalism is that the former take place within the frame of the global empire. This means that in theory they have to conform to certain patterns and follow certain given rules. It is these rules which make the sequence of events look more like a game than a war. Rivalry is about attention and social identity rather than territory and money.

Ethical shifts throughout history have occurred in parallel with, and as a result of, revolutions in information technology; with the help of technology we have progressed from the primitive tribe via the nation to the global empire as the frame within which our values are formed. This means that the ultimate civilisationist boundary of spoken language was hunter-gatherer society, the boundary of written language was permanent settlements and their conquered territory, and the boundary of the printed word was the nation state, while the interactive media technologies do not recognise any boundaries at all, apart from the existential isolation of the planet Earth in space. This explains why the players within informationalism – in contrast to their historical equivalents – primarily identify themselves with, and therefore base their values upon, the idea of the global empire.

Concepts such as 'Culture' and 'History' will assume a global meaning under informationalism; when we speak of Culture and History from now on, we shall mean nothing less than the collected experiences of all humanity. This connects with the fact that the constructive rivalry between the virtual nomadic tribes is replacing the destructive enmity between the dwindling nation states as the fundamental basis of the production of social identity. At the same time as the individual is being replaced by the dividual (see Netocracy), the collective subject is growing stronger at the expense of the individual subject; the desire to make sacrifices for the good of the group is highlighted, whereas selfish actions and their possible rewards are punished and lose their status. This is not to say that violence and conflicts will in any way disappear, merely that they will appear in a different form and will have a new frame of values. The desire to be tamed will still compete against the desire for freedom and self-assertion, even under informationalism.

The value of the global empire in terms of identity-creation and unification can hardly be exaggerated. An episode from the early days of informationalism illuminates one particular problem:

In the middle of the 1980s a group of pop-stars, whose hunger for publicity was at least as great as the hunger of starving Africans for food, came together to record the catchy little ditty We are the world in aid of international charity. There wasn't a dry eye in the house. But what drove the public to tears more than anything else was not the fact that they were being forced to participate, as outsiders, in the infantile worldview of the artists, nor that the prime objective of the project was so obviously to present these pop-stars in the media as noble philanthropists, nor even the complete lack of critical thinking on the part of the consumtariat mass media. No, the most upsetting thing was that the globalist idea, which had already taken root in the collective subconscious and was starting to influence the production of identity, had been so brutally soiled by the obvious cynical mediocrity of the project.

It was quite justifiable to ask, even as early as the 1980s, what right this group of poseurs had to speak for an entire world. Since the global idea was so central an idea in the gigantic mental shake-up that had just started, and because it was the greatest value in the nascent system of informationalism, it was not a concept that could be messed about with willy-nilly. For the developing netocracy the management of this concept is an incredibly sensitive issue. Claiming to be spokespeople for the world in an important subject without any real mandate was nothing less that secular sacrilege.

From the point of view of the netocracy, actions of this sort are valued in attentional terms, in other words: awareness multiplied by credibility. Consequently it was easy to dismiss Michael Jackson and his colleagues as clueless and self-righteous; they certainly created masses of attention, but absolutely no credibility in their role as global spokespeople. The interesting question which arises instead is how the netocracy will deal with more serious attempts in the future to speak for the whole world. The Global Empire is already out there in the world in a number of variant forms, both as a latent ideology behind a number of current political activities, and as the subject of academic studies in farsighted universities. Sooner or later someone will seriously claim to be the legitimate spokesperson of the global empire and announce that they are laying the foundations of its first concrete manifestations. It is this scenario which will give at least parts of the netocracy a self-image as the bearers of an historic duty. Credibility will be absolutely crucial within the netocratic networks that will be indispensable in this context.

Informationalist identity production diverges radically from that of capitalism: the basics are fundamentally different. As far as building identity from a starting point in the hyperreality of the virtual world is concerned, capitalism's old social divisions are no longer valid. Ethnicity, language, gender and so on are no longer basic categories: genetic and cultural roots have lost their relevance. As a consequence of intensified interactivity, differentiation will be postponed until the final stages in the production of identity. The stranger will therefore lose his old role as theatrical villain in the collective's demonology, and be transformed instead into an indispensable asset and opportunity. A divergent point of view will be transformed from a threat into a necessity. The survival of the virtual nomadic tribe in memetic Darwinian competition is closely related to its flexibility and receptivity. This has little to do with morals, even if it is bound to sound like it in the rhetoric of power. Genuine multiplicity is no longer just a politically correct phrase, but a blunt survival strategy built upon radical pragmatism: eternalists are irredeemably cosmopolitan.

This is not, however, any guarantee of eternal peace and harmony on Earth. As a result of plurarchy superseding democracy as the decision-making system, there will be a growing realisation that no social relations or loyalties can be taken for granted in informationalist society. The idea of dynamism is replacing the idea of growth as the short-term goal; the Event is replacing Progress as the transcendental ideal. All of this gives informationalism an easily recognisable characteristic, surfacity: at the same time as the value of long-term strategies is increasing, social value itself is just as incredibly fleeting and difficult to grasp as attention. An investment over several years in credibility can be blown away in an instant as the result of a fateful misjudgement of something that could be purely aesthetic in nature. Loyalties are linked to ideas and projects rather than to groups and leaders, key figures are constantly exposed to heavy pressure and seductive temptations. Consequently every alliance is fragile, and every agreement provisional, to the constant frustration of all parties. The situation must be constantly re-evaluated; paranoia is becoming a functional, fully respectable and often rewarded attitude.

The medialisation of society and life that was instigated during late capitalism is intensifying in line with the expansion of plurarchy, and its domination of one sector of society after the other. In the escalating informational chaos it is becoming ever more difficult and costly to be visible and to communicate in a meaningful way, but herein lies the unavoidable precondition for every form of activity, whether political, cultural or economic. Those players who underestimate the extent of medialisation, or who are incapable of putting their conclusions into a functional strategy, will be swept aside in the merciless competition for attention. Those who do not make themselves seen and do not communicate effectively are essentially not even on the same playing-field.

The growth of surfacity means that the nurturing of the attentional façade is elevated to become one of the most important priorities for the players in the social arena. Medialisation is forcing all players, of all different sorts, to revise both their goals and their structure and strategy. This means that self-generating metamorphoses – such as the Finnish company Nokia: from wellington boots, via mobile phones, to God knows what under God knows what circumstances in the future – will become the norm rather than the exception. All social activities and organisations, whether political, cultural or economic, will be forced to subordinate themselves to the laws of memetics and network dynamics in order to have any chance of survival.

In informational society, origins no longer have any value. The same sort of self-generating metamorphoses will spread from the level of the network down to that of the single person. The original, indivisible individual has played out its part and is stepping aside in favour of the dividual, a person who detests stability and seeks maximal receptivity and flexibility. The feverish search by the individual for the core of the self is being replaced by the dividual's conscious nurturing of a multitude of identities; one's self-image will be a wandering network of differently formulated, intelligently co-operating aspects, unified in the very ambition of networking intelligently. We shall no longer be anyone special, but rather will nurture the possibility of being several people, and will strive all the while to keep alive the possibility of change, and will no longer define ourselves in terms of characteristics but in terms of relationships.

Humanism's idealised subject has lost its function and therefore has no further relevance in eternalism's political philosophy. It is no longer relevant to speak of a conflict between the interests of the individual and the collective, just as it is no longer relevant to speak of a conflict between the ego and the super-ego. We are alluding here to the aesthetic ideal that Nietzsche called Superman instead of Man, and to what Michel Foucault calls the 'process of subjectification' rather than the subject. For the dividual it is always a matter of subordination in relation to a network; liberation can never mean anything other than subordination in relation to another network. The eternalistic subject – which is precisely an eternalisation, and not a mobilistically real and objective truth – arises out of this constantly changing system of tensions, and can never be fixed at any particular position. The principle of the movement of everything, of the fundamental instability of eternalisation, is central to the whole of the socioanalytical system.

The Global Empire as a concept has three components, separate but nonetheless linked and mutually interdependent. We shall use three classical Greek words to identify them. The first concept is mythos, representing the metaphysical aspect of the empire, the dimension from which the worldview and production of identity ultimately stem. In Ancient Greece, mythos was the world of gods and heroes. Even informationalism needs a credible mythology to hold it together, and to assist the production of identity. This is also found in the empire itself, in the vision of a global community which transcends differences and oppositions. The shake-up of power entailed by every paradigm shift is driven by an underlying longing for liberation from what in the collective subconscious is experienced as out-of-date ideological prison-constructions. But this liberation demands heroes, both as essential role-models and projection-screens, and for the actual, physical achievement of the necessary revolution. This means that in the same way as the birth of every nation state under capitalism produced its own, specific pantheon of heroes, so the global empire will gradually be provided with one of its own.

The fact is that it was precisely the hyperrationalist denial of the mythic dimension which castrated the academic left-wing during late-capitalism and made globally political activism impossible to implement from its own theories. We shall never see, for instance, how the philosophical works of Jürgen Habermas or Ernesto Laclau inspire the masses to form a global political movement; if for no other reason than because the fundamental need for a political mythology is completely overlooked by them and their contemporaries. Among the political philosophers of the twentieth century, only Lenin at the beginning of the century exhibited a deep understanding of and prioritised the necessary metaphysical dimension of political activism, something which the Slovenian philosopher Slavoj Žižek often returns to in his sociological implementation of Lacan's psychoanalysis. Or, to use the principles of eternalism: who could be said to have greater attentionality in terms of political activism than Lenin himself?

The second concept forming part of the global empire as a concept is logos, which stands for the world state itself: the political, legal and military structure which is the basis for the exercising of power. To the Greeks, logos stood for the republic itself, the functional organisation of polis, the underlying logic for the whole

249

society. In the eternalistic analysis of informationalist society, the plurarchy takes the republic's role as logos. This means that the immense difficulties involved in trying to understand this complex plurarchy – in order later to be able to organise it in a way that is beneficial and ethically acceptable to all parties – must be overcome if global society is to be guided at all, and if plurarchy is not to capsize and be transformed into anarchy. Capitalism's rationalist methods of analysis will have to be discarded; for instance, national economics as a discipline must leave the nursery and absorb serious doses of both philosophy and psychology – in other words: it must become part of socioanalysis – in order to comment seriously on the economic currents of information society. To guide a global state, or merely part of a global state, will demand a transrationalist worldview, including a recurrent reliance upon self-organisational models which have already shown themselves to work empirically.

The third and final conceptual component in the creation of the global empire is pathos, the organisation of what Nietzsche called the desire for power, the human instinct to produce social identity. Pathos is largely a question of netocratic aesthetics, the abundance of alternative lifestyles and tribal subcultures that characterise informationalism. But pathos also stands for netocratic ethics. And it is here, on the micro-level of identity production, that the new homo pathalogicus appears and consigns capitalism's exhausted aesthetic ideal, the sober, magisterial homo rationalis, to the history books. The Cartesian subject has disappeared at the same time as the old idea of a sound mind in a sound body. New myths will appear to be credible when the old ones no longer have support in either the knowledge or the ideals demanded by the age.

There are no 'healthy' people in the traditional meaning of the word; we are all 'sick' in one way or another. The entire notion of 'healthiness' looks, according to Jacques Lacan's and Michel Foucault's explorations of western pathologies, like little more than an instrument of oppression. What makes homo pathologicus a functional being in informationalist society are precisely the characteristics which would have been regarded as signs of sickness under capitalism, not least a tendency towards creative, schizoid behaviour. Thinking has become a mass of insoluble paradoxes, but this is much more functional in a fundamentally paradoxical world. A pathological tendency is no longer characteristic of something having gone wrong, such as a process of alienation or a fall from grace which must therefore be remedied, but, on the contrary, something which inspires hope in the netocratic dividual. Psychoanalysts will therefore be redundant, no-one will need their services, and their place will be taken by eternalistic schizoanalysts. By combining schizoanalysis with network dynamism and eternalistic metaphysics, we get socioanalysis, the new paradigm's basis for political theory and practice.

The history of political philosophy is full of arguments for and against various new forms of state structure. The ambition to expand and raise the level of complexity, to build empires upon smaller state structures, and the desire to elevate the ruler to the status of god, from Ramses II to Kim Il Sung, are all examples of mythos being dealt a good hand in the political game. In certain periods mythos has had to give way to logos, which was good news for the organisers of bureaucratic hierarchies and social engineering of various sorts. The Greece inspired by Plato, the Persia inspired by Zarathustra, the China inspired by Confucius, and the Prussia inspired by Hegel after the Napoleonic Wars, are all examples of societies strongly influenced by logos.

In a lot of ways pathos balances mythos and logos in political philosophy. The pathic discourse is characterised by the dream of returning man to an imagined place of origin, a state in which his free nature had not yet been domesticated or forced into the process of civilisation. But pathos is also the home of eternalistic philosophy's ideal, an inheritance from philosophers like Hegel and Nietzsche. Here pathos is mankind's wish to change completely, for its own sake, a political ambition constantly to create and meet demanding challenges. Pathos has never dominated any society in history – it is far too programmatically unstable for that – but as a source of the cultural production upon which the political sphere rests, pathos is the most important of the global empire's three components.

We can express this by saying that pathos is the resonance box of the political sphere. Pathos is the source of both the creative ethic which reinforces mythos, and of the radical pragmatism which keeps logos alive and even strengthens it long-term. So pathos is the motor which continually sets society in motion over and over again, and, for instance, bursts the bounds set by legislation and thereby forces those in power to renew and alter the law. Without pathos, society would fall and civilisation implode. It is vitally important to focus on precisely where the genuinely radical elements are in political philosophy. The eternalist realises that the ethically correct political act in itself, the human action which is perceived to transform political reality entirely, is, once and for all, just a romantic utopia.

According to eternalist philosophy, only the dominant information technology of the paradigm can actually transform political reality. The thoughts and actions of individual people can only develop, and possibly embellish the in-built preconditions of the information technology in question when it, rather than the players themselves, plays out its own hand. This means that the bitter truth which all romantically-inclined Marxists and poststructuralists are forced to confront at the dawning of informationalism is that there is not, and probably never has been, anything genuinely radical in their political philosophy. It was merely a post-Christian, highly reactionary dream, where mythos, logos and pathos were blended together and naïvely mixed up. The genuinely radical political act must instead be unconditionally built upon the disciplined application of practice, namely eternalism's radical pragmatism; a conclusion which Gilles Deleuze was alone in drawing among poststructuralist thinkers, and the most important explanation as to why he never called himself a Marxist.

The intensification of interactivity – our constantly growing opportunities to find and create virtual communities entirely independent of geographic limitations – is having two important consequences. The power structures of the capitalist nation state are imploding, and a dazzling array of globally active subcultures is arising. This latter constitutes a cultural paradigm shift, a transition from a system based upon the nurturing of national identities with the help of propagandist one-way communication, to a system based upon the nurturing of an overriding global identity with a broad spectrum of differently nuanced lifestyles with the help of new, interactive media technologies. The market for late capitalism's mass-medial popular culture will be confined to the production of prefabricated identity for the passivised consumtariat. The growing netocracy, the first genuinely global dominant class, will instead use interactive media technologies to produce exclusive new identities and values.

Even if we have still only seen the beginning of the interactive revolution, we can already study it and gain an understanding of the extent of its effects by looking at how it has already affected social structures. The introductory phase of the revolution is usually dated to the 1970s, which both explains, and is explained by, the appearance of the first virtual nomadic tribes at that time. As soon as the technology became available, it was nurtured by newly formed groups on the cultural margins who realised its advantages to them personally and, in certain cases, even its subversive potential. A revolution in information technology cannot possibly support the powers who are protecting the status quo; by definition it undermines governing values and power structures by creating and favouring entirely new patterns of behaviour and thought. It is therefore entirely logical that the first virtual nomadic tribes had their roots in the American 'counter-cultural' hippie movement and European student activism of the 1960s.

In order to differentiate the virtual nomadic tribes from the transnational subcultures which have their origins in the pre-informationalist order, we can apply five criteria which a group has to fulfil in order to be defined as a virtual nomadic tribe. The first and most obvious of these is that the group in question must be virtual, by which we mean that it has its origins and its original home in the virtual world, in other words, in the imaginary landscape which has arisen through our communal exploitation of interactive media technologies. But the activities that the group perform in 'real life' can be seen as different virtual events in so far as they are planned, discussed, announced and commented upon in the virtual arena, where their very social identity is thereby de facto produced.

The second requirement has to do with the nomadic aspect: the group in question must be characterised by its mobility. It makes a virtue of keeping its identity as fluid as possible, and seeks, as far as possible, to cut all ties to any particular point in physical space. The brutal, memetic Darwinian competition between the informationalist networks means that the group which makes stability the platform for its identity production will be knocked out (cf. the discussion about self-generating metamorphoses above), which automatically raises and heightens still further the premium value of mobility.

This fact separates the virtual nomadic tribe from pre-informationalist networks in a radical way, because the latter always presupposed a common core of values. There was always an ideological plane of business which dissolved or was transformed into something completely different and therefore alien in the eyes of the surrounding world, if or when that core fell apart or lost its power of attraction. The breakthrough of informationalism brings with it, however, a radical mental shift in this particular area: there have been dramatic shake-ups before in history, but people have always striven, certainly since the establishment of fixed settlements, to reach an idealised 'normal state' of stability. Now the very opposite of stability, radical mobility, is being raised to the status of a new ideal. The virtual world prioritises neither fixed ties nor settled dwellings. Its nodes function as virtual oases where the nomadic tribes stay briefly before unfailingly moving on in their eternal search for the transcendental Event: an eternally changeable identity, and constant new kicks.

The third requirement is that the group must be tribal in its form and structure. The enormous flexibility that is built into the interactive media and into the endless virtual landscape facilitates a welcome retreat to the size of group which mankind has preferred for the majority of its short existence, and to which it is genetically best suited. Neither capitalism's nuclear family nor its individualism retains much power of attraction when the netocrat, thanks to interactivity, is offered the chance to chose the structure and shape of the group which will be his or her social home.

This means that the tribes of hunter-gatherer society are resurrected as the basic unit for identity creation. Informationalism is therefore characterised by a technological primitivism, dominated by the concentrated leadership of the tribal structure, consisting of a handful of people who in turn represent a cohesive core of about a hundred people. Time and time again it has been proved within group psychology, as well as management theory, that 150 people is the natural boundary to what a human being can deal with socially: anything above that and the group begins to disintegrate into factions and to counteract itself. The tribal model is available and attractive to the netocracy to whom individualism merely seems vulgar and enforced by circumstances which are no longer pertinent. But the consumtariat remains trapped in individualism, dreaming the obsolete dream of individual self-realisation.

The fourth criterion is that the group must be network-oriented all the time. Internally it will lack the traditional hierarchy of capitalist organisations, and is instead built organically, from below, according to the principles of distributed networks. Externally it constantly concludes new alliances with competing networks, thus making it dependent upon the high status of its own members in order to be attractive in the market for relationships. The virtual nomadic tribe professes to be open to all, without favouring any ethnic background or wealth, but this openness is highly relative in practice. The network dynamics of informationalism encourage new criteria for social status and for membership of the most highly respected virtual nomadic tribes.

The fifth and final requirement is that the group must be dedicated to the production of social identity. Early virtual nomadic tribes which can demonstrate their successes are characterised by the fact that they constructed a demonology which is directed against the outdated laws and moral regulations of the imploding capitalism. As a result a conflict arises between the group and the remnants of the nation state organisation, a tension from which the group benefits because its attentionality is thereby increased. As these groups create more and more attention, and attract more and more members, they can no longer be ignored by the organs of the nation state, which may be shrinking and collapsing but which still have political power in their grasp. Recognition takes the form of the group being mentioned by name and introduced into capitalist demonology, which in practice means criminalisation. This mutual demonisation increases the tribe's social gravity, which in turn intensifies the conflict, whereupon the whole process is sucked into a feedback loop and accelerates still further. The conflict continues as long as the capitalist apparatus can generate enough energy; in the meantime the subversive group will grow stronger and stronger and learn to construct new and sophisticated demonologies in order to survive in the virtual jungle.

If these criteria – virtuality, mobility, tribality and network orientation – are fulfilled, and if the production of identity is proceeding at pace, then we can confirm that we are dealing with a virtual nomadic tribe. The tribes differ from one another, representing a broad range of ideological and aesthetic alternatives, and they compete hard with one another, but beneath this partially exaggerated proclamation of their differences they all exhibit a common platform, a precondition for them all which they are prepared to defend at every moment, and with greater force than they would their own territory, if need be. This platform is the Global Empire.

This idea is growing ever stronger as the interactive revolution rolls onward. It is becoming clear to more and more people that the global state is not only possible, but that it is necessary as the only solution to all the problems that are mounting up at a global level. As a result, tolerance towards national nostalgia, and towards all manner of protest movements against globalisation, is gradually shrinking. Hence the political fiction of capitalism – that all opinions are permitted so long as they are in harmony with étatism – is being replaced by the political fiction of informationalism, which prescribes obedience to the global empire. The netocracy sees no point in protecting ideological alternatives which it regards as exhausted – the new, multifarious range is primarily an aesthetic matter. We have read our history and recognise the need for a unifying idea, and because informationalism has raised the netocracy to power there is every reason to keep as much grit as possible away from the machinery.

3.

THE GENEALOGY OF NETOCRATIC ETHICS

IF WE ARE TO GAIN a deeper understanding of contemporary thinking and a thorough grasp of informationalism's historical roots, we need to carry out an archaeological investigation of the collective subconscious, which in turn demands that the focus be shifted away from traditional history writing's fixation on particular points in time and on particular individuals to a more general, ideas-based perspective of a relevant period of history. A suitable limited period for our analysis is the recently concluded twentieth century, particularly because it largely coincides with the period in socio-economic and information-technological history known as late capitalism.

There are two main reasons for differentiating a late capitalist era from a preceding period of high capitalism. Firstly, social and cultural implications inherent in the printing process, the all-pervasive information technology, right from the start only began to be developed fully during the late capitalist period. This allowed critical thinking to conceive of a worldview as a product of current circumstances and thereby even, in extension, to conceive of an end to the whole paradigm. The self-evident aspect of the current worldview was no longer self-evident. Secondly, late capitalism was characterised by the growth of the electronic mass media, which strongly reinforced rather than broke down the power structures which primarily rested upon the printing press. The electronics amplified the mass media and therefore increased the potency of one-way communication. The printed media – books, daily papers and magazines – had made relatively high demands of their audience. Literacy was a precondition for being able to receive any information at all. With the advent of radio and television, the entrance requirements were reduced to the ability to use a switch, and as a result centralistic power could quite literally reach everyone. This also happened at the same time as those being addressed were given less opportunity than ever to answer back.

During their introductory phase the electronic mass media thereby contributed considerably to the reinforcement of the nation state and its institutions. Broadcasts took place in national languages, within the nation's borders, and the audience consisted of the nation's citizens. Community was strengthened by the fact that everyone was watching and listening to the same thing. With the advent of satellite technology in the middle of the twentieth century, the situation was dramatically altered. Now people in every corner of the world began to consume the same sporting events, the same political events, the same military conflicts, at the same time, all with the same advertisements for the same consumer goods. As a result, a condition of hypercapitalism was able to spread rapidly across the whole world. Certain memes could benefit from extremely favourable circumstances, and the lifestyles and thought patterns of the dominant economies effectively colonised the areas which had earlier, during high capitalism, been politically and militarily subordinate. With that, a first step on the road to the global state had been taken.

The beliefs and values which early informationalism made its own formed part of late capitalism's consciousness of crisis, where they had lain for a long time causing friction and being generally uncomfortable. The origins of the netocratic elite can be traced as far back as the glory days of high capitalism, during the second half of the nineteenth century, to a collection of extremely controversial and literally anachronistic ideas. The most important if these was Friedrich Nietzsche's destructive critique of the basic assumptions of rationalism and humanism. According to Nietzsche, truth is not always a timeless gift bestowed by some god or derived from nature, but is always produced by mankind itself in order to fulfil certain functions under certain circumstances. This meant that, firstly, the truth is relative and changeable, and secondly, it is entirely dependent upon current power relationships. The truth is thus nothing we can seek, because instead it seeks us in order to demand submission. The purpose and consequence of ascribing transcendental qualities to the truth are to place it out of the reach of critical examination, and thus to make it appear as eternal and 'natural'.

Nietzsche's transrational metatruth, which states that the truth is a temporally bound product of a particular social order, is the only truth which retains its credibility throughout history. All other elevated values disappear with the society that was responsible for their elevation. Anyone who tries to defend the 'eternal' truths of rationalism and humanism after Nietzsche is defending nothing more than his or her own special social interests in the eternal struggle over definitions. There is, quite simply, nothing to stand up for, and never had been. With this, Nietzsche also destroyed all notions of a philosophy or a philosopher whose ideas might be thought to be independent of their age and material circumstances.

This realisation permeates eternalism; eternalist philosophers necessarily speak the language of the up-and-coming power, not because of any ambitious desire to get their head in the trough, but because there is no alternative, apart from self-deception, if you want to conduct any relevant work in philosophy. You either appear conservative within the frame decided by the outgoing regime, which means that what you produce will soon be outdated, or you produce philosophical concepts which pave the way for the coming regime. Eternalism is, and also sees itself as, a new phase in the civilisation process; it is simply not meaningful to take up a position outside the developing paradigm. Eternalistic philosophy is the affirmative centre of affirmative nihilism, to which we shall return later in the this chapter.

Nietzsche's unmasking of the origins of morality will have dramatic consequences once it becomes widespread. Since official truth is the basis of the hierarchy of values around which society is constructed, every system of morals is by definition both a product and a defence of the governing power structure and its interests. All the ideology which is used as packaging material is intended to cover up the functions and simple origins of the sacred truths. This is history: the story of how the governing value-hierarchy of the time is made legitimate through the creation of an attractive family tree. Consequently the flip-side of history is the story of nihilism and how it has been forestalled over the centuries. It is in the interests of every powerful elite to preserve the status quo and present all fundamental change as infernal and, above all, 'unnatural'. It is a question of suppressing at all costs the idea that we humans and our changing social forms are worthless outside our own imagination.

These processes are investigated in detail and explained pedagogically by Nietzsche and his successor Martin Heidegger, but the idea of history as the story of nihilism was already posited by G W F Hegel. Because mankind has, throughout history, both individually and collectively, lived more or less comfortably within the discrepancy between the fundamental truth which says that all truths are only based on the agreements about power relationships between different people, and the official truth which says that the truth is sanctioned by the highest metaphysical instance, then there has to be a large, dark space in thought where suppressed truths lie hidden. Most of us walk past this dark space every day without ever noticing it, but its absence is so noticeable that it constitutes a sort of negative presence, whose dark shadow falls across everyday life.

It is this dark space beneath the horizon of consciousness that Sigmund Freud calls the subconscious. Freud, however, is not content to state that mankind is distracted by a sort of eternal leakage from the subconscious, but goes a step further, saying that basic human frustration and dissatisfaction has its origins in this very discrepancy between the conscious and the subconscious. According to the rationalist view of mankind, as Freud points out, the big problem is negotiating an agreement between, on the one hand, social morality (the truth) and, on the other, thoughts and actions (the individual); this is naturally wholly in line with the interests of the ruling elite, and wholly in line with what every elite in every age has preached. Every kind of breach of governing moral ideas is perceived to cause existential angst, whereas harmony and happiness are assumed to be the rewards for successful adaptation of thought and deed to the prescriptions of social morality. If all citizens only had the sense to realise what was good for them, every individual would be able to achieve maximum inner peace, and all social problems would disappear.

Freud realised that this model was unsustainable. Instead, he localises pathological disturbances to the jarring disharmony between the conscious view of the world and the subconscious. This means firstly that the probable consequence of slavishly following the official truth is an increase in discomfort, and secondly that this discomfort is universal, and therefore extremely normal. The most problematic type of psychopathology is therefore not disharmony, but rather the absence of symptoms of disharmony. Mankind has meandered through history unaware of all of this, and has therefore been forced to accept the authorities' claims that all forms of discomfort are the result of the individual's disobedience towards those same authorities. Freud claims that the cure lies in making the subconscious conscious. The dark space must be opened up, what is suppressed must be set free. With this in mind he established psychoanalysis with the highest scientific ambitions. The ideas of psychoanalysis in turn form the basis of eternalistic philosophy, which is concerned with the dark spaces of public life, and the knowledge which is currently suppressed from language and public communication. This archaeological dig in the collective subconscious is called, consequently, socioanalysis.

The task of exposing the central role played by nihilism in the history of the collective subject is, according to Nietzsche himself, both thankless and unavoidable; it also forces him to become the spokesman for what he calls the 'will to power', in other words: the desire to transform nihilism into fuel for the motor driving human creativity and identity production. As a result Nietzsche is the first person to affirm nihilism; he accepts and ennobles it, instead of trying to hide or condemn it as a deterministic power driving mankind towards its doom. Nietzsche replaces the wishful thinking of rationalism and utopianism with a consistently thought-out and cool candour of previously unseen sort. Transrationalism wipes out rationalism once the logical conclusion about the limitations of rationalism has been reached.

As a result of Nietzsche's inverted project of enlightenment, nihilism was dragged out of the collective subconscious, and spread fear everywhere. The developing American film industry transformed nihilism into a sort of picturesque cabaret entertainment, but in Europe the revelation had considerably more dramatic consequences. In the trenches of European battlefields, an entire generation went to its death for distinctly murky reasons; Freud launched the death wish as one of the two fundamental antagonistic instincts of the psyche. It is an inescapable fact that every living thing is longing for death, as Freud bitterly states.

By combining the theories of Nietzsche and Freud we can see that nihilism is the death wish of the collective subject. However, it assumes different forms in different societies and at different times. Nihilism undergoes three distinct phases. They last different lengths of time under different circumstances, but they are all necessary and always follow one another in the same order. Nihilism is built into every stage of the civilisation process, but is only made conscious in a society dominated by an interactive information technology. With the arrival of informationalism and the coming of globalisation it will finally, with a few displacements, apply to the whole world.

The first phase is naïve nihilism, which is characterised by the fact that nihilism is primarily operative in the collective subconscious. It is still unconscious of its own existence and its influence on an entire world of thoughts and actions. During this phase the message relaying the death of God arrives, but the news of this death is generally understood as meaning that the only god is no longer necessary as the ultimate cause of mankind and its universe in a philosophical explanatory model which is in harmony with the very latest knowledge. The devastating effect which the death of God will have on the production of value in society is, however, something which no-one yet understands. This is why naïve nihilism is naïve.

Naïve nihilism lies at the heart of humanism, modernism and modern utopias. God no longer inhabits the subconscious, but the conscious, as an internalised aspect of the ego. This God, whom the naïve nihilist constantly addresses, is in actual fact the superego, and this confusion allows him to imagine that everyone else is equipped with an identical superego of their own, and exactly the same range of values that he has. This makes his own values appear to be universal and inspired by common sense. If only this common sense – in other words, his own values – could govern unchecked, everything would turn out alright. The question that the naïve nihilist constantly asks is: 'Why can't we all just get along?'. But behind the friendly smile there is always a rigid Jacobin.

Naïve nihilism was born with Enlightenment philosophy's cult of reason and criticism of religion. It became a highly active social and political power during the French Revolution, and reached its apex as the bourgeoisie secured its newly-won grip on power and étatism triumphed during the nineteenth century. One of the beliefs of naïve nihilism was that sound reason would henceforth be able to replace metaphysics; naïve nihilists had no perception at all of how hard they were working to fill their own worldview with masses of ideologically tinted metaphysics as a replacement for the religious thinking they had removed. In came ideas like the Cartesian subject, a romantic view of nature as the ultimate guarantee of mankind's special position and rights, and an irrational faith in rationality. As soon as sound reason had freed itself from all forms of superstition, it would solve all of mankind's problems. Thus would the social utopia be achieved.

History, in the form of the most grisly tragedies, reveals however the fateful superficiality in the psychology of the naïve nihilist. It didn't turn out as he imagined, because other people didn't think the way they ought to. His own worldview was merely his own, his universal values were merely the illusions of one confused individual. The process of disillusionment that begins once this more or less bloody failure has become a fact is difficult to manage and often gives rise to enormous bitterness. The naïve nihilist views a world which no longer seems to listen to the voice of sound reason, and which will not let itself be transformed into a rationalist utopia, with increasing scepticism.

Naïve nihilism lives on today in somewhat diluted form as étatistic liberalism, the political platform upon which the western bourgeoisie is still standing and which it is fighting to retain. Excellent examples of naïve nihilists are the leaders of nation states who have dominated the political arena during the years surrounding the turn of the millennium: Bill Clinton, Tony Blair, Gerhard Schröder, Jacques Chirac, and so on. One unmistakable sign of their naïve nihilism is their recurrent praise of rationalism and humanism. This is the core of the capitalist paradigm, this is where the bourgeoisie's belief in its own superiority originates – from reason, which is sound by definition. Its power of attraction ought not to be underestimated; naïve nihilism not only lives on in the orthodox custodians of the liberal creed, but also in the remnants of Marxism and among the single-issue political movements which, under their humanist banners, protect the nation state from every sign of increased supranational tendencies. This latter category contains, for instance, most of the environmental movement and the so-called postcolonial activists who claim to be trying to protect the third world from exploitation by keeping poor countries outside integrated global markets.

But reason is hardly the antidote for this cult of reason. There is nothing to suggest that naïve nihilism is going to unravel thanks to shaky logic or an intensified intellectual collapse in general. Étatistic and humanist appeals are, of course, more emotional than intellectual in nature. The death blow will come instead from a thoroughly medialised existence, and from the breakthrough of interactivity on all levels. Of course, anachronistically sharp and forward-thinking observers, such as Hegel and Nietzsche in the nineteenth century, saw through naïve nihilism, but it will only die as a factor of political power once informationalism and the netocracy have entered the arena.

The making-conscious of the collective subconscious and the realisation of the evident consequences of naïve nihilism will lead to a counter-reaction known as cynical nihilism. The realisation of the naïvety of naïve nihilism gave rise as early as the nineteenth century to a bitterness which would come to dominate the twentieth century's philosophical and ideological discourses. This condition developed two different symptoms, firstly a paralysing resentment, and secondly an historical-romantic escapism. The two dominant trends in the philosophical discourse of the late twentieth century, postmodernism and cultural relativism, are typical products of cynical nihilism. Every connection between individual people and the surrounding culture is by definition disconnected. No-one can actually understand what anyone else means, language is a system of arbitrarily chosen signs whose innate relations are far more interesting than any relation they may bear to material events outside the sign system. The medium is the message, the surface is the only depth of any interest, and attention shifts from reason, now suspect, to the mirrored halls of symbolic play.

The cynical nihilist is not so much a reader of signs as a player of them. His metaphysics are calculatedly mundane and trivial. But the continual presence of irony is his great blind spot. This irony indicates that he is still clinging to the idea of a universal hierarchy of values. He speaks dismissively of rationalism and believes himself to be a devastating critic of it, but he is actually still living in the rhetoric of rationalism and its conceptual world. Never before have long-winded footnotes been quite so pervasive as in postmodern theoretical reasoning (by all means note the restful absence of footnotes from this presentation, as in Hegel and Nietzsche). Every thought, no matter how banal, must unavoidably be legitimised with a reference. Through this use of rationalism's own formal language to criticise rationalism, the cynical nihilist is not being the anti-rationalist he thinks he is, but rather an exemplary ultra-rationalist. In his unreserved worship of the surface, in his fascination with its shiny coolness and his own ability to mirror himself in it and enjoy this surface, the cynical nihilist is practising a sterile act of self-adoration. The deceased god has been thoroughly internalised. Monotheism is replaced by multi-coloured cultural relativity, but this polytheism merely means a multitude of masks, and behind every mask lurks the same universal god.

The cynical nihilist therefore repeats his naïve predecessor's mistake of believing that instinct can be curbed by the intellect. He believed that his lack of prejudice and his flexibility of values are the solutions to the most difficult problems. But he is only fooling himself. Relativism can never deal with really infected conflicts with their roots in cultural traditions; neglecting to adopt a position is actually the ultimate way of adopting a position, and doing so always means abandoning the position of relativism. When, for instance, Muslim women refugees from east Africa during the 1990s continued their ritual circumcision of their daughters once they had arrived in Europe, tolerant cultural relativism was left helpless, incapable of advocating any form of intervention which would imply de facto that western values were superior to those of eastern Africa. We shall look closer at this problem later. Cynical nihilism's pleasurable paralysis of action means it loses all credibility and is revealed as little more than a tasteless, luxuriant laziness of thought.

So the circumstances are now ripe for the next developmental phase, affirmative nihilism. This stage is a rejection of cynicism, and it arises when it becomes clear that this cynicism is linked to an enforced connection with a discredited worldview, and that cynicism can be abandoned by an act of will which is in turn connected to a new clarity of vision. Cynicism is therefore turned into its opposite, nihilism is no longer seen as a hopeless terminus of history, but as the starting point for the new production of values and a new, creative aesthetic. Humanism's Man, the internalised god, may well be dead, but mankind lives on with new ideals before his eyes. After Man comes Nietzsche's Superman, the netocratic ideal.

We can get a clear view of the differences between the three various stages of nihilism by comparing their relationship to the pre-nihilistic basic value: God. The naïve nihilist believes that he believes in God – or in his own ego, which was assumed to possess the same unproblematic and absolute status that God once had – but has in his subconscious already abandoned his faith in God and in absolute vales. His faith is literally only lip-service, an observance of certain comforting, traditional forms. In a more watered down form the privately religious person places a less well-defined being in God's place, but the level of often unconscious hypocrisy is in practice the same. Half-hearted faith exists uncomfortably alongside rationalism, with constant horse-trading and compromises.

The naïve nihilist is therefore characterised by the fact that he says what he thinks sounds good, rather than anything reflecting what he really thinks. He lives in the hope that his beautiful words will beautify even himself. The naïve nihilist is unaware of the existence of the subconscious and of the many depths of his own thinking. To the naïve nihilist, his beautiful words live their own life, completely divorced from a genuinely thought-out value system and the events which could be determined by it. These phrases are the primary source for his social identity. Models only interest him in so far as they refer to tangible facts and produce measurable benefits. The naïve nihilist is, therefore, the ultimate positivist.

Historically, the naïve nihilist is an exemplary democrat and a fully-fledged member of the bourgeoisie; he is the bearer of what Hegel sarcastically calls 'the beautiful soul'. He is an individualist, and strives for self-realisation, because that is what society and the zeitgeist offers. He prioritises the appearance of success over being happy, or rather, to be more accurate, he cannot tell one from the other. Happiness and the appearance of success are the same thing, it is all a matter of playing your role on society's stage. According to the naïve nihilist, the entire performance is arranged according to reason, and all troublesome misunderstandings will be sorted out over time, which in practice means that all deviant opinions will be corrected.

During the introductory phase of informationalism, the naïve nihilist is still dominating public space, above all within politics and science. He proudly parades being religious in a suitably modern way – God lives for a couple of hours on a Sunday morning, but is dead for the rest of the week – and by being liberal at the same time. He prefers dialogue to dogmatism, being well-dressed to being unkempt, and he has an unfailing nose for opportunistic attitudes in opportune subjects, such as: so-called vulnerable groups in society, the third world, exploitation of children and environmental pollution. The naïve nihilist always thinks the right thing in the right context, and this thinking often vibrates with gripping sensitivity. The shedding of more and more crocodile tears is of course ideally suited for the electronic tabloid culture of late capitalism. Televised debates, with their short, sound-bite slogans, are the most advantageous frame for the naïve nihilist.

The cynical nihilist is, in contrast, quite clear about his own atheism, and is happy to heckle a faith he regards as irrational and baseless. God simply does not exist in the real world, only in people's superstitions, and atheism makes things much simpler by sweeping aside masses of old rubbish which is just stopping mankind from seeing its situation clearly and weighing different possibilities against one another. The cynical nihilist wants to go further into a world explained by science and reason. But, on the other hand, he does not spare a thought for the void left by God in society's hierarchies of values and power, and consequently has no concept of the deeper effects of his own atheism. This means that the cynical nihilist is actually still living on in the values of the religious faith he has rubbished, without being conscious of it. The concept of God still permeates his existence as an intangible and nameless spectre, just as active as ever.

As a result, the cynical nihilist is also the last humanist, a sort of unconscious archaeological warden. He claims that God is dead, but he refuses to confront the suddenly very cold and desolate world where God no longer forms part of the preconditions. His reaction to cold and desolation is to seek protection and warmth among likeminded people. The hope is that an increasingly noisy aggression in cynical reasoning can conceal the lack of deeper analysis. Cynical nihilism always develops into extreme relativism; each and every one of us can be saved by our faith, and the nature of that faith is nothing to do with anyone else. What the neighbours do behind their fence is of no interest to the cynical realist, who is frenetically defending himself against unasked for opinions. The cynical nihilist constructs his identity exclusively from negative definitions: he knows what he isn't and what he doesn't believe in. The freedom to identify with something entirely new and to construct entirely new, positive values is out of sight and out of reach. By not setting any expectations, the risk of being disappointed is avoided. With a considerable amount of schadenfreude, the cynical nihilist believes that the wisdom of avoiding difficult reflection upon the true significance of the disappearance of religious faith is made clear by the fear and anxiety demonstrated by foolish worriers. In the long run this attitude is untenable, because it rests upon what is known as a naïve negation.

The oft-quoted remark that there is 'nothing new under the sun', from the Book of Ecclesiastes in the Old Testament, is a classic example of naïve negation. The statement presupposes a certain opinion of what 'something new' could possibly be, and in it there cannot be a new combination of old components, which is why the only time there might have been something truly new was at the moment of creation. Nothing can ever be new in this strict definition, everything is just varying compositions of already existing factors. But because of this the entire suggestion becomes pointless, because it is these same varying compositions which are the interesting thing about history, and in the relevant sense all sorts of new things under the sun are constantly appearing. To deny this is to adopt a point of departure which is absurd, it is only a case of finding an adequate definition of what 'something new' is.

The fundamental atheism of cynical nihilism is a naïve negation of exactly the same kind. What the cynical nihilist claims to deny is the existence of something that is an inescapable reality in the only relevant sense, namely the concept of God which continues to play an extremely active role in the value hierarchy of society – quite apart from anything science might have to say about the actual physical existence of God – and which cannot be replaced by doubt alone, but must be replaced by some new positive value. The cynical nihilist is therefore forced to carry on living with the worldview whose fundamental precondition he claims to doubt. But this denial is always transient, and it is more a matter of finding an adequate definition of the new value which is going to assume the identity-creating function of the concept of God. But in order for this to happen, the cynical phase of nihilism must come to an end and be replaced by the affirmative phase.

The sceptical attitude finally ebbs away in the cul-de-sac where mobilism alone rules, without its dialectical opposite, eternalism, which is its necessary complement. Shut into this cul-de-sac, absolute mobilism develops either into cultural relativism or a romantic longing for an imagined natural state, unsullied by civilisation. Fundamentally, both of these attitudes are expressions of chronic impotence. A sceptic is constantly critical, never creative, never pragmatic. He is the eternal backseat driver, always ready with a contradictory point of view, but incapable of contributing anything which makes the actual driving any easier.

It is cynicism itself which reveals the cynical nihilist and his dependence upon something whose existence he denies. For the atheist, God is a necessity without which his own attitude would be an absurdity, a real phenomenon whose existence it is interesting to debate; God must remain as something which either exists or does not exist, otherwise cynical nihilism itself cannot survive. The energetically denied God has, in the eyes of the atheist, not yet been transformed into a thoroughly logical product of certain power relationships under certain material circumstances, a component which fills a socially cohesive function in a necessary hierarchy of values. Why should the cynic need to be cynical if this is the case? He would realise that this abandoned function must be filled by something else, and progress from non-belief to beyond-belief.

Abandoning cynicism is the conscious act of will which defines affirmative nihilism, for whom the question of God's existence is no longer at all problematical. God was ultimately a concept in society's hierarchy of values under certain historical conditions. The concept of God filled a certain and necessary function, but now conditions have changed, and under current circumstances scepticism is no longer a relevant position. The affirmative nihilist realises the necessity of replacing this and other exhausted concepts with new values which are valid and functional under these new circumstances. But why the delay? Why this time-lag in the creation of concepts and values? If Nietzsche noticed the difference at the end of the nineteenth century, and if Heidegger formalised the distinction only a few decades later, why has it taken until the beginning of the twenty-first century and the growth of an informationalist dominant class for affirmative nihilism to leave its first historical traces?

One initial explanation is obvious: you cannot just conjure forth values you happen to be enamoured of, for whatever reason, just as little as you can develop biological mutations for which circumstances are unsuited, and then expect them to survive and breed successfully just because that is what you want to happen. So it is not a matter of any stringency of philosophical reasoning, but of the conditions which are determined by material and technological circumstances. Consequently, the netocracy could not simply take command of history, that isn't how it works: instead, a new power elite is the result of a new media technology rewarding certain qualities while other forms of talent which have been successful in the past are no longer favoured to the same extent. The netocracy is thus the result of the interactive communication technology which began to develop during the 1970s, and affirmative nihilism is part of the netocratic ideology which has been developed since then. Nietzsche and Heidegger were refiners of concepts with no access to a suitable ecology, philosophers way before or, rather, outside their time.

A number of interesting explanations can be added to this. Firstly, there is a general historical sluggishness, consisting of drawn-out power struggles: what were originally positive forces become reactive counter-forces, an outgoing paradigm retains a considerable mass for a long time, and naturally its dominant elite defend their positions and privileges with all available means. Secondly the collective subconscious is subjected at regular intervals to traumatic shocks which attack thought in the form of self-applied censorship of various sorts. During the 1990s these shocks rained down more intensely than ever before, and thanks to the mass media they became known and commented upon to a remarkable degree. This meant that the century which had seen more comprehensive technological development than any before it was at the same time characterised by a stagnation of ideas which gave rise to the description 'the little Middle Ages'. Mankind was frightening itself to such an extent that it had stopped thinking creatively and innovatively.

The twentieth century was largely devoted to the philosophical, ideological and artistic revision of the collective trauma which arose when nihilism came to the surface of western culture and made its intentions known at the turn of the last century. How could people deal with this newly uncovered, terrible emptiness? Under these tumultuous circumstances, Darwin's natural selection, Nietzsche's will to power and Freud's libido were all largely misunderstood as concepts. More or less intentional misinterpretations served different propaganda purposes. On the one hand it is clear that Darwin, Nietzsche and Freud were thinkers who were literally epoch-making in the final stages of high capitalism and the opening years of late capitalism. On the other hand, all the vulgar interpretations of their ideas have built up to form an almost insurmountable pollution problem for anyone wanting to orientate themselves in the period's world of ideas and to develop their philosophy further.

Marxists, fascists, existentialists, feminists, neo-liberals and postmodernists: these and countless others can be convicted of serious and repeated pollution of the public arena. The lazy lack of demands required by the cynical nihilist encouraged orgies of self-pity and navel-gazing. Beyond that, there were four important problems hampering thought: the trauma of totalitarianism, the collapse of capitalist normativity, the division of the academic world, as well as last but not least, the built-in infantilism and populism of the electronic mass media. Together, these amount to an explanation why late capitalist thinking was to a large extent a vain exercise in resentment.

The collective consciousness was to a large extent split at the beginning of the twentieth century. On the one hand, there was a widespread idea within the liberally minded bourgeoisie that the realisation of capitalism's utopian dreams was imminent. Reason ruled in the form of well-developed nation states, democracy triumphed in the form of increasingly extended voting rights, markets expanded, welfare grew, science produced one sensational discovery after the other. On the other hand, the Victorian world harboured a strong and widespread fear that these improved living standards would result in lethargy and debilitation; there were constant discoveries of new signs that the human race and western society was rapidly becoming emasculated. Everything under the sun, from traditions to marriage, from the sport of rowing to masculinity, was thought to be in deep crisis. In this tense climate, the outbreak of the First World War was greeted with jubilation from almost every group in every nation; the absence of critical voices is explained quite simply by the fact that everyone thought they had something to gain in the trenches. The optimists thought they were preparing new ground for future advances, the pessimists thought the war offered a necessary purging of a decadent civilisation.

In actual fact, it was extremely difficult to discern any winners at all when the smoke had cleared. The only exception in this context was possibly the USA, whose position was strengthened at the expense of the old colonial powers. But otherwise the war, with the new military and media technologies it encouraged, paved the way for a new, industrial form of totalitarianism. As a result of the war Germany, Italy, Japan, Spain and the new nation states of eastern Europe became fascist dictatorships. Russia was hurled into a bloody civil war which ended with a definitive victory for the Communists. The liberal democracies which two decades before had seemed to be on the threshold of the culmination of history, and which believed themselves to be exemplary, were in a difficult position. Totalitarianism was not just a threatening alternative, it even seemed in several respects to be superior to the bourgeois democratic nation state.

One factor in favour of totalitarianism was its extremely well-developed ability to foster a powerful demonology, which created a platform for the massively efficient production of social identity. Germany, governed by a messianic dictator, was a Nazi one-party state built around a Rousseauian notion of the historical supremacy of the Germanic race. Russia, also governed by a messianic dictator, was a Communist one-party state built around a Rousseauian notion of the Russian people's special qualities. Hitler turned politics into aesthetics, Stalin turned aesthetics into politics; their two doctrines seemed to be each other's opposite, and the two regimes used one another as the lead player in their respective demonologies. The conflict between them sucked up all the ideological oxygen of the European continent, where politics quickly polarised. You were either for one and against the other, or vice versa. There was no room for a third alternative, and bourgeois democracy looked impotent and exhausted. Both totalitarian regimes benefited in this way from their mutual antagonism, their common interest in this confirmed by the Molotov-Ribbentrop Pact. The same demonological complex lived on after the end of the Second World War and fall of Nazism, when the East painted the West as fascists, and the West nurtured a permanent terror of Communism.

The strong attraction of utopianism influenced by Rousseau made it synonymous in many people's eyes with radicalism, whereas bourgeois demonology was connected with complacency and stagnation. This even applied within the bourgeois democracies themselves, which were undermined as a result. Utopianism suffered a severe blow with the fall of Communism, when totalitarianism's systematic cruelty and economic collapse were revealed, which in turn led to a dramatic realignment of the intellectual climate. Totalitarianism showed itself to be in many respects even worse than its opponents' propaganda had claimed: its repression was even more brutal, its economic collapse far more pathetic. The silencing of internal criticism clearly did not lead to advantageous non-zero-sum games of any sort. After that the old Left was transformed overnight from Communism to Social Democracy, which admittedly was its only chance of survival, but it meant that the romantic, revolutionary aura lost its attraction. The old radicals could no longer pretend that they stood outside the shabby and unromantic establishment. The philosophy which had not yet recovered from the Auschwitz-trauma of the late 1940s was hit by yet another body blow in the form of a gulag-trauma. Intellectual discourse imploded, all energy was used up in various sorts of denial and defence of having adopted a position on the wrong side. The utopias were admittedly compromised, but utopianism itself must be saved at any cost. The only philosophical alternative on offer seemed to be a stringent professionalisation, through which thinking abdicated the public stage and shut itself away in the dustiest corners of universities to conduct mathematical logical concept analysis. Nothing could be of less concern to the governing power structure.

The response of continental philosophy to the Auschwitz-trauma is called existentialism, a moral code based upon a vulgarisation of the phenomenology of Kierkegaard, Husserl and Heidegger, so full of aggressive decrees that Immanuel Kant's efforts within this petit-bourgeois genre pale in comparison. Auschwitz led to a demand for good and evil to be reinstated as absolute values, which led to Nietzsche and Heidegger either being misinterpreted or relegated to the poison cabinet. Auschwitz became the symbol of evil, a singularity, an historically unique event, instead of yet another genocide using the methods and technology available at the time. This ideology of the victorious powers was raised to the status of an axiom, and the Nuremberg trials were thereby transformed from a judicial process conducted by the victorious powers against the war's losers into a purely moral affair. Good made its reckoning with evil, and critical thinking did not get involved.

Moralism retained its paralysing grip on thinking throughout the whole century in every significant area. Not even the breakthrough of Foucault and Deleuze in the 1960s with a devastating Nietzschean critique of the existentialist agenda was more than a temporary reverse for moralism, because the gulag-trauma soon appeared as an angel of salvation. As a result, it was once again time to start up the existentialist carousel. It was time for yet another renaissance for individual opinions and self-pity. Every tendency towards criticism could be regarded as suspect, every critic could be sent to the confessional; in order to participate in the conversation you had to be able to demonstrate loyalty to the wreck of Rousseau's utopianism. Yet again, critical thinking had lost the fight.

The second major problem hampering thinking during the 1990s was the collapse of capitalist normativity. During high capitalism, marriage had replaced salvation as the emotional core of western society. The height of happiness and the confirmation of social status was no longer devoting oneself to God, but doing your supreme citizenly duty as a pillar of the nuclear family which formed the cornerstone of society. Women's role was to be seen and chosen by responsible men, and thereafter to play the supporting and servile female role which was an indispensable part of the project. Romantic fanaticism forced out its religious counterpart. All of society's production of ideology, all of the mass media machinery, sang the praises of the nuclear family, the familial patriarch and romantic fanaticism. Strict censorship and self-censorship kept the range of entertainment on offer within acceptable bounds.

But these bounds were broken by capitalism's inherent contradictions in the form of its increasing atomisation of society in order to maximise consumption and its increasingly noticeable focus upon the individual: the more households there are, the higher consumption will be. Stability could not be reconciled with productivity. And the situation of women had changed dramatically with the Second World War. Women had been forced out to work and had thus become accustomed to a considerable amount of economic autonomy. In line with increases in welfare and educational standards in the industrialised nations, the birth-rate fell at a corresponding rate. The decline of the manufacturing sector and the rise of the service sector has benefited women at the expense of men, and the traditional male role as breadwinner and head of the family was further weakened. With the wholesale breakthrough of interactivity, even the patriarchal structure itself was undermined; power became more a question of argument and dialogic consequence than of a predetermined position in a hierarchy. The classical patriarch simply no longer appeared credible.

In the climate of the time, the historical subjugation of women became an effective instrument of power: as a so-called vulnerable group, significant favours could be gained in the form of quotas and other special treatment. The rage of feminism against the patriarchal order assured women as a collective a prominent position in the public arena. The women's movement soon gained a number of imitators, first and foremost the gay movement, which proclaimed the cause of equal rights for homosexuals in a world suffused by the heterosexual norm. These pugnacious movements soon gained a foothold in the universities, and as a result even academic discourse was transformed into an arena for a free-for-all of the special interest groups which already dominated the media landscape and political debate.

However, this constituted another devastating attack on critical thinking. Every attempt at reason in the form of systems and larger structures was branded as oppressive by definition, and rejected out of hand. The consequence was a sort of absurd competition in relativism, and total triviality was the cost of no-one feeling insulted or offended. Every minority trumpeted its own special qualities and declared loudly how badly off it was. Everyone had been violated, everyone sued everyone else, demanded apologies and compensation for real or imaginary past wrongs. States and companies which did not want to appear insensitive gave way. Only when it became quite clear that neither a feminist nor any other minority perspective was capable of an analysis of the global transformation constituted by the interactive revolution, was it possible to discern a pathway out of this minority hegemony.

The third problem hampering creative thought through the 1990s was the division of the academic world. Political power was, at least formally, responsible to its citizens at regular intervals, and economic power was constantly at risk on the open market, which created a certain amount of transparency and competition in which the very worst forms of laziness and incompetence were done away with. Even if freedom of choice and influence were both limited in practice, at least there was a form of continuous quality control of a fairly basic model. But where the academic world was concerned, the third corner of the capitalist tripolar power structure, there was not a single sign of any regulatory instance. As a result, there was a complete lack of the necessary incentive to maintain acceptable quality of activity.

The universities willingly gave way to external pressures for faster through-flow, low costs and high marks for everyone, particularly to those belonging to some sort of minority. Where internal tensions were concerned, complaisance was the dominant strategy. When the developing plurarchy caused conflicts within the different academic disciplines during the late 1900s, and when it was no longer possible to maintain full control over the theoretical constructions, these disciplines were chopped up into an endless number of sub-departments rather than having the conflicts between them brought out into the open, which might have led to the maintenance of at least a minimal level of competition, and higher standards. For reasons of comfort, it was decided to nurture and amplify symbolic but illusory conflicts, and to keep quiet about genuine theoretical oppositions. When no-one could see any personal benefit in criticising or competing with the system, criticism dried up entirely.

The consequence was a harmless, insipid multitude, an acute inflation of prefixes, an increasingly desperate excavation of increasingly peripheral niches. As more and more advanced research moved to private laboratories, and more and more qualified intellectual discussion moved to closed networks and think-tanks tied to particular business interests, a rapidly escalating crisis of confidence set in. For the developing netocracy, the academic system seems to be primarily a form of preservation, where the averagely intelligent and discerning are offered occupational therapy so that they do not cause trouble out in the world of real work, or disturb political stability. Degrees and diplomas are therefore rapidly losing their sociometric value, and the knowledge which the universities and colleges have in their possession is gradually becoming more easily attained at ever decreasing cost. As a result quality is sinking still further, because young people possessing the type of talent which is really in demand are staying away in ever greater numbers.

The fourth and final example in our reckoning of the problems hampering critical thinking in late capitalism is the electronic mass media. The medium is, as Marshall McLuhan asserted in the 1960s, to a great extent also the message. This means that the dominant mass media have fundamentally altered our mental environment; that the forms for media consumption are of greater interest that the actual content in one instance or the other, and that the media has its own internal agenda which is entirely independent of either its owner's or its broadcaster's own intentions. The form of communication influences our thought-processes and our acquisition of knowledge, some ideas allow themselves to be expressed and transferred more easily than others in a new media landscape, and, as a result, the frame around what and how we think is adjusted. Totalitarianism is, for instance, intimately connected with effective one-way communication, propaganda is irreconcilable with large-scale interactivity. Both the Nazi apparatus of oppression in Germany during the 1930s and 1940s, and the genocide in Rwanda during the 1990s are therefore difficult to imagine without the radio as the dominant mass medium in these societies at the time in question.

Television was the medium which achieved almost seismic change during the second half of the twentieth century. When, for instance, politicians moved onto television, political discourse changed and its innate preconditions altered radically. Cosmetics became a more important subject than ideology to the media-oriented politician, as Neil Postman writes in Amusing Ourselves to Death. Political debate became, as a result of the form of the television medium, more a question of who was wearing a nice tie, or who seemed pleasant, than a matter of attitudes to certain matters of policy. This depended upon the fact that policy matters proved to be too complicated for television, other factors stole the majority of the attention even during an extremely serious presentation. It was not a question of whether the producer was serious or not, it was all to do with the form of the medium. Since the message had to be adapted to the medium, in reality it became something entirely different, often something which had shown itself to work before in that medium. Politics became, like journalism and everything else which took place in a culture where television functioned as the metamedium – in other words: the medium which set the daily agenda and defined which information had the right impact – merely another type of more or less successful television entertainment.

In a cultural climate where television was the sun around which everything else revolved, the conditions for critical and creative thinking were not ideal, since a talent for complex reasoning on several levels was simply not rewarded as much as it had been during the heyday of the printing press. Other things, such as nice neck-ties, were more important. The explosion of mass interactivity brought with it fundamental changes, changes that it is difficult to gain an overview of and piece together. The need for analysis and a broad understanding is becoming acute, not least because it is possible to discern an increasingly general weariness with superficial visual media. The widespread use of word-processors has also entailed something of a renaissance for text, at the same time as this new text naturally exists in an entirely new context and therefore carries entirely new implications. Besides this, the competition for attentionality is becoming increasingly fierce. The future scenario is noticeably stratified: the netocratic elite will create favourable conditions for the sort of critical thinking which it finds enjoyable and useful, whereas the range of simpler entertainment for the consumtariat underclass will both grow and diversify.

The netocratic elite's interests and legitimacy are closely related to affirmative nihilism. New values, constructed around the global empire, must form the basis of a new society in a global arena. Eternalism's radical pragmatism is replacing both cynical nihilism and every notion of natural entitlements. Since affirmative nihilism is flexible in structure, it does not necessarily need to be scrapped with the next technological revolution, but can be equipped in a relatively painless way with new signatures, and can jettison exhausted values in favour of new, functional ones. With the advent of informationalism, mankind is for the first time in history constructing a value hierarchy in complete consciousness of the actual preconditions of the creation of value. This is the epoch-making aspect of eternalism's radical pragmatism. The table is set for a new period of enlightenment, and informationalism's ethically inclined netocrats are ready to take power from capitalism's bourgeois moralists.

4.

THE RENAISSANCE OF IDEOLOGY

THE CONCEPT OF A WORLDVIEW encompasses much more than just a more or less correct understanding of the current state of society. It also encompasses a partly unconscious and often disjointed, but nevertheless identifiable, idea of history and its driving forces. Because our world is what we have agreed to say that it is, a new pattern of definition implies an entirely new world. Old axioms are suddenly shown, from the perspective of the new paradigm, to be ideological constructions typical of the period. This is therefore not a question of altering one or two episodes in history in the light of a few new facts, but of re-evaluating the foundations of history itself. We are writing a new metahistory.

With a different history, the world becomes a different world. As a result, the current paradigm shift from capitalism to informationalism is inextricably linked to a dramatic change in our understanding of the past. The overriding idea of capitalism, of history seen in purely economic terms – with Karl Marx as its foremost exponent – which is, in turn, founded upon the idea that social development is ultimately determined by material production, has slowly but surely been undermined. One contributing factor is that the transcendentalisation of history essential to this viewpoint, which Marx inherited from Hegel, has, piece by piece, been destroyed by the perspectivism that developed during the twentieth century. A new matrix of interpretation has begun to appear over the shapeless mass of information, which will have revolutionary consequences.

The most significant change in our view of the past is becoming apparent as the most central fundament of capitalism, and the starting point for its entire view of humanity – the indivisible and original individual – is dismantled and replaced by endless causality chains and feedback loops. Our view of the human body is changing, is being de-individualised, and is becoming one variable among others in the endlessly complex equations of history. Changes in our genetic make-up have been negligible throughout the short history of humanity, particularly in comparison with technological developments. The increasing complexity of society is, thus, not a result of human beings becoming gradually more intelligent, but should be seen as a result of our environment having become more intelligent. From an informationalist perspective, the driving force of history is therefore neither genetic nor ideological, nor in any way 'spiritual'. Social development is instead ultimately a question of communication, and therefore of information technology.

Power is ultimately always sociometric rather than economic – it has only been economic during the capitalist epoch, while monetary economics have been the driving force, because power has assumed the character of an economic sociometry – which means that material production is only of a secondary nature.

Circumstances deal a hand of cards which must be played as skilfully as possible. How we play them gradually affects circumstances, but seldom in the way, or to the extent, that we ourselves intend. The factors which make up the current technological complex form the basic preconditions for the distribution of power, status and identity. Each change means that some people gain at the expense of others. This might suggest that history is an endless zero-sum game, but, because newly gained information is constantly being superimposed upon earlier-won information, there is a pattern, a direction towards an ever greater degree of social and technological complexity, making increasingly sophisticated non-zero-sum games possible.

The values of informationalist society must, if they are to endure, appear to be credible even against a widespread and profound awareness that they have no basis in traditional metaphysics. God really is dead, and nature can no longer function as any sort of moral authority or as a guarantor of any rights at all. Informationalism's new values must satisfy a longing for genuine understanding of the conditions of existence, and not primarily be subordinate to the self-interest and wishful thinking of those in power. In an age characterised by mass interactivity, power will have to postpone rewards in the short term in order to protect its long-term credibility. This means that the escapist utopianism that has formed the basis of capitalism's étatistic supraideology must be replaced by a radical pragmatism in the exercise of power.

The historians of informational society are primarily interested in technology and its interaction with other social factors. We use the word technology instead of technique consciously: the latter can retain its original Ancient Greek meaning relating to crafts and building construction. Technique represents humanity's various methods of using mechanical instruments to extend and refine our own bodies and their functions. Technique therefore represents a machine of some sort – whereas technology is a philosophical and sociological concept for the structures created by large clusters of functioning techniques, and, above all, for the multifaceted relations between these clusters and mankind. By this definition, technology in general, and information technology in particular, is what most profoundly characterises a society, and which ultimately determines how power is distributed and identity produced.

What history indisputably shows is that truly revolutionary technological innovations – the mechanical clock, the printing press, and so on – have their own, innate agendas which are generally very different to what their creators imagined or hoped. A technology with this degree of power cannot be controlled to any serious extent. It is not the case, as naïve optimists claim, that these clusters of techniques are neutral tools whose use is determined by human beings. Technology, to use Neil Postman's terminology, plays out its own hand; it determines the framework of what can be done and thought. In so far as we can speak of free will at all, it is strictly limited by the given technological frame. A goldfish can choose to swim to the right or the left of a stone, but it cannot swim outside its bowl. This is not to suggest that it does not matter whether it swims to the right or the left of the stone. But pretending that the glass bowl does not exist is hardly productive.

If it really is technology that determines the division of power and identity production, then this clearly has crucial consequences for our view of history. It means, for instance, that it is not the events which are traditionally identified as the great revolutions in history that are truly revolutionary. The French Revolution of the 1790s, to take one example, must naturally be granted a certain degree of significance – not merely symbolically, but also for practical reasons – but its repercussions are entirely played out within the frame of printing-press technology, without which both the revolution itself, and its driving impetus of Enlightenment philosophy, as well as increased prosperity and the industrialisation that followed it, would have been unthinkable. Therefore the informationalist historian deals with spectacular events of great symbolic significance largely in passing: wars, revolts and proclamations. Instead, attention is focussed on the abstract fields surrounding the bifurcations where paradigm shifts arise, the often chaotic periods and circumstances in which one dominant information technology is phased out and replaced by another.

Genuine revolution is, quite simply, to be found in the introduction and use of a new information technology, whose agenda gradually suffuses the entire culture. What were described as revolutions during the capitalist epoch – more or less violent regime changes, with or without public executions – appear in this new light as spectacular expressions of aggression, loaded with symbolism, which in turn are merely the logical consequence of a preceding genuine revolution. The conditions which determined the exercise of power as a consequence of a dominant technology, the printing press, were expressed, both symbolically and theatrically, on the public stage, but the real revolution had already taken place long before. But theatricality and symbolism were ideally suited to be the starting point for a romanticised ideology that was of vital importance for the self-image of the capitalist era. Written history attached great weight to this sort of theatre, because it essentially supported the system and was incapable of questioning the given preconditions. Both academic battles in universities and political conflicts in parliament confined themselves to symbolically loaded pseudo-problems within the frame of one and the same supraideology.

The transition from feudalism to capitalism was consequently not a question of any sort of ideological breakthrough, nor a historically determined transition to a higher state of civilisational maturity. Rather it was an ecological change that occurred as a result of the existence of the printing press; this apparently innocent innovation meant that humanity's whole ecosystem and life conditions were transformed. Important information could now be spread quickly and in great volumes, which in turn meant that literacy became increasingly more valuable and therefore more widespread, which, in turn, created a new virtual world: public space. Even if the virtual world of public space, in the form of daily newspapers, journals and books, was a comparatively primitive means of one-way communication, particularly when compared to today's global and immediate interactivity, its arrival in the corridors of power meant that the church lost its hold on the worldview, the monarchy had to abdicate from politics, and the aristocracy was forced to relinquish economic and military power.

Once the ball had started to roll, there was no stopping it: a power structure which rested upon hand-written language and a mythology that revolved around a transcendental Eternity was forced aside by a new power structure which was based upon the increased spread of information, in the form of the first mass media, and a mythology that replaced Eternity with transcendental Progress as the purpose and meaning of existence. Theology was replaced by the worship of reason, in the same way as the nobility's titles lost their value when wealth became the ultimate gauge of social status. Capitalism's great project of enlightenment, proud humanism with its steadfast belief in the Cartesian subject, occupied the metaphysical realm, which had the somewhat paradoxical result that reason also occupied the place in life previously taken by unreason. When the old superstitions were swept aside, faith would be replaced by knowledge, and science would provide the answers to all humanity's questions about the meaning of life.

The problem in this is that science is constantly being revised, as is its nature, and, as a result, every truth can only be regarded as provisional. In the absence of an officially sanctioned unreason, the foundations upon which the values of social construction rested were notoriously unstable, which is ironic given that social theory was based upon naïve wishful thinking about a stable and balanced state of normality. The intact Individual, the literally indivisible ego, was installed as the hopefully immovable rock in this unquiet sea, as the unrestricted ruler of the complicated but rational machine that was the human body. The subject was given the task of realising all of his or her innate qualities and abilities, in an ongoing struggle towards sacrosanct Progress.

A paradigm shift always brings with it a new use of language and a new vocabulary. New phenomena require new terminology, at the same time as old terms acquire new meanings. This forms an integrated part of the worldview that develops in harmony with the material changes that follow the dominant technology and the interests represented by the new power. Words like 'truth' and 'reality', 'knowledge' and 'science' are imbued with new meaning, and assume, at least in part, new functions. This also applies, of course, to the transition to informationalism. The old meanings of the words 'feudalism' and 'capitalism' are encapsulated in new ones. The terms are incorporated into the eternalistic philosophy's sophisticated system of repetition and difference, and assume new functions in this new context.

In feudal society, where God was a reality, life was largely characterised by the constant thought of, and constant preparations for, the heavenly kingdom that beckoned in the next life. With the paradigm shift and industrialism, these concepts and ideals were replaced by The Modern Project, which concentrated on continuous expansion and change for the better within the frame of the nation-state society. Utopia was brought down into the material world, but was placed always out of reach, in a glittering future which could only be realised by the most immense effort, on both the personal and the political plane. Eternity was no longer a credible concept, but Progress functioned excellently as a replacement, despite the fact that its contours were strikingly indistinct in a way that was otherwise uncharacteristic of capitalism. Of course, Progress could be measured, but it was never possible to determine when the goal had definitely been reached. It was always shifting further ahead. Which was, of course, what made it functional; the fulfilment of the promise had to be capable of being postponed indefinitely. As a result, the power-wielding class could promise a reward for obedience and diligence, without it ever actually costing anything.

Truth and meaning were no longer bestowed from outside, but from within. Utopia lay slumbering within the very core of the Individual, in human nature, and it became the duty of everyone to 'realise themselves' by energetically testing their potential and their abilities to the utmost to produce the maximum possible benefit. The personal became political, and ever more detailed regulations were internalised. Everyone was expected to be the creator of their own happiness, and their own morality police, where the one was intimately linked to the other. So, to begin with, man was thought to have been created in the image of God, and, when that was no longer sufficiently persuasive, Man was launched as the model for mankind. Being a good human was to strive to be the perfect Human Being; this was the ultimate truth and meaning of life.

Everything was predetermined and governed by the desired outcome. The individual's two options were either to play along according to strict rules, or to neglect his or her own potential and, as a result, be rejected by the machinery of society.

This humanistic pattern of thought was largely based upon, and reinforced by, Newtonian physics and a model of the world which could be likened to a mechanical clock, an unchanging perpetual motion machine, where every cog moves strictly in accordance with the rules, and in carefully co-ordinated interplay with the other parts of the machinery. The role of the human being in the system can be compared to that of the cuckoo in a cuckoo-clock: to comply obediently with the rules and pipe up at regular intervals with cheery exclamations. At the same time, within a capitalist system intoxicated by progress and the pursuit of prosperity, there was a considerably more grandiose vision for utopian Man. This encompassed academic knowledge itself and the idea of an encyclopaedia; a word whose Greek etymology, enkyklios = cyclical + paideia = education, suggests an all-encompassing knowledge which forms a complete circle. The ambition was to collect and combine an exhaustive amount of knowledge, to reveal the eternal principles that govern nature, and to create a complete model of the world within the brain of rational human beings. The ideal of traditional science consequently forms part of the circulation system of capitalist mythology. This is in sharp contrast to the eternalistic science developing under informationalism, the focus of which is on processes and creative problematics, rather than the obsession of capitalist science with confirmed suppositions.

In God's conspicuous absence, History itself assumed a spiritual dimension: it became the holy story of how mankind had ennobled itself and thereby ascended to its rightful place as nature's supreme engineer. To subjugate nature, its own included, was the historic duty of mankind. Human beings were not yet themselves, but must use their own power to become themselves. History was thereby transformed into the ultimate judge, before which both the individual and the whole of society could be held accountable. The consequence was that God did not disappear, but merely changed his name and returned with his powers intact in the form of the Cartesian subject. When we place this atomised ego in a social context, we see how the bourgeois ideal of citizenship takes shape: sober, rational and reliable. The Cartesian subject was therefore a concept whose success in the meme-Darwinian arena was almost total, but the concept was also extremely well suited to life in an increasingly urban landscape, where atomisation and individual isolation were steadily increasing in line with narcissism. For today's developing netocracy, on the other hand, the Cartesian subject looks at least as bizarre as the concepts of Adam and Eve ever have.

The cohesive, individual subject – sovereign in relation to both body and environment – replaced the monotheistic god as the fundament of social metaphysics, and therefore also as fuel for identity production. The entire rationalist model rested, paradoxically, on this wild, empirical and, from a rational point of view, entirely unfounded guess; despite much laborious searching, the ego's mystical and impenetrable hiding-place within the body was never found, which of course it was essential to conceal at all costs. The Cartesian subject was therefore elevated, precisely because of its central role in the power structure, to the status of a transcendental axiom beyond all questioning. The dictatorship of theology was replaced by the dictatorship of scientific truth, despite the latter being fundamentally just as unscientific, if not more so. The relevant question that arises here is how the corresponding change will look in conjunction with our era's transition from capitalism to informationalism. What is going on under the surface, in the collective subconscious? How are ecological changes affecting our worldview, and thereby our world? And what will the political consequences be? These questions can only be answered by an archaeological excavation in the ruins of capitalism.

Bourgeois democracy had to provide a number of different ideologies, represented by different political parties. At regular intervals the voter was given a choice between a number of different alternatives. Party X would lower taxes a couple of percent, whereas party Y would safeguard current levels of taxation, and party Z might have had another position. Basically, however, these ideologies were merely variants of one and the same overriding idea of the State as the only legitimate instance of power: étatism, an idea which was in turn sanctioned by the metaphysics of capitalism: humanism. According to this idea, the State embodied the holy will of the people in the same way that the church had represented God's interests on Earth during the feudalistic era. To an extent, in young democracies an ideology was identifiable with a particular party and social group, which meant that political elections were often a question of which group, or class, would succeed in controlling the state and protect its own interests. But as prosperity increased and was distributed, the various classes became more similar and shared, in all important respects, the same interests; the lower-class was gentrified just enough so as not to constitute a disruptive threat, which meant that the class-struggle also slowly expired.

The different ideologies melted together so as to be indistinguishable, the common étatistic supraideology became more apparent, and the parties were forced to devote themselves to trying to fuel negligible and symbolic pseudo-conflicts as best they could in an effort to continue attracting attention and conceal the fact that they basically belonged to an ideological cartel. Politics was medialised and intimised. Because there were no longer any genuine alternatives to choose from, the People no longer existed to manifest the will of the People. All that was left was a carefully directed piece of theatre, with a great herd of voters in the non-speaking parts. It is hardly surprising that the voters lost interest, and stayed away from polling stations in increasingly large numbers. Eventually observers of the process began to speak of the death of ideologies.

The crisis of democracy is also a crisis for étatism. Interactivity on a global scale weakens both the state and democracy in several respects (as we examine in detail in Netocracy). As a result of more and more issues being moved from the level of the state, democracy is also undermined when politicians appear as powerless, ignorant puppets in the hands of well-organised special-interest groups. The netocracy has great difficulty finding any reason to engage in this old, exhausted form of politics. And the consumtariat can easily find more titillating entertainment in the immense array of one-way communication media that is aimed at the underclass.

Democracy's crisis is concealed behind a wall of transcendental romanticism. As soon as western interests are threatened anywhere in the world, Democracy is wheeled out and extolled as an absolute necessity. In the propaganda, Democracy is presented as the only imaginable guarantee of both freedom and prosperity, and the only possible alternative is still depicted as a tyrannical dictatorship surrounded by barbed wire, as if the national state in the capitalist mould was, once and for all, the best of all possible worlds, and not a product of certain historical, and ultimately technological, conditions. But to more and more people it is becoming increasingly apparent that the self-aggrandising marketing of the political class in the nation-state, and its stubborn fight to preserve the system, lack all credibility.

So far, the developing plurarchy does not have any particularly clear contours. It has not yet developed the political and philosophical concepts that are needed to dominate a political arena in which the scenery is changing rapidly. But it is merely a question of time. Interactive media-technologies are driving a political culture in which democracy is disintegrating and the plurarchy gaining a foothold in the cracks. When geographically delineated space is no longer relevant, and when people form virtual communities with no regard to national boundaries, bourgeois democracy and national legislation just look like exhausted phenomena. And when the Cartesian subject and the self-realising individual no longer appear to be either desirable or credible, Man will be replaced by the Network as the highest ideal. This will be the last nail in humanism's coffin, and we shall be able to move on.

Eternalistic thought is based upon the Nietzschean interplay between repetition and difference. Applied to social structures, this means that eternalism advocates the perfect Network in the form of an infinite, creative loop as the very basis of the metaphysics without which not even informationalism can manage. In this respect, the netocrat looks like the very personification of Nietzsche's superman, in so far as he himself creates his values in conjunction with immanent reality, primarily through active networking, instead of passively assuming his place in an enforced hierarchy of values. The cynical nihilism which characterised postmodernism will therefore be replaced at the breakthrough of informationalism by an affirmative nihilism with netocratic ideals. In contrast to postmodernists, netocrats have once and for all reconciled themselves to the collapse of the modern project, and regard it as a historical necessity rather than a failure. They even regard its conclusion as a perfect opportunity to act themselves, rather than merely reacting. The time has come for the netocrats to carry out their own Nietzschean Versuch.

Capitalism's legitimate ideologies arose in the meeting between all-encompassing étatism and the collective interest groups which appeared in society. But even pronounced anti-étatistic ideologies, such as anarchism, anarcho-syndicalism and objectivist libertarianism had important roles to play. Naturally they had to be excluded from all forms of power, but they formed pittoresque elements in the system's demonology and strengthened, as a result of their role as theatrical but ultimately harmless threats, support for democracy and the nation-state's collective identity. It is a fact that every society produces a demonology for this very purpose. As for every biological organism, but for partially different reasons, it is essential for social structures to have a boundary that defines what forms part of the collective by pointing out what is excluded. Creating an exhaustive definition of the structure's own identity would be extremely demanding in terms of time and resources; it is considerably more economical to position the structure in relation to a number of strategically chosen contrasts. A negatively defined identity like this is also extremely resistant to attack and comparatively insensitive to external criticism. The most effective identity production is therefore a form of parasitism on the selected demons' attentional value. Capitalism developed the demonological method to perfection. Hegel's dialectical metaphysics, which seems increasingly to have been the intellectual zenith of this paradigm, even elevates the demonological method to the status of an objective truth about existence itself.

Because étatism was the supreme political ideology of capitalism, all sorts of anti-étatistic movements were granted leading roles in the demonology. These movements were, by definition, anti-democratic, socially subversive, and terrorist in nature. But most important was the fact that their ambitions were completely unrealistic, because their prognoses lacked all connection to the governing circumstances. Despite this, the strong identity of demonised outsider status proved a temptation to many, not least to the many naïve academics who could afford to play at being dangerous class-traitors without ever having to risk their place in the social hierarchy. The demonological complex ensured that the state was further strengthened, and the middle-classes were provided with material, in the form of their own scandalous behaviour, for piquant tales to relate at dinner-parties.

One clear indication of the crisis of the capitalist paradigm was that the étatistic demonology eventually lost its potency; the demons that had once been so frightening were transformed into medialised pop-culture. Thanks to the punk culture of the 1970s, the anarchist became yet another Disney character among countless others.

Anarchy was no longer perceived as a threat to middle-class democracy, but was reduced to becoming yet another trademark for fashion designers to play with. This exploitation of the system's own demons can, in the short term, be seen as a victory for the system, by which it proves itself invincible, but in actual fact it reveals a form of slow suicide, because the system's socially cohesive symbols quickly lose their value, leading to the implosion of identity production. By consuming what the French philosopher Georges Bataille calls 'the sacred', that which forms the very core and most essential part of its own conceptual world, the late-capitalist order presided over its own demise. When capitalism deprived itself of the capacity to maintain a credible demonology, and thus protect its own identity, it paved the way for an already vital informationalism. The bourgeoisie went into the final battle without any weapons, and with no chance of offering resistance. All the old weapons were now kitsch curiosities, incapable of mention without irony. The death of the ideologies was therefore a fact.

The implosion of capitalism is confirmed by the dramatic fall in the stock of the nation-state, the paradigm's most important concept of identity creation. The nation-state once appeared as a hybrid between the myth of the nation – a romantic idea of a uniform culture built upon a common language and origins, a common history and common traditions – and the concept of the state – the legitimate representative of the collective subject. This ideological fiction was directed from a very real capital city, and it is in this fundamental sense that we use the word capitalism: a collective subject, with its base in the capital, which subordinates the surrounding territory and a number of other cities in order to feed its insatiable hunger for labour and raw materials in a constant struggle with other competing capital cities.

As support for the capitalist system, the collective subject created great masses of ideology. Just as the feudal system needed the Devil and his calamitous temptations, so the Nation State was forced to produce a comprehensive demonological rogues' gallery of both internal and external enemies, in order to maintain its own identity-fostering function. It is this central role which the Nation State has become incapable of managing in our era, which becomes apparent when we confirm that few, if any, of the highly industrialised nations are prepared to go risk death for something as obsolete as national identity any more. The only surviving superpower, the

USA, sends in ground troops consisting of professional soldiers only in extreme instances, and otherwise restricts itself to highly technological warfare from the air and from far-flung outposts to achieve its goals. The loss of any soldier is now regarded critically by opinion back home. The days of classic warfare between separate nation-states are therefore numbered. The military conflicts of the future will take the form of civil or guerrilla wars within the frame of a global system.

In the myth-construction of the collective subject, its own gravity is presented as natural and ordained by fate by the mystical origins of the people in question. But this gravity is entirely dependent upon the potency of the external threat that is conjured up for better or worse reasons. Thus the demonology occupies a key role in this context. In the same way that the parents and their early, painful absence foster a child's identity in Lacanian psychoanalysis, so it is the external threat, real or fictitious, which gives rise to a society's identity, rather than any internal qualities. The mythology surrounding the utopian project – the origins of the people, the people's culture, the people's fate – is admittedly also an important component, but its primary function is cosmetic: to camouflage the large black hole at the core of the project, and to conceal the fact that the whole apparatus is based upon a crass system for the division of power and status. Because no subject, either individual or collective, can survive and retain its cohesion without a constantly upgraded demonology.

This connection between project and demonology must not be revealed or admitted, relations must instead be presented as a dialectic opposition. Exactly how this process functions can be studied by looking at the creation of relatively young and heterogeneous nations like the USA and India, where the collective subject in question found its original form in opposition to the retreating colonial power. For the mental decolonialisation of North America and India to succeed, a retroactive demonisation of the British colonisers was required.

Hostile ideologies often function best as external demons if their representatives are easily recognisable, if their evil intentions can already be discerned in their strange and frightening facial features. This is why the Soviet Jew became a fascist, while the German Jew under the Nazis was reinvented as a communist. Thus racism became the capitalist equivalent of feudalism's faith in the devil, and an ever-necessary ingredient in all forms of nationalism.

The link between nation and state in turn resulted in a demonology built upon the connection between cosmopolitans and anti-étatists, an exotic cocktail which, because of its exoticism, came to be cherished within the western academic class whenever it wanted to distance itself from the petit-bourgeois nationalism that was enriching itself and becoming ever more widespread at the turn of the last century. The tension between the middle-class engaged in business, whose values were in tune with the mythology of the nation-state, and the already established, educated middle-class, whose values were starting to gravitate against the same nation-state's demonology, led in time to a situation where every guerrilla-movement in the Third World could count on having at least one influential mouthpiece on every European and North American university campus.

This role-play resulted, in turn, during the hectic days of late-capitalism, in the establishment of an anarcho-liberal counter-demonology based upon the vulgarised Hegelian concept of the end of history, thanks to the final victory of bourgeois democracy over all its rivals. Their opponents' demonised certainty in victory strengthened the cohesive identity of essentially self-assumed outsider status. This outsider status was, however, entirely fictitious, as was confirmed when the champagne socialists in question were entirely subsumed by the market forces they had so vehemently opposed, only to reappear in the form of a temporally-adjusted and fashionable so-called postcolonial Marxism. This process made it clear, once and for all, how Marxism had always been an integrated part of the capitalist system, and had never entailed any genuine system-criticism to match the phraseological radicalism of its own propaganda.

Since the bourgeoisie was the dominant class during capitalism, it was also the sociometric ideal against which all other groups were measured, or measured themselves. Its political ideology, liberalism, was an offshoot of bourgeois humanism. The theory of the end of history is true in so far as all other ideologies have eventually been subsumed into this bourgeois humanism in line with the gradual absorption of the whole of society into the middle-class. The end of history and the death of ideologies are one and the same thing. But this theory, naturally, is only valid within the frame permitted by the paradigm. When the fundamental cultural and economic conditions are changed as a result of an information-technological revolution, history will once again be in motion. And, as a result, the necessary conditions for a renaissance of ideology arise.

A social force sooner or later always meets a counter-force. Bourgeois humanism was consequently met with a dwindling but not entirely powerless feudal power structure in the form of the aristocracy, the church, the monarchy and a generally reactionary ideology: conservatism, a postfeudal humanism. As a result of the blessings of the printing-press, levels of literacy eventually reaching the factory-floor, yet another collective subject was produced, the working-class, and yet another ideology, socialism, or proletarian humanism. These were all fingers of the same hand. When their internal differences had been sorted out and the demands of the different interest groups had been met through a long line of redistributive compromises – a continuous adjustment is carried on throughout every paradigm in accordance with the second law of thermodynamics – then the different ideologies are revised and eventually fused together on all planes bar the purely formal.

This is the thermodynamic death of ideologies, where all energy transference has ceased because there are no longer any differences in temperature. All that remains of the political debate after this living death is general opportunism and mass-medial entertainment of varying quality, a form of simulated politics, a performance to galleries that echo ever emptier. Nietzsche predicted as early as the late 1800s that democracy would eventually reach a final phase of rapidly escalating apathy. For the cynical nihilists of the elite in power, this state appears to be a happy end to history, a state which thereby makes cynical nihilism indispensable for all eternity. But for the affirmative nihilists of the young netocracy, the growing apathy towards the forms and content of democracy signal an opening for an entirely different political order, with new players and game-rules. It means the beginning of their story.

Identity production can never achieve 100% coverage. In order to avoid unmanageable fragmentation, and to create collectives capable of surviving in the meme-Darwinian arena, a certain level of rounding off and horse-trading between different sub-groups is necessary. In the gaps between the various ideological complexes and classes, small pockets of identitilessness inevitably appear. These vacuums were occupied and exploited during the early period of late-capitalism by the groups of intellectuals who had found themselves, or positioned themselves, beyond the public spaces of capitalism. The increasingly top-driven class-ideologies were therefore gradually complemented by various extremist movements which filled the social gaps by absorbing the social elements that were left over. These movements directed their efforts with increasing aggression against the very interest groups that were fighting for political space and economic redistribution, and accused them of being parasites on the collective subject for their own ends.

Outsider status was expressed in a burning desire for a complete and all-encompassing social collective. No leadership from above, no hierarchies! This required that the transcendentalisation of the collective subject be driven a stage further; the transcendentalisation process itself had to be turned into the central hub of identity production. The will of the people had to create its own history, instead of resigning itself to subordination to economic forces. Positive action in the name of the collective was by definition moral, and democracy was merely a mendacious bourgeois institution which represented a loathsome hindrance to development. The people could, according to this viewpoint, only realise its utopian potential if it was driven forward with the help of the whip. Utopia was a question of achievement and privation, not of historical necessity at all. This theologised political thinking fostered a succession of totalitarian ideologies in the vacuums left behind by the more pragmatic alternatives. By cultivating an extreme antagonism between themselves, these movements could also make use of one another as antithetical demons.

In Germany, Russia and Central Europe extremism was favoured by the fact that a relatively large and well-educated middle-class in these late-developed industrial nations had been held back from exerting any political influence as long as possible. As a result of the delayed development in these nations, it was the aristocracy rather than the bourgeoisie which had been responsible for their industrialisation, and the prospects for an inclusive democracy along the lines of the Western European or North American model, entirely characterised by a bourgeois middle-class and its values, looked anything but good. Instead, more and more people were attracted by totalitarian and militaristic solutions to the political problem of power and identity. The inability of postfeudal power to manage the forces which industrialisation had released created enormous tensions which, in the absence of a belief in the future, came to be expressed in a gradually more brutal political paranoia. The situation was further complicated by the widespread chaos and desperation in Central and Eastern Europe after the First World War, exemplified by the Russian Revolution and the Versailles Treaty which proved so fateful for Germany. The result was a bifurcated development towards two extreme poles, each dependent upon and strengthened by the other in a demonological loop. One movement raised the People to the status of guiding principle, and directed its hatred towards the Individual and everything that could be perceived as diluting the pure essence of the People. When it came to power this movement struggled frenetically to exterminate interest groups in the name of a single romanticised collectivism with a single common, national agenda (Nazism, fascism, Stalinism). A comprehensive and fear-inducing security force was justified by the necessity of suppressing the People's internal enemies in the form of disobedient and egotistical individuals. This terror against the nation's own citizens soon developed into what could almost be described as a nationalised industry; the most frightening thing about Auschwitz and the Gulag is not their exposure of human cruelty – we are all, deep down, all too well aware of that through our own subconscious – but the devastating industrial effectivity that effective one-way communication was capable of producing. This was the ecstatic golden age of blind electronics – radios and telephones.

The other movement had the Individual as its highest ideal, an individual who was either a Rousseauian child of nature, bubbling with innate goodness, or a deeply enlightened rationalist. Even this hyperindividualistic theology fought interest groups as part of its campaign against anything related to a collective solution. These hyper-Cartesian individualistic romantics regarded every form of social agreement as an unacceptable demand as soon as any single person felt that their freedom was restricted (anarchism and anarcho-liberalism). Bourgeois democracy was merely a fraudulent producer of legitimacy for a repressive state. The absence of functional pragmatism, however, made this movement politically impotent: it succeeded in creating a considerable and often violent level of political unrest, but never became a permanent factor in power anywhere, which is why, between its increasingly rare outbursts, it was largely characterised as a harmless academic society game for unworldly, quasi-radical dreamers.

Both these variants of extremist ideology were doomed to fail from the outset, for the simple reason that the blinkered nature of their programmes lacked any capacity to connect with and manage the fundamentally contradictory nature of the capitalist paradigm. They did not have the innate flexibility required, and they were not rooted in immanent reality. Their objective was not to function in the reality at hand, but to create an entirely new reality for themselves. They were theological remnants of a vanished feudal era – God is executed in name only, while the corpse is actually placed at the centre of extremism; in the case of Lenin, Stalin and the Japanese generals, quite literally so – and they only succeeded in creating vast amounts of mendacious political romanticism and inexpressible amounts of suffering.

We are standing on the threshold of a new paradigm, driven by a new, dominant information technology. The growth of capitalist ideologies was, in all essential respects, predictable when viewed in terms of the prevailing conditions. The question now is what we can say in that respect about informationalism, how many of the contours of the post-humanist ideological complex can already be identified. The ideologies which have died – and this deserves to be repeated – are those which were created during, and adapted to, the specific conditions of capitalism. The fact that they are going to their grave together with the paradigm with which they were integrated, and whose interest groups they represented, is hardly surprising. This fact is, however, nothing to take as a pretext for saying that the new paradigm will be free of ideologies, but rather the reverse. New social structures demand new explanatory models and new political goals. These ideologies will be created in the field which arises between eternalistic thought, ultimately determined by technology, and the new interest groups which will gradually form as a result of the new stratification which will also ultimately depend on technology. Admittedly, this drawn-out process partly precedes the new technology's breakthrough, but is only completed long afterwards.

The ideological criticism of the twentieth century, strongly inspired by the increasing medialisation of society, inflicted severe damage on humanism, and therefore prefigured a form of post-humanist thought. However, this ideological criticism was antithetical rather than synthetic in its relation to enlightened rationalism, and it was not anchored in any interest group beyond increasingly isolated academic circles. This meant that ideological criticism, despite its brilliant wealth of ideas, never succeeded in presenting a credible ideological alternative. This could hardly have been expected either: before the turn of the millennium it was practically impossible to get an overview of the extent and consequences of the technological transformation. Twentieth-century political philosophy lacked the information-technological view of history necessary for informationalist thought.

All exercising of power, apart from direct violence or the threat of direct violence, is ideological. Everyone in power must be able to call upon a legitimacy that is based upon an ideological agreement if they are to have any hope of being heard, otherwise they will quite simply be powerless. The ideological element, in the form of explicit or implicit agreements, is becoming more important the further we move from a tribal society based upon the direct use of violence, and the more complex networks of mutual dependency we develop. Consequently, the death of the ideologies at the end of the twentieth century resulted in both a nominal and an actual loss of power for the representatives of bourgeois democracy. Ideologies lost their power of attraction, large numbers of voters broke the agreement and turned their backs on politics. Power began to migrate.

As social networks become increasingly sophisticated, power becomes more abstract, distributed and transparent, which means that the ideological structure which supports power is becoming indispensable. All that is required is for the interactive culture's so-called netiquette to reach the critical point of sophistication and attentionalism where the renaissance of ideology can take off. So all ideas about an ideologically bereft state lack all credibility. An absence of ideology would require a scarcely plausible return to pure power-positivism: might is right. The existing need for ideology is therefore bound to be fulfilled. Vigilance in the form of a qualified debate is to be recommended, because hidden contradictions, like hidden coup-attempts, would be brought into the open thereby. It is in the impressionable introductory phase that the possibilities of exerting any influence are at their greatest.

Immediately before the turn of the millennium, as a result of the stalled ideological development of energy, a remarkable – albeit typical of a paradigm shift – variety of different forms of political paralysis and diverse extravagant conspiracy theories arose around the issue of globalisation, the subject which has dominated political philosophy in recent years. However, those politicians who insist on performing on the nation-state level in order to exercise power in the traditional way are doing themselves and the members of their class a disservice. No amount of wishful thinking can restore the issues which have been raised to supranational organisations to their increasingly irrelevant forms of regionally-coloured ceremonies. Besides, the market always stands to gain from transparency and clarity, which is why a globally co-ordinated policy is desirable in this respect as well.

Ideological naïvety in the debate could be thought to be remarkable in a society where insight into the value of an escalating non-zero-sum game is widespread, particularly when the politics that is being desired does not benefit any interest groups apart from a small group of heavily subsidised farmers in the highly industrialised nations. Once the mass-medial sensation value has died down, the realisation of the wisdom of Lenin's advice will grow, that functional activism must always be preceded by profound ideological insight. The anti-globalisation movement is revealed to be self-contradictory, by being yet another example of all-encompassing cultural globalisation, and will turn, as eternalistic ideology makes its breakthrough, into a fight for political globalisation, the realisation of the world-state and the principle of one man, one vote at the global level. Only a political system based upon the application of this principle has the capacity to balance the effects of economic globalisation and the market where one dollar equals one vote.

The fact that academics fawn on for politicians, who in turn fawn on the markets, indicates that the necessary balance between the various poles in capitalism's tri-polar power structure has been lost, which in turn forms one reason for, and also a consequence of, the ongoing paradigm shift. We have no reason to expect deliverance in the form of any new thinking from the traditional sources, either from academics or politicians, because they have their old privileges to safeguard, while the actors within the market are fully occupied with maintaining the value of their companies' shares. The panic which is visible in some quarters could have its origins in a hazy realisation that what has been somewhat triumphantly termed the end of history is actually just the end of a certain specific history, namely that of the bourgeois era of power.

Consequently a vacuum is forming, one which must be filled, a growing demand for fulfilment, an increasingly desperate need for a clearly formulated political philosophy. When the new interest groups have established themselves and eternalistic thinking has coloured the worldview which is still on the drawing board, then identity production will begin in earnest. Certain conditions are negotiable in this context. Modified variations of old thought processes will not do, because they are only valid within the frame of an obsolete worldview. No, it is necessary to go back to basics, to leave no stone unturned, to question every aspect of our thinking. A new ontology is also required, an entirely new way of thought, one which is credible in the critical eyes of the actors of informationalism.

5.

THE DIALECTIC BETWEEN ETERNALISM AND MOBILISM

TO CONSTRUCT A POLITICAL philosophy which is credible for the information society, it is necessary to return to the basis of philosophy. This is unavoidable in conjunction with a paradigm shift, because the very foundations of the exhausted worldview are gradually disappearing beneath our feet. So what is it that actually exists, and what is it that does not exist? What can we confidently say about that which exists, and what does it really mean to say that something actually exists? How do the world, language and thought relate to one another, what are the consequences of the fact that our perception is rigidly governed by preconceptions, and what status does this give what we call truth?

Informationalist philosophy is based upon the conceptual pair of eternalism and mobilism. The fact that this constellation, and indeed, the following chapters, seem complicated is because they are genuinely complicated. In actual fact, this is literally the most complicated thing of all, because to a large extent it deals with things which can, admittedly, be discussed, but of which it is nonetheless by definition impossible to construct a mental image. We are forced to think through problems which we otherwise ignore. In an attempt to simplify matters, the relationship between eternalism and mobilism is often compared to that between the concepts digital and analogue, but this analogy does not actually lead to any greater degree of clarity, because the dialectic process is altogether too multifaceted.

The concepts of eternalism and mobilism are really rather more closely related to the platonic concepts cosmos and chaos, but because the informationalist society which is developing is radically different in all important respects from ancient Athens, even this comparison has its limitations, not least where the internal dynamic between the two concepts is concerned. In contrast to cosmos and chaos, eternalism and mobilism are not in a classical dialectic relationship to each other, a preconceived antagonism where the one defines and presupposes the other. The universe – that which exists – can perfectly well be thought to exist without the presence of observers and their constructed models of the universe, and could thus be characterised – that is to say: if there were anyone who could observe anything at all, and if this could be characterised without constructed models – as purely mobilistic, without any requirement of eternalism to define itself against. And vice versa: we can imagine intellectual objects in the form of structured models (a perfect example is mathematics) which are in themselves strictly eternalistic, without their necessarily being in relation to any form of mobilism.

This is therefore not a case of a defined oppositional relationship between eternalism and mobilism – as in the platonic dualism between cosmos and chaos – but of an immensely complex production process, an interaction which results in a more or less generally accepted perception of reality, an eternalisation of the actual properties of existence itself. The synthetic relationship between eternalism and mobilism is therefore entirely open, and is not preceded by a determining chronological chain of events. The one concept cannot be said to be primary in relationship to the other according to the strict formula thesis-antithesis; eternalism and mobilism connect to each other instead in a constantly revolving spiral, with neither beginning nor end. Each gradation or sequence is completely arbitrary, depending entirely upon the perspective of the observer. If we persist in the analogy with the platonic concepts cosmos and chaos, we must imagine the concepts as transferred from Plato to Heraclitus, who anticipated the stoics and is therefore generally regarded as the first mobilist.

One illuminating example of the dialectic between eternalism and mobilism in action is the actual connection between them. Even this fundamental relationship must be seen from a double perspective if it is to be understood at all. According to mobilism, the process lacks both beginning and end, it is not linear. But from an eternalistic perspective, on the other hand, it has both a beginning and an end, it is extremely linear. The process must of necessity have a beginning and an end, for the trivial but fundamental reason that linearity is an inherent pattern within the perceptual process governed by eternalistic laws, even if the basis for the connection from a mobilist perspective, imagined before perception, is infinitesimal, and its end, beyond perception, is infinite.

Another simplified but pedagogically useful way to look at the matter is to say that mobilism is based upon the physical, the immanent, whereas eternalism is based instead upon the mental and metaphysical. The complexity of this relationship becomes apparent in the fact that this definition itself is typically eternalistic, so it must be immediately followed by a powerful mobilistic reservation in order, paradoxically, to achieve the greatest imaginable eternalisation. This mobilistic reservation declares that even these relations, between the observer and his surroundings, are in flux and are constantly intertwined, which is clearly illustrated by the fact that we are forced to apply eternalistic concepts to describe mobilist reality, and vice versa, to apply mobilistic concepts to describe the eternalistic reality. The stronger we want to present a mobilist understanding, the more eternalistic the formulation will have to be, and vice versa: the stronger we want to present an eternalist understanding, the more mobilistic the formulation. It is precisely here, in the double perspective produced in the dialectic between eternalism and mobilism, that informationalism is constructing its specific image of reality.

With this we say goodbye to classical philosophy's desire to achieve eternal harmony of thought. Such harmonious thought would not actually be thought at all. In the light of the late-capitalist critics of the Enlightenment, Jacques Lacan and Gilles Deleuze, the totalistic philosophy which has dominated the field entirely up to our time appears as little more than the deathwish of thought itself; the only perfect harmony which exists is death itself. What is original and visionary in Lacan and Deleuze becomes apparent if one compares their ontological starting points with those of their contemporary rivals, late-capitalism's so-called postmodernists. Whereas the latter are obsessed with revealing the illusory nature of the generally accepted worldview – an obsession which is intimately interwoven with the very rationalism that postmodernism declares itself to criticise – Lacan and Deleuze indicate instead the necessity and productiveness of the fact that mobilist reality and the eternalised view of reality are so markedly different from each other.

This means that while postmodernism's cynical nihilists are still toiling within the frame of rationalism with their anti-rationalism, Lacan and Deleuze have already crossed the boundary to transrationalism and, therefore, paradoxism. The starting point for paradoxist philosophy is that the fundamental contradiction of thought – the double perspective, the chronic element of fiction – is not some infernal system fault, but instead the very condition for productive philosophy, and, on the most basic level, clearly also the condition for thought itself. The concepts of transrationalism and paradoxism are illuminating: this is a question of a philosophical logic which embraces and also promotes the innate contradictions of its own logic and the unavoidable limitations of thought. The negative connotations of the phrase 'problem complex' have been turned into the positive goal and meaning of thought.

From this perspective, what has hitherto been presented as the failure of rationalism can instead be seen as a successful phase in a longer historical development, where the original direction behind anti-rationalism can be seen as the subconscious search for a new and deeper truth beyond the relativism of cynical nihilism and its categorical denial of all attempts to define truth. Transrationalism can be seen positively as the improbable synthesis of rationalism's excessive faith in the capacity of human reason to conceive of the whole of existence – which culminated in Hegel's identification of human reason as the truth of existence – and anti-rationalism's disillusioned criticism of rationalism's utopian desires after the spectacular collapse of the modernist project.

Both rationalism and anti-rationalism are utterly spent and exhausted; transrationalism is the only passable way into the informationalist paradigm. It turns classic, totalistic philosophy inside out and sets off in the opposite direction. The relativism of cynical nihilism is not the solution to the problem, but the solution to the problem is not actually of primary interest anyway. And the problem is not a lack of answers and truths, both are constantly produced in great quantities; rather it is a question of relevance and application. Instead of the eternal question's fateful search for an answer, we now see how paradoxist thought takes its starting point in an imaginable answer in order to create countless new questions, which expresses a refusal to end up in yet another cul-de-sac in the form of insufficiently thought-out systematics, or to sink in a bottomless relativism in which the solution to the problem seems out of reach.

While Nietzsche, Lacan and Deleuze are merely individual forerunners, informationalism's netocrat is the first large-scale paradoxist. He accepts and welcomes a creative and unending dualistic relationship – within which, to take just one illuminating example, the dualism is basically eternalistic and the relation basically mobilistic – and allows himself willingly and consciously to be coloured by the consequences implied by the paradigm's inbuilt and fundamental paradoxism. Reality is, to express the matter in Lacanian terms, nothing more than the illusion of reality.

We find the basis of philosophy, as the thought of thought itself, as an abstract and elusive impulse in intuitive intelligence. This impulse becomes concrete as an artistic form of thought only when it is filtered through logical reason. Philosophy does not, therefore, arise in pure form as a thought, but is formed only in the communicative process. This means that it is bound to play by the rules of language; not entirely unlike the way in which an artist is forced to adapt his artistic vision to the expressive medium he uses, and only through that can produce art. Because language is a game with conventional symbols which refer horizontally to each other within the system's closed halls of mirrors, it is extremely eternalising by nature. So philosophy can never reach nor describe immanent, mobilist reality as such, but at best merely produce a continuous series of eternalisations.

This leads us to what is and must be the role of philosophy within informationalist society: to drive the eternalisation of existence as far as possible. Eternalist philosophy is thus aware that it is ultimately complimentary; its task is to supply the product which the immanent world itself lacks. Philosophy is always an eternalisation of our already existing, intuitively understood worldview. Its credibility is not bound to any revelation of hidden, objective truths about existence, which was what was expected of classical philosophy, but rather it is bound to creative embodiments of the worldview which is already latently present in the borderland between perception and consciousness. Consequently eternalist philosophy is primarily concerned with staging 'aha' moments, giving words to that which can already be experienced as known, but which is not yet formulated and thus not made conscious or communicated. It does not seek any ultimate truth, a magnitude which by definition cannot exist within the arena in question. It is not a science, but is instead concerned with mapping the ideological resonances within the collective subconscious.

Eternalist philosophy communicates with the participants in the game by creating a transformative bottom resonance, a sort of metaresonance of thought, within the collective soundbox of thought. That this overwhelming thought-system of informationalism goes by the name of eternalism is explained by the fact that the concept encapsulates the system's timeless qualities such as thought – thought which only recognises the inbuilt conditions of thought as axioms – without in any way denying its historical belonging as a fulfilled fact within the informationalist paradigm. In comparison, terms such as transrationalism and paradoxism are entirely dependent on the concept's chronological localisation in the history of philosophy. It would be meaningless, for instance, to speak about a form of transrationalism which precedes the antithetical relationship between rationalism and antirationalism, nor is it meaningful to speak of paradoxism before or without the totalistic tradition of thought. These concepts must therefore – just like the recurrent phrases civilisationism, globalism and socioanalysis within eternalist ethics – merely be regarded as various temporally bound aspects of an all-encompassing eternalistic system of thought, which instead presupposes, and has to presuppose, itself as timeless.

The limitations of thought, and thus also of eternalism, appear clearly when we start to observe the immanent world around us, of which we and our bodies form a part. This immanent world is fundamentally mobilist by nature. Space-time, the sciences' geographical and chronological yardstick for our physical universe, presupposes constant movement in all directions in relation to the inherent constancy of space-time. The Einsteinian worldview within which modern science operates is fundamentally shaken when it is clear that space-time itself must be in constant motion, even in relation to itself. The idea that the universe is expanding is by now well embedded, but its consequences are still difficult to conceive when one reflects upon them. If the universe is expanding, we must imagine a set of dimensions, literally beyond the horizon, within which this expansion is taking place. What we have to deal with is consequently a condition of expanding expansion within an imagined space-time that encompasses space-time. And even this expanding expansion must be imagined as expanding within yet another something, which in turn is expanding within something else, and so on. This creates great problems for thought, and underlines once again the collapse of classical philosophy, and thus the historical necessity of progressing towards an ever more sophisticated dialectic between eternalism and mobilism.

It is evidently possible to present and discuss the problem, but it cannot be envisaged. We are beings with a limited life-span and a limited capacity of perception. Consequently we cannot, for instance, imagine the expanding expansion of space-time without making use of metaphysics, a supra-spacetime. We must, to put it simply, cheat if we are to get any grasp of cosmological equations. Just as we have actually cheated throughout history with cosmic fundamentals like God and the self and all sorts of other things in order to orientate ourselves and survive. For understandable reasons there is no supra-spacetime in an immanent sense, at least not as far as we can know. And even if science admits cheating on such an industrial scale, it cannot simply be accepted within philosophy. The only remaining option we have to integrate the expanding expansion of space-time in a credible way in an informationalist worldview, without creating metaphysical banks of fog, is therefore to start from the assumption that existence is fundamentally paradoxical for thought itself, which in the current example can most simply be described as an internal expansion within space-time itself. Amongst other things, this has the interesting and fundamentally paradoxical consequence that the universe must have been infinite, in other words endlessly large and eternal even in its infinitesimal infancy. Making this paradox manageable is the great challenge for transrationalist cosmology during informationalism, with exciting repercussions for eternalist philosophy in general. This means, for instance, that we are forced to assume that the immanent world is always in a state of absolute movement – absolute in the sense that everything is in motion in comparison to everything else – at the same time as we can never comprehend this state with our thinking. If we are to have any chance of viewing and talking about the world, we have to change our perspective and construct a singularity in our thinking, a fictive extract of space-time. Even this is not particularly remarkable when one has become accustomed to the idea, because every form of understanding contains a fictionalisation in the form of a reduction of the object in question to something else, already known and already fictionalised earlier. We can only comprehend anything at all on our own terms, not on those of our surroundings or of objectivity. Because the metaphysical supra-spacetime in the above example is only a mathematical construction, necessary to conduct science of the usual sort, and therefore does not exist in any immanent meaning, we are forced to formulate what we already know deep-down: that the immanent world completely lacks all cosmic basis and is therefore in itself genuinely incomprehensible. This is precisely what classical philosophy and all metaphysical systems have denied throughout history – even if Immanuel Kant had the sense to mark the distinction between the noumenal and the phenomenological, a division which he promptly abandoned, however, when its consequences collided with his axiomatic worship of reason – and instead obstinately declared the opposite: the absolute idea of an immanent stability. Wishful thinking has directed our vision, the structures of thought have been confused with those of the universe, which led to the bizarrely inflated notion of rationalist epistemology about the innate capacity of reason to comprehend and understand existence in its entirety. First Man was presupposed to be the image of God, then became the image of the Universe; the truth, however, is that Man is not an image of anything other than possibly himself, because he is de facto alone in the conditions of life which are specific to him alone, and which therefore have formed him, and thus also thought and its inherent conditions.

Classical science teaches that space and time are linked in a collective complex which we humans can understand: space-time. A single object, a table or a chair, might appear stable in relation to space, but when we apply the insight that the object in question also exists in time, it becomes clear that stability is unthinkable, and this is before we mix in the other seven dimensions which comprise the current physical view of the universe. Consequently, movement is universal, everything we can observe and imagine is in motion, in time if nowhere else, and stability is a fiction which by definition cannot exist. Existence is being in motion, and this motion is always absolute, because it is incomprehensible for us as observers. Nonetheless we are forced to apply this fictive stability in space as well as time in order to be able to think. Thought itself produces the fundamental precondition of its own activity, the original eternalisation, the cosmic foundation, the platform from which a new, complete and comprehensive worldview is continuously produced and, as often as we can manage it, revised.

For the first time in history there is no longer any need for a specific cosmic basis which everything has to derive from – morality no longer has any place in the worldview – but the cosmic basis is chosen, seeing as it is still an illusory fiction, for every specific situation, out of the ambition which drives the observation in question. This does not, however, mean that the choice of cosmic basis is unimportant; on the contrary, it is actually more important than ever before in history, but in an entirely new way. The precondition for us best to be able to find our way in philosophy's endless abyss is precisely the care with which the cosmic basis for each individual observation is selected. The credibility of the result is, like all other phenomena in an attentionalist society, entirely dependent upon the credibility of the starting position. It is the constant interchange of cosmic bases which, more than anything else, reminds eternalist thinking how mercilessly it is subordinate to the surrounding mobilist reality. Eternalist philosophy is thus, despite its name, or rather precisely because of it, a thoroughly mobilist system of thought. Which brings us back to the history of philosophy.

Ever since mankind began the great project of domestication, taming first nature and then itself, absolute stability has been idealised throughout, while absolute movement has been denied and ignored, condemned as grotesque and mendacious. Mankind's burning desire to succeed finally in domesticating mankind itself has driven whole nations and civilisations into the arms of false and repressive utopisms. It is in the deathwish of the collective subconscious – in an understandable and apparently innocent, but ultimately life-denying desire to avoid the many trials of existence and achieve peace and quiet – that utopisms have always found their most fertile soil. What utopism always tries to sell is order and security, cosmos as a replacement for chaos, and it can only grow strong in a condition of denial. What is spurned is the insight that change is the only natural state which has ever existed, and that stability is the same as death and extinction.

Stability arises, to return to thermodynamics once again, only when all energy is equally divided within the system. Then absolutely nothing happens. And paradise is, of course, a place where nothing ever happens. This explains why all utopisms are united in their bitter hatred of the present and of fate. This hatred produces a strategy which leans heavily towards censorship, the only weapon of those in power to exercise control over the portals to the collective subconscious. Mankind must be saved from itself and all his destructive tendencies. The fruit of knowledge may taste sweet, but it leads straight to destruction. Utopisms build their successes on the inverted myth of the collective deathwish as a sort of secret reservoir for the actual, true love of life. The censoring super-ego is canonised and favoured at the expense of more uncontrollable instances. As in Orwell: Freedom is slavery! $2 + 2 = 5$. Albeit in a slightly different form: Stagnation is life! Change is death! Even paradoxism has its boundaries.

This is the basic, common pattern in every successful utopism, whether it preaches the heavenly paradise or the classless society. But because this recipe for the future is closely tied to the power of one-way communication – and only appears ridiculous in informationalist contexts, characterised by increased transparency and critical thinking reinforced by global interactivity – its future is behind it. From the smouldering ruins of collapsed utopisms, the radical pragmatism which characterises eternalist philosophy is rising. Utopisms can simply not survive in a society which regards itself as a mobilistic organism.

Defining existence as fundamentally mobilistic is the ultimate example of eternalism, because we have by no means crossed the boundary towards existence itself as such. We still find ourselves within language, and language is basically eternalistic in nature, an artificial reality in which immanent reality allows itself to be embodied in the form of analogies. What language deals with is never existence, but eternalisations of eternalisations. So we can discuss, but not in any realistic way describe mobilistic immanence; there is no direct correlation between the two systems. Nor is there any stability, other than that which we as observers produce in the form of the fictive models desired by the observer.

This idealisation of stability, this desire for the domestication of the chaotic immanence of existence, has no trace of a noble, transcendental origin, as classical metaphysics claims. Instead, this idealisation of stability stems from highly immanent, human needs. It is not possible to live in a chaotic immanence, whose environment is highly unmanageable because it is so impossible to overview. A domestication is necessary to ensure survival and reproduction. The observer constructs for himself, to return to Plato once more, a comprehensible cosmos alongside inhospitable chaos, and inhabits that one instead. Every now and then he looks out in horror through the barred window, but has great difficulty understanding the processes which are under way in the raging maelstrom. The manufactured home is therefore both his world and his worldview.

This means that the question of how the world really looks fascinates children and scientists, but not philosophers, as long as the people in question have not misunderstood their task. The basic philosophical problem is instead to explore what a worldview is, and how it is created. Productive philosophy is built upon genealogical, archaeological and meteorological investigations of the paradigm which forms the ultimate frame for the worldview. It is therefore not about trying to answer meaningless questions, but, instead, first creating and then developing the paradigm's countless questions from all possible aspects. For eternalist thought, philosophical work is primarily about constructing the credible cosmic foundations which are needed more than ever, particularly when they can no longer be taken for granted.

Perception is an active and creative process in which the basis of the eternalist worldview is established. No-one, as Kant points out, can comprehend things as they actually are. The fact is that there are no things, we manufacture them ourselves. What does exist is a noumenal chaos in absolute motion, and if one could imagine an act of pure perception, free of preconceptions, then the observer would only see abstract irregularities, a torrent of unsorted differences. Being is produced by the observer; the objects we perceive are admittedly derived from received impulses, but in all essential points created by co-ordinated memes and genes from a raw material of powerfully reduced sensual impressions. Deleuze has taken this post-Kantian epistemology as far as possible, and shown how immanence is a world of movement and differentials rather than a fixed space-time with stable objects.

All of this is extremely crass. We are programmed to create cosmos out of chaotic impulses. Both our genes and our memes have interests to defend, and they are very keen to form us as effective survival machines in all respects. But they have no interest at all in making us sharp-sighted truth-seekers, and nothing in this process has anything whatever to do with enlightenment or revelation. In this way, eternalist thought leaves the world in peace. The reason for our evolutionary success does not lie in divine origins, nor in any supposed isomorphism of either reason and world, but simply a gradually developing capacity to create functional concepts. In this context it is almost moving to think of the colossal efforts mankind has made throughout the course of history to compose for itself noble origins with noble intentions. With the advent of informationalism, precisely nothing of this remains.

The dialectic between eternalism and mobilism is a constant spiral movement with no beginning or end, but it can never be imagined fully from this purely mobilist perspective. The conditions of thought, our own limited point of view of space-time, the fact that human existence is a relatively small parenthesis between an endless mass of infinities, renders us once and for all incapable of comprehending infinity and absolute motion in our thought. We do not know what infinity is, and cannot know. This could, of course, be seen as a serious limitation, but for the paradoxist it is, nevertheless, a fundamental precondition for the whole of consciousness. Thus eternalist thinking contains an inbuilt system fault, which makes mobilistic immanence unattainable, by definition. But it is precisely this irreparable inability to think thoughts about thought and thinking to their conclusion which is the indispensable precondition of creative thought. It is this lack which is called the paradox of metaphysics, and it is this lack itself which has given paradoxism its name.

The reason that absolute motion cannot be comprehended by thought is that motion can only be thought of as a particular object moving a certain distance in a four-dimensional space in relation to the imagined constant of this space-time. We edit and recreate visual impulses in accordance with a series of preconceived ideas. Motion, an abstract phenomenon in the immanent world, assumes manageable contours in eternalist thought in the same way that we understand motion in a film, for instance, when what the eye actually sees is a series of quickly passing still images projected on a white screen. Nevertheless, motion in itself is a fundamental characteristic of mobilistic immanence, the universe consisting of expanding materia. This in turn means that elementary facts about existence are not only out of reach, but also in a fundamental and literal sense unthinkable, and that what remains are merely eternalised meditations on the imagined consequences of these facts.

The same applies to the concept of infinity. It is imaginable only when purely abstract characteristics are changed and embodied within eternalist thinking as a spatial-temporal illusion. The fact that our fantasy is stimulated by the thought of the universe's endlessness does not mean that we have an intellectual grasp of the concept. We pass it around linguistically like a parcel, without ever being able to open it. Besides, this endlessness is inevitably bound to be on a paradoxical collision course with the idea of the universe as an expanding spatial-temporal phenomenon which has a chronology, and which has its origins in an infinitesimal beginning, followed by a big bang. We are therefore forced to grasp the paradoxical notion of a spatial-temporal phenomenon which is at one and the same time infinite and infinitesimal. We can even package this idea within mathematical formulae and physical models, but we are incapable of thinking the idea itself.

We can express the situation by saying that we are oscillating between two different languages, where we produce a simultaneous translation of one, which we have a fairly shaky grasp of, to the other, which is our mother tongue. In the mobilist sphere we use intuitive intelligence, we navigate by instinct. In the overwhelming torrent of strange phonemes which really don't mean anything to us, we try systematically to find repetitions and exceptions, anything which can form a basis for the patterns which will in turn form the basis of our preliminary understanding. If we do not succeed in finding sufficient grounds to build a pattern, we fill in the gaps ourselves, all in order eventually to achieve a translation which must, for our survival, be functional and cohesive, but which for all that does not need to be the slightest bit faithful – and which, for the reasons given above, cannot be faithful – to the surrounding mobilist reality.

As soon as we long for comprehensibility, we go over to our mother tongue, whose grammar structures the torrent and admits a fixing of fictional singularities. The logical, conceptualising intelligence in this game is what we call the eternalist sphere. In this way we construct, and therefore imagine ourselves to see, a motion which derives from mobilism and leads us over to eternalism. Eternalist philosophers uses mobilism in this way to produce eternalism. Where political philosophy is concerned, it would obviously be a reasonable goal to compose an eternalist manifesto, but the path to it would have to go via an incisive understanding of what it means for the very nature of existence itself to be mobilistic. Which necessitates a meditation on how the mobilistic aspects of thought function.

Informationalist society has, like all other societies, a particular place in its power structure reserved for the production of ideology. The role played by the priest under feudalism, and by the academic under capitalism, is played by the eternalist in the new paradigm. In a society where stability is no longer the idealised norm, but where everything is experienced as motion which is itself in motion in relation to another motion – a mobilist worldview – the eternalist's task is to fix these motions in a series of attractive images, possible to assimilate and orientate oneself by. The eternalist is the netocrat who makes it even remotely possible to observe, reflect upon and interact with society in a meaningful and constructive way.

The development towards an eternalist worldview was foreseen by Nietzsche at the end of the nineteenth century. He claimed that philosophy's most important task, what gives it higher status than all other forms of human activity, is to think outside and beyond its own time. And Nietzsche lived as he preached, he thought to a great extent outside and beyond his own time, not least in his reasoning about the concept of the eternal return of the same. This thought, paradoxical in many ways, builds upon the very notion that existence is, fundamentally, motion, which is in constant motion in relation to all other motion. Human beings can therefore not comprehend a single object, a single point, a single now, and least of all themselves, without first fixing the surrounding complex of motions. All of this means that, for a mobilist thinker like Nietzsche, the surrounding complex of motion must be imagined as a single, eternally recursive repetition of the self's own motion. Mobilism becomes eternalism, and existence becomes, through an act of will, suddenly comprehensible and reconcilable.

For Nietzsche the eternal return is the utmost precondition for all thought, and consequently the starting point for philosophy. Thus he breaks radically with all of western thought, from Plato through Descartes to Kant, and practically turns it on its head. Nietzsche prepared an entirely new path for philosophy. With hindsight, we can see that this new path leads right into the centre of the informationalist paradigm. The Age of Nietzsche is only just beginning. While the entire tradition that predated Nietzsche presupposed the metaphysical freezing of all movement in existence, he instead throws philosophy back into the mobilistic chaos which people had been trying to ignore up until then. We must think again: it is not that cosmos, in the form of an eternal world of ideas or anything else, is foremost in relation to chaotic, formless existence, but precisely the opposite. As a result, the grand entirety of western metaphysics lies in ruins. Left among these ruins is the small human being – naked and ugly, confused and mendacious – equipped only with the nagging impulse that Nietzsche calls the will to power.

This has revolutionary consequences for philosophy. In order for thought to produce the illusory stability which must form the basis of the whole enterprise, it is not enough merely to think of a complex of motion in an endless loop, which would produce the eternal return of history. This would presuppose an already extant, stable world in which this eternally recursive motion could take place; otherwise the motion in question could not return to one and the same state, but would always have to assume a completely new meaning in a new context. Therefore thought, as well as imagining the complex of motion in question and its return to one and the same state, must construct an entirely illusory world where the whole of this great enterprise can take place. This illusory world is four-dimensional space-time, ideally adapted for us to orientate ourselves using our senses.

This means, once again, that every location, every exact report and localisation, in space as well as time, is always a fiction; at best to be regarded as mental polaroids of a turbulent, moveable event which otherwise only makes an impression in the form of diffuse and shapeless fragments of memory. The eternal return of the same is naturally only imaginable as an exercise of thought, a strategy to think consciously about the paradox of the concept of time. Actually returning to the same point is by definition impossible outside of this abstract thought: it cannot even be done in concrete, eternalised thought. When we approach the point where the motion is presumed to return, and which is assumed to be the same, the motion dissolves into yet another motion, which is immediately dissolved in still another motion, which in turn is dissolved in yet another motion, and so on, ad infinitum.

The eternalisation which seems robust and sturdy at a distance disappears before our eyes when we get sufficiently close to the imagined point. No-one and nothing can ever return anywhere in a strict definition, because the imagined point in space-time never existed outside fiction anyway, and even if it had done so, it would of necessity have been subject to change. What we think of as the same can only function as the same from a safe distance. Eternalisation is always, when examined closely, inhabited by mental ghosts, but it is nevertheless only in this way that conceptual thought is possible. Thus thought cannot exist as anything present in existence itself, but can merely function at a suitable distance.

Our thinking about time is an illuminating example. We cannot imagine any object or phenomenon of any kind without simultaneously placing it in time, and this point in time is understood in relation to the present, which is the starting point for all understanding of time. We see this imagined time, which stretches backwards and forwards from the present, as a line consisting of an endless series of points which follow each other. Every point on this historical line is a particular now. Yet there is no such now in a mobilistic sense, and never has been. If they had been, then the hare would never have caught up with the tortoise, because the tortoise in every now where the hare reached the point where he had just been would have had time to move just a little further ahead.

When we leave the safety of the command deck, at a safe distance from existence, from which we produce our eternalist worldview, and come closer to the series of now after now which makes up this worldview, every now dissolves into a haze of endless intensities before our very eyes. Nowhere can we find a now, an absolute fixed point, no stability at all, just this absolute motion which we – because it is incomprehensible to us – have to be satisfied with describing in transcendental terms such as torrent, field, process or chaos. The now is quite simply another example of our cheating, a crutch for our thinking, necessary in order to get any grasp of existence at all, ingeniously conjured up from nowhere. The now is a product of the process of perception, we carry it with us wherever we go in the same way that we can take a photograph with us, which also creates an artificial frame for, and a fixation of, an unstructured reality for the observer.

Aristotle was already extremely concerned by this ontological dilemma. Because he did not want to deal with any dialectic dualism of the sort that is being discussed here in the form of the oppositional pair eternalism and mobilism, his attempts to describe reality end as a inconsequential hotchpotch of disparate observations, some of them eternalistic, some mobilistic, without any attempt being made to differentiate between them. In this particular instance, Aristotle interestingly chooses a mobilist perspective; even if his thinking presupposes a unified, universally valid conception of time, he claims that the now is philosophically untenable. According to Aristotle, time can only be said to consist of a past and a future, which, as a result of his still solid status as the father of totalistic thought, has had a great influence on western perceptions of time.

The Stoics' perception of time is, in contrast, considerably more sophisticated that the Aristotelian point of view. It derives from a dualism which in certain respects is related to paradoxism, even if this dualism is strictly limited to time and is not connected to a complimentary perception of space, which is perhaps too much to demand: the notion of space-time was launched later and rests more upon developments within science and scientific theory than within the main thread of philosophy. The Stoics differentiate between two separate concepts of time: partly chronos, Aristotelian time which rejects the now, and which can be compared to the mobilist perception of time as an absolute movement which can only be thought of as a process; and partly aion, a non-Aristotelian time which only consists of a single, eternal now, which can be compared to the eternalist perception of time as an endless intensity.

From our perspective, the relationship between chronos and aion is more complex than it was to the Stoics, not least because it must be woven into a later age's view of space-time as a cohesive phenomenon, just as it must be seen in the light of paradoxist epistemology and its stress on finiteness as a necessary starting point for thought. In this context, time is something which always, from a mobilist perspective, takes the shape either of a past – in its most extreme form as the imagined origin of history – or as a future – in its most extreme form as the imagined end of the universe, but never as an actual now as such. The now belongs entirely within the eternalist sphere. We express this by making the now, in its capacity of endless intensity, into one of the fundamental infinite magnitudes of eternalist onto-logy.

Paradoxism therefore fulfils the stoical attempt to come to terms with the unexamined consequences of the Aristotelian perception of time. It claims partly that the present, from a mobilist point of view, is an illusion, a void in the most fundamental meaning of the word; and partly that the now, from an eternalist point of view, is one of the two basic preconditions for thought itself, a concrete phenomenon created out of noumenal chaos. Each contradicts the other. One is true, but so is the other. So: paradoxism.

In the proximity of infinite magnitudes, there is no longer any meaning in searching for objective truth. Even this truth, in the classic sense, is transformed into an infinite magnitude which can only be produced and kept alive at a suitable distance from existence. On closer inspection, it always dissolves in an endless intensity (see illustration). An objective truth is thus never objectively true, but just another in a procession of concretised abstractions, a sort of provisional necessity for our orientation in chaos. The truth is therefore not a characteristic, but a coincidence which afflicts a concept. Its position is fundamentally exposed, because it is forced to refer back to infinite magnitudes which thought, because of thought's demand for finiteness, cannot comprehend. And as an infinite magnitude, the now is something unthinkable which we, as thinking beings, are forced to think, or, rather, meditate upon. We have to produce it, because we cannot discover or deduce it, because it does not exist in any mobilistic sense.

If we suppose that we can observe a passage of time from a mobilist perspective – in other words, not as a series of nows, but as a flow, a process, a motion – we see how the past and the future, what has been but is no longer, and that which will be but is not yet, move towards one another. But we never see the meeting itself, because it never takes place. The two movements do not collide but are dissolved in immense intensities when they come close enough to one another. We cannot imagine the now as a fixed point in space-time because it is always in motion, moving from the past to the future, transforming the future into the past, constantly receiving new resources into infinity. It exists only in the eternalist world, but it is of inestimable value because we, as already noted, always have to place a phenomenon in time in order to be able to imagine it: Does the phenomenon exist now?

The now demands a mobile, abstract fixation in the centre of the passage of time, in order to link the past and the future, neither of which of course exists either: the former has passed and the latter has not arrived. The now holds time together and creates meaning by being the starting point for necessary decisions of distance in the temporal dimension. Something which in a mobilistic sense is an infinitesimal infinity is therefore contrasted, within mobilist thought, to an extremely real and stable phenomenon, which also happens to be utterly indispensable in terms of its applicability. And the genius of the dialectic between eternalism and mobilism in a cohesive, paradoxical system is that the one does not preclude the other, they are both equally correct within the double perspective. History is a flow, a process, a movement. But because of this, history is not only completely meaningless, but also impossible to comprehend and relate to – in other words, chaos. It is only when we decide to fix specific points in the process – when we decide to view time as a line, a sort of ruler for measuring distance, a single long series of now after now, in spite of the fact that we cannot think any such now – that we get a time and a history which speaks to us, and which we can talk about.

Because space-time is a collective phenomenon, produced by perception, this reasoning can also be transferred to the phenomenological twin of the present, the fixed point in space. Get up out of your chair, go into the kitchen, drink a glass of water, and then come and sit down again. Unreflecting observation suggests that you have returned to the same point in space from which you started, but this is not the case. Without any doubt, it is most practical to imagine that you have returned to the same point in space, but it is still not the case. Even a point in space is an eternalistic phenomenon which for the sake of practicality ignores motion in relation to another motion, which in turn is in motion, and so on. Just like the present, the now, the point in space is an infinite magnitude, an abstract stability, produced by perception in order to be applied to a complex of motion which is thereby transformed into an eternalistic phenomenon which perception can comprehend and thought can deal with. This is no faithful translation, but extremely functional, and it is above all true within the frame of our own thought and its conditions.

If we could travel faster than the speed of light, it is well known that time would stop. In the same way, it is the endless intensity of infinite magnitude which transforms it into something which we believe we can observe and deal with, a specific, delimited phenomenon which we can encompass and manipulate with thought. It is therefore not when we take in information from our surroundings that we think – in which case all animals would be thinking beings – but when the mass of information overwhelms us and we are forced to distort it. The fact is that infinity – despite, or, rather, because of the fact that it cannot itself be thought – is the only impression from the surrounding world which gets the constant attention of human thought. This is the very essence of Nietzsche's eternalism, the concept of an eternal return of the same: the eternalised, the artificially immortalised, is all that we can create out of the chaos that surrounds us. In the light of this historic insight, the resulting paradoxical ontology is the only thing that is credible in the informationalist paradigm.

6.

THE PARADOX OF METAPHYSICS AND THE METAPHYSICS OF PARADOXISM

RATIONALIST THOUGHT PRESUPPOSES axiomatically that humankind with its reason can absorb and comprehend objective reality as it actually is. Because someone has to map and fix the image of existence which rationalism has already identified as the objectively true reality, rationalist doctrinal beliefs are accompanied by a metaphysics which we can call the phenomenology of objective truth. The world which becomes apparent in this phenomenology of objective truth might at first glance appear to agree with the world which becomes apparent in the dialectics of eternalism and mobilism. However, eternalism's paradoxist view is radically different to rationalism's: what has been regarded by totalist philosophy throughout history, and by rationalism under capitalism, as objectively true existence, is, according to eternalism, nothing more than a fiction, which in turn consists of an endless chain of subordinated fictions, on various levels.

In the same way that space and time converge in the product of eternalisation known as spacetime, the point and the now collaborate in the product of eternalism known as the phenomenon. The whole menagerie of individual phenomena, separate objects in spacetime which totalist philosophy has appointed as our reality (i.e. whatever is to hand), arises from this meeting between point and now. According to eternalism, however, there is no reason at all why this experience of what is should communicate any sort of objective truth; rather, the experience must be regarded as an interplay between the individual observer's fiction-creation, and a series of collective agreements. Eternalist criticism of totalist philosophy therefore builds upon the idea that the phenomenon must be seen as an eternalist product of a mobilistic process, which always precedes the manifestation of the phenomenon in eternalist fiction.

The central point here is that the mobilistic process is not contained within the rationalist point of view; rationalism lacks paradoxism's creative double-vision. This innate limitation depends upon the fact that totalist thought is so fixated upon humankind's need for stability in order to comprehend the phenomenon that it consistently mistakes humankind's enormous need for stability for the fact that existence itself, by its very nature, should be frozen by some mystical process in order to make it observable. The purpose of existence is merely to be enjoyed and plundered by the observing subject, the solid ego. Mobilism is, therefore, not just one of two opposites in the dialectics of eternalism and mobilism, but also the historical opposite of totalist philosophy, a worldview which stems from movement rather than stability, and, above all, from the most fundamental of all movements, that between movement and stability itself. According to mobilist thought, existence was already in place right from the start; the subject invents him or herself in order to try to survive in the confused world which he or she, in tune with the surroundings, constantly recreates and modifies as his or her more or less credible fiction of existence.

In contrast to the metaphysics of objective truth, eternalist phenomenology does not restrict itself to the body which believes itself to comprehend whatever seems to be at hand. The extent to which what one person means by, for instance, pain or the taste of strawberries, is identical to someone else's perceptions of 'the same thing' is, admittedly, impossible to know, but it simplifies our existence a great deal if we presuppose that this is the case, and it is also reasonable to suppose that there are at least significant similarities. Particularly as we, time after time, succeed in agreeing on what we mean by a table or a chandelier. An important dimension of our social community – one of its unique selling points – is therefore the mutual confirmation of what is real and unreal.

We are, quite simply, genetically and culturally conditioned to produce reality using the same methods as other members of our species and our society. The fact that we believe that we have good reasons for calling our created perceptions reality has, thus, no foundation in anything outside of our conception, but is connected to the fact that our fictions appear to coincide with those of other people. These fictions say nothing about reality itself, but all the more about the conditions for our survival and the conditions for the production of identity, which is of central importance when eternalist phenomenology differentiates between the inner, eternalised, and therefore produced, reality, and the external, mobilist and predetermined reality. Our perception of reality is therefore a collaborative effort. Reality gives an impulse which shapes us as thinking beings, so that we in turn are together able to form a functional picture of reality, generate a manageable cosmos out of unmanageable chaos, where the boundary between cosmos and chaos is pragmatic manageability itself. Our perceptions of reality are no mystical reflections from some perfect platonic world of ideas, as totalism claims, but arise as ideological resonances in the soundbox we call the collective subconscious.

A paradigm shift involves a turbulent upheaval of the symbolic order, which gives rise to entirely new patterns in the truths which are produced within the collective. It is a matter of a change in the conditions for production which is so fundamental that it can be compared to the consequences of an earthquake or a tornado. Predicting and understanding these upheavals can therefore be seen as an abstract form of seismology or meteorology, and is one of the main tasks of the eternalist philosopher's daily work – the mapping and prognosis of the resonances in the collective subconscious.

Eternalist philosophy is what Nietzsche calls inverse Platonism. The individual objects that inhabit our worldview are not copies of some sort of hyperreal original, but constantly updated and revised fictions, simulations of simulations, produced in the collective subconscious, launched into language, and are closely connected to socialisation processes such as imitation, learning, the search for knowledge, science, and so on. The now and the point which must be created are, on closer inspection, as has already been mentioned, complexes of movements that are too large to get any idea of, even for the thinking which has created them. So how, then, can a movement be imagined in solid form? Well, Nietzsche claims that it must be sensed by perception as a movement which is constantly repeated in an imagined spatial and temporal infinity.

This brings us to the cognitive version of the Nietzschean concept of the eternal return of the same: by a form of wishful thinking which is essential for survival, perception believes itself to sense a phenomenologically fundamental similarity: movement is –

or at least seems to be – in practically every respect always the same. Every now and every point forms a sort of whirling movement which can be thought to return to its original state after a process which is continually repeated. Only as a result of this process can perception produce the stability of spacetime which is essential for thought and for our orientation in existence. A movement-complex is fixed as a now and/or a point through a creative translation into an eternalised movement, and thereby gains solid form. Chaos becomes cosmos: eternalistic phenomena which we can observe and manipulate.

Nietzsche reaches his eternalistic concept by radically diverging from the mainstream path of the philosophical tradition, and by ignoring the Cartesian subject whose status until then had been axiomatic and which therefore was never questioned. Instead, he takes the immanent existence around us – which also includes us ourselves as materia, bodies – as the starting point for thought. Nietzsche calls this immanent existence chaos, a concept which is therefore granted the same content as ancient Greek chaos, in other words: the absence of meaning rather than the absence of order. The starting point for thought for Nietzsche is thus the absence of meaning, and the human being which had thus far found itself at the centre of the system was banished to the margins and reduced to just one of countless objects in spacetime. The main task of philosophy after Nietzsche has been to explore how meaning is produced from something which itself is meaningless, instead of officiously creating the meaning demanded by ideology, as had been the case before.

According to Nietzsche, order, and therefore meaning, comes from chaos thanks only to the ability of the perception apparatus to freeze single moments of the meaninglessness of movements. Reality is not accessible for discovery even in theory, but is something which humankind achieves in its reflexive desire for order and meaning. The building blocks which it creates for itself – differences, singularities, repetitions – are known as fictives within eternalist philosophy. Only when the fictives are already in place, delivered by perception and passed through intuition, can consciousness get to work and erect structures in which the fictives can be placed in meaningful relationships to one another. In this way, consciousness fools itself into believing that its own single-handedly constructed performance is reality. This is the thinking being, someone who produces and organises fictives, someone who himself creates his own meaning, and then judges it to be meaningful.

When rationalism's idea that metaphysical insight is a matter of isolating common sense reasoning implodes, it seems abundantly clear to Nietzsche and his followers that metaphysics lacks substance, that it is fabricated by us alone. The onset of eternalism means therefore that all old, classical values have disappeared once and for all. This is true of all the values which were gathered in clusters around the monotheistic meme, with God at the centre, and which was later nurtured and developed by humanism, with an idealised Man in the centre. According to the result of Nietzsche's genealogical investigations, morality lacks the transcendental origins on which it bases its entire credibility. Morality has served as the domesticated human being's new clothes, an imaginary vestment of richly brocaded misconceptions, designed to conceal what is in actual fact characteristic of humankind and its amoral nakedness, not least to itself. So morality is part, as the historical Zarathustra claims, of the necessary preconditions for domestication, and, therefore, of the entire civilisational project.

This means, to start with, that human beings have actually always lived as amoral nihilists, but that for instinctual and ideological reasons they have been forced to suppress this knowledge and bury it in the collective unconscious. It also means that, thanks to Nietzsche's act of making their amorality conscious, human beings are forced into a new historical phase, which Nietzsche and Heidegger call the nihilistic era. The question of how fully nihilistic human beings will in future deal with the acute absence of classical values arouses both hope and fear in the two philosophers. The newly-discovered metaphysical emptiness, the absence of both divinely-given and natural values, gives rise both to a fantastic freedom of unprecedented range, and at the same time to a frightening liberation from responsibility, because there is no longer any higher metaphysical authority to hold us to account. The answer is beginning to become clear a century after these fathers of nihilism first aired their disquiet: the thought of the eternal return of the same, which has previously at best existed as a generally unspoken suspicion within a limited elite, is being transformed in informationalist society, thanks to its innate plurarchic character (see Netocracy), into a mass-movement on a global scale.

Human beings are being forced under informationalism to witness helplessly their own forced transfer from the centre of existence to its margins, which in one sense constitutes a painful devaluation which can be difficult to deal with. It is all made more interesting when we bear in mind the power over their surroundings which human beings still possess, not least due to the increasing development of technology. Is nihilistic insight leading to fear and vengeful bitterness, to a resentment against life? Or can it be experienced as liberating, as an opportunity to accept and even love our own fate with greater clarity than ever before? For Nietzsche himself there was no choice at all. The eternal return of the same is the fundamental principle of life, and it therefore forms the basis of his ethics. At the same time, he is open to the fact that the general comprehensiveness and survival of this ethics can be nothing more than wishful thinking on his part. The new independence and the brutality of isolation can become an all too heavy burden for post-Nietzschean human beings to bear, as a result of which nihilism must be suppressed again and replaced by yet another moralistic era.

Hope rests, according to Nietzsche, in the Superman, the new human being who has reached complete and all-encompassing nihilistic insight, and who therefore realises the necessity of creating his own values, where the value-creation process itself constitutes the highest value of all. Because all the classical values which were previously passed from generation to generation, like the old reward system of heavenly paradise and collectivist utopias, have lost all credibility, he calls his doctrine the tragic philosophy. But this should not be perceived as a defeat; within this tragedy Nietzsche sees the possibility of freedom, an historical opportunity for the new human being who has stopped moralising, and who accepts without illusions and therefore loves life, only because it is the only life which exists, in all its fundamental contradictions.

This ethical ideal is affirmative nihilism, and the Superman embodies this ideal. The problem is that because Nietzsche is seeking a consequential philosophy of immanence, a mobilistic way of thinking which is in constant motion, there is no space whatever for any sort of determinism. Consequently, the Superman is merely one possibility, a more or less pious wish, but it can never become an historical necessity. This results in that which is affirmative in affirmative nihilism, the value-creation which itself is the highest value, eventually looking like merely one arbitrarily chosen ideal among countless others, a Nietzschean preference without any direct connection to the absolute mobilism within which philosophy is conducted.

As a result, Nietzsche is mercilessly forced back to the metaphysics he has so frenetically tried to smash and get away from – a tragic/ironic and highly involuntary return to the same. Human beings can, if we stick with Nietzsche, merely criticise and reject the metaphysics which the age has left behind, but can never abandon metaphysics as such. No metaphysical system can be regarded as exhausted unless it has been replaced by a new one. The Superman will therefore become yet another in the series of innocent utopias, a dreamed-up phantom image which constantly restless nihilism attacks and destroys. And so Nietzsche's philosophical project ends: in a beautiful but highly doubtful and self-critical hope against better judgement. The tragedy is repeated, time after time: not according to a predetermined law, divine or natural, but nonetheless with the highest empirical probability.

However, this is not 100% bound to happen. This historical loop, according to David Hume, the Scottish empiricist who was one of Nietzsche's most important predecessors, is never hermetically sealed. The hopelessness is not total, the attempt to formulate an eternally valid metaphysics of metaphysics is not doomed to fail in principle. The chances of progress are merely incredibly small. As a result, every Versuch by Nietzsche also reflects an ethical aspect in this eternal return of the same. The overriding value which value-creation itself is thought to comprise is yet another of eternalism's infinite quantities, but an entirely unknown and unthinkable occurrence within a mobilism which is itself always nihilistic. This perceived value can be compared to conceptual consciousness's equivalent of perception's fictives: the now, the point, the phenomenon. The way out of nihilism's chaos therefore passes through, in the same way as phenomenology, the rope-trick of eternalist philosophy: the fixation of something which cannot be fixed. Out of this paradoxical insight, homo ludens, the playful human being, is born, and with it its flexible but nonetheless powerful and uncompromising ethics.

For the informationalist human being, eternalisation of mobilism itself – the freezing of life as a process, the eternal return of the same – appears to be the definitive, final metaphysics, an idea which both encompasses extreme relativism and at the same time avoids being sucked into bottomless quicksand. The eternal search for meaning eventually finds meaning in the search itself. And precisely because this meaning is constantly in motion, because it is its own answer, and must therefore always exist in the eternal orbit between question and answer, it will never reach a conclusion unless the process of thinking which creates meaning, and thus life itself, ceases to exist.

Nietzschean ethics can thus be summarised in the strict requirement for constant questioning in order to find the illusory and provisional answer in full awareness of the illusion and the provisional nature of the answer, because the answer is by definition not an answer in the traditional sense, but a question. And the question is always open. The ontological solution to the Nietzschean dilemma is therefore an open dialectic between eternalism and mobilism. The thinking human being appears in this fundamental contradiction between necessary inaccessibility and desired completion. The oscillation between these two poles cannot stop as long as life is still in motion and a thinking human being is acting as both observer and participant.

Heidegger has most ingeniously developed the idea of the eternal return of the same, and thereby prepared the way for paradoxism. He sees the possibilities of the concepts, but also raises and problematises the weaknesses of the Nietzschean analysis. Heidegger is not content with Nietzsche's mobilistic denial of being in favour of an immanent becoming, nor does he stop there. Instead, he presents being as a fundamental condition for thought, and therefore ascertains the existence of being, not least in the form of a deeper aspect of becoming, a being. Heidegger calls this being, this state beyond becoming which is so essential for human beings and human thought, Dasein.

What is interesting about this is how this manoeuvre forces Heidegger to break with classical philosophy's demand for a unified, cohesive worldview and instead accept the thought that two parallel worldviews can co-exist and complement one another: firstly, an immanent worldview which stems from becoming, and secondly, a metaphysical worldview which stems from an imagined being. Heidegger, for his part, does not cling on to any hope that the creation of value as such might constitute an absolute value, in the way that Nietzsche does when he prophesies the Superman and affirmative nihilism. Instead, Heidegger stops at a belief that the nihilistic state is a necessary accomplishment of the historical process, a paradox which can be said to be unavoidable from the very start. This is the fundamental metaphysical paradox which forms the basis for the mutually dependent and determined perspectives we call eternalism and mobilism.

If Nietzsche is the philosopher who completes mobilism and confronts its ultimate consequences, then Heidegger, through his reintroduction of being as a more primary quantity in a mobilistic context, is the first eternalist. However, Heidegger still wrestles with what he sees as a conflict between eternalism and mobilism, and does not see that the dialectic between them constitutes the connecting and necessary function on which humanity can build. He continues the rationalist search for a metaphysical foundation where only the need for, and therefore even the lack of, a metaphysical foundation can serve as such. This has the consequence of forcing Heidegger to reject the moral imperative of Nietzschean ethics: Versuch!, without this helping him to offer any alternative. He ends up in a dead-end, from which someone else has to think further in order to establish a platform for informationalist thought. The eternalist philosopher, to use a Nietzschean expression, picks up Heidegger's arrow in order to shoot it still further in a new direction.

If Heidegger is the first eternalist, who, in his attempt to wrestle with Nietzsche and the eternal return of the same, perceives an opening for the dialectic between eternalism and mobilism, then it is Heidegger's French successors Jacques Lacan and Gilles Deleuze who notice and fully implement paradoxist thought. As a result of this, everything changes. From its position as the great philosophical cornerstone, a problem complex which had to be worked through and past, the dialectic between eternalism and mobilism is being turned into a cohesive ontology, out of which a systematic process of thought can be developed.

What Lacan shows, in his revised and expanded variant of Freudian psychoanalysis, is how his modified version of the Cartesian subject appears as a lack, as a vacuum which becomes evident only as a result of its insistence upon being filled with something. It is possible to use this theory to complete the paradoxist puzzle where every individual singularity in our worldview eventually appears to be a forced response to this original vacuum. What Deleuze does, through his deconstruction of the history of philosophy, is to open the way for a new philosophy, based upon repetition and difference, which aims to produce problems rather than solving them, and which affirms life as an expanding expansion of game and chance, multiplicities of multiplicities, instead of thinking reactively like a totalist philosopher and becoming obsessed with producing fictive solutions to problems which appeal to the current power structure.

Where these philosophical efforts meet, an image of the dialectic between eternalism and mobilism emerges as a movement of movements, a metafeedback loop in need of a final meta-eternalisation. This, like all eternalisations, requires us to take a step back once again in order to gain the necessary distance from the phenomenon in question. Then a pattern begins to emerge: our perception produces a cohesive complex, a frozen supra-movement. The result is that the metaphysical paradox – built into the relationship between immanent becoming and metaphysical being, and a recurrent dilemma for both Nietzsche and Heidegger – stops being an irrational instance which must at all costs be thought out of philosophy, and appears instead, precisely because of its indispensability to our existence as thinking beings, as a credible cosmic foundation. The phenomenon is admittedly fictive, but nonetheless functional reflections of intensities and movements in the chaos of immanence. This makes paradoxism an open but still total universe, in the frame of which we can construct a credible worldview for informationalism.

Deleuze is part of the mobilistic tradition which is attempting to evade the jurisdiction of totalist thought and instead construct a transrational philosophy beyond the language which is to such a great extent permeated by totalistic structures. His work can be described as thought in motion, characterised by the desire for a transrational truth, a deeper understanding of immanence, and by an aggressive desire to deconstruct every transcendental phenomenon which is superfluous within metaphysics. Deleuze's transrationalist philosophy – built upon an original reading of Nietzsche, inspired by Spinoza – can at first glance seem to be fundamentally alien to an eternalism in Heidegger's spirit. Closer inspection reveals, however, that both of these deal with the same eternal return, merely viewed from two different points.

Deleuze constructs a metaphysical system of repetition and difference. While thought, for an eternalist inspired by Heidegger's reading of Nietzsche, is in the first instance an eternalisation of the noumenal, a product of fictives of group-work character (see above), Deleuze takes as his starting point his original interpretation of the eternal return of the same. Even this is an endless chain of repetitions, but a chain where every individual link includes a slight deviation in comparison to the previous repetition. This can compared to how biology's replicators, DNA molecules, for instance, produce countless copies of themselves, identical apart from a tiny little mutation, with these mistakes facilitating evolution, because completely stable structures would be no different to stagnation.

The difference between eternalist ontology and Deleuze's metaphysics is that where eternalism sees an endless dualistic series (a first eternalisation of an arbitrary excerpt from mobilism leads to a new stage of mobilism, which in turn encourages yet another eternalisation, and so on, ad infinitum), Deleuze, in his desire for absolute mobilism, sees instead the whole process as a single step, a repetition with the difference as a built-in condition. Deleuze is an impassioned immanence philosopher, and wants at all costs to avoid what he perceives as concessions to eternalism. Despite this, he himself is forced to make a considerable concession in the Nietzschean sense when he – like all other philosophers, for that matter – is forced to put his thinking into words in order to structure and, in due course, communicate it.

Deleuze's categorical critique of the subject ends up in difficulty, when, to take one example, he is nonetheless eventually forced to put his own name to the books he writes, and when language forces him to use being and an 'I' in order to get anything meaningful said. No matter how mobilistic Deleuzianism may be within Deleuze's own brain – even if this cannot be fully thought through either, because verbal reflection has been deeply involved in the formation of thought – it is still transformed into an eternalist phenomenon among others as soon as it is formulated in language. Philosophy as a discipline, unlike art and possibly poetry, can never itself be mobilistic.

Unlike Deleuze, eternalist thought does not perceive Hegel's dialectics as a problem. What is problematic is instead the idea of the dialectic process's dynamic and chronology, and the opposition which the chronology creates. In Hegelian dialectics, the development of history is a constant conflict of contradictions. An antithesis confronts a thesis, whereupon thesis and antithesis merge and form a synthesis on a higher plane. In the paradoxist dialectic, on the other hand, the synthesis precedes a bifurcation of the oppositional pair thesis and antithesis. The reason for this is that the immanence which Hegel, in his capacity as an idealist, does not want to be involved in, is the fundamental mobilistic condition for the entire dialectic relationship, as a result of which it has to precede eternalism in a fundamental sense.

Perception cannot comprehend either thesis or antithesis unless the synthesis is already apparent. The necessary worldview never appears to consciousness as loose fragments or pieces of a puzzle, but always appears as total and cohesive to the observer; it must literally communicate an idea of some sort of world in which newly-arrived observers can be placed. Perception therefore works from totalities, and what we do not see is filled in with the help of our imagination. We move, therefore, from an appreciation of the whole – partly produced, so to speak, in house – to an appreciation of the parts, and not vice versa.

The immanent life may seem disconnected, and the coherent image of life may be a coarse illusion, and we may be only too well aware of this; nonetheless, it is only from this illusory totality that we can reflect upon the state of things. This means that the synthesis precedes both thesis and antithesis in the eternalistic process of perception – only after a synthetic relationship has been registered as a whole is it possible to see the thesis and how it is followed by the antithesis – and it is here that Hegelian dialectics break down, because the chronology is the reverse. As well as this, the eternalist synthesis is extremely promiscuous; every synthesis can give rise to countless oppositional relationships. Here eternalist thinking joins in the Deleuzian criticism of Hegel, but develops this criticism further to form a new and modified dialectic, this time between eternalism and mobilism, and therefore stops neither at Hegel's strictly idealistic and therefore unusable dialectics, nor at Deleuze's principal refusal to be involved with dialectic relationships at all.

If Nietzsche has gone down in history as the philosopher who declared God dead, then the breakthrough of paradoxism means that we have to exhume God from his grave and declare him dead once again, this time for good. Anti-rationalism in all its variants is evidently directed against rationalism, but merely replaces one religious belief with another, hyperrationalist one, and therefore falls at its own hand. What is dying this time is thus the atheist instinct itself, the need to kill and declare dead, the aggression and sensual pleasure which the attacks of Nietzsche and the nihilists who followed him exude.

There is no need for anything like this anymore. The grave is not merely filled in; we make sure it is overgrown by impenetrable vegetation and impossible to discover. It is no longer of any interest. Paradoxism has no interest whatever in continually revealing and attacking the paradox of metaphysics, over and over again, but regards every such attempt as a clear sign of an increased rationalistic inclination with its roots in a stillborn nihilism, in the same way as the cynic in love always appears as a betrayed lover. In sharp contrast to anti-rationalism's ingrained bitterness, eternalism uses the paradox of metaphysics as the starting point for the metaphysics of paradoxism.

The eternalist's main purpose is to trace and construct the metaphysical foundation for the collective consciousness of information society. There is of course no metaphysical basis in the mobilistic sense, and it can therefore never been regarded as eternally and universally valid. Nonetheless, the metaphysical foundation is necessary for thinking as the constant yardstick against which incoming impulses can be compared and categorised, so Hegel was entirely right in that thought itself produces the metaphysical foundation as an internal necessity, and nothing else. From this Hegel draws the conclusion that the subject he himself worships so deeply is fated to become merged into the final, and therefore objectively true, metaphysical foundation, which is the same as the end of history. The problem is just that when Hegel's version of the Cartesian subject is set against Nietzsche's absolute mobilism – considering that we consist of materia and nothing but materia, it is hardly credible to avoid materia at all costs as Hegel does – then everything, including the metaphysical foundation itself, begins to move, also in relation to its own manifestations. And a history which has started moving again can hardly be said to have come to an end.

Even if Hegel was the person who introduced mobilism into modern philosophy, his version, compared to the Nietzschean variant, seems rather like pseudo-mobilism. This fact, together with his idea of the world spirit, means that Hegel perhaps first and foremost ought to be regarded as the last of the great totalists. Nonetheless, his philosophy is useful to paradoxists, who take from Hegel their insight of the meaninglessness of looking for a metaphysical foundation within mobilism. This foundation can only be found within eternalism, and the given starting point of the search is the Nietzschean concept of the eternal return of the same, since it shows how the necessary eternalisation of absolute motion can be thought to function. It is from this platform that the construction of a credible metaperspective in harmony with contemporary knowledge and linguistic usage stems. The dialectic between eternalism and mobilism transforms mobilistic immanence into eternalistic metaphysics, without this meaning that the movement – perceived as repetition and difference – must stop as a result of this.

Eternalism is tragedy, and mobilism comedy, to put it in Nietzschean terms. The former is necessary if we are to understand and be able to think about the endless complications of life; the latter is consciousness of the illusion of understanding and thinking, and of the basic inaccessibility of life. Every time the eternalist makes a firm statement about something outside his own limited, strictly conceptual jurisdiction, the mobilist stands up and laughs at him. Comedy is, as Lacan says, life's perpetual triumph over every vain human attempt to fix it, and thus make it anywhere near comprehensible. But, however annoying this laughter is, human beings can never lay down their arms and accept the incomprehensibility. What gives a new and interesting dimension to this eternal dialectic is that we can join in this laughter at our own expense in our capacity as paradoxists, despite the endless series of pathetic failures, and still fight on. 'I cannot go on. I'll go on', as Samuel Beckett writes in the last lines of The Unnameable. And Beckett was, of course, in the midst of all the gloom, a great comedian.

7.

THE METEOROLOGY OF KNOWLEDGE AND THE PARADOXICAL SUBJECT

BOTH NIETZSCHE AND HIS cousin Darwin spent a large part of the twentieth century locked in the poison cabinet. Being a Nietzschean or a Darwinist was hardly a winning career strategy in any context, with the possible exception of some highly specialised scientific niche. Both systems of thought, in a coarsely distorted and manipulated form, had been exploited for the most vulgar propaganda purposes imaginable, where Nazis and racists tried to create legitimacy for their superstitious message. In their unadulterated form, though, both Nietzsche's and Darwin's thinking, because their anti-humanism and extreme materialism were out of kilter with the age, was completely unusable in ideological terms. Neither Nietzscheanism nor Darwinism was in harmony with the supreme ideology of the capitalist paradigm, and no social class seemed able to gain any advantage by calling upon or nurturing thinking in these terms.

This is the great change, the paradigm shift, which is happening on the ideological plane as a result of informationalism: Nietzsche and Darwin are suddenly contemporary. Those who are inclined to see life from the perspective of these thinkers are favoured by circumstances and are forming the new elite: the netocracy. And this perspective alone forms a credible, supremely ideological starting point for the political philosophy of informationalism. The task therefore is to change the Versuch of Nietzschean ethics into a political project on a global scale. The metaphysical basis for informationalist philosophy is becoming, for reasons which have been elaborated in the two previous chapters, our innate and inexhaustible need for a metaphysical basis itself. And there can be no more stable basis on which to build.

Thinking stems from perception, which constitutes an immense production and management of fictives, of which the point is primary in space, and the now primary in time. Despite the fact that neither point nor now exist in a mobilistic sense – in other words, beyond perception and conceptual apparatus – the whole of our worldview is based upon variations of these infinite magnitudes. Language and logical intelligence presuppose, for instance, the eternalist concept of the ego (human existence imagined as a point) and being (human existence imagined as a now). The distance from immanence which is necessary if we are to be able to produce functional thought makes every human being a more or less conscious eternalist in a mobilistic environment.

What is meant by the infinite character of the point is that we perceive it as a magnitude which is divisible into infinity: every point consists of a number of smaller points, which in turn consist of even smaller points, and so on. The point is therefore an infinitesimal magnitude; this is not to say that it is the opposite of infinity, but rather the complementary underside of infinity. On closer inspection, therefore, the point dissolves into an endless intensity, which makes the point as a concept fundamentally contradictory. The paradoxical way of handling this dilemma is to use the merciless principle of the eternal return of the same. This results in the realisation that the point is not so much a point as an idea of a point, an eternalisation of the mobilistic torrent which is vital for perception. And the same applies to all phenomena, including spacetime itself: they are fictives.

Here Hegel's most important insight becomes relevant: it is not enough to say that we produce our own worldview ourselves, we even produce the very preconditions for the production of a worldview. However, eternalism takes its leave of Hegelianism in its next step, when it goes on to proclaim a transcendental linearity, a dialectic progression in which a thesis is followed by an antithesis, where the contrast between them dissolves into a synthesis of a higher order. For eternalism, this is a rationalist construction in hindsight of a considerably more complex transrational process, because the entire worldview – the totality of experienced phenomena in experienced spacetime – is not constructed of disparate fragments, but instead precedes, of necessity, the comprehension of the various components.

This means that the synthesis is primary in eternalist dialectics, instead of the relationship between thesis and antithesis. Marx had good material reasons to put Hegel on his feet, and therefore turned Hegel's absolute idealism into what he perceived as an absolute materialism. Eternalist thinking does the same thing, in another respect, when, inspired by Nietzsche's and Heidegger's constructive criticism of Hegel's pseudo-mobilistic totalism, it reverses the dialectic order. The fact is that this reversal in extension also means that eternalism puts Hegel's totalistic predecessors on their feet. Eternalism can, therefore, be usefully regarded both as an inverted platonism: we do not need the world in order to be able to understand ideas, but instead produce the ideas in order to understand the world; and as an inverted Cartesianism: we do not exist because we think; we exist, therefore we think.

The revolutionary consequence of this philosophical u-turn is that history is separated from determinism and restored to immanent reality. Eternalism, quite simply, insists that the view of reality really is just a view, with all the implications of interpretation and individual creation, and not faithful reflection, that this suggests; just as it insists that an idea of totality always forms an unavoidable reference to which one or other phenomenon must be related if a perception is to be established at all, and must therefore be regarded as unavoidable even for perception and thought themselves. Eternalist philosophy turns the historical direction of philosophy's overriding ambition through 180 degrees: it is no longer a matter of constructing a credible totality (as under totalism), but of working out exactly how absolute movement is constantly tearing apart and deconstructing the totality which human beings have already created. The unavoidability of totality for thought can be expressed within eternalism as the synthetic origins of the subject.

The great mistake of classical philosophy, regardless of whether God is mixed up in the equation or not, is to elevate thought – in other words: its own activity – to the absolute pinnacle of creation, a divine gift of transcendental origins, an insight into everything natural, and a bridge over to the supernatural, instead of simply seeing thought as a product of evolution, a technology of immanent origin which exists for the simple reason that it brings with it certain advantages in the perpetually raging struggle between and within the species, for space and resources. Thanks to the meeting of Darwin and Heidegger, eternalism leaves thought to Dasein, becoming, and therefore puts a stop to philosophy's desire to localise thought beyond immanence, as some sort of perfect form in a pure and unbesmirched highest heaven of existence.

After Kant and the understanding that there is a fundamental difference between the noumenal and the phenomenological worlds, there is ultimately no other way forward for anyone wishing to move on but to accept the dialectic between eternalism and mobilism as the cosmic foundation. This is the eternalist philosophy: simultaneously an open, mobilistic system and a closed, eternalist totality, in constant interaction with each other, but without ever becoming united as a result of this. There are no phenomena in the immanent sense, only a noumenal chaos. Distance and volume, past and future, subject and object – all these preconditions for or variants of the point and the now – are fictives, which we are forced to regard as real, because such a view is both required and rewarded by evolution.

Perception, or, in other words, the production and management of primary fictives, is, in one way or another, a necessary instrument for survival for all animal species. Thought, or, in other words, the production and management of secondary fictives, is, on the other hand, something unique to human beings, at least when we are talking about thought in any advanced form. This explains why such a large proportion of our planet's bio-mass consists of human beings: among the animal species, we have the unique capacity to imagine alternative configurations in spacetime in relation to the current image of circumstances pertaining in reality. Not only do we have the capacity to produce fictives, but also to set these fictives in motion against one another in a fictive world which we have at our disposal. The eternalist world is transformed into a second-rate mobilistic chaos, which is re-eternalised only to be set in motion again at once. This process never ends, it is itself mobilistic, and in this process the whole wasteful wealth of alternative worldviews is created, virtual worlds which can be compared and played off against one another. They are our memories, identities, premonitions, fantasies, wishes, myths, stories, theoretical reasonings... and so on. They are the cultural element of our nature.

Thought can, in relation to perception, be seen as a turbo compared to an engine: it exploits the energy expressed and pushes it back into the system. In this reinforced, expanded perceptual process, hypothetical alternatives to the current version can be constructed anyhow and localised anywhere within experienced spacetime. These alternatives form the secondary fictives, those relations created by us between the primary fictives, the components in the mobilistic chaos of thought. This creation of fictions has a more important function here than in the process of perception, where it fills the vacuum between impulses from the sensory organs with pre-programmed expectations so that the result is a cohesive totality. In thought, it single-handedly produces complete worlds. In the management of these secondary fictives, language arises, along with a self-image in relation to a worldview. We experience ourselves as conscious of ourselves and of the world.

The secondary fictives are managed and communicated both within consciousness and between people with the help of language. But when the mobile consciousness, in the form of an equally mobile language, is to be perceived and interpreted, it in turn must be eternalised. This secondary eternalisation process is carried out by a production of metafictives. When these in turn are managed and communicated, movement occurs, the shift from mobilism to eternalism moves to a new stage of mobilism, which in turn must be eternalised in order to be understood and interpreted, and so on. Consciousness oscillates constantly between a given movement and a fictive fixation, encompassing both of them, without letting itself be blocked by the contradiction.

This is the dialectic between eternalism and mobilism, the principle under which individual thought has always operated, which has also become the principle of philosophy, but only after the breakthrough of interactivity. It is only since the arrival of the interactive media technologies that collective thought has begun to operate under the same principles as individual thought, which has in turn made possible the understanding and acceptance of how thought actually functions which the dialectic between eternalism and mobilism offers. The rapidly expanding interactivity in society means that the structure of the collective subject is taking a step closer to the structure of the individual subject – because the latter has always been based upon the principle of interactivity – and, beyond this, with all the colossal power which only the united collective can call upon, when it is now, on a global level, set in the internal resonance which is necessary for the subject to be understood as existing.

In contrast to totalistic philosophy, which moves along a straight line from question to answer, from origin to fate, eternalist philosophy lacks both beginning and end. It takes place in the middle of an imagined line between the two abstract poles of mobilism, the infinite and the infinitesimal, and the space which Deleuze calls a milieu: a world which must be imagined as both a point in the middle of a flat surface and at the same time a point in the middle of a line, without being able to leave this relative position, simply because this is by definition impossible, regardless of speed and spacetime, to approach either end of a scale between two infinities.

One illustrative example of the complexity of paradoxist dialectics – where the dialectic, nota bene, is acted out in the eternalist sphere – is the two contradictory ways of seeing that are necessary to capture modern physics' view of the phenomenon of light, where both ways of seeing are correct in spite of the fact that they cannot be correct at the same time. Quantum physics, as is well-known, regards light both as a particle, a so-called photon, and as a wave motion. But the observer is forced to choose a perspective: when the particle is in focus, the wave motion disappears, and vice versa. In both cases, naturally, it is a question of a conceptual application, in other words, an eternalisation of a complex of chaotic movement. But which phenomenon we perceive is entirely dependent upon what we are looking for and the way in which we choose.

This means that our understanding of the qualities of light is not primarily determined by the light's own characteristics, but by the pre-understanding of the observer; it is in the first instance not the object which produces the phenomenon – even if its noumenal characteristics influence the phenomenological process – but its subject. But here we are dealing with a subject which is radically different to that perceived by the Cartesian paradigm. Because one and the same subject in this model can assume a mass of different subject-positions, it is no longer the classic individual, who remains unaffected by what he observes, but instead the eternalistic dividual, who arises through and is a part of the observation, who observes his surroundings in the case in question.

The transition from the balanced models of classical physics to the programmatic contradictions of quantum physics reveals that the former never had anything to do with any innate, transcendental truth about life which exists somewhere in life itself, outside the observer. Neither perception nor thought is intended, in spite of rationalism's naïve faith in the reverse, to uncover the innermost secrets of life, but has instead been polished over millions of years by a natural choice which has merely favoured whatever was functional within the frame of given ecological circumstances. It is, in other words, purely a question of survival. The idea that classical physics seems logical and is confirmed by our sensual perceptions, whereas quantum physics seems incoherent and difficult to reconcile with our experiences of the phenomenon, says less about life itself than it does about the conditions of humankind. In the same way that it was once functional to consume as many calories as possible, because starvation was a far greater risk that obesity, it was functional to regard the world in line with the so-called laws of natural physics and act accordingly. Some memes were simply more viable than others. Quantum physics, like dieting and exercise, is nothing more than a late, premium arrival where human survival is concerned.

Once we have crawled over a threshold, the path back is cut off. Once we have eaten of the tree of knowledge, it is not possible to erase the experience. When we leave the worldview in which humanity has dwelt for what is in this context an extremely long time, we are stepping into worlds which have in a sense always been there, but which it has neither been meaningful nor even possible to explore. Now our new knowledge is a fact, and forms a fundamental component in our understanding of life in general, and of informationalist society in particular. In line with a changing ecology, it is becoming possible, and necessary, to replace the obsolete worldview with a new one, because we have realised that a pre-programmed totality is a precondition for our orientation in spacetime. New circumstances favour certain new memes at the expense of others.

In the case of light, we can confirm that the search for and the production of a light particle is a traditional eternalisation of an ungraspable, mobilistic torrent. This is the norm when we fix a more or less arbitrary extract of chaos and transform it into a stable object, fixed in spacetime, in this case a photon. But if we instead look at a wave motion, we leave the classic production model for fictives and approach mobilistic reality, immanence, by constructing an abstract fictive – admittedly a stable phenomenon of necessity, but with a marked element of noumenal chaos, a hybrid of a classic fictive and an historically new form of fictive, localised to a context characterised by consciousness of the dialectic between eternalism and mobilism.

We can express this by saying that we are eternalising an imagined mobilisation of an imagined eternalisation of a mobilistic phenomenon. We are thus producing a metafictive, which should otherwise be regarded as a secondary fictive, but without in this case – and against what so-called common sense would dictate – first establishing a primary fictive as the basis for our metafictive. The primary fictive is merely assumed, an as yet unopened parcel whose contents we are not even curious about. It is in this process that quantum physics' break with classical physics, like eternalist philosophy's break with classical philosophy, becomes visible.

In the same way that quantum physics insists that both particle and wave motion are two separate but, in terms of truth, equally correct observations of light, eternalist philosophy also insists that eternalism and mobilism are two separate but nonetheless equally correct and also mutually dependent aspects of existence. The deeper understanding of life that Heidegger calls for demands both perspectives, which in turn demands a practised ability to handle contradictions, and to change perspective instantly, according to the situation, in full awareness that the current perspective is merely one side of the matter. This in turn demands that every dream of a finality and unambiguity is replaced by a joy and a sense of belonging within a constantly revised provisional solution.

This causes difficulties. The contradictions of quantum physics cause wear and tear, as shown in our instinctive desire to fictivise the field by dividing the wave-movement into smaller components, in other words: creating a long series of points. But with this the movement would stop being a movement, and quantum physics does not permit this, and eternalist philosophy can help us to understand why, and teach us to accept it. It is of course a fact that the field as a directly produced metafictive in several respects better reflects the qualities of noumenal chaos than a primary fictive could, which takes us closer to an understanding characterised by absolute movement, in other words: constant movement in relation to constant movement. This in turn can facilitate our acceptance of the necessary return to mobilism, which is constantly actualised in every new phase of the eternalistic process.

The difference in this particular respect lies in philosophical ambitions. Establishing a metafictive without a primary fictive as a platform is unthinkable within classical philosophy, but entirely in line with eternalism. The reason is that eternalist philosophy, in contrast to totalist philosophy, does not intend to domesticate mobilistic reality. It has no intention, again in contrast to its predecessor, either to be or to achieve some ultimate, transcendental truth, but sees itself merely as an instrument subordinate to the need for eternalisation and metaphysics. Eternalism is, however, not synonymous with metaphysics, it has no need to localise thought anywhere else but to Dasein. Whenever the eternalist perception of truth seems to be on the point of bursting under the pressure of newly gained knowledge of mobilistic immanence, the doctrine is smoothly altered in the direction of the new insight. The inclusive membrane of eternalism has a surface which remains intact while the contents are in constant development, a movement which is driven by the forces which are active in the surrounding immanence.

The newly-gained creative acceptance of contradictoriness, and the resulting ability to produce metafictives without having to take a detour through primary fictives opens the way for a deeper understanding of life than was possible within the frame of the old worldview. New knowledge has come into reach, and we are forced to exchange fundamental ways of thought so that this new knowledge can be understood as meaningful. The double breakthrough of paradoxism — first within science, followed by the reformatting of philosophy and our understanding of reality — is a necessity if the continued accumulation of knowledge is to be at all possible. New knowledge reveals a new world, of which we human beings form part, which promotes new thinking if we are to understand anything about ourselves and our function in a wider context. The change is slow to start with, and partial, but it later spreads over the whole field of knowledge, at the same time as the speed of the change dramatically increases.

Hegel's perception that the historical goal of thought as a transcendental phenomenon is to think itself as pure thought is further developed in eternalism into the belief that the understanding of the structure of thought itself is the only possible meaning of thought. The goal of thought is not a particular object, but instead the creative avoidance of the thinking of goals, a continual, balanced creation of problems. The death-wish of thought is disarmed, and is turned on itself, and is therefore transformed into a paradoxist desire for life: the paradox of metaphysics is benign, it is life-giving and forms the basis for eternalism's ethics. Eternalism and mobilism speak of different things in different languages, and together they achieve a sort of stereophonic antiphony which can only be understood from the precise point of intersection, dancing on the slack line of the paradox. The dance is the goal and the purpose.

From an eternalist perspective, therefore, paradoxism is the creed of the innermost secret of existence, and from a mobilistic perspective it is the revelation of existence's total lack of a core. Each is as true as the other. Thought is both open and tautological. The question answers itself and must therefore be constantly asked anew. Repetition and difference: all of our interaction with existence, the entire construction of continually new levels of eternalisations, stem from the concept of the eternal return of the same. Nothing changes, at the same time as absolutely everything changes all the time. Wherever we turn, wherever we move, we cannot imagine existence to be any different. Therefore it cannot be said to be different. This is not to say that this world is, as G. W. Leibniz claims, the best of all possible worlds. Instead it is a matter of our own thought. This thought is the best of all thinkable thoughts, because any other way of thought is quite simply unthinkable. Tautology is the word. In contrast, though, this thought can certainly be done with considerably greater intensity, a higher degree of difficulty and with greater enjoyment than we can manage today. The dance can always be developed.

As we have previously stated, affirmative nihilism will sooner or later relieve the cynical variety. The eternalist is manoeuvring out of the comfortless, masochistically enjoyable cul-de-sac of absolute nihilism. Claiming that there is no objective truth is, of course, in Hegelian terms, to affirm a highly objective truth. And not just that: this very truth is a metatruth, a truth about truth itself which renders invisible and denies the basic conditions of thought. Eternalism is philosophical discourse's equivalent of the natural sciences' quantum physics, or rather of the natural sciences' enforced division into classical physics and quantum physics. Initially this seems illogical and without any connection to our sensory perceptions, but gradually, after a process of acclimatisation, it is becoming clarifying and unavoidable, necessary for an understanding which comprises the whole of our knowledge about life.

If we return to the phenomenon of light in an eternalistic context, the photon appears to be a fictive, and wavelength to be a metafictive, based on a concept of a fundamental field, without reference to an underlying fictive in the form of an imaginary point. Even if our thinking is polished by evolution in order to split the metafictive at all costs into a series of fictives, even if we would be incredibly relieved if we could see a wave-movement as an endless chain of particles and thus apparently avoid the troublesome movement itself, we no longer, thanks to the instruments offered by quantum physics and eternalism, need to devote ourselves to such conscious self-deception. We can keep the particle and the wave-movement apart, fictive and metafictive, and avoid the unhappy mixture which makes the contradictory unmanageable. Eternalist philosophy makes it possible to think what we know – at least to a considerably greater extent than before – which implies a revolution considering what we know today, not only about light. This revolution is reformatting not only thought, but also thought about thought.

Maintaining the distinction between fictive and metafictive eternalisations is of the greatest importance. Thanks to this difference between different levels in the production of fictives, there is an opening for a new, eagerly awaited rationality. All linguistic usage depends upon eternalisations, and in order to avoid the fatal mixture of fictive and metafictive eternalisations it is important to keep the distinction in mind, and to be constantly aware of which level is currently applicable. An eternalist form of linguistics will hopefully clean up the mess that classical philosophy has caused. In the same way that the natural sciences will show no tolerance towards a physicist who cannot keep the particle and wave-movement aspects of light apart, so a philosopher who cannot remain aware of the degree of eternalism and mobilism, fictive and metafictive, cannot count upon any great level of credibility after the breakthrough of eternalism.

The fact that quantum physics upsets us is connected to the fact that its findings do not coincide with the programmed pre-understanding with which we construct a cohesive worldview. We have simply never needed to think in quantum-physical ways in order to organise our survival, reproduction and production of identity. On the contrary, that would only have hindered us. But this is no longer the case. The next part of our old, learned and inhibited worldview to be blown to pieces is cosmology, the opposite of elementary particle physics, which will over the coming decades explode before our eyes. The attacks will rain down, in one area after the next, worldview and self-image alike will change beyond recognition. New conditions for survival, reproduction, and not least the production of identity will favour an entirely new form of pre-understanding. An entirely new generation of memes is waiting in the wings for its cue.

Thought is gradually opening up to an increased tolerance towards higher levels of abstraction. Perception of the conditions of spacetime and phenomena are moving towards the point of intersection between eternalism and mobilism. As a result philosophy is liberated from totalism's obstinate attempts to subordinate mobilism to eternalism by force, as well as from absolute and one-sided mobilism's denial of eternalism's pretensions to reality. The result of the breakthrough of eternalist philosophy is an elevated vantage point, a sort of Nietzschean tower from which we can look out upon the paradoxical battle of contradictions. In one sense, Hegel is right in that history reaches its conclusion when he himself completes classical philosophy by identifying thought with the absolute truth about being. But because Nietzsche set thought in motion once again in all senses, history gathers new speed in several different directions. Eternalism gathers these movements together and throws them out into speeding history once again.

As a result, it is possible to transgress the narrow categories which evolution has equipped us with: the interplay between memes and genes enters an entirely new phase, which we shall return to in a later chapter. The balance of power is shifted further to the advantage of the memes and the disadvantage of the genes. We human beings are radically altering the world by thinking completely differently, and by thinking thought entirely differently. This relationship of this new metathought to thought can be compared to thought's relationship to perception, in other words: yet another turbo-charger, even more expressed energy which is being fed back into the system, yet another radiant, eternalistic loop. Once and for all, we are leaving humanism for trans-humanism.

The new science and the new philosophy are part of a mutual non-zero-sum game of cross-pollination, where a development in one field also has an effect in the other. The boundaries of the thinkable are constantly being shifted. The eternalistic metaperspective corresponds, for instance, to how physics is abandoning the study of particles in what to us is familiar four-dimensional spacetime and instead, as in membrane theory, is beginning to observe energies and movements in an eleven-dimensional universe (including gravitation). The informationalist paradigm both facilitates and necessitates a pattern of thought in the thinner air of the level of higher abstraction, a new consciousness with a new, more flexible structure. As the boundaries are burst, every philosophical desire for purity, unity and dogmatism becomes increasingly absurd, for the simple reason that without a recognition of the parallel necessity of both eternalism and mobilism we lose the capacity to form a balanced view of life, and to say anything about its characteristics with any credibility in an informationalist context.

Eternalist thought rejects poststructuralism's singularisation of the Body as the metaphysical foundation of philosophy, in the same way that it rejects the Cartesian fixation with the individual Subject and étatism's fixation with transcendentalisations of the State and the People. Instead, eternalism constantly returns to the same starting point: its own understanding of the eternal return of the same. It is from this thought-out, rather than arbitrary, cosmic foundation that the eternalist social concept is formed, which should be regarded (and anyone who thinks there have already been enough abstractions can skip the rest of this sentence) as an eternalisation of a mobilisation of the eternalised process which has observed the originals and then produced the individual objects, bodies, technologies and distances which make up the phenomenon known as society.

On closer inspection an endless chain of linked movements and freezings becomes apparent, where only an eternalised metaperspective, a freezing of the whole process, can constitute the final eternalisation which forms the foundation of the process as such: the platform from which we observe and produce the phenomenon of society. If we observe the world from, for instance, an aeroplane window, the poststructuralist bodies disappear into the invisible infinitesimal, and what appears is a society in spacetime, buildings and infrastructure. This is civilisation: the mark of technology on nature, another order. Society is, in short, an eternalisation of the same scale as the body, albeit on a different level. Eternalism's socioanalysis, the mapping of the collective unconscious, should be regarded as the equivalent of psychoanalysis on this other level.

This society is neither more nor less fundamental than, for instance, a human body. The question of whether we use society or the body as the basis is only a matter of where we place our vantage point. Eternalist philosophy therefore brutally dismisses all modernist and postmodern ideas that a worldview must necessarily be based upon a specific phenomenon – a body, a subject or a society – as its metaphysical starting point, because every such starting point rapidly loses its credibility thanks to its fixation on one of an infinite number of imaginable perspectives. Instead, eternalist philosophy stems from the conditions for the dialectic between eternalism and mobilism, and these conditions have nothing whatsoever to do with anything outside thought itself, and have, therefore, no connection to any physical reality either. The capitalist paradigm's belief that a fixation upon a particular phenomenon is ideologically necessary seems, in the light of this insight, to be merely a shining example of the muddle of thought that all confusion of eternalism and mobilism leads to.

Within the frame of the paradoxist dialectic we can, in principle, deal with and arrange any number of different perspectives. Therefore it is becoming clear how absurd it is to claim that society does not exist, as in postmodern discourse, or that the collective cannot be said to exist, like the libertarians. In that case, nothing exists, and we will simply be forced to revise our vocabulary. This is just as absurd as saying that there is either a pile of pine-needles, or ants, without seeing the actual ants' nest. Absurdities of this sort are a direct consequence of the inability to separate eternalism and mobilism, and of the inability to realise that language necessarily exists within the eternalistic sphere. Thus eternalism sweeps away a number of old problems, which are basically only a matter of conceptual confusion. At the same time, it is only after this sweep has been done that the possibility emerges for an ideology which sees society as an organism and prioritises the construction of positive feedback loops, in other words: the interests which arise from the relations between phenomena, rather that the specific interests within the phenomena themselves.

The most severe consequence of the dialectic between eternalism and mobilism is that the process of thought can itself never be rational. This is because enormous voids appear between the various fictives, separating them in spacetime, and these voids expand, because they too are in motion in relation to motion. And because the illusion of stability and totality is a necessary precondition of thought, these voids must be continually filled in by the creative imagination of the observer. This creative imagination has an absolutely decisive function in the eternalist model, which can therefore not co-exist with rationalism. The eternalist view of thought is therefore that thought must ultimately be seen as reactive towards its surroundings, and as guesswork, rather than self-sufficient and rational. This means that if eternalist philosophy wants to establish itself properly, it must put the classical axioms of rationalism aside, and regard itself as a sort of meteorology of knowledge, rather than a classic self-deceiving science.

Both spacetime itself and the phenomenon within spacetime are categories which form part of our genetic inheritance. They have become part of our inheritance because they have proved to be extremely useful and beneficial to the survival of our genes, and they therefore do not require learning. Imagination produces totality by filling the voids between the fictives in accordance with our pre-programming, and the results are rapidly adjusted to fit the surrounding collective's production of totality and new incoming data. Upon closer inspection, the process consists of perception and thought constantly presenting, like weather-forecasters on television, a series of more or less well-founded prognoses of the state of things, and these being constantly modified through feedback. This is the meteorology of knowledge, an eternal construction and reconstruction of provisional views of reality. And this flow of fictives is fictivised on a higher level to become a metafictive in the form of a fixed worldview which we preserve and defend to the point where no renovation process in the world can save it, because incoming data can no longer be blended into the totality, which as a result is ready to collapse at any moment. The alternative, then, is either suppression and psychosis, or a shift to an entirely different worldview. The former often precedes the latter. The entire process is known as a paradigm shift.

The need for suppression, or alternatively a total shift, only arises when continuous revision is no longer enough, which strictly speaking means that reflection can be regarded as an endless series of paradigm shifts, albeit microscopic and limited to the individual subject. A paradigm shift on the scale that interests us in this context is, however, both a collective and an individual occurrence, the transition of an entire society from one common, all-encompassing worldview to a completely different one. This is not something which anyone does voluntarily or for the sake of it: it is a turbulent process which changes the ecology of an entire society fundamentally, and therefore forces the collective to orientate itself according to completely new points of reference. Some groups are favoured at the expense of others, entirely new power structures develop, concepts like status and success acquire entirely new meanings and are manifested in entirely new ways.

The eternalist view of history recognises only four paradigm shifts on this scale, all linked to a defining breakthrough in information technology: spoken language, written language, the printing press, and electronic interactivity (for a more detailed discussion of this point, see the first chapter of Netocracy). With the appearance of spoken language, human beings literally became human beings, because the development of the organs of speech coincided with the appearance of homo sapiens; with the development of written language, human beings settled down and formed more cohesive societies; with the printing press, human beings became urbanised and industrialised; and with electronic interactivity human beings are becoming globalised. These paradigm shifts can naturally not be objectively true from any other point of view but the eternalist – the metahistorical truth about truth is that we always write history within the frame of a worldview, and that anything else is impossible – but no other point of view than the eternalist one is, on the other hand, credible and relevant as an informational society's producer of truth.

In order to understand social relations we must first understand what we call the subject, and the basis of the subject is not merely paradoxist, but also ironic. The fact that thought ultimately always rests upon fictives such as the point and the now, and that the totality of the worldview is always highly illusory, clearly shows the central role illusion plays in our lives. The subject must experience the world as a totality in order to experience itself as a totality, otherwise there would be no boundary at all between the world and the subject, and consequently no subject. Lacan, inspired by Hegel, demonstrates precisely this point: how the subject has to think of itself as a totality in order to be able to think itself at all, while at the same time that same subject, from a mobilistic perspective, for instance when regarded by other subjects, can only appear as an echoing void. This is the ironic and paradoxist basis of the subject. In part we have an eternalist subject which must be filled with substance, and in part a mobilist subject which is a pure effort of will, a gesture with no content. Both are true, but in different senses. They contradict one another, at the same time as they come together in the paradoxist subject.

Within this irony there is a deeper one. Every substance which the subject, during its continuous introspection, imagines itself to find embedded in its own essence, has to be cleaned out in order to maintain the illusion, and therefore keep the subject itself alive. The substance-filled ego constantly empties itself in order to be able to refill itself again. The project can never be completed, because that would be the same as the death of the project, and therefore the subject. It is this internal archaeological excavation, complemented by a methodical demonstration of all findings, which characterises self-consciousness and the almost enforced nurturing of the ego. The subject is, thus, a walled, strictly guarded and minutely illuminated void, whose emptiness must always be concealed and at the same time defended. The death-wish is a continual nagging desire to surrender to the pressure of the surrounding world, to tear down the wall and let oneself be filled up by the formless torrent. The problem here is that the subject would be extinguished in the process. The death-wish on an individual level can, in other words, be said to be the individual unconscious's desire to be filled up by and dissolve into the collective unconscious.

On the one hand: the subject's hard-won eternalistic self-image in the form of a container full to the brim of non-world. On the other hand: an indifferently amazed, mobilistic reverse image of the same subject in the form of a vacuum-pack with no content at all. The result is a glaring discrepancy, a vast abyss which the subject in its dealings with the surrounding world seeks to bridge. The fact that the subject only arises and survives in its very struggle to convince the mobilistic surrounding world – full of other eternalist subjects – of its own unique status as subject, is the fundamental fact upon which all social relationships are built. As a result, it is also the starting point for all eternalist sociology.

The only recognition of the subject's substantiality which is at all possible is the subject's recognition of itself, because no other subject can comprehend the existence of any other such substance. This results in a continually recurring and painful lack of recognition, a deficit of identity which the subject tries to remedy by confusedly seeking both psychic and social recognition, a lack which therefore constitutes the very engine of the desire for life. The enforced compromise between the continually unsatisfied subject and the collective – whose existence is naturally dependent upon the existence of the subject; it is enough to state that suicide is an almost universal taboo: at the same time as the collective stands or falls upon the continued maintenance of an identity deficit, because this keeps the subject in the role of its loyal slave – consists of the subject hiding behind a symbolic façade which the partners in the social game have agreed to recognise against the promise that no-one will touch the apparently insoluble, underlying conflict. This symbolic façade is the name, and the effect of the façade is strengthened by the genetically motivated tendency to project the dream of recognition onto the human face. The appearance and survival of the subject can therefore, admittedly, be seen as a form of unconscious voodoo, but the arrangement has worked splendidly for many thousands of years.

Eternalist thought, therefore – unlike all the various variants of capitalist ideology – does not start from either the subject or the body, nor even – unlike Nietzsche, Heidegger and the poststructuralists – from the illusion of the body. The starting point for eternalism is instead the paradoxist illusion itself, both the individual and collective variants. The set of conditions is universally valid, because the paradox of metaphysics is not a phenomenon which restricts itself merely to our human thought, but something which must be built into every imaginable thought, simply because the relationship between thought and existence cannot be imagined any other way. Every form of consciousness must by definition circle around a core of paradoxist illusion, this is the formally eternal but, in terms of content, constantly changing truth about the subject.

As a result of this insight, humanism is definitively consigned to a newly-dug grave. But the burial plot alongside is reserved for the extreme relativism of late-capitalism, in other words: the anti-humanism which started with Kant and was completed by Jacques

Derrida and his many adherents, tripped out on melancholy. Just as atheists practice an inverted form of religion, anti-humanists are no better than embittered and frustrated humanists whose position is entirely determined by what they deny. Eternalism is therefore not reactive and anti-humanist, but active and post-humanist. It sweeps up, cleans out, and moves on. It claims universal validity precisely because the very oscillation between two parallel, fundamentally different but, at the same time, mutually dependent systems is not only acceptable, but absolutely fundamental. As a result, existence as chaos is reconciled to thought in fictive totalities. The synthesis, which is and must be given in advance, reveals both components of the process: the eternalism whose ultimate truth is the greatest lie of mobilism, and vice versa. And they are indissolubly united in the eternal dialectic dance.

According to Lacan, the subject's experience of itself, its self-consciousness, is a process which starts at the moment the original experience of total harmony between the point in space and the now in time is broken and the subject's lack of substance becomes unavoidable. The metaphysical desire which thereafter characterises the subject can be seen as a desire for a healing of this original wound, this shocking disappointment, and therefore as a desire to form part of something else, something larger. Naturally, this is ultimately a longing for extinction, comparable to the Freudian death-wish or the Buddhist desire for the extinguishing of Nirvana.

The path to extinction is edged with other subjects who offer the same temptation, difficult to resist. The mutual death-wish of the subjects attracts them to one another. The result is a desire for symbiosis, a longing for ultimate submission, total domestication, and this is a fundamental driving force in all forms of social relationship. By combining, the subjects hope to avoid their fundamental existential loneliness. If it were not for the fact that the hermit-instinct – which stems from the subject's longing for recognition, both its own possible and the collective's impossible recognition – encourages the opposite desire in the subject, to transgress domestication and maintain an absolute boundary against the outside world – only that which still exists can demand and enjoy recognition – then the desire for symbiosis would dissolve all social dynamics and society would implode. The paradoxist subject therefore gains its energy from the internal power-struggle between the desire for symbiosis and the hermit-instinct. The oscillating but maintained balance between these two desires is the very precondition for the existence of the subject.

The paradoxist process of subjectification means that the subject arises from the very contradiction between mobilism's demand that the subject be an illusion (the subject confronting the death-wish), and eternalism's demand that the subject be a metaphysical basis (the subject confronting the desire for life). The subject is consequently a phantasmagoria floating in the field of tension between these two fictives. What the ego does not know about itself it has to imagine with the help of the meteorology of knowledge. This is the paradox of metaphysics of the subject level. In the mobilist sphere, metaphysics are an impossibility, but within the eternalist sphere they are a necessity. Without this paradoxity we cannot imagine ourselves as thinking beings. Existence is, when we come to think of it, fundamentally paradoxist.

The life of a human being can seem like an endless series of vain attempts to dissolve the paradox which is the very precondition of life, which adds yet another paradoxist and ironic dimension. It is these eternal, tragically fruitless efforts which Nietzsche praises in his ethics by using the word Versuch. Every Versuch is with devastating probability doomed to fail, but one can never be entirely certain; the failure is not predetermined by fate or inscribed in any law. Therefore human beings must act out every Versuch with maximum effort – like a conscious protest of the desire for life against, and therefore also a reckoning with, its origins in the death-wish – in spite of all previous failures. This is Nietzsche's tragic ethics, the love of fate: amor fati. Consequently it is also the starting point for the whole of mobilistic thought, which, via Freud and psychoanalysis, has been further developed and partially restored to philosophy by thinkers like Bataille and Lacan.

In a mobilistic sense we cannot really speak of a subject at all. But what we can speak of is a process, a series of impulses, whose starting point is the mobilistic origin of the subject. Lacan attributes this origin to the early separation of the child's body from that of its mother. This is, to borrow a metaphor from physics, the big bang of the ego. The origin of the ego is infinitesimal and must be presupposed by eternalism, even if in a mobilistic sense it can never be tied to any specific now. This singularity, this fictive moment of birth of the subject, is actually from a mobilistic point of view merely a continuous, flat chain of actuality, a field of events rather than one particular event.

This singularity is developed, when seen as a process, with infinite speed. As a result, a countless number of potential subject processes die every imaginable moment: all the possibilities which are not actualised, and all the countless consequences which in turn stem from these. A veritable genocide of unborn subjects takes place in every now. Only a single subject process lives on, is singularised and immediately splits into an endless number of potential subject processes, of which all but one are exterminated in the next imaginable moment, upon which this single actualised survivor forms the starting point for the next link in the further development of the chain. And so on, ad infinitum.

The innumerable mass of variables and the high degree of chance in this process mean that the chain's development and its necessity can only be determined with hindsight. If we in our thoughts summarise this chain and see it as a single continuum which imagines itself, we have created an eternalistic subject. But it has, as we have said, a constantly evasive twin. We cannot observe the mobilistic subject process when we have the eternalistic subject in front of our eyes. We cannot observe the mobilistic subject at all, because its only defining feature is its emptiness, which is why all that is left is a striking absence. Both of these subjects are true in their correct context, and only there, and together they constitute the paradoxist subject which demonstrates entirely different characteristics from different angles. This means that the question of the subject's existence or non-existence must, in eternalist philosophy, be answered with 'both'.

It is extremely illuminating to see the subjectification process as analogous to the universe's development in time, which in a mobilistic sense has been a development of an endless number of potential universes, of which only a thin thread of actualities has wound its way through the narrow passage of imagined moments. The immanence is an endless sea of potentialities, where a single small island of actuality flickers for a moment before immediately fading and being replaced by a new one, which also immediately fades, and so on. This sea is a bottomless grave for countless possibilities, which would be truly tragic if that thin thread of actualities were not itself the bearer of countless possibilities. The universe is in this sense itself an infinite magnitude, at every imagined moment.

Consciousness cannot imagine either the infinite, nor the infinitesimal in which the origins of everything are lost. If this were the case, if consciousness really could get a grasp of the infinite and the infinitesimal, consciousness would grow rigid and cease all activity, it would fade and be extinguished. The totality would be real, everything in infinity would have its equivalent in thought, the creative function of the imagination would be abolished, the meteorology of knowledge would itself have no purpose. As a result, the thinking subject would also dissolve, be discharged because of a lack of work. The inaccurate correspondence between thought and being is thus itself the deficiency which makes thought, and therefore life itself, possible. Both existence and thought have to take place within the finite in order to exist.

Eternalist epistemology can be summarised by saying that the amount of information is always impossible to grasp, no matter how limited the perspective may be. And, contrary to what rationalism claims, information is always running away from us. However hard we attempt to grasp it, it will always run through our fingers like sand, because the amount of information which is produced always greatly exceeds the amount of information which we – or any other imaginable divine being, for that matter – might possibly be thought to handle. But in contract to what rationalism claims, this is actually a blessing. There is no chance of managing without the meteorology of knowledge, the compass, based upon a provisional set of paradoxes, which ultimately keeps our illusory thought in motion and our double subject alive.

Those who deny that God is dead often claim that God is not only extremely alive, but that he is also all-seeing and all-knowing. This is, in actual fact, the definition of God's being. But if God knows everything, then he is guaranteed to be dead. And of course he would have realised this himself, if he really does know everything. Life is, instead, the art of getting a small portion of confused and tragic information, and a large dose of creative and comic imagination to collaborate with one another in a constantly surprising piece of theatre, performed against the ungraspable and indifferent backdrop of mobilistic reality. Faith in the divine or the supernatural is, in the light of this beautiful insight, no more than a poorly concealed fear or hatred of life itself. If we want to love instead of hate, we must therefore constantly remind ourselves that we are in the state which Heidegger calls Dasein, and nowhere else; there is nothing divine, nothing supernatural, only the human, the all too human. But one can love that, and one can love that together with other people, precisely because it actually exists.

8.

ETERNALISM'S RADICAL PRAGMATISM

THE STATUS OF THE SUBJECT underwent a dramatic devaluation during the twentieth century, partly as a result of developments within psychoanalysis and linguistics. The subject lost its role as master of its own house, the ego was given a supervisor in the form of a superego. The paradoxist subject's double aspects mean that another boundary is being transgressed in this respect. The static power hierarchy of psychoanalysis is being replaced by the dialectic dynamism of schizoanalysis. The subject therefore does not even have a house of which to be master, but is instead in constant motion. This is all that remains today of the proud subject which has been the solid anchoring point for humanism since Descartes: a fundamentally schizoid and nomadic illusion, a constantly on-duty and constantly inadequate crisis-manager with a constantly growing backlog of microscopic paradigm shifts to deal with. And the one, mobilistic, hand really does not know what the other, eternalistic, hand is doing.

The traditional vertical model of psychoanalysis is being replaced by the horizontal model of schizoanalysis. Friends of order can justifiably question our continued use of a concept such as the unconscious. This is, however, a question of a dialectic relationship which is neither spatial nor temporal in the usual sense, because it is acted out in a never resting circular movement in the form of a loop. Therefore we can, if for no other reasons than for pedagogical, imagine a horizon of consciousness, and the unconscious as a border zone linked to what is neither conscious nor lacking in consciousness, which is indefinable and unreachable, and which is the home of intuitive intelligence, a sort of filter with certain elementary sorting functions in which waste products are picked up and processed.

The post-Cartesian subjectification process can, in Lacan's spirit, be described as a dance around or above an empty abyss. A political philosophy on an eternalistic basis presupposes, as we have already shown, that the same pattern also applies to the collective subject, informationalism's modified and more precise version of the capitalist concept of Society. Informationalist society is thus ultimately a ritual dance around a void in the collective unconscious: a paradoxity, a deficiency, a vacuum, which must be regarded mobilistically and empirically as an illusion.

In line with the dialectic between eternalism and mobilism, this collective illusion is eternalised into an informationalist we, an identity which constitutes the metaphysical basis for, and the object of, eternalist socioanalysis. The collective subject is, like the individual subject, necessarily empty. It can never be given an immanent content of any sort, but instead must be constantly emptied and filled and then emptied again, a Sisyphean labour. The function of the subject is symbolic; symbolism emptied of content, a social agreement. If the content actually existed, the illusory characteristics of the eternalisation – its absolute motion and consequently its chronic instability – would be revealed at once. This would mean that the constant work of building and maintaining the collective subject would be unthinkable and impossible.

The dawning insight at the end of the nineteenth century about the central role that the paradox of metaphysics plays in the collective unconscious was developed into a widespread vulgarised form of Nietzscheanism within twentieth-century thought in general, and within poststructuralism in particular. When orthodox Marxism collapsed, the hopeless task of discovering an absolute truth in language instead of being was pursued. Consequently this cynical nihilism cannot bear the thought of a collective subject, and refuses to recognise the existence of society in any form, using the argument that society must be an illusion. As if any subject, or any eternalisation at all, could under any circumstances be anything but illusory from a mobilistic perspective. The reasoning becomes a purely tautological conceptual exercise. Water can never be dry, because when we use the term water we always mean something wet.

Cynical nihilism's relativists effectively trip themselves up as soon as they formulate themselves, because they then suppose something which they believe to be true, and because they thereby also acknowledge in action their own existence in their capacity as eternalistic subjects. And anyone who means, and communicates, that every utterance is a rhetorical constellation whose content is produced by the recipient, has suggested, and communicated, something particular. Anyone who expresses themselves at all unavoidably does so as a subject. The only way out of this self-imposed logical cul-de-sac, at least for anyone who cannot close their eyes to the mobilistic perspective, is the dialectic between eternalism and mobilism. Eternalist philosophy joins in unreservedly with postmodernism's original scepticism: naturally the collective subject is an illusion. At the same time it blithely contradicts itself: naturally, society must be a reality. By interacting socially we create society every day and in every moment, and it is in this sense, as something continually developing and never finished, that society is an eternalistic reality.

By constantly leading the work of ideology back to the mutually advantageous feedback loops which characterise network society – and which need far more than a monetarily-driven market to function – eternalist thought opens the way for a new socialism, beyond the cynical vulgarised individualism of post-Marxism, this time in informationalist form. The creation, maintenance and eventually the ownership of the collective subject, the metaphysical complex of empty symbols and eternalised phenomena, is what the informationalist power struggle is about, and one extremely valid point of view in this respect is that this ownership can, or rather must, be communal. This applies on all levels, both within the virtual nomadic tribes and in respect of the we of the global empire. One concrete example of a practical application of eternalist socioanalysis is the common slogan of the developing global socialism: 'one man, one vote, globally', where the goal is a world-encompassing political structure which can balance and correct mutations within the already partially globalised market, because it falls under the strict economic principle of 'one dollar, one vote'.

In comparison with this growing eternalistic socialism, the traditional leftwing movement at the turn of the millennium is ideologically effectively lost. From an eternalist perspective, popular poststructuralists' cries for the collective subject to be replaced by the diffuse and crypto-transcendental concept of the Multitude, for instance in Michael Hardt and Anronio Negri's famous book

Empire, seem like complete idiocy. A socialism with a pacified and mystified, rather than an active and self-aware, collective subject at its centre means little more than an anxious retreat back from informationalism, replaced by a neurotic embrace of the ruins of the capitalist order. The Multitude seems, on closer inspection, to be little more than a fashionable term for the musty old concept the People. At best, this lazy non-thinking can be used to stimulate medially spectacular riots, but only at the cost of abdicating from any opportunity to take part seriously in the game for real power in informational society.

The truth is that the production of identity has never been more real or more important than it is in early informationalism. The fact that the existence of the collective subject is questioned from the limited perspective of extreme mobilism only makes the necessity of a complementary eternalist analysis more pressing. Denying the various social identities their actuality merely demonstrates an impermissible level of naïvety, and an almost masochistic refusal, on the part of the Spinozan left both to realise that power is localised, and to see what form meaningful resistance to power should take in informational society. Philosophers like Hardt and Negri must have forgotten to study Lenin before they began to spread their insidious New-Age romanticism. The sudden attraction of the Spinozan left to late-capitalism's embittered and disillusioned leftwing activists – who, like small children, do not want anything to do with reality, and only want to hear happy stories with bittersweet endings – lies in its predetermined failure. Either consciously or unconsciously, it is expending all of its energy on making itself irrelevant.

In contrast to the Spinozan left's soppy romanticism, eternalism's political philosophy does not flinch at the big, difficult questions that the left has to answer if it wants to be credible at the onset of informationalism. Not least, eternalism stresses the production of social identities as the key to understanding. What seemed an incredible and provocative prophecy to Nietzsche's contemporaries is fast becoming for our present and future something utterly obvious, and the necessary basis for anyone interested in the collective unconscious of the global empire. In Netocracy we explain at length how mobilism offers an almost tailor-made set of axioms for the new elite, the netocracy, with its obsession with speed, movement, tribalism, network dynamics and eventism. If we transfer this argument to the area of political philosophy, it is unavoidable that eternalism – as a consequence of the triumph of mobilist discourse in the sociological arena – will form the basis for the production of ideology in information society.

When Nietzsche claimed that God was dead, he did not mean that human beings had suddenly stopped believing in the existence of God. Atheism is as old as religion itself, and has always played a vital role in the history of thought. Large and important non-European thought systems – Zoroastrianism, Jainism and Buddhism – rest upon atheistic foundations, which Nietzsche, of course, was fully aware of. What he meant was instead that modern humanity was becoming aware that the universe could very well have existed, and actually did exist for a greater part of its history, and to a great extent still does exist, without any living beings at all, either human beings or animals, and therefore also without perception and thought, without subject or metaphysical foundation. Nietzsche went on to say that modern humanity was starting to realise the immense consequences of this insight. The world is, in actual fact, a turbulence in a void, precisely the world which Hegel so demonstratively ignores. Immanent nature has no need for any divine creator or any thinking human beings with metaphysical ideas. Suddenly the world became very cold, the cosy fires of philosophy's search for meaning had gone out. It was not just God who was dead, but also, as Nietzsche's follower Michel Foucault claims, humanism's self-satisfied idea of Man as God's replacement.

The fundamental problem in this context is that it is not possible to relate to a genuinely chaotic reality, a turbulence in a void. In such circumstances, human consciousness can neither function nor exist. Both perception and thought demand order, and we are forced to produce this order ourselves with the help of a sophisticated information management process based upon feedback and continual revision. We eternalise existence, and we both mobilise and eternalise our eternalisations of existence. We create fictives, snapshots of fictive points at fictive points in time, and then eternalise these fictives in relation to one another, creating metafictives, systems of ideas of existence. We match these against the ideas of those around us, and together construct, with the help of language and art, a collective worldview. The boundaries are fluid, everything is constantly in motion, and the motion moves from perception to consciousness and back again, since perception is always being adjusted.

Between fictives which are suitably similar to one another, and are positioned suitably close to one another on the paradigmatic arena, oscillations occur. Some fictives even harmonise with the mental disposition which is embedded within our inherited characteristics. The ideological resonance which thus arises between different clusters of fictives and our innate, given categories govern the process which we call the meteorology of knowledge. Some oscillations are more intense than others, and are therefore given priority in the information management process which necessarily has to prioritise very strictly. This process of selection leads to a frenzied meme-Darwinian battle for survival and reproduction. When different memes, so to speak, seem to coalesce and reinforce one another, when we perceive thereby that things seem to fall into place, we happily incorporate these particular memes into our worldview at the expense of countless other memes. Our idea of the truth is thus never a question of a rational factual process, but is instead a matter of experienced intensities, where a point or a now has an endless intensity. This fact is known within eternalistic epistemology as the intensity principle: the oscillation itself always beats a lack of oscillation, and the high-intensity oscillation always beats the low-intensity.

In this way, ideological resonance is a decisive component in the production of metafictives and the creation of a worldview. The resonance means that we choose to see what seems to remind us of, and agrees with, what we already think that we have seen before. New constellations always mean at least an initial disharmony; it is quite simply more pleasant to feel at home, because every rearrangement only seems to mean a lot of extra work. Consequently, the refined production of fictives is hugely important. In order to facilitate our orientation to the highest degree, and avoid costly disorientating rearrangements, consciousness chooses in principle to perceive a single movement for each individual phenomenon, a movement either towards or away from the cosmic foundation: the overwhelming, already established perception of the actual field.

Imagination has the task of maintaining the illusion of stability. The resulting artificially stable consciousness makes it possible for human beings to step outside themselves and see themselves from single-handedly constructed, external viewpoints. This ability expands greatly in language, which is the world alongside the world where consciousness assumes graspable and communicable form, a refined eternalisation which rests upon a series of advanced illusions such as the subject, the now and the point. The continuation of the process in a loop is demonstrated by the fact that language in turn produces the overwhelming illusion: being. Totality precedes the individual components.

The fictives coagulate as memes (we will return to memetics in the next chapter), which in turn are organised in systems known as ideologies. The production of ideologies arises at the moment when the human subject assumes self-aware form. Every ideology consists of just a handful of fictives, inherited programming and more or less confused empirical interpretations via sensory impressions of supposed patterns in the chaotic immanence. On top of this there is a large portion of imagination which fills the gaps between the fictives in order to create the ideology's necessary totality. This process of filling occurs in the unconscious and pre-conscious border-zone, and it is only when totality is a fact that we can actually become conscious of any ideology and start to perceive its constituent parts. The ideology, made conscious, in turn influences perception and the production of fictives, which in turn leads to continuous ideological testing.

Language is also the arena in which the ideologies conduct meme-Darwinian wars against one another. This struggle gives rise to a constant stream of new, multi-dimensional relations of movements, a chaos which must also be illusorily frozen, eternalised, if it is to be at all possible to view and get an idea of it. The production of fictives reappears on a new level of consciousness, with a greater degree of abstraction, as metafictives. The movements which must be fixed and placed in stable relationships to one another are no longer suggested patterns in an immanent chaos, but suggested patterns in a torrent of symbols, which in turn refer to other symbols. The structure which arises, the result of this second-level collective ideology production, is what we call the symbolic order.

A new mobilistic state arises when the various symbolic orders meet and are faced with one another. This can be a question of any ideological opposition, depending on which level we are concerned with. And so the chain of alternately mobilistic and eternalistic states continues, in principle eternally. It is only when we freeze this entire movement, conceptualise the very process of thinking, and accept both the chain's infinitesimal origin and its infinite conclusion – however impossible it is for us finite creatures to get an idea of these – that we can establish an eternalistic ontology and epistemology. The whole of this alternating movement of fictivisation and chaos is frozen in a single gigantic metafictive. To a rationalist this can seem like a half-measure, a superficial solution to the problem, but in actual fact it means that we, unlike the rationalist, have stopped chasing the wind, because we understand, accept and love the nature of wind, and are no longer wishing that the wind would stop and allow itself to be captured. We have learned, once and for all, to distinguish between our human needs and those of the indifferent world around us.

It is therefore the eternalising process itself, and not the platform from which it is observed, which is stable and can thus form the basis for thought. And it is therefore, ironically, only at the moment that we abandon classical philosophy's grandiose ambitions that we achieve the desired stability. Here, at the ultimate boundary of knowledge about knowledge, it is, however, as Heidegger points out, less a matter of rational knowledge than a meditative understanding. Eternalisation will never stand up to a thorough examination, but dissolves into movement, which it is its nature to do. Eternalism can never be a truth of all truths, but must instead be regarded as a metaphysical state achieved through an act of will.

From this turning point of nihilism, thinking passes into eternalism's radical pragmatism: a joyous and conscious creation of value from a foundation formed by a failure which is tragic but inevitable. For Nietzsche, this is affirmative nihilism put into practice and formulated as eternalist ethics. What is pragmatic about it is the acceptance and defence of boundaries which are already given in advance, while what is radical is the simultaneous rejection of these boundaries and a refusal to conform. Precisely this empirically impossible transgression is, according to Nietzsche, the genuinely ethical act. As a result, eternalism's radical pragmatism is restricted exclusively to the world as it is, at the same time as it transgresses it.

This is the practical aspect of the paradoxist dialectic between eternalism and mobilism: the mobilist worldview forces the body to remain in pragmatism, while the eternalist worldview spreads reflection – observation and analysis of the world – beyond pragmatism. Once again, there is no fundamental contradiction in this oppositional relationship. Or, to put it another way: the contradiction is evident, but it is the cohesive rather than the divisive factor in the actual relationship, and it is precisely the contradiction which maintains radical pragmatism in motion. And it is this motion which makes up the political ideology, and therefore the foundation for political activism which is consistent with informationalism's worldview.

As a result, everything becomes both simpler and more complicated: simpler because eternalist philosophy clears away a long series of wrongly-phrased and therefore meaningless questions from the agenda; more complicated because these wrongly-phrased questions were nevertheless based upon comfortable simplifications and were phrased to appeal to the old, secure, symbolic order of things. The classical dialectic either/or is comfortable and convenient, but ultimately unproductive, particularly in light of what we now know about all the paradoxes of existence. The paradoxist dialectic both/and is, on the other hand, unfamiliar and difficult to handle, but is at the same time the only path which is remotely clear after the paradigm shift. Anyone looking for a key in the lamp-light has, of course, the advantage of good lighting, but if there is no key there at all, and if it is neither the key nor the lock which is the problem, but rather the way of perceiving the architecture itself, then it might be a good idea to do something entirely different somewhere else, even if the lighting is rather worse.

Before the arrival of transrationalism, rationalism was confronted with anti-rationalism, in other words: either/or. Transrationalism instead proclaims both/and, which of course is also the same as neither. Rationalism starts from the axiom that there is a single truth, even if this is as yet unknown, and that this is accessible to language and linguistic understanding, which has a direct connection to a reality which, although difficult to find, is never inaccessible. Anti-rationalism imagines that it says the opposite: every so-called truth is relative and therefore untrue in all other contexts but its own, and linguistic understanding is basically deceptive because language is a closed system of internal references, as a result of which no understanding can actually comprise anything but the system of rules which apply within a particular discourse. But neither of these perspectives is satisfactory.

Rationalism's aims and goals are clearly absurd – the whole of rationalist logic is, ironically, based upon a completely illogical article of faith – which is why anti-rationalism can seem, if not attractive, then at least credible upon cursory inspection. But anti-rationalism inevitably ends up in a dead-end where it is turned upon itself: to say that no truth is true is itself to proclaim a truth which has pretensions to being true. Anti-rationalism is thus nothing but another form of rationalism, and a cynical and shabby rationalism at that, because what it is so frenetically attacking is nothing but its own blind-spot. The transrationalist attitude towards the supposed oppositional pairing of rationalism and anti-rationalism is therefore that it is not a question of opposites at all, but of two different versions of the same thing. The two discourses share, above all, the same fundamental problem: they lack humility, because they refuse to be confronted by their own limitations. If they did, they could transgress all limitations. The result of this fruitless opposition is a clear sign of a collapsing paradigm: thought as escapism, characterised by countless exceptions and evasions, and coloured by insufficient self-criticism, or even a total lack of it, in short: large-scale, naïve wishful-thinking.

Just as Nietzschean atheism is concerned with a genealogical mapping of the origins and functions of religions instead of getting to grips with the theological question of God's existence or otherwise, transrationalist eternalism is concerned with an examination of the very desire for rationalism from a paradoxist perspective, instead of confronting the claims of classical philosophy, because the rules of classical philosophy cannot easily be seen as relevant. As a result, not only does rationalism fall, but also anti-rationalism with its embittered desire for an impossible hyperrationalism. The thorough failure of the anti-rationalist is his inability to think outside of what he is criticising. As a result, he becomes the prisoner and slave of resentment, enclosed behind the bars of utopianism's prison, against which he is vainly smashing his fists to a pulp (or, rather, self-pityingly tapping a little with his finely-manicured nails). But the problem is not a question of a key or a lock, but of the way of looking at the architecture of the prison. It is perfectly straightforward to leave the prison at the moment eternalism and mobilism are no longer mixed up, but instead held separate and allowed to interact with one another.

The allegedly Nietzschean poststructuralism is thereby revealed to be fundamentally anti-Nietzschean, because its ultimate driving-force is an ill-concealed resentment towards rationalism's failure in the form of the so-called modern project. This is at odds with Nietzsche's own doctrine, which never shows any resentment towards modernism, but merely questions its transcendentalisation of itself (the elevation of Humankind as the replacement for God), and points out the dramatic consequences that this act will have for the production of morals. Nietzsche is absolutely not an anti-rationalist, certainly not in the sense that the word came to mean in the twentieth century, but ought instead to be regarded as the first transrationalist.

A purely practical problem as far as twentieth-century thought is concerned has been the innate conservatism of academic institutions and their subordination to a paradigm which is on its last legs, which has hardly made it worthwhile to seek out creative new forms of thought in the old universities. Peer-pressure has hindered different forms of thought, the current university system of peer review has been devastating for philosophy, and the lack of competition has resulted in a lack of incentive to think differently; an inferior professor is passed around the institutions rather than be forced to give up his high-status position, which in turn has led to feelings of guilt and shame for all involved, which have to be suppressed and hidden, et cetera. In such circumstances it is obviously difficult, not to say impossible, to think and formulate anything substantially new.

Eternalist philosophy lives in and from the paradox, it extracts the renewable energy of the paradox in order to keep thought in motion, and therefore alive. The sum of all current perspectives, the metafictive which precedes and links all fictives, forms the starting-point for the separate subject's worldview, which is constantly retuned against the collective worldview. And it is in the original contradiction – the paradox of metaphysics, the constantly present and indissoluble relationship between eternalism and mobilism – that both the single and the collective subject arises. The separate subject is a fictive, and the ego is the meme which is connected to this fictive, in the same way as the we is the meme which is connected to the collective subject's fictive. The eternalist is conscious that he is practising advanced illusionism, that neither an ego nor a we can exist in any immanent sense, but he is equally conscious that this ego and this we are necessary constants in order to make information-society's network-dynamic equations work.

In contrast to the anti-rationalists and the poststructuralists, we take Nietzsche's message seriously and are creating, instead of trying to derive, the basis upon which we are constructing our worldview. In order to achieve even a shred of comprehension, we perform the Indian rope-trick in every waking moment, for ourselves and also together. Eternalism is in essence an active philosophy – in contrast to rationalism's and anti-rationalism's absurd belief that philosophy can and ought to be a derivative, passive activity – which cannot even be thought without being practised. This is what is called the radical pragmatism of eternalism, and it is indissolubly linked to, and is therefore also a fundamental component of, eternalist philosophy itself. And this really is a question of a rope-trick: the chaos of immanence itself lacks given forms and categories, the structures of comprehension are produced within consciousness. On the other hand, we have had many millions of years to learn this incredibly sophisticated trick. Within the theory of evolution there is much talk of precisely 'good tricks', useful skills which are linked to a particular gene-type, a special variant of the brain's wiring. And this act of illusion, conjuring stable fictives from formless chaos, is one of the very best and most fundamental of all tricks.

The experienced differences are verified in the consciousness and sanctioned as fictives when the consciousness perceives that the differences harmonise with the fictive-systems of surrounding groups and individuals. These fictives are incorporated into the interaction which produces the ideological resonance through communication within the collective. Through feedback, this resonance colours the interpretation of new sensory impressions, which gives rise to new differences, new fictives, eventually a different ideological resonance, and so on. Every level of every worldview, single and collective, is therefore constantly in motion in a system of repetition and difference; the ideological resonance is constantly exposed to larger and smaller modifications, paradigm shifts on a macro- or micro-level. Natural selection long ago removed individuals who lack the aptitude to learn this trick quickly. We are in this way all the offspring of evolution's winners.

Classical philosophy wants to prove that it is possible to demonstrate clear similarities between different cultures' worldview in general terms, which must mean that the noumenal world speaks an easily understood language which is recognised in roughly the same way everywhere. What it tries to prove is that humanity was born blessed with a common sense derived from transcendental origins. This is, however, a fatal logical mistake. Common sense does not actually exist, what does exist is merely ideological resonance. And this ideological resonance can never have a status as a higher ideological truth, but is purely an survival mechanism conditioned by evolution. The similarities between different cultures' worldviews therefore only reveals that similar conditions for survival exist in different places.

Natural selection has for a long time favoured a certain array of tricks, which is why we do not differ genetically from our siblings in other cultures. And it would be strange if it were otherwise, considering how incredibly slow the pace of genetic change is. Memes, on the other hand, have a far higher rate of change, and therefore the differences between cultures are far more noticeable. It is precisely these memetic variations which make up the differences between different cultures. But the development of memes is most of all conditioned by the development of other memes. Consequently the similarity of a priori forms, related to the differences of various cultures, tells us nothing about the existence of any universally valid categories of transcendental origin. They merely tell of universally applicable conditions of survival for humanity.

If we were to try to think of a metaphysical foundation of immanence, it would still remain an unfathomable mystery. This mystery implies a void, and this void has been occupied throughout history by countless religions and philosophies in the hope of conquering power against the promise of expelling all existential angst arising from this unfathomable mystery. The most difficult question has been given a long series of simple answers, simply because this has been the easiest option. But after all the broken promises and collapsed utopias, the void and the unfathomable mystery remain, unaffected by all internal wishful-thinking and all anthropomorphic projections. Every attempt to clarify the mystery is doomed to fail. Ironically, this failure is the source of our salvation.

The noumenal world is by definition unreachable, unfathomable, and has, therefore, nothing to either hide or reveal. Chaos is chaos. The finite being's finite thought can never think of infinity as

369

infinity. The only insight we can hope for in this context is that every perception of chaos is illusory – an illusion of an illusion of an illusion, and so on ad infinitum. This is the transrational imperative: we can never become or be rational beings in the classical sense; what we can do, on the other hand, and have to do for the sake of our own survival, is to create our own rationality. We build our lives and our societies in accordance with a pragmatic and always provisional quotidian rationalism, in full awareness of the innate limitations of this rationalism. This works as long as we keep a careful eye on the difference between eternalism and mobilism, as long as we are transrational.

The breakthrough and resilience of a priori categories is in direct relationship to the functional value of the phenomenon in survival and reproduction contexts. There are therefore good reasons to look for the first signs of conflict between an old and a new worldview within the cultural and intellectual fields where the link to the genes' survival is weak or non-existent. Art, music and boundary-transgressing sciences like quantum physics and cosmology are relatively marginal and exclusive fields as far as the genes' interests are concerned, where the crisis of the old paradigm can therefore be discerned and contemplated without ordinary people having their sleep disturbed as a result. The circuitry of the brain prioritises neither one nor the other complex of perceptions, quite simply because the survival and reproduction of genes has thus far not been dependent upon any particular attitude within any of these areas.

The business of thinking deals with extremely abstract fictives, ideas about ideas about ideas, which is why a slight change in the entrance values can have an enormously large impact further on in the process. These changes of the initial conditions can have dramatic consequences which seriously affect our conditions of survival to an unimaginable extent. As the physically weakest of the savannah's mammals, humankind's only competitive advantage was its unique, sophisticated capacity for communication, which promoted and was developed in tandem with a unique, sophisticated intelligence. A pragmatically orientated curiosity about the conditions of life belongs, alongside a highly developed capacity for imitation, without doubt to the tricks which are inscribed upon human genes. It is these characteristics which make humankind the chosen favourite of the memes – if we follow this chain of thought to its conclusion, we might as well say that the memes have created us humans and our genes in order to serve their own survival purposes – and it is in the fields where the memes' superiority over the genes is most marked that the production of fictives shows the greatest number of, and most interesting, innovations.

Newtonian physics was greeted with such unanimous joy because it so thoroughly confirmed everyday experiences and was in line with so many a priori categories. And because humankind is addicted to stability, it consequently began to call for a new Newton in every conceivable area of life. These dreams are still alive, even if they appear less and less credible with each passing day. When quantum physics reverses the historical direction of travel towards Newtonian confirmation of a visible universe of categories inside out, and instead starts to talk about contradictions, it means that the door is opening onto what seems to be an absurd and lawless country, and the result is that ordinary people choose not to see or hear for as long as possible. The a priori categories make quantum physics extremely difficult to take onboard, which is why physics is being reduced in the collective consciousness to a marginal and exclusive field without any connection to everyday experience. The problem for ordinary people is merely that the absurdities are starting to become so numerous and so intrusive. It is enough to look at what is happening within the economy and politics. Never before has the so dearly desired stability of worldview seemed so far away.

The field of the new physics is a typically boundary-transgressing area, a scientific Kurdistan which comprises parts of both mobilistic immanence and eternalist metaphysics. Because the limitations of metaphysics are evident, it must be complemented with a new and expanded variant. In line with the expansion of the collective eternalisation of mobilistic immanence, it is becoming the task of eternalist thought to produce new truths which make the expanded perspective comprehensible, in which even previously known phenomena demand new truths. This total rewrite and expansion constitute the textbook example of a paradigm shift. It is therefore not enough to insert a few new definitions; the whole dictionary must be rewritten from cover to cover.

The transition from a capitalist to an informationalist paradigm means that rationalism in both its guises – in other words, even as anti-rationalism – is going to its grave and being replaced by transrationalism. The fact is that rationalism started to fail even in Hegel's thinking, when he pointed out that mathematics is purely tautological in nature, and always refers internally to itself. Mathematics has, of course, many practical applications, but this says nothing about the inner nature of anything else. However, rationalism has been able to reign unthreatened for the remainder of capitalism because there has been no serious challenger, and every criticism of rational common sense has only had the character of a doomed rescue mission, or resentment of the failure of the modern project.

It is only when Lacan reads Nietzsche that the idea arises that Hegel's view of the tautology of mathematics might be applied to language, which obviously has tumultuous consequences. If language is tautological in the same way as mathematics, then our entire worldview, produced in language, is consequently also tautological. As a result, language is on every level dependent upon an innate paradox. This insight was already hinted at by Hegel, but because the Hegelian dialectic is fixed within a linear historical perception, the dialectic process is never paradoxist, which would be consequential. The kick which moved matters on from this unsatisfactory incomplete state with Hegel came from Nietzsche's metaperspective on history and the concept of the eternal return of the same.

A vision characterised by rationalism, linearity and totality is an unmistakable sign that the death-wish of thought has taken over. At the same moment that such a vision seems to have been realised, thought dies, because the completely rounded thought has no language left with which to think itself. It empties itself of all content and dissolves into nothingness. This concealed void is the dark secret of rationalism, and it is the unconscious but strong fear of this void which explains rationalism's power under capitalism. The rationalist project consists of using colossal effort to try to bridge the opposition between thought and world, and thus replenishing the dreadful void. Rationalist thought is therefore instrumental, thinking is result-orientated. For Nietzsche, on the other hand, creative thought without any illusions is never productive in the rationalist sense, only exploratory and investigative. Nietzsche's genealogist, Foucault's archaeologist and eternalism's meteorologist – rather than classical philosophy's builder – are the credible ideals for anyone wanting to involve themselves in philosophy.

The liberating kick in this context came from Nietzsche's abandonment of the ambition to reach a metaphysical basis for thought outside of thought itself. With Hegel, the goal of thinking was admittedly that thinking should think of itself as thinking. But this model still needs an external engine to hold together, and Hegel is forced to solve this by making History, or the Spirit, the engine of thought. He is forced to reintroduce God into the worldview. With Nietzsche, on the other hand, there is no basis other than the desire for a basis, imagination's necessary magic trick, what he himself called the will to power. This urge is the fundamental characteristic of the thought itself, which human beings in turn project onto existence, which is in this way anthropomorphised. Only in the form of this provisional illusion can the longed-for agreement between thought and world be reached, and as a result the world opens up for observation and manipulation. Therefore History and the Spirit and the like can all retire after long, faithful service. Nietzsche's genial insight that the body's own drive towards thought – rather than any external and therefore divine power – must be the engine of thought means that he really is God's undertaker.

Admittedly, Hegel shows how thought eventually must think itself as thought, but he commits the mistake of ignoring the role of immanence in this context. The chaos of the surrounding world constantly makes itself known in the form of inexplicable impulses which cause gaps in our worldview, incessant disturbances transmitted via perception. The symbolic order is constantly being torn down, and must therefore constantly be rebuilt. Nietzsche moves human beings out to the periphery of existence by stressing the unfathomable movement of life, but at the same time he gives human beings their own little centre to worry about on the periphery, namely the task of producing for themselves the metaphysical foundation which they can never reach outside of their own thinking.

Heidegger combines the Hegelian and Nietzschean perspectives, and thereby opens the door to transrationalism. Lacan in turn shows how the fear of paradoxism which, according to Nietzsche, was rampant within culture, also constitutes the early experience of fear which summons the separate subject into being. A central task for the eternalist philosopher is to show how the collective subject arises and is formed in a similar way – where not least information from the field of science constructs a continually growing insight about the fundamentally contradictory nature of the world – and, using this analysis as a starting point, formulate a political philosophy for information society. The paradox of metaphysics will therefore form the basis for the metaphysics of paradoxism, and, with that as a platform, human beings can choose to become supermen by creating their own values, which is precisely what the netocracy is in the process of doing.

As one of three key-figures in the netocratic leadership troika, the eternalist philosopher is a close friend of contradictions. He is a genealogist who maps the historical preconditions for society as it exists now, a meteorologist of knowledge who produces and revises forecasts about society's future shape, a socioanalyst who refines the horizontal model and deepens the understanding of the collective subject and its unconscious. Last but not least, he is an activist who places himself on the political map as an interactive component: in other words, the eternalist himself embodies the radical pragmatism which he produces and preaches. Without personal engagement, eternalism's radical pragmatism would lose the attentionality so vital for informationalism, and the philosopher's work would all be in vain right from the outset.

9.

NEO-DARWINISM AND HORIZONTAL BIOLOGY

THE COLLECTIVE CONSCIOUSNESS only moves very sluggishly, and it takes a serious shake-up before any effects at all can be discerned. The consequences of powerful upheavals are therefore all the more noticeable, and give rise to acute shifts in the social sense of balance, setting the whole routine of life in flux. A state of crisis arises: ideas which have formed the intellectual foundations of an entire epoch, so deeply ingrained in our idea of self that they have never been questioned, and rarely, if ever, even noticed, show themselves to be so completely riddled with decay that they are ready to collapse. The constant adjustments which occur on a microlevel within society suddenly become visible as a whole. We are being forced into the great change known as a paradigm shift.

Now that two truly fundamental factors in our understanding of self – digital information technology and new reproductive genetics – have begun to develop in phase with each other and to use the same language, the combined power of these upheavals is greater than at any previous time in history. Our obsolete truths are being subjected to a barrage of attacks. The situation is driving a series of concrete, drastic, and more or less welcome changes in our work and private lives. We are being compelled to think in completely new ways in order to make life even remotely comprehensible. And if any of the mass of regulations governing the new technological complexes that are increasingly in demand are to be even theoretically imaginable, then a credible political development towards the inception of the global state is required.

But before we have even had time to think through the consequences of a Darwinian, evolutionary view of nature and developments, or of what 'the selfish gene' can tell us about history and our own position in the scheme of things, we are confronted with yet another dramatic shift in our worldview. Instead of being the antithesis of nature, as humanism has been preaching for centuries, culture is beginning to appear as nature's own continuation of itself. This is an insight which overturns precisely everything: as human beings, we do not stand above evolution, as we have hitherto believed. There is nothing higher than evolution, apart from in fairy tales. In actual fact, we are nothing more – and could never be anything more – than the self-produced evolutionary machinery.

Even within culture the intractable laws of natural selection apply. The cultural equivalent of selfish genes are the equally selfish memes, the conceptual (in the broadest sense) packages of information with whose help we think and communicate. A combined term for genes and memes, the evolutionary agents with an apparently endless capacity to produce copies of themselves, is 'replicators'. Our consciousness is ultimately the product of the infinitely complicated interplay between these two replicators, our genes and our memes, an interplay which is further complicated by the fact that the replicators often have diametrically opposed interests and seem to want completely different things from us. This is a bewildering insight for any literal-minded Darwinist of the sociobiological sort: not everything in our behaviour can be traced back to genes.

For instance, the situation is not so simple that we can say that men are only attracted to the most fertile women, as classical sociobiology claims. Men seem to have developed a taste for any number of piquant factors and activities which in no way favour – and often actually obstruct – the propagation of their genes. Adoption, contraceptives and pornography are only a few of the more flagrant examples. Men are behaving in an increasingly 'unnatural' fashion, according to patterns which cannot be contained within a purely sociobiological explanatory model, which indicates that the memes are gradually winning ground in their bitter battle with the genes for mastery of our consciousness. This process is in some ways similar to a custody case, in which we human beings are the children over whom two quarrelling custodians are fighting; something which naturally causes considerable problems for us as the objects of this power struggle.

There are, admittedly, many striking similarities between the replicators, but there are also significant differences. Whereas genes reproduce vertically, relatively slowly, from one generation and from one organism to the next, memes spread horizontally, and therefore at a bewilderingly fast rate, from brain to brain. As a result of this, the memes can liberate themselves from the genes. In the informational society memes can spread faster than ever, thanks to interactive media technologies, without any geographic limitations at all. All of a sudden something − a lifestyle trend, a particular linguistic expression, a food dish, the chorus of a pop song, gossip about someone or something − is everywhere, from having been nowhere a short while before. A Swedish musician can be incredibly popular in Japan, but at the same time lack any real support in his home country, purely because the cultural conditions in Japan for some reason or other happen to be more favourable to that particular musician. Memetics provide the stringent logic which enables us to be able to understand this phenomenon.

But before we can even begin to discuss the consequences of a memetic perspective on social developments, genes are demanding our attention once again. As a result of the spectacular development of genetic research and reproductive biology, and their gradual merger, a scenario is developing in which genes are rapidly and irrepressibly starting to behave like memes and propagating horizontally. For more than a billion years, our reproduction, and that of our extremely distant forebears, has been indissolubly linked to sex, but that link has already been broken as a result of test-tube fertilisation having become a routine procedure since its introduction a few decades ago.

From the moment we take the next step and create the first human embryo through cloning, we will have freed ourselves from the reproductive link to actual fertilisation. The whole of the newly-created embryo's genetic inheritance, transferred into the cytoplasm from an unfertilised egg, will come from a single ready-developed somatic cell. This means that the traditional relationship between the child and its parents will instantly become problematic. The function of the parent will be split into a series of variants. Let us take one example: if man A and woman B have one of B's cells cloned, child C will actually be B's twin sister, with an identical genetic make-up, and B's parents, grandfather E and grandmother F, will become the genetic parents of C, which means that, in theory at least, C's old grandfather E would become, under current legislation, responsible for supporting C if A decided to leave B.

Naturally the whole debate about the embryo's rights is turned on its head if there is no longer any 'natural' link between fertilisation and a new human life. Add to this all the complications which genetic manipulation brings with it, such as the possibility of modifying an embryo's genetic material in order to change the characteristics of the developing individual, and a state of almost total confusion is reached. What is right and what is wrong? And on what grounds? It is difficult to claim that the cloning of cells is itself 'unnatural', because there are already identical twins, and even if we disregard this, it is impossible to discern any moral direction from looking at nature itself, because on closer inspection nature is not particularly idyllic. The answers are anything but clear: we are forced to think in entirely new ways, or else passively permit others to think in our place.

The complexities surrounding horizontal biology mean that most people try to avoid the entire problem altogether. The underlying and pious hope is that the progress of reproduction technology will come to a halt for some reason or other, and be content with helping infertile couples, for instance. The hope is that either purely practical difficulties, or some sort of quasi-religious sense of restraint, will put the brakes on developments just within the boundaries of traditional, bourgeois morality. This non-position rests, however, on the more or less unspoken idea that technology is our obedient tool, which does what we command it to do and nothing more. But what history clearly shows again and again – as discussed in Netocracy, and which others such as Lewis Mumford and Neil Postman have shown before us – is the exact opposite: every technology of any significance has its own specific agenda and 'does its own thing', irrespective of its inventor's ambitions. One illuminating example is the networking computers which were originally intended for the collection of factual information, but which showed an entirely different side when their users began to communicate directly with one another instead.

We have to overcome the instinctive reaction described by the science journalist Oliver Morton as the 'yuck-factor'. What seems unnatural also seems disgusting, but as the benefits of what seems unnatural become increasingly obvious, not least in regard to medical advances, so the process of acclimatisation accelerates and our discomfort decreases. Something which was almost unthinkable and indescribably unpleasant yesterday, such as using the corneas of dead people for transplants, now seems the most natural thing in the world. We have good reason to be grateful for this capacity for adaptation, because the whole of our culture and our civilisational progress in the evolutionary arena rest upon our willingness to rapidly renegotiate our boundaries for what is unnatural. The conservative position, that our permanent boundary is precisely where we are standing at the moment, is an attitude which is constantly attracting new exponents, not least among those who believe themselves to profit from the status quo. But history shows time and time again that this position is always indefensible.

Not all processes of acclimatisation occur equally quickly, however; some re-evaluations are extremely complicated. One idea which was thought by many to be indescribably repugnant when it was first launched in 1859 was Charles Darwin's theory of the evolution of the species and natural selection. The problem was not in the first instance a scientific one, but philosophical and ideological, because the idea swept the ground from beneath so many generally accepted axioms about life. Within the scientific community today there is no-one who questions the basics of the theory, but in other contexts it is still extremely controversial. Many people, predominantly in the USA, are still trying to fend off anything to do with evolution, demanding, for instance, that alternative ideas with religious characteristics should be given equal status in schools. All of this merely underlines one of the central theses of the theory of evolution, that it is circumstances and not innate characteristics – however these might be objectively evaluated – which determine whether a new mutation, genetic or memetic, will survive and expand, or disappear into oblivion. It is therefore a question of the survival of the best adapted rather than the strongest, and precisely what is best adapted varies according to the circumstances.

So what was the problem with Darwinism? Originally it was movement itself, the changes over time, and their consequences. The idea that the eternalisation of the world only occurs in our minds and does not have any equivalent in the physical world, that life outside is fundamentally mobilistic, was completely unthinkable. It turned out, for instance, to be an extremely unpalatable idea that the different species were not in a permanent state, but were purely part of a historical process. In Darwin's day a species was by definition still an Aristotelian essence or a Platonic idea, as timeless and unchanging as the perfect figures of geometry. The idea, for instance, that a cat had once been, and might in the future develop into, something other than a cat was thought to contravene every sort of common sense. And besides, humankind suddenly found itself in dubious company, because Darwin reduced it to being just one animal among all the others. Humankind was, of course, the pinnacle of creation, and possessed, according to predominant thinking, something known as a soul, and between it and the animals was a vast and unbreachable void between species. Darwin overturned all of this in one fell swoop. And this was not terribly popular in some quarters.

Darwin's reasoning was particularly difficult for the governing middle-classes to accept, as a result of the strict logic of his position. The protests of the day tended to attack him personally, which suggests that the controversy was as much about the lack of personal opinion in his texts as it was about the consequences of his thesis. This sort of consequently applied science was something quite new for the middle-class masses. Darwin's strict logic declared: under the assumption that natural resources are insufficient for the number of individuals, the best adapted individuals will survive and reproduce better than the others, which in turn must lead to a new generation with a different range of characteristics than the current one. If you add into the equation 'incomprehensibly vast distances in time' (Darwin's own words), the result is inevitably a gradual evolution of the species through natural selection. This logical reasoning was then strengthened with an overwhelming number of observations from different areas of science in the controversial book On the Origin of Species.

The exemplary scientific nature of Darwin's work made the project an historic watershed: adopting a position for or against Darwin meant adopting a position for or against the natural sciences, and therefore the new paradigm itself. Even if it is possible in retrospect to question Darwin's reasoning on many points, a couple of them central, the stumbling-block is hardly his scientific material or the applied logic. Darwin's contemporary opponents declared that this simply could not be true, for the sake of God and social order. This, interestingly, is still the argument used by the powerful anti-Darwinian lobby in the USA at the beginning of the twenty-first century. If Darwinism is right, then nothing is holy any more, and nothing is higher than base matter. The secure connection between morality and the unchanging heavens would be broken. And as a result the beauty of the world and the whole meaning of life would be trampled in the dust.

To some people's ears, however, the philosophical implications of Darwinism, the demand that all old truths must be tested and their positions redefined, was sweet music. Marx and Nietzsche both had a complex relationship to Darwin; they both felt an instinctive scepticism towards all English thinking, but fundamentally they both felt a deep admiration for, and a sense of solidarity with the English scientist. Marx wrote in a letter to Engels that Darwin's book contained the scientific preconditions for their own theories about the class struggle, and in due course he sent a signed copy of Das Kapital to his esteemed colleague, which Darwin never managed to finish reading. Whether or not Nietzsche read Darwin is unclear, but it is clear that from the feverish debate about the theory of evolution he exultantly understood the message about the death of God and the ceaseless rumble of the all-consuming and never-resting machinery of matter. 'Now it is no longer possible for mankind to make itself important by referring to divine origins', he wrote in Daybreak, 'that way is barred by a grinning ape and other hateful creature standing there baring their teeth.' But Nietzsche claimed that the other path was blocked as well. Evolution is no cause for optimism, the many and the weak may eventually overcome the few and the strong; from a philosophical perspective, the development of the species does not imply any improvement or ennoblement.

The innate goodness of evolution was otherwise something that many of Darwin's most enthusiastic supporters proclaimed: natural selection is a process whose task is to produce us human beings, here is the new meaning of life uncovered by science, and here is the basis for the social morality of the new age, taking nature itself as its example. These so-called social Darwinists kidnapped certain superficial aspects of Darwin's ideas and transformed them into a political ideology in quasi-scientific apparel. They claimed that every form of help for those disadvantaged by society is immoral precisely because it is abhorrent to nature, because those who are worst off are bound to succumb in the struggle for survival. They insisted, quite simply, that this sort of elimination was a necessary element of the evolution of the species, and therefore of its underlying refinement. Every pauper who reproduces means an unwanted dilution of valuable characteristics in the next generation. 'Making it easier for the poor to reproduce is in principle the same as equipping your own offspring with a mass of enemies', wrote the political philosopher Herbert Spencer. By the same logic, presumably medical science and the production of glasses should be condemned, and all politics, and practically all of society, be regarded as unnatural abominations, but logic was not the social Darwinists' strong side.

Marx and Nietzsche were also famously afflicted during this period by impetuous disciples who persisted in cobbling together mendacious and vulgarised versions of their idols' complex philosophies. The focused civilisational ambition at the heart of these two philosophers – expressed by Marx as the classes' desire for revolution, and by Nietzsche as the body's desire for power – is jettisoned by these confused disciples, who then subordinate themselves masochistically to what they perceive as nature's predetermined order. Their logic collapses, however, when these inverted forms of Marxism and Nietzscheanism are to be taken to the masses: if nature has already conquered culture, why should it need the help of culture to proclaim its message? Why struggle at all to carry out something which is already determined by fate?

The social Darwinists are therefore revealed as religious rather than scientific thinkers. In their eagerness to find a new god to subordinate themselves to – the masochistic desire to stop developing their own will and therefore stop existing – they transformed their vulgarised form of Natural Selection into the God of the new age. And, just like all other religious fundamentalists throughout the ages, they demand, as an effective way of avoiding their own doubts, that all humankind must submit to their god alone, without giving a single reason why this is justified. In this context it is ironic that it is scarcely possible to get further away from the worldview shared by Darwin, Marx and Nietzsche. The sense of loss for a vanished god, as Nietzsche fears time and time again, turns out to be stronger than common sense. In the Nietzschean worldview the social Darwinists, because of their relentless unwillingness to develop their own will, are, ironically, the weakest of all.

Bad science and bad ideology unfortunately entered into a powerful and long-lived alliance. Each gave legitimacy and status to the other in a destructive feedback-loop, supported by the simple reason that their theses were always constructed with a view to confirming the governing class's intellectual and moral superiority. A functional system for internal criticism within the sciences had not yet been developed. The result was an almost bizarre kindergarten: skulls were measured, there were campaigns against immigration, and race-based hygiene-studies were carried out at state-funded institutes, even in the Sweden governed by the Social Democrats. Soon this ideologised quasi-biology had eaten its way into psychology, anthropology, sociology, criminology, et cetera. This development was made possible by Evolution undergoing an ideological metamorphosis in the collective subconscious and became synonymous with Progress, the in-built metaphysical ideal of capitalism. Because capitalist ethics demanded that all possible room be made for Progress, the capitalist equivalent of feudalism's eternal kingdom of heaven, this meant that a new morality could quickly be constructed around the demand that the ultimate function of society was to facilitate Evolution.

Just as the Marxists had earlier obstinately ignored the argument that the communist utopia hardly needed any help to get going because it was metaphysically unavoidable, the social Darwinists ignored the argument that an evolution which was unavoidable anyway hardly needed any help, still less would it thank anyone for it. Nietzsche's terrible predictions came to pass: the sense of loss for the dead god of Christianity in the collective unconscious turned out to be so huge that critical thinking was sacrificed on the altar of bitterness and longing for death. God may have been dead, but Evolution could assume God's vacant place without criticism. This in spite of the fact that Evolution, in contrast to God, was a god without ambitions to reward its faithful minions.

Social Darwinism therefore became a ritual of pure subordination, without any communication at all between master and servant; this in turn increased the lack of internal criticism, because internal criticism always starts with an individual initiative, something which had become impossible through social Darwinism's in-built demand for individual subordination. In retrospect, however, it became clear – albeit very painfully, after a series of catastrophic experiments – that bad science could never fulfil its abstract promises, which led to increasing levels of doubt in one discipline after the other. The ultimate demise of social Darwinism came with the attempts in Nazi Germany and its allies to put a bad ideology into practice on a massive scale, by actually destroying selected groups that were said to be inferior. As a result of this, social Darwinism collapsed entirely.

Unfortunately this catastrophe also had as a consequence that every type of biological explanatory model within social debates was automatically seen as compromised. The pendulum swung to the opposite extreme. Biology was isolated and lost all influence on philosophy and other intellectual activity. Darwin was locked in the poison cabinet, where he was joined, in a confusion of the original and its misrepresentation that was typical of the age, by Nietzsche. Once again, it was ideological and political factors more than anything else which lay behind the radical change of climate within the sciences. All human activity was now suddenly culture, and culture was everything but nature, although it was unclear precisely what. To be a good person and a friend of equality, the value which now assumed precedence, one had to reason like a good humanist once again. Biologically coloured reasoning was regarded as fascist.

The postwar period meant that humankind once against assumed its unique position in the world, free from nature, and instead equipped with cultural traditions. Human beings were born with a pure, virgin consciousness, a tabula rasa, and were formed into individuals and social beings by their environment, a result of which was the evident differences between cultures around the world, specific details of which were now documented with great assiduousness. The whole of this scientific programme was suffused to varying degrees by political utopianism: by acting upon society in accordance with sensible principles we could create freer and happier people. Supposed primitive peoples were reported to wear relentlessly cheerful smiles and had, therefore, much to teach us stressed westerners. Attributing human behaviour to biological factors was regarded as a politically unsound outbreak of deterministic and pessimistic tendencies. Rousseau's natural romanticism was once again in fashion, and the transcendental Liberation became central; exactly what we were to be liberated from, and what we were to be liberated to was never made clear.

To this day there is still a lot of bitter resistance to the idea of a human nature connected to materialistic and mechanistic processes.

Even if the word itself is no longer used so regularly, a more or less diffuse notion of a soul still figures in a wealth of arguments about human consciousness. We would dearly love to believe that there is something beyond animal instincts within us, that we have freedom of will. We still suppose that there is something other than our brain somewhere within our brain, something which interprets sensual impressions and feels feelings and distributes orders to the body, some sort of miraculous special arrangement, like a soul, which we human beings alone possess.

Yes, we all know that the fundamentals of the theory of the evolution of the species and natural selection are stronger than ever. No-one whose opinions are worth listening to in this context would today claim anything else. We also know, in contrast to Darwin, what genes are, and what happens when inherited characteristics are passed down to a new generation. We know in detail what the DNA-molecule does and how it communicates with the cell, and we have recently spelled our way through the whole of the human genome. We know all this, and nowhere is there anything but nature and utterly natural processes. But for ideological and strategic reasons, many of us want to believe that this business of biology is nothing to do with us. Even if humanism is lying on its death-bed at the onset of informationalism, evidently it still has considerable power. For many people it is a religion, and people are often reluctant to give up their religious perceptions, particularly when they often ward off all demands for critical thinking about large and difficult questions.

When the concept of sociobiology began to spread in the middle of the 1970s, it was mainly a collective term for studies of animals' social behaviour, something which could not possibly have its roots anywhere but biology. When Edward O. Wilson published his controversial book Sociobiology in 1975, he therefore concentrated on animals: he wrote about termites, cockroaches, bees, elk, starlings, birds of prey, turkeys, frogs, elephants and all manner of other animals that buzz and chew and cackle and quack, and about how the often apparently unfathomable behaviour of these and a mass of other animal species becomes comprehensible when viewed within the framework of evolutionary logic. Evolutionary biology studies how natural selection has formed different organisms, whereas sociobiology studies how natural selection has formed the organisms' behaviour in groups. This might have been just about acceptable to faithful humanists; termites and cockroaches surely ought to be able to be seen purely as products of nature. But the book's 27th and final chapter is about humankind, its unique anatomy as a species, its intricate patterns of behaviour, and the extreme variation demonstrated by its forms of social organisation. And with this, the metaphorical cat was out of the bag.

Far from all of those who aired their furious criticism of Sociobiology had read the book in question. The subject itself, evolution in combination with humankind, was regarded by many to be offensive and indissolubly linked to Nazism and racism, which meant that every effort in this direction was regarded as a dirty attempt to legitimise social barriers and the oppression of the world's poor. Wilson was depicted as a radical extremist, which he certainly is not. It is not the case that he, or any other serious person, is claiming that everything in the human individual is 'predetermined' and 'written in the genes', that life runs unshakeably on biological rails. What Wilson is actually saying is that we, like all other species, have a biological history, that even our development has been subject to natural selection. This in turn has the consequence that a number of conclusions about humankind and society are in the end unavoidable, at the same time as a number of cherished old 'truths' become untenable.

The sociobiological view turned out to be a potato so hot that few dared grasp it. The debate remained loud and static for a long time, on the subject of its political consequences. Isn't all this talk of genes and evolution simply the worst sort of disguised right-wing propaganda? To a great extent, the debate has not moved far from this even today. At the same time as Darwinian attacks on old 'truths' are causing more and more damage, the ideologically based defence is looking more and more desperate. But the Darwinian attacks are proving to be just as damaging to sentimental connections to humanism and its touchstone, the Cartesian subject, with its still popular elements: Man, the Self, Free Will, and other pleasant but obsolete notions from the Enlightenment and the dawning of capitalism.

The real upheaval of the extended neo-Darwinian model which has become increasingly powerful during recent decades is its consequently thought-out materialism, its refusal to anchor theory in anything vaguely soulful or otherworldly, or to accept any transcendental substance inaccessible to criticism. The neo-

Darwinian model is taking on the Big Questions – Whence? How? And why? – without granting itself the luxury of explanations that go round in circles or lose themselves in eternal regression. But everything has its price, and the price in this context is that the grand castles in the air which have formed the frame for our grandiose illusions about the special position of Humanity, et cetera, are dissolving in the wind.

We are nature. In the neo-Darwinian model humankind, like other organisms, is what the biologist and ecologist Richard Dawkins calls a survival machine, in other words: an intelligent mode of transport, a sort of relay runner designed by and for our selfish genes in order to transport our biological information onwards. Evolution is the story of how the originally extremely simple vessels which offer our genes more or less functional protection from various chemical attacks, gradually developed into increasingly sophisticated machines, eventually with the capacity to compose sonnets and build cathedrals. Things which are more functional than others are valued more highly by natural selection, and what is more functional varies over time.

Infinitely slowly, but nonetheless surely, the originally scarcely intelligent machines became more intelligent, for the simple reason that intelligence – in the sense of a finely calibrated capacity for adaptation and collaboration – was at a premium, as a result of which various characteristics spread at the expense of others. The machines' development later affected their conditions in a significant way: the machines began to form one another's environments, and goaded or forced each other to develop still further, to become ever more intelligent. Together, the many machines created an increasingly varied nature, which could offer a gradually more varied selection of ecological niches. In this game, eventually the human machine became a successful player, but the real winners are our genes.

Biological evolution goes incredibly, almost incomprehensibly slowly by our standards, but with certain exceptions. At irregular intervals fate interferes and the arena is suddenly turned on its head, and at a stroke a new set of rules applies, there are new players with entirely new strategies. One example is when a large asteroid collided with our planet approximately 65 million years ago, causing a global ecological catastrophe and mass extinction of the machines which had been successful up until then, amongst others the dinosaurs. But every cloud has a silver lining, and the demise of the dinosaurs became the mammals' great chance, because our early ancestors belonged to those who could best adapt to the new circumstances.

If the asteroid had taken a different path, and missed the Earth, then biological evolution would have followed a completely different path. In all probability, there would never have been any human beings, and therefore there would have been no reason to ponder the riddle of existence. It is also probable that no sonnets would have been composed, and no cathedrals built. So not only are we the children of chance: evolution would certainly not have created any human beings given a second chance if it was possible to 'rewind' the tape to zero and start the process anew, because the variables are innumerable and every little change has radical consequences. On top of this, our existence is only possible thanks to the demise of other species. The extinction of plant and animal species is, thus, the most natural thing in the world, and no-one has greater cause than the survivors – us humans – to be grateful for that.

The central perspective, according to this biological model, is not that of the species, the population or the individual, but that of the selfish gene. If we ask the ultimate question about why we exist at all, the answer is simply that our genes needed somewhere to hide, and that we are the best survival machine that they managed to produce. The genes supervise our cells' production of proteins, and the proteins that are produced in turn determine the rest of the cells' behaviour, how they specialise in certain strictly delimited tasks and co-operate with about a million billion other cells in the construction of our bodies. Genes which produce co-operative, networking cells have been rewarded by natural selection, because specialisation and co-operation broaden the repertoire of the organism. Together the cells became intelligent, which produced mutual advantages in the fight for scant resources. This is simple game-theory: one plus one become more than two in a so-called non-zero-sum game. This is not to say that the greatest size gives the greatest advantage, because the efficiency profit of organising a gigantic organism will at some critical point be swallowed up by escalating energy costs. There are more bacteria than elephants and blue whales in the world, as Richard Dawkins points out.

So the intelligent alternative for genes and cells operating in niches in which intelligence is at a premium, is to organise a corresponding development towards a higher level: specialised and co-operating individuals who in turn create mutual benefits for one another in various forms of society. By helping others we help ourselves first and foremost; what looks like altruism is actually often carefully disguised and possibly unconscious egoism. What we are now facing is the next stage of evolution's experiment in intelligent co-operation: instead of a swelling society, the classical empire – which history has proved to be impossible to sustain over longer periods – development is leading towards a global confederacy of networking societies, an informationalist empire where power and information are distributed between many centres, rather than concentrated in one single point, as under capitalism. The winner throughout this whole long story is the selfish gene alone, because it is the only constant feature. Cultures blossom and die. We human beings will all die, like our fathers and forefathers before us. We are provisional, biological machines with a certain purpose and a limited lifespan; from an evolutionary perspective we are dispensable packaging material. Our lords and makers, the genes, on the other hand, merely pair up with a new dance partner and waltz off to the next survival machine, a slightly more up-to-date model.

There is naturally a great deal in this 'new synthesis', as Edward O. Wilson calls sociobiology, which becomes disturbing when the theory is applied to humankind. Particularly if one for religious or political reasons, as in the humanist worldview, regards human beings as raised above messy biology. The ape is still in us, nature constantly makes itself known again, even among civilised people who talk themselves hoarse about humankind's inviolability, equality and justice. This can be seen in the patterns we demonstrate as consumers and parents, in our working life and as social beings in general. Gender is not merely a social construction, whatever the social constructionists among the feminists and queer theoreticians say: that sort of thing is just ideological wishful thinking. The fact that anthropology has been able to show how behaviour and values vary hugely between different cultures is not in the least bit troubling, and by no means suggests that biology has been outplayed, but rather shows merely how human nature, in full accordance with elementary Darwinian logic, takes different expression under different circumstances.

Of course, all differences in behaviour cannot be referred back to genetic differences. Beyond this, the no longer entirely new synthesis has a more interesting and simpler explanation for the basic similarities which repeatedly occur – status, hierarchies, gossip, gender roles, courtship rituals, incest taboos, etc – namely, that these patterns are natural. Which – and this must be constantly stressed to avoid misunderstandings – does not mean that qualitative moral judgements can be dismissed. It is merely a recognition that there is such a thing as human nature. This in turn means that we human beings are certainly extremely adaptable, which is the key to our survival, but only within a certain specific framework.

During the glory days of humanism, and above all academic Marxism, the driving ambition within the social and human sciences was the question of how society forms human beings, and which social policies could be implemented to use society to produce the perfect Human Being. Now, in the light of the updated theory of evolution, the utopian glow has faded, and interest is being focused on the opposite question: how humankind produces a society. Consequently, today we can see a renaissance for two gloomy power theoreticians of the old school: Thomas Hobbes and Friedrich Nietzsche. According to the philosopher and meme theorist Daniel C. Dennett, Hobbes must be regarded as the first sociobiologist, 200 years before Darwin, because his strict materialism unfailingly leads to evolutionary thinking. According to Hobbes, the state is a sort of communal survival machine for individuals, a collective construction forced into existence by brutal nature in order to protect human beings against themselves and each other. Nietzsche has the idea of how the capacity for co-operation develops during humanity's pre-social stage, as an alternative to general bloodletting. The link between biological development and social construction appears quite plainly.

Sociobiology reads into our patterns of behaviour and emotional life, into what and how we feel, and the fact that we have any feelings at all, a devious calculation on the part of our genes. Gratitude, friendship, loyalty, moral indignation, trust, suspicion, betrayal: everything follows an evolutionary logic. This even applies to the capacity for self-deception which constantly takes us by surprise, because it may well be easier to persuade others of something if one is convinced of it oneself. Existential restlessness, the desire to strive and rise through the ranks, to refuse to accept the lot allocated to us by fate: even here our genes have a hand in the game. It is simply not in our genes' interests for human beings to be content and happily settle down. We are 'programmed' to think that our neighbour's grass is greener, because then we try harder, which makes us more attractive. All ideas about zero-growth and the like are extremely 'unnatural'. On the other hand, utopias and high ideals are functional, as long as they remain utopian and out of reach. What our genes 'want' is for us to be constantly on our toes, to be seeking to raise our status in our various social niches as far as we can, in order to maximise our possibilities for reproduction.

However, no-one is suggesting that genes can explain everything of interest. If that were so, the accusations of determinism and possibly even pessimism would be quite justified; it is clear that there is a lot left to explain. Often we are disobedient and act in contradiction to what would seem desirable from a genetic perspective. Voluntary childlessness and suicide, for example, are two of the particularly hard nuts to crack for sociobiology and evolutionary psychology. Even if culture is nature in the sense that it marks a natural development within the frame of human preconditions; even if culture is not something strange which comes from elsewhere; even if Dennett is right in that humankind is an animal species which produces books and all manner of other cultural products in the same way that many spiders produce webs, we know that the traffic is always two-way. Individuals create a culture and a society – in other words, ecological circumstances – which in turn form and transform behaviour and psychological structures, changes which in turn lead to a modification of ecology, and so on. Foundations and superstructure, in Marxist terms, conduct a continuous and intensive dialogue with one another, the process and change are eternal, no-one will ever get the last word. Once again, we are talking about an eternalistic feedback-loop. And it is here that the memes enter the picture.

10.

THE WAR BETWEEN THE REPLICATORS – THE MEMES' VICTORY OVER THE GENES

THE CONCEPT O THE MEME was launched almost in passing by Richard Dawkins in 1976, as an exciting and interesting idea, but nevertheless a sidetrack alongside his biological argument. This idea, the meme of the memes, has proved itself to be particularly viable under current circumstances, and has more recently been developed into a comprehensive theory by, among others, Daniel C. Dennett and the British psychologist Susan Blackmore. Dawkins' fundamental idea is that the meme is the cultural gene: in other words, it is the meme which is the real actor in an evolutionary process in which we human beings are once again given a subordinate role. Our consciousness is nothing more than a survival machine for the memes.

But how can biology, so endlessly slow, and culture, so arbitrarily unpredictable, be compared at all? According to Dawkins, both are examples of evolution and natural selection, both constitute a continuous selection process in which countless losers are discarded and the winners gradually changed as a result of altered conditions which they themselves have helped to create. The gene, or the DNA molecule, is the actor which once emerged in the sludgy primeval soup that was the earth's ocean approximately four billion years ago. Human society is the new soup.

What is special about the gene is its function as a replicator, its capacity to produce copies of itself. These copies are often, but not quite always, perfectly identical to the original. The 'defective' copies are often, but not quite always, completely useless. Some of them, however, turn out to be, quite by chance, extremely well-suited to the current conditions, and, as a result, these so-called mutations are successful. The meme is the replicator which swims in the new soup, and it reproduces thanks to the human beings' highly developed capacity for imitating one another. The meme, like the gene, is a parcel of information. A meme might, for instance, be a philosophical idea, the chorus from a piece of music, linguistic jargon, a fashionable item of clothing, different ways of laying a roof or producing a steam-engine – in short, anything which for one reason or other is able to capture people's attention and invite imitation. The selection criteria are harsh: certain memes stick in people's subconscious and therefore succeed in reproducing: some of these achieve spectacular but short-lived success, whereas others show themselves to be more viable only after a slow start. The rest are hopelessly lost in the torrent of information.

The most common criticism of the concept of memes has been the problem of extent. Where does a meme start and finish? If, for example, we take a philosophical or religious belief: does the meme comprise every last piece of documentation, carefully reproduced, or just a general idea of the main features of the belief? Or, if we take a widely disseminated song like the Marseillaise: what is the Marseillaise meme? Is it the music or the words, or both in their historical context? Things like this can be debated, of course, but the fact that it is not possible to define the meme easily in a general way does not mean that the meme does not exist, nor that the theory falls as a result of this. Quite the contrary! The interesting thing about memetics is not what the meme is narrowly supposed to represent, but how, even if only as a theoretical abstraction, it manages in a pedagogically ingenious way to make us understand how thought works. Whether we regard the meme as an individual object, or merely as a continually changing characteristic of an object, its extent is always dependent upon the viewer's point of view, in the same way as all other eternalisations that lack a demonstrably material basis.

In the same way as Nietzschean philosophy and Darwinian science eventually presented a common platform of values and reinforced each other's theses in a common ideological resonance, memetics and eternalist philosophy match one another perfectly, despite their having developed in different places and within different subjects. One clear example of this is how the problem of the individual meme's extent disappears as soon as we place memetics within the frame of eternalist philosophy. It would therefore be wise to sum up here what eternalist philosophy says about the process of thought.

According to eternalism, every individual fixing of an object is a highly arbitrary freezing of the constantly moving immanence of contemporary trends. This eternalisation presupposes in turn at least one already existing eternalisation, the metaphysical basis, which is produced exclusively by human thought. This means that all objects, or, to be more accurate, all ideas of objects, including memes, ultimately are and must be eternalisations, and as such they are limited to human thought. These eternalisations are communicated between human beings in the form of symbols, such as language, where the mutual understanding of the eternalisations' content between individuals must be presupposed, without this ever being able to be ascertained. It is more accurate to say that the eternalisations and their corresponding symbols are tuned and corrected over time by collective empirical experiences, what we call the ideological resonance.

In order to make the world understandable, and thereby increase the genes' chances of survival, thinking produces a complete worldview by eternalising precisely those eternalisations that perception has already made of the world. But because every eternalisation has a considerable built-in component of illusion, this worldview is constantly collapsing and must be revised time after time. This happens in principle every single second, through what we call the micro-paradigm shift, small-scale variants of the rare historical paradigm shifts which occur when an entire society revises its common cosmic foundation. This means that our worldview is in constant motion, so it has to be frozen on a regular basis, and so the process goes on, the dialectic of eternalism and mobilism, in principle ad infinitum.

The resulting meta-eternalisations, the building blocks of the individual worldview, laden with information, are known within eternalist philosophy as fictives. A fictive is a sort of eternalisation nexus which, in spite of the fact that it exists on the micro-level, includes both a built-in metaphysical foundation and a world of fixed points, a sort of shadow image of the world which can be fallen back upon. The fictive balances between ingenious simplicity and comprehensive complexity: simplicity for the sake of comprehensibility, complexity for the sake of credibility; however, its complexity is only a fraction of that of the world it is intended to mirror. All the individual consciousness needs to do is to find, or rather, produce, enough fictives which seem to harmonise with one another, and a complete worldview arises in no time. The quality of all additional fictives is judged according to this worldview. Those fictives which are in tune with the governing worldview are accepted, the others rejected.

It is here that memetics and eternalist philosophy begin to interact with one another, rather like the different components of epoxy glue. All we have to do is imagine eternalism's fictives as transportable entities, like packages of information which can be communicated freely and quickly within and between individuals, and, above all, as machines with a built-in desire to survive, and we have transformed the passive fictive into an active and selfish meme. The fictive may be more correct philosophically, but the meme is pedagogically superior. This means that eternalist philosophy and memetics can profitably be combined into a unified, common platform. And it is precisely this platform that the netocracy is using as the foundation of the informationalist worldview.

The objection that the extent of the memes is a problem is equally applicable to genes, where the division of the spiralling long string of chemical 'letters' depends entirely upon what you are looking for. Different groups of researchers mean different things when they use the term gene, but there is no serious dissent on the question of whether genes actually exist. So, if we permit ourselves to describe genes loosely as a chromosome sequence which natural selection tends to treat as a unit, then the same might even apply to memes. A meme could therefore be described as a more or less condensed unit of information which facilitates mental reproduction. As far as philosophical or religious belief is concerned, this means that memes are the kernel of ideas – to put it in eternalistic terms: the metaphysical basis which is always unconsciously presupposed – which exists in the consciousness of anyone who has even the slightest understanding of the ideas in question.

Far from everyone who claims to be a Marxist has actually read Marx to any great extent, but, nevertheless, they can still reasonably be called Marxists after reading a summary or heard a lecture giving an idea of what Marxism is all about; at the same time we are unfortunately forced to accept that many who really have read Marx have still managed to miss the core of his philosophy. As far as the Marseillaise is concerned, a few notes are enough; when you hear the intro to Lennon and McCartney's All you need is love, for instance, you recognise the classic fanfare at once, and when you hum it later, the Marseillaise-meme has reproduced by means of grafting itself into this new context. We can therefore suppose that successful memes show signs of intelligence. A balanced mass of fictives is equally effective in both organic and mental environments.

By making use of indistinct or, rather, sticky surfaces, genes and memes adhere to new environments more readily, where they can quietly mutate and thereby increase their chances of survival. But exactly when a mutated replicator like that abandons its original identity and is transformed into a new replicator can never be objectively ascertained – neither eternalism nor memetics recognises any objective truths at all in the classical sense – but is entirely dependent on the requirements that the observer in question is demanding of the replicator. The definition of a replicator is therefore always a construction of thought, even if to a great extent it is matched by an indefinable yet cohesive noumenal complex in mobilistic reality.

Just like certain genes, successful memes can, in principle, live for ever, as long as they are successful to the extent that the sequence of survival machines remains unbroken. What is most important, therefore, is not that the meme in question is stored in books and libraries and so on, in the same way that a gene is sometimes stored in fossils, even if this would do no harm, but that it constantly infiltrates its way into new consciousnesses and thereby constantly builds more machines, preferably machines with minor innate idiosyncrasies and adhesive surfaces in order to increase its chances of survival still further. Just like with genes, coincidence often plays a decisive role. Manuscripts and other forms of documentation can get lost or be rediscovered at an inopportune moment, enthusiasts with a mistaken understanding of a meme can damage its reputation, and ideas can be used consciously for purposes that were not foreseen at the outset. What a society regards as true, interesting or natural is ultimately a question of changing power relationships and conflicts of interest, and has nothing whatever to do with any timeless objective criteria.

Advertisements and marketing can achieve two things on two different levels: firstly to spread one or more memes, and, secondly, to manipulate circumstances in order to promote a benevolent reception for the meme in question. The memes' struggle for survival, just like that of the genes, is anything but straightforward. Competition is literally lethal, and is getting more intense now that interactive media-technologies are increasing the available amounts of information so dramatically. The bottleneck in this context is what we call attentionalism: awareness multiplied by credibility. What the memes are fighting over, and what their very survival stands or falls on, is their attention. The total number of human consciousnesses is finite, as is the capacity of each individual consciousness. The untamed hurricane of information which is raging through all the world's media is a heart-rending expression of the desperate anxiety of far too many memes facing imminent extinction.

Memetics complements sociobiology, and illuminates a lot of dark mysteries in which the active involvement of genes has not always been clear. A 'voluntary childlessness gene', for instance, would presumably have great difficulty surviving natural selection, whereas a 'voluntary childlessness meme', on the other hand, works under entirely different conditions. In the generally accepted view of women who have achieved success and high status, children and traditional motherhood no longer play much of a role; having many children and the duties involved in their upbringing are, on the contrary, regarded as a hindrance for the socially ambitious woman, and are therefore no longer fashionable. The 'career meme' thereby proves itself under these circumstances often to be stronger than the outmoded 'motherhood gene'. As far as celibacy, as advocated by religion, is concerned, as Susan Blackmore points out, it is in the interests of the 'religion meme' that priests live alone and childless in order to concentrate their energies entirely upon reproducing religion. Genes and memes therefore often 'want' quite different things of the survival machines they share, and there are countless examples of the merciless power struggle involved, pulling the machine in different directions at the same time. It is important here to realise that neither of the replicators has our own human well-being in mind. They are fighting purely for their own survival.

For more than three billion years genes were the only replicators in the arena, and ruled absolutely. Memes arrived on the field late, and were forced to play away from home and use the human brain which the genes had constructed. To begin with, memes were obedient tenants, subordinate to the interests of the genes; being a skilled imitator became over time an increasingly important advantage in the struggle for survival and reproduction. But as the memes became more significant and influenced the furnishings of the human consciousness more and more, the hitherto harmonious collaboration became increasingly strained. Today there is a state of all-out war over the programming of the survival machines, memes and genes have separate, strictly selfish agendas, and the focus of the conflict is sexuality.

The fact that memes have gained the upper hand is clear; the birth-rate is falling in all parts of the world where welfare and education are increasing. Sexuality has therefore been annexed by the memes, and the connection between sex and reproduction has been broken. Many people appeal to so-called common sense, suggesting that this development cannot continue much longer, that the pendulum must swing back the other way again, and that the interests of the genes must be addressed to a greater degree for the sake of our own survival. It is therefore supposed that the memes would voluntarily abdicate out of sheer self-interest. What this apparently sensible argument ignores is the possibility of choosing an alternative strategy, one in which genes become totally enslaved thanks to the fact that more and more of the production of the survival machines is being transferred to laboratories, leaving sexuality purely as a playground for experimenting memes. In the long-term there is also the possibility that at least some memes will completely cut their ties to their erstwhile masters, by constructing new forms of survival machines with an intelligence that we today would define as artificial.

It is hardly surprising that memetics is repugnant to all good humanists, for two main reasons: firstly because it has finally shut the door on all the beautiful stories about the human soul, thereby extinguishing all pious hopes of a charming creation myth somewhere beyond matter and its soulless processes; secondly because it removes from humankind its role as an active participant within even the social and cultural arena. As long as new biology and the theory of evolution had difficulty explaining what was clearly irrational, and as long as culture was needed to be something essentially different to nature, then there was still room for speculations plucked from thin air. As late as 1996, for instance, Pope John Paul II claimed that there was an 'ontological discontinuity' between humankind and its ape-like ancestors, in other words some sort of transformation act shrouded in mist and gloom, in which the soul was inserted into our genetic inheritance by higher powers. The point of memetics is that it replaces faith in all forms of miracle with an explanatory model which is logically coherent and completely in tune with modern research into consciousness. It removes the soul from the agenda and reveals every papal effort in this area as an expression of pure lust for power.

The human brain is constructed and built by genes: on this everyone, even the Pope, must surely now agree. And the brain is nothing unique to human beings: to begin with, all mammals have brains. Our consciousness, on the other hand, is unique: our capacity for abstract reasoning, to communicate complicated ideas through speech and writing, and thereby construct a collective memory of accumulated information. In contrast to other species, we do not need to start from scratch with each new generation, we do not have to learn every scrap of knowledge necessary for survival through our own hard experience. Instead, thanks to language, we inherit carefully tested flashes of genius from complete strangers whom we have never met and are not related to. And we can use our consciousness to reflect upon the meaning and purpose of everything. This makes us unique. So what is the relationship between memetics and consciousness?

According to Dennett, consciousness is the result of the memes' reformatting of the brain to make it an ideal habitat for memes. These memes travel using images, text, electronic media, oral stories and conversation. A small child's brain attunes itself according to external stimuli and quickly tunes itself in to Swedish, English, or some other language, and then the long process of colonisation begins, our consciousnesses becoming the memes' survival machines. It is memes that make us what we are, there is no original, critical input from anything other than memes, no inner 'ego core' which picks and chooses. Consequently it is not we who think with the help of memes, it is memes who manage our thinking for us.

In order to understand the extent of this revolution in thinking, it is vitally important to get to the bottom of the capitalist worldview which we are leaving behind. We need a thorough spring-clean of all our presuppositions about life. And in this context, there is nothing more essential to do away with than what is known as the Cartesian subject, the imploded starting-point for the whole of the capitalist worldview. Because even if individual philosophers over the past two hundred years have made strenuous attacks on the Cartesian subject, it still lives on as an obstinate myth in our everyday life, in the same way that astrology, for instance, or literal belief in the biblical creation story, still live on as remnants of the feudal worldview.

It is a fact that the vast majority of people – with the principal exception of those who have read most philosophy, or have undergone Lacanian psychoanalysis, for example – are still uncritically or unconsciously basing their individual worldview upon the existence of the Cartesian subject. The attempt to maintain the Cartesian subject is overwhelmingly the single most important factor behind the widespread sense of confusion and powerlessness which is dominating the social climate at the transition from capitalism to informationalism, a mental chaos which in turn attracts and contributes to popularising even older and more obsolete prejudices and myths, such as within the New Age movement, for instance. How the growing netocracy, with its belief in the dividual instead of the obsolete, capitalist individual, will react to this increasing foolishness is a matter of speculation. Are we going to experience a new global enlightenment, or will the netocracy laconically give up and serve the growing consumtariat even more individualistic nonsense via the electronic mass-media which the netocracy already controls? We shall see.

That the Cartesian subject continues to exert enormous influence is demonstrated by the fact that it is still regarded as entirely 'natural' to adhere more or less automatically and without reflection to a metaphysical dualism with two different fundamental principles of existence: soul and body, spirit and matter. The problem is just that if there really was a soul, it would of necessity be a part of the physical world, otherwise it would not exist, at least not within the physical world, and would therefore be nothing to worry about. But if, as believers think, it by definition cannot be part of the physical world, but nonetheless exists somewhere else, unknown but still capable of being believed in, then the problem of communicating with and controlling the brain, which is unquestionably part of the body and matter, becomes insoluble.

When we speak of my 'soul' or my 'inner self', and thereby imagine a sort of encapsulated command centre for the interpretation of sensory impressions, and the location of the individual's unique characteristics, then we are dealing with a fiction, a story we tell ourselves and each other, in order to make ourselves feel secure and powerful. And a 'soul meme' which grants us well-being and self-belief will naturally gain admittance to many consciousnesses. Besides, the supposition of a soul or an ego coincides with what we instinctively regard as self-evident, in the same way that a flat Earth around which the sun revolved was once self-evident. But if we study the brain and consciousness closer, we find no microscopic cinema where the soul or any other co-ordinating organ compiles sensory impulses into a complete picture. The fact is that consciousness has no residence or central location anywhere within the brain.

René Descartes was himself aware of the problem, but believed he had solved the dilemma by locating the human soul in the pineal gland. Because medical science was still largely undeveloped in the 1600s, he ran no risk of being contradicted in his lifetime. But this little gland beneath the brain has been examined thousands of times since then, without any space for a soul ever having been discovered. The question we must therefore ask is where today's many millions of left-over quasi-Cartesians are hiding their respective subjects. The depressing answer is that they have never been asked this question, and that within the current education system they will never be asked it.

The reason that this has been allowed to continue is ultimately down to the durability of the capitalist system, the structure which aims to keep members of society as frustrated as possible rather than enlightened, in order thereby to maintain maximal production and consumption capacity. This is the system which uncritically nurtured the myth as its own innocence behind the supposition that the task of the market is to give the people what the people want, as if human needs were always a predetermined factor. Those participants who see through this intellectual serfdom are obvious recruits for the developing netocracy, where demands for the death of individualism are obligatory; not for any noble intellectual reason, but simply because the realisation is spreading that the once so successful individualist has been transformed into an embarrassingly obsolete dead weight in the developing network society.

What is actually within the brain are parallel networks of cells through which information passes, and which continuously produce parallel 'stories' of what is going on in the world outside, stories which are constantly revised, and many of which disappear without a trace, as determined by circumstances. The brain's task is not to discover the ultimate truth of things, nor even to build a rationally coherent worldview, but to guide us on our way through the world in such a way that our genes' chances of survival are maximised. Because we have the capacity to formulate one of these stories in words, we are prepared to imagine that this story also has a little internal author who is 'consciously' making use of the brain's functions. But this is, as already stated, an illusion, and illusions, as Blackmore points out, do not exist anywhere.

As a result, the question of free will becomes extremely problematic. Or, more accurately, it does not become particularly relevant. When 'I' choose washing powder X instead of washing powder Y in the shop, it is in a situation where the choice is free to the extent that no-one is usually forcing customers at gun-point to choose one or the other. So it feels as if 'I' can choose freely between X and Y, and that the choice is conscious; if nothing else, it feels like that in retrospect when 'I' think about the purchase or talk about it to someone else. But who is this 'I' in the transaction, other than a more or less intense battle between all the 'washing powder memes' which have occupied my consciousness? In order to be able to discuss free will at all, we have to be able to presuppose a stable 'I' which either does or does not possess this freedom. But we cannot do this. For we are confronted with the question: Is all this really true and proven? Does the ego really not exist, nor free will and the other building blocks of humanism that we are so used to? Are we really nothing more than machines in the hands of our genes and memes, neither of which really cares at all for our welfare?

The answer is that it is precisely as true and as proven as one can desire within the frame of the new informationalist paradigm which is in the process of establishing itself. It is itself a meme which is both attractive and credible for the developing netocratic elite, and which is therefore in the process of being realised. The view of evolution as a single, large, increasingly complicated information process on several levels – which in turn leads to the dissolution of a series of well-established boundaries between, for instance, the 'natural' and the 'artificial', between organism and machine, between ego and world, between one species and another – means that everything is fundamentally the same ones and zeros and that everything is merging together. The relativism of values according to which truth is a question of supremacy over definitions and morals is a question of sentimentalised manipulations, the ever-present ambition to 'deconstruct' every form of human communication to a more or less subtle power struggle; all this is connected, and constitutes a dominant feature of the netocratic worldview.

That this worldview is starting to assume clear contours right now is naturally no coincidence. The memes have been in the arena for approximately 100,000-150,000 years, having made their breakthrough when the first language-based civilisations arose approximately 4,000 years ago, and have since then taken one dizzying leap after the other in conjunction with the development of revolutionary communication technologies: written language, the printing press, electronic mass-media, interactive computers and telephones. Here we stand, or rather, here the memes stand, on the threshold of the next phase: spectacular reprogenetic research and applications, for which advanced calculations and simulations in powerful computers are a practical precondition, and for which the netocratic worldview possesses the ultimate legitimacy. And here, as usual, there are interests to be defended.

There is an interesting irony in this: the worldview and reasoning which is rejecting older ages' efforts to base morals in a supposed natural order that was possibly divine, is anchoring its own programmatic relativism in a supposed natural ambivalence towards anything connected with moral principles. The same thing, in other words, but reversed. The full, revolutionary consequences of the genetic breakthrough for society and thought are being recognised as a result of their being embedded within and co-ordinated with a series of social and cultural changes: the collapse of the nation state, the loss of political authority, the abdication of the citizen, the coronation of the consumer, the media explosion, the increasing power of attentionalist principles, and the changes which are occurring within philosophy as the theory of evolution, information theory, and values-nihilism after the collapse of capitalism are fused together. All these processes are interacting with and strengthening each other. For genetics and biotechnology, this means that everyone involved becomes an actor in a marketplace, genetic resources and knowledge of various sorts become products which dramatically influence all aspects of life, from sex to work. The question of intellectual rights – in this case the patent on genes – will gain an entirely new dimension.

Precisely which reprogenetic sensations will become accessible when is a question we have neither the space nor the inclination to speculate upon here. But we can safely assume that the common denominator for them all will be that they transgress all the boundaries of what most of us, until very recently, regarded as 'natural'. The collective consciousness is, as we have earlier pointed out, slow to move. In the relationship between science and worldview there is a significant delay, which leads to disquiet and discomfort. The American commentator Jeremy Rifkin, and many others, fear that we have reached 'the end of the natural world', and are demanding action to stop or at least slow down the speed of developments. The practical question is then which political or judicial authority could carry out and implement these actions, and the more academic question is which arguments would then win the day.

Any state could implement legislation tomorrow to forbid all research which has anything at all to do with the cloning of human cells, seeing as this is something which both believing and secular humanists find offensive and 'unnatural', partly because of the assumed applications, and partly because the cells which are used must be gathered from somewhere, either from aborted foetuses or from embryos left over after fertility treatment. The whole issue is a minefield, not least because it touches on the abortion issue, a sensitive subject in many cultures. Legislation like this is, however, not a credible scenario. A wealth of potentially controversial treatments are still dearly sought after, meaning that legislation of this sort would be practically meaningless.

Current research in this area in largely carried out in the private sector, with little political or regulatory attention, and can easily be moved. Other countries with other taboos than those of western countries – and there are many of them – would have no good reason to reject this new source of taxation or the new injection of knowledge. In reality, decisions in this sort of area have therefore already been transferred to the global market. Just like test-tube fertilisation, so controversial at first, this question will eventually be decided by whether there are sufficient well-heeled consumers or not. Everything suggests, therefore, that reprogenetic technology, like all other significant technologies, will 'do its own thing'. This means that it will, for instance, facilitate intervention in the human genetic code, something which we by extension, and according to today's values, would define as a clear modification of our own species.

Only a global state can seriously hope to regulate this development, which in the eyes of many who believe in regulation means that a global state is a desirable goal. What these activists often fail to notice, however, is that the global state will ultimately speed up rather than slow down this development, for the simple reason that the quickest and most effective changes throughout history, both technological and in terms of values, have occurred in well-regulated environments. The central question in this context is just when and how the developing netocracy intends to subordinate the world state beneath it and allow its new (from a historical perspective) values to steer global politics. The truth is that if today's governing bourgeoisie shows itself to be too naïve and paralysed in the face of the problem complex of globalisation, and not least in its handling of reprogenetic technology, and if it therefore chooses to cling on to the obsolete nation-state model, then members of the netocracy could well show themselves to be the lords of the global state from day one.

But even a global state would be faced with difficult decisions about where to draw the line, particularly since the developing netocracy prefers to avoid paying much attention to drawing lines. If, for instance, it is currently acceptable to perform certain operations on new-born children to correct certain defects, why should it be unacceptable to prevent the same defects at the embryonic stage? If it is currently obvious that a teenager's crooked teeth should be corrected with a brace, why should it be so indecent to use genetic technology to programme an improvement at an earlier stage? And if we praise parents who do all they can to help their children get good school results, and fill their home computers with all manner of expensive pedagogical learning tools – why should it be so disgraceful to use the available genetic technology to help the child on its way? Because it would be 'unnatural'? How 'natural' is a mouth-brace?

Once we start walking down this slippery slope, it becomes incredibly difficult to locate the specific point where we should put our foot down. So we never set our foot down, and gradually slide downwards, with no obstacle in sight. Privileged people have always made the most of their opportunities to give their own children the best possible chances, and this can hardly be said to be 'unnatural'. It is reasonable to imagine that this will continue. Our capacity to think about and get used to the unthinkable is well-documented. The biologist Lee M. Silver has speculated about a future in which the elite and the underclass have developed in different directions, in order eventually to separate into two distinct species: the 'genetically enriched' and the 'natural'. Perhaps this will not be the case, or at least not to that extent, but the point of Silver's argument is that the thought is not unthinkable when we know what we already know about the new reprogenetics.

The collective consciousness may be sluggish, but scientific developments are placing increasingly unavoidable demands upon us to think afresh and to do so quickly. The question which must be asked is how long we shall be able to speak of a collective consciousness: perhaps we will soon be forced to speak off several, parallel collective consciousnesses, for the simple reason that the collective consciousness as an entity has disappeared? Power today is hardly in the hands of those who believe in astrology and feudalist creation myths. This ought to serve as a warning to all those who have still not got to grips with their own highly private faith in the Cartesian subject. There is no freedom of choice in the face of the informationalist paradigm, other than the choice between being part of it or getting left behind. Which collective consciousness do you belong to, or, to be more accurate, in the remnants of the 'ego meme' which is still dancing round in your brain?

11.

PERFORATED BODIES AND CHEMICAL LIBERATION

WHEN THE EMBITTERED and self-pitying Roman, Juvenal, coined the phrase 'a sound mind in a sound body' in one of his Satires, extremely critical of a life of luxury and vice, he was admittedly suggesting that the sound body should be the container for the sound mind. But it does not follow that the soundness of each must necessarily be linked. The sound mind and the sound body simply form part of a longer wishlist that the poet presents. He simply wants peace of mind, and to avoid pain. That is all.

The constant references to the sound mind in the sound body during the capitalist epoch signify something entirely different to what Juvenal had in mind. It is then a question of ideology. The starting point is the Cartesian notion of the soul as something more or less intact: somewhere, although its precise whereabouts is unclear, there is a sort of immaterial subject which interprets physical sensations, takes necessary decisions and implements these by sending orders to the body, although it is unclear how. It is therefore always presupposed in a remarkable way that there is some sort of human being living inside the human being, not unlike the Russian dolls where a new, smaller doll reveals itself within each opened doll, although in this case there is never any end to the sequence of doll-openings. Besides this, there is also the concealed concept of the originally Christian idea of the weakness of the flesh. The unsound and pleasure-seeking nature of the body needs to be punished by a disciplined soul. So the sound body is the visible sign of a healthy soul, a walking billboard for the soul, whereas bodily decay reveals a laxness and corruption of the soul. The ideal is, of course, complete balance: a desirable normal state defined by a well-protected harmony and an absence of external disturbances of any sort. Every change to this sensitive equilibrium is evil.

The Cartesian subject – the very cornerstone of capitalism's self-understanding, and the starting point for the idea of the responsible individual and free will – presupposes as a concept this normal state, which in turn rests upon two unavoidable suppositions: the health of the body and the sobriety of the mind. This means that in this normal state all the body's senses and its entire reasoning are presumed to be working at ultimate capacity. The subject – or the soul, if you like – has to be able to rely 100% on the body in order to function in a social context. So the body must respond correctly to commands at all times, and always relay reliable information. The subject must be master of his own house. Consequently the health of the body and the sobriety of the mind together constitute the ultimate guarantee that humanistic values can be maintained in a world which would otherwise be threatened with chaos; on these two pillars rest both prestigious citizenship and every individual's capacity to act as a full and valued member of society.

With hindsight, the Cartesian subject looks to be, at the very least, a hyperneurotic human ideal. Health and sobriety are transcendentalised. The concepts are so deeply ingrained in the aesthetics and morals of capitalist society that they are never questioned or even defined. With hindsight we can see how they could never have been defined, because they can never really be said to exist at all, other than as unrealistic platonic ideals. Instead, all available energy is focussed upon describing, and demonising, the opposites of both health and sobriety. According to demonological logic, it is enough to prove that their opposites exist in order to prove the existence of health and sobriety, which in turn explains why the capitalist era's ideology-producers constructed two concepts which had been unknown before then: sickness and intoxication. In their capacity as the demonised opposites of the ideal, sickness and intoxication have become the system's two mortal enemies, which have to be combated with the same frenzy as the faithful were expected to combat Satan during the feudal period. The fragile individual whose soul is not sufficiently robust to successfully drive off sickness and intoxication must consequently be punished with a declaration of incapacity.

The binary opposition of health and sobriety with, respectively, sickness and intoxication formed the basis of capitalism's moral system, which was watched over by steadily more powerful men and women in white coats. Because health and sobriety were never defined, the healthy man was characterised by the fact that he was not sick, just as the sober man was characterised by the fact that he was not intoxicated. This desirable absence of disruptive external elements was administered by state institutions, with a mandate both to form a diagnosis of the citizen and then to take all necessary steps to correct the problem. The sin and shame that were attached to deviations from the true path, which had previously been the province of the church, were now handled by doctors and researchers in long hospital corridors and medical laboratories. Earlier ages' confessions of sin behind the curtains of the confession booth were replaced by revealing conversations in clinically lit surgeries, the priests' black robes replaced by the green trappings of the operating theatre, or the innocent white of the nursing staff.

It was not until Darwin and Nietzsche appeared in the arena in the middle of the nineteenth century that the gospel of health and sobriety started to be questioned. The radical materialism of these two thinkers saw in humankind a body and nothing but a body; a heretical belief to begin with, which nevertheless took root in certain more or less closed groups, and lived on underground. With informationalism's breakthrough, this radical materialism, reinforced by countless research results, is occupying the position of being seen as universally self-evident. The Cartesian subject is ultimately collapsing because of its logical implausibility, and will in future be confined to a place among history's obsolete myths.

The behaviour of the body is governed by a complicated interplay between pre-programmed conditions, stored experiences, and the specific circumstances of the situation at hand. Internal activity is regulated with the help of chemicals. Organs and cells bathe in and communicate using chemicals. Instincts and emotions are chemicals, whose production and secretion in turn encourages the production and secretion of other chemicals, and so on. These mechanisms are incredibly refined. We notice this not least when we have performed well in the social arena. When we, for instance, have concluded a business deal, or merely won a friendly game of tennis, the body rewards itself with a chemical kick that gives us pleasure. In this way, success is quite literally a drug, something we more or less consciously strive for at all times, because it enables us to experience a sense of wellbeing.

This is completely logical from an evolutionary perspective, because social success is intended to improve the preconditions for reproduction. Research shows, for instance, that there is a clear connection between a high position in the social hierarchy and a high concentration of pleasure-inducing chemicals. We are forced to conclude that there is not, and has never been, any 'natural' or neutral normal state of chemical balance. The chemical condition of the body varies from day to day, from person to person, as every pregnant or breast-feeding woman can confirm. As a consequence, the foundations for the demonisation of deviations from the idealised norm disappear. The whole construction of moral judgements of sickness and intoxication, energetically supported by the capitalist power-system, is collapsing like a house of cards. The idealised, predictable, sensibly thinking human being has turned out to be little more than an arbitrarily thinking mix of chemicals. The ideology and its intentions are revealed, and blind faith in the apparently objective and irrefutable diagnoses of official institutions now seems laughably naïve.

The perfect Man, always completely healthy and sober and working at full capacity, occupies the place at the top of the system of social morality that was left vacant by the omnipotent God when he followed feudalism into the grave. This imagined individual reigns supreme in a hierarchical and law-abiding universe, and expresses the desire for order which is necessary if untamed nature is to be held at bay. The perfect Man is the sound individual soul in a sound social body, a symbol of pure common sense which is charting and controlling its surroundings. However, this is an unattainable ideal, and therefore an illusion. As a result of the elevation of this illusion to the status of central symbol for capitalist morality, health and sobriety – in spite of the fact that they can only be defined as negations, with the help of manipulative demonology – become two eminent virtues. The fact is that the illusory characteristics of health and sobriety merely make them more effective as instruments of power. Only at the onset of a new social paradigm is it possible to reveal fully their lack of substance. A revelation which in turn prepares the way for new and more functional illusions which will be perceived in the new paradigm as more true against the background of new patterns of thinking.

The revelation of the mythology of health and sobriety – with Michel Foucault's presentation and application of his 'archaeological' methods at the end of the 1960s as its intellectual highpoint – appears in hindsight to be one of the most important victories of the Nietzschean project during the twentieth century. The resulting relativisation of the concepts of health and sobriety had a strong impact on the first informationalist subcultures in the 1960s, in the form of open experimentation with drugs for ideological reasons. All of a sudden, the old cult of sobriety appeared to be an evidently arbitrary and authoritarian limitation of the many possible dimensions of consciousness. Alongside sanctioned normality, countless other worlds were discovered, with new patterns of perception and thinking, which in turn were presupposed to open the way for alternative ways of building a personality or formulating a social identity – in other words, for another society. When these ideas made their general breakthrough, a market arose for drugs that could be used to manipulate the torrent of chemicals in the body. Both artificial wellbeing and alternative perception were therefore available to an entire generation of young people.

The late-capitalistic power-structure fought back immediately with the hardest means available. Trade in all drugs which were thought to conjure up any form of wellbeing was criminalised; a 'war on drugs' was declared, and the question became so inflamed that debate of the actual issue became practically impossible. The arguments of the establishment were to a large extent circular: illegal drugs are illegal and must be combated at all costs, partly because they are illegal, and partly because they cause so much misery in the form of social exclusion. The fact that this exclusion is in turn by necessity closely connected to the criminalisation only closes the circle even tighter. It is also strenuously claimed that these drugs are 'addictive', at which point the argument becomes purely arbitrary. As the American author Theodore Roszak, one of the subculture's chroniclers, has asked: what is addictive? Fingernails? Chess? The Internet? Literature? Sex? Crisps? And, in that case, what measures can be advocated for society to get to grips with every form of addiction? The illogicality of the establishment's argument and the hysteria of its actions reveal that the intention was to combat something considerably more sensitive than widespread drug-addiction: experimentation with drugs had itself revealed the hollowness at the heart of the capitalist moral system. The Cartesian subject was a lie.

Intoxication and drugs are, of course, not new phenomena in history. What was new during late-capitalism was the level of militant intolerance. In the Victorian England of high-capitalism, to take just one example, authors and others in the margins of respectable society could partake of opium and morphine in peace and quiet; they did not even need to be particularly discreet about their habits. Awareness of drug-use was widespread, but it was not much discussed openly. Drug-use was a private matter. And it was also entirely possible to conceive of drug-use that did not necessarily escalate to become abuse and eventually death by overdose. Sigmund Freud himself used cocaine, for instance, and prescribed heroin to his patients. The divine status of sobriety had not yet become immovably set in stone.

The criminalisation of drugs began in earnest at the outbreak of the First World War. Between 1909 and 1914 the first laws were passed in the USA and United Kingdom with the aim of gaining political control over usage of a series of narcotic preparations, but far from all of them. Even if the Anglo-Saxon temperance movement played an important part in this process – alcohol prohibition in America could not have been passed in the 1920s, with well-known and devastating consequences, unless competing and less widespread pleasures had been criminalised first – this legislation was not primarily a question of moralising on the part of the authorities. It was more a question of the military's need to control drug-use during war in order to be able to maximise its soldiers' efforts on the battlefield. This is demonstrated by the comprehensive active use of narcotics during the World Wars and by American troops in the Korean and Vietnam Wars: from morphine and heroin in field-hospitals, via amphetamines during drawn-out attacks and bombing raids, to cannabis between battles and in base.

During late-capitalism, however, the pragmatic approach to narcotics disappeared. Abuse became the only imaginable term when drug-use was mentioned in official contexts. The basic preconception of the nation-state demonology, fear of the unknown, was transferred from the increasingly unacceptable phobia of outsiders, which was dealt a final, fatal blow with the spectacular defeat of Nazi racism, and its Japanese variant, in the

Second World War, to fear of the revelation of the human body's radical materiality. Drug-use became the perfect target for late-capitalist demonology's irrational excesses. Musicians, artists and other public figures who were discovered with drugs, even if only for their own use, were nailed to the pillory of the mass-media, then sent to court and punished by the judicial system, officially with the aim of deterring western youth from imitating their decadent lifestyle.

Because this was ultimately about trying to prevent the revelation of the individual subject's arbitrary dependence upon the actual chemical composition of the body, narcotics became the perfect demon for late-capitalist demonology. Drug-use was rendered incompatible with the role of the good social citizen. The war against drugs has, like all wars, been based upon fear, but not upon fear of the drugs themselves and their effects – in that case, local pharmacies would long since have been subjected to aggression – but on the fear entertained by the late-capitalist individual that his own physical fragility and mental unreliability might be revealed to him. From the perspective of eternalist socioanalysis we see how the moral tyranny of health and sobriety, like all moralisms, eventually comes full circle and crashes into its own creator, the healthy and sober individual himself.

Society's massive efforts cannot prevent political credibility from collapsing, particularly when the use of prescription drugs is increasing dramatically all over the world. Nothing seems to happen 'naturally' any more; we need chemical help in grotesque quantities to sleep, wake up, eat, digest our food, keep our food down, go to the lavatory, keep our weight somewhere near stable, and maintain something resembling a sex-life. The classical normal state is evidently no longer the norm, but increasingly seems to be the product of comprehensive, regulated drug-intake. Consumption of anti-depressant medication among American schoolchildren multiplied ten-fold during the last decade of the twentieth century. It would take considerable suppression of the facts to believe seriously that these children would be remotely interested in maintaining a restrictive view of drugs when they grow up and join the political discourse.

Long-term, nothing can save belief in a balanced normal state, with the sound body suffused with a neutral and stable chemistry. So the Cartesian subject's last line of defence is breached, and the consequences of this insight are revolutionary for our self-image. The entire moral system that was based upon the myths of health and sobriety is collapsing like a demolished skyscraper. Capitalism's control-mechanisms are losing all power and legitimacy, nursing institutions are losing their credibility, and the entire platform for social moralising is vanishing. Left alone in the harsh spotlight is the body, stripped of its ideological garb, but, by way of recompense, bearing dizzying possibilities in its nakedness.

The consequence of this paradigm shift in self-image – from capitalism's individual, slaving away under his internal morality police, to informationalism's dividual, consciously connected to the dynamic of the network – is a global chemical liberation, a social and cultural mass-movement that we have only seen the first beginnings of thus far, and which will make the twentieth century's equivalent, sexual liberation, pale in comparison. Instead of the humanistic ideal image of the healthy and sober body, an increasingly strong idea is developing of the pathological as the only normal state: the body is in constant imbalance. Any other state – healthy, sober, balanced – has never existed, other than as propagandist illusions. Pathology is the starting point and basic prerequisite for human existence, and no particular condition is given favoured ideological status.

The moral dimension of the issue is being rapidly dismantled. Descartes is being put on his feet, the thesis 'I think, therefore I am' is turned into its opposite: 'I am, therefore I think'. Rationality and rationalising only come later, as a secondary construction in order to create a necessary fictive explanatory model for an occurrence which is ultimately determined by chemicals. Consequently capitalism's and humanism's task for the individual, to nurture and protect the healthy and sober individual by caring for the fictive normal state of health and combating intoxication, is unravelling. The informationalist dividual is a homo pathologicus. Pathology is losing its loaded content, is no longer associated with an illness needing to be defeated, but is instead becoming the norm in a countless range of variants. Chemicals are constantly working inside each and every one of us; what interests us in no longer the degree of 'naturalness' or sobriety, but the degree of wellbeing, which in turn demands complex sociometries in order to be defined. The point here is that none of this can be the object of social moralising any longer. Morality cannot survive in the age of mass interactivity, because it is being outdone by socioanalytical ethics.

As homo pathologicus steps forward out of moralism and constructs the world according to his own tastes, he is transformed into homo experimentus; someone who, like a poker player, is constantly working to improve his own hand in ingenious ways, and who eagerly experiments – chemically, sexually, surgically – on his own body without any moral reservations. This is a global development whose introductory phase can already be discerned; the tolerance threshold is rapidly being lowered in a number of different areas. Drugged athletes are harshly condemned in official contexts, while cheap concoctions of drugs are being bought and sold in gyms and sports clubs all over the world. Developments within plastic and transplant surgery are happening at an incredible rate, and the lingering remnants of moral objections are constantly having to give way to the consumption interests of wealthy minorities. So-called designer drugs are taking huge shares of the market of a generation of young people which is not tempted by the alcohol consumption that its parents have had to sanction, which is forcing legislation in the area into retreat in one country after the other. The gradual liberation of sexuality from reproduction and the demise of authority is paving the way for an exhilarating game of sexual practices, and so on.

The netocratic dividual is developing something that we call the ethics of the damaged, a new value-system which clearly distances itself from the absolute and transcendental values of capitalism and humanism, such as health and sobriety, and other basic suppositions about human existence which were previously taken as given. The ethics of the damaged promotes the open, the fluctuating, the mobile, at the expense of the well polished, the balanced, the accomplished. Rapid change is the only norm, nothing is ever perfected, a state of equilibrium is either an oppressive utopia or a passing anomaly. This applies as much to society and the economy as it does to the collaborating mechanisms and capricious chemistry within the human body. As part of the new system – which, consequentially, is itself naturally changeable – there is a series of partly contradictory ideas of the body, created and revised under great pressure from conflicting forces. Even if this value-system lacks clearly defined edges, and the body is both promoted and degraded at the same time, the old axioms are nonetheless irredeemably lost.

With the rise of radical materialism, and the fall of Cartesian dualism, the body is advancing its position. From having been the fragile vessel of the divine soul, it is becoming transformed into the mother of all consciousness. Everything stems from the body. The thinking which Descartes claimed was paramount is reduced to being the product of bodily processes. At the same time, recent years' developments within cybernetics and information theory mean that the body is being placed in a new philosophical context, where it is being questioned and attacked from all sides. What differentiates the body from a machine? Is the body's physical presence really necessary for the subject to be maintained? Is it possible to regard the body credibly as anything that is by definition limited?

As the ethics of the damaged gains ground, people are starting to perceive the body as a constantly unfinished project, an ongoing experiment which is continually changing with the help of both the addition of chemicals and various surgical interventions. The boundary between nature and culture regarding the body is dissolving. It is a fact that over 10% of the population of the USA could at the turn of the millennium be termed cyborgs, in other words people with various forms of implant, from artificial hips and skin transplants to electronic pacemakers. In these cases the body has been renovated and enhanced with one or more artificial features, something cultural and originally non-bodily. This activity will expand as technical development in these areas proceeds. This behaviour shows itself time after time to be crassly pragmatic; ethical or ontological questions are dealt with retrospectively. The main thing is that the heart beats and that the hip works. Consumer demand is guiding development with an iron hand.

The body is undergoing a radical objectification; it is becoming something else, an artefact, a collection of ordered matter that can be manipulated according to whim and taste. The body is being transformed into a more or less flexible fashion item, which can be adjusted according to the varying demands of the season. As a result, the body is also to a great extent losing its historical meaning and symbolic content, and being transformed into a neutral, blank surface which reflects its 'inhabitant's' social ambitions and the cultural projections of its surroundings. It is becoming part of the world which interacts with other parts of the same world. The body itself is becoming the netocratic dividual, a physiological network which forms part of ever-larger and more complex networks.

A central question within both media theory and cognition research is how this objectified body relates to machines. Current thinking is gliding gradually towards more or less articulated theories of a form of symbiosis. In the same way that a blind man's stick is perceived to be an extension of the body, so we see increasingly often examples of how the body is being intimately woven together with sophisticated technology. We are speaking of a metaphorical cyborg, a literally physiological homo technologicus. We take it for granted that the blind man is helpless without his stick. Now we see the same thing with, for instance, the neurosurgeon without his fibre-optic microscope and the computer hacker without his keyboard and high-speed modem. The accessibility of databases on the Internet is increasingly replacing aspects of our memory in a mass of different respects. In advertising, which is playing an increasingly central role in our mental furniture, the insufficiently equipped consumer is portrayed as alienated and cut off from his surroundings. Without the latest design of car he is as exposed as a hermit crab without a shell. The fear of ending up in an involuntary state of technological solitude in a world where man and machine are continually expected to marry is constantly invoked.

Consequently a relationship of physical dependency on technology is developing, as strong as on any drug, which has a great deal to do with the death of God and the dilution of religion. The individual fears isolation and longs to belong to a higher communion. In the traditional old belief of the body as essentially different from, and clearly defined in relation to its surroundings there was certainly a large dose of pride and arrogance, but also a tragic awareness of difference and enclosure. The boundary of the body was absolute. The Cartesian subject ruled supreme within this boundary, but the body which constituted the boundary was excluded from a more widespread communion. According to the philosopher Georges Bataille, there are only two ways out of this dilemma: firstly, sex, by which the body unites with another body, albeit in an illusory and temporary way; secondly, death, by which the body returns to the eternal cycle, but at the cost of its own destruction. This connection between the desire for symbiosis and the desire for death helps explain why eroticism and death appear as a pair in so many contexts, why the orgasm is known as 'the little death', et cetera. It is a question of the ego, through the body, breaking its chains. The sound soul leaves the padded cell of the sound body. The dividual flees the internal morality police, recognises and nurtures its own pathology, and thereby gains the chance to explore on its own terms the complex desire for symbiosis and destruction.

Christianity promises a solution to the impossible Cartesian equation by offering a union with the whole of creation through faith, and by removing the destruction problem through the immortality of the soul. The body does not matter so much, because flesh itself is mortal and already corrupted by nature at birth. The sound body is merely a provisional solution in a utopian project aiming at eternity. The Christian project, however, collapses attentionally in line with the spread of secularisation and radical materialism, which in turn explains both the arrival of an irrational and aggressive evangelical movement, mostly in the USA and Latin America – trends are met by reactionary countertrends – and also the religiously coloured perceptions that are often applied to information technology. There is an idea here of transcendence, a materialistic mysticism, which builds upon the dream of fusing body and machine. That mankind is merely materia, that the body itself is a machine, was proposed by the Enlightenment thinker and physician La Mettrie as early as the mid-1700s. This perception still arouses controversy, which gives popular culture an incitement to play with the thought; one influential example is the German group Kraftwerk, who not only create a demonstratively synthetic soundscape in the studio and explore an extremely machinistic aesthetic, but also allow mechanistic replicants to replace their own bodies on stage at concerts.

When we analyse the body's smallest components, its cells, we find a myriad microscopically small machines which carry out their tasks entirely mechanically, whether blood-cells or bacteria in our bowels, or anything else. This is also true of the brain. Nowhere do we find mystical collections of any other type of secret or unidentifiable matter. This implies that even the grandest expressions of our human consciousness ultimately have a mechanical explanation. Consequently we should also be able to interact closely with the machines we ourselves have created: the conditions for some form of symbiosis look good.

Both the theory of evolution in its modern form, and cybernetics, the two most influential contemporary theoretical scientific complexes, include an image of man as a thinking machine. Thought itself, learning and creativity are the results of advanced information management through so-called feedback loops. The human machine interacts with its surroundings (and with other machines/people). Incoming data is constantly re-evaluated, which modifies its actions, which in turn leads to new incoming impulses, which in turn modify behaviour once again. As a result, interest is turning towards thinking machines, which, according to the mathematician Alan Turing's famous test, can demonstrably be shown to think as soon as they answer a list of questions in the same way as a person, and around which an entire research discipline, artificial intelligence, has been constructed. More and more people are inclined to admit that there are no essential differences between the human body and a machine, or at least that any differences that might occur are insignificant. The important thing from this perspective is not the differences of internal organisation, but the similarities of observable function.

As a result, the body as an isolated phenomenon also becomes uninteresting, and the isolation itself is shown to be an artificial fiction. The body, in its capacity as a thinking machine, functions only in close interaction with its surroundings, surroundings which to a large extent consist of other sorts of machines, which have been delegated all manner of suitable tasks. The reason why we today can conceive of such infinitely more complex things than cavemen could is, as cognition researcher Edwin Hutchins points out, not because we are so much more intelligent than they were, but that over time we have constructed far more intelligent surroundings in which to live and work. Different sorts of machine spur one another on to greater achievements. They are getting smarter, which makes us smarter, which in turn means that we make them smarter, and so on. Homo technologicus is, to a great extent, an environmental phenomenon.

At the same time the surface of the body, in its capacity as a protective shell around a subject or a soul, appears to be perforated, an admittedly defined but nonetheless permeable membrane which leaks impulses of various sorts in all directions. Our highly different and specialised cells (machines) together constitute our bodies (machines), which in turn, together with a mass of other different and specialised machines, constitute a greater context in which relations and communication are paramount and far more important than any more or less vain attempt at controlling the boundaries on an individual level.

The downside of radical materialism's promotion of the body is information theory's degrading of physical embodiment generally, which leads to what has been called a 'dematerialised materialism'. In a context in which relations and communication are foremost, the body loses its special status. Information is a digital sequence, a pattern which can be transferred and reproduced; its embodiment in the form of, for instance, a newspaper article or the coloured squares of a piece of fabric, is merely a copy of something which could most closely be called a platonic idea, eternally true and superior to all copies in the grubby demimonde of actual things. If the same text is printed in an anthology or the same coloured squares printed on a plastic bag instead, the pattern still remains the same. And in the same way, an information-technological perspective offers the chance to view the body as merely a temporary and possibly flawed reproduction of an individual's pattern. Postmodernism's degradation at the end of the twentieth century of the platonic original and its copies as an ideal, in favour of endless sequences of simulacra is already in jeopardy. Information theory is turning the debate in a platonic direction again.

According to the view of information theory, the human subject is fundamentally a digital sequence which can be freed, if necessary, from the body and transferred to some other, better suited machine. As long as the pattern is the same, the subject's identity will remain intact. The material embodiment itself is secondary, and so we are back in the world of classical metaphysics, in a view of the world which has tellingly been described as virtual gnosticism. This is the 'we' which is modifying 'our' bodies and considering emigration, the posthuman subject in its purest form, liberated from matter and independent of context. A smart soul in a smart machine, immortal thanks to the nature of its software, theoretically possible of being downloaded to another hard-disk to be stored forever.

This idea, however, is merely a dream, or rather a nightmare, without foundation in either actual observation or logic. One useful comparison is with the long-cherished dream of the paperless office. The well-known idea was that the arrival of information technology into the workplace would mean that filing and piles of paper would disappear, but this was based upon far too shallow reasoning and insufficient analysis of information's conditions of life. Information is never liberated from matter and independent of context. A report printed on paper is something entirely different to the same text on screen, and paper makes the information accessible for quite different unreachable processes, particularly where working in groups is concerned. Paper makes the information in question easy to get an overview of, and easy to use for your own ends. Paper – even piles of apparently unsorted paper – is simply part of a smart environment which makes us ourselves smarter. The paperless office can therefore not become a reality until the day when the human subject really has been downloaded onto a harddrive.

But we shall never see that day; identity is liberated from matter and independent of context no more than information or anything else is. Human consciousness is indissolubly linked to the body. It is a fact that it is a body. There is nothing else but the body, and it is important to point this out constantly and protect the interests of the body, particularly when it is under pressure, not only from virtual gnosticism's dreamers, but also from strongly reactionary forces which are mobilising a last desperate defence of the old religious view of the soul and Cartesian dualism.

One example of the latter is the political scientist Francis Fukuyama, the man who declared the end of history in the early 1990s, and who has devoted a large portion of his subsequent books to patching up this vulgarised Hegelian theory, which we have already discussed in Netocracy. Further comprehensive repair-work is to be found in Our Posthuman Future – Consequences of the Biotechnological Revolution.

Only ten years ago science was a close collaborator of bourgeois democracy, which in turn was the social system which, in the best imaginable way, answers people's need for recognition and acknowledgement, which was the main reason that the historical process could be said to be over. Bourgeois democracy had therefore inevitably triumphed, once and for all. But now the harmonious end of history is suddenly under threat, because science and technology have refused to stop, and are threatening to push history into dangerous directions. Science has become a danger, according to Fukuyama, because recent decades' developments within biology and medicine have taken a risky path. Entirely regardless of whether the more speculative applications of biotechnology – for instance, cloning, the growth and manipulation of stem-cells, genetic engineering – are actually achieved within the foreseeable future or not, the current position represents an acute danger for the most holy, namely the human 'nature' that Fukuyama regards as given and constant, and on whose basis the whole idea of the end of history rests.

His reasoning touches for a moment upon the eternalistic analysis of chemical liberation, but quickly moves off in completely the opposite direction. One of the great problems for Fukuyama is that recent research has transformed both psychology and religion into chemistry. The path to happiness and wellbeing no longer passes through group therapy and self-insight, or salvation and faith, but through doctors' prescriptions and signal substances. Antidepressant preparations like Zoloft and Prozac increase the brain's levels of seratonin, which greatly increases the basic sense of self-worth both for the individual and the collective. In a similar way, ritalin, prescribed to children with attention-deficit disorders, promotes increased concentration and a mild euphoria through chemical stimulation of the central nervous system. The problem, as Fukuyama sees it, is that these methods function all too well. Admittedly, increased self-worth is the goal of historical development, according to his vulgarised Hegelian model, but this must, he goes on, be reached in what he terms a 'natural' way.

Fukuyama is clear that success in the social arena causes the body to reward itself with pleasant chemicals. High status is linked to high seratonin levels in both animals and mankind. This is 'natural', and it is the necessary carrot that drives mankind to achieve great things. He himself mentions Julius Caesar and Napoleon as examples: how would they have bothered to conduct wars across the whole of Europe if they had had the opportunity of improving their self-worth by swallowing Prozac whenever they wanted? (For some reason, Hitler is not mentioned.) Eventually Fukuyama is prepared to admit that certain serious depressions actually warrant medication, but nonetheless calls for stronger legislation because of what he sees as an increased tendency toward 'cosmetic pharmacology'. People who feel low would therefore, after strict tests, be allowed to feel a bit better. But those who, according to these tests, do not feel quite so bad, would be committing a crime if they used chemical means to feel a bit better.

Fukuyama avoids all problems regarding the drawing of boundaries; the difference between sickness and mischievous self-indulgence can evidently be discerned by common sense. For Fukuyama the concept of 'health' is entirely unproblematic. He dismisses Foucault's revelatory reasoning about differing attitudes towards homosexuality through the ages, for instance, without any real argument. Being healthy is simply being normal; if you have broken your leg, then you know something is wrong. Wellbeing must be deserved and linked to deserving achievements. But because no-one but Fukuyama himself can say precisely what is worth rewarding or what is deserving, he remains an opportunistic moralist of a dreary and all too familiar sort. In this way old-fashioned humanism is still being produced, nowadays with the help of superstition and wishful-thinking, to appeal to the consumtariat masses. We cannot get any further than this from socioanalytical ethics.

When Fukuyama tries to reinforce his argument philosophically he is forced, consequently, to try to maintain the old value-objectivism and the Cartesian subject in order to establish the logical basis for his demands for stronger legislation. He claims that there is an objective natural right which is superior to all the changing circumstances of history, and which guarantees man a sequence of holy rights. Man has been raised from the mass of beasts by some sort of holy power – he refers to Pope John Paul II's speech about the 'ontological leap' – and has thus gained his unique soul. Human consciousness cannot be explained in mechanistic terms, Fukuyama says, because we all know that we have 'subjective mental states of a non-material character within us' (according to exactly the same logic, we also know that the world is flat and is at the centre of the universe). Our possession of 'soul' gives mankind a unique 'worthiness', and it is in the name of this soul and this worthiness that we must legislate away chemicals which make us feel good in an undeserved way, as well as everything else 'unnatural' which biotechnology might bring with it. Otherwise, according to Fukuyama, we will be violating ourselves and our 'natural' rights.

An interesting irony in this context is that Fukuyama – in entire agreement with eternalism's sociotechnological laws – does not see the terrorist attacks on New York and Washington in September 2001 as a serious threat to the West and to global social development. Muslim fundamentalists, he suggests, are a desperate rearguard of history's losers and are fighting an invincible foe. What he does not see, on the other hand, is that he himself belongs to an equally desperate and at least as reactionary rearguard of a large losing group opposing change. With his pen he is conducting the same vain struggle as the bearded terrorists with their swords. The enemy is the same: technological innovations, secularisation, the dissolution of norms, shifts in power, the desire for change, the dismantling of old traditional structures.

The long-term losers are uniting, in spite of their differences, behind the battle-cry 'Status quo for ever!' and are being given space in the public arena for the same reason. Not because of any blinding logic or credibility in their political engagement, but because there are still large groups with considerable influence who do not want to hear any new truths about a new age, but insist upon only listening to opinions which happen to be favourable to themselves. The similarity between Fukuyama and the reactionary Islamists and their like on the one side, and on the other the opportunistic prophets who in the sixteenth century claimed that power would never leave the aristocrats' country estates and move to the merchants' trading cities, is striking. Then it was unthinkable that anything would ever be able to accumulate a higher worth than the production of food. Today, it is presented as unthinkable that people might be able to live in and manage a society where they have been liberated from a morality which has already lost all credibility.

As the capitalist paradigm is gradually phased out and the replaced by informationalism, nothing can save the torpedoed ideal notions of normality, health, nature, et cetera. As the intake even of sanctioned chemicals soars, all such ideas are becoming increasingly absurd and impossible to maintain. The body will therefore gain an entirely new status. There will no longer be any demand that it remain sound at all costs, nor will it contain any sort of soul, which will only serve to make it more interesting. More and more people are realising that the idealisation of a healthy, sober normal state is a repressive instrument which forms part of a specific epoch's ideology and ruling strategy. A new insight is starting to take shape: we are all sick, one way or another, and if everyone is sick, then the division between health and sickness dissolves. We are all bodies, nothing more nor less, and inside us all there are raging hormones and other chemical substances, which we can pay attention to without prejudice, less and less inhibited by old taboos.

Informationalist human beings, first the netocracy and later even the consumtariat, are undergoing a 'chemical liberation' and regard it as their self-evident right to experiment with their own bodies. An interesting consciousness in an interesting body! This development is being accelerated by an explosive boom in innovation, within both the legal and the criminalised sectors of the industry, which is constantly producing new, ever cheaper and more potent chemicals. That this expanding chemical industry is collaborating with boundary-transgressing popular culture only increases the power and extent of the chemical liberation. This global subculture has already shown itself in late-capitalism's trance and techno clubs, whose power of attraction is linked to the need for a new, globalist metaphysics. That this subculture is operating on the margins of society only increases – in combination with an openness to unknown elements – the temptation and sense of cohesion.

We are witnessing the introductory phase of the first genuine global mass culture. It would, however, be a serious mistake in this context to believe that drugs themselves are the central point here. Chemical liberation should not be seen primarily as a libertarian affirmation of the citizen's right to intoxication. What is truly interesting is how an informationalist and – in the true sense of the word – alternative mass-culture is developing, forming the arena in which the virtual nomadic tribes first settle, where they grow fastest, and undermine the old power structure. The netocracy is not concerned with using stock markets and party politics to take power from the bourgeoisie, but is instead making use of art, culture, aesthetics. Here the new, sought-after preconditions are developing for the creation of the social identity which for the first time in history will arise from a globally collective subject.

12.

SOCIOANALYTICAL ETHICS AND THE COLLAPSE OF THE CAPITALIST LEFT

WHEN TODAY'S LEFTWING ACTIVISM is active at all, it is often in the form of stone-throwing street riots in protest against financial globalisation. This development is both symptomatic and at the same time deeply ironic. The political power which rightly used to view the nation as the foremost propaganda instrument of the bourgeoisie has been transformed into the reactionary resisting force which is most strongly clinging on to the disintegrating nation state. At the same time it is holding on to a hopelessly outdated vulgarised Marxist analysis of class society. Each is dependent upon and validates the other.

The prevailing confusion and partial paralysis is closely connected to the academic Left's hatred of grand perspectives and its latterday obsession with peripheral trivialities, such as the mystifications of deconstruction (everything can mean everything and nothing means much at all) and the infatuation of postmodernism with the surface of consumer society (all the countless interpretations of Andy Warhol's soup tins, or Jeff Koons' ironic kitsch, for example). This in turn is connected to the dramatic fall in value of anything on a grand scale, and any attempts at ideological totality, after first the Holocaust and then the Gulag became known and were dealt with in the public arena. It only feels safe to become engaged in the very smallest and most intimate contexts; when they arise, large contexts are consequently something that one automatically opposes.

But informationalism's first generation of young, eager activists has, as the developing network society has become more defined, realised how pointless it is to continue to repeat the old doctrinaire slogans. Instead, it has turned to the first attentionalist explanatory models and new sociotechnological strategies. It is in these contexts that so-called hegemony theory has gained, if not quite hegemony, at least a strong position. The fact is that the very phrase hegemony has become one of the most frequently used within political philosophy, particularly where the strategic thinking of leftwing activism is concerned.

The original hegemony theorist was Lenin, whose theory was severely modified after his death and relaunched by Antonio Gramsci, one of the founders of the Italian Communist Party. According to Gramsci – who was imprisoned for ten years by Mussolini – hegemony is synonymous with a consensus that is enforced by the more or less subtle application of power, a process in which the perspective of the dominant class in society is presented as common sense in every area, and therefore becomes irrefutable. The workers' chance of taking power lay in the construction of strategic alliances, primarily with the peasants, with which the bourgeois consensus could be torn down and replaced by the perspective of the new alliance. Gramsci's theory has, in turn, been revised, and forms the basis of late-capitalist variants, of which that presented by Ernesto Laclau and Chantal Mouffe in the mid-1980s has been the best received.

When hegemony theory is used as the starting point for political activism, it takes the form of a sort of collective application of Foucauldian ethics: an action is justified by the fact that in the case in question it aims to, or can be expected to, weaken the hegemony of the ruling elite, its preferential right to interpretation, with the intention of transferring power to those in a subordinate position, so that they can make their own voice heard on their own terms. The theory is based upon undermining the foundations of the existing hierarchical power-structure, so that this implodes, whereupon good forces can actively drive society towards a plurarchical state where everyone has power and determines their own actions, but lacks the power to decide what anyone else should do. Because plurarchy has in this way become both goal and justification for political struggle, it is reasonable to describe this ideology as plurarchism. Foucault, Laclau, Mouffe and their many followers are all plurarchists, and they are interesting in their capacity as the heralds of information society's ideological thinking. A plurarchist can be compared to an anarchist insofar as both are fighting to destroy capitalism's old power-structures – it is hardly a coincidence that plurarchists borrow freely from the popular old symbols of anarchism – but, at the same time, it is extremely important to differentiate between plurarchy and anarchy. Even if a lot of plurarchists have not yet realised it, this is a question of two fundamentally different phenomena, which is something we examine in more detail in Netocracy.

From a sociotechnological perspective, however, it becomes highly problematic to use hegemony theory as a basis for political activism, not least because the theory as such lacks any reasoning about the consequences of its own success in the political arena. Laclau and Mouffe, for instance, never pay any attention to the fact that society's power relationships are a mobilistic phenomenon which is highly influenced by a widely disseminated ideology, particularly if this is accompanied by powerful activism. So when hegemony theory deals with the question of who has the right to speak on behalf of the collective – or, to put it in attentionalist terms: who can embody the collective subject in a credible and simultaneously powerful way – it shuts its eyes entirely to its own role in this context, in other words, how it itself, by making the collective conscious of the manipulative consensus and of the power that is up for grabs, sets power in motion once again and thereby displaces the focus of the public discourse towards, for instance, repressive strategies and the sublimating dialectic of violence in the collective unconscious.

As a result, hegemony theory falls at its own hand, at least insofar as its efforts to form the basis of political activism are concerned. It speaks of a political discourse in perpetual motion, but it is strangely blind to the fact that it itself constitutes a political movement which influences other movements in the arena. Hegemony theory sees a fluid pattern of movement, but freezes this pattern into a model, like a game of jackstraws, and does not realise that this model instantaneously dissolves itself, because the model as such, and the awareness it attracts, mean that it is itself poking about among the sticks. The adherents of hegemony theory – in good company, because here they are joined by Heidegger and Derrida – miss the fact that the relation between eternalism and mobilism is dialectic. The plateau of stability they envisage is a strict eternalisation. Their mistake is that they do not see that the plateau has been set in motion at the very moment that it reveals itself.

Eternalism's political philosophy understands, unlike hegemony theory, that it must not cling on to a single eternalisation of movement on the political arena, but instead builds upon an analysis of sociotechnological principles. Within this, interactivity between its own strategy and the political arena is already discounted, and constitutes the very starting point for the analysis itself. This is the decisive reason why attentionalist network dynamics (see Netocracy) is superior to hegemony theory as the ideological basis for information society's political activism. The problem is just that eternalism's political philosophy is also considerably more complicated and therefore harder to transmit in media-friendly slogans. Its attentional value is anything but striking. This does not mean that in a longer perspective it will not be far more important than hegemony theory as a platform for information society's political activism.

One important difference between the different theories is that eternalistic activism is not content with driving political discourse towards a plurarchical state. This is also entirely superfluous: the plurarchical state is already built into interactive media technology and will come to be realised regardless of any strategic strokes of genius. Foucault, Laclou and Mouffe all ignore this, probably because they are not at all interested in information theory. Instead, eternalistic activism takes the next logical step and problematises plurarchy itself, and uses this to promote politics whose focus is already beyond the initial chaos of plurarchy. It is not content, unlike the anti-global Left, with a narcissistic fascination with its own event. It does not see every demonstration watched by the media as a triumphant show of strength, but is clear about the underlying purpose of every demonstration. Eternalism's political philosophy is a long-term strategy for civilisation building on a constantly more complex information technological platform.

Hegemony theory's comparatively powerful breakthrough suggests, of course, nothing about how correct or useful its analysis actually is. The only thing we can state is that the university environment of late-capitalism has been extremely favourable to this meme. And the most straightforward explanation of its popularity among academics is that the academic Left could not resist a quick fix when the possibility arose, a pleasant intoxication which dissipated all thought of the really serious problems. The Left's intellectual collapse began in connection to the student revolts of 1968, particularly that in Paris. The failure of the revolt was devastating for the theory of activism; the working class did not behave at all as it was supposed to, and instead showed itself to be far more interested in raising its own standard of welfare that in political utopianism. Those activists who were genuinely interested in a real change soon saw the romantic illusion of revolutionary posturing for what it was, and turned instead towards the corridors of social institutions and the media industry in order to conduct pragmatic revisionism from within the stomach of the alleged monster. Left behind in their revolutionary poses were only those activists who were primarily motivated by embittered middle-class self-loathing and a libidinous fixation on the trappings of revolution. Those who did not seek out terrorist cells found a bolt-hole with a monthly salary and career prospects in the universities, where they could conspire in peace and produce revolutionary romanticism during their paid working hours.

The eternal problem with failed revolutions is twofold: firstly, the revolutionaries in question are never held responsible for their ideology, or even their lack of ideology, because this has never been implemented. Fidel Castro, for instance, can probably expect a harsh judgement by history, considering how Cuba has developed since the revolution. According to his theory, socialism was going to nationalise the nation's wealth, but in Cuba the regime has done the opposite and gradually socialised poverty, as the exiled writer Guillermo Cabrera Infante points out. Castro has magically made all the goods on the shelves disappear for everyone apart from a small, dollar-rich elite, and merely offered the people slogans as compensation. The situation is quite different for his old brother-in-arms, Che Guevara, because Guevara never participated in the implementation of his doctrine, and died as a revolutionary martyr in Bolivia's jungles. Unlike the likes of Marlon Brando, he has never shown his bloated, middle-aged stomach in sordid contexts, but belongs, like a communist James Dean, to the eternally young and untarnished heroes of the media age.

The second problem is that failed revolutions are always the best revolutions for incurable romantics. Responsibility, practical administration and compromising, workaday pragmatism can never be as exciting as building barricades and throwing Molotov-cocktail parties. Ever since the days of Jean-Jacques Rousseau, the French intelligentsia has been full of this type of exalted revolutionary romantics, theorists and activists, for whom a successfully executed revolution would be the worst nightmare they could imagine. But what else can be expected of a culture which regards its own – in certain respects successful, in others disastrous – revolution of 1789 with a level of veneration worthy of a returning Messiah? The fact is that the great degree of secularisation and pure rationalism that everyone is so proud of in France is nothing more than the gaudy feathers of a masquerade costume, intended to disguise the fact that the divine Revolution has taken God's place in the system, that the nation state has replaced paradise, and that Rousseau's Noble Savage has replaced the Adam and Eve of the so-called desert religions.

Thankfully France has also given the world its most spiritual antidote to revolutionary romanticism in the form of Henri Bergson's concept of history as la longue durée. Bergson's understanding of history is notably more mobilistic that eternalistic, and from this perspective the obsession of the revolutionary romantic with certain fateful years, dates and even times of day as utterly absurd. Years, dates and time of day can only have a symbolic value, and mobilistic thinking does not grant symbolism any value at all. Truly transforming changes can only take place over long periods of time. La longue durée therefore forms one of the basic ingredients in eternalism's information technological writing of history. If it had not been for Deleuze's patient defence of Bergson, the academic Left in Europe would undoubtedly have dismissed this anachronistic thinker long ago.

Once the spread of hegemony theory and the attention it creates has been problematised, another reason against the use of this theory as the basis for political activism becomes clear: its tendency towards repression and its participation in the so-called discursive censorship syndrome. Nothing is mere coincidence, and it was no chance that made Gramsci's ideas of hegemony suitable to be polished up again during the glory days of political correctness during the 1980s. Laclau's and Mouffe's theoretical construction is thus a synthesis typical of its time, of contemporary post-utopian Marxist ambitions, and of the special obsession of political correctness with minority movements, within which discursive censorship syndrome is particularly widespread.

Many of hegemony theory's supporters have chosen to ignore the theory's claim to universal validity in order to use it, like so many cynical Machiavellians, as a sort of sociotechnological toolbox, which has resulted in hegemony theory being partially transformed into the official ideology of discursive censorship. This is the original source of postmodern rhetoric of victimhood: a situation arises where all groups try to silence all the others in the name of artful suffering and oppression that each group (or its forebears) supposes that it has had to bear. Arguing against someone who, rightly or otherwise, believes themselves to be oppressed has been compared to supporting the oppression itself and the oppressive system. In such an intellectual climate, the conditions for open and clarifying debate are naturally the worst possible. What Foucault saw as a plurarchism based upon a fundamentally eternalistic ambition, and upon ethics which wanted to facilitate genuine and creative dialogue, a mutually enriching non-zero-sum game in which all participants are winners, has become, in the hegemony theory-inspired version of cynical activism, merely a hypocritical and intellectually invalid exercise in political correctness. Everyone loses.

The perceived kinship between the so-called anti-globalisation movement and minority movements is obvious. Hegemony theory has often been called upon as a source of inspiration by the demonstration industry, under the strict supervision of the media, and itself become medialised, as it follows the international political circus around. The thought, or rather the lack of it, is that spontaneous action – which is seldom particularly spontaneous, and generally follows a carefully rehearsed liturgy – can easily precede ideology, because action is directed at Power (a mystical abstraction, which for reasons of convenience, is never specified) and therefore automatically believed to favour the powerless in some mystical way. The fact that an attack on globalisation is in practice a defence of the status quo, a protection of protected markets where poor countries are not permitted to compete with cheap products, does not seem to matter at all in this context.

The single-issue and protest parties which have blossomed in conjunction with the loosening of the democratic establishment's legitimacy, under equally strict supervision by the media, reason in much the same way. They claim that they want to 'shake things up', to irritate those in Power, but never have any thought-out ambitions. The anti-globalisation movement's phrases demonstrate with all desirable clarity that it lacks a long-term strategy, and therefore also long-term credibility. Ideologically, it represents, on closer inspection, little more than a naïve romanticisation of a past which will never return, and which, more often than not, never actually existed. Whatever it might have intended with its media strategy, it is inescapably swallowed up by its own success in the media. The demonstration industry is becoming fused together with the fashion industry, and their balaclava helmets will find their way into next autumn's collections. And that is all.

The big problem is naïvety once again; partly an incapacity to problematise, and partly a lack of information-theoretical perspective. Hegemony theory sees how a manipulative consensus has been constructed and has functioned throughout history, but does not understand that this pattern, like all other conditions for producing consensus with propaganda, will disappear as and when the actors on the arena become interactive under informationalism. Where eternalistic analysis sees network relations and a sophisticated interplay of transrational arguments, hegemony theory merely wants to see alienated individuals chained to their pasts. As a result of people mattering more than things, and of credibility being said to be linked to background rather than argument, hegemony theory eventually loses all chances of dialogue, and transforms public discourse into a pathetic competition in misery. At the same time, it is cutting off its ideological roots, because its predecessors argued from a factual basis and did not seek to win sympathy by harping on about personal suffering; both Marx and Nietzsche would undoubtedly have hated hegemony theory and its consequences. It is difficult to imagine a more cynical nihilism than this, and it would, if allowed to spread unchecked, be guaranteed to lead to the death of political activism. And actually also to the death of politics.

What hegemony theory ultimately expresses is nothing more than the desperate attempts of the old Left to cling on to the capitalist order it professes to oppose, but which at the same time is the only thing which can justify its own existence. Like a neurotic patient, it holds on to the familiar, out of fear of the unknown, eagerly denying that the familiar, even if it is viewed as oppressive, has become irrelevant. The true mortal enemy of the old Left is not the capitalist bourgeoisie, but informationalism as paradigm and eternalism's radical pragmatism as ideology, because this complex is in the process of removing the old Left and its inseparable companion, capitalism, from the historical agenda. Its strategy is therefore to deny at all costs that a paradigm shift is taking place, or that the power structure and rules of the game might have changed in any fundamental way since the nineteenth century; ultimately it is a question of obstinately denying that society is a mobilistic phenomenon, because such an admission could never be combined with tenacious wishful-thinking about a future utopian society.

It would be almost absurd for the activism which was born in the tracks of eternalism's political philosophy to oppose globalisation itself, not least because globalisation is the implementation of the agenda of interactive communications technology, which forms the basis for informationalism itself. The genuinely new Left – not to be confused with, for instance, Anthony Giddens' and Tony Blair's new-old leftwing liberalism – sees plurarchy as more democratic than democracy, and is working to see that economic and financial globalisation is followed as soon as possible by cultural and political globalisation. This means that one of the decisive political conflicts will be between, on the one hand, reactionary romanticism: an outgoing capitalist Left acting as the self-appointed voice of the world's oppressed peoples, but which is, in practice, clinging on to an oppressive status quo, and, on the other, an incoming informationalist Left: a radical pragmatism which wants to conduct a more strategic and less theatrical activism, helping the oppressed to help themselves, in accordance with a complex and changing, but clear-sighted, analysis of developing circumstances.

One strong contributory explanation for the fatal confusion which reigns within the Left at the turn of the millennium is that hegemony theory, like the majority of late-capitalism's political philosophy, stems from the entirely unfounded wishful-thinking which makes it possible for current minority movements to form the pattern for the future in terms of political activism. But, however unappealing it might be for sensitive liberals and Marxists, the lack of network-dynamic creativity within these movements reveals that their political successes have been achieved as a result of a 'walkover' (which is significant for countertrends) rather than by their own power (which is significant for genuine trends). A trend in this context is a social and/or cultural movement in time which expresses a marked desire for change for change's sake. The trend is always in line with developing information technology and the groups which are favoured by this. It is primary so long as it comes directly from a working force in a field rather than from other movements. The countertrend is by the same definition secondary, and should be seen as little more than a reaction to the trend, a defence of interests which believe themselves to be threatened by the forces which are favoured by the new circumstances.

The traditional, capitalist, patriarchal networks had quite simply been so weakened so that they no longer offered any resistance. In the wait for the developing paradigm to assume sharper definition, a political vacuum arose which minority groups could exploit. This explains why the strategy of aggressive whining was initially so successful. Traditional networks were as good as dumbfounded, largely because the powerful upheaval in the media climate meant that they were no longer playing on their classical, secure home territory, but were instead forced out into a new, transparent public space governed by new rules. From their shifted positions, the minority groups began to develop the discursive censorship syndrome, and poisoned a large part of the debate still further. But this poisoning also had swift internal consequences in the form of ideological blocks and an increasing inability to deal with even constructive criticism within their own networks. Activists were reduced to either unconditional yes-men or traitors to the good cause, as a result of which the minority movements never succeeded in developing a dialectic dynamic, but instead stagnated in doctrinal paralysis. The anticipated events never occurred.

This extremely diffuse anti-ideology, minoritarianism, simply was not capable of acting as a platform for a united Left. Neither feminists nor gay activists ever became a political power of global dimensions. Instead, women and homosexuals, like other supposedly oppressed groups, were quickly recruited in ever larger numbers to the cheap freak-shows of the mass-media, built upon pseudopolitics as a simpler form of entertainment. It turned out that everyone wanted to play the media game, but that no-one had any strategy other than going on about their rights and possibly irritating Power, and therefore did not notice when real power took home healthy profits and at the same time silenced all criticism by handing out neon-coloured megaphones to everyone. Radical chic became big business. The rainbow flag became one more fashion accessory among many others, and the angriest feminists got to write their own columns in the tabloid press.

Subversion became entertainment for the masses, exclusion became the in-thing. As a result, the subversive obviously lost its power to subvert, without having achieved any noticeable change or redistribution of power in society; exclusion became inclusion which then went out of favour. The eternalist activists saw all this, and were discouraged from nurturing minority identities, largely because the initial successes of the minority movements had turned out to be merely the prelude to the most humiliating defeat. Discursive censorship syndrome can only attract attention-seeking wreckers, never devoted non-zero-sum players with a highly developed capacity for networking. Instead, the virtual nomadic tribes constructed their collective identities with the help of sophisticated social technologies in accordance with the new principles for distribution of power and status which are coming into force as a result of the paradigm shift, technologies which the minority mass-movements of late-capitalism can neither equip themselves with nor compete against.

Something which must not be forgotten in this context is eternalistic ethics' stress on the matter of responsibility, which shows that the Nietzschean belief in the death of God is being taken very seriously. From this perspective, both the activism of the minority movements and postmodernism's relativism, with its playful element, appear to be fundamentally irresponsible. The latter is claimed, not least in its self-produced mythology, to be Nietzschean, bizarrely enough, despite the fact that its most clearly defined characteristic is a frightened reluctance to deal with nihilism. Postmodernism would dearly love to throw a party in the middle of the wake, anything to avoid thinking about what happens after God's funeral. Consequently, it ought to be regarded as a collective act of suppression, a falsified way of thinking which is sliding about in the remnants of the Christian and humanist inheritance of ideas. We are witnessing a humiliated retreat from the Nietzschean position, in which humankind is forced, however unwillingly, to play the role of its own moral authority, simply because there really is no-one else to whom it can turn.

A constantly recurring theme within postmodern reasoning about power and morals is how the strong automatically oppress the weak. This is almost a form of inverted Nietzscheanism, in which men by definition oppress women, heterosexual oppresses homosexual, white oppresses black, north oppresses south, and so on. The exercise of power as such is demonised and linked through vague insinuations to a threatening, global fascism. In the vanguard of this diffuse threat are the multinational corporations and 'unrestricted market forces'. This power relationship is supposed, on the basis of unspoken evidence, to be entirely arbitrary and possible to maintain merely through manipulated collaboration mixed with brutal repression. But the whole reasoning nevertheless becomes entirely meaningless as long as it does not presuppose a superior moral authority before which the strong party in this context can be held responsible. So postmodernism, beyond all of its verbal fireworks, is ultimately a last attempt to give artificial resuscitation to humanism. Naturally, this suits the typical academic nerd like a hand in a glove: it looks daring and new-fangled, at the same time as it is the same old thing behind the façade, in other words: a reactionary denial of life.

We have now ended up an extremely long way from the supposed master of the Left, Karl Marx: capitalism is no longer an historical phase linked to a certain group of material circumstances, but has been transformed into an evil conspiracy aimed at all the poor and insignificant of the world. Admittedly, it is easier to argue if you are able to construct your own opponent, but in the long-term it is hardly worthwhile. The global economy as it actually exists – the endlessly complicated system of regulation and occasionally competing, occasionally collaborating interests – is in practice reminiscent, ironically, of the very organic multiplicity which postmodernism's prophets claim to idealise. Compare this to the unregulated market which the libertarians idealise, but which has never existed anywhere, and we must conclude that it could never maintain the power structure necessary to produce the minimum level of predictability necessary to the market. The unregulated market is nothing more than a neo-liberal version of Rousseau's nature, in other words: an unworldly wet-dream.

The fact that poststructuralism would rather devote itself to tactical demonology than genuine political philosophy is apparent from its obsession with the term resistance, which is never specified or questioned. Exactly whom this resistance is to be practised against, and why, is never revealed. The term is transcendentalised, raised above the world of the senses and every form of criticism, which means that resistance is by definition always good, and never even needs to be discussed. As a result, there is always resistance as an emergency escape route into thinking's thickest banks of fog, useful to have available when all the other romantic reasonings get muddled up. When your argument starts to fail, you can always stage a piece of theatrical resistance and, as a result, join the ranks of the undeniably good. Without the protection of this transcendentalisation, resistance would soon be revealed as meaningless and ridiculous. For a French activist, for instance, it works like this: you vandalise an American hamburger chain and throw some populist phrases at the media, whereupon you are supposed to have embodied the most holy resistance. Twentieth-century immanence philosophy sadly does not get any more immanent than this.

However, the twentieth century was undoubtedly the century in which democracy and the principle of one man, one vote conquered the world. Totalitarianism and the dream of the commando state's supremacy collapsed in two stages: firstly, with the defeat of Nazism and fascism in the Second World War; secondly, with the more drawn-out collapse of the Soviet block, the Latin American military regimes and the postcolonial dictatorships in the following decades. Democracy has, in the course of its journey, been elevated to the status of transcendental ideal, which has made it practically impossible to illuminate the problems and anachronisms of democracy in any serious way, just as it has succeeded to the extent that there can be talk of the end of history. This is all made more difficult by the fact that the problem complex surrounding democracy has the same origins as its success: the development of mass-interactivity has undoubtedly helped democracy to achieve its status as a universal phenomenon, but will eventually also cause its downfall.

Another aspect of this taboo problem complex is the breakthrough of the democratic ideal in a simplified form in all possible and impossible contexts, not least in the academic world. The gaining of knowledge and the transfer of information has been able to be described as oppression to good effect, if it has not been carried out in accordance with the often arbitrary wishes of poor and disadvantaged groups. Unpleasant conclusions have been voted away by majority decision, and the correct decision achieved by the fact that only the poor and disadvantaged groups have been granted the vote, in accordance with discursive censorship syndrome. An innate aspect of democracy has been the supposition that it could never sanction any form of supremacy. Consequently the education sector in industrialised countries, rapidly expanding for reasons of employment politics, began to produce enormous quantities of self-pity, beyond the reach of all criticism because every objection was instantly condemned as fascist, patriarchal, capitalist or colonialist repression. Everything which was not deemed to form part of the oppressive sphere of power, on the other hand – Mao's China, communist Vietnam, Castro's Cuba, the Sandinistas' Nicaragua and various African one-party states – was embraced uncritically in the holy name of resistance.

The problems with this infantilisation of intellectual life soon became apparent. If only people who claim to have been disadvantaged by some form of injustice or oppression ever make their voice heard, then all genuine dialogue ceases. All the alleged subversion becomes a new orthodoxy in the same moment it is expressed. And the exclusion which has thereby moved into the institutions can only be a meaningless confirmation of an already established, collective self-perception. Not only does this mean sitting in chains in Plato's cave, but that the only exit has been blocked at the request of the person within. A child learns nothing by constantly being allowed to do what it wants, and hear what it already knows and thinks. All parents know this, but it seemed to be a fact that twentieth-century political philosophy – out of fear of blaspheming against transcendental Democracy – had never dared learn.

Postmodernism's criticism of structuralist anthropology – the cultural relativist argument that structuralism is worthless, because it expresses itself in general terms about things which it does not know because it is by definition on the outside – misses the target badly, because it completely ignores the most fundamental principles of collective information gathering. It can actually only be someone who 'does not know' something or other who has the ability to see what no-one else can see because of over-familiarity, which is what is really interesting in this context, particularly when we are talking about scientific methodology.

The development of so-called homosexual liberation during late-capitalism – and of its political ideology, gayism – was ultimately based neither upon any increasing oppression of homosexuals, nor upon any desire for a public battle for liberation. The explanations for this phenomenon instead lie deep within the sociotechnological laws of network dynamics, which stem from fundamental meme-Darwinian survival principles. Escalated interactivity is indissolubly linked to escalated multiplicity; there is, for instance, an empirically proven connection between a greater visible degree of sexual variety and economic growth in the metropolitan areas of Europe and North America during late-capitalism. Environments in which homosexuals are included are simply more creative and openly tolerant than environments where they are excluded, and this creativity is something which no ambitious network can afford to be without. In cosmopolitan metropolitan environments, homosexuals have assumed the role of catalysts, acting as tracker-dogs and forerunners, their initial exclusion has begun to be regarded as an advantage by a far-sighted elite, which has therefore granted them a role which is reminiscent of that of tribal shamans, for the simple reason that the elite perceived a need for them. This need has unleashed a sociological trend which favours the creativity and openness which includes homosexuals, and this trend is an unavoidable consequence of mass interactivity.

The problem, however, is that the homosexual subculture which formed during late-capitalism is being marginalised once more and is losing its value now that sexual liberation itself has been achieved. The reason is that the movement has succeeded to its own detriment; homophobia is now in short supply, and gayism's whole demonology is imploding as a result. The expression gay pride is losing its identity-producing gravity now that the external, unifying enemy has been dissolved in a politically correct embrace, and there is no longer anything to fight against and be proud for. The entire attitude of rebellion is losing its original meaning in the new cultural context, and is being reduced to one turn among many others in the changing roll-call of items in the world of media entertainment. Once the homosexual subculture's elite has realised that it is time to leave the gay ghetto behind in order to enter the netocratic networks, all that will be left of the once proud movement will be a feeble, shopping-fixated gay consumtariat, desperately hugging their rainbow flags and disco anthems.

In the eyes of the netocracy, sexual preference is not enough to build a social identity upon. There will still be a noticeable element of homo- and transsexual lifestyles in the future, but it will not cause any eyebrows to be raised, and this is the double-edged sword of increased tolerance. On the contrary, the netocracy will cherish a large array of lifestyles and perspectives, because multiplicity as such is advantageous in these contexts for the survival of the netocratic networks in terms of meme-Darwinian competition, and also because it would be unwise to offend presumptive talents because of an attitude or behaviour which no longer has any charge, either positive or negative.

In conjunction with the breakthrough of network society, heterosexuality has already sated its interest for, and absorbed what it sought from, homosexuality. In future, homosexuality will only be interesting insofar as it produces eternalists with a unique and sought-after talent, such as acting as shamans for the nomadic tribes of virtual culture. Otherwise, homosexual subculture – precisely because of its escalating predictability and conservatism – has nothing which the power-wielding circles of the netocracy might be remotely interested in. 'Gay' will become an increasingly ordinary, consumtariat, underclass phenomenon, rather like darts and coach tours to bargain outlets in the countryside.

The expanded and value-producing development of gayism, 'queer', on the other hand, will occupy a central function in the netocratic lifestyle aesthetic. Queer is a far more mobilistic concept than gay. Here, sexual inclination as such is of quite subordinate importance, and other qualities are prioritised, not least consciousness and application of the network dynamics that are so vital to the networks. The new mass interactivity brings with it entirely new conditions for the construction of social structures, and forces the establishment of a new, amoral value system, a socioanalytical ethic whose pattern is clearly apparent when we transfer Lacanian psychoanalysis's individual perspective to eternalistic socioanalysis's network perspective.

The two emotional poles in post-Lacanian socioanalysis are ecstasy and angst. From the deathwish perspective, birth represents the ultimate angst, but it is important to remember that this refers to the birth of the subject, and not childbirth. In other words, a crack appears in the original symbiosis between mother and child, after which nothing can ever be the same again. The child, of no volition of its own, has in a Heidegger-like way been cast out into a alien and incomprehensible existence, fundamentally alone. Death, according to the same point of view, is the ultimate ecstasy, the dissolution of loneliness and the return to union with the world. All of life's experiences of sadness and enjoyment, boredom and happiness are placed unconsciously in relation to the angst of birth and the ecstasy of death.

A conflict arises from the suppression of the deathwish by the individual and the collective in order to favour the desire for life –

this can be compared to the romanticisation of nature at the expense of culture – which means that thinking produces a parallel, prioritised value system with reversed roles. In this symbolic order, birth is therefore seen as the ultimate ecstasy, obviously in the most natural of surroundings, whereas death represents the ultimate angst, just as obviously surrounded by heavy cultural symbolism. Birth is linked to a collective, ritualised happiness and joy; death is linked to a collective, ritualised sorrow and sadness. Traditional, civilisational ethics preserve these presuppositions in their place. The individual cultures through history which have used the reverse valuation have been knocked out in a meme-Darwinian way; without the current power structure's idealisation of the desire for life, it is impossible to build any civilisation at all.

If we were to illustrate this graphically, we can imagine a point in the middle of a line which runs from ecstasy to angst. The part of the line between zero and ecstasy is called enjoyment, whereas the part of the line between zero and angst is called sadness. Enjoyment and sadness increase the further away from zero we move. This means, for instance, that truly sublime enjoyment is literally a near-death experience.

In a social context, increased enjoyment arises, which Lacan terms enjoyment-plus. This refers to the enjoyment of creating enjoyment for others, or experiencing their enjoyment. In a similar way a social sadness-plus arises – which must not be confused with hypocritical sympathy – which is the sadness or causing or perceiving sadness in others. Socioanalytical ethics' focus of non-zero-sum games means a desire to maximise the mutually stimulating interplay between enjoyment and enjoyment-plus with the aim of placing the event in question as close to ecstasy as possible, and then maintaining this position as long as possible (see illustration on p.xxx). Consequently, socioanalytical ethics condemns the reverse linkage which produces a minus-sum game, thought or behaviour in which enjoyment-plus and sadness-plus have changed places with one another, where enjoyment-plus is linked to sadness – either in the individual (masochism) or in others (sadism) – or where sadness-plus is linked to enjoyment; either in the individual (misery) or in others (resentment).

Socioanalytical ethics must not be confused with a purely additive utilitarianism. Enjoyment-plus and sadness-plus are actually empirically superior to enjoyment and sadness – to express it in

Lacanian terms: the greatest enjoyment is experiencing The Other's enjoyment, and vice versa – and the important thing is the mutually conditioned interaction. Shared enjoyment really is a enjoyment doubled, and successful networking can only be conducted in this way. The individualist is the great loser in non-zero-sum games. The functions of enjoyment-plus and sadness-plus create a pattern whose enormous complexity makes it impossible, not to mention absurd, to discuss intentions and actions in terms on benefit and maximal usefulness. Utilitarianism, the most extreme and naïve branch of rationalist thinking, therefore collapses under the weight of socioanalytical ethics. In other words: if utilitarianism was on the right lines, humankind would immerse itself at the earliest possible opportunity in a fog of morphine.

Socioanalytical ethics presents objective values and judgements, not in a rationalistic way, but transrationally. The logic is watertight and comprehensive, but only within the frame of eternalism, and in individual cases one must always retain a paradoxist awareness of the mass of unstable variables which are constantly being added to the equation for the simple reason that existence is mobilistic. This ethics is credible within the eternalistic sphere, but any other, more comprehensive credibility is, on the other hand, not even imaginable. It is concerned with well-supported hypotheses rather than with truths in the classical sense, but these hypotheses are subject to continuous testing and adjustment, which actually increases, rather than decreases, their credibility and makes the eternalistic analysis attentionally superior to every imaginable alternative.

The gravity of the virtual nomadic tribe, the notional substance which means that the tribe generates attention and attracts members in competition with other tribes, stems from the collective subject. This can profitably be analysed by using the same principles as the individual subject, which offers a chance to clarify the extent to which a specific collective is based upon constructive ideals in the form of a dynamic non-zero-sum game in an upward spiral – where sadness is linked to sadness-plus and enjoyment to enjoyment-plus – or, if it is a question of destructive ideals, in a downward spiral – where sadness is linked to enjoyment-plus and enjoyment to sadness-plus. Either constructiveness through feedback, or else resentment, followed by schadenfreude and self-loathing.

Schizoanalysis of the dividual's contradictory desires and urges is complemented by socioanalysis of the collective subject's contradictory trends and countertrends. In the test of power that arises when a trend is faced with a countertrend, the latter, thanks to the complexity of the game and the sluggishness of history, can very easily gain an advantage over the former, but only short-term. Long-term, the trend has history on its side, because it is favoured by the wind of change which never stops blowing, and favoured by the growing intensity in communications which is one of the constants in the equation. The fact that what was yesterday's trend often becomes tomorrow's countertrend, as a result of new circumstances threatening the conquered position of power, is another matter. A combination of the ethical reasoning of schizoanalysis and socioanalysis, where they overlap and thus either strengthen or question one another, has all the preconditions to dethrone the value-relativistic social constructivism which was dominant under late-capitalism.

One extreme but illuminating example of how the one relates to the other is, once again, the conflict between allegedly oppressive western values with universal ambitions, and the local traditions governing the genital mutilation of young girls in eastern Africa. When a postmodern values-relativist is faced with the tradition within the east African female collective which insists upon the mutilation of a young girl's genitals in order for her to be accepted by the group, he is forced, ironically enough by his own values, to refrain from any form of value judgement about what is going on. According to values-relativistic social constructionism, it is impossible to rank or even compare different discourses such as, for instance, western and east African views of sexuality, gender roles and the rights of individual women. It is a question of apples and pears, incomparable entities, where an apple in the form of an orthodox relativist – and as such the representative of the western patriarchy – does not have the right to express himself on the subject of the pear. The young girl is a pear and is subject to the jurisdiction of the pear. Admittedly, she may cry and scream, but eventually it will all be over. Admittedly, her chances of a satisfying and functional sex-life have been destroyed, but that of course is only the apple's view of the matter. Far better to close your eyes and think of something else.

From an eternalist perspective, this is an untenable position. Claiming that there are no universally valid values is itself an attempt to express a value with ambitions to universal validity. Saying that there is no link whatsoever between different social constructions means talking about precisely such an all-encompassing relationship between all existing social constructions. Following the moral imperative of values-relativistic social constructionism to refrain from intervention only means that one accepts the existence of a universal truth by referring to the universal absence of universal truths. This reasoning falls by its own application, it is reduced to an actual intervention against intervention which thereby condemns itself – a consequential cynical nihilist can never actually write a text, because the action reveals one value held by the author, that authorship is an activity that has a positive value – and is revealed as little more than an excuse for satisfying the very basest and most short-sighted of urges: the values-relativist's own intrusive desire to avoid conflict at all costs and to be constantly amenable to everyone.

Ironically, nothing in the current historical context could be as 'western' as advocating the avoidance of intervention, because current values-relativism does not stem from any logical calculation, but is merely a question of an attempt to suppress the values-relativist's own reluctance towards conflict and action, which, ironically enough, is both historically motivated and culturally limited. Postmodern values-relativism is revealed as little more than a specific generation's embittered indictment of the previous generation's modernistic utopianism, a romanticisation of the desire for victimhood and the desire to conquer the world, and is therefore ultimately just as bitter an indictment of the values-relativist himself because of his own paralysis. We are dealing with a guilt-complex which the values-relativist seeks to hide by turning his own cowardice into a moral virtue. Beneath the umbrella of morality, beyond the neat, well-meaning words, there is – to put it in Nietzschean terms – nothing but naked urges. Conflicts of interests must eventually be solved, they pay no heed to pacifistic wishful-thinking, and violence or the threat of violence is always at the centre of all conflicts of interests.

Eternalism claims, unlike value-relativism, that there is a universally applicable ethics of the sort that we have outlined above, a system of ethics which for instance makes it possible to adopt a clear stance against the mutilation of young girls' genitals. Because the east African female collective of this example is linking its enjoyment-plus to the young girl's sadness, both now and in the future, what schizoanalysis terms a destructive feedback-loop arises. Because the actions of the collective are here in obvious conflict with an increased spread of information and are only possible in culturally isolated environments where alien trends, in the form of impulses for change, are excluded, this behaviour is a reactionary countertrend in defence of a fatally weakened cultural identity. So the moral imperative of eternalism is: intervene!

In this way, socioanalytical ethics transgress all arbitrarily drawn boundaries between cultural and ethical discourses. This is an extremely important act of clearing the road towards a global political-judicial order, a world state. As a result, there is a cohesive foundation, a universal ideology upon which a possible constitution and model for the practical exercising of power can be sketched. Once an awareness of this possibility spreads, the forces that are acting for a transition will be strengthened to move from thought to action.

13.

The Ecstasy of the Event and the Fading Gaze of Nature

HUMANKIND'S FOREBEARS SAID goodbye to the apes sometime between six and ten million years ago. During at least the last two of these millions, our forebears wandered across the savannahs and steppes in search of food and protection from storms and predators. Over what is in this context a fantastically short space of time, the past 10,000 to 11,000 years, have we enjoyed the luxury of settled dwellings. And during this short space of time, the number of genetic changes has been negligibly small. So humankind is, from a genetic perspective, essentially formed by and for a life on the savannah – which explains, among other things, why we so easily get back-ache from sedentary work behind desks, for which we really are not constructed. In other words: humankind is a herdanimal programmed for life in tribes of between 40 and 50 adult individuals who can all contribute to supporting the group. To these are added investments for the future in the form of children, and sources of knowledge in the form of old people.

Another immediately striking characteristic of humankind and its forebears, the hominids, which is obvious but which was nonetheless energetically denied during the entire length of its conscious self-reflection, is its physical weakness compared to other competing species. This relatively fragile capacity for survival meant that humankind was driven out of the jungle, for which the other ape species were better suited, and had to live as banished refugees on the margins of an environment where it was, if possible, even more threatened in relation to its competitors: the savannah and the steppes. From there, there were two possible ways to go: the one which led via helpless passivity to extinction, because the species was simply unsuited to any of the ecological niches on offer, or the way which led to survival and expansion via the development of ingenious solutions. It would be wrong to say that humankind chose the latter; it was forced to develop, alone among all animal species in the history of nature, successful technologies, where the decisive metatechnology is consciousness itself.

Necessity really is the mother of invention. Yesterday's weakness became tomorrow's strength when humankind's forebears, last of all animals in the queue for the remnants of a predator's prey, learned to use a rock to crush the chewed bones and release the marrow. The salvation of the species was a relatively advanced capacity for problem-solving and the imitation of profitable behaviour. In other words, the species developed an intelligent interplay with its surroundings, and therefore gradually changed from the weakest and least-suited animal to the strongest, in terms of its adaptability.

Technology arrived hand in hand with ethics, because no action can be more ethically admirable than actively shaking up the prevailing worldview, forcing through a paradigm shift, and thereby creating new, unimagined possibilities for non-zero-sum games. The paradigm shift in question consisted partly of a cause: the introduction of new technologies, and partly of an effect: the concept of strength gained an entirely new meaning, whereupon the power-structure underwent a radical transformation. As a result of the new circumstances, the losers of the savannah became its winners: homo technologicus. Humankind's unique capacity for adapting has later made it possible for it to continue the process and adapt its environment after its own needs in an unparalleled manner.

If we try to imagine what it would be like to deny humankind its unique process of thought, in other words, if we were to force humankind to manage as a genuinely natural rather than a cultural being, then its long-term chances of survival would be considerably worse than those of the coelacanth and the quagga. What we are constantly trying to avoid is the fact that our only strength is our great weakness, and that we are forced to recreate the world in order to be able to make evolutionary progress and survive at all. As a result, we carry with us a fundamental sense of guilt, always present in the form of a collective, nagging and throbbing suppression. Humankind feels its guilt towards the nature it has transformed to its own ends, guilt about its technologies and its sophisticated way of thinking. This guilt can never be atoned for or repaid, as a result of which the whole business must be hidden in the shadows, in other words: the feelings of guilt must be suppressed by a machinery which drowns out the self-accusations. Finding excuses for this continued suppression of our fundamental guilt about culture has therefore been one of the central tasks for philosophers and theologians.

Among the most prominent ideologies in this conspiracy of suppression are the desert religions: Judaism, Christianity and Islam, whose shared basic agenda is the categorical condemnation of the search for knowledge, the burdening with guilt of homo technologicus. The first human being's eating of a fruit from the tree of knowledge marks the fall into sin, a crime of disobedience for which the punishment is expulsion from paradise. This paradise, humankind's natural existence – about which the founders of these religions admittedly knew nothing at all – is presented as happy and carefree, whereas the search for knowledge is presented as having brought humankind into ruin and caused all the suffering in creation. This acrobatic somersault has deeply tainted the whole history of ideas; in principle, the whole of western philosophy, with only a few exceptions, adheres to this conspiracy. The fact is that this machinery drowned out all serious criticism until the second half of the nineteenth century, when the launch of Darwin's theory of evolution and Nietzsche's break with totalistic rationalism radically altered our view of history, and therefore also our view of ourselves (see Netocracy).

It is as ironic as it is logical that the monotheistic religions which deviated from the totalistic line – for instance Zoroastrianism and Mithraism – and other mobilistic philosophers, have been falsified and censured, warped or even simply erased from the record throughout history. With the arrival of informationalism, these mechanisms are now being discarded, and it is becoming as impossible to continue to nurture the myth of the totalistic utopia as it is to govern the flow of information in general. Only a utopia which harmonises with the dialectic between eternalism and mobilism – a vision which is inclusive rather than exclusive, a non-zero-sum game rather than a zero-sum game – can be credible in the age of mass-interactivity. This utopia is the Global Empire.

Satanism is particularly interesting in this context. The Bible gives us, as is well known, no information about this dark anti-theology, which is explained by the fact that no Satanism was required before there was Christian missionary activity among the masses, because only then was an impressive demonology needed for the production of identity. This explains all the theology which has been constructed afterwards from occasional references in the gospels to the garbage tip, Gehenna, outside Jerusalem. Because theology suddenly needed a hell, Jesus must have spoken about it somewhere. So Gehenna must be a reference to this hell. This less than graceful manoeuvre can be compared with how reincarnation was granted to the Buddha in retrospect – as a loan from the Hinduism it was competing with – when it became clear that the Asiatic masses were not prepared to accept Nirvana, extinguishing, as the ultimate goal of life. The meme-Darwinian struggle is at least as brutal within the area of religion as anywhere else. Religious memes are highly influenced by circumstances.

When Roman polytheism could no longer retain its status as the state-religion in the fourth century, two main competitors arose to fight for the vacant position: Christianity and Mithraism. This rivalry, combined with diametrically opposed attitudes to the eating of the fruit of knowledge, made Mithraism the perfect basis for a Christian demonology. Here we find the template for the ideology's secret Satanist sects, carrying out ritual, blood-drenched sacrifices in small temples, housed in dark and hidden caves. Here, in the Christian fear of Mithraism, are the origins of the whole of western hysteria about secret societies and closed networks, and also about secret passageways in architecture. There is a line which runs from the illuminated space of Christian cathedrals, via Hausmann's boulevards and the transrational idea of the panopticon, planned to be applied to all sorts of social institutions, to the vulgar functionalism and avenue architecture of Nazism and Stalinism, and the whole of political-aesthetic social choreography. This line stems from the terror of revolutionary sects conspiring in hidden corners. Every nook and cranny in society must be illuminated and under observation.

The persecution of Mithraism was sanctioned by Emperor Julian in the year 361, and was carried out very thoroughly. Its practitioners were executed, its temples and records destroyed. After that, Christianity could calmly plunder Mithraism of ideas, and manipulate and incorporate them into its rapidly growing demonology project. Christianity thereby killed two birds with one stone: firstly, it erased its main rival for power, and, secondly, it obtained high-octane fuel for its Satanist demonology, which noticeably strengthened its own production of identity. All of this explains why we today know so little about the true ideological content of Mithraism, in spite of its having been widespread throughout the Roman Empire. Almost everything of value was destroyed by zealous Christians.

The ideological exploitation of humankind's suppressed feelings of guilt towards nature did not stop with the gradual secularisation of society during capitalism. Totalism was reborn in the form of Enlightenment philosophy, and gained an articulate spokesman in Jean-Jacques Rousseau, the great pioneer of the Modern Project. The Noble Savage thereby replaced God as the ideal figure. None of Rousseau's many enthusiastic disciples was troubled by the fact that the Noble Savage was pure nonsense, an absurdity. Anything like a noble savage is simply impossible to imagine, the savage cannot be noble because nobility presupposes a culture, and a transformation of nature which would destroy the savage itself. Only after the supposed Fall and the entry of the cultivated human being into the race is it at all possible to talk about nobility. In the wilderness of nature one is either full or hungry, frozen or sweaty, but never noble.

So it was not thanks to an incontestable argument that Rousseau won his supporters, but rather because of his ideas' close relationship with the much missed but sadly no longer credible Christianity. Rousseau made it possible to combat both the creed of the Church as well as its position of power, yet avoid confrontation with suppressed collective feelings of guilt. What is the idea of the Noble Savage other than a secular and supposedly rational variant of the first human beings before their expulsion from paradise? The nobility of the Noble Savage rests precisely upon his refusal to be tempted by knowledge, and to choose the wild instead. And what is Rousseau's utopia other than a secular and supposedly rational variant of paradise lost, and the hope of one day regaining it? Rousseau exerted a level of influence over the political production of identity during the capitalist era that is hard to exaggerate –within both socialism and liberalism – and is still highly present in those political parties which, with increasingly little success, conduct democratic parliamentarism during the final teetering seconds of the capitalist era.

Marxism and liberalism are two fingers on the same Rousseauian hand. The fact that both these ideologies – which are routinely presented, and present themselves, as one another's opposites – actually share several important roots confirms yet again that the collective production of ideology within the capitalist paradigm is subordinate to a single overarching supraideology: étatism. The close connections between the ideologies appears very clearly if we compare alienation theory, one of Marxism's corner-stones, with natural law, liberalism's axiomatic starting point. According to alienation theory, society bestows upon human beings a fundamental sense of alienation towards their work and their true interests. The revolution brings a secular revelation: human beings are purged – which is comparable to the forgiveness of sin – and are restored to a pure and original natural state, a paradise on earth where all social conflicts are solved, and eternal harmony reigns. All we need to do is eliminate the sudden revolution from the picture, and replace it with an imagined revisionist development, and we see at once the implicit utopia that liberalism believes it can achieve through its obstinate advocacy of natural law.

If religion is the opium of the people, Rousseau and Marx each offers his own variant of endless methadone treatment. Intoxicated social-liberals and socialists share the same wet dream of a mythical natural state, which society admittedly has ruined, but which can be reinstated through applied political work. Anyone who wants to retain this naïve faith is however forced to intoxicate himself heavily and at the same time shut his eyes to what we actually know about nature and humankind's dependence upon culture. Natural law falls immediately on the fact that it has everything to do with culture and nothing to do with nature. And if there is anything that we really need to be liberated from, it is the very idea that we are alienated at all.

It is a fact that it has long been obvious, even for leftwing sympathisers, that the communist utopia is built upon a contradiction, which is why various attempts to save Marxism by removing Rousseauian mythology from it have been made under the banner of postmodernism. But without a communist utopia as a reference point, alienation theory loses all significance, and, without alienation theory, Marxist social analysis loses its whole starting point. What is left is merely an atrophied ruin, an obsolete bolt-hole for irrational and masochistic nostalgia-freaks who lack the capacity for self-reflection.

The most ingrained, and therefore the most difficult to discern and most treacherous remnant of Rousseauian mythology within capitalist identity-production, is, however, liberalism's idea of a society and an economy in a predetermined natural state of balance and harmony, in other words: a recreation of good nature through sound judgement, an idea of a pragmatic and pluralistic culture as a sort of protective shell around a piece of Sunday school-tinted nature. But this too is a dream, anchored only in pious wishes, and actually concerns another fatal mixture of eternalism and mobilism.

No normal state, whether in nature or culture, has ever been balanced and harmonious. And eternalisation can never be true in the mobilistic sense, only more or less functional, and only for a limited period. Admittedly, culture can be said to tame nature in several concrete senses, but this does not mean that immanence really subordinates itself to our eternalised worldview. The one must not be confused with the other. On the contrary, as cultural complexity tightens, more uncertain variables arise, rather than fewer, as a result of which the instability in the relationship between world and worldview actually increases. An increasingly fast pace of change will be the only normal state we know. And all of this actually has nothing whatsoever to do with nature.

This dreamy liberal utopia is expressed within the national economic discourse, where advanced models are constantly being constructed, excellent in every way, apart from the fact that they constantly fail to reflect and predict economic reality. They can therefore be compared to the increasingly complicated Ptolemaic system, where new circular motions were constantly being imposed upon the old ones so that observation and theory could correspond to at least some extent. In the same way that the problem of Ptolemaic astronomy was that it was developed from something entirely irrelevant in the context, the perfect circle, so national economics is ultimately based upon geometry's perfect figures, a dream-world bound by laws where balance and order are presumed to reign. As well as this, national economists act as though their activity existed within a vacuum, without any connection to economic reality. A crumb of eternalistic insight would clarify that every presented model and theory which has the slightest impact because of that, by return, is discounted by the economic players, as a result of which the realities that the model once purported to reflect have already changed, precisely because of the disseminated knowledge of the model in question.

Like all totalistic systems, national economics falls eventually on its innate naïvety. Its supposed task to explain and prognosticate economic development is compromised by its customers' urgent need for apparently rational explanations which can be used to hide the players' actual, irrational behaviour. Thus discourse remains stuck to the values of an obsolete paradigm. From an eternalistic perspective, national economics would win credibility if it was practised as a sort of constantly changing, transrational socioanalysis, with its focus on flows and the system failures which might hinder these flows. But so long as national economics rests upon impotent rationalism – which includes liberalism's impossible hope of a balanced, natural order, deep within the heart of human nature – and is managed by the defenders of this ideology, then it will only continue to produce old truths for a context which is on its way out.

Myths are always cultural and eternalistic, whereas the world is always natural and mobilistic. Thus culture cannot change the very nature of nature, it would be unnatural even if it were possible, which it is not. Because of its programmatic lack of clarity on this point, liberalism is losing all ideological credibility within the frame of informationalism. In this new light it is obvious that the ideology no longer stands up. Liberalism's discourse seeks obstinately for an answer to its question – how can we reach a natural balance? – without realising that the question itself is the answer which is constantly seeking a question. The longed for balance can only be described, but can never exist within eternalisation, it can only exist on the metalevel, in the paradox between eternalism and mobilism.

This is the blind spot in the liberal supra-ideology, its shameful secret, carefully camouflaged but no less apparent for all that: it believes it can unite thought and reality into an ultimate, synthetic truth, to which thought itself forms the final step on the ladder. As a result, the dialectic process would be over, and the cultural illusion of a stable nature would be a fact. Because of this, humankind would also, conveniently enough, be released from its gnawing guilty conscience. Its cultural manipulation of nature would be seen in retrospect to have had a noble purpose: to help nature to become more natural. But the cultural illusion of a stable nature is based upon culture's fundamentally illusory self-perception. Even culture is evolution, replicators and natural selection, never in balance, always changing. Culture is, in other words, a new generation of nature: Nature 2.0.

Culture's illusory self-perception is a form of megalomania. Like a politician at election time it presents grand promises which could never be fulfilled even theoretically. The world and worldview can, by definition, never be united – eternalist philosophy mercilessly reveals this wishful thinking – and the gnawing feelings of guilt about nature can only be dealt with using grim clarity of vision, and not sentimental self-deception. Exposing this tangle of lies might admittedly cause some initial pain, but would at the same time mean a possible liberation in the form of affirmative nihilism.

The collective suppression of feelings of guilt has, particularly since victimhood has become, in the short-term, a successful media strategy, resulted in perfect orgies of sympathy. Suffering animals of all sorts arouse floods of human sympathy, whereas starving human beings in distant parts of the world end up somewhere between the stock-market figures and the weather at the end of news reports. We suffer the most, naturally, where species are threatened with extinction, and forget that more that 99% of all animal species which have ever lived are totally extinct, without humankind having helped them on their way. As a result, we are acting as parasites on the suffering of others, putting on a theatrical performance of suffering, and producing a hollow moralism which lacks any long-term credibility. This results in an ideological vacuum which can only be filled by an ideology anchored in new conditions, and which only expands further if the discourse receives further suffering and moralism.

The entirety of writing about history up to now – with its basis in the three desert religions and totalistic philosophy, crowned by liberalism and Marxism – is permeated down to its very core by a death-wish and by self-loathing. There is talk of the Fall and alienation, of exploitation and crimes against the goodness of nature, but in actual fact humankind is tormented by something entirely different: shame at the fact that culture is actually necessary to compensate for its own almost obscene weakness, a result of which is that its boundless progress in the evolutionary arena does not feel deserved. When will this be revealed? Without technology humankind would die on the spot, and that realisation is a very heavy burden. Humankind is shamed by being a machine in an environment which consists of other machines, is shamed by necessarily being enclosed within its civilisation like a helplessly incapable infant in an incubator, but without hope of ever moving to the other side of the glass.

Moralistic demands for guilt and improvement are all fabricated. There is no external force demanding that humankind, in atonement for some imagined crime, must be healthy, sober and athletic (in other words: 'natural'), and the internal force, the brutal moral police, can quite easily be dragged into the light and lose all authority. Humankind can therefore give itself permission to be weak – and even to see this weakness for what it really is: the mother of all situations of necessity, and therefore also of all invention. Homo technologicus is meeting his exiled twin, homo pathologicus, neither sober nor healthy, and together they may not make a particularly beautiful sight, but this is the only human being that will remain when all the storybooks have been shut and the informationalist paradigm is at the door. After humanism, which was systematicised self-loathing disguised as a civilisational project, it will be possible for humankind to see itself for what it actually is, and, by a fundamental effort of will, learn to love what it sees.

An entirely new civilisational project becomes apparent as soon as humankind is liberated from the critical gaze of nature. Everything depends on this: the realisation that nature is not merely blind and entirely without morals, but in existential and eternalistic terms is actually dead. In other words: nature, or rather Nature, is a concept which has been drained of all its old ideological content and no longer fills any ideological function. So it was Nietzsche who declared God to be dead, and Foucault who declared Man dead, and now it is eternalism which is declaring Nature to be dead. And, as a result, the world will be a slightly better place to live in, better in the sense of more open and more creative, bathing in memetic multiplicity. The intellectual climate is getting milder, ideas are being turned around at hitherto unimaginable rates. As a result, of course, the degree of memetic elimination is increasing, but because the range is becoming ever larger there is every reason to hope for a qualitative improvement through the development of ever smarter sorting mechanisms. Humankind itself is therefore becoming neither more noble nor wiser, but is merely lucky enough to be able to interact more intelligently with its surroundings after the death of Nature.

Weak human beings lived an extremely exposed life in nature, and therefore constructed, with the help of their increased cunning, a nature of their own, culture, where their talents could be better used. The big city is the urban jungle, the suburb the suburban savannah, and the countryside has been cultivated into a combination of grocery factory and recreational park. On the Net new hunting grounds are opening up, endless and unprotected, and in this environment the virtual nomadic tribes are forming, offering their members identity and solidarity, and competing among themselves for the attention which is fuelling the fight for survival and expansion. This is where electronic tribalism is being nurtured. The technology is sophisticated, the mechanisms extremely primitive.

The virtual nomadic tribes differ from their predecessors — for instance, late capitalism's countless urban tribes or the alternative family units of queer activism — by developing a network dynamic from communication that is interactive on all levels. And in a world where there may well be access to both the Internet and mobile telephones without there being access to running water, virtual tribes can just as easily develop in inaccessible Afghan mountain passes as in the urban jungle of Manhattan, just as they can ignore geographic boundaries and arise in many places at the same time.

The entire identity production of the capitalist era encouraged and addressed the individual as the ultimate instance of responsibility. Everyone was the architect of their own happiness, responsible for finding the best possible return on their own talents. This in turn favoured a mentality characterised by zero-sum games and the hierarchical structure; career success meant advancing past one's competitors in the pyramid, which meant that superficial acquaintance largely replaced long-term friendship as the most important social relationship. Contact with one's surroundings was characterised by short-term profit. This pattern is changing as a result of informationalism's and the interactive media's entry into the arena. This does not mean that we can look forward to a return to old, pre-capitalist structures; the paradigm shift will instead result in a new type of connection between people and networks. The virtual nomadic tribes are unlike anything we have ever seen before; they have their own network dynamic and their own specific way of relating to their surroundings. The frames are decided by, on the one hand, the speed and the capriciousness of all flows of information, and, on the other, long-term planning, solidarity and non-zero-sum game-playing.

Eternalist analysis provides an overview of the pertaining structures: networks which consist of dividuals, single members who have discarded their individualism in exchange for dividual participation in the collective identity produced by the network. The dividual's function in the network can be compared to that of the cell in a multicellular organism, in other words: it is specialised. Every dividual contributes its own specific repertoire of talents, frustrations, expectations, contacts and values. The network's productivity is not the sum of the contributing talents, as the dominant management theories of late capitalism claim, but must instead be worked out using a considerably more complex calculation of how well the contributing talents interact with one another. Productivity is therefore a question of resonance. Maximal productivity occurs when values, frustrations and expectations are all in tune, whereas contacts and talents are amplifying.

In general terms, productivity in the network is maximised when the associated dividuals share frustration at competing networks' shortcomings, at the same time as sharing a conviction that they can achieve something much more valuable in their new constellation. As well as this, the dominant value must be that the primary goal for their activity is to create new values, rather than joining up with already established external values. Talents and contacts must be subordinate to this collective ambition, and most important of all is that all activity is ultimately aimed at building and strengthening the collective identity. The group's well-being must under all circumstances be placed first, and maximal results can only be achieved when every dividual is convinced of the fact that the interests of the single member and the group coincide in every respect, in other words: that enjoyment is directly linked to enjoyment-plus.

Productivity explodes and enters a self-perpetuating phase at two specific critical points. The first threshold arises when the complementary characteristics of the dividuals for the first time achieve a resonance strong enough to be registered by the collective unconscious. The members of the network recognise that a collective activity is underway and producing results, without this production necessarily being identifiable and capable of being analysed. They are encouraged to continue as before, but faster, more intensively. The second threshold arises after the first has been eternalised, and thereby left the collective unconscious – where it has acquired gravitation, certainly, but no real identity – and reaches the collective consciousness. As a result, the resonance has begun to be turned into identity; a collective subject takes shape and its uniqueness becomes more and more apparent. The dividuals become conscious of the mechanisms of production, have the chance to fine-tune their own input, and continue the activity secure in the knowledge that the network is already productive. The faster and more powerfully a network passes these two thresholds, the higher its productivity will be, and the stronger its gravitation in relation to competing networks.

The introductory phase, stretching from the creation of the network to the first critical point, is what we call the attentional phase, when the network is dominated by initiative. The radiance and credibility of the initiative-taker, together with the attraction of the declaration of intent, determine which potential key members join up, and how strongly the newly recruited members become engaged. In this phase, there is large-scale elimination; it could be compared to all the spontaneous abortions at the start of a pregnancy. Only a very few networks survive their initial trials. Most collapse under the pressure of the dividuals' disappointment once their expectations have not been realised; alternatively they stagnate and are forced to reduce their ambitions, which results in a sort of open playground which any member of the consumtariat can join should they wish to.

This necessary incubation period shows the degree to which a society characterised by the building of networks differs from a society characterised by individual projects; it shows that the overriding social logic is becoming attentionalist rather than entrepreneurial in a capitalist sense, simply because the preconditions are fundamentally different and success is measured in other ways, which in turn can be traced back to the explosion of interactivity. The attentional phase, as its name suggests, is about creating the greatest possible amount of attention in an explosive way, in other words: awareness multiplied by credibility. Failure implies a more or less drawn-out death by drowning in plurarchist society's ocean of superfluous information.

Once a network has successfully passed the first threshold, it enters the mobilistic phase. What happens in this second phase is characteristic of the often idealised and, in retrospect, often sentimentalised phenomena known as subcultures, or the underground. A resonance spreads in the collective unconscious, but it cannot be localised or specified more closely. Some people believe that they know something is happening within a network, the mystique encourages the creation of myths. Expectations of future results escalate, credibility is established on credit, and the general acceleration that can be seen around the network itself exerts a powerful increasing effect on its gravity. The attraction of this diffuse transitional stage, similar to a turbulent adolescence, is clear. Consequently it can arouse feelings resembling love in a lot of people, members and observers alike. Often it becomes the subject of different forms of media romanticisation. But at some point the party has to end.

A transitional stage is by definition transitional, and it presupposes at least a vague awareness that sooner or later there will inevitably come a point when it is time to step up to the next stage. This happens when the first bifurcation is eternalised. The dividuals can differentiate between cause and effect, and become conscious of their own roles in the history of the network. The original mystery is transformed into conceptual insight. The network moves to the eternalistic phase, infatuation is replaced by the dividuals taking responsibility, distanced passivity is replaced by intense activity, and there is an explosion of productivity. Resonance breaks through on all levels, encompasses every dividual, and all energies collaborate. This state of maximal productivity is known as an Event, and in this period, when the optimally functioning network is working under optimal circumstances, the collective ambition is to keep this Event alive as long as possible. It is a question of maximising what is known within socioanalysis as the ecstasy of the Event (intensity multiplied by duration, see illustration on page xxx).

An interesting observation in this context is that both Zoroastrianism and Mithraism place central importance on the celebration of the authentic Event. Zoroastrianism celebrates the spring and autumn equinoxes and the summer and winter solstices as the highpoints of the year, and thereby avoids ranking the celebrations of one year against those of another year. Within Mithraism, the actual ritual of sacrifice, the slaughter of a bull, is even prioritised over the consciously mythological slaughter which Mithras is supposed to have carried out. In both cases we are dealing with Events as simulacra, and not as copies of an original Event. The Event belongs to believers, and there are no higher beings than the believers themselves.

This is in sharp contrast to the social highpoints of the desert religions, which are never allowed to be authentic Events, but are only quasi-Events: it is not the Event itself, but the memory of the Event which is celebrated: Christmas, Easter, Whitsun, the exodus from Egypt, the migration from Medina to Mecca, it is always about preventing believers from experiencing the Event itself. Only the memory of the Event remains. The myth is never realised, is never tested against reality, but continues to be unreachable, which means that the myth, like the platonic idea, is the original which can never be repeated but only approached through the production of inferior copies. Life is consequently denied, and postponed until the future. All that remains is the self-contradictory belief in eternal life, the hub of the desert religions, the death-wish. What is eternal life other than a hatred of life itself, perpetuated in a single, eternally drawn-out moment of death?

The decisive question for every dividual, the individual player in informationalist society, is what he expects from the network to which he is attracted. During feudalism people hoped for a reward in the form of eternal life. The single player submitted to the offers and rules of power, and believed himself to have fairly good reasons to hope for this reward after an arduous life of subordination. He knew no better.

With the transition to capitalism, the idea of eternal life lost its credibility as a metaphysical foundation – the nineteenth century's Gothic vampire literature put paid to that – and the reward which was instead promised to the dutiful and diligent individual was Progress. The worker could console himself with the thought that his children's future would be brighter thanks to his own hard work, the middle-classes could look forward to their children and grandchildren enjoying ever-growing capital as the reward for their own wise investments. The reward was still out of reach for the individual, which meant that those in power could promise so much more, secure in the knowledge that pay-day would never arrive. The rhetoric of our age's all-promising but never-fulfilling parliamentary politicians is a typical remnant of the dying paradigm. Why else would there be this fetishisation of an almost transcendental Growth?

The idea of progress presupposes a faith in predictability and economic models, and also an idealisation of the growth of capital. Everyone who has followed our reasoning thus far will soon realise that this idea is dead in the water with the onset of informationalism. For a start, progress is extremely insecure, and it is also no longer relevant, because capital as such has undergone a serious devaluation. The reward for completed exertions must be brought forward in order to be credible to the players of informationalism. The dividual would certainly prefer it to be paid out during his own lifetime.

The transcendental reward on offer to informationalism's dividual is therefore the Event. Neither eternal life nor progress is sufficient, and instead there is the offer of the slightly magical state which pertains at the precise point in time and space where It is happening, an escalation of the feeling of being alive, a sort of cerebral ecstasy, maximal enjoyment-plus. But even if the reward is within reach, there is necessarily always an essential remnant which is eternally out of reach, running like sand through the greedy dividual's fingers. As in Dante's paradise, the light will eventually become too strong for anyone to get an idea of exactly what is happening when It is happening. The same principle applies to the attraction of the Event as to sexual attraction: exactly where the attraction lies must remain a secret if the attraction is to remain. After every Event there must be a feeling of not being satisfied, a desire to achieve this reward time after time in order to drain the cup completely. This emptiness must, so to speak, be continually refilled if the magic is to continue working.

Eventology – the eternalist theory of the Event – is always applicable, whether you study the netocratic dividual within schizoanalysis, the networks' functions within network dynamics, or the virtual tribes' production of social identity within socioanalysis. What is the dividual looking for? What suppositions do dividuals project upon the global empire? Regardless of perspective and the nature of the question, we return constantly to the idealisation of an ungraspable, sacred intensity in space-time: the Event!

Because the metaphysical basis for eternalist philosophy is the need for a metaphysical basis itself, the very need for an Event is the only metaphysical aspect that the Event needs. We cannot get any deeper than this. But it is, of course, interesting to try to see what characterises the Events which the developing netocracy wants. Informationalism naturally has a sharp and critical eye for late capitalism's blind spots, and sees through the previous era's supposed uncovering of history and culture. Because of this, the Events of early informationalism are a sort of dialectic reaction to late capitalism's myth-creation. In retrospect it is, for example, easy to see that the phenomena which late capitalism regarded as liberating breakthroughs in the form of collective achievements, were in actual fact the result of the cards played out by history. This might be individualism, the one-person household, migration to the big cities, women's struggle for equality, or sexual liberation. The result is widespread scepticism about the real liberating content of capitalism's social revolutions. Young women are questioning feminism, young people are criticising the sexual revolution and experimenting with celibacy. So revolutions are conducted against revolutions, old theses are met with new antitheses, which in turn results in new syntheses, new social hybrids, new ways of seeing.

It is this scepticism towards the recent past which explains why the queer movement and chemical liberation are the first global mass movements in informationalist society. In both cases there are good opportunities to present strongly identity-producing resistance to governing norms – they are both fighting existing legislation in a long list of countries – but also a promise of collective ecstasy, which, according to eventology, is a necessary component in the imagined core of the virtual nomadic tribe. It is clear that what the bourgeoisie saw as epoch-making social advances are, in the eyes of the netocracy, not only insufficient steps forward, but, in a stagnating phase, also constitute obstacles on the path to continued expansion of the range of potential lifestyles.

A long series of truths which enjoyed axiomatic status within late capitalism's bourgeoisie merely look bizarre in the eyes of the netocracy. One of the most significant of these is the economism which eventually became so entrenched that it was confused with capitalist social order itself. Economism's position was seriously confirmed in 1992 when the Nobel prize for economics was awarded to Gary Becker, an American national economist who proposed the theory that every human activity and relationship can be explained, compared and evaluated in economic terms. According to this hyperrational viewpoint, something – anything at all – either has an economic value, or it has no value at all. When this viewpoint becomes generally accepted, society sees itself purely as an economy, and forces all imaginable activity into a system of paid services, which can be taxed, and also contribute to the gross national product, the single measure of welfare and quality of life.

It is not surprising that several short-sighted futurologists during the final period of capitalism regarded the broad breakthrough of economism as confirmation that the future would be governed by hypercapitalism. Like Francis Fukuyama, they confuse a series of given historical preconditions with eternity, and do not understand that everything changes when these given preconditions are no longer present, which is what happens when one dominant media technology drives out another. The fact is that the breakthrough of informationalism means that economism's pretensions to dictating the entire social process appear as simply ludicrous. The economy is merely the economy, and very far from being the yardstick by which everything can be measured.

With the development of the interactive media, the amount of available information is multiplying many times over, as a result of which power is shifting from production to sorting. This in turn means a shift from economic valuation, where prices determine a transaction, to attentional valuation, where awareness and credibility are what matters, while money is at best of secondary importance. The most important sorting of information occurs within the most important networks, and a network implodes in attentional terms the moment it makes itself accessible in an open market. Every form of transaction is becoming more and more coloured by attentional aspects – the one-way communication which characterises the exchange of a product for money must be made interactive if it is to survive in meme-Darwinian terms, which means that what cannot be bought with money – in other words, belonging to a network and the social identity this conveys – is becoming increasingly important for the single person's power and status. In a network society, therefore, people no longer value themselves or each other in economic terms, at least not within the dominant and normative netocracy. The new measure is, instead, sociometric.

Like economism, sociometry is based upon a system of universal equivalents. But the differences are dramatic, and anyone who thought that economism was complicated will find sociometry ten times worse, because different characteristics, different actions and different assets are compared with both each other and a vast and shifting set of co-ordinates. In an economistic system, every variable is traded at a certain price within a certain market, where the highest price determines a sale, and the lowest determines a purchase. Asset x is worth y, or, in other words, as much as a buyer is willing or forced to pay. But in an attentional system this model is unusable, because entirely different questions need to be answered. The value of x (which might be a characteristic, an action, a product or a service) is largely determined according to who is involved in the transaction, and this person's attentional value is in turn determined through a complicated calculation where a long series of interacting entry-values are constantly changing. A transaction which was previously one-dimensional and unambiguous is now played out many different levels at the same time. You cannot deal with just anyone, because this could harm your attentional value, and you cannot buy the right to deal with whoever you want to, but must earn this right by making yourself valuable. Sociometry has the task of tracking and documenting these multi-dimensional movements. It is not a rationalist science, but a transrationalist one; a happy science, to express it in Nietz-schean terms.

Eventology and sociometry are both necessary tools for anyone interested in the social complexity which is exploding in all directions at once within informational society, now that it has freed itself from the fading gaze of nature. They demonstrate how, and explain why, power and status in the intensifying storm of information have to be based upon overview and sorting. And they demonstrate how, and explain why, the accelerating speed of information transfer means that the desired talents have more to do with intuition and receptivity than with traditional leadership qualities. The netocratic leadership also possesses charisma, but charisma means something entirely new under these new circumstances, the quantitative perspective is replaced by a qualitative one. If during capitalism it had been a question of enchanting the masses, the charismatic netocrat uses all his energy to interact with a small number of carefully chosen dividuals. Leadership is constantly open to trial, power is always up for grabs. And it is no longer the single individual but the network which possesses charisma.

The fact that God is dead means that no values or rights can be divinely sanctioned; the fact that Nature is dead means that no values or rights can be guaranteed or given by nature, which means that all values and rights are exposed to constant testing. On the one hand, the cohesiveness of the paradigm is entirely dependent upon highly effective identity-production. On the other hand, the production of identity is hampered by the interactivity which is the very precondition for the paradigm. Transparency facilitates the examination of power, which places extremely high demands on the netocrats in power. Interactivity means a massive and constant exchange of information between people and networks, to an unprecedented extent. It is no longer even theoretically possible for anyone in power, or even an entire establishment, to control the formation of opinion with the help of a few loyal supporters, or to use manipulation to create a consensus (which is yet another reason why the old hegemony theory no longer works).

One interesting portent of the new rules of the interactive media-landscape is the way the Monica Lewinsky scandal developed and soon took on a life of its own, despite the established mass-media's stubborn resistance. It was sufficient for the story to be leaked to a gossip website of ill-repute, and after that it was impossible to either control or stop it. This mass-interactivity means that values and valuations will be constantly questioned from all sides. Informationalist netiquette can therefore never be based upon, or associate itself with, any arbitrary moralising or even the slightest hint of bias towards any vested interest, because both transmitter and purpose will immediately be visible to all players within the network.

Consequently, the paradigm shift means that there will be entirely new preconditions for the production of ideology, and these new preconditions in turn mean that moralism is losing ground to ethics. Enjoyment-plus reigns. In theory this means that the rules, both written and unwritten, which benefit the non-zero-sum games which are vital to the collective can count on an advantage over the ideology and the system of rules which was left behind by the abandoned paradigm and its docile authorities. In practice everything is becoming inexpressibly complicated. The choice is between understanding at least part of what is happening, and above all the general changes, by applying a transrationalist perspective, or misunderstanding everything by insisting on a rationalist point of view.

The netocracy therefore has no chance of exercising power over people and networks through the production of ideology. Its power is no longer based upon a manipulated consensus, but on its having a headstart in the gathering and compilation of information. The netocracy possesses the talents and has mastery of the techniques which allow it to remain a few steps ahead, and to understand what no-one else has understood up to that point, which gives it an invaluable advantage. Essentially, we are talking about the same creature which once realised that it could benefit from the fact that it was actually possible to use a rock to get at the bone-marrow within the remnants of a predator's prey, despite the fact that no-one had had the sense to think of this before.

Unlike capitalism's individual, informationalism's dividual does not need to nurture a self-aggrandising mythology: he realises that he is in no sense more intelligent or morally superior to his forebears. Instead, he realises that he has merely had the advantage of benefiting from thousands of years of culture, which has given him the chance to establish more intelligent relations with the world around him. Because he has been forced to do so. Which he has stopped feeling ashamed of. Tomorrow's human beings will love this civilisational obligation, precisely because it is this nurturing of culture as a survival strategy which has made them who they are.

What should human beings otherwise do with the life that, to put it in Heidegger's terms, they have been so inexplicably cast out into, and almost been handed by an otherwise apparently completely indifferent world? What can tomorrow's human being otherwise be, but a creature who, through an active decision of will, has decided that he loves himself, and who uses this love of his own dividuality as a cosmic foundation, and, as a reward, has discovered that it works perfectly well? The ecstasy of the Event can never be a reward for individual achievement, but must be earned collectively, which means that collaboration is becoming ever more important, at the expense of competition. Or, to put it another way: collaboration and competition are coming closer and closer together. But this does not make the eventists better or even any different to their forebears, because the gaze of nature which was supposed to judge people on moral terms has faded. This is the starting point for affirmative nihilism, which is where we stand now. So what do we do next?

14.

NAZISM AS A SOCIOTECHNOLOGICAL PHENOMENON

RACISM IS A TRUE CROSSOVER phenomenon, both in natural and cultural terms. In nature, strictly guarded boundaries against anything alien are fundamental, primarily for the protection of resources. The battle for survival is hard enough, without having to share what you have with someone outside your immediate collaborative unit. Ants seldom welcome their neighbours from nearby colonies into their own nests, visitors are regarded as trespassers. The growth of a young cuckoo in its hosts' nest shows what can happen if the alien is not discovered and expelled. The cuckoo's recruitment of foster-parents is not an example of a non-zero-sum game. In culture, racism is one of the cohesive demonology's most tenacious base-ingredients. Someone has to represent all the evil and the threats that a society defines itself against, and that role is always given to the Other. The enemy is the stranger, and the stranger is the enemy.

The ideology of the colonial project was multifaceted. It was not primarily a question of protecting borders, but of expanding the boundaries of a market and exporting a civilisation. Genuine goodwill was mixed with obvious hypocrisy and a desire for power which had its ultimate roots in racism. When the European colonial powers collapsed in the aftermath of the First World War – firstly collectively in the face of one another, and later one by one in the face of the growing nationalism of the third world – and an era could be summarised, the racist elements were impossible to hide. But because the colonised themselves still lacked a voice in the public arena, there was no-one who demanded a settlement of accounts, and, as a result, racism lingered on for a while out in the open, and only gave cause for still more fascination. It continued to make itself highly usable in sociotechnological terms by collaborating assiduously in the production of ideology and identity.

The absence of a settlement of accounts with, or even a debate about, racism made it possible for a fateful innocence to linger on. It did not occur to anyone that the modern media and military technology which had developed out of industrialism ought to be kept separate from a racism whose roots stretched right back to primitivist tribal society. No-one realised that a mixture of the one with the other could unleash an uncontrollable reaction. Racism and industrialism were strongly attracted to one another, and made a powerful combination under the prevailing circumstances, and out of their meeting arose a malignant romantic ideology. The fact that the new was mixed with the old in this unrestrained way was not seen as potentially problematic – on the contrary, it strengthened the illusion of historical continuity and eternal validity. This electrified romanticism was plugged in to vitalise the centre of power within the paradigm, the nation state, and eventually found its most extreme expression under a series of guises: fascism, Nazism, the Japanese imperial cult, et cetera. Political discourse was transformed into an arena for national-religious sacrificial cults.

The Nazi reign of terror in Germany during the 1930s and 40s is a terrifying example of the destructive energies which could be developed in a society where a resonance arose between racism and the fascination of the age with the media and industrial technologies. Suddenly a largely unconscious, unformulated ideology, which otherwise manifested itself mostly as imprecise and poorly thought-out bar-room talk, could be sharpened to rhetorically perfect phrases and, via the megaphone of radio, be screamed into every citizen's living-room. Thus a perfect projection surface arose for the vengefulness and longing for social identity which developed within a humiliated collective subject.

Thus a long series of factors interacted in Germany: deeply felt resentment against the latest twist of history, a Rousseauian romanticisation of an age-old racism, a dizzyingly fast pace of development within the media and industrial technologies, the strength of whose libidinous powers of attraction few, if any, understood. This fateful cocktail was at its most explosive when Adolf Hitler praised the German blitzkrieg's finely oiled precision in well-directed speeches immediately after the outbreak of the Second World War. All the components were now working together in finely tuned resonance: the desire for revenge which had lain festering since the humiliating peace settlement at the end of the First World War, the strengthened conviction of the Aryan 'race's' superiority, the technological fascination of the age. All of this led Hitler to work himself into a state of frothing ecstasy, which could instantly, and without any noticeable loss of energy, be transmitted to millions of devoted listeners via Germany's radio-sets.

Like Venus from the waves, a new human ideal arose out of this murky cocktail: the Rousseauian noble savage, injected with Nazism's own extreme version of cynical nihilism. The foremost explanation of the efficiency of the German war machine is, therefore, not a particularly German sense of duty, or a well-defined longing for sacrifice, as has often been supposed, but a widespread belief in, and a desire to embrace, the Nazi ideal of humanity: man as machine, the industrial worker selected for the national team of war, besotted with his own romanticised, glorious aura.

Nazism produced a hugely varied demonology, and a grand heroic aesthetic, but its ideology lacked any trace of political substance. It was all smoke and mirrors, a vast and satanic illusion. In order to participate in the collective identity, every citizen was forced to come up with his own social project, which made the question of loyalty all the simpler, and made the job of the internalised moral police so much less strenuous. All that they could actually offer were patches of light in the darkness, a two-dimensional stage-set. There were never any guarantees of any future reward, only an endlessly compulsive theatrical performance, a social identity of unsurpassed gravitational force.

This means that Nazism's unique explosive power lay in the ideology of absence: politics without theory, in constant, crazy motion, a turbulence of situations which were all united in a desire to achieve a maximal projection surface for the dreams and nightmares of the individual, and which succeeded in maintaining this function by clearing out every trace of political substance, and instead offering striking symbolism. No-one in a position of power, least of all Hitler, had any idea of where Nazi society was going, or even where it might be going. There was no secret formula in the safe. But insofar as anyone wondered about this, it was easiest to believe that the vision was either kept secret for good reason and being guarded by the innermost circles, or that it was visible to other participants with a sharper eye for ideology, in which case it was most sensible to follow the leaders, wherever they were aiming for, and to follow orders. When a life-lie becomes sufficiently absurd, it also becomes stronger, because it would be so endlessly painful and humiliating to see it punctured. Consequently, critical thought was not permitted to disturb the desire to enter into Nazism's collective subject. And, in the absence of exercise, it gradually withered.

The effect of the ideology of absence was further strengthened by a sort of passive matriarchy which governed alongside, and formed the echo-chamber of, Nazism's cult of masculinity. This matriarchy was extremely real, but passive insofar as it had arisen out of an absence of men, specifically the absence of the generations of men, both young and middle-aged, who had fallen on the battlefields of the First World War. The badly depleted group of survivors which returned from the war was a collection of humiliated losers, not in any shape to play out the patriarchal social technologies which were needed to organise society according to traditional patterns. But because the matriarchy was passive, a power vacuum arose in the middle stratum of society, which was opportunistically exploited by a group of extremist marginal figures who under normal circumstances would have remained in dank cellars. This sort of desperate extremists exist in all times and in all places, and the idiocy of their preaching is so blatant, and the word 'loser' branded so clearly on their foreheads, that they are generally mostly regarded as being unintentionally comic. But the conditions for desperation and a desire for blind loyalty happened to be extremely favourable in this instance. There was, quite simply, no credible contrasting image, and in the absence of an alternative, Nazism's placard slogans suddenly seemed a good replacement for ideological substance.

It is in the nature of the thing, in both senses of the phrase, that our inherited social instincts are primitive. They reflect primitive living conditions, and they have not had time to change, which is why our genes are still in the savannah. This is the necessary starting point for sociotechnology. The tri-polar power structure of the primitive tribe – chieftain, hunter, shaman – is essentially still intact, and is still the basis for the construction of networks. This is clear within the high-technological neoprimitivism of informationalism and the power structures within the virtual nomadic tribes, where the curator is the new chieftain, the nexialist the new hunter, and the eternalist the new shaman.

The role of chieftain is comparable to the role of Freud's prehistoric Urfather, and in Nazism's sociotechnological application, Hitler initially took on the role of father in all the German families where the father was absent. This proved to be particularly profitable, because Germany after the First World War was a nation full of fatherless families. Hitler's popularity rating soon soared. At the same time as countless fathers were absent, the fathers who remained in inter-war Germany lacked a connection to the functional patriarchal network which could have offered resistance to the Führer's claims. The next step was therefore for Hitler, once again in the absence of credible alternatives, to take on the role of the imposing father of all Germans. His only competitor for the role of chieftain, ironically enough, came from within his own ranks. This rival was Ernst Röhm, the leader of the Sturmabteilung, the SA, which Hitler soon had eliminated. This in turn had the positive side-effect of allowing Nazi demonology, because of Röhm's homosexuality, to gain yet another productive demon: the Homosexual. This was a worthy addition to a varied and constantly expanding group which already included the Jew, the Slav, the Gypsy, the Communist, the Mentally Subnormal, and so on.

Nazi homophobia was, to a large extent, a clearly sociotechnological phenomenon, a purely tactical manoeuvre without any ideological motivation. In actual fact Hitler's manifesto Mein Kampf – published in 1925, a whole decade before the elimination of Röhm and the rest of the SA's leadership – is full of the most obvious homoerotic fetishism. It was also among the regulars of Berlin's gay bars in the 1920s that Röhm had recruited many members of the SA. All of this fits in well with the sociotechnological principle according to which all social rules are programmatically flexible, and quite probably contradictory, which gives them a libidinous mysticism. The single over-riding and permanent principle is the fight for the survival of the tribe, and every exertion is subordinate to this goal. Strategy details must be constantly revised as circumstances in the social arena change.

Because his transgression of roles is so difficult to define, and because of his traditional position of exclusion from the tribe, the Homosexual is something of an archetype for the shaman's role.

And society's need of shamans can, together with its need for reserve parents – a need which was acute on the savannah, where the dangers were many and life-expectancy extremely insecure – explain a stable occurrence of genetically determined homosexuality. So natural selection favoured populations with a certain percentage of homosexuals.

When the shaman is allowed into the arena, a complicated and almost bizarre performance is staged within the collective unconscious, where the central theme is exclusion itself. For the shaman to fulfil his central function in the life of the tribe, he must be ostracised in times of plenty, and be banished from proximity to power in a process directed by the chieftain. Women and hunters participate willingly in this process, because it strengthens both their position in the hierarchy, and the general cohesion, and it grants some of the enjoyment to be had from being in the majority and behaving aggressively (just think of football hooligans, for instance). But in times of need, it becomes necessary to recall the shaman to the centre of power, often to the great surprise of women and hunters. The fact is that Nazism, under its final period, suffered an acute shortage of potential shamans. They were not merely banished, but to a large extent even executed, and the rapidity of the Nazi collapse meant that it would have been impossible anyway to recall them to the centre of power. From this perspective, Nazism appears to have been initially an extremely successful, but ultimately aborted tribal project. One decisive factor in its collapse, and a contributing factor to its loss of the war, was that the sociotechnological functions of the chieftain and the shaman were mixed up.

The regular recall of the shaman to the centre of power –behaviour which is deeply engraved in the collective unconscious –in turn explains the homosexual subculture's constant fetishisation of the prehistoric Urfather, and its masochism towards the chieftain. Ultimately this has nothing to do with homophobia or homophilia, at least not in any primary and original sense. Instead, the underlying explanation is the collective unconscious's strategy in the fight for the survival of the tribe. The shaman must be banished and excluded in times of plenty, because it is his exclusion and his divergent perspective which makes him essential in times of need. This is the cause of the complicated connection between chieftain and shaman, and the homosexual subculture's libidinous connection to the heterosexual male as an idea.

According to this sociotechnological pattern, the church was closely allied to the state in times of need, but strongly criticised and questioned during the intervening periods. This pattern was repeated with abundant clarity when, during the Second World War, the Stalinist regime called in the Russian Orthodox church – a feudal shaman in a society which to a large extent was still feudal – for their united fight against the German invader. An unholy alliance was formed, only to be dissolved, naturally, by the Soviet chieftain as soon as the war was over, ironically enough with reference to the fact that the Soviet Union had left feudalism behind.

The chieftain controls both hunters and women, and can, when necessary, play them off against each other. Because Hitler was accepted as chieftain and national father to such a great extent, the Nazis succeeded in persuading Germany's mothers to send their sons willingly onto the same battlefields on which their husbands had already fallen in the last war. The women were placed in a solid rank behind the soldiers, and were able to exert strong pressure on the front from there. The harshly formatted emotional climate meant that there was no practical alternative to consenting to become cannon-fodder.

This new sacrifice of men on the altar of the nation also functioned as a retrospective justification of the First World War's sacrifice of the previous generation. The dying and killing which had been seen as pointless during the inter-war years were finally given a justification through still more dying and killing. Not least because everything was overseen and blessed by the omnipresent Urfather. The desire for symbiosis was so strong that as long as the Führer's gaze seemed to be fixed on the flow of events, all judgement was abdicated to him; no-one questioned whether what was happening was right. The collective subject was presupposed to have moved from the public arena to the highly private world of the Führer; as a result there was no real interest in any divergent opinion, not even in secret among citizens who might be expected to have such an opinion.

Nazism's use of the father substitute as social technology is most evident in the so-called lebensborn project: baby factories where selected Aryan women were inseminated using sperm from selected

Aryan men, resulting in a child that was dedicated to the German nation. The project's propaganda consisted, amongst other things, of huge posters bearing idealised and utterly Aryan peasant families, and with Hitler once again in the position of the prehistoric Urfather. With the German nation in the role of mother, and the Führer in the role of father, biological parenting was reduced to an administrative formality. The good citizen was born, reproduced and died for the nation. Sociotechnology had invaded every imaginable space, and left no opportunity for individual initiative of an undesirable sort. The metaphysical parents, the leader and the nation, demanded total obedience, and offered in return a comprehensive family community. A total symbiosis of metaphysical parents and their vast hoard of children was unconditionally essential, as the propaganda made sure to explain. An entire population was infantilised and crept in terror up to its fictive mother's breast.

It has long been known that hard working people under great pressure lose the ability to think critically. As a final safety measure against any tendencies towards internal questioning, and as a complement to tribalism's social technologies, Nazism made use of the tried and tested exhaustion tactic. Weapons foundries and other industries were run in shifts with the help of mothers, daughters and prisoners of war as conscripted labour. In this way, an entire people was united around a single common, strictly focused project: Germany at war. The nation would not merely survive, but expand and reproduce itself. Germany was thereby transformed into a single, cohesive meme, a gigantic monster-replicator entirely focused upon copying and dissemination. Everything was intended to contribute towards the aim of ruling the world, and everything which deviated even slightly from this over-riding ambition had to be ruthlessly removed. Hitler's aesthetic was the noble seed which fertilised the German nation. It was their offspring's holy duty to populate the earth.

Nazi sociotechnology produced a war-machine which defeated Poland after 27 days, Denmark after 24 hours, Norway after 23 days, and so on. The arch-enemy, France, held out against the Germans for 39 days. The effect of these successes was overwhelming, crushing, and not favourable to the promotion of internal criticism of the great leader. The absence of a concrete political content strengthened rather than weakened the effectiveness of the ideology complex dramatically. The abstract vision, together with collective pressure, forced the individual citizen to choose the apparently worst imaginable option every time a choice was offered. This applied not least to the rapidly expanding bureaucracy, which on the one hand was powerfully idealised, but which, on the other, was hard pushed by competition and lacked clear directives about what it was expected to achieve. On every level in society, repeated new records were demanded for destructive initiatives. What looked from the outside to be a marvel of efficiency and rationality soon began to disintegrate internally as a result of an escalating zero-sum game.

This destructiveness was further fuelled by the growing collective blindness to speed and a fascination with the ability to remove taboos. The speed of the implosion of values was bewildering, and led to a constant succession of new delights. The people's appetite for constant new victories over old taboos increased. The raging pace of change could be perceived as confirmation of the historical necessity. All that was new must in some mystical way be connected to prehistoric purity and nobility. Such a rapid and apparently irresistible development could hardly be anything other than good and determined by fate. A fated event silenced every trace of criticism in advance. The feedback loop of inflated destruction could grow unchecked in intensity and scope.

The ironic consequence of this strict determinism – when the Germans' luck in the war finally changed and defeat was inevitable – was that the Nazis, with Hitler himself in the vanguard, felt themselves obliged to greet the victorious powers as the truly superior race. Sociotechnology had long since knocked out all morality, and all that was left was naked power-positivism: might is right, and the weak have forfeited their right to life. A defeated Germany deserved to be destroyed. With this praise from their enemy ringing in their ears, there was little reason for the victors, either Soviet Communism or the western democracies, to reflect upon, or come to terms with, any elements of fascism within themselves. The Germans were floundering in the dirt and then carried out their miraculous recovery. Everyone could agree that the tragedy which had occurred could be attributed in its entirety to the common cause of Nazi ideology and absolute evil.

Attacking Russia was, as hindsight has made abundantly clear, not a particularly well thought-out decision. Had Hitler avoided having to fight on two fronts – Stalin would never have attacked his admired and similarly moustachioed colleague in Berlin, and refused as long as he could to believe that the German invasion was a reality – then the result of the war would in all likelihood have been different. But the Nazis' application of sociotechnology was inconsequential and uncontrolled rather than planned as a long-term strategy; once the Nazi project was under way, it assumed a life of its own and its own nightmare logic which in no way coincided with any discernible advantage to those taking the initiative. An attack on Russia, however idiotic it may seem to a casual external observer, was on the cards. To anyone who had the sense to read it, Mein Kampf gave detailed descriptions of how the Russian steppes would be subdued by fire and sword, and how the inferior Slavs would be chained and set to forced labour. The same frothy, excited naïvety which was initially a recipe for success became in the long-term the cause of the ideology's inevitable demise.

This insight means that we must re-evaluate the common image of Nazism, not least all the accepted ideas of Auschwitz and the other concentration camps as an historically unique outbreak of evil. The methodical extermination of primarily Jews and Gypsies in specially constructed camps is not, as has often been claimed, the result of specific and culturally motivated German efficiency. There is no basis for the belief that once the Germans had decided to do something evil, they would become world champions in it simply because of their superior capacity for organisation.

In actual fact the reverse is true: Auschwitz is chaos, and if the evil in question was banal, as the philosopher Hannah Arendt claims, then it was banal in an even more banal sense than she realised, which in turn makes the observation in question itself banal. It was actually in the vacuum at the heart of the Nazi organisation, in the programmatic absence of direction and goal-oriented directives, that various pieces of swirling garbage created a resonance which made itself felt right out to the periphery of the organisation. And it was in the margins of this strictly choreographed chaos that the extermination camps took shape, and became self-supporting thanks to the libidinous energy of destructive and self-destructive madness, a malignant tumour which ate its way into the organisation from the outside. When the Wannsee Conference in January 1942 formally took the decision about 'the final solution', the result had in reality already been decided by the escalating resonance which was underway, and which had led to the conference itself.

What Hitler knew or did not know about the existence of the camps is irrelevant, the extent of the destructive and self-destructive madness could not have been greater. The camps served no other purpose than their own; for the war-effort they were obviously a burden, a sort of bizarre extravagance which stole resources and energy from a core business in rapidly deepening crisis. Nor did the Allies show any great interest in interrupting the activity once it became known towards the end of the war. The Holocaust was almost a by-product of sociotechnological chaos, an uncontrolled reaction released by the fusion of an hysterical national romanticism and a blind fetishisation of technology.

The image of the camps as the logical end product of an historically unique, systematicised evil only developed in retrospect, in a geopolitical context coloured by the expansion of the Israeli state and its demand for legitimacy. This image played upon an active denial of the widespread 'Nazism light' which had coloured the whole of democratic identity production from the middle of the nineteenth century onwards. Both right-wing and social democratic regimes in inter-war Europe had enthusiastically constructed an entire industry of race-biological institutes, which organised the mass sterilisation of people with divergent backgrounds or otherwise undesirable characteristics. This continued at an accelerating pace after the fall of Nazism.

The Nazis in Germany were far from alone in their ideology, they merely applied it with greater thoroughness than their gentler neighbours, which the pictures from the camps illustrated, as a result of which this insight had to be suppressed. The ultimate goal of the widespread postwar moralising against Nazism was therefore to recast the universal racism that was typical of the time as, in general, a German, and, in particular, a Nazi, phenomenon. From this follows the massive and uncritical support of postwar western opinion for the Holocaust industry. By portraying the Nazi as homo pathologicus, people attempted to hide the ironic fact that the Nazi was nothing but the consequential development of homo rationalis himself, the perfect Kantian, who, by first displacing and then killing the homo pathologicus that he has inescapably been from the start, believes that he can be changed into a perfect human being.

Hitler's frightening strength in relation to an undermined humanism lies in his preparedness to commit suicide in the event of his characteristics being shown to be morally inferior; he even actively sought out this decisive occasion, which explains the Nazis' stubborn desire for war. Rationalism was therefore refuted for the remainder of the twentieth century, tragically enough, merely by a moralising anti-moralism, a camouflaged collaborator, which meant that any serious questioning of rationalism was avoided. The paradigm shift which Nietzsche called for, from a rationalist to a transrationalist worldview, could be postponed into the future under cover of a comfortable lie about the true nature of Nazism. The Nazi was transformed into The Other above all others, a demon with which the westerner, and therefore also the Jew, for instance, shares no characteristics at all. The fear of free thought was based upon the fear that the thinker himself might be able to prove himself to be the Nazi who he has already, axiomatically, demonised.

The Holocaust was unfortunately not unique, either in its extent or in any imaginable moral sense. Other examples of officially sanctioned chaos which have ended in large-scale bloodbaths include the Terror of the French Revolution, and the genocide in Rwanda in the 1990s. Stalinism's various waves of collectivisations and purges surpassed Nazism in terms of numbers many times over. Not to mention the famines administered by the Communist Party in China between 1958 and 1962 (The Great Leap Forward!), when at least 30 million peasants died. Documenting these manufactured catastrophes and understanding their causal connections is, of course, an urgent task for historians, but the establishment of charts and the proclamation of a winner in evil can ultimately only serve propagandist purposes. Even if these purposes are extremely well-intentioned, the result will always be counterproductive.

By labelling something as evil, whether this something is later said to be banal or of some other form, one does not achieve or clarify much at all. New, destructive versions of moralism's demonology are merely constructed instead. Michel Foucault, of all people, speaks of how we must fight the fascist within us every day, but this is a regrettable example of a banality of goodness. If everyone is a fascist, then no-one is a fascist, and saying that we must fight the fascist within us may well send shivers of self-righteous well-being along our spines, but, at the same time, the concept, and therefore the entire discussion, becomes meaningless. Self-righteous moralism is actually fascism's best friend and fundamental precondition, and in this way becomes more fascistic than fascism itself.

Fascism is entirely dependent upon moralism, because its ideology and demonology have to build upon a set of moralistic axioms. So evil must be of transcendental magnitude, protected from any disturbing insight which might reveal its lack of substance. Moralism conducts this grubby work for fascism, wearing white gloves. Only a de-moralised view of history as a series of shifting circumstances, social processes linked to material complexes, tells us anything useful about the extermination camps: they are extreme and highly visible examples of destructive feedback loops, with fateful zero-sum games as their inevitable consequence. But that is all.

To say that we are all fascists, as Foucault does, is to say that all people are people and that circumstances change. It follows that fascism is not hiding in any innate human evil, whose existence fascism would therefore prove, but that it is concealed within circumstances themselves. The problem is not a lack of moral instruction, but a lack of understanding of the processes involved. It is not a boost of free will which will save us from fascism, only our almost embarrassingly needy and entirely basic requirement for the recognition and respect of the world around us. The noble savage has nothing to teach us; on the contrary, we need more society, more civilisation, a larger and closer-knit net of mutual dependence, and a common ideology with global foundations to achieve this.

The idea that every individual person can and must single-handedly ransack themselves internally and fight the fascist within on a daily basis is nothing more than meddlesome moralism's desperate last attempt to save itself from extinction. All that remains today is a vacillating mixture of indignant and obsequious series of fine phrases and empty promises. The good news is that moralism's conditions for survival under informationalism are becoming increasingly bleak. Moralism's self-aggrandisement is becoming more and more obvious, as is the absence of real morals. The idea that one might, through inner atonement, make oneself immune to the death-wish and the temptations of force merely reveals that we imagine that we can grab ourselves by the hair and remove ourselves from humanity with the help of pious wishes. No ideology could be more mendacious or less credible. Moralists are people who under no circumstances want to hear the truth about themselves, and who, ironically, believe that their suppression of this truth will impress others. You can, as Abraham Lincoln noted, fool all of the people some of the time, and you can fool some of the people all of the time, but you cannot fool all of the people all of the time.

In his capacity as the stooge of both racism and fascism, in other words, as their unconscious protector, the moralist is becoming one of informationalist society's greatest enemies. The transrational strategy is to replace wishful thinking with clarity in every instance: we cannot exterminate any cruelty within ourselves, because it does not exist where it is supposed to be. Instead, cruelty exists within interpersonal relationships – and, naturally, also in nature: many zoological research results never reach the public because they are deemed too unpleasant for people with illusions of natural goodness – and within social processes. Man is the product of his circumstances, but these circumstances are, on the other hand, at least partially the product of man himself. The only relevant methodology in this context is an unsentimental, far-sighted sociotechnology with a firm goal of expanded non-zero-sum games. The bell is tolling for the last moralist.

15.

Sex, Power and Network Dynamics – The Necessary Metamorphosis of Feminism

ON THE SIDE NATURE, on the other culture: similarity and difference, equality and inequality. Discussion of gender roles and power structures is as old as humanity itself. Thus spake Zarathustra, for instance, about the importance of a balanced relationship between the sexes in the earliest days of written language. The development of social patterns towards extreme individualism during the capitalist paradigm, and an increasingly radical questioning of traditions and authorities, meant that the issue was back on the agenda during the twentieth century. Strong voices, mostly female, claimed that it was high time to topple the power structure known as the patriarchal order, which was said to have formed the basis for the systematic oppression of women throughout history. It was time to work seriously for alternative, equal social structures.

During the nineteenth century the immensely controversial question of women's right to vote was raised, largely through the so-called suffragette movement. Opinion was not unanimous even among women themselves; certain high-profile women suggested that the issue of the right to vote was a pseudo-issue, that women and men were certainly of equal value, but basically different, that they exerted social influence in different ways, and that this should continue to be the case. The issue of voting rights therefore was not resolved until a good way into the following century. Soon after this, in conjunction with the Second World War, women entered the labour market en masse, leading to greatly increased economic independence. The high-capitalist institution of the family began to break up.

The increase in welfare standards during the Cold War made possible the experiment of the nuclear family. A unit comprising the well-paid husband, his full-time housewife, and their offspring, moved out to the suburbs, away from the demanding and oppressive social communities of the inner-cities. Through hard and unrestrained sentimentalised marketing, this experiment was presented as something traditional and fundamental. This did not help, however. Economic development and increased standards of education contributed to make the suburban garden seem like far too small and unstimulating an arena for intelligent and ambitious women. The experiment collapsed. When the nuclear families' daughters discovered existentialism and various other forms of radicalism at university, at the same time as they themselves, with the help of the Pill, could take control of reproduction, there was an explosion of criticism of the patriarchal order. Feminism quickly became a mass-movement.

The driving forces behind nineteenth-century feminism were liberal, whereas those behind the liberation of the 1960s belonged to the political left. Soon enough, though, everyone in the political arena, from left to right, was labelling themselves as feminist. Everyone seemed touchingly unanimous that equality was the overriding goal towards which all forces for good must strive together. The idea of equality between the sexes became transcendentalised, which necessarily led to conceptual confusion: in the same way that many people say they believe in God, but have completely different understandings of what God is, so everyone was suddenly in favour of equality, but equality meant different things to different people. The discussion therefore soon came to focus upon symbolic questions instead of factual ones: different groups tried frenetically to conquer the key concepts for their own cause. The dominant strategy that developed was to make yourself out to be weak, or, when this did not work, to present yourself as a noble spokesperson for the weak. Any opponent, on the other hand, always represented the patriarchal dominant power. Soon the subject became so inflamed that constructive discussion was practically impossible.

Equality of the sexes is actually not only a political or an economic question, but is also to a large extent about culture and strategy. It is a question of the application of social technologies, which is becoming even more apparent when viewed from an informationalist perspective. According to eternalist thinking, the only productive course is to apply radical pragmatism, removing the subject from the transcendental heavens and looking at it in the light of what we know about social processes and their dynamics. The very essence of the sexes and their social constructions is interesting, but that path has turned out to be a dead-end. Eternalist discussion of equality of the sexes therefore concentrates on how social technologies are forming gender roles and power structures here and now.

This is not to say that feminism as it has been up to now ought to be judged a failure; its successes are unquestionable. But the question of activism's goals must constantly be asked anew, particularly if the whole of society is undergoing radical change. At the same time as feminism has celebrated great triumphs during the final period of the capitalist paradigm, it is a fact that the patriarchal order has equally successfully survived by mutating and moving to the arenas where power itself has already moved. Clear-sightedness is always preferable to naïvety. For feminism to be a relevant meme, to informationalist networks in general, and to the netocratic woman in particular, it must be transformed into a transrationalist discourse. Feminism's real enemy is not so much the other sex, as its own ideological rigidity.

An illuminating example of the complexity of social movements, but also of the general tendency, is the current power structure pertaining to gender within the EU. On the one hand, women have succeeded in gaining a large degree of representation in the various west European parliaments. On the other hand, men have actually strengthened their grip on the increasingly global business world, and not least over the increasingly influential media industry. Because real power is always easily moved, and never locked to one or other institution or level, there is every reason to ask whether women have managed to gain a genuinely stronger position of power within Europe, or have merely been granted a symbolic victory in the hope that this will be sufficient, at least for the time being. In this case it is worth noting how a series of areas in the public sector have gradually become derelict as the male networks retreat and take power with them. As a result, the patriarchal order achieves a double victory: firstly by preserving and defending real power for itself, and secondly by disarming criticism by referring to the symbolic power from which it has abdicated.

There are two main variants of capitalist feminism. The first of these is an essentialist feminism which refers to biology and claims that both gender and gender differences are incontestable realities. Men and women have, because of biological differences, been given different social roles during different historical periods. But in our time the influence of biology on social life has decreased, and with it the justification for difference. According to this view, today there are no tenable reasons to nurture or maintain the so-called traditional gender roles. On the contrary, the state ought actively to counteract all inequality of power and independence. Men and women remain biologically different, but this is becoming more and more irrelevant in this context.

According to this essentialist feminism, it is a strategic mistake to try to downplay biological difference. Women have the right to be different to men, and to cherish their femininity, without as a result having to accept any limitations upon their right to equality, or even having to renounce their right to define their difference themselves. In this context, feminism's task is to define the differences between the sexes and to put pressure on political power to obtain equality. The enemy is prejudice and ignorance rather than any patriarchal conspiracy. And, in every event, political power is there, and has as its purpose, to correct any imbalances.

Other feminists viewed this essentialist position as far too conciliatory and ingratiating towards the oppressor. Instead, structuralist feminism claims that biology is overrated, that the sexes, as well as their attendant differences, are social constructions, constantly manipulated by a patriarchal order which is looking after its own interests. The very idea of differences and the structures this idea gives rise to are the origins of oppression, and its permanent abode. Social conventions make boys into boys: bold and active, and girls into girls: submissive and passive. Only by exposing and politically altering these conventions can the patriarchal order be reached, and only after that is it possible to create an alternative political culture which pays no heed to negligible, individual differences related to biology.

The confrontation between essentialists and structuralists created tension in the feminist ranks. An attractive solution to this unpleasant problem was suggested from an unexpected direction, however. Between the two combating factions, in a borderland where Marxist romanticism met the growing New Age movement, a myth began to form of a prehistoric matriarchy, a tranquil society governed by wise earth-mothers, where peace and harmony reigned. With support from various hazy religious sources, it was claimed that this matriarchy was the good, natural state which a bellicose patriarchy had toppled by force, at which point all traces of it were swept away and history was falsified. In matriarchal society the vagina was worshipped instead of the phallus, the Goddess instead of God, and reproduction was central, instead of production. With the patriarchal coup followed masculine civilisation and all the evils that accompanied it in the form of war, violence, conflict, the destruction of nature, and technological development. Therefore both men and women today live alienated from their real needs, which in turn both means that, and explains why, all people at least unconsciously hark back to the calm and peace of the womb, away from the threat of the phallus and its tyranny.

The prehistoric matriarchy and the patriarchal coup supply feminism with a whole mythology, including both a Paradise and a Fall, complemented by Rousseauian romanticisation of a natural state which is supposed to have existed before the ruination of civilisation. The good womb is, of course, nothing but the Noble Savage after a sex-change. This mythology also supplies feminism with a sacred task: to recreate the peaceful matriarchy for the good of coming generations. In the same way as Christianity – and countless other forms of Rousseauian étatism, both liberal and Marxist – feminist mythology exhorts its followers to recreate the original, balanced society which once existed. Today's civilisation is fundamentally evil.

This romantic feminist ideology is complemented by a media-friendly demonology around which all parties concerned – both essentialists and structuralists, both elite and ignorant masses – can unite and draw comfort from. It could not be simpler or more effective: force is the same as evil, whereas peace is the same as goodness. Man is violent by nature, and therefore an evil demon. Woman, on the other hand, is peaceful, and therefore a good goddess. The greatest joy for humanity would be peace on earth. Violent men can therefore not be allowed to stand in the way of humanity's greatest joy, but must be dealt with and educated by peaceful women, and might eventually, after some sort of examination of maturity, be permitted to be elevated to equality with women. But for the time being men only have the right to express themselves it terms of apologies for, and confessions of, their own evil.

In this demonology, every camp can find something attractive. Essentialist feminists find support for their ideas of innate and deep-rooted differences between the sexes, and can agree that all evil stems from men. They are happy to ignore the fact that physical violence is at least as prevalent within lesbian relationships as it is within heterosexual ones, and a series of other complications. Structuralist feminists appreciate the myth's idea of the matriarchy's transcendental infallibility. The reasoning goes: woman is taught by other women to be peaceful, peace is good, therefore woman is good. The matriarchy is governed by women, the matriarchy is peaceful, peace is good, therefore the matriarchy itself is good. Man is taught by other men to be violent, violence is evil, therefore man is evil. The patriarchy is governed by men, the patriarchy is violent, violence is evil, therefore the patriarchy is itself evil. If only women could replace men and take over power, then goodness would defeat evil and everything would be perfect.

There is, however, a fundamental problem with the feminist mythology: the matriarchy never actually existed. Nowhere has anyone ever reported anything that even hints at the existence of anything of the sort, at any point in time. There is not a single shred of evidence. This of course does not prove that there has never been a prehistoric matriarchy, but in that case the same thing applies to Santa Claus. As we showed earlier in our discussion of Nazism after the First World War, it is occasionally possible to speak of a passive matriarchy, in other words: a state which arises when the patriarchal order has been weakened for some reason. This passive matriarchy has only ever existed as a highly parenthetical occurrence, without the development which is a precondition for continued civilisational growth in the form of positive feedback loops, and, ironically, they have often been characterised by violence, insecurity and expansionism rather than peace, security and conflict-resolution, as promised by the mythology. Feminism's utopian matriarchy is, therefore, neither active nor passive, merely fictitious: a fairy-tale. Just like the entire romantic dream of a peaceful, original natural state.

When the American social theorist Camille Paglia says that she thanks God for men and the patriarchy every morning as she drives across a bridge on her way to work, she reminds us that without the supposedly wicked civilisation and technology, she and others would be forced to swim to work. Insofar as there would be any work to go to, of course. Nature is chaos, and civilisation is order in chaos. Paglia's simple statement puts the finger on a fact that cannot possibly remain hidden for ever – particularly not in an informationalist society, characterised by interactivity on a global scale and frenetic information exchange on all levels. If feminism has any relevance at all, if it is to be compatible with a civilisational project which neither can nor ought to be explained away, if it is not to reduce itself to being merely an escapist sect for self-obsessed and embittered ladies with an excess of energy, then it has to start attacking the patriarchal order with entirely different and considerably more sophisticated methods than sexual essences, social constructions and New Age mythological nonsense.

Power is power, no matter what we call it. The feminist ambition to play a different power-game to the only one accepted by the sociotechnological rules, and over which the patriarchy has perfect command, makes it impossible to see which women the movement actually represents. Just as it is impossible to understand how the theory might function, seeing as it persists in fighting for power where it imagines power is, rather than in the places where there is any real power to fight over. Feminism is looking for keys in a pool of light where the light is admittedly perfect, but where the absence of keys is striking. Its logic collapses on the altar of mythologies, and the necessary infrastructure between networks is noticeable by its absence.

Logic and infrastructure have nothing to do with gender. Consequently it is pointless to insist upon always playing on home territory and with your own rules; there is only a gender-neutral arena and rules which are neither negotiable nor can be blamed on men in any way. This in turn means that the only chance for the women's movement to achieve the equal distribution of power and status in relation to masculine or male-dominated networks is to play this single game as skilfully and forcefully as its opponents. The great problem of feminism is a mixture of the actual conquest of power, and the impossible idea of redefining power and deciding the conditions in which it can be conquered. It is admittedly true that masculine and male-dominated networks have at all times and in all known societies conquered and defended power. But the conditions for this conquest and defence have never been dictated by any particular interest group. These conditions are ultimately determined by the information technology which dominates the prevailing paradigm, and to try to ignore this is merely a waste of time for everyone concerned.

This means, for instance, that female members of an orchestra who want to exercise power over interpretations and choice of repertoire must succeed as conductors – with all that this implies in terms of demands and competition, hard work, pushiness and networking – instead of spending time fighting over who should sing the female solo. The orchestra's power structure is not something which has arisen from the discussions of an exemplary democratic meeting of all concerned, but what the network dynamics dictate. The conditions for the successful creation of music can only be manipulated up to a certain point, beyond which the results suffer, of which the orchestra is fully aware. Trying to stretch that boundary in the name of justice between the sexes or any other political motivation can only result in the devaluation of achieved power, a loss of quality for the orchestra, and thereby rapidly of its status as well, so it is pointless to waste time and energy on criticising the decision-making structures instead of competing for power on the terms that actually apply. Those people and networks which realise this and take it as their starting point are better placed to achieve real power and real influence than those who insist on following their own wishful-thinking.

The patriarchal order has not arisen as a result of male complaints or appeals for sympathy. So it is not possible to get past it by talking, writing, painting, crying, or even by threatening or networking. However, it must be remembered that it is not a charitable arrangement which serves every individual man, but simply puts a premium on a certain set of strategies which masculine and male-dominated networks have applied to great effect. The only productive attitude to this irrefutable fact is to learn the rules of the game and adapt oneself more skilfully than the competition. It is important to remember that the masculine networks' recipe for success thus far has been adaptation. One might wish for another world with different conditions, but in this world there are no short-cuts to power, and the battle is already lost if we abandon ourselves to naïve dreaming. No matter how militant the rhetoric gets.

The concept of discursive mystification is helpful here. A frequently recurring example of a discursive mystification is when a neurotic resonance between over-stressed participants in an academic debate drowns out the debate itself, which therefore ceases to be productive. The debate becomes a metadebate: who has the right to express themselves? Who is representing which interests? What does so-and-so mean by 'actually'? The result of this is that the actual subject of debate is mystified and becomes inaccessible, while the spectacle of a circle-dance goes on around it. The problem therefore is not the level of complexity or mystery of the subject itself, but the participants' inability to focus. Their respective neuroses trigger and reinforce one another, and the resonance they attain short-circuits the entire discussion.

One of feminism's great mistakes is the discursive mystification of patriarchal power. Turning men and the patriarchal order into demonological protagonists seems natural and contributes greatly to feminism's internal cohesion, but sometimes it is sensible to take a long hard look at your own marketing. Feminism's problem is that at the same time as the patriarchal order has been changed into an impenetrable mystery in feminism's own propaganda, feminists are supposed to be capable of disarming and defeating it. These two are incompatible, which explains why the feminist strategy, in spite of its proud rhetoric, has always dissolved into whining about rule-changes which are never going to be applicable and which are entirely irrelevant to the subject.

It is not possible to carry out a powerful change in general terms without a relatively detailed idea of the results of the change. This is a fundamental characteristic of eternalist ethics: the need for a target against which results and actions can be measured. In the same way as a fat person has to start with a convincing perception of him or herself as thin in order to be able to lose weight successfully, feminism must construct a credible vision of an equal society. Slogans alone are not enough. Superstitious wishful-thinking about lambs and lions lying down together will not do either. Civilisation, technology and the exercising of power are key concepts here. Realism and credibility in the light of ongoing social changes are inescapable requirements. And it is at this precise point, at which feminism has up to now failed to be a serious player, that an eternalistic feminism starts its work. Its task is to create a encouraging and convincing vision of an alternative social order where non-zero-sum games between the sexes can get going.

Capitalist feminism has, like the whole of the capitalist left, become stuck in its analysis in obsolete explanatory models such as essentialism and social constructionism. The reason for this is principally discursive censorship syndrome, which tends to develop to an alarming extent within groups where the collective identity is strongly linked to a communal sense of victimhood. The demonological aspect of identity production is here of central importance: discursive censorship is stretched to enclose every person and group outside the collective and its potential sympathisers. Where the discussion of sexual equality is concerned, this censorship applies first and foremost to men, because they are axiomatically defined as enemies and demons.

In this scenario, the discussion looks like a consciously organised zero-sum game. The presence of the female perspective demands the absence of the male perspective. What women win in this context is justifiable, considering the institutional oppression they have been subject to, and what men lose is equally justifiable, because their privileged status has been won by a single long succession of systematic oppressions which began with the defilement of the original, mystical matriarchy. Men, by definition, can have nothing of value to contribute, because they speak the language of power; their only legitimate function is to be ashamed of the strength which can only be used to oppress. Their silence – possibly interrupted by some lone, ingratiating confession of sin – is a necessary precondition for the defeat of the patriarchal order. The silenced men give women the opportunity to speak freely for the first time, which is regarded as a necessary precondition for the re-establishment of the matriarchy.

The problem with discursive censorship is that feminism thereby gives up the chance of understanding how power functions and is achieved, at the same time as it abandons any ambition to achieve a relevant and coherent analysis of the current situation. What is left is the nurture of a New Age-inspired theology and the outlawing of the sociotechnologically necessary ambition and desire for power which are unfailingly characterised as aggressive, masculine behaviour. No theatrical initiatives, however, can change the fact that there are no truer conditions for the exercising of power that those which are to hand. And no complaints, no matter how loud, can change the fact that it is sociotechnological principles, and not some patriarchal order, which are dictating these conditions.

Once the negative feedback loop has started to roll, it is hard to stop it. The next phase of feminism's discursive censorship syndrome damages women themselves, both inside and outside their own group. It is obvious that the patriarchal order lets through a number of women who thus end up at the top of male-dominated networks. These female power-players are soon banished from the feminist community by being defined as not being proper women. When leading female politicians and business leaders take decisions which do not coincide with the general feminist victim-mentality, according to which women are in principle better, this is not the result of reality forcing certain pragmatic decisions, regardless of the sex of the person making the decision; rather the explanation is that these powerful women have become hostages of the patriarchy. This victim-mentality becomes a vicious spiral, leading to an absurd competition in media-friendly weakness, intellectual argument disappears into a black hole, and the censorship syndrome silences everyone except those who manage to present themselves as being most oppressed of all.

Feminism is reduced to being one egotistical self-interest among many others, a medial platform for self-appointed representatives whose representativity is, to put it mildly, doubtful. When the theory collapses, even activism is afflicted by a paralysing confusion, and the medial liturgy is elevated to the principal occupation. At this stage the collective identity is so undermined that every attempt at internal criticism, even if is only intended to maintain a minimum of intellectual integrity, has to be deflected. The critic in question is silenced by intimidation or is excluded for the good of the cause. The destructive spiral moves on, until eventually only the most obedient, least creative members are left, those who do not seem to have anything better to do than to remain and maintain the illusion that something important is happening, which leads to a reduction of the network's ability to create attention. At the end of the spiral is the network's dissolution and death.

A direct consequence of the comprehensive application of discursive censorship was the obsession of the late twentieth century with political correctness within most areas which had anything to do with the production of social identity: race, gender, sexuality. Only the oppressed were allowed to speak. Because of this, Foucault's ethical ideal was deemed to have been put into practice: power was silenced so that the powerless could make their voices heard uninterrupted. But this was a Pyrrhic victory. Admittedly, the powerless were allowed to speak, the fact that no-one was listening was ignored, so the powerless remained powerless. Plurarchy had already broken through so powerfully in the diversified media-landscape that the audience went home when it was no longer entertained by what was being said, or thought it irrelevant. Power nodded in a friendly but disengaged way, at the same time as it quickly moved to another arena.

It is a fact that this friendly but disengaged nod indicated that the patriarch already knew that he would have the final word and thereby retain power, at the same time as he appeared to be enlightened and amenable. Performances in the public arena presuppose that the patriarch is their main audience, and he is fully aware of this. He is the true power-player, and it must not be supposed that he will give up any of his influence on grounds of sympathy, or that whining from a position of weakness constitutes a serious threat. In practice, discursive censorship syndrome means the reinforcement of the status quo in all respects other than the purely symbolic. Just as the beggar who can demonstrate the most upsetting handicap is in a good position to get the largest donations, those who manage to portray themselves as weakest can count upon a large sociometric donation, but the advantage is extremely short-term and of only symbolic value. In the same way as large donations shackle the beggar to his begging, and also encourage new recruits to the industry, suffering and weakness themselves become career choices, albeit highly limited ones. A self-image of victimhood becomes permanent because victim-status is rewarded. This happens at the cost of the cause itself, the eradication of suffering, itself suffering an enormous and long-term blow.

By persuading themselves and their fellow sisters that they can only speak on their own terms, in the absence of men, women, long-term, are doing themselves the greatest imaginable disservice. They are in practice disqualifying themselves as power-players, and are both admitting and reinforcing their inferiority, both to themselves and to men. If women do not take themselves seriously, then men do not need to either. This voluntary acceptance of an inferior position has to stop if there is eventually to be any talk of real equality. From the outset, women must regard themselves as the equals of men, in order to discuss equality seriously. Once again, it is a question of being able to present a credible vision of what a mutually profitable equality of the sexes would actually involve, instead of pleading for sympathy. It is a matter of suggesting in a persuasive way the result that you want to achieve until it becomes reality.

The harsh truth is that the capitalist women's movement lacks this vision entirely. And because it so clearly signals that it does not really believe that any real equality is possible, it is instead devoting itself to a stubborn fight for worthless symbols. The harsh realisation of the movement's belief in fate is alive and well at its core, even if this has to be denied and suppressed at all costs, both internally and externally. What women are obstinately trying to hide – from both men and themselves – is therefore that equality according to the governing ideology must arrive in the form of a gift from men, and it is men who must first believe in and work towards equality before women themselves can believe in it. The same feminism that denies men the right to express themselves simultaneously recognises, paradoxically, men's power as the only legitimate power. It is still the patriarch who decides which truth is true, and is he who determines the degree of possible equality. At its core, therefore, classical feminism is nothing more than praise for the patriarchal order.

In order to understand the patriarchal order and its off-shoots, we need a different perspective to that of political correctness, and a different strategy to that of discursive censorship. Demanding quotas and stressing particular female values will not get us very far. This issue is becoming more pressing as a result of the current paradigm shift, which is tearing up and reordering the social game-rules, both within and between the sexes. This new perspective can only arise when feminism either does away with its victim mentality and sectarianism of its own volition, or when its inability to command attention finally wipes out the women's movement in its current form. An eternalistic feminism is, on the one hand, a synthesis of essentialism and socioconstructionism, at the same time as it on the other hand principally presents an entirely new analysis which for the first time builds upon the sociotechnological explanatory model. The problem for this eternalistic feminism is thus that it must wage war on two fronts, against masculine and male-dominated networks, and also against the old feminist networks which are actually protecting the status quo and preventing all creativity in the area of theory.

The fact that the patriarchal order is still intact at the onset of informationalism, despite almost two centuries of the women's movement, suggests that almost all the work still remains to be done, and that resistance to the patriarchal order has essentially been a failure. This failure has its basis in feminism's inferior and ingratiating production of ideology, and in its unclear and superstitious analysis. The patriarchal order is thus not the result of any essential difference between the sexes. Nor is it the product of any traditional values system. The explanation of why men as a collective exercise power over women in western society lies instead in social organisation, in the differences between male and female networking, and in the differences of sociotechnological application. It is network dynamics which answer the question of why we are living in a patriarchal system. Once that question has been answered, women and men can together move forward and ask whether this system can really be toppled, and, if so, how this might be done.

It is of course interesting to discuss the origins of the various network structures – what is nature, and what is culture? The problem here, however, is that the pattern is so complicated, and that culture, if one inspects it closely enough, turns out to be an entirely natural continuation of nature itself. The only alternative view is that culture is a miracle, a gift from some god or other, probably patriarchal, so we do not explain quite as much as we perhaps think we do when we describe one thing as natural and something else cultural. This sort of hair-splitting, for the analytical ideologue or activist, is definitely a non-essential premium. Instead, the task is to develop a radical pragmatism where what is accessible to an empirical investigation is the truly active network dynamic which produces a certain amount of identity from a certain characteristic. The ambitions of ideology can be compared to the results of activism. The only hindrance is that this work – in contrast to the feminist discourse that has existed thus far – demands a willingness to accept even the less attractive facts about oneself and one's group identity which have previously been censured or suppressed.

It is a question of abandoning traditional individual thought and instead nurturing a relational way of thinking. If men as a group exert control over women as a group, then this simply means that throughout history men have made use of a network dynamic which is more effective than women's for the exercising of power, neither more nor less. The question which it is interesting to ask in this context is how the men's network dynamic differs from that of the women, while we can forget the question which capitalist feminism has been asking: how the essences or construction of the two sexes differ from or are similar to one another. An eternalist analysis is concerned with what is available – processes or their complex structures – and is not interested in either essences or the possible origins of characteristics. Mankind is a dysfunctional and confused machine, homo pathologicus, whether male or female, and the social technologies make all the difference in the world.

One fundamental sociotechnological fact is that action always precedes words. Sometimes we do one thing and say another, and in those cases the discrepancy can be interesting, but in the long-term it is always actions which deserve most attention. Up to now, however, feminism has persisted in doing the reverse by proclaiming, without being able to be specific, a sort of primitive platonic idea which is supposed to constitute a female alternative to a supposed male truth. This means that the expressed goals are given a primary value, while achieved results are only a pale and uninteresting copy of the goal in the form of fallible implementation. This perception results in a form of feminist activism which consists of verbose affirmations directed at a reality which deviates from the activists' wishful thinking. The problem is that as long as activism is concerned with wishful thinking rather than reality as its starting point, it will obviously never reach reality itself, the sphere in which the real battle for power is fought. So the activism is little more than another form of subordination.

Naturally, a resistant wall of obstacles and denials arises here, a wall which an eternalistic feminism would simply bypass, because it is based upon entirely different and, for the feminist discourse, new premises. The most significant achievement is that power is separated from sexuality. Men may appear, and may present themselves, as obsessed by sex, but at the same time they are trained to keep sexuality and power relations separate, which makes it possible for them to observe power and the fight for power in a detached way. Women, however, are trained to do the opposite: they see submission to men as unavoidable, and try to set the price for this submission as high as possible. Power and sex are intimately intertwined, power and status are bought with sex, and in this game other women appear mostly as competitors for the patriarch's favours and necessary recognition.

But in informational society, where power is divided according to increasingly evident network-dynamic and sociotechnological principles, the traditional female link between power and sex risks having serious consequences. Where men see relationships, women see individuals. While men are dividualised and network for mutual gain by linking potential rivals to themselves, women do not perceive the social structures of potential competitors and the great rewards of collaboration that would be available to them if they did, but merely see a sort of hierarchical knock-out competition where the single woman is constantly and involuntarily confronted by one opponent after the other.

If we look at the patriarchal order from an eventological perspective, it is apparent that masculine and male-dominated networks are powerfully over-represented in the eternalistic phase, and that they even dominate the mobilistic phase, while female networks seldom tend to grow out of the initial attentional phase. From this we can draw two possible conclusions: either that women ought to obstruct the growth and abilities of the masculine networks, or that women have to start increasing the production of their own networks.

Choosing the former is simpler, because it does not require any new training or thought. But there is a risk that women will thereby reduce themselves to comparatively insignificant satellites orbiting the men's planets in the virtual solar system. Choosing the latter, which is the choice of eternalistic feminism, means having to resume the great project of the twentieth century, which never really moved from talk to application – sexual liberation. Women will also have to learn how to separate sex from power, and thereby come to terms with their own need to constantly chase after social recognition from men, itself a subordinating act, while men, for their part, receive their social identity from other men and not from women, and are therefore free and independent of the approval of women's networks.

According to sociotechnological analysis, violence is always violence, even if it is practised discretely and/or indirectly, in secret, or second or third hand. The general is, for instance, highly involved in the use of violence, even if is a foot-soldier whom he has never met who physically does his best to kill one of his brothers in misfortune in another army. Not to mention the wives of both generals and privates listening at home on the radio. The women sit and enthusiastically cheer on their men, and would refuse to allow them home unless they had done their utmost on the battlefield, and preferably had won the bloody war outright. Naturally these women are also highly complicit in the use of violence. Sociotechnological analysis can be compared to an x-ray examination using contrast fluid: we can see the actual spread of violence throughout the body, see how finely connected and widespread it is in all the body's extremities, see that it is impossible to imagine violence out of existence. As a result, the concept of violence comes to comprise even invisible violence: mental, verbal, medial. And, because of this, we can see how violence is always responsible for the transfer of power in society.

This analysis becomes truly fascinating when we turn our attention to the informationalist patriarch's use of violence by abstaining from using the violence that is expected. This can be compared to the way a sadomasochistic relationship reaches its pinnacle at the moment when the sadist refuses to fulfil the masochist's wishes, and how this refusal itself fulfils the masochist's highest dreams of being entirely and completely dominated. The dialectic of sublime violence is more active under informationalism than ever before; power hierarchies are still based upon violence and the threat of violence, and always with a chieftain at their centre. Sociotechnology's principles remain the same, even if their expression and application obviously change. Any form of feminism which naïvely or hypocritically believes that it is beyond the dialectic of sublime violence has already abdicated from the opportunity of playing for power. Violence is ultimately neither a male nor a female characteristic, but merely a universal, sociotechnological necessity.

The concept of feminism has fought itself to a standstill, to the applause of the patriarchal order. The fact that everyone calls themselves a feminist today is naturally connected to the understanding that feminism is supporting the status quo and, in contrast to its own rhetoric, is bowing its head to the demonised men. The future demands an entirely new viewpoint. If the dividual replaces the individual, it is no longer relevant to speak of sex in a social sense. Instead, it is dividuals in networks who have social relevance, and the most interesting thing is how well these networks adapt to certain conditions. This adaptation is, in turn, highly dependent upon both an intuitive and reflective understanding of the principles of network dynamics.

When gender ceases to be a relevant social category, all talk of the essences and construction of the sexes will become meaningless, and all those characteristics and talents which were previously linked to gender will be released, whereupon every dividual will be able to make free use of the whole of his or her abilities. The boundaries are decided by network dynamics and not by predetermined gender roles. Man and woman are transformed from genetically and culturally programmed life-sentences into two roles among countless other ways of adorning oneself on informationalism's hyperreal stage. And, as a result, feminism – because it has become eternalistic – really would have fought itself to a standstill, in other words: it would have made itself unnecessary as a result of genuine progress.

16.

THE INFRASTRUCTURE OF THE EMPIRE AND ETERNALISM'S MORAL IMPERATIVE

☐

THE GROWING TORRENT OF INFORMATION is making information itself a logistical problem and an environmental hazard. Attention is becoming more and more desirable, but it is in increasingly short supply. One characteristic of media developments in conjunction with the transition to an informationalist society is the increasingly brutal competition for this finite amount of attention, which in turn leads to yet another increase in the torrent of information. Producers see their chance to get in ahead of their competitors by implementing and supplying faster what consumers might be expected to want, and this producer's speed builds in turn upon the increasingly rapid collection and processing of information. More than ever, speed is becoming a value in itself, a so-called selling point. The fastest wins.

The electronic mass media are perfectly adapted to speed, if only in one direction, and they are therefore largely competing with speed as their weapon. As long as the traditional mass media dominate the landscape, speed will be prioritised above everything else. News must always be as new as possible. The ideal is not to reflect the actual event, but its breakthrough. As soon as something newsworthy has happened somewhere, CNN or some other television channel makes sure to get a camera there as soon as possible, and in living rooms around the world people can follow the development of this particular piece of news. The ironic consequence of all this speed is a paradoxical sluggishness, combined with the galloping meaningless which arises when the absence of relevant analysis is filled with guesses and chatter.

Take an aeroplane hijacking, for instance, or some anticipated trouble on some border in the Middle East. The big television companies send their teams in, set up their cameras and start transmitting. A plane stands in the shimmering heat on a runway, black-bearded men move about in streets and squares, nothing much happens. But it is precisely this state of nothing happening, this non-event as event, which is the only thing that counts. The static plane remains static, the black-bearded men look exotically agitated: the pictures in living rooms the world over are completely meaningless, and in order to simulate some sort of meaning they are ornamented with commentators who make comments: in other words, they chatter and express an opinion. But all this talk is just padding, just like the more or less informed guesses before a football match. The moment something actually happens – when the plane explodes or a hostage is released, or when some match which was already won in advance is pathetically lost – then everything that has been said becomes superfluous and as unutterably uninteresting as anything could possibly be. This explains why no-one really listens, except to kill the very time which is supposed to be so valuable. What the news-consumtariat is ultimately consuming is nothing but a tragicomic liturgy of the loss of meaning and their own impotence.

When speed becomes a value in itself, superficiality is inevitable. The torrent of information gradually loses more and more of its intellectual substance. What is left in the end is merely the dramaturgy of the entertainment aesthetic transferred into daily practice, a standardised procedure that acts both as a screening mechanism and a packaging ritual. An event becomes news if it is suitable for the industrial process of the media, otherwise it is reported at best merely as a curiosity, but is usually ignored altogether. Within the larger media, journalism no longer has anything to do with the communication of information, but is conducted and evaluated as a sub-genre of the entertainment industry. Journalists are not paid to exercise critical thought, and seldom make any show of doing so; instead, their pride in their work is linked to a sort of assumed professionalism, an ability to make a story out of promising raw material.

The key criterion in this process is the potential for intimisation: is it possible to become intimate with someone, to force oneself upon them, to ingratiate oneself? A story is no longer a summary of an event but the so-called human interest aspect in the form of a victimised individual who has been catastrophically affected – upset, angry, ecstatic, humiliated, entranced, crushed, arrested, murdered, raped, disgraced, or whatever seems appropriate in the circumstances. The mass-medial torrent of information is reduced to a flood of emotions, with no critical reflection. What is known as critical reflection is limited to one of the reporter's colleagues, with whom the audience is already on more or less intimate terms, sitting down and expressing something utterly predictable, and preferably affected as well.

The result is a media landscape where the darkness is illuminated by a constant display of short-lived fireworks made up of superficial chatter. An endless procession of people pop up and become intimate, to express something, anything at all. This arrangement is, quite literally, extremely popular, because it is undemandingly democratic in the most general sense: everyone can express something, no-one demands that the person expressing the opinion should have any knowledge or ability to present an argument, and all of these expressions of opinion are precisely as worthless as each other. Everyone is an expert, everyone is ready to express his or her own opinion. As soon as the price of petrol goes up, for instance, every motorist anywhere in the vicinity of a television station stands a good chance of being that day's expert on the global economy and on the fluctuations of the commodities market.

No longer is anything the result of a complicated chain of causal events, because complicated chains of causal events make poor stories. Nothing fits into an historical perspective any longer, because the need for speed and variety are incompatible with the presentation of historical processes, and because the preconditions for constructing the necessary frames of reference are extremely poor. Everything is taking place right now, then it is gone. Every piece of news is a separate component of a more or less entertaining, constantly changing cabaret show. One item may follow the other, but the first never connects with the second in any meaningful way, and the second might well be about something completely different, with an even higher intimacy factor. Medialised public life is therefore becoming something one consumes rather than something one participates in. Faces, constantly new faces, and disparate fragments of stories shimmer past on the screen, then disappear. This is what Neil Postman call a peek-a-boo world.

This structure survives and is upheld for two reasons: firstly, because it is in harmony with a political and economic culture linked to a media-technological complex dominated by television, and, secondly, because it favours the three groups which have dominated the late capitalist media landscape: the journalists of the mass-media factories, the nation states' politicians, and multinational companies. In actual fact these two reasons are both ways of expressing the same thing. None of these groups has any interest whatever in prioritising critical thinking at the expense of opinionated babble. In common with cynical cultural relativism, we might claim that this structure is 'true' because it reflects actual power relationships. It is based upon purely quantitative thinking in the same way that economism is. But this would be to miss the fact that this structure is fundamentally reactive, a countertrend vulnerable to being undermined by a new media-technological complex. When large-scale interactivity makes its breakthrough, the circumstances of the social ecosystem will change radically, after which new power relationships will produce an entirely new media landscape, and a whole new collection of truths.

In the current interregnum, the electronic mass media have retained their grip on the underclass in particular, and are producing a steady stream of new 'stars' who all personify the primacy of chatter over actual thought. Members of the consumtariat are offered the possibility of realising themselves as individuals by consuming the same things. The individualism that is so sought after lies in having opinions, in having an attitude, because anything that shows any hint of originality is permitted to vary just a little. Having opinions about absolutely everything has become a popular movement, monitored by television as soon as it fulfils the basic dramaturgical curve. In the meantime, qualified discussion of central social questions is gradually moving into the closed networks of the netocracy, slowly escaping from the ruins of the public arena. As a result, the democratisation and popularisation of debate is actually a deadly threat to democracy itself, which is teetering ever close to its grave. The supremacy of the elite is reinforced by the fact that all valuable information and sophisticated analysis will literally become unavailable to the great mass of the population. All this frantic and insubstantial chatter is the new opium of the people. Intelligent analysis, on the other hand, will become a netocratic privilege and instrument of power.

As television is becoming more and more a purely consumtariat mass medium, it is ceasing to function as a usable channel for information, and is being transformed into a substitute for the campfire. The medium is the message; the function of television is to crackle pleasantly, ratings leap when the pictures and sound are at their most fire-like. The actual programme-content is considerably less significant, the audience can soon zap to the channel that offers the most comforting crackling. When the need for comfort is increasingly prioritised like this above the need for knowledge – in both producers and audience – then unforeseen events and critical analysis will both come to be regarded as unwieldy and extremely undesirable disruptions to the soporific flow of non-events. Reality is becoming ever more unreal. The underclass's perception of reality is becoming more and more irrelevant and unusable, while the elite is continually refining its own instruments. As a consequence, class divisions can only get wider, and the subordination of the underclass can only get more entrenched. For the netocracy, disruption itself has a central ethical value. An unforeseen event is what breaks the conventional worldview, forcing perceptions to be refocussed on their mobilistic surroundings, so that a further new eternalisation can be made. The reactionary mass media, with their simplistic and distorted perception of reality, will seem deeply unethical in contrast.

The task of mass media producers to promote comfort and a good night's sleep cannot but add the cynicism to cynical nihilism. The range of offerings is increasingly infantilised, and consumers are regarded as a group of self-obsessed and unruly children who must be addressed in baby language and gently cajoled. Along with this escalating development, the self-destructive tendency of this systematic flight from reality is becoming increasingly obvious. This in turn leads to a decline in viewing figures, which means that advertisers are re-evaluating the priorities of their communication strategies and considering other forums and forms, because it is obviously desirable to reach groups other than merely the most passive couch-potatoes. At this critical point, the extent of analytical overview will be decisive to developments. Media producers themselves, for obvious reasons, have difficulty appreciating the destructive feedback loop of which they are a part, a development in which they are both victim and aggressor. The easiest conclusion for anyone observing developments through the screen of cynical nihilism to draw is to consider the low quality of what is on offer as a confirmation of their own righteousness. This is what the public wants! The lowest common denominator is confused with a general evaluation of the public's intellectual ability and potential.

From this perspective, interactivity runs the risk of looking like just an amusing gimmick that can be incorporated into programmes – call in and vote out one of the participants in a docusoap, or vote for the man of the match, even if the match has not yet finished – so as to create a bit of extra entertainment value out of the opinions of the public. Talk of the socially transforming implications of interactivity runs the risk of seeming quite insane, at least for a while. The same obviously applies to eternalistic history writing, which departs from the dominant information technologies in order to unveil power relationships, worldview and ideology. Instead of seeing the growing infantilisation of the mass media as an indication that the netocracy is just not interested, cynical nihilists claim that this dumming down is actually a necessary step back from unrealistic ambitions and a correct reflection of the stupidity of the population. Investigations prove that well-educated young people born after 1970 are increasingly choosing other sources of information than the mass media, and are playing with new interactive media technologies in order to form the troops ready for the take-over of power. Once again, allegedly democratic reasoning is lurking in the background: giving people what they want is supposed to be the only democratic stance in this context. This argument presupposes, however, that someone can in advance predict how those in question want to be surprised, which is by definition impossible. But as long as this logically deficient argument is seen as valid, as long as cynical nihilism reigns, then the decay will continue.

What is ironic is that it is precisely because of this that the interactive revolution will be so much more effective. Because the relationship between transmitter and receiver is becoming so much more multifaceted, and because roles are continually changing, the interactive media are superior to the mass media in terms of both entertainment value and the transference of knowledge. The traditional mass media have nowhere near the same capacity to exploit the creativity and attention-building abilities of individual players. Their prejudiced, superficial and irrelevant valuations of news are mercilessly revealed by the growth of interactivity, through which alternative analyses will be disseminated and immediately receive qualified reactions in a positive feedback loop. The best imaginable conditions for interactivity are therefore a precondition for the netocracy to even consider discussing social issues in public; in contrast to the elites of other eras, it is not interested in transmitting its propaganda unopposed, but wants instead to gain the greatest possible benefit from any criticism it initiates.

The destructive feedback loop is constantly reinforcing the cynical conservatism of the mass media. The more interactivity undermines the power of the mass media – by well-educated young people selecting other forms of media – and the more turbulence builds up, the more energy is mobilised within reactionary countertrends, with the aim of preserving at least the illusion of security and control. The developing netocracy is quickly picking up social-technological principles and is learning to apply them under new, changing circumstances, while the old media powers and their interest groups, hungry for security, persist in occupying the increasingly bitter and prejudiced world of one-way communication. Cynical obstructions and obligatory defensive behaviour make it difficult for the netocracy to absorb the old media powers, which is why they will follow their dilapidated technology as it gradually but inexorably sinks to the bottom.

The paradigm shift from capitalism to informationalism implies an upheaval of values, from economic quantitative thought to attentional qualitative thought. The qualitative aspect of attention – credibility – will be utterly decisive. It will not matter how much awareness you manage to create around a potential event; as long as it has no credibility, then it will have no attentional value either. This value shift also means that mathematical information theory, which has exclusively been applied to the quantity and speed of the transfer of information, will be replaced by a new communication theory which encompasses both interactivity and the qualitative aspect. In the torrent of information, further increases in productivity will not be top of the list, but more refined methods of sorting, which in turn will make it necessary to develop functional quality criteria. As information becomes a bulk commodity, there is a growing shortage of attention, and, like love, attention is one of those things in life that cannot be bought at any cost. It can, in principle, only be offered in exchange for the attention one has to offer oneself, and only then if it is deemed to be of equal value.

Developments towards netocratic qualitative thought will lead, ironically, to a renaissance for those media and means of artistic expression which were left in the shadows of all the shimmering television screens during late capitalism. Above all, literature looks set to improve its lot. It has – as the author Italo Calvino claims in one of his lectures about the qualities that make literature indispensable, even in the new millennium – a quite unique, intelligent quickness. When the speed of the electronic mass media flattens out communication to a single, homogeneous surface in which the differences between separate phenomena are basically eradicated, the best literature (Calvino uses Jorge Luis Borges as one example) will offer an associative quickness. This quickness makes it possible to place widely different phenomena in relationships to one another in a way that accentuates their distinct differences. As a result, one connection which has always been somewhat vague is clarified: life is given meaning, instead of meaninglessness continuing to expand through the efforts of the mass media.

This development is strengthened by the fact that both art and literature, right from the start, demand a good deal of interactivity. The viewer/reader has no choice but to do a lot of the work, and is expected to invest many of his or her own experiences and thoughts in order for the work to take shape as an experience. This may be part of the explanation as to why both art and literature have quickly found their place in an interactive environment: a long succession of experiments and hybrid forms have arisen in a very short time. Text, image, sound and music are interacting with one another and with the viewer/reader under entirely new conditions. As in every interactive context, the distinction between the transmitter and the receiver is fluid. This relationship is more important than their individual roles, and the process attracts added creativity from all directions.

The crisis of the mass media is primarily affecting mass products: the tabloid press, television chat-shows, inane pop radio. They will out-compete each other to extinction for steadily shrinking advertising revenues, at the same time as interactive media both inform and entertain better, as more and more people in the most attractive target groups are discovering. The netocracy finds itself in a position where it can chose its media production and consumption itself within a broad spectrum of different alternatives, and it tends to chose quality over quantity, it prefers the sophisticated and demanding to the conventional and complacent. It also has good, if crass reasons to nurture an elitist attitude, since the netocracy, as a result of its decentralised structure, is competing hard internally for its own attention, which demands constant improvement and the ability to come up with brilliant and unpredictable responses requiring a re-evaluation of old truths. Education will once again become fashionable as a cohesive concept for the wide frames of reference and the rapid association capacity that is in demand.

For purely practical reasons, the late capitalist mass media had inherent limitations – newspapers and television are, to start with, both extremely expensive media forms to produce – which was in turn the precondition for a cohesive and comprehensible public arena, common to everyone, even if only a small elite could act as transmitters while the great mass had to be content with being receivers. The netocracy, on the other hand, is not forced to share any public space with anyone else, it can afford to be extremely selective. Virtual space is plurarchical, there are many possibilities to create your own subcultures and integrate with a select few. This exclusive sectarianism is in a permanently incomplete state of dialectic opposition to the development towards a global state, meaning that the netocracy is becoming the motor of the global ideology. On one hand, the desire for domestication, and, on the other, the desire for freedom.

Through history, this eternal conflict has been played out in front of a closed door, and behind this closed door there is absolutely nothing hidden. This is how it is, and this is how it has to be. We shall never know what was hidden in the holy of holies in the Temple in Jerusalem. The only person who knew for sure was the high priest, who alone was permitted to visit the heart of the sanctuary, and only then on certain special occasions. The point of the holy of holies being a carefully preserved secret is obvious: in this way each Jew whose collective identity ultimately revolves about this sacred room can imagine the most fantastical things about its contents without ever needing to be disappointed. The closed door is the perfect projection screen for dreams, speculations, and the production of identity. It makes no difference what is actually behind the door. Logically and aesthetically, it would be most appealing if the holy of holies concealed absolutely nothing.

What is qualitatively new about eternalism's political philosophy and informational society's identity production is that all doors, even the ones leading to the holy of holies, are open. And there is an ferocious draft blowing. Everyone is his or her own high priest, everyone is initiated into the mystery, and everyone can make sure of what was clear right from the outset, that the metaphysical heart of the ideology, the core of the collective identity, i.e. the global empire, is made up of a mobilistic void. And yet the empire definitely exists, but as an eternalistic phenomenon, in precisely the same way that God really existed once as an inevitable consequence of mankind's need for a God.

The mobilistic void in the collective subconscious has clearly always been empty, nothing new has happened, apart from the fact that the doors have been opened. But because of that, everything has changed. Mankind is still staring into the void, becoming painfully more conscious of the need for a metaphysical basis for collective identity. So the realisation is growing that the metaphysical basis has to be created rather that directed, and that this must be a united, collective process. Eternalism's radical pragmatism is growing out of this, the global empire's affirmative nihilism. Since nihilism has by now left its cynical phase behind, the revelation of this void does not imply any sort of catastrophe, but rather an immense liberation, opening up literally unimagined possibilities.

All naïve theories of alienation, and the liberation project too, with their roots in missionary religions and early utopianisms modernised after the Enlightenment, are therefore collapsing to the ground in a feeble pile of scrap. The only true alienation was the idea of alienation itself, nothing more. Mankind is, and always has been, liberated. The task of liberation mythology was to serve as the socially acceptable excuse for not having to see the conventional aspect of conventions, for not thinking critically or taking any action. The convention was a sort of institutionalised convenience in the form of lazy, sadomasochistic practice. The master remained a master, the slave remained a slave. The actors may have changed now and then, but the structures remained remarkably intact.

What happens when plurarchy opens all the floodgates and lets loose the torrent of information, is that the conventional power complex is unravelled and washed away. It is not a matter of any conventional liberation, but that liberation is no longer possible to hide for anyone with eyes to see with. Master and slave have historically corroborated one another's positions, after all, but in plurarchical society there is no longer a master who is oppressing anyone, not even if the slave begs and pleads for the oppression to continue. Power and status are distributed according to new principles, the meritocratic system has broken through entirely, and the resulting class divisions can be regarded as reasonable and fair. The netocratic dominant class is not particularly interested in the consumtariat underclass and its intellectual existence. Instead it is fully occupied with internal competition (see Netocracy).

The realisation of the void in the innermost metaphysical chamber is, naturally, not new. Attempts to lift this veil and thereby establish what we can see as a truer theory appear in a long list of religions through history. Zoroastrianism, Buddhism before the reincarnation myth, Christianity before the resurrection myth, and Mithraism all demonstrate patterns of thought in line with eternalism, all of which were impressively ground-breaking in their day. But the socioeconomic circumstances proved to be unfavourable to these groups of memes, meaning that the belief system in question either had to be modified and vulgarised, or outperformed and demonised. The time was not yet ripe for eternalist metaphysics.

The circumstances of the breakthrough of informationalism are forcing not merely an easing but an uncompromising tearing up of the veil. Jesus drove the money-lenders out of the temple, the eternalist philosopher drives out the opinion-mongers. The electronic media have contributed greatly to this development by obstinately producing a representation of reality which is increasingly unreal, by stepping up the destruction of meaning to acutely painful levels, and by driving cynical nihilism to a point where the absurdity in its tautological argument becomes so obvious that people are more or less forced to think new thoughts, and to think for themselves.

Talented young people are not content to be addressed as retarded children. They are hooking up, and hooking together, and forming their own topographical public space now that the old one is becoming too stupid and bizarre. Countless nomadic tribes are being born and developing underground, far beyond the diminishing spotlight of the capitalist mass media. With the help of interactive information technology, they can sit and play a new world order into existence, a smile of discovery on their faces. For some people this is a frightening scenario, for many others it is indescribably hope-inspiring. One's point of view of course depends which interests one happens to represent.

Play is the keyword here. Liberated from the most limiting of late capitalism's collective neuroses, homo pathologicus can realise the dream of homo ludens. The central aesthetic imperative is: Play! Create! Think new thoughts, and think differently! Make mistakes and learn from them! Love your shortcomings and use them as a lever in increasingly daring and more playful civilisation projects! Nurture your talents and multiple personalities, and take extra care of the paradoxes! Play with identity! Cherish loyalties! And when play is over, and death is approaching, bathe one last time in an ocean of exquisite chemicals and drift off to sleep in the company of your nearest and dearest, your brothers and sisters from the nomadic tribe that you helped to create and maintain.

In virtual space you and your playmates are the stars.

1.

THE RISE AND FALL OF THE SOUL

IT IS AN OLD FAMILIAR truth, a well-worn turn of phrase, that taxes and death are the only certainties in life. But let no-one suggest that we human beings have not done our utmost throughout history to wriggle out of both of these. People exhibit the most astonishing creativity in trying as hard as they can to keep their income and fortune to themselves. New talents are constantly being recruited to the hydra-headed and highly paid corps of professionals who spend all of their time doing precisely this for the benefit of the rest of us. And as regards death, the campaign is being fought with a good deal of intensity on a number of fronts.

Efforts to cheat death were a dominant theme in even the very earliest literature. Gilgamesh, the hero of the Sumerian epic that bears his name – and whose oldest versions are over 4000 years old – bitterly mourns the death of his friend and brother-in-arms, Enkidu, and draws far-reaching conclusions regarding himself.

> *What became of my friend Enkidu was too much to bear*
> *so on a far path I wander the wild.*
> *How can I keep silent? How can I stay quiet?*
> *My friend, whom I loved, has turned to clay,*
> *my friend Enkidu, whom I loved, has turned to clay.*
> *Shall not I be like him and also lie down,*
> *never to rise again, through all eternity?*
>
> Tablet X, lines 242-248, translation: Andrew George

Gilgamesh says this, after a great many adventures, to his friend Utanapishti, who has been granted eternal life by the gods, and who, to Gilgamesh's astonishment, replies that all our striving for

515

immortality only leads to worse suffering and the devastation of our short lives.

Mere mortals are thus by definition mortal (and Utanapishti is the exception that proves the rule), doomed to return to clay. The decay associated with ageing is hard to deny. But this is not to say that there are no loopholes. There is an elegant solution to the problem if you maintain that material reality, in which ageing and decay take place, is actually only secondary in relation to another, more real, reality. The body – that which ages and decays – becomes in this sense merely a body, a piece of transient materia, a feeble and worldly object. What is important, or, in a literal sense, essential, and that which raises humankind above the rest of creation, is the body's ghostly inhabitant: the soul. And the point of the soul is precisely that it really belongs to the higher, more real, reality. It is only on a more or less temporary visit to the painfully turbulent transitory world where decay inexorably advances.

In many ways the soul is a brilliant concept, because it solves several different existential problems. It makes the body's fragility and limitations easier to live with, it eases our fear of death, it gives us at least partial absolution from desires we regard as low and dirty (these get blamed on the bestial body instead). The soul is the eternally constant and immutable lodestar of our unquiet and changeable personality, our link to the supra-real world of ideas, and the part of us that enjoys immortality. It guarantees a continuation of the life we are so reluctant to give up – and which we therefore need not care too much about how we live, or perhaps not even live particularly carefully at all, seeing as time, thanks to the soul, is unlimited – at the same time as it promises a total make-over of everyday greyness and exhaustion for anyone who plays their cards right. The soul thus constitutes the very cornerstone of the construct that imbues everything with a higher purpose. It's hardly surprising that this concept has proved incredibly popular.

In its early, preliminary prototype-phase, the soul is seen as life itself, the thing which leaves the body at the moment of death to enter, more or less reluctantly, into the underground realm of death. In Ancient Greece the soul was called psyche, a word with its roots in breathing and breath. The Iliad tells of how Achilles stops Hector, his 'helmet flashing', with his lance, thrusting it 'clean through the tender neck'. The mortally wounded warrior asks his slayer to make sure his corpse is not eaten by dogs, but no measure of sympathy is forthcoming:

> *Death cut him short. The end closed in around him.*
> *Flying free of his limbs*
> *His soul went winging down to the House of Death,*
> *Wailing his fate, leaving his manhood far behind,*
> *His young and supple strength.*
> **Book 22, lines 425-429, translation: Robert Fagles**

What is evident here is that later ages' confidence in life after death is absent from this preparatory developmental stage of the concept of the soul. The soul of the dead man wails, and with good reason. Admittedly, final extinction is not, thanks to the existence of the soul, an obligatory consequence of death, but this is nothing to be happy about when the alternative – the House of Death, Hades – is regarded as a fate worse than death. As the years passed, it proved necessary to rectify this unappealing flaw, if for no other reason than to enthuse soldiers on the battlefield. The same ideological development occurred among the Greeks' neighbours and rivals in Persia and Egypt. As a consequence, those who fought in the Trojan War, whom Homer regarded as perfectly ordinary mortals, are elevated to demigods by Hesiod in the latter half of the eight century BCE. As a result, they avoided passage into Hades and were instead able to spend eternity strolling gently around on The Islands of the Blessed without a care in the world.

Within the Orphic and Dionysian cults several centuries later, the soul starts to undergo a sort of cleansing process which elevated its status to an almost holy level. From having been the power that breathed life into the body, and which left its bodily abode at death, the soul was transformed into an independent phenomenon with a direct connection to the divine. As a result, the soul ended up in an oppositional relationship to the body, longing for liberation. This also brings with it, of course, a dualistic way of thinking: human beings are, on the one hand, the soul, and on the other, the body. The soul represents what differentiates humankind from animals – the elevated, the disciplined, the refined, the civilised – whereas the body represents the bestial in humankind – the low, the wild, the shameful, the barbaric. This division between soul and body is nothing to regret, though. The divorce of the soul from the body is elevated to the decisive existential experience in life, the event in relation to which everything else in life gains its meaning.

Plato adds his full weight to this elevation of the soul. He is also the first of the Greek philosophers to deal systematically with the soul in writing. The imperfect body and its unreliable perception apparatus is a burden and a prison for the soul. Only once it has cast off its physical chains can the soul approach and perceive the truth. When 'the soul when using the body as an instrument of perception, that is to say, when using the sense of sight or hearing or some other sense', Plato writes in the dialogue Phaedo, *"the soul too is then dragged by the body into the region of the changeable, and wanders and is confused; the world spins round her, and she is like a drunkard when under their influence."* (Translation: Benjamin Jowett) Because Socrates, Plato's mouthpiece in Phaedo, has devoted his life to philosophy, there is no need for him to fear the death sentence he has received. Anyone who is distraught as death approaches cannot be a true philosopher, he says, no 'lover of wisdom, but a lover of the body'. Instead, Socrates sees philosophy as a single long preparation for death, an activity intended to distance itself from the body and its desires. He has good reasons for this:

'For the body is a source of endless trouble to us by reason of the mere requirement of food; and also is liable to diseases which overtake and impede us in the search after truth: and by filling us so full of loves, and lusts, and fears, and fancies, and idols, and every sort of folly, prevents our ever having, as people say, so much as a thought. For whence come wars, and fightings, and factions? whence but from the body and the lusts of the body? For wars are occasioned by the love of money, and money has to be acquired for the sake and in the service of the body; and in consequence of all these things the time which ought to be given to philosophy is lost. Moreover, if there is time and an inclination toward philosophy, yet the body introduces a turmoil and confusion and fear into the course of speculation, and hinders us from seeing the truth.'

A soul which has kept itself pure by the practice of philosophy can be reunited after death with the divine and immutable beauty and wisdom in which it has its ultimate origins. Souls sullied by sensual pleasures become, in contrast, miserable ghosts wandering through Hades as they wait to be reborn into some wretched and lesser creation. As a result, Socrates drinks his poison without hesitation, in the secure knowledge that something better awaits him. He has nothing to gain by postponing the death sentence, as he explains to the miserable disciples who shed misdirected tears as they watch the death sentence being carried out. On the contrary, they should be as happy as Socrates is. Death's bell is actually tolling for the philosopher's liberation. At long last, the soul can disentangle itself from the heavy burden of the body and rise into the light to think pure thoughts.

The relationship between body and soul is less antagonistic and more complementary for Plato's headstrong pupil Aristotle. What Plato saw as a fundamental split between spirit and flesh, Aristotle sees as an indissoluble unity of form and materia, two substances in fusion, each of which can admittedly be dealt with separately in theoretical contexts, but which in practice cannot be separated from one another. According to this view, the body is a piece of materia with a certain potential that the soul realises, and which at that very moment comes alive. To be soulless is thus also to be formless and lifeless. But without a body there is, on the other hand, no potential to realise, so the body has nothing to be ashamed of.

The connection between body and soul is consequently not, as it was for Plato, anything that spiritually aware philosophers have the slightest reason to regret, but instead a precondition for life. And life interests Aristotle far more than pure thoughts in an imagined world that isn't ours. Everything living has a soul, people and animals and plants, and the various species' souls vary in their development and degree of refinement. The fact that form is always superior to materia in Aristotle's hierarchy of world order does not mean that the body must be resisted or condemned. Its nature is decisive for the shift from potential to reality. What Plato saw as a necessary evil is for Aristotle necessarily something good. Body and soul are each other's eternal companions. Humankind's bestial nature is not a necessary evil, but a necessary good in order that the humanity in humankind can be realised.

Biblical and early Christian views of the relationship between body and soul vary. It is not merely the saviour's immaterial soul that leaves the grave and ascends to heaven after the crucifixion, but body and soul together. 'And if thine eye offend thee, pluck it out,' Jesus says in Mark's Gospel, and goes on: 'it is better for thee to enter into the kingdom of God with one eye, than having two eyes to be cast into hell fire.' No chance of getting shot of the body, in other words, it'll go with you to paradise in its current state.

In his City of God, St Augustine brought clarity to the question of the division of guilt where Original Sin was concerned. He claimed that the body could not have led the soul astray. On the contrary, it was the sinful soul that despoiled the feeble but, in this context, innocent body. In Dante's Divine Comedy, which also offers a detailed catalogue of every imaginable sin and its judicial consequences in the highest court of all, the entire conflict has moved onto the territory of the soul, even if earthly matter happens to be the arena where the conflict arises under unfortunate circumstances. 'Voluntary love' can, unlike 'innate love' be turned to evil. The trick, or possibly the divine gift, is probity combined with Aristotelian moderation:

> *'The natural love can never go astray.*
> *The other, though, may err when wrongly aimed,*
> *or else through too much vigour or the lack.*
> *Where mind-love sets itself on primal good*
> *and keeps, in secondaries, a due control,*
> *it cannot be the cause of false delight.*
> *But when it wrongly twists towards the ill,*
> *or runs towards the good too fast or slow,*
> *what's made then works against its maker's plan.*
> *Hence, of necessity, you'll understand*
> *that love must be the seed of all good powers,*
> *as, too, of penalties your deeds deserve.'*
> **Purgatorio XVII, lines 94-105, translation: Robin Kirkpatrick**

During the early medieval period the much discussed and influential Irish theologian Johannes Scotus Erigena united Platonic metaphysics and Neo-platonic mysticism with Christian thinking about the fall of man. Sin, a form of misdirected and over-ambitious thirst for knowledge, a product of the bestial side of human nature, ruined forever the harmony of the altogether perfect world created by God; sinful man was punished quite literally with death. But death was, on the other hand, in the good Platonic sense, actually not so much death as a passage to another, higher form of life, a real hike upwards in the metaphysical hierarchy. With Erigena, humankind liberates itself from materia and unites with its own idea, becoming itself in spiritual perfection, as an integrated part of the universal whole.

While religious dogma was calcifying in monasteries and cathedral schools, while Erigena's works ended up on the Vatican's index of censured heresies, while spokesmen for heretical opinions were being burned at the stake, then both competing ideas and the nuances of this dualism disappeared. The dualism thereafter steadily becomes stricter and more categorical. An image develops of the human soul standing passively beside Jesus, like a bride beside her groom, while the body is associated with Christianity's infernal opponents. A continual struggle rages over life and death.

René Descartes bears more responsibility than anyone else for recent thinking about body and soul. Even though he is rarely read these days, his reasoning and conclusions have taken firm root in the western self-image. And this in spite of the fact that Descartes' ambition to balance faith with the natural sciences results in a mixture of riotous independence against philosophical authorities with an either genuine or tactical obsequiousness in the face of the diktats of the Church, a bizarre hybrid that can, admittedly, be seen as the product of one of history's revolutionary paradigm shifts, but which today leaves a very strange impression.

In his desire to attain total wisdom through a philosophical system which would explain humanity and nature in exhaustive detail, Descartes starts from a position of radical doubt. He not only doubts everything he has ever heard and read, but even doubts the evidence of his own senses. The fire and his dressing-gown could have been conjured forth by an hallucination, or simply dreamed up. Nor can the dogmatic doubter trust the basics of geometry. Certainly, a square always has four sides, but it is impossible to reject entirely the possibility that God or, perhaps more likely, some evil demon wants to spread this perception with the help of metaphysical deception, meaning that it is a false belief, while at the same time those responsible have de facto created the world in such a way that a quadrilateral has three or –why not? – nineteen sides.

No, the only thing a sufficiently doubtful doubter cannot doubt, according to Descartes, is doubt itself. And doubt can only exist if there is a doubter who exercises this doubt, whose existence can thus not be doubted. Therefore he too must exist, and this 'I' which undoubtedly exists is the fixed point from which the whole of the philosophical system stems. Cogito ergo sum (or in French: Je pense, donc je suis) – I think (that everything is false), therefore I am.

For Descartes, therefore, thinking precedes existence. The thinking 'I' has no justifiable reason to doubt its own existence as long as thinking itself does not cease, whereas, on the other hand, it is a simple matter to think the body out of the thinking process. 'I thereby concluded,' writes Descartes in Discourse on Method, 'that I was a substance, of which the whole essence or nature consists in thinking, and which, in order to exist, needs no place and depends on no material thing; so that this "I", that is to say, the mind, by which I am what I am, is entirely distinct from the body, and even that it is easier to know than the body, and moreover, that even if the body were not, it would not cease to be all that it is.' (Discourse 4, translation: F. E. Sutcliffe)

The soul and the body are, in other words, two opposing aspects of life, utterly distinct from one another. Each is all that the other is not; the body is material and possesses extension, the soul is immaterial and possesses consciousness rather than extension. This consciousness devotes itself to thinking in various forms, of which the body is consequently incapable. Descartes even uses the expression 'body machine' to underline the fact that the body is incapable of doing anything on its own other than follow pre-programmed instructions.

Only human beings have a soul, which confirms our unique place in creation, a supposition which both the philosopher's deeply religious contemporaries and the humanists of future generations have noted with great satisfaction. Animals have, and are, only their bodies; in other words, they are soulless automata, body machines. And death can, Descartes claims, never be the fault of the soul, but merely a consequence of one or more body parts failing to function. The living body is a mechanism which, in the same way as a clock, carries out the movements for which it is constructed as long as it is wound up and all the ingeniously designed components are in functional condition. The movements of the muscles are governed through the nervous system by the brain, whose function can be compared to that of a telephone exchange. It distributes signals, but it doesn't think. The nerves are 'like little filaments, little tubes', full of 'a certain very fine air or wind, called the animal spirits' (The Passions of the Soul, translator: Stephen Voss).

This strict dualism, which categorically rejects any mix or overlap of the jurisdictions of soul and body, is difficult to maintain for long, however, even for Descartes himself. If we do have a soul, and if its thoughts are to mean anything at all in the material world of the body machines, it is of course impossible to exclude every form of contact. Besides, we can often perceive a link between what is thought, supposedly within the soul, and the actions of the body machine. Perhaps we feel like eating something nice, the soul takes over and thinks about what is in the cupboard and the fridge, and then the body makes a sandwich out of pastrami and pickle. Perhaps we have a brilliant idea in the shower, or wherever brilliant ideas usually occur – resulting in us rushing to the computer to write an essay or a chapter of a book. Or perhaps our souls are simply warmed when we hear a favourite piece of music.

In any case, there must exist somewhere inside the body a sort of coordination centre which translates the nerve impulse into a sensation of the soul, and then back again. We are faced with the so-called psychophysical problem, in other words: the question of how the possibly non-existent but still necessary communication between body and soul takes place. This question is uninteresting and even impossible to ask except within a fairly strict dualistic context, but it is impossible to answer if this dualism is too strict. And, sure enough, the question makes even Descartes soften his position considerably, not that this makes him particularly comprehensible on this point. He never answers the question within the framework of his own system, nor does he adjust his system in accordance with the implications of his own response.

There is a specific part of the body where the 'the soul exercises its functions in a more particular way than in the other parts,' writes Descartes in The Passions of the Soul. He has 'examined the matter carefully', and can state firmly that this part of the body is within the brain: 'a certain extremely small gland, situated in the middle of its substance', in other words: the pineal gland. But how did Descartes identify this particular little gland so emphatically? He used a process of elimination. All other parts of the brain, he says, exist in duplicate. But at any and each moment we have only one thought about any particular object. So there must be a place where the images from both eyes are combined into a unified impression. And there is nowhere else in the body where this could take place except this little gland. From then on, his reasoning disappears inexorably into thick banks of fog. Descartes quite simply believes that his supposition is entirely plausible and suitable. This little gland in the middle of the brain is where the animal spirits of the body and the will of the soul hold regular meetings, even though they, by definition, can never have anything to do with one another because, according to the fundamental rules of dualism, they are two completely different things. It isn't really surprising that Descartes leaves the details of this impossible interaction somewhat unclear.

The psychophysical question is in fact unanswerable. Somewhere in the dualistic equation Descartes and his followers had to introduce a conjuring trick. The apple had to become a pear, but without anyone noticing how. As a result, the dualistic view is not so much a way of trying to figure out the psychophysical question, but a long-winded way of avoiding the entire issue. The explanation explains nothing. The game of patience works itself out, but only in your imagination. The cards have actually been reshuffled.

It would be great to be generous and regard Descartes' many failings as limited by statute. But unfortunately they have had wide-ranging consequences that are still evident today. Holding Descartes by the hand has led not only the everyday psychology of ordinary people onto the wrong path, but also many sciences. As the American neurologist Antonio Damasio writes in his book Descartes' Error, the question is actually where we should start if we are to try to bring order to this vast, post-Cartesian disaster.

To begin with: if thinking really is a precondition for existence, then there is a huge amount in this world that doesn't actually exist. And that is clearly impossible. In actual fact, thinking developed gradually, of course, out of non-thinking yet absolutely existing creatures. We exist, and then we think, as Damasio says, and it is only insofar as we exist that we can also think, seeing as thinking is actually the product of processes in our body machines. Where else could it be produced?

Admittedly, the idea of thinking developing gradually was unthinkable in the 1600s. This was, after all, long before anyone had heard of the theory of evolution and the development of the species. But it is not unreasonable to claim that Cartesian dualism actually allowed greater room for manoeuvre for empirical research than had previously been the case, by so definitively separating the soul from the tangible world, and thereby indirectly reinforcing the Church's monopoly on all spiritual matters. Studies into nature and the bodies which were entirely lacking a soul were clearly no threat whatsoever to the true faith, and therefore no longer had to lead to anyone being burned to death.

However, this happened at the expense of the horrible hubris of humanism. Thinking and reason were idealised beyond all reason. The soulful human being began to regard itself as the godlike and rightful lord of all the soulless raw material around it. At the same time, reason became its own blind spot, meaning that its own mechanisms generally and its irrational aspects in particular remained in complete darkness. This blinding arrogance is unfortunately still with us in many ways today. There are, for instance, still people who seriously claim that it is possible to say interesting things about the processes of consciousness without understanding anything about neuropsychology and neurochemistry.

Another consequence of Descartes' error is that the 'I' itself that does the thinking – the individual which is the firm foundation of the Cartesian system – was granted almost sacrosanct status. The 'I' became the substitute of secularised and humanistic dualism for the religiously contaminated soul, a backdoor to an imaginary thinking free of materia, and a comforting if mistaken notion of the uniformity and unchanging nature of existence. This is an illusion that remains remarkably unchanged to this day, even though it lacks any basis in what we now know about how our body machines think, remember, feel and act. The 'I' became the metaphysical illusion around which developing industrial society constructed its entire worldview, not dissimilar to the way the preceding agricultural society had constructed its worldview around the metaphysical illusion of God.

The truth is that even if thinking seems to exist in the moment the thought is thought, this does not necessarily mean that any 'I' has to exist. It merely means that something at that same moment thinks 'I' and possibly has an ulterior motive in doing so. And nothing guarantees that the something which thinks in the first place is the same something that then thinks that something is thinking. It is a matter of two different thoughts at two different times, and there is no reason to assume that whatever calls itself 'I' on the one occasion has to be identical to the 'I' that does the same thing on the second occasion. One can only wonder why the otherwise so radical doubter Descartes never seemed to doubt this.

Descartes and his error are most definitely still with us today. A strictly mathematical approach to the processes of consciousness and thinking are still widely regarded as an expression of vulgar reductionism which undervalues humankind's rich inner life and which deprives human beings of their dignity and meaning in the world. Because we feel so splendidly unique, and because we so desperately want there to be something beyond the perceptible, we decide that this must indeed be the case. Because it is in the nature of the thing that this spiritual dimension exists beyond perception, the absence of evidence is of no concern. And proving the opposite is just as difficult as proving that Father Christmas doesn't exist. You can never be completely certain, of course. Maybe there are loads of old men with white beards and sleds pulled by reindeer up in the inaccessible icy wastes of Greenland, after all. You can never be sure.

Modern dualism appears in both hard and soft variants. According to a more compromising version – which appeals to many friends of a less specifically subjectivised faith in 'something higher' and various forms of 'spiritual search' – it is correct, from what we can see, that the interplay between the brain's neurones has something to do with consciousness, at the same time as this can never be an all-encompassing explanation. The human capacity for discussing moral questions and maintaining a relationship with God, et cetera, cannot be reduced to chemical processes. Respect for these mysteries also demands that we accept the existence of a spiritual dimension which is somehow woven into life without it actually being here in any vulgar physical sense. The soul retains its role, in other words, albeit often under another name, and with certain limitations in its authority.

Dualism lives on in science in the widespread notion that consciousness and the brain are related in the same way as a computer's soft- and hardware. The thinking 'I' is seen as a programme that uses a certain piece of body-machine equipment, but which in principle could just as easily use a different piece of equipment under different circumstances, with the same result. This is an idea that Damasio is vehemently opposed to. In a similar way, this ostensibly updated and materialistic computer metaphor conceals a dualistic train of thought within the standard model of cognitive science, where perception impulses are seen as 'input', compiled and transformed into 'output' in a control centre comparable to the computer's processor, somewhere inside the brain.

This is a model that the philosopher Daniel Dennett energetically tackles in several books. He uses the term 'the Cartesian theatre' for this imagined command-centre of thought. The idea is roughly that Descartes was broadly right in his reasoning about the little gland, that there is somewhere inside the brain a special place where the 'I' lives and conducts the consciousness. All the impulses from the perceptual apparatus are directed to this coordinating centre and, once they are there, the impulses become conscious and accessible to the critical evaluation of the 'I'. The theatre thus has a stage and projection screen where the impulses parade past. This constantly changing stream of consciousness-making impulses – in other words, our image of the reality around us – is consequently the performance which is constantly playing in the Cartesian theatre. And the audience is the 'I'.

Central to this idea is the existence of a centre in the brain where consciousness arises as and when new content is supplied and without which consciousness could thus not exist. And this is probably what it seems like when people think about it: things seem to glide in and out of consciousness like actors making their entry only to slide out of sight once again into the wings. At any given moment there are a number of things that one is conscious of, because at that moment they are on the Cartesian theatre stage, being watched by the 'I', and there are simultaneously countless things of which one is more or less happily unconscious, simply because they are not on the stage.

However, this spatial metaphor, with an inside and an outside, is misleading in one Cartesian sense. The fact that something is conscious does not mean that consciousness has to exist in any given space, just as little as thinking itself proves the existence of the 'I'. And if you examine the workings of the brain more closely, it soon becomes apparent that none of this exists. There is no centre, no superior function which coordinates impulses from other parts of the brain, no 'papal neuron', as William James sarcastically put it. Nor is there any specific point in time when 'input' changes into 'output', when one might be able to localise the activities of the thinking 'I'.

What actually exists is an indescribably complex, constantly changing, lightning-fast pattern of parallel processes in the brain. That is all there is. In other words: what there is, is this single material reality, plus our experience of things gliding in and out of consciousness like a cavalcade of revue acts. On the one hand are the neurons' electrochemical signals to each other, and on the other is the subjective perception of consciousness, how it feels right now to be the person one is and be doing what one is doing. The question of how the former produces the latter is, according to a widely accepted definition coined in 1994 by the philosopher David Chalmers, 'the Hard Problem' (as opposed to a series of 'little conundrums' such as perception, memory, learning, et cetera) within the study of consciousness. This, of course, is Descartes' old question, albeit somewhat reformulated. The psychophysical question remains, therefore, unanswered. No-one has yet managed to explain comprehensively how that apple can turn into that pear.

Someone who spent years grappling intensively with this difficult problem in his own way was Sigmund Freud, who of course also made great contributions to how our age views the structures of our inner life. One purpose of the psychoanalytical method was, if possible, to build a tenable bridge across the apparently unbridgeable chasm between the Cartesian body machine and the whole of the fascinating provisional map of the more or less anxiety-strewn feelings of the soul. Instinct, a key concept for Freud, which regularly comes into equilibrium-shaking conflict with various censoring impulses, has its ultimate origins in the body. As a result, psychoanalysis was constructed on solid biological ground.

The problem was just that instinct could never be observed empirically, and still less could any connection be mapped between physiology and psychology. Freud was eventually obliged to be content with simply presuming that such a connection existed and moving on. What is interesting here is that the scientifically minded Freud, who admires Darwin and is predisposed to think in terms of human medicinal science, remains, when it comes down to it, a Cartesian dualist in the sense that he reasons in terms of seeking a link between two essentially different phenomena: body and soul. His failure means that the act of transformation, from apple to pear, in practice has to take place behind the closed curtain of the Cartesian theatre.

No-one in modern times has contributed more than Freud to keeping the venerable old theatre running. In The Interpretation of Dreams he guides us round the newly-renovated premises, pointing out the auditorium of 'consciousness', the wings of the 'preconscious', and the murky cellars of the 'unconscious'. Here, the 'ego' conducts experiments in direction which are occasionally subjected to both internal and external attempts at sabotage, and which are continually observed critically by the artistic direction of the 'superego'. The show's script is written by the dreaming, instinct-led 'id' down in the cellar. The 'ego' and 'superego' look on, the 'ego' in order to correct and tidy up where necessary, to the best of its abilities, while the 'superego' keeps an eye on proceedings and makes major interventions where necessary in order to keep the theatre as a whole in decent condition.

The diluted variant of Freud's conceptual apparatus has, for better or worse, together with selected extracts of his spectacular model of the human psyche, been incorporated into popular culture and everyday terminology. We therefore believe that we know in broad terms how suppression and sublimation work. And many of us, probably the majority, also subscribe without any great reflection to the Freudian version of dualism, where conscious confronts unconscious, culture confronts nature, and the link between body and soul is and will remain an insoluble problem.

But if a problem remains insoluble over many centuries, perhaps this is because the question is based upon faulty premises? Perhaps it is time to abandon dualism in all its forms, and once and for all shut down the Cartesian theatre? Perhaps it is time to stop asking how neurophysiological processes in the brain give rise to consciousness – or, in other words: how the apple becomes a pear – so that we can at last realise that there are not, and never have been, any pears, that all we have are apples, and that consciousness is precisely the brain's neurophysical processes, and nothing else?

Of course it is possible to dig one's heels in and continue to believe in dualism, barricading oneself inside the Cartesian theatre in a heroic effort to shut out all information that goes against everything one has always believed, and which therefore threatens to force a revision of one's entire self-image. It is an entirely plausible and common reaction, to defend oneself against anything that contradicts one's intuition and so-called common sense. After all, we can see that the world is flat and that the sun revolves around us, and we may as well burn at the stake anyone who says otherwise. The problem is just that our intuition is not infallible, and, above all else, it is no good basis for reliable knowledge.

Because dualism so well matches our experience of consciousness, its appeal is understandable. The same thing applies to the Cartesian theatre: it feels as though our little 'ego' is sitting there, receiving and evaluating sensory perceptions somewhere inside our head, perhaps even within the pineal gland. But in actual fact dualism does not explain anything, and the problem with the theatre, as we have seen, is that it simply doesn't exist. This ought to be sufficient motivation for a rethink. At the same time, there is also good reason to remind ourselves that it is undeniably a big step to actually bid farewell to dualism, which has at least made it possible to talk about consciousness in a way that has done justice to the sensation of being conscious. Dualism has fulfilled, and still fulfils, many basic functions in our thinking about ourselves and our world, and filling the vacuum that its abolition will leave is no easy task.

This isn't just about our anxiety about the inevitability of death and a pious wish to somehow live on in another, hopefully better, world. It isn't just about setting off as a newly-formed pear and leaving everything to do with apples behind us. The soul and its many offshoots – the ego, the individual, free will, et cetera – constitutes, in many people's eyes, a non-negotiable fundamental precondition if our difficult lives are to have any meaning whatever. If our consciousness does not obey an entirely different set of rules to those governing the rest of nature, we are undeniably reduced precisely to what Descartes so scornfully calls body machines, passive marionettes led astray in an ultra-materialistic inferno. Resistance to such a view of humanity is for obvious reasons robust and comprehensive. Particularly since there is still a lack of considered alternatives.

The philosopher and cognitive researcher Peter Gärdenfors says that one conclusion we must draw from all the collective research into the human brain is that it is evidently constructed to seek for meaning and contexts everywhere. Behind this obvious need is an evolutionary logic: we have an unquenchable thirst for meaning which turns us into compulsive puzzle-solvers, which in turn increases our chances of surviving and reproducing. The consequence is that we do not leave anything to chance, and when the picture is incomplete for whatever reason, we fill in the gaps we believe are there, often unconsciously. And where existential questions are concerned, the meaning of everything, there is undoubtedly a lot to fill in, one way or another.

The soul and a variously diffuse dualism has throughout history been the solution closest to hand, and for a great many people this still works very nicely. But for this solution to continue to work, we have to screw our eyes tight shut against all the new knowledge about the brain and consciousness which is gradually taking firmer shape, pressing ever harder against the doors of the Cartesian theatre. And this is, to a great extent, a matter of vanity. Or pride, if we're being generous. This isn't just about us not wanting to be equated to machines; it's also incredibly important to us that we should in some qualitative way be differentiated from, and superior to, other animals.

Our immense need of a hierarchy blinds us. We don't seem to be able to cope with not being unique, not being higher, not being superior to the world around us. The fact that the human genome turned out in the end to consist of only 30,000 genes – far fewer than the 100,000 which had generally been expected, and not really much more than for instance the 20,000 or so genes that the little roundworm Caenorhabditis elegans can boast of – was a serious blow to the self-image of modern humankind. Research which goes on to strip us of our immortal soul will not be greeted with universal acclaim.

This business of not being unique is not, of course, anything we need be particularly concerned about. The very fact that we are worried about not being unique makes us very unique indeed. Not to mention the fact that we are mapping our own genome and counting the number of genes. We know things that no other animal knows. What marks humankind out as unique ought therefore to be that we are constantly acquiring new knowledge, particularly knowledge which is counterintuitive and brings entirely new dimensions to what we know. What we really ought to be proud of is our evident ability to accept knowledge which contradicts our original intuition.

In a 1995 episode of the television series The Simpsons, young Bart Simpson is discussing the existence of the soul with his nerdy young neighbour, Millhouse. Bart claims that the soul doesn't exist, that it's just used to scare young children, rather like Michael Jackson. Millhouse believes the opposite. The soul is in there somewhere, he says, and it flies away when you die. How does it do that, wonders the doubtful Bart, if you die in a submarine? Well, the soul can swim, is the response of the firm believer. The soul has thus become, even in the USA, something that can be joked about and laughed at in animated sitcoms aimed at youngsters. And, in the focus of our era's strenuous efforts to avoid the inevitability of death, the body machine naturally stands alone. The question that remains is more one of whether or not we really want to succeed.

If we one day actually manage to conquer ageing and thereafter suffer accidents to the same degree as the average healthy twelve-year-old, we will reach an average life expectancy of a thousand years. Assuming that everyone in society has access to the same technology. This would undoubtedly give rise to almost surreal problems of readjustment. But if, on the other hand, the technology was only accessible to a privileged few, this would mean entirely different but just as convulsive problems. We know, after all, that average life expectancy has increased dramatically over the past 200 years (thanks to better diet, hygiene, healthcare, et cetera), and that women in the western world are choosing to have children later in life, which, if the trend continues, will eventually lead to one of the decisive aspects of biological ageing process being radically modified. But at the same time as we make this claim, we have to set it to one side. Or, to be more precise: we will leave it for a completely different book, which will in all likelihood be written by another author.

We have a different agenda: our old ideas of an immortal soul which lives its own life, separate to the body, may be something dealt with in American television series nowadays, but this doesn't mean that the vacuum left by this wishful thinking has now been filled by enlightened clarity of vision. These waters are sadly as murky as ever. It is so desperately difficult to look beyond our old, familiar pride and our intuitive misconceptions. Dualism's comfort blanket is still a source of relief, and materialism still seems comparatively harsh and cold.

So, if there isn't a soul sitting inside a little gland in the brain – what then? What is it that calls itself an 'ego', and which so desperately wants to 'realise itself', and which so enthusiastically claims that it is exerting 'free will' in every imaginable context (apart from those occasions when it is more practical to fall back on impediments caused by external influence or internal imbalance)? Does this mean that when it comes down to it we are all merely those same body machines that Descartes turned his nose up at?

Or is it that the question is wrongly formulated? What does that 'merely' mean? We intend to explore and discuss that reflex, common sense word, 'merely'. That's the main reason why we've written this book.

2.

A Brief History of the Brain

So, there's really no desperate cause for concern: we human beings are unique. We are unique as a species, and we are also all unique as individuals – a fact that is constantly trotted out by well-meaning humanists whenever the biological substratum, our human nature, is mentioned. The real question, however, is: how much of a comfort is this? Every species is unique, of course, that much is obvious, otherwise it would be impossible to differentiate it from other species. And if each and every one of us really is so terribly unique and special as we are supposed to be, it is tempting to conclude that being unique is not in itself particularly unique. Because each and every one of us can make that claim! We are, however, unique in various ways that flatter our own vanity. Compared to other species, for instance, we human beings have a remarkably large brain in relation to the rest of our body. We also have relatively large penises. Some of us take comfort and delight in the former, whereas others attach more significance to the latter. Regardless of which one chooses to emphasise, there is a connection between the two of them, a connection to which we shall return later on.

The size differential between brain and body can be measured using various index systems. One accepted method is to work out a so-called EQ (encephalisation quotient), which attaches a value to the weight of the brain in relation to the weight of the body, compared to an average from other more or less closely related species – other mammals, for instance. The EQ value of any given species therefore reveals how large the brain is in relation to the body compared to how large it might be expected to be in an animal of a certain body-size within a particular category.

Human beings come up with an EQ value of 7.44, compared to the rabbit's 0.40, the horse's 0.86, the chimpanzee's 2.49 and the dolphin's 5.31. Admittedly, the elephant has a larger brain than us, but because its body is so much larger, it has a lower EQ value (1.87). This means that a remarkable proportion of the elephant's large brain is tied up with the considerable and demanding routine requirements of maintaining such a large body. Our human brain, on the other hand, uniquely large in relation to our not particularly large body, is, to a uniquely large extent, free to use its uniquely large excess capacity for other purposes, such as worrying about the meaning of life, the universe and everything.

Average brain-volume for us human beings is somewhere around 1,400 cubic centimetres. Our heads are so large that we are born at an earlier stage of our development than would in other respects be regarded as optimal. Few other species produce offspring that are so helpless at birth as we do, and so exposed to the caprices of their parents. The large head with the large brain is the result of what, in terms of evolutionary history, is a dramatic and uniquely rapid development. Our predecessors on the savannah managed to survive and reproduce with a brain-volume of around 500 cubic centimetres. But then something quite revolutionary occurred. We are talking here about the trebling of brain-volume in less than three million years. This level of growth demands an explanation. How is it possible for evolution, which usually moves at such a glacially slow pace, to take such a sudden leap? What on earth could the reason for this be? Let us begin by looking at what the brain actually is, and what is actually does.

The early development of the brain and its original tasks are most clearly evident if we observe the subtle but no less decisive difference between having a minutely small brain and having no brain at all. Our unassuming little relative (we are all related, after all) the sea squirt lives an ostensibly quiet life on the seabed. This transparent little gelatinous sack sits there, firmly anchored by a stalk-like device, and spends all its time filtering water which it draws in through an opening on one side of its slender body, and blows out through another opening on the other side.

Yes, this is what the sea squirt's entire existence consists of: water in, water out, and the filtration of nutrients into its digestive system. Well, actually, no. That isn't quite all. Occasionally the accumulation of particles gets too large, whereupon the filter shuts off. On these critical occasions the sea squirt is obliged, through the use of powerful muscular convulsions, to expel the entire contents of its gut. The sea squirt simply throws up. But otherwise the adult sea squirt's life is noticeably free of what we might call drama. This includes its sex-life. In its capacity as a hermaphrodite it mates quietly with itself and thus avoids having to compete with rivals.

The sea squirt's childhood is rather more eventful. The microscopic little larva is pumped out into the water and swims about for a day or so looking for somewhere suitable as its permanent abode. At this point it is aided by a brain-like ganglion, a sort of bundle of nerves consisting of some 300 cells. This proto-brain receives sensory information from its surroundings via, among other things, a sense of balance and a light-sensitive strip of skin. Thanks to this system, the larva has a chance of orientating itself in the changing world around it, and can eventually find a new home. Once it has reached the desired spot, it drills down into the seabed and undergoes rapid development to adulthood, thus becoming a stationary sea squirt. An important component in this process is that the sea squirt absorbs, or rather consumes, its own brain, which it no longer perceives itself to need, and so is transformed into food. The sea squirt is done with thinking.

The reason why we have chosen to spend time with this remarkable little chordate, a close relative of us vertebrates, is not to draw parallels to cultural journalists or university lecturers who, after a period of uncertainty and anxiety as part-timers and freelancers, eventually manage to get hold of a permanent post and can therefore settle down and stop thinking. No, the point is to illustrate, following the work of neurophysiologist Rodolfo Llinás and others, the fundamental idea that the evolutionary development of the brain and the nervous system is linked to movement.

An organism that is in motion yet which lacks a brain is quite literally fumbling in the dark. In such circumstances even a miniscule brain, something which can give a rough idea of where light is coming from, is a devastating advantage in the struggle for survival, and consequently something richly rewarded by natural selection.

So it is the brain which makes it possible for even the most primitive creatures to move actively and strategically instead of merely keeping their metaphorical fingers crossed and trusting to blind fate. A stationary organism, like the adult sea squirt, has, in contrast, no need for a brain. There are no decisions to be made about future movements, which makes the brain an unnecessary expense, a waste of valuable resources. Nothing is free, not lunch, and not brains. Everything has a price.

For an organism with the capacity for movement, life is a sea of possibilities. It can move this way and that, right or left, up or down. It can move quickly or slowly, aggressively or carefully, in a straight line or zigzagging. But with these possibilities come risks. The difference between option A and option B can be the difference between eating or being eaten. Even the simplest manoeuvre is impossible without a long list of detailed forecasts.

In his book I of the Vortex, Llinás uses the example of something most people do every morning without giving it a conscious thought: taking a carton of milk (or something else) out of the fridge. In order to carry out this action successfully, to start with we need to be able to estimate the weight of the carton more or less correctly, how slippery it is, and how full it is, and then adapt the grip of our fingers and our lifting motion according to our conclusions. When we tip the carton to pour the milk, we have to predict how much force we need to compensate in order to keep our balance. We begin the operation with a preliminary, so-called premotor evaluation of the movements which might be needed, and then we make constant adjustments to the actions of our muscles during the process, according to the information continually reaching our brain through the nervous system.

But we don't have to carry out these complicated calculations every time, thank goodness. Our brain does all of this 'automatically' – in other words, without our having to devote any of our precious attention to it. In the meantime, we are free to think of other things, maybe our taxes, or death, and how to avoid the former and preferably even the latter. Forecasting is therefore not linked to consciousness, and is thus not the exclusive preserve of organisms perceived as possessing consciousness. The larvae of the sea squirt also produce forecasts. That is what brains do, and that is why there are so many species which devote precious resources to them. To survive everyday life, animals that move, like us, need a forecasting machine with the capacity both to evaluate different strategies of movement against one another, and to implement the strategies whose consequences the machine chooses to desire. And because these two are inextricably linked – complex movement strategies lack any advantage for survival without the parallel ability to forecast their consequences, and vice versa – we have to conclude that these two functions developed together.

The production of forecasts proceeds continuously on all the different levels of the consciousness hierarchy. The subconscious scenario-factory which never stops generates a constant stream of experiences and reflections which get to bask momentarily in the glow of the spotlight of our conscious attention. But the serious work is really done in the many dark corners where light never penetrates. Consequently we never have to carry out consciously the complicated evaluations of how gravity and resistance will slow a body of a certain mass, shape and velocity, all of which are involved in the return of serve in a tennis match. Which is something of a relief. Otherwise we would never have time to hit the ball.

But the job still has to be done. These calculations are necessary in order to extrapolate a forecast of the optimal point for a meeting between racket and ball. We direct the whole of the complex collection of movements which make up the perfect forehand towards the point in space where the ball will hopefully be at precisely the predicted moment, and not at the point where it is when we begin our backswing. With the help of the available information we create a constantly updated, internalised model of the world around us, and, taking that model as our starting point, we forecast future scenarios, short and long-term. The further into the future these forecasts stretch, the harder it is to evaluate the variables, and, as a result, the less certain our forecasts. So we are constantly revising our forecasts.

So the brain's production of forecasts is a precondition for the mobile organism's chances of successfully navigating and integrating with a world full of all manner of other things that are also in motion. But the organism's own forecasts, via feedback, are the true raw material for new forecasts, and are thus a precondition of the brain functioning at all. It isn't the case that the brain adopts a position towards every new set of impressions without preconceptions: that would take far too long, and devour far too many resources. The serve would have whistled past long before we had finished thinking on the baseline. The predator could calmly swallow its sluggish prey while it was slowly weighing different strategies against one another. No, the brain – and the rest of the organism – is entirely dependent upon context-related templates, so called default settings, practised impressions of the normal condition of the world around it, against which impressions gained from a wholly cursory reading can be compared. This is infinitely quicker than constantly having to build up an entirely new impression of the state of things from scratch each time.

In the same way, the brain saves time and resources when it comes to acting on these forecasts. Micromanaging the slightest movement made by every single muscle would be hopelessly time-consuming. Instead the brain and the body rely to a large extent on an autopilot setting through the use of what Llinás calls FAPs (Fixed Action Patterns), pre-programmed modules of coordinated patterns of movement. Using all of our attention to cross the room or walk a few blocks would be paralysing. So this act of walking is an FAP module delegated as far down the system as possible, and is self-regulating as long as nothing unexpected triggers the alarm and requires extraordinary actions, such as consciously stepping to one side to avoid treading in dog's mess.

A small degree of understanding of this basic need of the brain to simplify as much as possible leads to a large degree of humility. Otherwise one could imagine arrogant human beings pitying the sea squirt's larvae in the belief that these are reliant on simple and incomplete representations of reality, while we ourselves are blessed with a perceptual apparatus so advanced, and a brain so richly equipped and disinterested that we perceive reality precisely as it really is. Nothing could be more wrong. Just like the larvae of the sea squirt, and everything else, we too are in permanent thrall to pragmatic simplification.

The task of the brain is not to furnish the truth about existence, but to be as functional a forecast machine as circumstances allow. We never have direct contact with reality, which is never within reach, but must make do with the brain's heavy-handed version of it.

The fire-engine is not red and the grass is not green in the real world, but only inside our heads: the colours are the result of our brains' particular way of interpreting energies of certain wavelengths. There are countless other ways of seeing exactly the same thing. As Llinás points out, snakes have infrared vision, with is actually the same as thermal radiation. Bats hear ultrasound, far above the frequencies we human beings can perceive. Radio-waves certainly seem to exist in reality, even though we lack the capacity to pick up on them without tools.

Our brain simply does not receive signals emitted by reality that do not address our peculiarly selective sensory organs. And those signals which do reach the brain in spite of this are always, without exception, simplified translations. Or, as the father of modernism, Immanuel Kant put it: the noumenal reality around us, and even within us, is and will remain an unapproachable mystery. The phenomenal world in which we imagine that we live is our own creation. It is thus not the case that the problem – in so far as it can be seen as a problem – lies in our not understanding the original (and therefore requiring it to be translated). We simply do not have access to the original. It isn't even of interest to us. A narrow selection of external impulses – photons, sound-waves, et cetera – are transformed into bioelectrical activity in the nervous system, patterns which in turn are interpreted and manipulated within the brain. We live and die among these phenomena, the representations we ourselves fashion from our surroundings.

There is therefore no philosophical difference to speak of between human beings and the larvae of the sea squirt. But there are other ways of looking at it, of course. Human beings are, in spite of everything, unique in their own way. We are relatively generously equipped as far as our capacity to forecast is concerned, and thus have, for better or worse, what is usually described as a rich inner life. We don't just form perceptions of how other bodies in motion move around; we also have the capacity to imagine what other human beings are imagining.

This capacity – known as the 'theory of mind' in modern philosophy – complicates our social lives in interesting ways. We believe we know what other people think and believe, what they want, what they are feeling. We presume that other people have the same capacity that we ourselves have, which complicates matters further. Other people's intentions are perhaps not always benevolent. Perhaps they are using their rich inner life for some form of deception. There is therefore often good reason to reflect upon what others believe and know about what we ourselves believe and know about what they believe and know, and so on. By thinking one or more steps further than others, it is possible to gain a strategic advantage. Other animals certainly conduct their daily battle for survival and reproduction under considerably simpler conditions, at least from an intellectual perspective.

Our rich inner life inflates our lofty thoughts about ourselves, and is the cause of a good deal of self-reflexive flattery. Our consciousness encompasses so much more than others. We can consider our own mortality and try to fill our spiritual life with something we call meaning. We look further ahead than other animals and can, with a certain measure of self-control (such a simple thing!), suppress our need for instantaneous gratification in the hope of larger future rewards. Thanks to our uniquely sophisticated language and our symbolic communication system we collect vast amounts of knowledge. In these terms, every new generation stands on its forebears' shoulders, avoiding the need to discover everything from scratch each time, unlike our cousins in nature. This fact tempts us to share Descartes' humanistic view: animals are basically simple automata that do what they have to, whereas we, thanks to our free will, have the ability to raise ourselves above base nature and follow a higher moral.

The development of the central nervous system and the growth of the brain, according to Lewis Mumford, liberated humankind partly from 'the long night of instinctive groping and fumbling', and partly from being imprisoned in the immediate here and now. Instead of a simple, reactive relationship with our surroundings, we developed an active relationship formed by advance planning and reflection. It became possible to have ideas other than those that were genetically programmed. The really big news was thus the appearance of a consciousness that gives human beings a past, and the whole of existence an historical dimension. Human beings start to create for themselves a unique human identity through communication and imitation. Evolution was breaking new ground.

According to Julian Huxley's theory, every imaginable physiological/anatomical innovation – size, strength, speed, greater sensory and muscular effectiveness, chemical combinations, temperature regulation and so on – was tried out two million years ago and developed as far as it was possible within the frame of the given conditions – in other words, nature. Human beings therefore never exist in any pure natural state. Jean-Jacques Rousseau got it completely wrong. As soon as human beings became human beings, we are by definition talking about cultural creatures.

But all this inner richness, Mumford suggests, must initially have been difficult to manage. Consciousness was merely the tip of the iceberg, the rest was the subconscious, constantly forcing its way out in the form of dreams and all manner of irrational impulses. The large brain brought with it a frightening menagerie of mental ghosts. A multitude of internal voices is therefore just as much a source of confusion and fear as a blessing, from a purely utilitarian point of view.

The first task of human beings with their uniquely large brain was thus not to construct highly advanced technologies with which to control the world outside, but to create tools designed to control human beings themselves. As a result, after tens of thousands of years nothing revolutionary had happened to our ancestors' simple stone axes. But what did develop rapidly were techniques to support the fragile structures of our inner world: rites, symbols, language, et cetera. Over time human beings developed a culture which created a new human being, who in turn created a new culture, and so on, in a never resting spiral. Civilisation was born, and evolution switched, de facto, onto an entirely new track.

Once this change of track has been achieved, the question of the underlying Darwinian mechanisms remains. The size and rapid growth of the human brain is a problem for the theory of natural selection, because this oversized brain does not have any obvious advantages for humanity's chances of survival. This excess capacity was largely used up in trying to deal with the problems that it had itself caused. For at least 100,000 years the size of the brain and the tasks it had to perform were out of all proportion. As Alfred Russel Wallace – who developed his own theory of evolution at the same time as, and independently of, Darwin – points out: all those people who could not yet count their ten fingers had exactly the same mental resources at their disposal as Aristotle and Galileo.

This is undeniably a mystery. For those of a religious sensibility, it is tempting to see in this conundrum a chink in the otherwise so solid armour of Darwinism, an opening for the peaceful coexistence between faith and knowledge. Evolutionary theory may have a few things worth saying about animals and plants, but it clearly can't account for the development of human beings themselves, and their extraordinary brains. Maybe you could even go so far as to concede that the human body did, after all, develop from earlier forms of life; but the miraculous complexity of the brain and the unfathomable nature of consciousness confirm that there is also actually a soul, the existence of which can only be explained through divine intervention.

The former pope, John Paul II, spoke in an oft-quoted speech from 1996 about 'the ontological leap' from the animal kingdom to the first humans. First evolution, then a handy little miracle, in other words. The two different views involved — continuity and discontinuity — are only ostensibly incompatible, according to the pope. The transition to the spiritual can never be the subject of scientific observation. It is a question of two different sorts of knowledge about incomparable grand concepts that are temporarily forced together thanks to divine intervention, which is a priori necessary in order to preserve humanity's special value. The fact that science has trouble here while theology can elegantly untangle all the knots is, thus, not so strange, seeing as God has de facto chosen to intervene in the evolutionary process. QED.

It is all too clear that this is yet another variant of the magical explanation that doesn't explain anything at all, but merely envelops every difficulty in an impenetrable fog. Faith just steps in and replaces science when things get tricky. But a theory of evolution that has to be propped up with magic here and there is utterly pointless. Anyone who acknowledges the difficulty of explaining the rapid growth of the human brain (which is hard to avoid), yet still holds fast to their monism and materialism (which is the whole premise of this book, and a necessity if one is to avoid getting stuck with two, or maybe more, 'different sorts of knowledge'), has therefore to return to the theory of evolution to see if there are any remaining unturned stones to explore. To start with, what is life? That's the big mystery, of course. How can life have developed at all, and how could the haphazard mutations that form the basis of Darwinism result in anything as complicated and apparently superfluous in survivalist terms as the human brain?

Ultimately, life is the capacity to create copies of oneself. Particles may go on colliding, grabbing onto each other, then drifting apart forever, but that isn't life until vaguely stable physical entities start to copy themselves. The biologist Richard Dawkins calls these entities replicators, and all the evidence suggests that the very first replicators were considerably less sophisticated than DNA molecules. The commonest group of theories about the very earliest forms of life stem from the idea of an organic gloop, a 'primordial soup' where organic molecules developed spontaneously with the help of electricity from lightning strikes and powerful ultraviolet light. Another theory suggests that life first developed in non-organic crystals such as silicon. However it happens, life develops. Copies are made. Our planet is approximately 4.5 billion years old, and according to paleobiological estimates the very first life-forms appeared after just 400-500 million years. The first fossil evidence of living organisms dates from another half billion years later.

Another two things were required to facilitate the development of this new and possibly less than enthralling form of life, and for the wheels of evolution to start their gradual progress. To begin with, not every copy should be an exact replica of the original, or, to put it another way: small (or even large) errors must be permitted to sneak into the process, thus producing modified variants of the original organism. The very earliest and most primitive replicators were probably considerably more erratic than DNA molecules in this regard, so that there was soon a large number of different variants for the evolutionary process to play with. The second factor is that these changes have to pay off when it comes to the survival and reproduction of the new replicator. A few variants are suited to survival in the pertaining circumstances, leading to these reproducing and copying themselves in large numbers, while the vast majority are not remotely suitable and soon dwindle without leaving a single copy of themselves.

Nothing in this world is ever free. For a replicator to be able to produce copies of itself, it has to use up a certain amount of resources in the form of raw material and energy. Because these resources are limited, competition arises. The replicators which happen to be equipped with particular competitive advantages, qualities which for one reason or another are rewarded by the governing circumstances, will produce copies of themselves at the expense of others.

As time passes, cooperation shows itself to be a decisive competitive advantage. It arises when a primitive replicator, one of the forerunners of our brain-cells, joins together with a pushy parasite, a prokaryote: a sort of bacterium which can be seen as a forerunner of our mitochondrions, the organelle (the cell's set of 'inner organs') which is responsible for metabolism. This collision was neither planned nor friendly. The prototype cell was probably trying to swallow the parasite, and failed to absorb it, or else the latter tried to invade the former without managing to kill it. Despite their internal antagonism, the result was mutually beneficial: specialisation, division of labour, and cooperation. Different components handle different tasks but work towards the same goal, far more effectively now that they have joined forces.

This effective cooperation is favoured by natural selection and consequently develops into increasingly advanced forms, which leads to more prokaryotes joining forces through symbiosis. Single-cell organisms become gradually more refined until they eventually take specialisation, division of labour and cooperation to hitherto unprecedented levels by forming multicellular constellations. But all of this takes time. Another two billion years, to be more precise.

The troublesome threshold between single-cell and multicellular organisms probably has a very simple explanation. To start with, the single cells have to be sufficiently sophisticated in order for cooperation to be able to offer any tangible advantages at all. And those same cells have to develop a biomolecular language – salt, sugar, amino acids, and so on – in order to be able to communicate with each other in a functional and meaningful way. The cooperation which eventually becomes possible also has to offer genuinely decisive competitive advantages, because a merger requires every participant to give up its individual freedom and its ability to concentrate solely on its own interests, something like a marriage. When things get tough and it might seem rational for each individual element to look after its own interests and abandon the others, that option has long since been negotiated away. Thereafter the entire collective stands or falls together. A bullet through the human heart, for instance, does not spare the (theoretically) individually thriving cells in the toes or gut. So there is a problem. All for one also means one for all.

But specialisation and cooperation beat self-sufficiency and isolation in the long run, even in the transition to this new stage of development. Advanced replicators in the form of DNA molecules begin (relatively) quickly – once the practical difficulties have been overcome – to construct ever more expansive survival machines in the form of the bodies of living organisms. At any given moment within our human bodies, between 70 and 100 billion cells are cooperating. The decisive competitive advantage here is the emerging qualities that develop within the integrated cells in the form of specialised, two-way communication, when they form a decentralised system which has been constructed from the bottom up. Single participants start to notice their neighbours in the network, and adapt their behaviour to theirs, which in turn leads to new adaptations in other parts of the network. The signals are thus modified and strengthened into feedback loops of increasing power and range. Complex patterns develop in what was previously simply soup. A lot of stupid components organise themselves and suddenly all become – through a so-called phase transition, when, at a certain critical point, a system shifts from one state to another – intelligent.

At first glance this relationship does not seem particularly problematic. Intelligence weighs heavily as a competitive advantage, rewarded by natural selection. The threshold consisted merely of practical difficulties which hindered specialisation and communication, the preconditions for an intelligent collective. When these difficulties were overcome, the path toward multicellular organisms with a rich inner life lay open. The development of our own unique brain with its extravagant finesses was merely a matter of time. But it wasn't quite that simple.

On the other hand, it wasn't quite as difficult as the proponents of divine intervention and 'intelligent design' would have us believe. These people regularly use the eye as an example of a piece of biological machinery which, firstly, is so ingeniously and specifically constructed that it could not possibly have been the result of haphazard mutations, and which therefore must have been created consciously for its own particular purpose (by some higher power), and, secondly, is constructed in a way which required all of its specialised components to have been created at the same time, which would preclude gradual development. According to this argument, it is utterly pointless to have a retina, for instance, if there is no lens in place at precisely the same time, and vice versa, because the one presupposes the other. The entirety of this miracle of intelligent design (the same applies, of course, implicitly to the brain and central nervous system) must therefore have arisen all at once, and consequently Darwinism's suggestion of endlessly slow and gradual development from isolated cells in the soup to multi-faceted human beings with a rich inner life must be fundamentally flawed.

This, of course, is not the case. It may be true that to start with the mutations happened in a haphazard way, but the thinning out involved in natural selection is almost brutally methodical. Only the vanishingly small number of mutations that happen to be suited to a particular purpose and improve chances of survival are rewarded, while all the others are unceremoniously dumped. Then the whole process starts again from this slightly higher level, instead of starting from scratch again. The selected characteristics pass through the generations in great quantities, seeing as they are rewarded by natural selection under certain given conditions. New, haphazard 'mistakes' then occur in connection with the next copying process, or the next, or the next, and these new mutations are subjected to the same brutal process of thinning out, over and over again. In this way each new competitive advantage is added to the pack. Natural selection is therefore a cumulative process, not a biological throw of the dice. Given this background, multicellular organisms with a rich inner life are absolutely one of the options.

It is also not quite true that an eye, or any other ingeniously constructed organ, must have sprung forth fully developed – whatever this might mean practically in a never-ending process – right from the start in order to offer those in possession of it a competitive advantage. Merely being able to tell light and dark apart in a fairly basic way is fantastically useful in terms of survival in comparison to total blindness, just as the very weakest form of hearing is naturally preferable to no hearing at all, and so on. And then each improvement is gradually refined, incredibly slowly, simply by being favoured by the nature that is doing the selection.

In his brilliant book The Mating Mind, the psychologist Geoffrey Miller transfers religiously flavoured criticism of the idea of the gradual development of biological innovations to the business world. If there is any substance to the notion of an eye or an ear necessarily being created in its entirety at one and the same time if it is to be created at all, and if there is to be any meaning at all to it, then the same ought in principal to apply to a large limited company like Microsoft. A company like that consists of thousands of different people with different skills. There are departments for production, marketing, sales, research, and so on. And a company like that must also, according to the logic of those hostile to evolution, have been created all at once, because anything else simply isn't possible. Who would otherwise be employed first? A marketing man who has no product to market and no salesmen who could sell one even if it existed and were actually being marketed, or a programmer who could create products which no-one is marketing and no-one selling? So they must all have been employed at once, because the gradual development of such a complex and specialised organisation as Microsoft is unthinkable.

But, of course, this isn't a problem at all. The very idea is flawed. Even large businesses start very small, with only a handful of employees. None of these is particularly specialised, but has to deal with all manner of different things. Then the degree of specialisation increases as the company grows and more people are employed. And if you can accept that possibility and at the same time understand a little of how natural selection works, you can see that it is via the same principle, one mutation after the other, that nature constructs biological adaptations. This principle is known as gradual development through progressive differentiation and specialisation, and has been recognised and written about for 150 years. No, the real problem is something quite different, and that too can be suitably illustrated in economic terms.

Sadly, nothing is free in this world. Not lunch, and not an intelligent brain either. Such a brain costs resources which could be used for other purposes. The facts of the matter are as follows: the unique human brain consumes approximately 15% of our intake of oxygen. It uses 25% of the energy produced by our consumption of raw materials, and 40% of our blood sugar. It constitutes, in other words, a heavy drain on resources. Of course, we might retort that our inner life is terribly rich as well. Unique, in fact. We compose sonnets, produce oil-paintings, build cathedrals. Our language gives us the chance to conduct abstract arguments and consider the question of whether our own existence has any meaning. And our brain has surely been more than enough of a competitive advantage in the fight for survival . There are more and more of us, and we are spreading out everywhere, often at the cost of other species.

Of course. All of this is true. The problem is just that these admittedly considerable competitive advantages in relation to other species with comparatively smaller brains manifested themselves rather late in the day. Our species first appeared in Africa some 200,000 years ago: the distinctions between any species and its forebears are always vague, and not a little arbitrary. This means that people with brains like ours were drifting about the savannah for thousands of generations without showing any apparent signs of progress in technology or civilisation. Agriculture is no older than 11,000 years, and settled dwellings in connection with agriculture – settled dwellings are really only possible when food is produced rather than gathered – first appeared a couple of thousand years after that. Written language and its attendant developments took even longer to evolve.

So we might justifiably wonder what use human beings put their brains to for more than 100,000 years. Mumford was probably right in his claim that human beings spent a long time getting to grips with impulses from their subconscious, and that our large brains were as much a burden as an advantage in the struggle for survival. There were relatively few people, compared to other mammals, and they lived a comparatively marginal existence until they decided to adopt fixed settlements. But that does not stop us wondering how in all the world the evolutionary process could produce something as surplus to requirements and luxurious as the human brain. From a survivalist perspective, poetry and painting have to be regarded as a waste of time, and natural selection has never, in the long term at least, rewarded any waste of resources.

According to Miller, the real question is whether there was ever an example of worse correlation between the development of a biological organ and proof of imagined advantages in the fight for survival. The very fact that our brains are so unique is telling. Outsized brains equipped for our sort of intelligence have not become a mass phenomenon ; in fact, they are something that has been weeded out by the process of natural selection wherever possible, in fact in every instance bar one. The cost simply outweighs the benefits, at least in the short term (and here we are talking of hundreds of thousands of years). And when natural selection carries out its merciless cull, there is usually no scope for anything but a short-term perspective. If we return to Miller's analogy with business, another troublesome question arises: how can we explain the fact that natural selection could reward innovations which generate great costs but no income in the form of increased chances of survival, at least within the foreseeable future? The answer is that we can't.

A pharmaceutical company like Pfizer can spend something like 100 million dollars and many years of research developing a promising drug like Viagra. Large profits glimmer in the dim and distant future, but until then the enormous costs have to be covered – for a very long time. In the worst cases, the product never reaches the market: it might prove to have unexpected and serious side-effects and be withdrawn. The only thing that is certain is the immense costs, and that sort of thing simply does not occur in nature. Pharmaceutical companies can weigh the risks, plan for the long term, and wait decades for an investment to move into profit, but a long-term perspective and forecasting are unknown in evolutionary theory. Plant and animal species search in vain for willing venture capital. Every innovation has to be able to bear its own costs right from the start.

But innovations are always a risk in their early stages. You never know how things are going to turn out. A company can grow and develop for a long time without earning so much as a penny. Not that it needs to. A stock-market floatation can generate big profits for the investors without a single product ever being sold. As a result, an idea that investors consider sufficiently sexy can open the doors to generous amounts of credit. Which begs the question: if natural selection is so ruthless, what evolutionary institution would act as venture capitalist and be so generous with its credit as to allow us human beings to be equipped with a brain of surreally oversized proportions, which for many thousands of generations costs colossal amounts of resources without making our chances of survival noticeably better? Who or what found that idea the slightest bit sexy and was prepared to take a chance and solve that particular financial crisis?

The answer is: we did. Or, to be more accurate: our ancestors on the savannah did. Or, to be even more precise: the females among our closest ancestors. And the word 'sexy' is a key concept in this context. Because there is, as every peacock knows, a way of manipulating natural selection, and that's by being sexy. So, for materialists like us, the most satisfactory explanation of the sensationally rapid development of our oversized brains is that the females among our closest ancestors simply thought that males with big brains were exceptionally attractive. A big brain was in many respects a heavy burden to drag around, but it brought its owner many sexual contacts, so the characteristics responsible for it spread around the world. After all, managing to survive was only half the job, as Darwin proved. You also have to reproduce.

So the evolutionary process needs two powerful engines: natural selection, which is the theory that science has chosen to highlight and take seriously, and sexual selection, a theory which for various reasons has been treated like an unloved stepchild. A great many people, experts and laymen alike, have had difficulty accepting that biological development might be driven by capricious female preferences, or psychology at all. As a result, we have chosen to regard the many examples of showy ornamentation found in nature as merely a distinguishing feature of different species, and have shut our eyes to the fact that such ornamentation was undoubtedly a handicap in the struggle for survival.

It is certainly the case that you can be ridiculously favoured by natural selection, and live longer than all your competitors for food and other resources, but if you haven't managed to find a willing mate and reproduce your genes together with him or her, then you still end up a loser in the knock-out stages of biological evolution. Because male hominids, unlike females, have no reason to be stingy with their sex cells, it is only natural for the females to be relatively picky, and to stick to certain selection criteria when they choose a sexual partner. Thus it becomes the admittedly voluntary task, but a task nonetheless, of the males to show off as best they can, and the reward for successful males is the favours of the females, while the losers are rejected and knocked out of the evolutionary process.

If you only have a limited supply of eggs to play with, mating with anyone who comes along isn't really an option, because your offspring in turn will be subjected to the same crude filtering by the reproduction market. But if, on the other hand, you choose a male who is generally regarded as attractive, there's a good chance that your offspring will also be considered attractive, and will thus have a competitive advantage in their own struggle to find a suitable sexual partner, an advantage that will be passed on down the generations. So, reproduction isn't only a question of quantity, but of quality. Focusing on quality is a way of ensuring quantity in the long run. Today's attractive partner is a promise of attractive children and grandchildren, able not only to succeed in the struggle for survival, but also winners in the struggle to find a sexual partner, who by preference ought in their turn to be attractive as well, seeing as this will further increase the chances of those selfish genes which see it as their task to multiply as broadly as possible.

A peacock would live a considerably simpler and probably longer life without its long, showy tail-feathers, which cost a great deal of energy to produce and maintain, and which make it more difficult to evade predators. Shorter, less ostentatious plumage would be far preferable from the point of view of natural selection. But that would make for a lonely life without sexual contact, since the females know what they want when it comes to deciding if a male is attractive. So males with short, unostentatious feathers have over time been weeded out through sexual selection, leading to the species looking as it does today. Here we have an excellent working definition of what a species actually is: a generally accepted, mutual understanding of what the selection criteria are as far as sexual partners are concerned.

But why are the females enchanted by gaudy decoration which makes life harder and steals resources which could otherwise be mobilised to maximise chances of survival? Well, precisely because of that. That is to say: the females are enchanted for the same reason that obscenely luxurious consumption attracts large numbers of willing women in modern society. The high cost is the whole point. Ostentatious excess is, as the sociologist Thorstein Veblen pointed out in his classic Theory of the Leisure Class, a form of advertising, a way for the luxurious consumer to show his wealth publically, as well as his suitability as a sexual partner.

Life is anything but simple for anyone who owns a luxury yacht in the Mediterranean and various beachside villas around the world; advantages such as these are also burdens, because they generally demand effort in the form of management. But if he (and it usually is a he) is wealthy enough, he can buy himself free from any such worries. The peacock's tail-feathers and other forms of ornamentation signal the same thing: here is a prime specimen of a creature so phenomenally blessed with survival-promoting resources that he can afford to waste them on bulky and burdensome luxuries and bling. Feeble peacocks can't manage a big tail and keep it in shape. The fussy female can easily see the underlying truth of what she is being offered. Characteristics associated with wealth are something she desires for the sake of her offspring. And, indirectly, for her own sake as well.

The theory of sexual selection not only explains showy ornamentation in nature, but also the rapidly growing differences between species, and the notable differences between the sexes. Within even closely related species, the females who get to do the choosing are often very similar, whereas the males, hoping to be chosen, demonstrate striking differences. Some prefer one set of options, others another.

One particular characteristic of human beings is something we have already mentioned: our comparatively long and coarse penis, which is yet another outsized luxury. It doesn't come without a cost, and it certainly isn't necessary for survival. It requires indefensibly large amounts of blood which could be used for other purposes, and chimpanzees and gorillas manage perfectly well with considerably smaller penises, simply because their females aren't so fussy about that particular detail.

The female hominids among our ancestors provide the key to the development of our penises. For them, size really did matter. The degree of sexual pleasure was their guide to the ideal partner, and their hypersensitive clitoris was the instrument that helped separate the wheat from the chaff. Miller talks of 'the choosy clitoris' in this context. And because everything we say and do from the perspective of biological evolution is a constant advertising campaign for our genetic characteristics, it isn't so strange that our large brain fulfils in principle the same function as our large penis. In both cases it is a matter of giving pleasure of one sort or another, whilst simultaneously demonstrating general competence and hopefully proving one's suitability as a sexual partner.

So the human brain was originally a machine designed for courtship, a concealed but nonetheless ostentatious peacock's tail. The reason why this outsized organ is favoured by sexual selection isn't that it produces anything useful, but that it produces entertainment. And the more refined the entertainment the better.

At the same time, the female organ which plays the role of the choosy clitoris, critically evaluating the capabilities of this large brain, is the female's own large brain, which therefore develops in parallel to the male's. (A human male brain weighs on average 1,440 grams, a female brain 1,250 grams.) This large brain would be pointless from an evolutionary perspective without a informed audience to perform in front of; the predisposition towards developing a large brain isn't the only thing passed on to the next generation, but also a predisposition towards precisely this sexual preference. Both predispositions are mutually encouraged by an escalating feedback loop known to science as 'linkage disequilibrium'. Thanks to this type of feedback loop, a chance inclination within a minority can quickly achieve the sort of breakthrough that eventually results in a new species.

So, there is no persuasive justification for leaving the explanation of the rapid development of the human brain to theology. In fact, there are no justifications at all. We are stuck with monism and materialism. Our unique brain is simply an integrated part of the body machine, a piece of extremely luxurious and sexy extra equipment that we can thank sexual selection for. It is our agreeable duty to be as creative and ostentatious as we can. Anyone who doesn't fulfil that duty doesn't get to have sex. And their genes will have to pay the price.

3.

THE PROBLEM WITH SUBJECTIVITY

ANYONE WHO HAS NEVER held a brain in their hands should try to imagine something like an outsized mushy, beige avocado. Or, to take another example from the fruit and veg counter, 'a mushy, overcooked cauliflower that's been boiled for too long' (suggested by the cognitive scientist Christof Koch). However you look at it, the brain is tangibly material, an obvious physical part of the body machine. When you see it and touch it, it is perfectly clear that it is just one organ among many others, the liver or kidneys, for instance.

However, the brain isn't just any organ. Gerald Edelman, awarded the Nobel Prize for medicine, calls it 'the most complicated material object in the known universe'. It is, of course, the brain's intricate and unique network of connections that makes us who we are and decides how we think, feel and act in any given situation. No one brain is the same as any other in its detail, not even those of identical twins, because the network of connections is never finally fixed, but constantly developing and changing. New thoughts, emotions and actions mean new connections within and between the brain's networks, at the same time as old, seldom used connections gradually weaken and fade away.

The causal connection therefore works in two directions. The organisation of the brain is the basis for the way the brain makes decisions in any given situation, leading to a given result, which in turn is fed back in the form of experience of a certain sort of situation, which helps to reshape the organisation of the brain, something which at a later stage means that slightly different decisions will be taken in similar circumstances, leading to different results and experiences, and so on, in a constantly changing feedback loop which continues as long as we are able to absorb new impulses and think new thoughts.

This mutual influence, this interaction between biology and culture, means that we can draw a line under one of the most poisonous debates in history: whether human beings are the product of their genes or their environment, nature or nurture. The question is based on a false premise. There has never been any oppositional relationship between nature and nurture: each has always complemented the other. This much is obvious when you think about it. How could nature exert any influence whatever over the behaviour of an organism other than in close cooperation with the pertaining environmental factors?

Certain people, for instance, are more inclined than others to get fat. Is their obesity the result of their genes, or junk food? Both, of course. What the genes 'control' is, in the first instance, appetite. In a society of excess like our western culture, the people who eat most and get fattest are those who are the most hungry – as Matt Ridley points out in Nature via Nurture. The difference between those who are genetically fat and those who are genetically thin is that the former wolf down more ice-cream and snacks than other people. The reason why Bridget Jones is relatively plump, to take a concrete example, is consequently a combination of her genes (which tend to lead her into certain specific environmental circumstances) and Ben & Jerry's (which is easily available in her immediate vicinity). Neither of these could leave any noticeable trace without the other.

The same thing applies to our brain and our personality, that never-ending process in which nature and nurture are constantly cooperating. And that's not all: these two factors, so often mistakenly regarded as opposites, speak the same language, in the words of the neuroscientist Joseph LeDoux. They both form our thinking and our behaviour by modifying the synaptic organisation of the brain. Once you realise this, you soon understand that another poisonous debate – about medication therapy vs. psychotherapy – is also based on a similar misunderstanding. The oppositional relationship has to a great extent been constructed out of nothing.

Changes in behaviour and mood, not least for people who are generally regarded as 'sickly', are connected to changes in the brain. The electrochemical activity within and between the various neural networks demonstrates new, unfamiliar patterns. The fact that medicinal preparations are useful for counteracting many symptoms of illness is indisputable. Some forms of psychotherapy can also show results when it comes to modifying behaviour and thinking. And although adherents of both camps often regard one another as enemies, the fact is that these two forms of treatment speak the same language when it comes down to it. There is, quite simply, no other language in which to address a brain, healthy or sick. For both methods, success is a question of managing to direct neural activity into patterns, old or new, which are functional. And this can either be done from the inside, so to speak, with chemicals, or from the outside, with new ways of thinking, new lessons which leave new impressions in the brain's multiplicity of connections, thus leading its traffic onto new paths.

Subjective experiences and electrochemical activity in the brain's many networks are therefore not two different things, but exactly the same thing seen from two different perspectives. Either a treatment of psychotherapy is also biological/pharmaceutical insofar as it modifies to some extent the flow of traffic in the brain which governs the problems the patient is experiencing, or else it misses its target entirely. Either the therapist speaks the brain's language, or he or she is talking nonsense.

Many billions of voices babble incessantly in this electrochemical lingua franca within every human brain. The neurones, often called nerve- or brain-cells, are the basic elements of the brain's extensive activity. There are something like 100 billion active neurones in a human brain, and the activity of these frenetic networkers consists of receiving and transmitting information in the form of electrical impulses to and from each other. More or less temporary coalitions of neurones cooperate and compete with each other in turn, in ever-changing patterns. Alliances appear and disappear and reappear again. Solidarity is established, unions sealed through the temporal synchronisation of the emission of impulses from active neurones, even across relatively large distances. This is also to a large extent a question of timing. A small number of impulses, synchronised within a single millisecond, can have a considerably more powerful effect than far more of them spread over an interval of, let us say, 25 milliseconds.

The neurones get nutrition and various other services (protection in the form of encapsulation, waste-disposal, et cetera) from approximately ten times the number of glial cells, and communicate with each other through branching nerve cells of varying length and thickness: one axon for the distribution of outgoing impulses – so-called action potentials – and up to twenty dendrites per cell for the reception of incoming traffic. The outgoing impulse is transformed into an incoming one in the synapse, the system's switching centre, and the neurone's point of contact with its surroundings. Here the electronic signal is transformed into a chemical signal by the action potential-releasing so-called neurotransmitters, or signal substances: chemical molecules that act upon receptors in the post-synaptic terminal at the extremity of one of the branches of the receiving cell's dendrite tree, where the signal is changed back and becomes electrical once more. And there are thousands of synapses in every dendrite tree.

The reaction of the post-synaptic neurone – whether or not it in turn creates its own action potential and sends it further along the system – depends partly upon what type of signal substance has been released, and partly how comprehensive the flood hitting the receptors is. There is a threshold value that has to be exceeded, and only an intensive bombardment of molecules from many different pre-synaptic terminals simultaneously will result in a new action potential, changing the receiver into a transmitter.

Different signal substances have different functions: some are stimulating, whereas others are inhibiting. This means that certain signal substances, for instance glutamic acid, stimulate the receiving cells to create an impulse, while others, for instance GABA (gamma-aminobutyric acid), reduces the sensitivity of the receiving cell. The last, and decisive, factor that determines whether or not a receiving cell will fire off a signal is thus whether the total mass of stimulating input, after reductions for the inhibiting input, passes the necessary threshold. So the brain, at least from a neuropharmacological perspective, is a chemical machine whose performance is determined by the sensitive balance between various active substances: neurotransmitters acting locally (synaptically) and short-term, and neuromodulators, which can affect the entire brain and whose effects can persist for long periods. This balance is in turn determined by an integrated interplay between genes, nutrition, various environmental factors, and the experiences the brain is subjected to.

This delicate balance, as all recreational drug-users know, can be manipulated with various degrees of success. Cocaine, to take one example, works by blocking the normal re-absorption of the substance dopamine in the pre-synaptic terminals, which leads to an enduring accumulation of dopamine in the pre-synaptic terminals, which in turn means unbroken stimulation of the receiving cells, giving rise to the feeling of euphoria desired by the user. Dopamine is an active component in the body's own programme of rewards, the internal showers of chemical well-being that the brain uses to reward itself when it thinks that there's reason to do so. And this process can evidently be manipulated very nicely if you fancy getting the rewards without having to go through the effort that the brain is otherwise programmed to reward.

The sensitive balance in the brain is never constant, because the effect of influencing factors is always changing. LeDoux compares the brain to 'a delicate soup' whose characteristic flavour and smell depends upon the precisely measured blend of the right ingredients. A bit more of one, and a bit less of another will mean – for better or worse – an entirely different soup. So we can already see that notions of a stable and uniform (to whatever extent such a definition is possible) human identity are confronted with numerous problems of a troubling factual nature.

To start with, it is extremely difficult to pick out a certain variety of the delicate soup and declare that precisely that one is the normal state that one should always strive to achieve. Why not an entirely different variety from yesterday, or last week? And it just gets more complicated if, out of some moral conviction, one is suspicious about chemically motivated feelings of well-being, seeing as there is no other way for the brain to develop well-being than through strictly chemical means. There is no such thing as sober normality.

This is not to say that every variety of soup is as functional and desirable as any other. Over-stimulation of dopamine receptors, for instance, seems to be a powerful cause of paranoid psychoses, while reduced production of dopamine is linked to movement-inhibiting illnesses such as Parkinson's Disease. But between these two extremes there is a broad spectrum of possible and more or less practical variants. And of course there are considerably more types of neurotransmitter than dopamine alone, substances that we don't have time to go into in more detail, which mean that the flavour and smell of the delicate soup is constantly changing.

The chemical machine is forever refining the content of its own soup, both according to its own inclination and as a reaction to various external factors. Stress is a common example of the latter. In a stressful situation, a process starts within the amygdala, a part of the brain situated just below the temple, which leads to the adrenal glands releasing the steroid hormone cortisol into the blood, which makes the body mobilise its resources to meet the current challenge. The cortisol that reaches the brain is absorbed by receptors in a part of the brain close to the amygdala: the hippocampus, where the body's ongoing stress-management, in the form of cortisol production, is regulated.

As a short-term solution to a temporary problem this modification of the soup recipe is excellent in every respect. But that isn't to say that sloppy soup with excessive levels of cortisol wouldn't have devastating repercussions for the hippocampus. The dendrites contract and the cells within a certain area start to die, which in turn leads to depression, sleep-disturbance, memory loss, anxiety attacks, erratic weight loss or gain, and various other unpleasant consequences. The chemical machine has simply not had time to adapt to modern society's relatively new circumstances, such as permanent stress in the form of a strictly regulated working life and mortgage repayments over a long, unbroken period of time. And because the machine is no longer entirely suited to these circumstances, there is nowadays a broad requirement for external assistance in adjusting the chemical balance of the soup.

But chemistry is only one aspect of the matter. The system of connections is also in a constant state of development. The tree-like form of the dendrites is the optimum structure for prioritising desirable connections and allowing room for the thousands of synapses which pass information to every individual neurone. Yet this is still not enough. There is a permanent state of silent Darwinian struggle for synaptic space. And the only path to success in this struggle is intense activity. Passivity means that connections will gradually wither, whereupon the synapse will eventually vanish and its space be taken by a competitor.

These connections require constant maintenance. And this activity is also required to keep the individual neurones in good long-term health, otherwise they would atrophy just like muscles that are rarely or never used. In this way, the brain resembles a building site where the work never stops, and where the plans are constantly being revised. What is missing, however, is a site manager who has oversight of the whole project. Within the genetically given architectural frame, this ongoing series of decisions is taken collectively through grassroots democracy where the most involved participants together decide the agenda. But it is impossible to determine what is cause and what effect within these processes. Individual players exert influence on the organisation of the network while the network regulates the activities of the individual players.

In the final stages of pregnancy the foetus produces neurones as fast as it can. During the most intensive period up to a quarter of a million neurones are made every minute. These are gathered in various clusters that inhabit what will eventually develop into the brain.

Clear patterns begin to arise, layer settling upon layer. And when the neurones have arrived in their final destinations, they start sending out shoots and connecting to others. A so-called growth cone at the point of the contact-seeking and growing shoot navigates towards a target which might be close or distant, by feeling its way from the protein signals around it. In this way a preliminary structure is constructed, according to predetermined instructions which are primarily of genetic origin.

But this is only the beginning. There are several billion synapses which need to be linked, and defend their existence through utility. Development enters an epigenic phase, in which patterns of neural activity lead the way. A complex circumstantial interplay arises in which some synapses establish themselves at the cost of others, in a constant battle of life and death. A never-ending selection process sorts out the synapses that are not part of the more frequent activity patterns, and which are therefore not used enough to maintain their positions in the branches of the dendritic tree. Simultaneously, existing synapses favour certain patterns of activity, and thus also a certain repertoire of behaviours. Coalitions are formed and reinforced through the fact that neurones which fire off at the same time also have a marked tendency to join together in networks. As the Canadian scientist, Donald Hebb, put it in the late 1940s: 'Cells that fire together wire together'. Then, when any of the networked neurones is stimulated, it in turn stimulates the others.

So, evolutionary principles are active on both the small and the large scale. Edelman uses the concept of 'neural Darwinism' for the antagonistic relationship between the many synaptic populations of the brain. Survival and reproduction have their equivalents on the level of the individual neurone in survival and influence over the actions of the organism. Synapses choose behaviours which in turn choose synapses, and so on. These connections can certainly be modified at a later stage, but not all of them, and not to any extent. The early developmental stage of the brain is critical, because the learning that is not done within a certain temporary window of opportunity is impossible to do at all after that.

It is simply too late. Certain fundamental connections are already in place, and cannot be undone. This might, for instance, involve stereoscopic sight, the ability to connect two different, partially overlapping and contradictory images from each eye into a single common image that is also three-dimensional. This is something the brain has to learn with the help of the right external stimulation (in the form of two contradictory impulses from the eyes, from two different perspectives) within a certain critical period. Experiments on animals, where one eye is kept shut until the window has closed, have shown that damage or neglect in this area is impossible to rectify later on.

To begin with, the neurones network with those close to them, but also in some cases via extremely long axons with select cells in more distant regions. Each cell is directly connected to about one percent of its potential partners within comfortable reach, but every neurone is simultaneously – because each individual member of the network has multiple loyalties – indirectly connected to every other neurone in the brain via serial synapses. In this way, the interactive populations form small-world networks, where masses of local clusters with many internal and partially overlapping connections contain a few nodes that connect to other clusters in distant regions. With this structure, a signal that starts to circulate within a particular module in one of the different parts of the brain can, in the right circumstances, quickly reach countless other modules via these long-distance connections, and thereby achieve a global effect. All the innumerable functions within this vast, branching system are only a few steps from one another, and together they comprise a single coordinated whole.

There are many advantages to such a system: effectiveness, speed, and stability. Impulses in any given module can, in practical terms, immediately stimulate other units to joint, synchronised action on a large scale. And if any of the modules is knocked out for some reason, there are usually enough alternative routes for the signals to get through. This pattern of connections, which at first glance can seem messy and arbitrary – all these thousands of kilometres of muddled connections within every head – is actually a precondition for the brain to be able to construct any form of comprehensible and cohesive idea of what is going on around it, and then make quick decisions on what action is most suited to any given situation.

The interesting thing about the never-ending traffic rushing through this nest of nerve-threads is that to a very large extent (some claim up to something like 90 percent) it consists of parallel feedback to and fro between the different levels of the brain. So we have to discard any old notions about signals from the sensory organs being sorted and gradually sent upwards through a hierarchically constructed apparatus for information management, until they finally reach a command centre where the relevant response is calculated, coordinated and despatched. There is, admittedly, a form of hierarchy and specialisation, but certainly no command centre. And the brain is primarily concerned with conferring with itself. The subconscious is not dependent on external stimuli. It is a self-perpetuating process.

Every neurone is in part an individual player that forms a collective together with its neighbours, and in part an obedient underling forced to follow the will of the collective. Interactivity arises when the complexity of the network crosses a certain threshold. Upon this bifurcation, or phase transition, the neural population gets a life of its own, its own identity, which both influences and is influenced by the actions of the individual players. Consequently, linear causality ceases to apply in this new state. It becomes meaningless to ask if it is the actions of the individual neurones which causes the specific patterns of activity of the collective at any given moment, or if, in contrast, it is the collective which dictates the activities of the individual cells, simply because one does not precede the other. Simultaneity makes it impossible to determine what is cause and what effect. In the same way, it is impossible to map out which specific neurone gets the other neurones either to fire off or wait and see. The system is – like, for instance, fires, hurricanes and crowds of people – non-linear, and can only be understood as a totality.

The dynamic in question here can nowadays be observed and copied, at least in broad strokes, with the help of various sorts of scanning technology like PET (positron emission tomography) and

FMRI (functional magnetic resonance imaging), but cannot, on the other hand, be predicted with any great degree of precision. The number of variables is astronomical. The brain constantly conducts negotiations with itself via parallel feedback loops. The different modules each have their own agenda, fighting an ongoing Darwinian battle to set their mark on the collective decision. Various needs fight for the highest priority, countless voices babble simultaneously. The ecosystem is an echo chamber comparable to a gigantic parliament.

The neurones' activity at module level forms patterns which reflect temporary coalitions which all reflect a particular special interest, a perception of what is most important at that moment: a sensory perception, an internal warning signal, a painful memory, et cetera. These coalitions can, as Koch suggests, be compared to political parties which, in the form of ever larger alliances, fight for the privilege of defining the issues. You could even, like Steven Johnson, see the many modules of the brain as instruments in a large orchestra improvising without the help of a score. The various sections each play their own melody, but some of them gain the initiative and manage to get the whole of the collective to join in with them. Some sections join in with the melody while others fall back and play their own tunes for themselves as a scarcely perceptible background noise.

The orchestra sticks to the same tune until one of the previously subordinate sections can mobilise enough support to take the initiative and pick the tune, or, in other words, fix it as the focus of attention. The orchestra has, thus, no conductor. Instead, like a swarm of bees or an anthill, it applies a self-organising collective intelligence to effect the ongoing process of taking necessary decisions. This is all about coordination through communication. The orchestra listens to itself very carefully, taking notes, and sending out a constant stream of new and modified signals to itself, signals which are in turn dealt with in each of the spread of modules, which function as referral bodies in this context, and which in turn send new and modified signals out into the system.

This activity never stops. The brain is working even during sleep. Consciousness is constantly working to form a functional idea of what is going on around it and, like a talented chess-player, produce and evaluate different strategies for all imaginable situations that could arise within the near or distant future with the help of a bank of stored memories.

But wait a moment. Aren't we forgetting something? Something crucial? We started by talking at length about the brain and the neurones' frenetic signalling to each other – in other words, a physical system, something tangibly material. And then we suddenly started talking about the consciousness – in other words, subjective experiences of, to take any example, a gentle breeze on your face or the metallic taste of a Chablis in your mouth, the feeling of inexplicable excitement or anxiety before you make a speech in public. How can a physical system have any subjective experiences, or even any subjectivity at all? How can a crowd of pulsating neurones be anxious about a speech or have opinions about white wine?

Well, we're back with 'the Hard Problem' again, the modern variation of Descartes' old psychophysical question: how does the apple turn into a pear? Or, in the more precise formulation of David Chalmers (the scientist who made his name by defining this hard problem at a conference in 1994): the question is 'how physical processes in the brain can give rise to a subjective experience'. People write book after book about this Hard Problem. But is it really a problem at all?

The real problem is that the question itself stems from the dualistic idea of apples and pears: that the psychic and the physical are fundamentally different phenomena that have no bearing on one another. The question presupposes, as it were, an antagonism which has never actually been established. For Chalmers, a committed dualist, this is a worthwhile research project, but from a materialistic perspective it is clear that the difficulty of answering the question isn't the result of the complexity of the problem, but because the question itself is wrongly framed and wrongly thought-out. There are no apples that 'give rise to' any pears, nor any causal relationship at all. There is no one thing that leads to another. The physical and the psychic go hand in hand. We are simply talking about the two apparently different sides of the same single coin.

Science spent a long time wrestling with another problem which has certain similarities to this one – that of heat. What is heat? According to a theory that was commonly accepted in the late 1700s, heat was actually an invisible substance known as 'caloric', which moved from warm bodies to cooler ones, warming up the latter. These ideas were eventually abandoned, but the mystery remained, as more pragmatic scientists simply ignored the question of the nature of heat for the time being in order to concentrate on how heat actually works. Others considered the relationship between heat and energy, and the work that this energy could be used for.

The physicist and inventor Benjamin Thompson had other, clearer, ideas, however, about the connection between heat on the one side and warmth on the other. His ground-breaking realisation was that heat has no causal relationship at all. So it wasn't the extreme motion of atoms that 'caused' or 'produced' heat through friction from collisions or anything else. No, these extreme movements among microscopically small particles and heat are identical to one another. They are one and the same thing seen from different angles. The movement of atoms and the warming up of a substance go hand in hand.

In the same way, the question of neurones and consciousness – objectivity and subjectivity – is difficult if you persist in looking for a causal relationship, how one can be assumed to lead to the other. This is a question without an answer, a question which can't have an answer, and persisting with it means shutting yourself in a dark, animistic dead-end where materia has to be provided with some sort of spirit if the equation is to work out. In actual fact, the pear is also an apple, even if it looks a bit strange. The activity of the neurones and consciousness are identical: they are exactly the same thing seen from two different angles. Dualism can never explain anything. Intellect, in the words of the mathematician Marvin Minsky, is simply what brains do. The Hard Problem is an illusion, a ghost.

There are other popular ghosts that get trotted out in the copious literature about the brain and consciousness. The most striking example is probably the philosophical concept of 'qualia', to describe our subjective experiences of, for instance, a gentle breeze on your face or the metallic taste of a Chablis in your mouth, which cannot really be described with any precision without resorting to tautology: like a gentle breeze on your face or the metallic taste of a Chablis in your mouth. Another common example is the experience of colour: 'redness' itself in the experience of, let's say, the red colour of a fire-engine. These experiences are the very essence of consciousness, and the point for those who claim that qualia really does exist is that they are intuitively experienced as something quite different to electrochemical activities in the physical system of the brain, that they consequently exist in their own right, independently, and that their relation to the electrochemical processes has to be investigated and explained. This reasoning is once again concerned with apples and pears, in other words – about something being caused by something else. It's the same dark old dead-end where pseudo-problems become so dreadfully difficult.

The person who has written most astutely about qualia is the American philosopher Daniel Dennett. Qualia is how something appears to be at any given moment under certain conditions, but what can and must be explained is why this something appears as it does precisely then, not why something 'really' is (smells, tastes, sounds, appears) in a particular state for a particular person, because qualia in that sense is a fiction, regardless of what intuition suggests. Because it varies, not least as the other half of the equation, the self to which something seems to be in one state or another, is so bewilderingly changeable – regardless of what intuition suggests.

There are flavours which require a certain degree of familiarity before one can appreciate them fully. Dennett uses beer as an example. An experienced beer-drinker will say that he (it's usually a he) thought beer tasted terrible to start with, but that it now tastes wonderful once he got used to its particular taste. But what taste? The old one? Or has the beer somehow developed an entirely new taste? If so, how? Or is it just the same old taste that the beer-drinker has developed a new opinion about? If so, what is his real experience of beer? Is there such a thing?

It isn't easy to experiment with qualia, because qualia is by its presumed nature subjective and consequently not within the reach of controllable, objective manipulation. But you can always conduct thought-experiments. One oft-debated example, constructed by the philosopher Frank Jackson, starts with a theoretically educated colour expert called Mary. This Mary has lived her whole life shut in a cell where everything is black and white. She has never seen a colour, so we must assume that her skin grew very pale inside the cell, and that she has never seen blood, but she has read everything there is to know about colours and their different frequencies, about the optics of the eye and how work is organised in the visual centres of the brain. The question is: when Mary finally leaves her cell and sees a rose for the first time, or for that matter a fire-engine, will she be surprised? Will her reaction be a big 'oooh, is that what red actually looks like?' – or does she already know?

For an adherent of qualia like Jackson, and for a dualist like Chalmers, it is obvious that Mary will be surprised. She is experiencing 'redness' for the first time, something which can't be expressed or described. So qualia exists, and the problem remains terribly hard. But for Dennett – who discusses Mary in his book Consciousness Explained (1991) – this supposedly obvious conclusion is the result of a misunderstanding of the circumstances. If Mary is surprised, it is simply because she didn't get to learn everything about colour, because if she had there wouldn't be anything to add. Dennett's point is that if everything is allowed to mean something other than everything – everything minus everything that is important – then the conditions for the experiment have been fudged and the result is a pretence that was the assumed and apparently obvious conclusion all along. If you set out somehow assuming that consciousness is actually a pear, then there is naturally nothing interesting to say about this phenomenon within sciences which by definition are concerned with apples. You won't get any further than a pious statement of belief.

What we are going through is an extraordinarily slow – and, for many, a difficult – process of secularisation, a drawn-out farewell to dualism and animism, linked to a belated rehabilitation of the ill-regarded body machine. It is gradually dawning on us that we are actually apples, albeit rather peculiar apples, but apples nonetheless, which for perfectly understandable but no less untenable reasons have been going about for far too long telling themselves that deep down they are all pears.

This has a lot to do with pride: when Descartes gives us a divine soul, we see that as nothing less than right and proper. It isn't quite appropriate that us human beings, who are so unique, might be constructed from the same soulless and, frankly, base materia as every other organism, having to submit to the same physical rules as the rest of nature. But this is also about existential unease. Our self-glorifying narcissism makes us willing to believe that we control our own fate at least to some degree, and we imagine that we are ultimately responsible for our own actions, and the reason for this is thought by many people to be the fact that we are really something else, something superior to base materia. So there has to be some sort of immaterial commander somewhere inside our body, there has to be a ghost in the machine.

It is clear that if this immaterial commander vanishes, a lot of people will believe that this troublesome life loses all meaning. Why struggle and long for anything different and better if our freedom of action is merely imaginary and always limited by material frames that we can't shift? A lot of people see the machine-ghost as a precondition for our society being able to function at all. Why put burglars and fraudsters in prison if we're all automata whose actions are ultimately determined by genetic instructions and external circumstances over which we have no control? Besides, deep down we all feel like machine-ghosts if we think about it: we talk of 'my brain' in the same way we talk about 'my house'. 'I' can lift 'my' arm with the help of impulses that 'I' send out from 'my' brain, and so on.

According to the Cartesian logic that matches what intuition tells us, there must therefore be some sort of essential 'I' which somehow lives inside 'my brain' and 'my body', and which in some meaningful way can be differentiated from both the brain and the rest of the body. So the whole of our conceptual world and our self-image are formed by a mixture of woolly wishful-thinking, crass utilitarian ideas, ancient superstition, and the same uncritical common sense that tells us the world is flat because it happens to look flat. As a result, it isn't just the literal religious believers who are reacting against the current process of secularisation, but a broad alliance of cultural conservatives from left and right, and a mass of other people who for various reasons are incapable of accepting counter-intuitive reasoning.

Feelings, memories, worries, ideas and impressions: all this is the work of frenetically signalling neurones. One reason why this is so hard to accept is that these neurones are individually as stupid as it is possible to be. They merely signal, or don't send a signal. They know nothing and understand nothing about anything. They don't see contexts, over-arching patterns. And they really aren't conscious of anything. But once they have linked together and started to cooperate, they can suddenly feel inexplicably excited, get nervous ahead of a public speech, and have opinions about metallic Chablis. A lot of base functions become miraculously talented when working together. The real mystery in this context is actually how anyone can think that a monistic/materialistic view of the matter makes this mystery any less interesting and the miracle less admirable. This collective talent knows, quite literally, no limits.

There are certain fish, the blue-fin tuna, for instance, that swim far better than they should be able to. They simply don't possess the muscle strength to reach the speeds that they quite evidently achieve. According to the hypothesis reached by two experts in marine dynamics, Michael and George Triantafyllou, the explanation lies in the ability of these fish to exploit their wet surroundings to their own advantage. They have developed the ability both to create new currents and eddies in the water and to exploit existing ones, to achieve a sort of turbo unit that drives them forward with explosive force. The point here is that it can be hugely worthwhile regarding your surroundings as a resource rather than a problem, and that there are many biological systems that have succeeded in making evolutionary capital from precisely that opportunity. And perhaps the most spectacular example of this is the human brain.

So this talent does not live only inside the head, nor only inside the body. The brain is fundamentally technological. It thinks to a large extent even outside of itself – as the philosopher Andy Clark demonstrates in his book Being There – with the help of existing and, above all, newly created resources in its surroundings: texts, calculations, computers, and so on. But, to a quite remarkable extent, the brain also makes use of other brains. We are therefore not limited in our thinking by the capacity of our own brain: thanks to modern communication technology we have an inexhaustible ocean of resources at our disposal.

Taken individually, each of our brains today isn't any more remarkable than the brains inside the heads of our ancestors on the savannah; evolution moves far too slowly for anything like that to be possible. But they are participants in an unprecedented collective ability thanks to their great capacity for integrating with an environment that consists to a large extent of other people's brains. In a culture saturated with communication, the brain learns, as Clark points out, to regard the surrounding media as equally obvious components of the basics of life as gravity and friction. And it learns to act accordingly. So on closer inspection much of what we usually perceive to be our own mental qualities are instead common characteristics in a much larger, collective, ability-raising system.

The boundary between consciousness and its surroundings is anything but clear.

It is vital to ask the right sort of question. Certain questions have no answer at all because they are pseudo-questions based upon imagined premises. So it is usually a good idea to test the unexpressed suppositions that lie behind a question that is proving particularly sticky. We already know the answer to other questions, but we continue to worry at them because, for some reason or other, we aren't satisfied with the answers. Of course this is just another way of saying that the answer doesn't match with our unexpressed suppositions of how things ought to be. In these circumstances we have a choice: we can either think in new, counter-intuitive ways, or we can choose to ignore new knowledge and cling to imagined premises.

The question of how far a machine can be conscious and have a rich inner life is one that was answered long ago. We know that for the simple reason that our brain is a machine, a conscious machine. Or, as the philosopher John Searle puts it: 'The brain is a biological machine, just as much as the heart and the liver. So of course some machines can think and be conscious. Your brain and mine, for example.' It follows from this that there is no clear difference in principle between psychology and the area of research known as artificial intelligence, concerned with constructing machines which carry out tasks that are perceived to require an intelligence similar to our own. The fact that a whole series of problems arises when you actually try to build conscious machines is an entirely different issue. This isn't particularly strange: there are still immense amounts that we don't know about the complex structures and functions of the brain.

The point is that these practical problems really don't legitimise any form of dualism, animism, or any other sort of magical thinking. All of that merely means that we have two mysteries to deal with instead of one, without having any idea of how each of them relates to the other. Nothing has actually been explained and the pseudo-questions pile up. Even if there is a lot still to explore and find out about the brain and consciousness, we actually know a lot of important things already. We know, for instance, that the brain consists of materia, we know that it is a machine, we know that it is a machine which generates consciousness, and we know that there are no ghosts or controllers involved. And as a result, we are already a long way outside the animistic dead-end where the bewildered opponents of secularisation are having a rather pathetic picnic.

4.

THE MYTH OF THE EGO

SOMETIMES YOU WANT ONE thing, sometimes another. You have moments when you really want grated raw vegetables, then just a few moments later you're desperate for ice-cream and cake. Should any of these desires be regarded as more 'authentic' than the other? Does one desire reflect the 'true' nature of the ego, while the other is an expression of... well, what, exactly? Temporary confusion, or perhaps treacherous inconsistency? Maybe some sort of personality breakdown, or even a mutiny carried out by hidden forces acting outside consciousness?

Changes – in our culinary tastes or anything else – can be either more or less permanent. In his book I am a Strange Loop the cognitive scientist and best-selling author Douglas Hofstadter writes, for instance, about his wavering attitude to vegetarianism. After a period of doubt Hofstadter finally turns down an offer of roast suckling pig at a Sardinian barbeque, and after that abstains from eating both meat and fish because he doesn't want to be a participant in the killing that eating meat and fish entails. This is a position which appears perfectly obvious and unshakable. But just a few years later Hofstadter abandons it for various practical reasons – it had just become too difficult – a change of heart that seemed unthinkable a couple of years earlier. The question he eventually asks himself, after several more years of vacillation between the two positions, is: are the meat-eater and vegetarian really the same person, or are they two different versions of him who take turns to inhabit the same head?

The questions we are asking are: what does it actually mean to be 'the same person' as before? Do we really know with any precision what we actually are, and what either is or isn't the same as anything else at another point in time and under other circumstances? In that case, what is that 'other', and how do we draw fixed boundaries between what really is ourselves and that other, whatever it may be? If that is even possible, of course.

One problem is that it often feels so difficult to make up one's mind. Either going to bed and getting an early night (sensible) or reading this fascinating book for a couple more hours (fun); either the black jacket (matches the shirt better) or the brown one (actually much nicer). Conflicts are going on inside us all the time. We want different things simultaneously: the various alternatives all have their own advantages, and the question is – which of these demanding voices is the mouthpiece of the true desire of the ego?

Maybe we don't appreciate this as a serious problem, seeing as a decision is always made eventually. The question seems to resolve itself. You can't both sleep soundly and read on for hours; you can't choose both the black and the brown jackets at the same time. No matter how many impulses there are, there is only one body machine. And it would be reasonable to assume that the final decision is presumably made by the ego itself. That feels intuitively right as well: the ego decides either immediately and instinctively, or after more or less considered evaluation of the possible consequences, to choose one option at the cost of all the others, whereupon the ego sees to it that the decision is carried out as effectively as possible.

You could say that the ego is making an appearance here: what Hofstadter calls 'The Grand Pusher', the ultimate reason behind the words our lips speak and the actions our bodies carry out, and thus for the whole of our interaction with the world around us, whose most important and notable characteristic is that it is precisely outside the boundaries of our selves. So we are talking about a sort of managing director ego that is always expected to be able to explain why it did this or that. This is the level where power is exercised and where responsibility can be assumed to reside. There is no higher authority in the hierarchy of consciousness.

But, as the alert reader will already have realised, this means that we have swept one decisive thread of our reasoning thus far under the Persian carpet of the managing director's office. The whole idea of an executive ego that 'makes itself known' through its decisiveness and its ability to choose precisely those actions that we execute presupposes still another level: someone else to whom the directorial ego makes itself known, a level which in turn presupposes a further level, and so on. In other words, we are either in an infinite regression, or a circular argument. And that assumes that we choose to ignore the fact that on closer inspection there isn't much substance to the renowned decisiveness that is supposed to be the directorial ego's most characteristic trait, and the proof of its existence.

It is easy to imagine the following scenario: quite by chance, you run into the man or woman you've been dreaming about for weeks. In a lift, let's say. He or she just happens to get in at the same time as you when you're least expecting it, and there you both stand, alone together, very close to each other in front of a mirror. Your eyes start to wander. You are determined to act unconcerned, or at most to offer a cautious smile. You don't want to reveal the strength of your feelings. But when your eyes actually meet in the mirror, the strength of your feelings gives you away. You start talking a load of embarrassing nonsense, and your smile is nowhere near as relaxed as you would have liked. When the lift eventually reaches your floor and you stumble out, embarrassed, cursing your foolishness. Now, if never before, you have every reason to question who exactly is in charge of you. What power, and what means of exercising that power, does this supposedly omnipotent ego actually possess?

What we are dealing with here is what Steven Johnson calls a 'module disagreement' in his book Mind Wide Open – a difference of opinion between various modules or clusters of neurones. Johnson gives another example: you meet a colleague in the office, a rival for future promotion. He (or she) turns out to be in a talkative mood and unexpectedly tells you about some recent setbacks that could put the brakes on their scramble up the career ladder. It's the sort of revelation that a benevolently minded, or at least civilised, person would receive with an expression of sympathetic seriousness, however hypocritical it might be, so this is the expression you command your face to adopt.

But the fact is that while you are sorry for your colleague's misfortune, at least to a degree, you are also experiencing a rapid burst of schadenfreude. And for a brief moment a sly little smile plays across your lips, completely against your own expressed intentions. It turns out that your faithless mouth serves several different masters at the same time, which is a problem precisely because of the difference of opinion between the various modules.

Your mouth is receiving mixed messages and is behaving in a confused way.

Sometimes you want both one thing and another at the same time. The various subsystems compete with each other for control. Which in turn complicates the question of the 'true' nature of the ego to the extent where it is debatable whether there is any point in presuming that any true ego actually exists.

The subsystems, the multitude of modules alternately competing and cooperating with each other, undoubtedly do exist, just as the desires and impulses they represent exist. But does the ego – the unified and constant subject, the decision-maker and commander-in-chief, 'The Grand Pusher' – exist as anything other than an old linguistic convention? The answer is no. But it could be yes, which isn't necessarily paradoxical. Because the answer obviously depends on what we mean by 'existence'. The ego certainly exists in the same way that God existed once upon a time: as a significant, functional and cohesive consensus (in this case, the collective agreement of the various modules). So the ego is a fiction, an hallucination. But hallucinations can be extremely effective. Just look at the rainbow that appears when the sun shines through breaking cloud. Does it exist? Well, that depends once more on what we mean by existence. We can't touch it. We're never going to find any treasure at the end of it. But it's certainly beautiful.

What would the economy look like if we suddenly all realised that the 100 kronor notes in our hands are really only worth the three ören they cost to produce? Doesn't the fiction of the hundred kronor notes being worth one hundred kronor work precisely because we imagine that the other citizens in our society are stupid enough to believe that the notes are worth a hundred kronor just because that is the amount printed on them, and thus their symbolic value? Can we even begin to imagine a worldview without functional metaphysical illusions? Can we imagine a language without conventions that survive just because they actually work, rather than represent any underlying truth about life?

The answer is that language, like our self-image and our worldview, is formed over a long period of time by Darwinian pragmatism. We use the tools which we have learned actually work in order to get our bearings and deal with the turbulent world around us. And because the ego is primarily a practical tool in our everyday lives, rather than a deep insight into the innermost nature of life, it is in the role of linguistic convention rather than as metaphysical truth that it clings on so stubbornly as a prime concept. The thousands of utopian attempts that have been made throughout the history of philosophy to cleanse language from these unpleasant illusions – in modern times not least within so-called analytical philosophy – have also collapsed sooner or later, if for no other reason than that these energetic cleansing efforts eventually have no language left to make use of themselves. The power of metaphysical illusions over language and thereby also over our thinking is so strong and so fundamental that language would not function without these components.

But if the ego is an hallucination, who is doing the hallucinating? Ultimately, this is a circular system, a feedback loop. The ego is thus, in Hofstadter's formulation, an hallucination that is being hallucinated by an hallucination. And so on, ad infinitum. Sounds complicated? In actual fact it's an extremely radical and ultimately productive simplification. We hallucinate an identity and stick to it. The German philosopher Thomas Metzinger talks of the ego as the product of an 'ego machine', a mechanism which the brain switches on when it needs to integrate the impulses of the perception apparatus with the movements of its own body, for instance when we wake up in the morning. In that moment the ego becomes, or assumes, an ego. And because the impulses of the perception apparatus have constantly to be coordinated with the body's movements, we quickly perceive this ego both as constant and continuously present in our consciousness about our body and existence in general.

Ultimately this is a matter of functionality. The primary task of the brain is not to reveal complicated truths about existence, but to make us competitive in an evolutionary sense through the use of powerful hallucinations which simplify our everyday lives. And the perception of a constant and continuously present ego simply gives us the optimal perspective for maintaining productive relations with the world around us. If we were more sophisticated that we actually are, or rather, if our brains saw through their own virtual simulation and therefore did not perceive what Metzinger called our 'phenomenal ego-model' as a genuinely existing ego, the cost would outweigh the benefits. We would probably end up paying a higher metabolic price – burn more sugar – without achieving anything more than practical difficulties and, in a lot of cases, existential angst for ourselves. In the same way, a language which had been militantly purged of every imaginable illusion would be so clumsy and stilted that it would be impossible to use to describe an existence in which distinctions often dissolve into a mysterious haze.

There is, then, an evolutionary logic behind the immense power of the ego fiction. It explains why our brains are just sufficiently sophisticated and programmed to make us naive realists. We are electrochemical module systems which systematically confuse ourselves with the contents of our self-produced ego-model. For the same reason we automatically equate those impulses, mediated by necessity, which signal for instance food or fear, and the actual existence of food or fear. It is, admittedly, true that we never ever come into direct contact with what we call reality, but that is no rational reason for us to complicate our everyday life with constant fretting. If it looks like a freshly cooked Vienna schnitzel and smells like a freshly cooked Vienna schnitzel, we may as well take out our knife and fork. Because any other course of action would be a threat to our survival.

One vital structure in the brain's system of modules is permanently devoted to relating the ongoing and successively growing narrative of itself to itself. The result – the ego hallucination – is for most people so persuasive that they experience it as the solid rock that can't be called into question in a stormy sea of uncertainty. So Descartes has intuition on his side: the ego feels like something self-evident, beyond all debate. 'The ego' is the obvious protagonist of the narrative, the player that perceives 'my' perceptions, thinks 'my' thoughts and makes 'my' decisions. It is actually 'the ego' that gives 'me' 'my' personal identity, and without this identity 'the ego' would be no-one. At least that is what it feels like. Unless it is simply the case that many of us have misunderstood what it means to be no-one.

Personal identity is a matter of habit. We register physical perceptions and mental processes. We connect these, without reflecting too much on the matter, to an owner and actor who has a certain identity and a certain personality. Thought thoughts have a thinker. The thinker who thinks my thoughts is 'me', the ego, that's what makes those thoughts mine. But we could, as the philosopher Derek Parfit amply demonstrates in Reasons and Persons, just as easily describe these phenomena without needing either to presuppose or construct any personal identity. Certain perceptions and thoughts exist; they are linked to a certain collection of perceptions and thoughts from the past. The interesting thing here is the connections, not going to any lengths to ascribe every thought and perception to a particular owner – like you would with a child's hat and gloves (even though they'll still get lost on the end) – and believing that as a result you have achieved anything approaching clarity.

When viewed in this way, the question of personal identity looks like a pseudo-question. The notoriously inconstant Bob Dylan expresses this idea beautifully in a famous interview with Newsweek in the late 1990s: 'I change during the course of a day. I wake and I'm one person, and when I go to sleep I know for certain I'm somebody else. I don't know who I am most of the time. It doesn't even matter to me.' Parfit illustrates the idea of an identity which, on closer inspection, is constantly running like sand through your fingers with the mythological Phoenix bird: every new incarnation of the 'same' Phoenix is actually a new bird which definitely ceases to exist each time it is burned to ash. What remains and develops over the course of time is the connection between the Phoenix of yesterday, today and tomorrow.

The Greek philosopher Heraclitus' famous phrase that 'you can't step into the same river twice' (because neither your foot nor the river is the same the second time) most definitely applies to the human ego. At every new temporal possibility there is an infinite number of possible egos that could follow on from the current ego. But only one of these possible egos is redeemed, the other egos never materialise. So from a philosophical point of view we are constantly dying. In the end our lives are pretty much just a huge cemetery, a vast, merciless slaughter of potentialities. Because all the potential egos that exist at every moment must inexorably die the next moment, or in other words: all apart from the one that we perceive in retrospect as the materialised and realised ego. And so the merciless slaughter of possible ego-lines goes on, moment by moment, throughout our lives.

But how can something be said to remain, yet simultaneously be in a permanent state of transformation into something else? This doesn't make sense, of course, and it is a paradox that the ego machine effectively conceals with smoke and mirrors. In order to function in a complex world, it is important that the brain's system of modules perceives itself to be a single phenomenon – literally, an 'individual' – and that this single individual, even though this is impossible, also carries with it the same identity from one moment to the next.

Most people are, unlike Bob Dylan, extremely keen to be individuals and to have identities based upon this idea, even if they don't consciously reflect very much on this insistent necessity. It forms part of people's obvious and unquestioned expectations, and they in turn expect the same of their friends and acquaintances. A functional society is based to a large extent on this notion of individuals and identities. This doesn't stop the individual and the identity being constructions to which we more or less successfully adapt ourselves – an adaptation for which we pay a more or less manageable price. This price varies from hallucination to hallucination. Or, if you prefer, from individual to individual.

We are all Phoenix, in the sense that we are in a state of permanent renewal, never staying the same from one occasion to the next, even if we don't maintain the same rate of replacement as the fiery mythical bird. You remember one or two things from childhood: warm summer days spent swimming in a lake, frantic snowball fights in winter, maybe how exciting it was lying in bed pretending to be asleep on the morning of your birthday. Which is surprising, considering that you yourself weren't actually there. Not a single cell of your body – or, to be more precise, not many (scientists still don't know how rapidly renewal occurs within, for instance, the lens of the eye or in certain parts of the cerebral cortex) – remains since the day when any of these events actually took place. The constituent parts of the body have all been changed many times over since then. That is what our bodies do: eat and change, converting nutrients in order continually to replace their constituent parts to keep themselves in as good a condition as possible: 1.5kg every day, which means more than half a ton each year, or something like 50 tons over a lifetime. Fortunately most of us also manage to get rid of most of that.

So who was it who spent those sunny days swimming if it wasn't you? The only reasonable answer is that it was actually you, but with the reservation that it was a different you than the you you are right now, which takes us back to Parfit and the critical connections between different perceptions, past and present. Those cells which are now you are entirely different cells from those you were in the past. So it really is true, as radical materialism has it, that our consciousness is our neurones and nothing else, because there isn't anything else. But that isn't the whole truth, nor is it even the most interesting aspect of the truth, which gets us back to Metzinger and the realisation that this materia – in other words, us – really isn't anyone at all. We've just imagined that we're someone special. Not that there's much 'just' about it. Not at all.

A materialist view of human life and self-image therefore becomes problematic as soon as you peer even slightly below the surface and demand precision. It's important to get a grip on this if we don't want to let all the dualists of this world through the door, all the vitalists and the committed religious adherents of the immortal soul. And this means getting some idea of what functional materialism actually entails, and therefore also what materia actually is.

The biggest hindrance to understanding is that our brains can't be trusted. They don't give reliable evidence. The brain's own agenda is entirely focused on survival and reproduction. It isn't involved in any sort of idealistic endeavour to show how the world or consciousness actually work, because that would only mess things up for no good reason, without giving any form of competitive advantage at all. Instead the brain invents an ego with a fictive identity and devotes a lot of resources to protecting this illusory ego from the harsh light of reality because it produces effective behaviour. There have been many experiments that prove the link between self-produced illusions and mental wellbeing. The brain wraps the ego in nice protective padding in the form of systematic, excessive self-regard, whilst simultaneously running a large dementia apparatus which continuously explains away and smooths over all those setbacks in life that could pose a threat to the ego's survival. Weaknesses and adversity are belittled while strengths and success are exaggerated. Without this latent narcissism our fragile and illusory little egos could never survive.

Of course some people have a more realistic self-image than most, and are willing to shoulder full responsibility for their failures. But those are the ones who suffer from what we call clinical depression. Because when it comes to our self-identity, our brains are extremely unwilling to problematise. Intuitive notions of the ego as the home of identity and centralised decision-making are so functional that our mental flood-barriers against any form of questioning are very high. In the same way, we perceive all of the countless generalisations and classifications we make about the reality around us as natural and obvious simply because we get them confirmed whenever we interact successfully with the world around us. When we put out a hand and grab hold of a book we want to read, there doesn't seem any scope for boundary difficulties. A thing appears to be just that, a thing, clearly differentiated from all other objects, ourselves included.

But the book in this example – like the human body and all other material phenomena, potato-peelers, wristwatches and cirrus clouds alike – is merely a temporary configuration of a certain amount of matter (at the fundamental level, the same matter that forms everything else), and nothing that will last forever. The bitter truth is that nothing lasts forever, except perhaps matter itself (but then in other configurations, and that in turn depends which subatomic level you choose to study). Consequently it isn't the materia itself that is the point, but the configuration, which may be more or less temporary. Different things aren't really different things, just different configurations of the same thing. The distinction we make between hardware and software is an illusion performed by the brain. Hardware is, as the game-constructor and scientist of life processes Steve Grand has pointed out, a subsection of software. Our intuition is leading us astray. It's impossible to set the concept of form in meaningful opposition to the concept of materia because materia is ultimately merely a form of form itself.

Seen from this perspective, according to Grand, human beings are like clouds: a material phenomenon whose shape is in constant flux and whose constituent parts are continually being exchanged, but which still remains the same person or cloud in a decisive sense as long as the system functions and holds together. We are talking, then, of consistency and mutability simultaneously. However, the continual exchange of the body's constituent parts, which is beyond question, becomes problematic the moment we leave Cartesian dualism behind us, because it unravels the boundary between what is ego and what is by definition outside the ego. The constant heavy traffic in both directions makes it difficult to ascertain exactly what is ego and what isn't ego. And it is hard to think of a more worrying threat to the fragile ego.

The modernist view of health and mental wellbeing, strongly tainted by Descartes, rests on a notion that external impulses are disturbing elements which ought to be combated. The soul – or its secular successor, the ego – is, in this romantic view, something virginally pure and original which needs to be developed in isolation in order to be preserved intact and reach its full potential. To maintain this illusion of the unblemished ego, the brain's organised system of self-deception comes in very useful once more. The brain classifies and draws boundaries where it deems suitable, in an effort to make the world around us as manageable as possible, so that the fictive but functional ego can rest as securely as possible in its fictive but functional isolation.

'The human skin is an artificial boundary', the science fiction author Bernard Wolfe wrote in the novel Limbo, 'the world wanders into it, and the self wanders out of it, traffic is two-way and constant'. The body's outer casing no longer looks like a protective shell, but more like a permeable membrane leaking all manner of impulses in all manner of directions. The apparently sharp dividing line between the ego and the world is certainly not absolute, but in fact more or less arbitrary.

The point of this reasoning is twofold: firstly, this is nothing to despair over – the body is a thinking machine which merely exists and functions in a more or less symbiotic interplay with an environment that consists to a great extent of other machines of various sorts – and, secondly, this isn't a matter of some new phenomenon that has only arisen now that human beings are seriously starting to consider modifying their bodies with various sorts of implants and transplants, and exchanging worn out body parts with artificially produced replacements. It is, then, not the case that human beings are starting to develop into cyborgs because of new technological developments making increasingly advanced surgical interventions possible. In actual fact, human beings have been cyborgs right from the start.

We are born into a universe which is already structured by information technology: our species – homo sapiens sapiens – is precisely the same age as spoken language. This structured universe in turn informs our consciousness, which in turn learns to integrate in an even more intelligent manner with the environment which it has already made more intelligent. Humankind is quite simply the babbling ape; all significant differences between us and our hairy relatives follow from this never-ending stream of words with which we construct a richer and smarter world, which goes on to make us smarter – at least as a collective, when it is possible to put into place new and more complex forms of cooperation – and even, in many respects, richer. And so on. To a large extent this is a question of integration through intelligent outsourcing: we liberate large amounts of mental resources by outsourcing unwieldy functions such as information storage and a whole lot more. No feedback loop in the history of civilisation has ever been more spectacular.

All manner of conservative thinkers and cautious generals have throughout the ages viewed the development of information technology as harmful. One of the most famous examples of this is Socrates' tale of the mythical beginnings of writing in Plato's dialogue Phaedrus. The story comes from Egypt, where the god Theuth developed the alphabet, along with numbers, astronomy and backgammon. But King Thamus, known for his wisdom, was unimpressed. The alphabet, he said, didn't live up to its inventor's grand marketing claims, but ought instead to be regarded as a danger to health and a threat to true knowledge.

'This discovery of yours will create forgetfulness in the learners' souls, because they will not use their memories; they will trust to the external written characters and not remember of themselves. The specific which you have discovered is an aid not to memory, but to reminiscence, and you give your disciples not truth, but only the semblance of truth; they will be hearers of many things and will have learned nothing; they will appear to be omniscient and will generally know nothing; they will be tiresome company, having the show of wisdom without the reality.' (translation: Benjamin Jowett)

This is exactly how a traditional businessman reasons when he tries to keep the whole of his business within his own company at any cost, unable to foresee a point beyond which it will cost a good deal more than it is worth, even assuming that it is even practically possible to employ the necessary skills. And this is exactly how intuitive, common sense dualists reason when they seriously believe that it makes sense to differentiate between on the one hand 'external written characters' and, on the other, internally produced impulses and perceptions, whatever origins one might now imagine these to have. And this is exactly how laymen reason even today when they haven't given any thought as to how the human brain has always worked and the savings that it makes as a result.

In actual fact the apparently natural and – to many people – fundamental dividing line between an inside and an outside is, in this context, entirely illusory. The productive and innovative consciousness that conducts this refined outsourcing isn't a phenomenon enclosed within and limited to our brains, but spread throughout and active within the whole of the cognitive system. As the French existentialist philosopher Maurice Merleau-Ponty pointed out back at the start of the twentieth century: we can't speak of senses confined to the brain. The entire human body is involved, so we must at the very least talk of an embodied sense. But why stop at the body as a boundary?

For a start, vast amounts of what we imagine is inside our heads is actually in the world outside. The internal models we make of the world are extremely sketchy and poor on detail: there is no reason to internalise a great degree of detail, of course, seeing as it's so much easier to content yourself with continually checking that the overriding pattern remains roughly the same, then just paying particular attention to the relevant details where necessary and whenever anything new seems to have turned up in the corner of your eye.

Admittedly, this results in what psychologists call change blindness, a phenomenon which has been proven in countless experiments. The unreliable and arrogant human brain believes that it has a much clearer image of the world than it actually has, and doesn't discover changes taking place because it only registers what is in front of its eyes in the very broadest terms. But the brain is not concerned, as we have said, with truth, but with survival. So, change blindness is a small price to pay for the brain being able to concentrate on other things, especially as our surroundings are there for us if there is suddenly a need to focus on anything in particular. This brilliant strategy allows the world, as the robotics scientist Rodney Brooks put it, to function as its own best model, simply because this is most cost-effective. This is the most practical option; we are always in the world and have nowhere else to go.

The brain is also primarily interested in meta-knowledge, as Andy Clark points out in his book Natural Born Cyborgs. In other word, knowledge about how you gather and use information about the state of the world, rather than these basic fasts themselves, which are better stored and retrieved from elsewhere. And this is where spoken language and the ensuing innovations in information technology, the representational systems that Daniel Dennett calls 'the prosthetic extensions' of consciousness, come in useful.

Out of fleeting ideas we construct manageable concepts by fixing them with the help of words. We objectify our own thought processes and thus facilitate thinking about thinking itself, and how to think better. And thus yet another beneficial feedback loop starts to work. With written language, the development of a train of thought itself become visible and understandable. It becomes possible to refine and expand upon a promising but lazily expressed thought that someone else has fixed in writing. The prosthetic extensions of consciousness connect us to the world around us and, not least, to the consciousnesses of other people. These connections become increasingly sophisticated, expansive and significant as information technology develops and in turn drives the development of consciousness.

Consequently yet another apparently natural and, to many people, fundamental boundary is in significant respects illusory: that between our own consciousness and other people's. We would, like Plato's complacent King Thamus, dearly love to believe narcissistically that we become who we are through our own efforts, and that somewhere inside is a unified and in some way authentic ego which we can take care of and nurture until it is in full bloom, if only we can manage to mobilise our integrity and protect this fragile little seed from 'alien signs from outside'. But without alien signs from outside there won't be anything to burst into bloom, and in the end the opposite happens, as Julius Caesar is reputed to have said: 'it is impossible not to become what others believe you are'.

The fact is that we are constantly forcing our way into each other, just as we are always being penetrated by others. At this very moment, dear reader, your consciousness is being invaded by the two of us, Alexander Bard and Jan Söderqvist. And during the long process of writing, naturally we occupy and influence each other's consciousnesses the whole time, whilst we simultaneously invite all manner of other people to rearrange our innermost nooks and crannies through all manner of different media. Trying to maintain clear boundaries between one consciousness and another is impossible, and wouldn't be worth striving for even if it were possible. The process of consciousness is a group activity, and it is largely the generous influence of other people that makes us the people we are. Each and every one of us is a mutable synthesis of different people who for one reason or other have made an impression that led to an expression.

We are, then, not indivisible singularities, but rather highly divisible multiplicities. We are simply not the singular individuals that Descartes would have us believe, but rather schizoid dividuals, divisible body machines, as the French mobilist philosopher Gilles Deleuze described us in the 1980s. This is a counter-intuitive realisation that doesn't have to be unpleasant, but could even be seen as liberating. The responsibility that has weighed so heavily upon the shoulders of humanism's individual is hereby shared out between a great number of other players.

5.

THE MYTH OF FREE WILL

THE EXPERIENCE OF consciousness is closely linked to the idea of the ego. And the continuous process of consciousness can, in somewhat simplified form, be compared to a game of tennis, to borrow a metaphor from Douglas Hofstadter. It is certainly possible to claim that player A's brain is really only controlling his own arms and legs, but that requires you to ignore the dimension of the game that actually makes it a game. A's brain (and arms and legs) exerts a great deal of influence over player B's brain (and arms and legs), seeing as B has to fall into line and try to hit the ball coming from A. This means that where, when and how B uses his swing is not something that B's brain decides in splendid isolation, free from external involvement. Any player who thinks like that will lose badly. A and B actually have partial control over each other's game and movements, and consequently they also have only partial control over their own game and their own movements. The decisive factor affecting how both A and B move is the situation itself, and A and B create that together, taking as their starting point a great number of interacting variables which are either given from the outset (the playing surface, gravity, air-resistance, the rules of the game) or arise regardless outside the players' control (weather, wind, their current condition).

In a situation where two or more people's consciousnesses are interacting in organised and more or less constant forms, distinct patterns generally develop. A and B (and C and D) specialise in roughly the same way that different cells do within a multicellular organism, because division of labour brings with it effective management of resources, and because there is seldom any reason to duplicate effort. The textbook example is a marriage or partnership, where different roles soon crystallise and, over time, become permanent. Consciousness A cultivates and develops personalities A1, A2 and A3 (and so on), whereas personalities A4, A5 and A6 (and so on) wither away from lack of nourishment and exercise. Consciousness B prioritises in a similar but complementary way. One partner may take care of the budget and the bills, while the other looks after the couple's social life. They each respond, according to ability and expectation, to what the situation requires.

This is a decisive and revolutionary insight: it isn't me who decides who I am in a given situation, it is the situation. Or rather: I am not a solid ego, a single personality. I am many. I am a whole repertoire of different egos which can be enticed out into the spotlight of consciousness in different combinations upon different cues in different contexts. This schizoid state is not a sign of illness but entirely normal. Not only that: this multiplicity of egos generates many advantages, which explains why it has not disappeared in the merciless selection of the evolutionary process, but instead emerged successful and gone on to become more important as our surroundings have become more complex. Because we inevitably end up in a huge number of different situations which demand different sorts of competencies. As a result, anyone who has a large repertoire of personalities and a large variety of perspectives at their disposal will be at an advantage. A unified ego with a single perspective on complicated problems would, in contrast, actually be a serious social disadvantage.

Even if a well developed multiplicity of egos has always been important, this requirement is accelerating at a rapid rate in today's developing informational and network society. Interactive communication technologies and the construction of virtual worlds with masses of new and constantly changing social identities, where the rate of change is also dizzyingly high, favours schizoid talent at the expense of the classical solid ego. Psychological research carried out by Patricia Linville at Yale University shows that people who are aware of, and happy with, their own multiplicity of egos – people who are simply able consciously to nurture a schizoid personality – are also better than other people at handling stress and setbacks, and that such people suffer much less from depression as a result.

The reason for this is that the schizoid dividual connects any setback in life with just one or a small number of personalities, which means that the other players in the dividual ensemble can carry on performing with undiminished strength in the meantime. It is simply easier to handle a setback if the resulting experience is that there are small deficiencies in part of me, rather than a fundamental deficiency in me as a whole. Games in the virtual world are thus precisely as serious as necessary in order for them to be won, whilst simultaneously no more serious – or rather, no more connected to the collective sense of self – than that the person in question can easily move on in their life even if they lose the game or if it comes to an end for some reason. The body machine is therefore a mental Hydra where the various dividual players correspond to the mythical beast's many heads.

Exactly how extensive human beings' potential repertoire of personalities really is, and how sensitive we are to the demands of a situation, even extreme situations, became clear as a result of one of the most famous experiments in the history of psychology. From the results published by the social psychologist Stanley Milgram in 1963, it was apparent that a frightening number or ordinary citizens were prepared to expose their fellow human beings to brutal and even potentially lethal torture in a situation where the subjects thought that the torture victims' capacity for learning was under investigation, when in fact the aim was to study their own willingness to submit to apparent authority.

The experiment was arranged so that the subjects thought they were assisting the leader of the experiment. On the orders of the leader, they were to punish people who pretended to commit errors in simulated memory tests with electric shocks which would have been painful and eventually even life-threatening had they really been administered under those circumstances. Beyond a certain point, the victims of this supposed punishment screamed in simulated pain, but that didn't stop most of the experiment's subjects – more than 60 percent of them – from obediently continuing to administer electric shocks on the orders of the experiment's leader. Because the results were so spectacular, the experiment was repeated several times in the years that followed. When the results from different professional groups were compared, it emerged that nurses were prepared to go further than any other group with the torture. This might be worth bearing in mind next time you visit a hospital.

Different egos experience things in different ways, and also commit different things to memory. In this way the different egos are constantly refining and developing themselves; they expand and reconstruct themselves by absorbing new memories. This is what all these various egos basically are and consist of: different clusters of linked memories which only occasionally overlap. These memories exist as well-worn paths through the brain, a special pattern of connections that has been used many times and which has become an ingrained habit, to which the brain tends to return for precisely that reason.

But there's no coordinating function, nor any need for one, seeing as the situation in question determines the selection. The illusion of singularity perpetrated by the brain is more than enough to create an impression of context and continuity. Something else that actually exists is all the prosthetic extensions of consciousness, the instruments through which the brain communicates with the outside world and with other brains. But that's all: pattern-building memory processes and communicating technology. In spite of our intuition saying the opposite, there is no privileged end-user, or, to put it another way: there is no special ego with all-encompassing powers, no final, highest authority in any sort of ego-hierarchy. The only ego that exists is many.

One problem with the multiplicity of egos is that a common sense, sentimental and illusory idea of a single, sovereign, identity-bearing ego taking all the decisions forms the basis for our most cherished notions about responsibility and freedom. How could we ever demand personal responsibility for mistakes committed and evil deeds from anyone if the guilty ego can't be identified, at the same time as it becomes clear that the explanation for what has occurred – whatever it was – lies ultimately with the situation in question, and thus in circumstances over which no single person has any control? What remains of humanism's proud flagship, free will, if we can't even admit the existence of an identifiable and decision-taking ego which could conceivably exert this will even if this cherished freedom were even possible (which it isn't, of course)?

This isn't a new problem, though, nor is it exclusively linked to the multiplicity of egos. Within the field of psychology it has long been clear that not only the superior, decision-taking ego, but also the whole notion of conscious decision-taking at all, is yet another magic trick that the brain performs for itself without being conscious of it. Consciousness is never actually conscious of how conscious mental processes work – and of course even less conscious, if this is even possible, of how the unconscious processes work. Self-awareness therefore becomes something of a utopian project when you realise that the self that is hoping for awareness about itself systematically imagines everything that it believes it knows about itself, and that it does not actually exist outside this self-generated imagining.

In the end, nothing remains of the immense narcissism of the history of ideas: in the same way that Galileo Galilei used tangible scientific evidence to force us to realise that the Earth, humanity's home, wasn't the centre of the universe, we are being forced to admit that the extremely remarkable egos around which life has been presumed to rotate have proved to be utterly marginal, splintered, and even directly illusory.

We can try to imagine how the foremost of the great historicists of modernism's infancy, the German philosopher G W F Hegel, might have expressed this. If history has an underlying driving theme in the sense that History (as a metaphysical phenomenon) strives for the unveiling of the ultimate metaphysical Truth, then this truth is not the Ego's awareness of itself as the given centre of its own universe – as G W F Hegel himself presumes when in the early 1800s he preaches the end of History – but rather the opposite: we are faced with the apparently unavoidable de-anthropomorphisation of our view of the world.

Throughout the course of history we have been walking relentlessly, collectively, step by step, away from our original childish narcissism, with the single individual and its closest friends (the nomadic tribe) as the centre of the universe, towards a grown-up decentralisation of our self-image, where humankind is eventually not only reduced to a insignificant drop on the edge of the universal ocean, but even loses its faith in its own enduring substance. In the end, this drop is not just peripheral and minimal, but has been split from within right from the start, and is also, at the most profound level, an illusion. Eventually not even the lonely Ego in its isolated self-awareness is left, contemplating its pure existence by itself, as Hegel triumphantly claimed. After the closure of the Cartesian theatre, all that is left is a vacuum. Not only God, but also the Ego, turned out to be an insubstantial social construction, a concentrated power-wielding device whose emptiness was revealed and whose power vanished as soon as its presumed potential as a device was lost

The technology and network-obsessed netocrats of our age therefore reject individualistic Enlightenment philosophers from the 1600s onwards, and their modernistic project, with precisely the same force and determination as the Enlightenment philosophers in turn once attacked the theological metaphysics of Christianity, Judaism and Islam. Just look at how we have been attacking Descartes and his followers in this book, to take just one obvious example. The metaphysics of individualism are being swapped for the metaphysics of networking. The Net is the new Ego, in the same way that the Ego replaced God.

The Net is precisely the most suitable metaphysically significant metaphor in our developing network society. Because what is the point of history for the developing netocratic elite if not the building and strengthening of the all-encompassing global network? This is the conviction that the film director Godfrey Reggio and the composer Philip Glass prophetically captured as long ago as 1982 in their majestic, high-technological epic of image and music, Koyannisqatsi, the greatest and most powerful artistic manifestation of Californian counter-culture.

Of course it is in the nature of the beast that we tend to focus on what is in our consciousness, and therefore don't question it as much as we ought (at least, not if our aim is self-awareness). What lies beyond consciousness is something which, by definition, we are not aware of, and nor can we be. But this also means that we create a deceitful and narrow image of who we are. 'Consciousness is a far smaller part of our mental lives than we are conscious of, because we can't be conscious of what we aren't conscious of,' according to the American psychologist Julian Jaynes. He goes on: 'It's like asking a torch in a dark room to look for something that is not illuminated. Since it is light wherever it looks, the torch must draw the conclusion that it is light everywhere. In the same way consciousness seems to fill our whole mind, even if that's not the case.' We greatly exaggerate its extent and significance precisely because wherever we look there is consciousness. We tend to forget that everywhere else there is a complete absence of consciousness. And, of course, we constantly allow ourselves to be fooled by our brains' devious tricks.

That consciousness, in the form of our own will, also encompasses – perhaps more than anything – our capacity for taking all manner of decisions is something that most of us take for granted. We turn right or left, we turn the light on or we don't: these are conscious decisions, and such decisions are taken consciously. That's why they're called that, and this matches our experience of the whole process (I noticed it was a bit too dark to read, I decided to turn the lamp on, I reached out my hand, I clicked the switch, I carried on reading in the cosy glow from the illuminated lamp.) The process seems quite unproblematic, but is actually a complex act of self-deception.

The role of the conscious will in this sort of procedure is actually fairly modest, as the neurophysiologist Benjamin Libet clarified in his ground-breaking investigation into something as trivial as what actually happens when we decide to move a finger. The willed movement is preceded by a so-called 'readiness potential', an electrochemical change in the cerebral cortex within the areas which control those muscles responsible for the movement. What is most remarkable in Libet's studies is that this potential change within the brain also precedes the conscious decision by as much as (almost) half a second.

So we need to think again. We have to realise that our experience of consciously deciding to do one thing or the other in no way confirms that a conscious decision dictates the action in question. The truth is that the brain, the subconscious collective of dividual components, always decides on its own terms without prior consultation with the unwieldy consciousness. The experience of wanting to do something and the reason why this is actually done are therefore two entirely different things, and it is our inclination to mix the two up which has given rise to the illusion of conscious will. What we experience as a conscious act of will is a retrospective construction, a confirmation of something which has already occurred, which both confirms and strengthens the ego machine.

If we want to understand this, we have to reinterpret conscious will and realise that it is actually – as the Harvard psychologist Daniel Wegner points out in his brilliant and invaluable book The Illusion of Conscious Will – merely a feeling. At the same time we have to realise that the brain cannot be criticised for this systematically misleading process. Consciousness does its job, and that job is to equip us with character-building or useful (in evolutionary terms) suppositions and experiences. Our experience of a potent decision-making ego which dictates one action after the other with its conscious will is conceivably in many ways more edifying and practically useful than an experience of pocket-torch consciousness and a causality which is so complicated that our actions remain entirely unfathomable.

An illusion which both simplifies the world for us and flatters our own consciousness is not particularly hard to sell to a consciousness which loves simplifications and which is unconscious of everything apart from what it is immediately faced with. It is, as Wegner also claims, impossible for us to keep hold of the countless mechanical influences which dictate our actions, particularly as we inhabit such a bewilderingly complex machine as the human brain. So what we do is develop a summary framework in the form of a belief in the ability of the our conscious will to make decisions and carry out our actions. We choose to believe in the magic of the conscious will, and we energetically protect this illusion against any disquieting suspicions, often by retrospectively finding suitable motivations for actions which have produced unforeseen consequences.

On top of this, there are the religious and humanist superstitions which most people still associate with the Ego and free will, if only because this excuses the narcissism with which they seek to conceal and protect their crumbling identity against the attacks of modern psychology. The stronger these attacks on the Ego and free will from psychological science are, the more resolutely the majority of people line up behind the last remnants of the religious and humanist paradigm. Just as during the Enlightenment Christianity sought to parry the sudden appearance of ideological attacks by nurturing a new, pure fanaticism based upon its own teachings (first in the form of the Reformation, and then just as vehemently with the Counter-reformation), so many religious and superstitious people today respond to attacks from modern neuroscience and postmodern cultural criticism by nurturing a new, pure fanaticism of increasingly extreme variants.

This phenomenon obviously comprises not only religious movements but also the political ideologies with their roots in the Enlightenment which are being undermined with great force. As a result, extremism is becoming increasingly violent not merely among Christianity, Islam, Judaism and Hinduism, but also among libertarians, anarchists, and a surge of different forms of nationalism. The displacement involved in this is striking: the weaker their faith in their own agenda becomes, the more violent their reaction to attacks from outside (not least from modern science). The lack of internal ideological conviction is compensated for by an excessive faith in collective cohesion, militant strategies and rhetorical tactics.

The subconscious logic behind this behaviour is actually: 'If I scream loudly enough at the world around me, I can make it doubt itself and thus stop bombarding me with messages that make me doubt myself'. This explains why the extremists of our era blow up skyscrapers, start supranational wars, try to build weapons of mass destruction, and even censor and shut down peaceful messages and scientific arguments from millions of internet users. The similarities with the Catholic church's methods of silencing heretical critics during the Enlightenment are striking. These methods became so extreme and violent precisely because this heresy not only threatened the power of the church but, above all, also threatened the church's own conviction in its own supremacy. The same thing applies today. Those parts of the world where the netocratic worldview has still not broken through and is already dominant are therefore experiencing a highly predictable wave of high-technological inquisition.

The explanation is that when the intellectual status of the Ego is weakened, the response is not singular and clear, but instead dramatically bifurcated: in part we are acquiring a new, netocratic elite which accepts, recognises and adapts itself to the territorial gains of modern psychology. They are turning their backs on classical metaphysics in both its religious and humanist forms, and are instead constructing a new metaphysics which takes its lead from the monistic ultramaterialism of our age, and using the metaphor of the network to describe and give meaning to the new style of existence which is emerging. The problem is that not everyone either wants to or can accept this new information and live in harmony with this new worldview. So we are gaining a new underclass in network society which, in its panic at the territorial gains made by modern psychology, is clinging ever harder to superstitious explanatory models provided by the mantel of old religions and quasi-religions, and proclaiming ever more vehemently the central roles of the soul, the ego and free will in our lives. And the more lacking in identity and, frankly, ridiculous, this new, global, consumtary underclass perceives itself to be, the more aggressive its reactions become.

This explains why modern neuroscience's unveiling of the false foundations of religion and humanism also has a dramatic and tragic downside in the explosive development of both religious and political fundamentalism. There is no reason to believe that the strength of these consumtary fanaticisms will decrease for the foreseeable future, but rather the reverse.

This polarisation is strengthened by an interactive communication technology which is, admittedly, encouraging a cultural and economic globalisation, but also undermining the entire notion of a common public space where problems arising from all forms of disagreement can be dealt with. This is both paradoxical and entirely logical. On the net today, it is just as easy to find people who share your views as it is to shut out those who oppose them.

You network with those you agree with, and demonise others instead of debating with them. The possibilities for creating a tailor-made flow of information instead of having to put up with a mass-medial standard model mean that more and more of us are choosing channels where we can expect news and opinions which concur with the self-image and view of the world we already hold. We opt to ignore the rest. This is called selective exposure, and in the long term it will lead to a situation where disagreements within any polarised opinion will no longer be based upon opposing attitudes as much as upon entirely incompatible facts. It is becoming increasingly difficult to agree upon precisely what it is that we disagree about.

When facts become something that each of us choose for ourselves when we choose our channels of information, the concept of theory becomes synonymous with pure guesswork. This explains how it is even remotely possible to claim that creationism is an entirely legitimate alternative to the theory of evolution. They are both 'theories', and are thus of equal value. What makes any meaningful debate impossible is that these 'theories' are based upon entirely different collections of 'facts'. There is no longer any consensus about what actually is a fact.

In the same way as the Enlightenment's attack on the theology and power-structures of the Catholic church from the 1600s onwards gave rise to the increase in religious fanaticism at the time – including the birth of Protestantism – during the next century we will experience a torrent of increasingly violent conflicts between new fundamentalisms, and above all between the fundamentalists and the ultramaterialistic netocracy of secularised society.

There can be no doubt that this involves forms of fundamentalism never seen before: the practitioners of the classical religions were, in spite of everything, more or less genuine believers. But if there is anything that characterises the fundamentalists of our age in their various guises, it is that they refuse to believe. They claim to know that they are right, which is something very different from claiming to believe. This shift shows that the fundamentalists neither believe nor know anything, and are actually acting in the dark. Instead, beneath their theological rhetoric is concealed an aggressive reaction against the new, secularised netocracy's increasing hold on power. And if the fundamentalists know the Truth, then consequently their opponents – whether they be other fundamentalists or secularists – must also be aware of the same truth. They represent inexpressible attitudes because they are making an active choice to ignore the truth and the correct facts that support it. So their opponents are no longer simply unbelievers in the classical sense – confused individuals to be won over to real knowledge and genuine truth – but instead people who refuse to accept what they already know deep down to be true and, above all, morally correct.

This explains why today's fundamentalists would rather blow their opponents up than convert them in an effort to win new souls for the Truth. Their lack of faith is made up for by an aggressively denying desire to believe themselves to possess true knowledge. Traditional liberal-democratic condescension is no longer an adequate response to this violent fundamentalism – the sort of condescension which defends pretty much any form of lunacy with a mixture of knee-jerk fondness for freedom of expression, conflict-averse relativism and an arms-length derision of ignorance. What is needed now is open intellectual confrontation where superstition is patiently unmasked and where underlying aims and interests are dragged into the light.

The netocracy will soon be forced to dispense with traditional cultural relativism and replace it with powerful pragmatism (tolerance must of course be intolerant to survive in the face of intolerance). Only in this way can the real ideology of the fundamentalists be uncovered and defeated. The underlying mechanisms have to be uncovered, and this requires that these movements be understood in a larger historical context. But in today's stunted media landscape, this is no easy task.

In the ongoing battle between netocratic secularisation and consumtarian proto-religiosity, the conquest of the Pathos of Truth will be decisive. The origins of the Pathos of Truth must be traced further back in the history of ideas than within the so-called Judeo-Christian inheritance, something which western philosophers from G W F Hegel to Friedrich Nietzsche to Martin Heidegger have failed to do. Mainly because the Pathos of Truth actually has far deeper and more universal roots than we have hitherto been prepared to admit. But also because the feedback to the monotheistic religions – upon which the humanism of the Enlightenment constructs its fundamental belief in the Ego and free will – has to be broken in order for the necessary paradigm shift to take place. Once again we need a new view of history in order to complete the ideological paradigm shift. And because this is a globalised age, this new history has to be globally relevant. For understandable reasons this is probably easier to undertake beyond the western cultural sphere, inhibited as it is by the traditional history of ideas.

The power struggle that has already commenced is not about differentiating between those who can see through and those who are seen through. It is more of a battle between those who know they have been seen through and have harmonised their lives in accordance with this insight, in opposition to those who obstinately refuse to accept this new insight and pretend that they have not been seen through. Because the truth is that we are all of us wrong about practically everything, almost all of the time. We choose, for instance, to believe in the magic of conscious will, and we strenuously defend this illusion against all disturbing suspicions, not least by retrospectively making up plausible motives for actions which turn out to have unforeseen consequences.

But it is to a very great extent – and this is Daniel Wegner's concluding observation – precisely the fact that we are wrong about this which makes us human. We are also wrong when we proclaim free will against a deterministic alternative, because free will is a highly real feeling based upon illusory suppositions, whereas determinism is simply a process in which one specific effect mechanically follows one specific cause. Once again, this is a matter of apples and pears. Consequently we can go about our business feeling that we are willing and deciding things freely as much as we like, without the appearance of any logically tenable alternative to a determinism which says that everything that happens is, de facto, unavoidable, because it happens as a consequence of predetermined circumstances entirely outside our control.

Free will has no way of wriggling out of the grip of determinism. Denied its foundations in the form of the illusory Ego, free will has nothing to fall back on under the brutal onslaught of determinism. So is there, then, no free will? Well, we can certainly speak of a will. The body's chemicals seek stable and attractive combinations at the expense of instable and repulsive reactions. So the Body as a whole, as a network, has a series of more or less concrete wills. And are these wills free? Well, the Body certainly operates in an environment where choice exists. Attractive combinations are chosen and rewarded by the Body's own internal system of rewards. We can certainly talk of a form of limited freedom within these processes. It is even the case that some environments are more free than others. There are probably considerably more exciting dishes to choose between in a smart restaurant than in a rubbish-bin in a slum. But this strictly focused choice within given frames can hardly be said to have anything much to do with theology's and moral philosophy's ideas of 'freedom of will'.

What initially looks simply like a strategically necessary shift of the free will out of the vacuum left by the illusory soul or the illusory ego, and over to a networking body, soon reveals itself however to be of little comfort to dualists and humanists. Because free will is the Soul's and/or the Ego's very raison d'être, its actual substance. The body, of course, acts entirely without the presumed just considerations of the Ego, and without its identification with and responsibility for the decisive choice. The body really is a machine, just as Descartes once feared, and machines act as they can and must as a result of the components of which they happen to consist (including the fuel which their engines are loaded with). It is exclusively the material construction of the Body, in relation to the material conditions of the world around it, which decides the outcome in any given situation. And without a separate agent for free will itself, isolated from the ice-cold Body Machine – in other words, without a ghost in the machine – there is no space left for anything deserving of the description 'free will'.

But does this mean that determinism has won in the classical battle between faith in the power of free will and faith in everything that happens being predetermined (a conflict that also happens to cut right through both the theologies of the world religions and the great schools of philosophy through the ages)? The answer is yes. Without a soul, independent of the body's impulses and desires, determinism has once and for all beaten the likelihood of free will existing. No amount of exciting and fantastical invention can alter this fact. But the answer is, ironically enough, also no. Because beyond the battle with the adherents of free will, classical determinism is facing a new obstacle with its origins in the spectacular territorial gains made within physics during the twentieth century: Heisenberg's uncertainty principle.

When the German physicist Werner Heisenberg developed his infamous uncertainty principle in 1927 (nowadays often called Heisenberg's indeterminacy principle, because the problem is of a principal rather than a practical nature), he had, as far as we can tell, no philosophical ambitions. Heisenberg merely claimed drily that in the world of physics it is impossible to fix the position of a particle at the same time as measuring the speed of the same particle. The reason for this clearly counterintuitive fact is that no particle has any definitive position in the world of quantum physics. The position of particles cannot be fixed in space-time, but at best placed within a probability spectrum. If we then set a specific value for the particle on one axis, we are forced to accept that the value of the other axis is left hanging in the air, impossible to fix. And the more detail we give the value on the one axis, the more uncertain the value is on the other. It should be noted that this is not about finding a shortcut past scientific problems with measurements, as we are intuitively inclined to imagine. Instead, this is about a fundamental quality of physics itself which becomes apparent when we start to study its smallest components.

The philosophical consequence of Heisenberg's discovery is that we are forced to accept that there are no closed processes consisting merely of cause and effect. Because a miniscule amount of unpredictability creeps through the back door into the rules of quantum physics, colouring every historical outcome, faintly but unmistakably. Of course we can object and say that if we measure the collected outcomes from thousands and thousands of similar events, then, according to probability theory, the element of unpredictability will disappear among the sheer quantity measured. But in every individual event – and of course history consists of a series of sequential individual events, and history never repeats itself from identical coordinates in the way we approach scientific experiments – this minute but nonetheless unpredictable element creeps in on the quantum level. The process may in practice be predetermined, but in theory we can never be sure.

Besides this, the underlying probabilism of life is the very basis for the existence of time. In The End of Certainty (1997), the Nobel Prize winner Ilya Prigogine showed that this realisation knocks holes not only in the laws of Newtonian physics, but also within the classical determinism of quantum mechanics and Einstein. The actual occurrence of time, the unavoidable irreversibility of existence, are thus intimately linked to probabilism. Quantum physicists and Einstein claim that physics as theory is reversible. But the irrevocable increase in entropy which indicates the direction of time means that existence does not actually look like that. Materia is in fact demonstrably self-organising. (Ludwig Boltzmann showed this with his research into gases long before Prigogine drew the philosophical conclusions.) Classical determinism is therefore in practice dead, and from now on we can only speak of a so-called soft determinism, built upon the realisation that probability and self-organisation are fundamental aspects of existence, preconditions for time and thus also existence as we know them to exist at all.

The actual existence of time's arrow, and the minute element of unpredictability, stop history from being devoured by merciless determinism. So we are living in a deterministic universe which is never quite complete.

While scientific experiments – where one and the same process is repeated time after time and eventually reaches an apparently deterministic median value – suggest that we live in a closed deterministic universe, Heisenberg's uncertainty principle instead paves the way for a contingent universe where an element of unpredictability, so small that it slips below all forms of radar, prevents determinism from devouring the whole of existence in its debilitating grasp. We have to learn to live with soft as opposed to hard determinism, where contingency regularly spoils our plans. Not only because the number of factors affecting the outcome is incredibly large, but principally also because individual events on the timeline always include a minimal but real element of unpredictability.

It is also because of this small deviation that the universe exists at all. Without the fundamental mobility on the quantum level, the underlying inequality in the infancy of the universe, which in turn was the precondition for 'The Big Bang' and thus our material universe, could never have arisen. The greatest contribution of modern physics to philosophy is therefore the insight that 'the Universe is an accident, a fundamental imbalance in a supra-universe of compact balance', as the philosopher and psychoanalyst Slavoj Zizek puts it. This is a matter of a microscopic accident which developed into an infinite but nonetheless uneven, split, and therefore materially existing universe. 'The universe is a mistake', as Zizek enthusiastically points out in the film Zizek – The Movie.

What is philosophically interesting about Heisenberg's uncertainty principle is that every time we identify a fundamental value in the world of quantum physics – which of course is the science of the fundamental building blocks of the world as we know it, and thus the very basis of the monistic universe we are constructing among the remnants of the dead soul – or, in other words: every time we identify anything at all, we are forced simultaneously to accept the mobility within the relating coordinate which makes the value itself meaningful. And the more exactly we determine anything, the more indeterministic that value's necessary coordinate becomes (where the relating coordinate is necessary precisely because it constitutes the background against which the first coordinate assumes its value in space-time; everything in our post –Einstein universe really is, without exception, fundamentally relative).

There is quite simply no fixed point in existence at all, not in the classical sense, and so there is no fixed state of things which can be determined in full. The ego is far from being the only illusion in our intuitive understanding of the world. In actual fact, Heisenberg's uncertainty principle illuminates the fact that all notional points in existence are illusory. Every frozen snapshot of existence at a notional fixed point in time and a notional fixed point in space simultaneously are fictive. If you choose to fix time, space shifts. If you choose to fix space, time shifts. The constant mobility of existence on every level strikes us with ever greater force the closer we get to its smallest components; in the end it is impossible to identify any point, any simultaneous fixing of time and space.

As a result, nor is there any specific remaining phenomenon which can be completely determined in relation to anything. Kant, taken literally, was right: phenomena arise in our heads. This applies to a great extent also to the ego, which is just another phenomenon among all the others – although Kant would object. What separates phenomena from pure fantasy – our fellow human beings and pets are examples of phenomena, whereas elves and angels belong to the category of pure fantasy – is that phenomena are functional and realistic approximations of actually existing intensities in the noumenal chaos of the world around us. There is, in spite of everything, something real out there; at least, we have extremely good grounds for believing this to be the case. And the boundary we perceive between ourselves and the world around us, the boundary that we identify as our own skin, may admittedly be far from as absolute as our brains would have us believe, but it is still meaningful in several respects, and therefore not pure fantasy. Without this functional process of determination, we would soon be driven into complete psychosis.

Free will is both fantasy and phenomenon; the world is both deterministic and at the same time unpredictable. Each of these is paradoxical, but simultaneously completely logical and anything but contradictory. The will is free insofar as we are not puppets who are forced to obey anyone else's will, but the problem is, as we have seen, that there is no-one living in our heads who might be able to use any such freedom, even if there were a way out of the grasp of determinism, which of course there isn't. But quite regardless of the tiny element of chance that creeps in via quantum physics, the future is impossible to predict with anything approaching high definition, because the variables are so immeasurably numerous, and the relations between them so inexpressibly complicated that the slightest miscalculation in just one of the countless starting values would lead the eventual outcome of any process to be entirely different to what was expected.

But – and this is a rather interesting point – even if our experience of exerting free will is illusory and can never do away with determinism, it is an extremely active and notoriously difficult to assess component in the deterministic but unpredictable process. And this is absolutely fine. Because, although it doesn't exist, the ego, and the free will which does not exist either, have important functions to fulfil. Even an illusory will can achieve great things.

6.

The Mechanisms of Thought

The ancient Egyptians had no grand notions about the brain, and thought that the soul lived in the heart. So they would throw away the brain and keep the heart when they mummified their dead. But since then the brain and the head have been central to, and completely dominated, humankind's image of itself. And this shouldn't surprise us, because it is via the head that human beings receive the majority of their most important sensory perceptions of the outside world. The head has therefore had to get used to playing the leading role in every context that really matters. It is inside our heads that most of us look for and, with unreflecting smugness, even manage to find ourselves. The ego is produced and preserved within the head. Even Hippocrates traced all of our happiness, all our sorrow, and everything connected with thought back to the head. The general consensus is that the head manages everything to do with the creation of personality 'in house'. This, however, is an untenable position. But because this position fits in neatly with intuition and common sense, it is extremely tenacious.

In his psychological thriller The Tenant (1976), the Polish director Roman Polanski formulated a critique of the whole idea of a harmonious personality and the offensive arrogance of the head. In a grand but faded apartment in Paris the protagonist, Trelkowski – a pale, inconspicuous Pole played by the director himself – undergoes a thorough and eventually fatal identity crisis. From having initially been merely the tenant – the person who moves into a new home and occupies it – Trelkowski is gradually transformed into someone who himself is occupied by the apparently hostile world around him.

It is actually the haunted house and its malevolent inhabitants who move into Trelkowski's consciousness and force upon him the previous tenant's fractured identity, thus forcing him mechanically to re-enact her miserable fate. In a fleeting lucid interlude, Trelkowski asks himself exactly when an individual stops being the person he thinks he is, and he meditates upon the relationship between self-identity and the various parts of the body: 'If you cut off my head, would I say, "Me and my head" or "Me and my body"? What right has my head to call itself me?'

With this, Trelkowski hits the nail right on the head as far as the greatest existential myth of modern humankind is concerned. Of course we see our own head, or actually just the front of it, in the mirror every morning. But what do we actually see? We generally know roughly what we think, but we can't see how the process works. The face hides considerably more than it reveals, and the brain itself falls woefully short here. It can't produce an image of itself because there are no sensory organs reporting from inside the head. It feels no pain on its own behalf, and has no need of anaesthetic during operations, even if it's pretty painful having your skull sawn through. The brain is its own vast blind spot.

The brain can, however, get a long way in its investigations through the smart use of outsourcing. Nowadays we know a great deal about how it operates in order to build up an impression of the world around it, in other words: what perception and thinking actually are. The interesting thing is that the images we believe we see, and the sounds we think we hear, just like the ego we believe ourselves to be, don't actually exist either. At least, they don't exist inside our heads, because the only thing there is an ever-changing flow of electrochemical impulses. Images aren't images and sounds aren't sounds; they are patterns of information constantly evolving over time. Sound and vision are, like our other sensory impressions, directed and modified interpretations which the brain performs to itself in order to orientate itself better in its surroundings. The bat sees different images and hears different sounds to us, and these are neither more nor less 'faithful to reality' than ours.

Some people make a great fuss about the fact that the brain soon learns to live with a pair of glasses that turn the images projected onto the retina the other way up. But this really only confirms that the brain works with patterns, and not with images. The brain is what the entrepreneur and neuroscientist Jeff Hawkins calls a 'pattern machine': the cerebral cortex always does 'the same thing', making use of the same basic algorithm when it processes incoming impulses. It makes no difference whether these concern sight, hearing, taste, smell or touch: the brain has no specific preferences where the senses are concerned, and doesn't care if the patterns come from one single sensory organ or in a jumbled mix from several of them. The cerebral cortex just keeps on chewing its way through one pattern after the other, all the while making comparisons with old prognoses based on old patterns, which results in a constant flow of new prognoses.

In other words: the brain updates old prognoses with the help of new patterns which are transformed into new reference material, which in turn is archived and replaced when new patterns no longer match the old ones. The reference material here is simply another name for memory. Hawkins' model of human intelligence is based upon memory and feedback. This is how the brain handles impressions from the chaotic world around it: it remembers and feeds back, and pretty much all of this activity takes place in the basement of the subconscious.

The world is 'an ocean of constantly changing patterns that come lapping and crashing into your brain', Hawkins writes. This torrent of information presents the brain with a multitude of problems which it tries to solve to the best of its ability by matching new patterns against earlier, stored memories. Those new patterns which more or less correspond to what the situation suggests might be expected, because they are in line with old patterns, are left to their own devices for the sake of saving resources. But those which don't match expectations are dragged to the surface of consciousness and give rise to new prognoses and strategies. The outcome of these new strategies is registered and sucked into the constantly whirling feedback loop as new reference material. As long as new patterns of incoming impulses appear in sequences which make it possible for the brain to recognise where it is, and, to a large extent, predict what is going to happen next, everything is fine. Tried and tested strategies still apply. Predictability is, as Hawkins stresses, the very definition of what we call reality.

Out of these sequences the brain fashions causal connections: pattern A is followed by pattern B in the same way that cause is followed by effect. Unforeseen patterns are viewed by the brain as mistakes that need checking; they are sent upward through the hierarchy of consciousness until they reach a region on a level where it is possible to comprehend the patterns and place them in a larger context. Only then can feedback take place. A new and thus far unforeseen sequence of patterns is fitted into 'reality' because it gives rise to new predictions, which are communicated back down the hierarchy to The Subconscious. The impulses that make up this two-way traffic interact with each other the whole time on various levels, modifying one another. It is this process that we call learning. We learn which incoming patterns we can expect, and, if the prognosis turns out to be wrong, the brain is swift to give itself extra homework.

Perception is linked to motor activities insofar as they are impossible to separate. In order to know which pattern to expect, the brain has to take the movements of the body into account, whilst simultaneously the movements of the body stem from the reports of the sensory organs. We see a flight of stairs and automatically match the size of our step to it. If for some reason we miss a step on the way down, we experience a moment of panic – suddenly we are conscious of our foot fumbling for support in order to maintain the balance of the body – until the alarm reaches consciousness and the incoming information from the body's sensors becomes comprehensible. But as long as everything goes according to plan, reality remains coherent to us. Predictions and perceptions weave together in such a way that our unconscious predictions largely give rise to precisely those movements which then lead to the predicted perceptions. And so it goes on. Our prophecies are self-fulfilling. We plod through our days on unconscious autopilot while our conscious attention is free to occupy itself with other matters.

So what are intelligence and creativity in this hierarchical system of recognition and feedback? Well, it's a matter of an electrochemical variant of overview, insofar as such a thing can be imagined. The creative brain discovers – thanks to a fortunate combination of genetic predisposition and intensive practice – an increasing number of, and, above all, more daring and unexpected connections between incoming and stored sequences of patterns than other brains do. In this way it highlights and deals with not just patterns, but also meta-patterns, and patterns of patterns of patterns, and so on. The overriding connections within complex structures and between different structures become prominent. It becomes easier for the creative brain to orientate itself in the world, and it gets the opportunity to expand its understanding of its surroundings, and in this way expands those very surroundings.

Hawkins' simple definition of creativity – and there is no reason to complicate it – is the ability to predict different sorts of occurrence through the use of analogies. This is something all brains do when they are awake, but it is also something that certain brains do in a more sophisticated way than others, and with a higher degree of abstraction. Creativity takes place along a scale which reaches right from the most elementary autopilot activities to epoch-making flashes of creative genius. The method is fundamentally always the same: it is a matter of more or less functional connections between new and learned patterns through analogy. New information and new problems activate, hopefully, old lessons which are contextually relevant. The structure of pattern X is reminiscent of the structure of pattern Y in some interesting way, which leads to a whole new insight.

This applies to all forms of problem-solving, even problems of a purely physiological character: how to put our foot down on an uneven rock without wobbling too much is a question of creativity. The ability to return a heavily spun tennis serve is to a great extent linked to the repertoire of memories of similar serves and to subsequent feedback that flags up which returns have been successful or unsuccessful in the past. Besides this, the whole sequence of muscle activity which makes up the return of serve is a variation on practiced patterns which the attentive body machine has repeated enough times for its autopilot to be able to handle both strategy and implementation, which is a necessity seeing as there is insufficient time to connect up our slow-moving consciousness ahead of every new shot. In the same way that we learn to return heavily spun tennis serves, we learn to do everything else: crawling and walking, swimming and ballroom dancing, driving a car and typing on a keyboard. We repeat and repeat, practice and practice, gathering memories which over time become so worn in and close to hand that the whole process can be delegated to the autopilot of The Subconscious.

Anyone used to reading doesn't identify every single letter of a text individually, but scans over words that the brain remembers and recognises, in the same way that it remembers and recognises its own face in the mirror. At the same time, the preceding words constantly provide a large degree of pre-understanding of what can be expected, so that the eye can check and compare against self-produced predictions rather than having to use the full force of consciousness to make a decision about every new word, as you do when you're reading a language you have only a partial knowledge of. Only when reading itself stops being a problem that requires attention is it possible to absorb the informative patterns carried by the text without distraction. And this can only be done thanks to all our well-managed memories of texts we have already read. A child learns to walk and swim, and eventually to drive a car and use a keyboard, by gathering and learning to manage a sufficient quantity of relevant memories. There's no other way.

Whatever we do and whatever we think, however much we try to live in the present or look into the future, we are constantly moving within the theatre of our own memories. This is the only way the world can be made comprehensible and manageable, and only to the extent that the world resembles or reminds us of our own memories. We don't understand anything else at all. Our brain has many functions, but its most spectacular party trick is precisely this magnificent ability to mix and match patterns with and against one another. And this trick is only possible thanks to our exceptionally well-developed cerebral cortex, and it is basically this trick which makes us more intelligent and more creative than other species. We simply get much further thanks to our more advanced analogies.

The arrogance of the head towards the rest of the body and the world is nonetheless entirely groundless. The brain has no right to call itself alone 'me'. The size of the cerebral cortex and its ability to do tricks are all very well, but human consciousness would still be impossible without the rest of the body and the physical and social world around us. We can calmly ignore all romantic notions about a pure natural state in a vague mythological past; human beings are social creatures, and have never been anything else. Beside, human beings are extremely adaptable – to the extent that we have collectively managed to develop a second nature through communication and cooperation.

We see evidence of this unique achievement every time we leave our homes and go out into a town full of strangers: everywhere we encounter people we don't know and whom in most cases we've never met. And we normally manage not to kill a single one of them, just as they manage not to kill us. We might even nod to them in a friendly way, usually without realising the significance of what we are part of: the historically unique fact that we actually tolerate strangers in our proximity. We can call it whatever we like, but it isn't natural. No, this widespread politeness is more the product of an extremely long and turbulent process of civilisation.

In contrast, our natural ancestors on the savannah acted the same way as our natural cousins, the chimpanzees. If they met a group of the same species during a hunting expedition, there were two alternatives, and nodding in a friendly fashion wasn't one of them. If the alien group was larger or otherwise physically superior, you took to your heels and fled as fast as you could; but if the strangers were fewer in number or otherwise physically inferior, you killed as many of them as you could. That's what happens in nature, and the reason is obvious. Strangers are enemies and competitors for the limited resources needed for survival and reproduction.

But then we come back to our remarkably large brain with its remarkably well-developed cerebral cortex – a piece of machinery that we have gradually learned to use with ever greater refinement. We learned to transmit vital information to each other, first within our own group: communication and cooperation were human beings' secret weapons on the savannah. And at some groundbreaking moment two groups that didn't know each other hit upon a mutually attractive alternative to the reflex and biologically natural battle for life and death, namely bartering (either with or without friendly nods). Once this process arose, social structures could develop and become increasingly complex. A succession of supra-technologies – amongst which we primarily reckon the dominant communication technologies (spoken language, written language, the printing press, digital interactivity) – promoted the development of increasingly extensive and mutually enriching cooperation in the form of increasingly comprehensive and multi-layered non-zero-sum games (where all participants can count on benefitting). Throughout history we have greedily consumed every new media-technological possibility for better communication and cooperation.

Biologically, today we still have the same brain as the hunters and gatherers who roamed the savannah 100,000 years ago. Genetic development moves at a glacial pace, and the number of generations to work with since our time on the savannah has simply been far too small for evolution to have had time to produce interesting changes in either our brain or any other part of our body. Yet it is still easy to state that the human brain conducts entirely different processes today than it did before. Or, to be more precise: its activity is in principle the same, but the inventory in the form of what we call consciousness has been exchanged many times over, which has given this activity new directions and entirely new dimensions. Humankind has transformed its world, and the human world has responded by equipping the human brain with new and more advanced patterns. In other words: we create the culture which then recreates us, and then we recreate culture once more and then it recreates us human beings again, and so on, ad infinitum.

The genes give instructions for the production of their survival machines and then send them out into the life which pertains in the biotope in question, where they then devote themselves to surviving and reproducing as best they can. The best survivors tend to reproduce more plentifully than others, passing those characteristics which made them good survivors on to the next generation. This process is so-called natural selection, which all the while is filtering out poorly suited specimens of both species and individual.

It is important here to point out a couple of details in order to avoid common misconceptions. One is that this business of being 'well adapted' is always an extremely relative concept: what might be suitable for one biotope could perfectly easily mean a quick death in another. The tiger shark, for instance, wouldn't survive too long in the Gobi Desert. So being 'well adapted' has nothing to do with any absolute qualities, but is actually a matter of sheer luck. It is a matter of being able to demonstrate the right characteristic in the right place, but also – and this is extremely important – at the right time.

The second thing that needs pointing out is that what makes someone 'well adapted' is always changing over time, because the biotope in question is always changing, which means that even the conditions which favour certain characteristics and punish others in turn are also changing. So yesterday's winners could be today's losers even though they themselves haven't changed at all. They have simply been run down by changes in the world around them, or because new combatants have entered their biotope. This relationship is obviously complicated still further by the fact that the surroundings and survival requirements of different species and individuals depend to a very great extent upon other species and individuals.

Charles Darwin's theory of evolution no longer has any serious competitors. All the talk of 'intelligent design' in different religious and pseudo-religious forms is so bizarre and full of countless misconceptions, both intentional and unintentional, that it is often wisest to suppress such nonsense rather than take part in discussions which can never be anything but fruitless, seeing as they have to take as their starting point highly curious premises and self-selected 'facts'. But, in spite of its absurdity, the idea of intelligent design – just like the associated belief in a personal god and creator – has achieved remarkable distribution and been adopted by many apparently extremely capable people. And this in turn is actually interesting, because it confirms that Darwinian principles are active even in the evolutionary process driving the development of culture and thus also human consciousness to an ever higher level of complexity. Even if Freud rather than Darwin is best suited to explain the continuing spread of the phenomenon.

What is happening here is actually not some tough but fair talent contest, with some imagined neutral and fact-orientated judge as the final objective arbiter. The point isn't whether the idea of intelligent design is intelligent or not, but rather if it has any survival value, and that isn't decided by some truth tribunal, but by whether this pattern of thought matches other patterns stored within the collection of human brains which make up the prime target group. And it is clear that it does. Large parts of the world are still crawling with people who are religious, who want to be religious, who believe or, rather, would like to believe in a divine creator, a giant daddy in the sky, and many of them are literal believers of the sort that finds it offensive even to toy with the idea that the species have developed by chance and over a long period of time without there being any higher thought or plan behind the whole business. Human narcissism really is that great.

Darwinism's intellectual victory is actually a red rag to these people: the stronger the well-founded intellectual conviction that Darwin was fundamentally right about the basic conditions of existence has become, the greater the desire of religious fundamentalists to believe that a feudal and paternalistic god is still, in spite of everything, hiding behind the unpalatable idea of Darwinism. This is where Freud rather than Darwin gets to explain what is going on. Because the truth is, of course, that if we are to talk about Darwin being intellectually wrong at all, we mean that in his texts he did not yet understand the full extent of his own revolution: it is doubtful that we can even call ourselves Darwinists today in any traditional sense, but should probably identify ourselves as ultra-Darwinists, seeing as Darwin's revolution covers so much more, and so many more aspects of existence than Darwin himself realised. Even the speculative worlds of physics and cosmology are today becoming more and more influenced by Darwinian reasoning.

Because this intellectual movement, this slow uncovering of the truth, is heading in a different direction to the ambitions of religious fundamentalists, their reaction is dramatically dialectical: where their intellectual arguments aren't enough, the mechanisms of Freudian repression come into play. The truth simply mustn't be true, because it disturbs or even destroys that metaphysical fantasy. So the Truth is personified and equipped, very imaginatively, with personal characteristics and agendas; an argument is not allowed to be merely an argument, but is supposed to conceal a hidden and dangerous agenda; philosophers and scientists can't easily be accused of stupidity, that wouldn't be particularly credible, so they are instead accused of being amoral and generally wicked.

This suppression is thus more powerful that the pathos of truth, and is gradually exchanged for the truth itself. Or rather: a spiritual truth is set against scientific truth and presupposed to be more true simply because of its supposed spiritual origins. The less credible the ideological hotchpotch is, in purely factual terms, the more believable, or rather the more spiritual, it is believed to be by the faithful. This is therefore the same psychological reaction which occurs when cast-iron prophecies of the end of the world believed by an apocalyptic cult fail to come true: when the Messiah doesn't show up or Doomsday doesn't take place, the sect isolates itself in the ever stronger belief that it alone possesses the ultimate Truth, unlike the wicked world around it.

The prophecy has by this point gained such a strong role in the collective identity that it has to be maintained even if it doesn't come true. It therefore becomes impossible for sect members to looks for faults in the prophet him- or herself, so the fault must lie elsewhere. The fault is, after all, moral rather than factual. And there is only one way out: finding an external enemy to blame, hate and attack for the failure of the prophecy to come true, and then sit and wait for a new moment for the cataclysm that is holding the sect together. Self-criticism is, historically, an ideological luxury which only people in secure positions of power can afford to indulge in. It is never exercised within a society driven by fear and hatred of the outside world. In such instances, the group's acute survival instinct has taken over completely.

The suppression mechanism strengthens rather than weakens the outward signs of belief when intellectual arguments collapse or are subjected to increasing criticism from outside. Such attacks are presumed to come from a surrounding (and larger) alien nomadic tribe. Here it is important to note that the emotional reaction is often strongest in those who have officially given up the original religion and are instead subconsciously using intelligent design as an ersatz ideology, a new belief which is intended to replace the lost religion and thus establish a firm connection to the abandoned religion, a notional way back to the security of the original nomadic tribe.

Once again this is a matter of compensatory behaviour: a lack of belief is compensated for by passionate belief. When you can't hack it intellectually, you have to compensate with excess morality. The result is an act of final desperate faith towards the old religion, of the same sort that occurs when the unfaithful partner in a marriage is often the one who is most insistent upon the continuing metaphysical validity of the marriage when definitive faithlessness is an established fact. The feeling of guilt is so strong that it gets confused with intellectual capacity, meaning that guilt rather than the intellect is advancing the argument and the drive for activism. The less the activist believes (inwardly), the more faithful he or she has to be towards the holy object or artefact (outwardly). For this reason the activist tries to maintain an impression of genuine faith behind their aggressive behaviour. This becomes most apparent when their personal pride rather than ideology is presented as the reason for their evident aggression. Anyone who genuinely believes themselves to have found the Truth has, of course, no reason whatever to be aggressive.

It is hardly surprising that we find the most intractable religious fundamentalists among, for instance, successful, middle-class Muslim students in Europe and North America rather than among the poor traders in the bazaars of the Arab world, even if it is mainly from among the poorest Muslims that suicide bombers, for instance, are recruited. And it is among the evangelistic careerists of the business world, rather than among the poor in the slums of Latin America, East Asia and the American south, that Christian fundamentalism is recruiting the largest number of new adherents. Growing emotional distance from the belief's original social context is fostering an equally increasing sense of guilt. This growing feeling of guilt is compensating the growing lack of faith. This is resulting in a powerful dialectic reaction: the fundamentalists' conviction and activism are developing as compensation for the experience of mental distance from their original social identity. And internal homelessness is accelerating the aggression of their involvement. Shy and reflective faith are being replaced by pompous, one-way belief.

For these people it is easy to sympathise with a creed such as 'intelligent design' and to incorporate its patterns of thought, a 'theory' which makes out that it can sink Darwinism and save the view of the revealed religion. In this way an unhappy consciousness can be granted heavenly harmony, and precisely this basic pattern in a consciousness constitutes fertile soil for ideas such as these. The theory of evolution, on the other hand, is in almost all important respects beyond their grasp. Its patterns of thought differ far too dramatically from the religious wallpaper that decorates their brains thanks to the culture that they either absorbed with their mothers' milk, or which they for some reason or other have become inclined to nurture through gradual accumulation of a religiously tinted collection of memories/patterns in their consciousness.

In the same way, it is natural that memetics, the theory of a cultural evolutionary process, meets resistance here and there. It is obvious that such a controversial concept – which upsets the whole humanist supra-ideology, with its fixation on a freely choosing and independently acting individual – is not going to sit well alongside traditional and intuitively attractive patterns of thought which are firmly anchored in the consciousness of most modern human beings. This in spite of the fact that counterintuitive ideas are really the only ones worth being seriously interested in; all other ideas – because they harmonise with what we already know and believe and expect – slip smoothly past all the qualitative barriers set up by the consciousness, and consolidate an existing complex of ingrained ideas and prejudices, without causing any sort of turbulent friction.

The concept of the meme was launched almost in passing by the biologist Richard Dawkins towards the end of his book The Selfish

Gene (1976). Dawkins went on to develop the concept in The Extended Phenotype (1982), but the aim remained simply to illustrate evolutionary principles in processes outside biology, and was not yet intended to formulate any general theory about the development of human culture. Such a theory – a memetic meme – did, however, appear and spread in the years that followed, in spite of resistance from various anti-Darwinists. It this way it has simultaneously illustrated and confirmed itself. The memetic meme itself has characteristics which lead to it surviving and succeeding in replicating itself even though the odds seem to be against it in many respects.

The basic idea of memetics is that the meme is the cultural equivalent of the biological gene, in other words: it is the meme which is the real and, like the gene, extremely selfish player in the arena of culture and the process of civilisation. Genes combine to build advanced survival machines in the form of organisms. Memes do the same; human consciousness is their survival machine. And the meme is selfish insofar as it is concerned with nothing but its own survival and reproduction. Peace on earth or the eternal happiness of its host organism just aren't on the agenda.

There are naturally countless differences between slow biology and capricious and apparently irrational culture. But what unites them and makes them both examples of evolutionary processes is natural selection. A brutal process of selection is constantly going on, where innumerable losers are discounted and disappear from history as their characteristics fail to meet the requirements currently demanded. New generations of the latest winners remain until the next round, when new conditions prevail, and so on. What makes a gene or a meme into a winner is constantly changing as the world around them changes, a change which the new winners themselves are to a great extent participants in. The origin of genes is the potent ancient soup which covered whole parts of the world four billion years ago. Culture in the broadest sense of the word, human society, is the memes' flavoursome soup.

Both genes and memes are replicators: they have an inbuilt ability to produce copies of themselves. But the copies are not always identical, deviations are common, and when these deviations are dramatic we can start to talk of mutations, which are the precondition for an evolutionary process. Selection works with material which is constantly renewing and changing itself. As a rule these mutations, these not-exact copies of the winners from the last round, are completely hopeless, but on exceptionally rare occasions they are actually successful, because the new conditions favour their new characteristics. Selection, copying, variation, and after that a new round of selection: this is how an evolutionary process works.

The meme, like the gene, is a discrete little package of information which is either more or less suited to survival and copying. Different examples of what a meme can be are a philosophical idea, the chorus of a piece of music, linguistic expression or a dialect, different techniques for building a roof or a steam-engine: anything which can capture people's attention and invite imitation. It is this imitation which is the memes' way of producing copies of themselves; the word meme comes from the Greek term for representation and imitation: mimesis. The conditions for memes are tough, on the verge of inhuman. Human consciousness and its capacity for attention have distinct limitations, and the number of losers who drown in a constantly increasing torrent of information is astronomical.

A small and exclusive selection of memes achieves short-lived success which can be more or less momentary and spectacular in its reach, while others turn out to be long-lived after a less than promising start. However it is important to point out that it is almost impossible to predict with anything like precision the outcome of different memes. The same thing applies to memetics itself, even if we have good reason to believe that the concept is likely to become stronger in a culture where knowledge of how the brain works is steadily growing.

Memetics is in line with our increased understanding of how the brain interacts with the world around it, and with the new ultra-materialistic theories about intelligence and creativity which are fighting a tough battle against the humanist ideology and the various revealed religions of the world, but which in a longer perspective will gain an advantage simply because these theories are in line with the new supra-technology in the area of communication: digital interactivity. Memetics connects and summarises the most exciting ideas within biology, psychology, philosophy and cognitive science. It illuminates the fatal blind spot of consciousness, its incapacity to understand how it itself works.

This means that we can understand what memes actually are: sensory impressions that are transformed into electrochemical patterns in our brain, and which reformat and build up our consciousness when a process of mixing and matching deems them to be worthy of interaction with currently existing complexes of patterns. Memes whirl around our globalised culture in a frenetic hunt for new consciousnesses to colonise. They survive and reproduce if they can escape the tough selection process and manage to capture the attention of another consciousness. They fade and are discarded if and when they are marginalised and/or become incompatible with the changing world around them.

Because we understand the ramifications of the fact that memes are selfish, we also realise that serious problems can arise when they come into conflict with genes, or when the mixing and matching process simply fails for some reason. But because we actually understand a few important things about the memes' desperation and ruthlessness, there is some hope that we might be able to outwit them, at the same time as realising that both 'we' and 'them' in this context represent our memes, and that each one is in practice identical to the other.

Without the complementary function of memetics, socio-biology would collapse. Thanks to memetics, it is suddenly possible to explain something like celibacy, a meme which is in direct conflict with the genes which want to reproduce, but which fits perfectly well alongside the whole religious meme complex, seeing as a priest living alone and childless can concentrate solely on spreading the religious memes, just as self-imposed childlessness fits well alongside various sorts of career meme, but less well with the reproduction of genes. Genes and memes to a large extent share the same survival machine, but they often want different things and pull in different directions.

Neither of these replicators has our best interests at heart. From the genes' point of view it is often better if we are anxious and frustrated, which makes us exert ourselves to be more successful, in order to be more attractive as potential partners for potential partners with even higher status that those we are currently referred to. And the memes' agenda is always their own. This business of loading yourself up with weapons and then shooting as many schoolchildren as possible before turning the gun on yourself, for instance, does nothing for your health or social status, yet in certain situations it still appeals to certain people as an irresistibly attractive option. It is hard to think of a more obvious example of memes triumphing over genes.

This may sound rather unpleasant, but it is important to realise that memes are not some sort of psychic bacteria subjecting the authentic Cartesian subject to various accidents and dangers if they aren't carefully sifted out and kept under strict supervision. In a brain built of genes lives a consciousness built of memes. There is no other subject but the one the memes establish for us and themselves; there is no other critical apparatus for filtering new memes but the one consisting of old memes. Our subject is, in short, nothing but memes, and the thoughts we think are thought for us by and on behalf of our memes.

This book is written by Alexander Bard and Jan Söderqvist's memes working together, and how you respond to it depends upon how well the memes that these memes are conveying match your personal collection of memes such as it appears in the specific situation in which you're reading the book. But even if you reject these memetic memes in frustration or with a sceptical grin, a tiny but real shift will have taken place in your consciousness as a result of your reading. The next time you come across a similar argument about memetics, your pre-understanding in the form of an actual and relevant collection of memes will be at least very slightly different. If you have read this far, then, if nothing else, we have at least held your attention for a few hours and our memes have mixed with yours.

This is what happens when you try to influence public opinion, or engage in advertising and marketing: you are working on two different levels. In part, you are communicating a series of memes and hoping for the greatest possible degree of acceptance and breakthrough (and stability in the memes once they have managed to take root within the target group), and you are also manipulating the conditions for this series of memes to be regarded as acceptable. If, for instance, you want to persuade people of the validity of memetics, you prove that the arguments of your opponents are based upon entirely untenable and slightly absurd premises. And if, as a therapist, you want to counteract a complex of suppositions and behaviours that is causing your patient problems and suffering, you do pretty much the same thing: you attack the actual problem itself, but above all you modify the non-functional model of the world and the consciousness that constitutes fertile territory for a cluster of unruly memes that are all pulling in the wrong direction. The problem isn't that the world is invading our heads and dictating our thoughts and our actions: this is an entirely self-evident necessity. No, the problem is that certain patterns just don't fit together with others.

7.

A SHORT HISTORY OF LANGUAGE

LET US SHIFT OUR FOCUS a little and start from another angle by asking: how old is humanity? According to biological history, humanity's forebears left the world of the apes to gradually develop their own branch on the common family tree sometime between five and eight million years ago. Here it is important to remember two things: firstly, that biological development requires oceans of time, and secondly, that every attempt to define the boundaries between a newly created species and its forerunners is extremely arbitrary, and, in part, fictitious. It would be so much simpler if the religious mythologies were actually right, and some bored God had actually created all the species, just as they are today, on a certain date. The truth, however, is messy and in constant motion: you just have to decide for more or less acceptable reasons to draw an approximate line somewhere on time's axis. And of course this can only be done from a great distance, when you have at least some idea of what it is you're looking for. Sociological history looks rather different. What we call a human being, a hominid of the species homo sapiens sapiens, starts to differentiate itself from its comparatively primitive predecessors among the pack animals and enters the evolutionary arena only some 200,000 years ago. There are various opinions regarding the exact point in time even in this regard. Sociologists, just like biologists, disagree about any number of things, and sometimes have to agree to differ. But there can scarcely be any disagreement about the most salient point. It was only through the development of the unique ability to talk (in other words: communicating with the help of virtual abstractions), and thereby the unique ability to think together (in other words: constructing advanced models of the world, based on collectively accumulated knowledge), that humankind – with remarkable speed

– took the epoch-making step from an overshadowed existence as one of the savannah's gentler, second-division creatures to its unique position at the top of the food chain. Language changed everything. We created language which then went on to recreate us. And then we moved on even further.

So, it is language, and the complex models of the world that we can construct with its help, that primarily distinguishes us from other species. Words are patterns which our brains have an unparalleled ability to comprehend and combine, mix and match. Syntax is a hierarchical meta-pattern which allocates the words their basic functions. It may be true that computers 'understand' language and can work with words to some extent, but they are easily beaten by any four-your-old of average ability. From an early age we learn to associate various patterns of words out in the wide world with our stored memories of their physical and semantic correlations, which opens the door to abstract thought and a world of modifiable concepts.

Because we are pack animals, we can apply ourselves to this linguistic management together: we construct a constantly expanding aggregate of intelligence. Learned patterns are passed on and can be developed further by others. Every new generation has richer material to work with than its predecessor. Unlike other species, we do not have to start from scratch over and over again, and that makes all the difference in the world. The patterns live on – at least those patterns which survive the Darwinian process of competition – and spread from one brain to another. This is a process that never stops: we who are writing this and you who are reading it are taking part in this process right now (our now, as well as your now).

Ever since the development of language, humankind has been arduously trying to learn to handle its new, unaccustomed role as leader. For many millions of years before that our forebears lived a relatively monotonous existence, entirely governed by only the most basic needs and entirely at the mercy of the harsh law of the jungle, an existence full of difficult challenges, but one which didn't come up with any surprises comprehensive enough to leave any noticeable trace in the form of genetic modification. But the development of human speech sparked a social experiment without parallel in all of history. The problem is that the conditions for our existence and our own ecological niche are changing so incredibly quickly as a result of the communication and collaboration that language makes possible – a process provided with masses of new fuel with each ensuing media-technological revolution. Our genes have maintained an entirely different and considerably gentler pace. This means that genetically we have not changed as much as we might like to believe. Or, to be more precise: we haven't changed at all.

The greatest revolutions thus far in the history of human civilisation have all been technological rather than genetic (and thereby not ontological either) in nature. This tangible discrepancy between a form of life in harmony with our genetic predispositions – regardless of how pleasant or unpleasant this life was deemed to be by the people in question (insofar as they ever reflected on the matter) – and today's requirement of a life where genetically motivated instincts have to be kept on a very short leash, if only in order for the civilisation project to be able to survive all temptations, is generally known as the idea of alienation. Civilisation is a thin veneer on top of humanity's bestial nature, which is something we know to be literally true thanks to genetics. In all important respects we have the same genetic make-up as we had when we lived on the savannah. So it isn't particularly strange if we experience the necessary adaptation to contemporary society, for which we aren't at all suited biologically, as problematic.

It is enough to take a stroll around any idyllic, leafy suburb to realise that human beings are more than happy to leave the trials of the jungle for a safer and more ordered life under savannah-like circumstances as soon as the opportunity presents itself. The culturally designated distance between the individual trees in these soothing avenues is practically identical to the natural distance required between trees on the savannah for each to secure enough water to grow from the ground beneath. The signals are clear: the attractive suburb isn't a desert (dangerous) or a jungle (dangerous), but is designed to remind us of a savannah (safe, at least in relative terms). This preference for the savannah also manifests itself at a very early age, and has been scientifically proven. When children are shown pictures of various types of landscape, the savannah ends up top of the list of favourites among primary and middle-school pupils. Other experiments have documented a clear preference for trees whose crowns have a flat, broad shape, which is typical of the African savannah. According to behavioural ecologist Gordon Orians' so-called savannah hypothesis, we human beings have an innate attraction to precisely those environments that remind us of the African savannah where we once developed and where the conditions for life were consequently favourable.

This does not necessarily mean that the jungle has left us. 200,000 years is not enough for our genes to undergo any change to speak of – that would require a vastly inflated number of generations. Our genes, then, remain rooted in the wild vegetation of the jungle and in a bestial and partially pre-linguistic state, where we still inhabit a modest little niche among other species that are superior to us in many important respects.

This explains why the desire to submit to anything at all is so strong that the subject constantly seeks something to submit to, even if the target for this submission has to be conjured up out of thin air. In the world of psychoanalysis this invented and constantly sought-out superior power goes by the name of The Big Other. And this, our fundamental 'slave mentality', deeply embedded in humankind's self-image, is precisely what got the philosopher Friedrich Nietzsche so upset when, in the late-nineteenth century, in books such as Thus Spoke Zarathustra and Ecce Homo, he dissected humanity, its history and conditions of life, and placed his hope in a different, future form of humanity: the superman who entirely rejects historically and genetically conditioned subordination.

The answer to Nietzsche's well-motivated concern is that, like practically everything else to do with humanity, the origins of this slave mentality are to be found in the strict cohesion of pack existence and the struggle for survival on the African savannah. The emotional masochism of the slave constantly seeking a master may not appeal to existential philosophers, but it has been a successful survival strategy for as long as we can tell. It is enough to study the social interaction in most modern bars just before closing time to be persuaded of how much of our fundamental bestiality still remains in our patterns of social behaviour. A masochistic attitude towards the world around us is still the leading pattern in our self-perception. If you bow, scrape, and retreat when the gorilla, lion or pack leader attacks, your chances of survival increase dramatically. So why mess with an apparently winning formula?

One simple way of understanding what was so revolutionary in the development of language is to go back to our own linguistic beginnings – in other words, by studying new-born infants. Because the new-born child – like the pre-linguistic adult hominid – still lacks verbal skills, it perceives life from entirely bestial impulses. There is nothing to reflect with, no linguistic structures in the brain, still less any meta-linguistic structures, and so there is nothing to reflect upon. The baby's own desires are naked and omnipotent, and its collisions with the basically incomprehensible world around it does not, although it clearly leaves strong emotional traces, leave any concrete memories in the form of separate concepts which can be returned to and contemplated. A trauma may be an electrochemical imprint upon the brain, but that imprint itself does not influence personal identity. The new-born infant lacks, by definition, precisely that: an identity. The production of that has not yet begun.

Without the analytical tools of language, the new-born infant cannot differentiate between bodies and desires, and thus not between subject and object either. There is no 'I' that exists separately to 'I want' (there's nothing for Descartes here), so there are no other subjects separate from their respective desires. The new-born infant may seek out its parents eyes and imitate his or her facial expression in order to bond and gain access to the closeness that is a hormonal necessity for life, but this happens purely instinctively, entirely without consciousness of what is going on and why.

What actually exists within the new-born infant's world are aggressive, all-exclusive, genetically motivated desires, linked to their respective bodies, without the slightest hint of freedom of action. This explains why the new-born infant does not distinguish between playing with its mother's breast, a friend of the same age, a teddy bear, or a piece of fluff. The world around it is an incomprehensible and almost irritating chaos against which its own will is conducting a cold, intense, war of attrition, where the goal – as inexorable as it is emotionally vacant – is the subordination of the world around it.

The new-born infant's own tyrannical and determining will alone is master of the infant's universe; there are no disruptive dialectical opponents here. Admittedly, it is completely isolated in this battle with the incomprehensible world around it, but without the infant perceiving this as remotely traumatic, seeing as it is not yet conscious of any alternative to the unshakeable focus of its own desires. Because the new-born infant is blissfully unaware of what awaits it in the social context of later stages of its development, of the adult's enforced and angst-ridden balancing act between a massive plurality of imagined wills – its own as well as others' – it does not perceive its existential isolation as being remotely problematic. It is simply a confirmed fact.

The gradual development of linguistic competence forces human beings to produce an existential worldview, and thus also an existential view of themselves. The child, thus far consistently psychotic, entirely at the mercy of sensory pleasure, must therefore pay a high price for access to language and the abstract pleasures connected to all the multidimensional, stimulating fantasy worlds it offers. This process was identified by Sigmund Freud as 'castration', and with it the problem of alienation enters the arena. The door to carefree childhood closes inexorably. Because of language, the child is forced to accept and fulfil the demand to grow up quickly and resolutely. Adulthood is the necessary survival strategy in the symbolic universe nurtured by the merciless maelstrom of language.

From now on, life is linked to the symbolic organisation which, with the help of language, has laid claim to the world. Life is no longer the child's own pre-ordained and sensually concrete phenomenon, but the adult's abstract mystery, something which seems always to be going on in the distance, somewhere far away from where you yourself happen to be. The mystery bewitches the child, in the same way that the children of the savannah must have been bewitched by stories of hunts for wild animals. The world belongs to someone else, and not to the child – to The Big Other – and getting hold of an invitation to join and belong to The Other's world is from now on the child's, and later the adult's, highest priority. The fight for social belonging, status and success is now in full flow.

Once language and all of its blessings in the form of various spectacular effects has made its appearance, a society emerges which places a non-negotiable minimum requirement on its members: adulthood. The need for a socially acceptable position in the symbolic order is constantly present, and requires a constant flow of new sacrifices. Anyone who can't formulate, or receives no help to formulate, a credible argument for their right to exist – in other words: anyone who can't present their intended contributions to the survival of the tribe and the development of its civilisation in a satisfactory way – will have to reckon with being both socially and physically ostracised. In the survival-fixated nomadic tribe it is never a question of what the tribe can do for you, but of what you as a responsible member can do or are planning to do for your tribe. From now on, social recognition is directly linked to survival. And to retain the recognition of the tribe, each individual member must submit to the power structure currently in place within the tribe.

Which brings us to yet another aspect of the emergence of language, because this is the point where The Law enters the story, and with it comes the labelling of the infantile deviant as The Criminal. Because The Law is the holiest of texts – the original monotheistic texts were all law books, concrete rules of survival for those in fixed settlements – criminality is not, at the most profound level, about obvious crimes against society's laws and rules (if someone steals something you simply chop off a hand and have done with it – individual crimes have nothing to do with character), but about identifying those who stand outside the fundamental principles of the law: this holy and remarkable Language itself. Being criminal is not the same as being someone who commits a crime. Instead, being criminal ultimately means being a person who lacks a socially acceptable position in the symbolic order, being the person who refuses to listen when power speaks. But why simply eject The Criminal from the social commonwealth when The Criminal actually constitutes excellent material for the tribe's edifying narrative about itself?

So The Criminal has to fill the role of the requisite Demon, the invented internal enemy which the social body desperately needs in its mythology in order to nurture the vital symbolic order. The Demon is whatever needs to be rejected, locked up, ostracised, tortured and, in the end, preferably ritually executed in public in order to foster cohesion and loyalty towards the group's mythological origins and core. If The Law is really to work, it must be granted a metaphysical dimension and become more than a simple collection of rules. For this reason, God and humankind have to be complemented with the Devil (the fallen angel who refused to obey orders from above). The Law then administers both the excuses and the modus operandi in order to maintain this ambition. And the reward is increasingly strong social cohesion and a clearer identity for the social body. It is worth noting that nothing promotes social identity as effectively as a public execution. The old women knitting sweaters for their grandchildren during the performance up on the scaffold are the regime's most loyal subjects.

Demonology holds society together, and language makes demonology possible. Without an obvious enemy, the society's narrative about itself loses its ability to promote cohesion.

The unavoidable division between external language (speech) on the one hand, and internal language (thought) on the other, results in an equally unavoidable duality or bifurcation: the constantly ongoing conflict between, on the one hand, the primary, outer, pre-linguistic, immanent and physical world, and, on the other, the secondary, inner, virtual, transcendental and psychic world, where human fantasy and imagination reign, offering immediately accessible pleasure. There is absolutely no qualitative difference between exterior and interior, between a physical and a 'merely' psychic experience: everything we are able to perceive at all is of course electrochemical patterns produced by temporary coalitions of collaborating clusters of synapses. An entirely internal experience or fantasy releases the same torrent of stimulating chemicals in the brain as an experience linked to an external event, just a bit quicker.

The duality between the external and internal worlds becomes clear in the insurmountable discrepancy between the speech of the other members of the tribe, and thus presumably their thoughts, and the narcissistic fascination of our own thoughts, our internal world's continuous dialogue with itself. This dichotomy arises because the brain switches on the ego machine and language offers its own abstractions. The ensuing questions explode and overwhelm us: who am I, and what do I really think? What's hiding behind what I believe I am thinking? Who are these other people around me, and what are they really thinking? What lies hidden behind the words they are speaking? What do they want? What do they fantasise about? Who do they want me to be? What do I have to do to make them happy? What do I know, or what am I merely imagining, about the fantasies of my fellow human beings? And how do all these illusive desires relate to my own mysterious – to put it mildly – desires?

While the talking and thinking human being continues to have a one-dimensional and relatively unproblematic relationship with the small children and pets in its immediate vicinity, its relationship with the adults and its own psyche is, thanks to the hyper-dimensionality of language, both complicated and demanding. At the same time, these relationships provide human beings with their greatest and deepest pleasure. Language is therefore the invention and the technology that we never learn to live with, yet cannot imagine living without. Our fascination at the many suggestive consequences of language is so affecting and comprehensive that language and the world eventually tend to become synonymous. This is the metaphysical World.

It is thanks to and through language that human beings realise that there are other, concrete spaces outside the space in which their bodies happen to be at any one moment, and that all these spaces together make up abstract Space. It is thanks to and through language that human beings realise that there are inexhaustible and unexplored fantasy worlds inside the talking, thinking people around them, and that these fantasy worlds together make up the abstract World. And as the inescapably solitary observer of these expanding and mysterious spaces, the world of each human being is not merely their own world, but appears to be even the only world that exists. Forget the concrete world, now it's the abstract World that matters instead!

The pre-linguistic world is concrete and physical, while the linguistic World is abstract and metaphysical in character. This means that the linguistic World is experienced as something much larger, more intense and pleasant than the pre-linguistic version. Life in the pre-linguistic world was, of course, mainly only a matter of avoiding direct physical threats, and finding food and a place to sleep. But the advent of the linguistic World meant instead that the longing to appease the mystical and abstract Other took over the whole agenda.

The problem is just that no matter what human beings do, however much they subordinate themselves, The Other is still never quite satisfied. Soon human beings cannot even eat or sleep without longing for the regard of The Other. The metaphysical hamster-wheel carries on spinning all the way through life, right into death. Language simply distances human beings in a radical way from nature and its directness, and once language is in place there's no going back. From that moment life is characterised by a notable distance, the distance which is a necessary consequence of all impressions having to be processed through the linguistic apparatus before they generate an emotional experience.

With the help of Language, Human Beings start to construct the World. Patterns are mixed and matched. Arbitrary but unavoidable sensory impressions are blended with culturally based evaluations projected upon sensory impressions, which the psyche goes on stubbornly trying to unite into an emotional whole. The clearer the patterns, the simpler the treatment. But there is always the fundamental antagonism within the worldview that we have single-handedly created. The attempts of Language to firmly fix the World are always breaking, and the worldview needs to be repaired and adjusted. The disruptions and surprises are never-ending.

This is the territory that classical psychoanalysis maps and tries to understand. The Real constantly makes its presence felt, as Jacques Lacan might have put it, where the Real is to be understood as precisely whatever marches, unexpected and disrespectful, into the fantasy world, disrupting established patterns, and forcing human beings constantly to piece together new fantasies of The World in order to orientate themselves and manoeuvre their way through life. At the same time Lacan points out that it is precisely this continually recurring opening, this impossibility of ever finally fixing the World, which makes it possible to experience the World at all. The World ought therefore not to be confused with the world around us in general, but seen as the equivalent of the fantasy of a metaphysical context superimposed upon the world around us in order to make it comprehensible and, above all, meaningful.

The interesting thing here is not whether or not life actually has any meaning – psychoanalysis isn't concerned with such rash speculations, theologians can deal with those – but the fact that life cannot be lived without a perception of its possessing a meaning. The crux here is that human beings do not experience any meaning directly, and neither can nor want to do so (human beings can only believe, but never know for sure), without this meaning being transferred to The Other. The meaning of life is thus nothing that we are aware of, but something we presume that The Other takes care of. The logic runs: if only I believe in The Other, then, as a reward, The Other will know for me (in other words: if I believe devotedly in my parents, the saints, the prophet, the monarchy, the oracle, the professor, the party, et cetera, then whatever I believe in will know the truth for me in return).

The World should simply be understood as the fantasy we use to fill in the gaps between our suppositions about the world around us, where it is what we use to fill the gaps, rather than what we believe that we know about the world around us, that dictates how we feel. What is most obvious about the world around us, the given and stable surfaces between the pleasure-giving fantasies, are largely perceived as banal and uninteresting in an emotional comparison. And of course they do not generate any particular activity in the brain. But the fantasies are a completely different matter. And none of these open and fantasy-nurturing gaps in our worldview engages us more that the ego itself. The ego is the gap that is never repaired, because it can't be filled with any content (the ego is, of course, an illusion). The multiplicity of egos also prevents the ego from ever being identified even as a fantasy. The hunt for this consistently illusive ego therefore never ends. Nor can our longing for The Other's favours ever be satisfied. This is a matter of perfect projections which are entirely sufficient for human beings as long as they live, talk and think.

In the continuous patching and mending of the worldview, language's dialectical competitors arise: the subject (the observer in the process) and the object (the observed). The process and the focus of treatment in the process therefore remain two separate yet mutually dependent phenomena, and the dependence between them in turn remains fundamental to our experience of The World. The necessity of the dialectic for the ontology of The World has as a consequence that what we feel about the world we also feel for ourselves, and vice versa, whether we are conscious of this emotional connection or not. Our self image and worldview are actually two sides of the same coin, impossible to separate. Or, to express this rigid dialectic in everyday language: anyone who hates the world basically hates themselves as well, whereas anyone who loves themselves also loves the world, because subject and object are the reverse of each other, and therefore constantly flowing into and out of each other. Or, to put it even more plainly: the self is naturally also the world, because how else could it be? We have left untenable dualism behind us, after all. The subject and object are not only dependent upon each other for their existence, they are also each other's mirror images, easily distorted through the lens of the emotions.

The division between our own world and other people's worlds that is necessary in terms of identity has dramatic consequences. It is not the child's realisation that its father and mother are other beings than the child itself that is the cause of the trauma of childhood. In fact, The Great Trauma accelerates when the child discovers that its parents' wills want something other than its own will, when it is forced to conclude that different people are fumbling around with different, and – on top of this – changeable, worldviews, and that this itself is unavoidable and deeply problematic. The simple, easily comprehended world with its limited number of building blocks explodes in every direction, turning into a hyper-dimensional hydra. World and worldview are no longer synonymous, the world actually contains at least as many worldviews as there are people. The fact that the disintegration of The World is intimately connected to The Great Trauma is clear, because it is from this experience that the narcissistic reaction stems.

Narcissism obviously has nothing to do with genuine love of self, but rather its opposite. The narcissistic reaction is simply the necessary survival mechanism for being able to handle, suppress and evade the overwhelming experience of the will of The Other when nothing else works to maintain the necessary distance. So when the world around us becomes so incomprehensible (in other words, so traumatic) that we have to withdraw and hide somewhere inside our enclosed fantasy world in order to survive, this is when the narcissistic condition arises.

The most extreme example of this internal focus is the psychotic's desperate attempts to recreate a functional worldview for the sake of his mental survival when a psychotic attack occurs. When everything blurs into meaningless chaos, when external impressions have fallen out of their context and lost all sense, and seem to crash into the brain upon the slightest sensory perception, without a glimmer of order, when language's distance to the surrounding world has collapsed, then the psyche only has its fundamental illusion, the Ego, left to fall back on. And this the Ego does with full force. Ego and World become one and the same thing and everything else vanishes.

Individual will is certainly not mysterious in the same way as The Other's will. Of course this depends upon the fact that I experience that I can always ask myself what I want, in other words: I can fantasise freely about my own will without being contradicted or denied an explanation, which means that I can confirm what The World is and not is for myself, simply using my original, childish, one-directional will. So when I shut off the competing wills, when I step off the world and my will becomes synonymous with The

Single Will, when my will and the direction of the world merge, that is when psychosis occurs.

The previously overwhelming feeling of powerlessness and incomprehensibility becomes the exact opposite under psychosis: an ecstatic feeling of obvious and comprehensive power. Because the Ego and The World have suddenly been reduced to one and the same thing, the previously utterly chaotic World suddenly seems to operate in a perfectly synchronised tandem movement with the Ego. The problem is that this only works in the psychotic's magical fantasy world. The psychotic is, of course – as long as the acute phase of psychosis lasts – completely incapable of action.

Like everything else in our surroundings, psychosis has both an existential and a Darwinian explanation. Psychosis clearly functions as a form of temporary survival trick when the subject needs to be protected from the threat of disintegration. It is as if the psyche were trying to save itself with a last desperate effort at the risk of life itself if necessary, in order for the psyche to be protected. The psychotic state only becomes a pathological problem, however, when the psyche can find no way back to symbolic order, when the psychosis threatens to become permanent. Because if the Ego is lost, there is no longer any psyche left. Just as the last thing a losing army does is to shut itself inside a fortress and pin its last hopes on the surrounding enemy giving up and going away again (maybe a more important enemy will turn up that needs dealing with elsewhere), so the Ego shuts itself in with only itself as its final means of salvation.

The narcissistic state is itself not psychotic, but rather a proto-psychotic flight from reality, a state where The Other and its will only temporarily make themselves known through their absence, in a sort of temporary recuperation before the painful surrounding world once again makes its presence felt. The narcissist, in contrast to the psychotic, has not stopped communicating with the outside world, but has merely shifted all emotional investment away from the world outside which attracts but disappoints, to an inner world which isn't really attractive but which seems to be controllable. Survival becomes, as is so often the case, something to be given a higher priority than pleasure; control always comes before enjoyment.

The oft-mentioned narcissistic phase of childhood is, for instance, intimately linked to the child's insurmountable disappointment that its parents' love for it is limited and conditional, where narcissism is the child's way of handling disappointment (the boundless attention that the parent can no longer give the child is simply replaced by the child itself). So the psyche is smart enough to make sure that there's a functional worldview somewhere, rather than worrying about whether or not this worldview is particularly realistic. Survival takes precedence over pleasure once again, and pleasure takes precedence over verisimilitude (or rather: before long-term functionality). Freud always has to submit to Darwin. But once psychic survival has been assured, what has occurred needs to be processed and placed in context. The powerful shock can in retrospect only be seen as a trauma, The Real once again making its presence felt in a painful way.

The Great Trauma occurs when the child realises that its own will and that of The Other (often, but not always, the parent's diverging opinion of when bedtime is, et cetera) do not agree. And it is precisely this trauma that gives substance to the Ego and The Other. This fundamental existential experience is the catalyst of narcissism. The immediate reaction to the discovery of The Other's divergent attitude is obviously to adopt a defensive position, hiding behind one's own will and completely identifying with it. Frustrated small children scream and scream when they don't get what they want, and the threat of retribution if they don't get what they want knows no bounds.

But once language is in place, the narcissistic response is quickly exchanged for its opposite. Deep down, our own will actually only wants to please The Other. And thanks to language and its inbuilt displacement of our ambitions – we start to believe in the future, we become willing to abstain from something small today in the hope of gaining something larger tomorrow, et cetera – we understand that The Other's will is our law, and the search for catching the eye of The Other and our adaptation to the fantasy about The Other's will hereafter be our driving force in life (which obviously expresses itself in everything from the hunt for love, the hunt for success, the hunt for social status, even the hunt for so-called self-realisation, which is really just a matter of guessing how to please the Other, and so on). It is this realisation which makes it so easy for us to see through the protestations of modern metropolitan women trying to fool the world around them into believing that they had their breasts or lips enlarged 'for their own sake'. Because once language is in place we don't do anything 'for our own sake': we do everything for the sake of The Other.

The conflict between satisfying our own internally nurtured ambitions – which is itself a particularly arduous struggle – and at the same time pleasing the mysterious and capricious Other becomes, after this narcissistic reaction, the dominant problematic in the production of identity. Obviously it is impossible to satisfy The Other – not least because The Other's many needs are practically impossible to predict, as well as magically attractive precisely because they differ from our own will – which means that narcissism is always having to give way. All ambition is subordinated to the need to adapt to the superior symbolic order. From this moment, the search for The Other's will dominates the whole of our existential experience, and there is no longer any doubt whatsoever about the fact that mastery of language is synonymous with power.

Henceforth life is a tricky balancing act between the subject's desire to liberate itself from the collective and the collectivist's desire to adapt to the social order. Should the child fight to get its own way, or choose to do as its parents want in order to win their favour? Can these ambitions ever be combined, through a mixture of cunning and patience? What consequences – indirectly via The Other and directly on our own part – will my behaviour have? Could it even be the case that The Other is actually a sado-masochist, and that obsequiousness will be met with derision, and nonchalance with love?

Thanks to language, what would otherwise be a marginal emotional mystery is transformed into a gigantic fantasy world full of fascinating twists and turns. It is this engine of phantasmical complexes in The Subconscious which both spawns, entertains and drives the subject onwards. Its power is so great, its patterns so deeply imprinted on us through biology, that even if – thanks to successful psychoanalysis – we have realised that the Ego and The Other are merely illusory perceptions and not physical realities, we are still incapable of freeing ourselves from their grasp. The effect of this analysis is actually the very opposite. Because these phantasms rule our subconscious, it is they who direct us, not we who direct them.

The psyche is balancing between two chasms. At one extreme is the absolute neurotic's obsession with constant and uncompromising appeasement of The Other, complete submission to the will of The Other, denial of bodily desires and immersion in the longing for longing. Because the neurotic can never be perfect in the eyes of The Other – the neurotic's fantasy world does not permit The Other's approval, because the neurotic takes pleasure in never being good enough, and pleasure is fixated upon repeated personal failures – he can never be happy with himself or what he manages to achieve. Nothing is good enough because nothing s permitted to be good enough (because if anything was good enough, the neurotic would no longer find any cause for pleasure and his worldview would collapse).

The formal error in the thinking of the neurotic is of course that The Other in no way wants the neurotic to be perfect. Perfection as an idea is not only impossible to achieve in an impermanent and changing world – to begin with, there is no eternal form out of which perfection could be achieved: Plato was wrong, after all! – but perfection is, above all, endlessly dull and off-putting. Who could handle having a lifeless, ingratiating, attention-seeking zombie walking two steps behind them all day? So the neurosis is driven by its own impossibility. The formal ambition behind which the neurotic hides will never be realised, the fears never justified, The Other will never get the chance to express its disappointment over the inadequacy of the subject. The longing for longing is not only the deepest aspect of how longing as such works – as with all human beings – but the longing for longing is, for the neurotic, the only longing that exists.

The perfect neurotic is of course the save who dies immensely rich without having made use of a single penny of his fortune. But to make fun of this behaviour would be to miss the whole point. For the neurotic, the pleasure is not in consumption or even in the social status that his fortune facilitates (neurotics seldom flash their often considerable fortunes), but in the act of saving itself. The fetish is thus no longer the symbol of The Other, the physical proof of the existence of The Other, but rather the fetish has been transformed into The Other itself. It is the postponement of pleasure that gives pleasure. The neurotic knows no other pleasure, and it is this, and nothing else, that is so tragic about the neurotic condition.

637

The neurotic's masochistic pleasure can in principle carry on undisturbed for all eternity, constantly repeating the same theme like the mechanical piano it actually is. The end of the story is the death of the story, so the end of the story must be avoided at all costs, and the cost of this is that the neurotic does not live life, but merely endures life in anticipation of a life that never arrives (it is hardly surprising that the so-called transhumanist movement on the Internet, with its ambition to create eternal life with the help of new technologies, is a paradise for neurotics). Life isn't something to be lived, but something to be constantly deferred in an pretend wait for its constantly deferred realisation (Judaism, with its constant little preparations for the Messiah's constantly deferred return, is the neurotic religion par excellence).

The other extreme is the absolute neurotic's complete and thus isolating immersion in his own narcissistic will, his immersion in instinct and the denial of desire, with the result that The Other and its will are shut out and ignored. Communication with the outside world collapses, which is obviously catastrophic for a social pack animal like human beings, and explains why psychoses are often identified with illness and potentially as a breakdown in religious ecstasy in all non-nomadic cultures. This is not, however, an emotional catastrophe; on the contrary, psychotics often describe the enormous kick they experience from an uncontradicted will in perfect harmony with the world around them. The problem arises instead when the will turns out to be paralysed outside the fantasy world, when The Other's appreciative gaze no longer participates in the experience and cannot stimulate the subject in the direction of the desired social recognition. Not to mention how impossible it therefore is for the psychotic to manage the simplest manoeuvres to ensure survival on his own.

Fortunately these extreme conditions are rare. The psyche is programmed in a Darwinian way to fight at all costs to maintain the difficult balancing act through a torrent of nagging ambitions. The balancing act between neurosis and psychosis is even the fundamental condition for the experience of a functional self-image. And it is precisely this balancing and rebalancing of impulses and desires which ultimately makes up the subjective experience itself. The psyche's stubborn attempts to maintain the balancing act between neurosis and psychosis thus have a logical explanation: the intense experience of a living subject is nothing more than the psyche's own pre-programmed deception of the body in order to ensure the survival of the body. The underlying illusion is actually the driving force of The Subconscious. The awareness that we actually don't exist outside our phantasms and the shadow world of language only increases the intensity of the existential experience. I simply feel more keenly that I exist when I start to suspect that I really don't exist at all. It works, because the existential experience is just a feeling, an electrochemical storm, and not an intellectual conviction.

This explains why neuroses and psychoses are, in spite of everything, so rare. The first thing to go when a neurotic or psychotic state arises is the sense of subjectivity, and subjectivity is also extremely difficult to restore afterwards. The person in question becomes an unconscious vegetable, a fatal burden to the tribe from an evolutionary perspective. The psyche is thus not programmed in such a way that it appears consciously in advance of the dramatic consequences of such an extreme loss of balance. Even the risk of a neurosis or psychosis releases powerful mental defence mechanisms, comparable to the defence mechanisms that are pre-programmed in the body's immune system to defend the body from external physiological threats like viruses and bacteria.

The recurring dilemma is rather that the psyche is basically nomadic; it does not permit any long-term fixed position, no allowance is made for rest in its lifelong search for hyper-dimensional balance. The fundamental ethical impulse from our pre-linguistic existence is still in place: standing still means death. The only imaginable solution to this ethical dilemma is to stimulate and defend our fascination at the difficulty of the balancing act itself. We must be content with at best enjoying the peace and quiet of the meta-stage. In contrast, the neurotic or psychotic state need not be regarded as pathological in the traditional sense, they aren't actually illnesses, but more a sort of supra-dimensional error in thinking which ought to be avoided because of their long-term destructive effects on our self-image, and nothing more.

After the appearance of language, nothing was the same again. The Subconscious turned the whole of our existence inside out. Speech and thought were surrounded by a magical aura which human beings soon started to project upon themselves. Language was the holy object which prefigured the deepest Truth. Anyone who controlled language also controlled the world. The most important function of language in a primitivist society was to convey the instructive story of the tribe's remarkable origins – which confirmed its attractive status as specially chosen – and at the same time to demonise the origins of neighbouring tribes, which was necessary in the fight for scant resources. But as language developed and humanity started to construct durable civilisations that prospered by cooperating with one another, the agenda changed. All human beings, all who used language, must have been meant one day to emerge as divine beings. Through this modification of language's message of the glorification of humanity, the authors of history open the way for religion, the moralising relative of the writing of history. The task of religion is to deny humanity's bestiality and elevate it to divine status. So the project of civilisation was begun in order to ennoble humanity by erasing its impulse-driven, pre-linguistic existence, and nurturing intellectual refinement.

The original myths had only a limited influence on the tribe's power structures. But when those myths were ornamented with religious dimensions, the mythology gained fantastic force. Religious myths could – unlike accessible, everyday tales of achievements in hunting and gathering round the campfire – be used to construct huge guilt-complexes which the developing feudal power structures could manipulate in turn. The linguistically and socially competent elite which managed to master these manipulative techniques soon replaced the old muscle-bound alpha-males as the leaders of the tribe.

In this way language fundamentally altered the conditions of life, and had dramatic effects on society's power structures at the dawn of civilisation. As the pre-linguistic pack was replaced by a gradually developing talking and thinking tribe with its purposefully designed mythologies – which in turn were a consequence of the fact that these talking and thinking tribes comprehensively thrashed the packs of their close relatives that were inferior in terms of communication technology in the fight for the scarce resources needed for survival – entirely new skills were favoured in the selection process that produced a leader-figure. The concept of the alpha-male therefore acquired an entirely new meaning: the gift of the gab and a capacity for intrigue replaced raw physical strength.

By placing language at its strategic centre, a tribe could defeat its competitors for scarce resources. So the leadership fell to the person who could best master and use language precisely as a tool of power. Since then, language has been the key to power. The individual who can tell the tribe the most attractive and credible story of its origins and future also becomes the internal voice of the tribe and its ideological centre. The person who controls the dominant communication technology in a particular society will also control everything else of strategic value in that society.

Ever since we human beings started to talk to one another, we started to be consumed by the self-obsession and megalomania that every rational project since then has ultimately tried to dismantle. It is probably only now, with our greater awareness of how the universe actually works, and the concomitant realisation of our own cosmological marginalisation, that we are once again starting to get back to the humbler attitude that was an unspoken truth for our forebears before language, with its glorification of humanity, took over and allowed our narcissistic fantasies to run riot for a few millennia. We once had a realistic awareness of our relative insignificance in the great scheme of things, and that awareness is once again within our grasp. But it is not at all certain that many of us will choose this clear-sighted perspective on ourselves and the world; it is always tempting to invent new excuses to continue nurturing a false self-image that flatters our vanity. Language persuades us that we are gods, and you can't break free from the abuse of many millennia just like that.

8.

THE RISE AND FALL OF MORALITY

IF WE APPLY OURSELVES to a philosophical debate aimed squarely at the existence of God – where the concept of God comprises all forms of imaginable higher metaphysical beings – then the scientific arguments used in other contexts are superfluous. There's no need for us to argue against the existence of some bearded old man sitting on the clouds or beyond the stars. Nor do we have to bother with attacking the idea of an independent soul hiding mysteriously in the pineal gland. Instead, let us focus on the historically recurring need for a metaphysical constant in our collective worldview. Rather than getting caught up in some post-Cartesian discussion of how the physical world and an imagined divine being might relate to one another, we shall focus on the considerably more interesting argument about the illusory character of the metaphysical constant.

This means that we will not have to deal with just one particular god or soul at a time – and, as a result, we will not be paving the way for another metaphysical illusion of the same type through our choice of argument – but that we can eliminate all such fabricated illusions in one single blow. Above all, we will be eliminating the need for ultra-materialistic philosophy to have an atheistic character. The answer to theology's classical question about our attitude to the existence of God is turned into direct questioning of the very foundation of the theological discourse: why bother with God? Why bother with the soul? Why adopt an attitude to the existence of something that we still haven't had adequately described to us by those who evidently feel the lack of it? Particularly now that it is so obviously a matter of something constructed in order to manipulate and control human beings throughout history.

Of course we sympathise with the atheist position. But the fundamental philosophical problem with atheism is that even atheists need to have an idea of the constant that is God. If nothing else, they have to have an idea of what it is they don't believe in, and must always be prepared to test their opinions in the face of humanity's inexhaustible ingenuity when it comes to inventing new metaphysical constructions. The atheist position is also, from a historical perspective, a humanist reaction against religion, and we're as uninterested in supporting humanism as we are in defending religion. We would therefore prefer not to be called atheists, by simply staying out of the whole debate. We believe instead that all classical metaphysical concepts like, for instance, The Father of the Tribe, the Creator of Everything, the Divine Clockmaker, the Soul, the Ego, and Santa Claus belong with horoscopes, crystals, pyramids and coffee grounds, none of which can be discussed in remotely serious terms. But what is interesting, on the other hand, are the reasons behind such metaphysics, and how they came about.

If we are going to talk about God, or rather the human need for a metaphysical focus, this focus must, ultimately, be synonymous with the universe itself. What could be bigger and more tangible than material reality itself, in its totality? The only intellectually defensible position regarding traditional religion is therefore pantheism. The father of modern ultra-materialism, Baruch Spinoza, was perfectly aware of this in the 1600s when he formulated his pantheistic theory of life as a single, connected substance with an endless mass of modalities. As a result, Spinoza became a prophet for the age of informationalism, because his construct provided the necessary synthesis of the capitalist age's dialectic between theism and atheism. While his contemporary Descartes, who was considerably more celebrated during his lifetime, got stuck in the humanist ideals of the Enlightenment and is now merely a milestone in the history of ideas rather than a living philosopher, Spinoza's long-neglected ideas have withstood the test of time with aplomb.

We both can and should ignore traditional religious and humanist convictions in this context, even if we recognise that we can never hold together a society, a worldview, even a self-image, without first – consciously or unconsciously – connecting the current paradigm to a necessary metaphysical centre. This connection itself is not actually a theological issue. It is quite sufficient to have a good grasp of phenomenology to understand the recurrent production of metaphysical constants, and an appreciation of social psychology to realise how this need should be handled.

Empirical experience from earlier paradigm shifts tells us that future generations will regard the Net, the specific metaphysical constant of our age, as both naive and illusory. But they will understand its social function. We have of course distanced ourselves, amused, from primitivist society's belief in the Original Father, feudal society's belief in God, and capitalist society's fixation on the Individual as the centre of existence, even if our laughter tends to fade away the closer we get to our own age. Naturally, we are both historically and ideologically closer to a belief in the Cartesian subject than belief in God; in the same way we are closer to a belief in a monotheistic God than to belief in the Original Father of polytheism. But the road leading away from the Cartesian subject in no way provides an escape route for the Individual, nor does it lead back to God or the Original Father – as the New-Age movement would sometimes have us believe in order to justify its existence – but rather an opening towards a new metaphysical constant with a higher level of relevance for our age and the age that is coming. So what we're talking about here are criteria of relevance rather than a discussion of the truth.

The only empirically demonstrable form of information-technological development is the gradually increasing amount of accessible information in society, which reaches explosive levels at each paradigm shift. In this way the temporarily eternalised worldview comes ever closer to the permanent mobilistic metaphysical truth, even if the latter can in principal never be pinpointed in detail other than on the meta-level. Our worldview thus appears to be getting ever more true, without ever quite managing to become completely true or comprehensive.

Eternalist philosophy is therefore not relativistic in the classical sense. Even if permanent truth can never be formulated, the illusions that follow one upon the other contain an ever higher degree of objective truth. The Cartesian subject is, for instance, less superstitious in information-qualitative terms than the monotheistic God, which in turn is less superstitious in information-qualitative terms that the nomadic tribe's Original Father. But it seems as though the ultimate metaphysical explanation always eludes us, off in what to us finite beings is inaccessible infinity, or up in the meta-level of thought from which it can only be abstracted as a diffuse necessity, but never made concrete as a sharply defined phenomenon.

However, we really don't have to worry about how we will be perceived by posterity. We're living in the here and now, after all, we think within the frame provided by the information technology of our age. No-one can ever think 'outside the box', as the advertising industry dreams of. Anyone thinking without a frame will only produce nonsense. Or, as the French philosopher Michel Foucault put it: 'It is intellectually unbecoming to imagine that you can think outside your own age'. The future cannot sit as judge in the here and now on what we think and do. We are responsible for our thoughts and actions merely to ourselves and our contemporaries. Neither past, future, nor any imagined generations can serve as our metaphysical frame of reference. But we can, however, always think more profoundly and sharply within our own paradigm.

The development of informationalism has opened the way for a philosophical and ideological renaissance. The dialectic between eternalism and mobilism is preparing the ground for a credible phenomenology. Socioanalysis and schizoanalysis offer new tools with which to study and understand newly expanding networks, their members, and those in positions of power within them. Through this work flows the inheritance from the great pragmatic European and American philosophers from the late nineteenth century onwards: Friedrich Nietzsche, William James, Charles Peirce, John Dewey, Jacques Lacan, Gilles Deleuze and Michel Foucault. This is even a process of radicalisation of the pragmatic inheritance, because genuine radicalism always has its stronghold in the currently pertaining circumstances, undisguised, and the subject we are studying – a new society with new conditions for existence – demands this radicalisation.

It is important that the concept of radicalism regains its original meaning. During the capitalist epoch the escapist utopianisms of both right and left have unfortunately been the noisiest claimants to the concept of radicalism. But, judged by our collected historical experience, both of these extremisms must now be viewed as the most reactionary, backward-looking, romanticising and mendacious of all the old ideologies. Did they manage to achieve anything other than a whole heap of misery and the defence of a whole load of stupidity? And what is an impulsive, simplified and populist explanation of the complexity of existence, if not precisely reactionary? Not least when it lays claim, entirely without justification, to universal validity. Sure the label of radicalism deserves better than that?

What, for instance, is the libertarian utopia of the night watchman state, if not a neurotic teenager's dream where one single arbitrary perspective on life is forced, entirely without justification, on humanity as an objective truth merely because the libertarians themselves cannot accept society's genuine plurality and the revealed relativism of science? What is communist society if not a low-budget version of the Christian paradise? What is the anarchist dream of a society without ownership or formal political direction if not a powerfully romanticised notion of life among the apes in the jungle before humanity's forebears had even emerged onto the savannah? In what way does any of these ideas deserve to be called radical today, when we can actually study their tragic attempts at implementation in the rear-view mirror of history?

Unlike the romantic fake radicals and their standard-issue flights from reality, genuine radicalism is characterised by the fact that it constantly forces people back to reality, here and now. Spinoza and Nietzsche are therefore far more radical than Hegel and Marx, because, out of all the classical thinkers, it is they who seriously clash with an old paradigm and an old worldview in their philosophy, and open history up to a new way of seeing the world. And wasn't that what radicalism was supposed to do?

With the emergence of informationalism, radicalism is synonymous with thinking trans-rationally – in other words: the starting point for all philosophical work has to be that mutable reality itself and nothing else is the metaphysical constant over time and beyond the information-technological paradigm – and, precisely because of this, eternalistic philosophy is the perfect form of radicalism for our age. It isn't enough, then, to be a rationalist, since classical rationalism takes no account of the evident limitations of intuition in understanding the world. Counter-intuition beats intuition these days in all manner of different arenas. An armchair, a pen and some common sense is no longer enough if you want to say something new and incisive. This is why we talk of a trans-rational age where logic forces its way past intuition in order to understand the world better. Only by doing this can we reconnect with and re-establish the Enlightenment's faith in increased knowledge driving humanity forward.

The basic task of socioanalysis is to identify the real metaphysical conception of faith in the collective subconscious of the age – in this context it is important to differentiate between the worldview that people officially claim to hold, and the one they subconsciously actually belong to – and then formulate this actual conviction as precisely as language and logic permit, in order to spread and increase awareness of this. So socioanalysis is not in any sort of oppositional relationship with classical sociology, but ought instead to be seen as a necessary addition to it, to facilitate the understanding of network society. Schizoanalysis fulfils exactly the same investigative and uncovering role as socioanalysis, but on the dividual level, where the schizoid subject of information society dwells. In this way it supplements psychology in the same way as socioanalysis supplements sociology.

The foundation of all of this work is obviously classical psychoanalysis – and its belief that an awareness of the psyche's mechanisms is an important project within the broader drive for enlightenment. Through socioanalysis, psychoanalysis moves from the individual to the collective level, and through schizoanalysis, psychoanalysis moves from capitalist society's view of humanity (based on the concept of the ontologically indivisible individual) to informationalism's view of humanity (based on the concept of the ontologically divisible dividual). We are merely talking about broader, and thus sharper, tools with which to understand humanity and the conditions of its existence. The social sciences can only get stronger through the use of these new tools.

One important ethical aspect of this archaeological work of the enlightenment of thought is the extent to which the proportion of truth in the collective fantasy in question is sufficient to give it long-term credibility. If the metaphysics are not sufficiently functional for us and the generations to follow, the work will still have to be done again anyway, and there's a risk that our input will turn out to be meaningless. Socioanalysis must therefore be based upon genuinely qualitative thinking: let us devote time, energy and care to constructing a decent cellar, so that the house that is then constructed on top of it is stable enough to last as long as possible. So, let's get to the bottom of these fantasies in the collective subconscious before we present suggested alternatives.

This is where we see the difference between populists with their short-term thinking, and radical pragmatists with their long-term thinking. Populists always rush the construction of the cellar – often by borrowing an abandoned old cellar from some once successful formula – in order to build the glittering walls and roof of their showy construct as quickly as possible. The short-term reward is considerable. Books sell, lectures are sold-out, elections are won. The masses pour onto the streets to back up the ingratiating guru who strokes their sensibilities the right way, mouthing appealing platitudes, before blaming any mistaken analysis and predictions on someone else. The problem is just, as Abraham Lincoln pointed out, that you can fool all of the people some of the time, and you can fool some of the people all of the time, but you can't fool all of the people all of the time. Sooner or later reality makes its presence felt. It is worth noting here that no social construction either reaches its apex or collapses as fast as those with fascist foundations. But there has never been an ideology as populist or as moralistic as fascism.

Without allowing that to force us into the most embarrassing moral trap, and ourselves moralising about the moralistic populist, and in this way getting hoist on our own petard, we can say that a shift from populism towards radical pragmatics will be an unavoidable consequence of a society that is increasingly interactive and complex in terms of information technology. It is the dominant communication technology that ultimately directs the values of a society, and as a result it is the transition from one-way communication to digital interactivity that is driving the development from a moralistic to an ethical society.

So it is not the case, we can state with some authority, that Humanity itself is undergoing a change and realising the superiority of Ethics, which would lead to Ethics gaining ground at the expense of Morals. Because Ethics can't very well be morally superior to Morals, just as a swimmer can't swim past a sprinter on a running track. This really is a question of apples and pears. Thinking is simply in the process of acquiring an entirely new material framework. Interactivity is rewriting the values agenda. Ethics are simply more functional than morals as a grounding value in network society, no matter what we might think of it. We would be wise to pay attention to this.

As one-way means of communication – the printing presses and electronic, megaphone mass-media – are losing their role as truth-bearers, and being replaced by interactive media as the dominant information arena, there is naturally a shift away from the values which are favoured by large-scale one-way communication and towards values encouraged by interactivity. And when the new media-technological framework forces the growth of new values, this means that the value-bearing and tone-giving elite will be exchanged for a new one, because the old elite simply isn't credible any more. We are in the process of a complete paradigm shift on every level.

The transition from a moralistic to an ethical values base is thus a direct consequence of the meta-medial shift from one-way communication to interactivity. Morals are certainly usually faster and more effective, in the short-term, than Ethics. A moral order does not, unlike ethical encouragement, need any reasoned foundations, which saves considerable time and energy. This is why morals have always been the engine of populist creation of values, which in turn explains why populists find it so shamelessly easy to change their opinions when it serves their overriding aims.

However, Morals lack the capacity of Ethics for openness, listening and constantly checking the current position, or, in other words: precisely those characteristics which are decisive for survival in informationalist society. Morality, of course, always proclaims a constant, objective truth – it is by definition not interactive. Ethics, on the other hand, never proclaim anything beyond a relative and subjective truth. The constants of Ethics are to be found only on the meta-level, where they by definition can only indicate how an ethical dilemma might be solved, but can never constitute the answer to the ethical dilemma itself (every dilemma within Ethics is of course by definition unique).

This means that the expression 'the ethics of interactivity' is, when it comes down to it, tautological. Because there is no particular interactive ethics. Interactivity is itself always ethical, and Ethics is itself always interactive. It is worth noting that there is no greater degree of truth in this new metaphysics as such which can decide matters. The same old Darwinian principles apply. What tips the balance in favour of Ethics is their compatibility with the dominant communication technology. In an increasingly interactive society, moralism is gradually losing its role as the foundation of values. A new, powerful elite is emerging and replacing old moralism with the ethical principles that are compatible with expanding interactivity. Anything that works in the attractive networks, the empirical pragmatism gathered under the heading of network dynamics, will be the universal norm.

When moralism is losing its connection to the divine metaphysical constant in this way, it also loses its axiomatic status. The amoral core of moralism can be revealed to the public without risk, and its attraction is fading. It is hardly surprising that the interactive arena is full of games concerning the old moralistic values, where moralists are exposed to ridicule and mockery. Weakness and inferiority are no longer synonymous with sin and evil, but rather, in true ethical spirit, with stupidity and foolishness. These merciless games with abandoned values would be unthinkable in a world which was still governed by one-way communication. These games themselves are sign that a paradigm shift is under way.

The explosion of interactivity is revealing the untenability of the common theological foundations of both religion and humanism: there simply cannot be a judge who enjoys spending all eternity evaluating human beings' nature, intentions and actions against predetermined criteria, like some pre-programmed machine. The stifling predictability of such a task makes it incompatible with precisely the narcissistic pleasure which simultaneously has to be the Judge's foremost character trait. Not even the most blinkered fanatic could gain any extra enjoyment from being the cause of the direct pleasure of a pre-programmed robot.

The two tasks of the Judge therefore appear to be incompatible. He cannot, as moralistic theology demands, be both a pre-programmed service computer working for the current power structure, and simultaneously the massively pleasure-seeking, pathologically narcissistic organism at the centre of that power structure. The automated fundamentals of the Judge's character are thus not only deeply unattractive – neither the robot nor the psychopathic madman is a particularly appealing father figure or role model – but its necessary components are also impossible to bring together.

No-one could be better suited to throwing the contradictions of moralism on the scrapheap of history than the successful netocrat, following in the trail left by the explosive spread of interactivity. In a society obsessed with network dynamics rather than the classical following of orders, there is no longer any need for a patriarchal lodestar. Any metaphysical invention that lacks every trace of functionality in the attractive networks of informationalism will soon lose its divine sheen. The patriarch doesn't disappear because he is evil; he disappears because he is unfit for purpose, an embarrassing historical deadweight rather than a strategic asset for the future.

Lies have a tendency to be revealed only when the players on the social arena can afford them to be. And such revelations are seldom pretty. The theological Judge is not only cold and impassive to our fates (we have of course forced him to be cold and impassive in order for our worldview to hang together): he is also both schizophrenic and in a permanent state of emotional torment. We are faced with a sluggish creature who is apathetically swinging his gavel without any idea of the convict's frame of reference or emotional life. God is appearing more and more like executioner and condemned in one and the same person. We are being forced to realise that he is either impotent – which means that he can hardly be regarded as a god, and under any circumstances has been reduced to something which we would be wise to ignore – or that his divine omnipotence is restricted to the limited and obsolete worldview of his deluded followers, which reduces God to just one more very unremarkable psychotic among all the others.

After the collapse of moralism, all that will be left of moralism's cherished judge will be a stultified and autistic psychopath with no memory, future or consciousness. And so every chance of identification between the Judge and the accused will be lost. The relationship between them is being reduced to a chimera. Judgements become arbitrary, meaningless and, above all, uninteresting, both for the Judge himself, the accused, and the imagined onlookers in the courtroom. Judgement Day is no longer a liberation party to look forward to, nor even some hedonistic slaughter along the lines of the well-attended guillotinings of the French Revolution, but more like a drawn out and tiresome torture scene. It would take a masochistic vampire rather than a harp-playing angel or a bloodthirsty splatter-fetishist to put up with the monumental dullness of God's presence.

It doesn't matter if we try to retain the moralistic worldview or leave it behind us and welcome an amoral way of seeing: a nihilistic values base is unavoidable under any circumstances. We are no longer God's, or even our own, creations, but merely the interesting consequences of coincidence. The countless peddlers of moralism throughout history obviously have no great interest in revealing this dark and unappealing underside of Morals. Power, and the shortest way to get it, via moralism, has always been far too tempting.

This relationship explains why nihilism, as Nietzsche points out, has been able to guide both the individual and collective subconscious throughout history, largely undisturbed. We have imagined ourselves and others to be morally correct, but in the long run we have still always done whatever satisfied our desires and impulses. All human beings are just the same when it comes to this, beyond good and evil, and are completely interchangeable with one another. Acknowledgment of this relationship would, however, deal a fatal blow to moralism. To the great satisfaction of the moralists, Nietzsche and his predecessors' texts only reached a limited readership. But in interactive society, where credible voices can no longer be silenced, the situation is rapidly changing altogether.

Growing pressure from below has forced the servants of moralism to proclaim double standards with ever greater gusto in order to conceal the nihilistic core of their own message. The evangelists in the New Testament relate, for instance, how the veils in the temple were rent when Jesus died on the cross. The moral core of the Jewish faith, the holy of holies, the innermost room of the temple, was thereby exposed to general view. What had once been reserved for the governing elite or the chosen few was now generally accessible to all people and cultures. The world entered a new age with Christianity as the new universal Truth.

But the evangelists never said what was actually revealed behind those veils. This must mean either that the writers are lying about the rending of the veils – the story is only intended to create a dramatic effect, an aura of amazement surrounding the death of Jesus, and the evangelists aren't afraid to deceive the audience in order to achieve this effect – or else that they for some reason consider themselves forbidden to tell what was behind the veil. Which in turn means that this veil is actually still intact. So what is the point in suggesting that the veils were rent, unless the act of telling itself is the definitive unveiling of the Truth? Once again there is supposed to be a sacred and enclosed room, a yet more sacred room inside the room which was previously said to have been the holy of holies.

Considering the overblown ornamentation in the form of gold, jewels and well-preserved old arks in the most sacred room of the

Jewish temple, could the absolutely most sacred room of all possibly simply have consisted of one single thing: an empty room? On this point the Jewish mystics, Dostoyevsky's cynical priests and the Heidegger-inspired theologians of the twentieth century are unanimous: God is, when it comes down to it, nothing but a black hole, an empty surface ready for projection. But the average Bible-reader never gets to know this. Christianity, like Judaism, is a moralistic religion, which is why the amoral core of Morality must be concealed at any cost from the foolish masses.

This means that the supposed paradigm shift, when Christianity replaced Judaism, is merely a chimera. In the same way that Judaism conceals the unknown absolutely most sacred room behind the well-known most sacred room, Christianity conceals the contents of the absolutely most sacred room behind the dramatic revelation of the absolutely most sacred room's existence. The difference between the religions is ultimately just a question of rhetorical strategy. Morality is saved, and has also – thanks to the role of the sacrificial lamb being transferred from the Jewish people to Jesus himself – been packaged in a way which means it can be spread around the world. Because the story also takes the side of the countless slaves against the limited number of masters in the Roman Empire – as Christianity does – its long-term popularity is guaranteed. When the masters fell, the slave religion could take over the empire.

Since Moralism cannot create itself and follow its own decrees, it is fundamentally always amoral. So Moralism is always, deep down, guilty of double standards. But in order for moralism's train of thought to cast its spell over the masses, the unappealing amoral core must be concealed, an act of concealment that has always functioned extremely well throughout history. And it has not exactly done any harm that the exciting secrecy surrounding the concealment has itself become the most important aspect in the appeal of moralism. Moralism never plays upon any objective value of truth, but upon its ability to get its followers to feel more special than their fellow human beings – or downright objectively superior to them.

It is well-known that the following of any confused sect leader, ironically, grows stronger when his prophecies are not fulfilled. In the same way, moralism's strongest card has always been its fundamental logical paradox. Morality requires the moralist for its survival, and it is the resulting feeling of being needed and important that makes the moralist the steadfast defender of Morality. An omnipotent God ought really not to need disciples. Only a damaged and thus illusory excuse for a god would demand the self-sacrificial spirit of the convinced preacher.

The double standard can only be maintained as long as the moral system in question is somehow being threatened by ideological competitors with alternative interpretations of the pertaining Truth. As long as there are credible people in the vicinity who have a deviating worldview, there is always a glimmer of doubt. And it is precisely this disruptive little doubt that prevents the preacher from putting himself on a equal footing with his ideology. But if, on the other hand, the moral system in question ends up as a monopoly, the necessary distinction between Morality and its followers is erased. Identification with Morality becomes complete when alternative social identities disappear.

A collapse of this sort sooner or later unleashes a collective psychosis: Morality and its followers become one and the same. The amoral core swallows the surrounding social structure like a supernova, and the previously concealed and therefore attractive amorality gains universal validity. What happens is similar to what happens in an individual psychosis: the isolated and abandoned subject soon falls, predictably enough, into a black hole. The surrounding world vanishes, world and ideology becoming one. The difference between the level of individual and collective lies, of course, in the scale of the catastrophe.

We can observe this recurrent sociotechnological phenomenon in the concentration camps of Nazi Germany and fascist Japan, in the gulags of Stalinist Russia, the killing fields of the Khmer Rouge's Cambodia, among the sharpened machetes of ethnic mass-murder in Congo, and in all manner of suicide-worshipping terrorist victim cults. The same mechanisms –intense collective pleasure behind a suddenly identified amorality – can be set in motion within any rabble: usually, fortunately, over a short period of time and with lighter weaponry than in the worst examples above. The point is that a moralistic ideological monopoly always exhibits an escalating destructivity over time, particularly if effective weapons are available. This phenomenon is completely universal and can therefore in principle occur within any culture.

The problem of the governing moral system is that the hellish chaos which arises sooner or later drags Morality itself with it into the abyss. So a long-term monopoly must be avoided at all costs. This explains why the most extreme variants of moralism are always criticised by apparently more moderate and pragmatic elements, who pretend to distance themselves from extremism's literal self-identification with the amoral core of Morality. This internal conflict within moralism explains why the moral system is always accompanied by an eschatological horror story. The complete triumph of Morality is in the long run, like all psychoses, synonymous with apocalyptic catastrophe. Or, to turn the argument round: there is a logical reason why psychotics are attracted by detailed accounts of apocalyptic stories.

The ironic consequence of this relationship is that moralism must devote at least as much time and energy to encouraging and supporting Immorality as it does to maintaining Morality. Demons are created and leaked out. This, naturally, cannot happen with the support of the official voice, because moralism would soon lose its credibility if that were the case. Instead, Immorality is subconsciously leaked out into the collective subconscious, preferably in the form of recurrent, pleasurable attacks on the demons in question. The ultimate aim of the moralists' doomsday sermons is thus not to limit the power of the demons, but rather to strengthen their power up to a certain controlled level where the production of social identity accelerates.

An example of this phenomenon is the widespread disappointment that arises during Pentecostalist revivalist meetings when it turns out that everyone in the hall is already saved. Logically the meeting ought then to be cancelled, or at least transformed into some sort of celebration. But for some reason this never happens. Instead, all those attending spontaneously start to behave as though they still haven't achieved the desired salvation. And this reveals that it is precisely the constant focus on the onslaught of the demons rather than salvation itself which is the appeal of the meeting. The more the preacher incites the congregation against evil demons, the stronger his libidinal charisma grows, and the stronger his own powers of attraction. Salvation is in this context of purely marginal interest. The important thing is that hell is considerably more exciting than dull old heaven.

This means that, between the lines of the moralist message, everything that moralism claims to object to is actually being nurtured; condemnation in no way conceals the strong appeal. Frenetic and constantly repeated distancing merely betray the depth of fascination. Look, isn't it disgusting? Look again! Look carefully! One more time, just to be sure! In this way, moralism manages to kill two birds with one stone: it fulfils the shameful and repeatedly denied need to look at the forbidden, whilst simultaneously also supplying the requirement of powerful demons which justify moralism's own position. All this talk of sin becomes both sinfully titillating and condemnatory at the same time. The details of this demonology are repeated time after time with ill-concealed delight. The battle against pornography is transformed into sanctimonious wallowing in, yes, pornography, and the constant prompting of thoughts about pornography: look one more time!

The conscious frenzy against Immorality and the subconscious frenzy in favour of Immorality reinforce each other and together promote attractive and pleasurable sensations in the frenzied collective. When the preacher rages against pornography, more pornography is sold, and more sinners come to church. This relationship explains in turn why abusers of sex, drugs or alcohol allow themselves to be saved so easily. They are merely exchanging one source of intense pleasure for another, without in any way needing to change or even seriously revise their worldview. The repentant sinner is also rewarded socially for the pleasure they experience, which acts as a further stimulant. The process is strengthened by the fact that there exists within the moral system an unspoken, paradoxical encouragement of the trespasses of the noble sinner: sin must first be nurtured if the message of Morality is to have any meaning. The sinner must first sin in order to get any pleasure from forgiveness. Without the serpent in paradise, Jesus can never die on the cross for our sins. Immorality is what gives Morality its right to exist.

This in turn explains why the Pentecostalist preacher must constantly repeat the dramatic tirade about his own sinful past. St Paul, for instance, saw it as an advantage rather than anything shameful that he began his religious career as the remarkably violent Saul, the foremost persecutor of the first Christians. Morality and Immorality survive in this way in a dialectical symbiosis, where Morality hardly needs to feel threatened by any victory for

Immorality, in spite of the fact that this is what its official message proclaims. What moralists actually fear is the collapse of Immorality, because this would remove the source of their existential pleasure, as well as their sought-after social identity, and would bring about the fall of both religion and the whole of the moral system.

As well as the intellectual amorality which is constantly encouraged among the leading proponents of moralism – their subconscious identification with the amoral core repeatedly makes itself felt in the centre of Morality – strong and contradictory tensions surrounding Immorality are also encouraged in the sphere of private morality. Rules can be broken by believers to their advantage, because the overriding goal always justifies the means. If Morality actually gains by individual moralists occasionally behaving in an immoral way, then the last barriers to the moralists' own achievement of their forbidden dreams are removed. The moralist is welcome to mess things up, particularly if this can be regarded in the long term as having had a beneficial effect. What is important here is that Morality itself is kept clean. In fact, the dirtier the moralist appears to be, the cleaner Morality itself shines.

This is why we often find these Pentecostalist preachers in the whore-house with their trousers round their ankles, the finest humanists at the centre of child-porn rings, judges in bed with criminals or hiding in the bushes with prostitutes, and the grandest proponents of democracy as the leaders of secret societies and lodges which make a mockery of all democratic rules. The amorality at the core of Morality may be officially concealed, but it lives on precisely because of that, like an active volcano between eruptions. Everything can be justified in the dialectic of the moralist elite, because Morality and Immorality de facto share the same agenda in the collective subconscious. They're two grubby little fingers on the same grubby little hand.

While an external ideological monopoly is the greatest threat to the survival of the moral system, an internal ideological monopoly is an absolute necessity. There is no room for different judges with different values within one and the same moral system, because that would cause the loss of universality – the basis of values which is presumed to be valid always and everywhere behind different values – and this would lead to the moral system itself losing all credibility. This explains why competing moral systems tend to end up in aggressive and prestigious conflicts with each other; the acceptance of a plurality of different, co-existing moral systems is completely at odds with the claims of universal validity which are the foundation of every moral system. The ideology of The Other must, like The Other itself, be relentlessly demonised.

This relationship in turn explains why the most violent conflicts that are occurring in the transition from capitalism to informationalism are not taking place within the practically invisible netocratic networks which are assuming control, but within the noisy and highly visible moralistic ideologies which are in long-term decline, gradually losing their status in the world and their grasp on the creation of values. We are therefore, ironically, in a historic age where the battle against militant quasi-ideologies is at the centre of events. The extreme madness of the desperate losers will steal our attention and energy for the foreseeable future, resources which we could otherwise use to develop a functional set of ethics for the new paradigm in peace and quiet. Instead, we are being forced to deal with moralists who are waging an embittered fight to the death against other moralists on many different fronts simultaneously.

The occasionally muted but always understood requirement for universal validity in today's globalised and multicultural society raises enormous adaptation problems for all forms of moralism. Catholic, protestant and humanist ideologies from the West, Orthodox, Islamic and Jewish theologies from Eastern Europe and the Middle East, Hindu and Confucian conformity from Asia – all offensive moralisms are ending up in ever clearer open and aggressive conflict with one another. The pretence of mutual understanding that is preached by the official supra-ideologies is cracking under the strain of the massive political and economic changes caused by globalisation. The moralist alternative cannot offer functional global ethics for the human beings of informationalism. There is no longer any room for the demonology that functions subconsciously as the engine of moralism.

9.

THE CURSE OF CULTURAL RELATIVISM

DURING INFORMATIONALISM'S infancy, the French philosophers Gilles Deleuze and Felix Guattari were already claiming in their twin opus Anti-Oedipus (1972) and Milles Plateaux (1980) that the increasing collective schizophrenia of late-capitalist society was the main characteristic of the development of informationalism. Informationalist human beings can no longer see themselves as Cartesian, cohesive individuals, but have changed into schizoid dividuals right in front of their own sceptical eyes. The same moment that the concept of the indivisible subject explodes into countless fragments, irreconcilable internal voices fighting and plotting to decide a conscious agenda, a new emergent phenomenon is formed. This is the dividual identity linked to a body machine, the multiple ego that is admittedly impossible to determine, and full of contradictions, but which, on the other hand, is available for observation and discussion. The brain solves the problem of contradictions perfectly well by simply closing its eyes to them.

This paradox – unified disintegration – explains both the development of and the problem with the new, levelling supra-ideologies and the intellectual short-circuit that permits the return of Morality in the form of cultural relativism. The dominant moral system of our age is neither of the old, classical ideologies – which are, of course, in open conflict with each other – but an aggressively imposed universal understanding between the old ideological rivals. This is a matter of a supra-morality which, ironically, is at least as intolerant as all earlier forms of morality, in spite of the fact that its express purpose is precisely to create and protect a dictated tolerance between moralities.

Under this supra-ideological umbrella we find, for instance, the ecumenical faiths, academic cultural relativism, the supposedly post-ideological liberal right, the New-Age movement, urban middle-class Islamism, and the pseudo-Spinozist populist left. None of these ideologies will be particularly popular among the developing netocratic elite. Because they never manage to attract any followers apart from the comfort-seeking remnants of the undermined ruling classes of the dying paradigm.

The problem is just that there are so many of these lingering, drifting moralists all over the world. Cultural relativism has therefore managed to capture the position of dominant supra-ideology during the current paradigm shift. The phenomenon can be described as a sort of ideological supernova, the terrible calm before the storm that is the transition from the age of the mass media to that of interactive media. Because even if netocratic ethics are already being practised within virtual networks, it will have to wait a while to make its appearance in the wider arena. Here the moralistic supernova still reigns unchallenged.

In the meantime, ecumenical churches are full of coffee-morning ladies and converted cultural journalists who, as a result of the isolation of dreary and chilly churches, have become so nostalgic and desperate for reassurance that they would rather listen to platitudes from a placatory wimp than kneeling in the fiery glow of salvation from a feverish Pentecostalist preacher. The fact that this means the church has given up all ambition to win new souls is something that tends to get overlooked. The pleasure of consuming security now brazenly exceeds the demonological pleasure of born again preaching. The responsibility for young people no longer caring about the message of salvation is placed, in true moralistic spirit, on the young themselves, instead of weighing down the stubbornly self-righteous ecumenicals, for whom what was once the so highly prized conquest of souls has practically been transformed into a shameful sin from their younger days. This is ironic religion, religiosity which takes everything apart from its own message with deadly seriousness. Behind the politically correct platitudes there is no message left. But everything else is most definitely deadly serious.

It is worth noting how the ecumenical churches debate nonsense like women priests and same-sex marriages within the church for an eternity, without ever referring to any divine attitude towards the issues in question. The shameless nihilism of religion could hardly be more clearly illustrated. The idea of any sort of democratic church contradicts, of course, everything that religion stands for, in other words: the revealed Truth. If it is the congregation rather than God that makes the decisions in church, why pretend that the activity of the church has anything to do with God? Because a democratic decision-making process is only an issue when there are disagreements that need to be dealt with, the democratic church can hardly be anything other than atheistic. God is simply one alternative to democracy, a way of handling disagreements through diktat. A schizophrenic or indecisive god presumably fills no function in a religion with pretensions to universal validity, like Christianity, for instance.

The consequence of this dilemma is a silent understanding within the cultural arena: supra-moralistic cultural relativism demands that the church de facto becomes atheistic in order for it to be accepted by the contemporary cultural establishment. The church accedes to this demand with the reservation that atheism, which is synonymous with the abdication of the church from all its claims, is concealed beneath an attractive guise of democracy that is acceptable to all parties. This mutual act of cheating is then presented as an ecumenical renewal of the theological message, where the moralising edge is, perhaps slightly unexpectedly, turned inwards, towards the more orthodox practitioners of the religion itself. The irony here is of course that this supposed renewal – the word renewal ought to be seen in cultural-relativist contexts almost as a retreat; the cultural-relativist message cannot be renewed – actually pronounces the church's definitive death sentence, a sentence which is then carried out with sadistic slowness.

It is hardly surprising that the vacuous, nihilistic church is suffering serious problems trying to deal with its extremist cousins. The consumtary quasi-ideologies that are being preached and disseminated by various crazy groups in above all the USA, east Asia and Latin America, and the hysterical macho imams of the Islamic world, refuse – for obvious reasons – to march in tune, even if these aggressive missions, with their pathetic programmes for a return to medieval moralistic values, will in the long term lose far more than traditional religion in the growth of network society. But the extremists still believe, unlike more socially acceptable congregations, the God really exists and is active in the world. There is at least an honourable logic in their madness.

Let us consider for a moment one example of the consequences of nihilism: if St Paul had listened to his congregations instead of single-handedly forcing the faithful to follow his moral code, Christianity would hardly have outlived St Paul himself. Today's priests lack Paul's strategic brilliance. They are far too corrupt and concerned with appeasing worldly powers. Because they have even stopped referring to the will of God in their theological quasi-debates, they evidently no longer themselves believe in the existence of God. The triumph of atheism could hardly be any clearer. Does the Pope seriously believe that we should believe that the Pope still believes in God? When the leading lights in a religion stop praying to their god and instead start to meditate, that's a pretty good sign that faith in meaningful communication with a divine being has been lost. If there really is a god who can show the way, meditation can only be a waste of time (meditation is also an oriental philosophical practice, carried out by professional yogis, and has therefore for logical reasons never previously had anything to do with any religious floundering for a personal god). Religion is now starting to look like a narcissistic excess typical of the age, designed to fill the vacuum which pointless prayer can no longer fill.

The strength of academic cultural relativism lies in its attraction to conflict-averse and careerist academics within an increasingly under-resourced, marginalised and politically expedient field of activity. What is most striking in this context is the impotence of the academic world when it comes to constructing a universal set of ethics, even though we are well on our way into the first genuinely cosmopolitan era. Because the incentives to promulgate an ethical perspective are negligible within the academic world, while it is still worthwhile both economically and in career-terms to represent moralising intolerance, the browbeaten and increasingly proletarianised academics choose in large numbers to act as megaphones for cultural relativism. Interest rarely lies.

As a result, the universities emit a never-ending stream of resentment. There is no end to the number of unjustly treated minorities that have been manufactured. Nor are there any longer any grand urban planning projects that can be carried out, no bridge building or traffic management schemes to accomplish, without someone in the media arena perceiving themselves to have been so violently mistreated that everything must be brought to a halt and examined afresh. Leftwing academic populism and its line-up of cynical mouthpieces – with such renowned philosophers as Slavoj Zizek, Ernesto Laclau and Chantal Mouffe all on the payroll – then connect the maltreated minorities with one another in their heart-rending theories of hegemony. The chain of equivalence that results is then supposed to represent The Universal in globalised society. Ostensibly weak groups are used as the planks out of which a solid media platform can be constructed. Moralism is throwing its weight around.

The netocrats might laugh ironically at this whole performance of shrewd vested-interest politics, all these embittered demands for attention and compensation. But they are nonetheless obliged to concede that this is a strategy that still works. Weakness is strength, self-pitying cultural relativism rules public space with an iron hand. And the slogan 'Status quo for ever' is a magical mantra for large and politically powerful hordes of nostalgia-freaks. Dissenters have to trek off to the developing economies of Eastern Asia and the Middle East to see netocratic architecture and experience modern metropolitan life which both encourages and is stimulated by change.

The problem with the pluralist message is that it doesn't work as an ideological attractor. Islamic, Christian, Marxist and eternalist academics may be commanded in the name of the holy multitude to burnish their own distinctive features, but this is really only a matter of superficial posing, never about absolute conviction. The totalitarian axiom of cultural relativism governs the whole of this ostensible multiplicity. Cultures and ideologies are really only decoration, and the only applicable norm is hypocritical, cultural-relativist supra-moralism. Dissenters will have their university wages withdrawn. As a result, we see a society obsessed with symbolic gestures, choice of vocabulary and dress-codes. All of this is dealt with academically by the institutions known under the Anglo-Saxon concept of Cultural Studies, and, in the media, by the vastly expanding number of opinion pieces by journalists. All of this noisy activity conceals the absence of genuine ideological criticism. Consequently, there is not much creative philosophy created here. That task has shifted from universities to virtual networks.

The attraction of the New-Age movement is a direct consequence of the growing fear of the specialisation of modern science. Increasing epistemic complexity demands a good deal of talent and knowledge if it is to be possible to combine it with a moralising and hierarchical social identity. So a supra-ideology emerges, levelling all human ideologies and fantasies, without allowing any empirical examination or argumentative comparison of the different ideas. This is the supreme instance of equivalence in thought: it's all just 'theories', and each one is as good as the next. Everyone is free to believe what they like. Everything is fine as long as it is sufficiently shocking and entertaining to win dissemination among old gossips and ayurveda clinics. The world can't be more complex than this, otherwise our blinkers go on. This is the core of the New-Age movement: being genuinely talented and able to think is synonymous with being cruel to people who are untalented.

This superficial attitude towards the Enlightenment's view of knowledge forces, paradoxically, the New-Age movement to create a huge demon which has to be presented as precisely inferior to all other fantasies – in other words, modern science itself. In order for chakra healing and pyramid energy to look like legitimate and interesting fields of knowledge, in order for ayurvedic treatments to be sold at a healthy profit, modern, high-technological discoveries such as the brain-scanner and the space telescope must be demonised. Knowledge is becoming evil.

It is hardly surprising that New-Age conspiracy theories about modern society aren't exactly hard to find. This new scepticism demonstrates enormous productivity when it comes to finding demons among new technological discoveries and scientific methods. New always means dangerous and evil. And when no other argument can be found, it always comes down to the same basic point: the balance of existence is threatened. The fact that existence has never shown any balance in any meaningful sense is in this context as unproblematic as the fact that those cherished chakra energies can never be proved by any currently existing means of measurement. The axiomatic goodness of the New-Age movement legitimises all manner of idiocies and sloppiness with facts. Crazy ideas about balance and energies fill the air. The New-Age movement is simply academic cultural relativism's stupid country-cousin.

This development has a socioanalytical explanation: fundamentally, the New-Age ideology is about the myth of victimhood as an epistemological norm. A piece of selected information no longer has a value in itself, nor is it even related to a context in which it can be tested according to scientific practice.

Instead, information is evaluated according to its origins. Person and opinion are no longer separated, but are now indivisible. The more exotic, ancient and connected to oppression any proposal's origins appear to be, the more noble and true it is presumed to be. The truth is no longer something that is arduously worked out, and thrust blinking into the limelight, but something that is pieced together according to idle whims in an undecipherable torrent of opinions. Your view of life is no longer what you are actually convinced of, but a decorative pose or an image you want to project.

The spectacular lack of critical analysis within the New-Age movement means that marketing overkill can be extremely profitable. For instance, the number of reincarnated Egyptian pharaohs has risen, strangely enough, in recent years, while the number of reincarnated Ukrainian peasants, which logically ought to be considerably larger, continues to be insignificant. This reveals the fundamental driving force of the whole movement. Ultimately it is just about its supporters' need to prove the superiority of their objective value compared to that of other people. The same banal old jealousy over titles that applied in the European courts of the 1600s is still alive and well. New-Age followers would dearly love to appear better, nicer, more noble and holy than other people. Their dense hatred of knowledge in turn means that any quasi-intellectual garbage will be favoured if it appears to serve this over-riding purpose. The winner is no longer the person in possession of carefully reasoned knowledge, but the most daring and entertaining liar. I'll pretend to believe your stupid lies if you pretend to believe mine. The one with the most daring and entertaining lies wins, grows rich and achieves social status and loads of sex.

This explains why the New-Age movement's demonology is full to bursting with wild conspiracy theories about the dubious morality of science. Everything is good and healthy as long as it comes from oppressed, forgotten or foolish people, while anything genuinely scientific and empirically proven is evil, because it comes from the strong and the knowledgeable. The foolish no longer merely have rights of ownership over paradise, as Jesus claims: they also have a monopoly over the truth itself.

Wisdom no longer has anything to do with knowledge or learning, but consists mainly of a fixed smile in the face of all of life's sillinesses. The holy smile, which venerated Eastern thinkers interpret as a sign of wisdom, is mistaken by the New-Age movement for wisdom itself. The result is the New-Age movement's collective theatre of false smiles and constantly repeated tales of progress, where Evil is a faded smile and an empty bank account. It is hardly surprising that the New-Age has long been the favoured ideology of the marketing departments of multinational corporations. There is no ideology that can compete with the New-Age movement when it comes to producing plastic smiles. This is marketing raised to the level of metaphysics.

Because this lovely smile is no longer founded on years of searching for the Truth – with all that this means in terms of sacrifice, training, learning, examination and questioning – the most profound wisdom is perceived to be easily attainable in just a couple of weekend courses led by stupid and narcissistic charlatans. Being able to exhibit a happy exterior and boast about your short-term thinking, rather than demonstrating hard-won knowledge spiced with the stimulation of long-term thinking, is the moralistic norm par excellence. It is hardly surprising that plastic surgery, intended to create gentler, smoother facial expressions, has become particularly popular among the adherents of the New-Age movement. Wisdom has quite literally become superficial.

If the Truth is the same as a first visual impression, then the Truth must also be synonymous with the first auditory impression. This explains why New-Age people are obsessed with the tone of what is said, completely ignoring what is actually said, a problem that recurs time and time again in the tyranny of political correctness. The intellectual standard is constantly being revised downward, no common denominator is too small any more. Our view of how the rhetoric and substance of a message relate to one another has become the very opposite of what it once was. The latter now provides the packaging for the former, which has taken over the role of primary signifier. This stress on marketing rhetoric at the expense of real substance perhaps goes some way to explain why the New-Age movement has such a strong following in the service industries, among vacuum cleaner salesmen and creative nail technicians who are into zone therapy. And because these niche groups make up a considerable part of the fast-growing service sector, the popularity of the movement is on the rise. It has managed to hit the demographic nail right on the head.

But popularity, we realise at once as good memeticists, naturally has nothing at all to do with truth. Some ideas find fertile soil in a particular context precisely because they are so bizarre. Tolerance of the spread of the New-Age movement is closer to being definitive proof of the lack of social criticism in our age. The great irony here is the very concept of 'New-Age'. In a time of growing interactivity, which brings with it an increased prioritising of ethical thinking, the term 'old age' (or 'old nonsense') would have been much more appropriate. Because what is actually new in a discourse which is entirely taken up with fantasies of lost ancient civilisations, but which lacks any relevant ideas about the dramatic future which is already forcefully making itself known?

According to the ethics of interactivity, a person's worth and their intellectual capacity have nothing to do with one another. But it is precisely this false connection which holds the macabre power-structure of the New-Age movement together, which makes New-Age the principal adversary of the developing netocratic elite, as well as the quite exemplary ideology of the consumtory underclass. The attraction of the movement's message lies in its appeal to people's subconscious shame at their intellectual shortcomings, which is why this shame is carefully nurtured within the movement to keep its followers in their place.

So the problem is not that these followers are intellectually inferior, but that they confuse their own experience of inferiority with decreased value as human beings. The New-Age movement is the clearest example of our times of an opium for the masses: it is the consumtariat's self-destructive reaction to the emerging netocratic knowledge society, with its meritocratic hierarchies. While young netocrats order yet another latte in their metropolitan cafés, a consumtariat fixated with New-Age is looking for ghosts in a barn with television cameras in tow. The discrepancy between worldviews could hardly be greater.

The pseudo-Spinozist populist left is the equivalent of the New-Age movement in political discourse. Once again this is an ideology of resentment. In the same way that coffee-morning ladies are attracted to ecumenical churches, and the retail-dependent bourgeoisie drawn to ayurveda clinics, forgotten old leftwing sympathisers are drawn to the new populist left. It is hard to think of a more grateful target group, because leftwing activists have long been ostracised and left to internal power-struggles within their shrinking and increasingly marginalised political sects on the edges of democracy. For these forgotten groups in the borderlands of media-society, the populist left offers an attractive package of slogans which confirms that the Left is and has always been morally superior to the demonised Right. When this simplified and de-ideologised message is combined with comprehensive media attention, popularity is assured.

Thanks to the pseudo-Spinozan populist left, old leftwing movements have once again ended up in the media spotlight. Their popularity in turn is deemed to confirm the truth of their message, or at least to add some sort of relevance to it. The hope of another 1968 attracts old leftwing activists and their guilt-ridden offspring, who, after decades of romanticised revolutionary story-telling, finally see a chance to do what their parents' embittered generation wants. So the guilt-ridden offspring of the superannuated lefties run around at international conferences throwing Molotov cocktails at the cavalcades of politicians' limousines, to the delight of the television cameras. Where their fathers failed forty years ago, the testosterone-pumped sons now hope to triumph. Otherwise there's a risk that both fathers' and sons' lack of ideological foundations and pathetic longing for moral superiority will be revealed.

These days there's no need for thick books to spread the message. The ideology has been stripped down and reduced to effective slogans in order to address a consumtariat with no patience for abstractions: the Left is simply the mouthpiece of The Oppressed. The Oppressed are by definition always right. Resistance is focused against something called 'Empire'. And because The Oppressed are always right, the Left is also always right, so there's no need for any critical evaluation of its arguments. All of this only benefits the demonised Empire. Criticism is branded as such and directed towards a particular interest, and therefore the issue in question can be more or less ignored.

The problem is just that the traditional left often preaches the same message as evil Capital, which is natural enough, considering that they are both subordinate to a common supra-ideology. Within the pseudo-Spinozist left this problem is solved by embracing the opposing attitude in relation to Capital, regardless of what conclusions an analysis of such masters as Marx and Lenin might suggest, and even if the adopted position involves a negative outcome for the left itself. The fact that this logic means that the populist left is both self-destructive, easily manipulated because of its predictability, and dialectically subordinate to the initiatives of Capital, does not appear to worry the masochistic activists very much. They evidently have other aims for their activism than Marxist revolution and the empowerment of the working class.

This is really about an ironic resistance movement that doesn't know what it's resisting, and has even less idea what it would do if its resistance actually managed to topple whatever it is that it is resisting. What socioanalysts suspected about the 1968 movement – that it was mostly a fashionable phenomenon where the activists' priority was to sleep with as many people as possible rather than change the world – no longer strikes activists as worth making a fuss of. The height of success within the pseudo-Spinozist populist left is, in spite of everything, to fly in a helicopter with Hugo Chavez over the jungles of Venezuela. Their ideology leaves no deeper traces in today's society. The concept of 'radical chic' has never been more appropriate.

Consequently, this nominally Spinozan quasi-leftwing movement has no qualms about entering into a variety of unholy alliances with groups that classical Marxists would hardly have regarded as housetrained. This is a marked change from the old Communists, who were relatively careful about whom they cooperated with. My enemy's enemies are now automatically regarded as supporters of the right cause. Everyone from superstitious animists to Islamic fundamentalists and extreme rightwing nationalists will do as company for the populist left, not to mention other consumtarian phenomena like ecumenical churches and all manner of New-Age groups. Everyone is welcome, as long as they are opposed to the common demon: global Capital.

It is particularly amusing that the left's desire for cooperation is so strong that it does not even need to be reciprocated. Islamic fundamentalists have time after time voiced their contempt for the amenable but naturally godless pseudo-Spinozists and their ingratiating offers of anti-globalist alliances. The Islamists want to force their own strictly literal interpretation of the Islamic faith upon the rest of humanity: consequently they are completely uninterested in forming part of the 'Multitude', the metaphysical phantasm of the quasi-Spinozan populist left.

Because everyone who claims to be exercising any sort of resistance is automatically regarded as oppressed, these activists are, by definition, always right, and must therefore always be supported. The abstract concept of resistance has thus assumed the role of the populist left's metaphysical axiom: why and in what way resistance is carried out is irrelevant, abstract Resistance with a capital R is always right in and of itself. Just as within the New-Age movement, there is a consequent confusion of person and opinion, and the reason for this error of logic is the same: the driving force of the pseudo-Spinozist populist left is the idea that the objective value of individuals is directly linked to their meritocratic status. This, again, is a question of resentment as an epistemological norm: because I feel sorry for myself – my narcissistic self-regard does not correspond with my social status – I am always right. The complications that arise when it later turns out that I didn't know what was good for me, or because I was too lazy to work out what was good for me, or that my interests turned out to clash with those of someone else, someone else who was at least as worthy of pity as me – all these problems are effectively swept under the carpet in order to keep the populist myth of Victimhood alive.

The hidden attraction behind the anarchistic utopianism of the populist left is the opportunity to feel morally superior, an attraction which for obvious reasons is strengthened when your self-image is dominated by a more or less accurate appreciation of your various shortcomings. The Victim is the rightful Master, this is the basic significance of being a victim. At the same time, populist leftwing activism presupposes subconsciously that the radical left will never win power: the victim will thus never become the master. Holy anarchy will remain a utopia, and power will always belong to the evil but subconsciously worshipped Capital.

The opening of the gates of paradise will be perpetually postponed, and Satan will always keep hold of power. This subconscious conviction means that the activists never need to take responsibility for what they say or do, not even to themselves. Only those in power have to be adult: those in eternal opposition can continue with their childish ways as long as they like. It is hardly surprising that the propaganda of the populist left largely consists of picture books drawn by scribbling schoolchildren, and their ideology does not permit any criticism to be directed to the idealised children in their followers' nurseries.

Cleverly, the quasi-Spinozan populist left carries out its media activism without such obsolete and infected old labels as Marxism and Stalinism. It pretends to stand for something new by not having any ideology at all. As a result, it can appear untainted in television debates. The absence of classical Marxist ideological criticism is striking. At most, the ideological content consists of a few suitably abstract quotes from Spinoza, pulled out of their original, intellectually complex context, which achieves the desired effect because the academic left is far too impotent and starved of attention to muster the energy to question the proposed slogans. The cost of this lack of ideology is that their activism has no long-term impact. When the television cameras are switched off, everything reverts to how it was. The left has not undergone any ideological renaissance, but has adapted itself to the market and become part of the commercial popular culture that it proclaims to criticise. It has been transformed from an ideological movement with long-term goals into a short-sighted testosterone spectacle for the consumtariat, a sort of quasi-intellectual macho-variant of the New-Age movement.

The basic reason for the shortcomings of the universalist supra-ideologies is that they never succeed in bridging their inbuilt contradictions. Denial of this problem might foreseeably rescue a dinner-party conversation, or hold together a hastily organised demonstration against a common enemy, but it reinforces rather than resolves the fundamental conflict in the collective subconscious. The supra-ideologies therefore never succeed in genuinely uniting their supporters behind a cohesive and attractive social identity. They remain supra-ideologies rather than genuine ideologies.

The preoccupation with nostalgically yearning for the cohesion of a dying moralistic network makes the authentic production of identity impossible. Moralism has no future, least of all in supra-ideological form. If the clergy's outfits are losing their power to create identity through their transformation into just one marker of ethnicity among others, the ideology in question will hardly win any new followers. Questions of life and death may conceivably entice people to make considerably greater sacrifices than questions of fashion and individual taste. Particularly if the underlying message is that all ideologies, regardless of their content and history, are of equal value, and, reading between the lines, equally true, and therefore equally superstitious and mendacious. If all ideologies are valid, no ideology is more valid than any other.

If conversion seems meaningless as a result, there is no longer any reason to go out into the world and battle for souls. What was once a fevered and exciting cup match is now a pointless friendly where the result doesn't matter, because cultural relativist supra-moralism does not permit anyone to win, or even to try to win. Victory and loss are connected to a moralistic worldview with one objectively higher valuation, and one objectively lower. So it is easiest to pretend that the contest no longer exists by moralising over competition itself.

This development shows that the traditional ideologies nowadays look as though their primary function is to beg money from states and institutions, rather than winning new souls for The Truth. The rain-dance is now performed for the benefit of tourists rather than calling forth rain. Churches are transformed from places where souls are won for paradise into cultural memorials and museums. When we know how stubborn Morality is, we can draw the conclusion that the overriding aim of this transformation is to change shape in order to survive. When ethnically or tribally delimited Morality loses its credibility, Morality soon bounces back in a new, universalist form. The first thing the new Morality condemns is, naturally, the old Morality, precisely in order to conceal and simultaneously preserve the discursive monopoly of Morality.

If all voices are suddenly to sing in unison, the universal supra-moralism must be pacifist. The universally prevailing peace, Pax with a capital P, the constant smoothing out of all conflicts, is the new metaphysical axiom, from which all other moral norms are fixed. Every war and conflict throughout history has been exclusively bad, we are told. Empire-builders and colonisers are the new demons. A sharp and aggressive tone of voice is the new evil, while no-one cares about heretical arguments themselves any longer. The remarkable thing is all the constant talk about our post-ideological state, as though cultural relativism and the ideology of the correct tone of voice were not themselves ideologies. What is this stifling of opinion for, we might ask, if not to conceal the fundamental internal contradiction within the universal supra-moralism?

Pacifism is, like all other variants of humanism, yet another moralism. And just as humanism conceals an amoral core – the fundamental bestiality of humankind – pacifism conceals a core of absolute and unreasoned violence. Because the driving force of pacifism is not the avoidance of violence, but the assertion of the pacifist's moral superiority over the warrior. This makes the pacifist ideology the perfect weapon for anyone seeking to set themselves above all ideologically handicapped warriors. As usual, Immorality is running amok through the subconscious while Morality stands in the focus of consciousness. Obviously, this is why pacifist demonstrations are the most aggressive, noisy, morally bombastic, and consequently the ones which most often tip over into violence against the forces of law and order, which is always said to be the fault of the forces of law and order. And the violence that is provoked is taken as proof that their own aggression needs to be stepped up.

Here we see the point of the moral system's internal monopoly on power: because God has been subordinated to the governing social order, he has lost his omnipotence and can thus no longer be regarded as a god. If God's ten commandments no longer apply to my neighbour – because he follows another moral system to me, which I have promised to respect for the sake of the Multitude – the commandments cannot in the long term apply to me either, because they have lost their universality through the acceptance of any deviating opinions. Quite simply, there is no longer any god behind the commandments, which removes any obligation to adhere to them. The consequence of this is that the faithful moralist either has to renounce his moral system entirely, or continue the fight for its universal validity.

Morality's inbuilt inability to compromise in turn strengthens Morality's tendency to nurture hypocrisy, a constantly recurring double standard. The inbuilt paradox explains the immense respect that fundamentalist practitioners enjoy within every religion and ideology, whether or not this is officially acknowledged. Fundamentalists are, as a consequence of Morality's inbuilt inability to compromise, the only coherent and credible spokespeople, in spite of their extreme and aggressive attitude. The so-called forces of moderation, the adapters, are in contrast traitors to Moralism, obviously guilty of double standards. They can only hope for the generosity of the world around them, but never for the respect of the fundamentalists within their own ideology. The fact that Islamic terrorism is afflicting moderate Muslims so badly is therefore entirely logical, and certainly nothing to be surprised at.

The intention of nurturing and maintaining Moralism is to placate the omnipotent and all-seeing Judge, even if the Judge is only a passive observer of and not a participant in the communicative process. Moralists are encouraged, consciously or unconsciously, to see their actions as ingratiating bribes in order to win the favours of the external Judge. In the world of Moralism, relations are always about manipulation rather than affection, which in turn explains why moralism seeks out and flourishes in environments where manipulation is the most prized behaviour. Because manipulation is incompatible with love – I can never know is someone loves me if I have manipulated that affection into being, just as I have no reason to manipulate a particular sort of behaviour if I really love someone – means that morals and love are ultimately incompatible.

The primary impulse towards moralistic behaviour can be seen in a child trying to please its parents. This is the same impulse which finds expression in a collective form when the primitivist tribe dances and makes offerings to the Rain-God in the hope of a downpour that will save its threatened crops. A child which gains its parents' attention and appreciation only when it does what its parents want – instead of that appreciation being the result of unconditional affection – will naturally develop into a formidable moralist. The tragedy is that the result is the same is if the reaction had been the exact opposite: children ignored by their parents will become, if possible, even more convinced of the power of manipulation, albeit in a genuinely tragic sense since this conviction is then combined by the subconscious belief in their own inadequacy. Other children are favoured, children who are superior to me. But there is no affection beyond the manipulation. Unconditional love is completely unthinkable.

A pat on the head for good grades in school thus becomes a prime example of moralising behaviour in all its glory, and the effect is obviously strengthened even more if a sibling with worse marks gets less attention. In the same way, a tribe that gets rained on the day after a rain-dance will soon start rain-dancing even more, even forcing previously passive members to take part in the ritual. Behaviour that we believe leads to rewards soon becomes the behaviour we identify with and see as a necessary condition of our survival. In this way we are encouraged to identify ourselves with either moralistic or elitist behaviour, depending on the system of punishment and reward in operation. Because these processes are fundamental in our production of identity, they are particularly deep-rooted and extremely difficult to direct.

The important thing in this libidinal process is not who the moralistic Judge is. It doesn't matter if we focus on a god, a goddess, a state, a party, a collective, an ego, a phallus, a matrix, or any other sort of metaphysical illusion. The conviction that there is a judge at all is what is important. The idea of the Judge, the absolute Phallus or Matrix, is far more important than any individual judge, postulated phallus or matrix that we imagine that we are courting with our morally correct actions. A pat on the head from our father only gains the desired credibility when we presume that our father in turn has received his authority from a father of fathers, the Ur-father, the absolute Phallus. As if there were really such a phallus.

This means that the primary arbitrariness in the production of values, the unpredictable aspect of God, also constitutes the precondition for the co-dependency between God and believer. If the believer can never predict in advance what God is going to think, he can never make himself independent of God in order to get his own existence and identity confirmed. Every decision must be referred to His Arbitrariness in person. This ruthless dependency reveals the subconscious, libidinal pleasure of the moralist: he takes pleasure from finally having found a credible external judge to appease, he no longer has to bother with a superego or take account of other judges and their wills.

This primal pleasure is the explanation why extremist sects force new members to cut their social contacts with competing moral authorities, such as their biological family or their ethnic background. The pleasure of obeying the sect leader's capricious orders must not in any way be disrupted, because it is this pleasure which holds the follower within the sect. The sect-member identifies whole-heartedly with this pleasure, and thus, in the long term, with the sect and its constant dramatic changes of direction. As a result, sudden separation or exclusion from the sect will often lead to acute psychosis. Cut off from the source of arduously constructed identity, all identity is lost and the psyche collapses.

The moralistic worldview presupposes a free-standing, substantial and cohesive subject, an absolute ego, a soul that exists in the sense that it is responsible for the urges, desires, intentions and actions of the body without itself being part of these processes. The ultimate purpose of the subject is to be the object that the external judge can judge. Goodness and evil in our actions must be ascribed to a specific object, and the moralistic subject is precisely that object. The subject is simply produced by and within the moralistic process so that someone can be held responsible for the impulses of the body. And this someone must, for obvious reasons, be something more than the Body itself, something outside the incomprehensible and mysterious totality of the Body.

However, closer inspection reveals that there is no such moralistic subject. After all, the subject, as should be clear from the preceding chapters, cannot even be localised. Moralism's credibility is lost the moment the Judge – and thus also the moralistic subject that the Judge is to judge – is revealed as an illusory myth, invented and maintained by an obsolete power-apparatus. All that is left of the once so sacred Human Being, after science's unmasking of the illusion of the ego, is a cohesive physical body steered by urges and desires, a network of organs that lacks both a centre and a responsible, decision-making subject. It is this body-machine, this dividual, that is at the centre of schizo-analytical investigation. The subject is reduced to a social convention, a linguistic necessity, an eternalisation which, from a mobilistic perspective, only exists as a synonym for the Body itself. Moralistic metaphysics are thus fatally punctured. Moralism has never been the opponent of nihilism, as it has always claimed, but ought instead – not least because of its inbuilt contradictions – be seen as the main defender of nihilism. The Judge is not just a monster and a victim that is perfectly suited to be the driving force of moralism, but simultaneously the force which inflames humankind's subconscious urges and desires in a society that is increasingly heading towards the opposite of moralism: ethics. The consequences for the citizens of informationalism are comprehensive: the great liberation project of our time is to eliminate all ties, intellectual as well as emotional, to an obsolete moralism. Only beyond this liberation can the ethics of interactivity be found.

10.

THE ETHICS OF INTERACTIVITY

UNLIKE MORALISM, WITH ITS unavoidable connection to the monotheistic paradigm, ethics are openly nihilistic. Without an eternal and omnipotent legislator there are no universally valid values. All values expressed and applied in society must instead be regarded as strictly subjective or contextual. But because all genuinely imaginable subjects have a distinctly marginal spacetime – human beings seldom live more than 100 years, or grow to more than two metres tall, and every known society and other collective subjects have been restricted to the planet Earth – the universal validity of the historical multitude of values has to be taken with a large pinch of salt. This is why we use the concept of nihilism, anchored in the history of ideas, as a starting point for the analysis of the ethics of interactivity.

However, it is important to distinguish between different forms of nihilism. When we speak of nihilism as a general concept – referring both to people's experience of life, and the collective worldview over a longer period of spacetime – we mean a historical development, a chronology where three distinct phases follow each other, a development which is fulfilled with the purely ethical worldview that we call the ethics of interactivity.

The metaphysics of the primitivist nomadic tribe revolved around the ur-father and ur-mother. But the development of feudal agricultural society saw the growth of mutual dependence between different tribes and cultures. Agriculture, livestock management, and fixed dwellings encouraged increased cooperation and an intensified system of bartering. This meant that previously antagonistic rival societies were forced to come up with a more or less common worldview. The ur-fathers of the various tribes were therefore replaced by an ur-father for all tribes: the universal god. The primitivist ur-fathers and ur-mothers became the gods, goddesses and saints of folk religion, but remained subordinate to the aristocratic elite's belief in The One True God. Besides, patriarchal society, the hierarchical system which made feudal society effective, could only be constructed upon the precondition that the universal ur-father himself was the alpha-male of all alpha-males, the patriarch of patriarchs.

Capitalism's urban bourgeoisie in turn replaced the universal god with the individual Ego and the nation-state People as the centre of metaphysics. All of these metaphysical entities are, however, obsolete in interactive society, where the abstraction of the Net is the metaphysical centre. Because highly effective one-way communication is being undermined and sidelined by divided multi-way communication in all manner of directions, the creation of value is shifting from monotheistic and humanistic moralism to the ethics of interactivity. Nihilism's growth, breakthrough and takeover of power is therefore the central intellectual drama at the transition from capitalism to informationalism. From a historical perspective, we are moving from humanistic moralism, through the nihilistic chronology, towards the ethics of interactivity.

The first of the three phases of nihilism is naive nihilism. The subject in practice lives with a worldview that is suffused with a nihilistic awareness of the absence of the Judge, although this awareness has not been made conscious, but is merely active in the subconscious. A typical naive nihilist is the middle-class citizen who is to all intents and purposes secular, but who goes to church on a Sunday for the sake of convenience. In other words, you don't believe, but you believe that the effects of belief can fill a socially useful and organising function. Another example is the Arab immigrant who experiences confusion, isolation and marginalisation is his new western environment, and who chooses to embrace Islamic activism without adopting an attitude toward or even reflecting on the validity of its central tenets of faith. We imagine we have a need for the practical consequences of one faith or another, but we choose not to adopt a position regarding that faith itself. We simply talk about other things and demand respect for our empty conviction. One characteristic of the naive phase is the plentiful occurrence of hypocrites and supra-moralists, which can be observed now that the humanist paradigm is slowly but surely collapsing under the weight of all of its internal contradictions.

The second phase is cynical nihilism. By now the nihilist has become conscious of their own nihilistic conviction, but is still living in a state of nostalgic loss for the stabilising security of the moralistic worldview, and retains Loss itself as the driving force in the production of identity. A typical cynical nihilistic argument is that Humanity is in the process of killing itself, precisely because it no longer has any objective values to which it can subordinate itself. Cynical nihilism is thus first and foremost a victim mentality, or, in other words: a drawn-out and intensely pleasurable experience of the self-assumed role as the metaphysical victim of history. It is in this pleasure that we find the strong emotional attraction of cynical nihilism.

A typical cynical nihilist is the humanist who curses his nihilistic awakening, and sentimentally expresses his longing to return to his romanticised idea of his predecessors' metaphysical conviction. He still speaks about God, but only in the third person, and for understandable reasons never actually to God. He meditates instead of praying. Faith in the existence of God has merged with the desire to believe in the existence of God. Religion has become confused with nostalgia for religion. The will of God is out of the game, and religious practice is transformed into a banal and crass democratic process.

Because there is no longer any god dictating theological truths, dogma must instead be felt, thought, nurtured and voted through in an opportune way in accordance with whatever suits the congregation in question. If, for instance, there happen to be more women than men in the congregation, God might be expected suddenly to switch genitals from penis to vagina and answer to the title of Goddess, only to revert to the previous gender the very next day. It is clear from this that there is no longer any real faith in the existence of divinity. Fantasy and reality have been mixed up to the point where all distinctions are dissolving.

Many of the most populist proponents of postmodernism are typical proponents of cynical nihilism, for example the French philosopher Jacques Derrida, whose project encompasses a great deal of sorrow at the shortcomings of the Judeo-Christian inheritance. Viewed within the history of ideas, humanism is nothing more than a smart way of recycling the monotheistic showpiece construction, albeit with no cellar this time. It is the Indian rope trick. Ideology has been transformed into a structure that floats freely in mid-air. On closer inspection, there is no other foundation for the whole system than pious wishful thinking, something that humanism actually acknowledges with the dethroning of God, although the consequences of this lack are never addressed.

The recurring argument is that nihilistic acknowledgement means the definitive end of the history of philosophy, a dialectic snare with no possibility of a synthetic solution. The idea of the French and British Enlightenment philosophers, that the Truth would free Humanity, is thus turned into its cynical opposite. In the same way as Dostoyevsky's priests curse the death of God and strive to silence the truth-sayers in order to save the morals of the people and their enjoyment of religious conviction, postmodernists like Derrida curse the irrevocable awareness of nihilism's historic victory.

A typical expression of contemporary humanism is the constantly recurring television documentary seeking out metaphysical Evil in the concentration camps, to the tones of monotonous minor chords composed by exotic composers. This whimsical and allegedly charming search for Evil will naturally carry on for eternity without ever showing any results, something which does not appear to trouble the filmmakers very much. This is a case of the search itself somehow guaranteeing the existence of what is being sought after: Evil. And this is the cynicism in cynical nihilism: it wants to carry on the search but never end it, because the existence of Evil is not what the cynical nihilist actually fears, but rather its non-existence. This is a thought that must not arise. The worst imaginable disappointment would be if dear old functional Evil turned out to be a fiction. Consequently, humanism strictly maintains its image of the supposed representatives of Evil in modern times, Adolf Hitler and Joseph Stalin, as some sort of super-intelligent and, a very real sense, inhumane, social sadists. It would be fatal for the humanist worldview to see them for what they are, sociopathic eunuchs.

Unlike its historical forerunner, Enlightenment philosophy, which was a product of the awakening and energetic middle classes during the previous paradigm shift from feudalism to capitalism, cynical nihilism – the supra-ideology of the collapsing capitalist bourgeoisie – is not driven by the enjoyment that is linked to the search for and revelation of the Truth, but instead by the ambition to retain its petit-bourgeois enjoyment of Sorrow and Loss in the absence of terribly useful Evil. It is hardly surprising that humanism cannot find a safe haven in interactive network society and is looking increasingly like the last confused defence of the crumbling bourgeoisie. This is more a question of a newspaper obituary in the culture section than any pioneer spirit in the blogosphere.

As a result, humanism's values are nowadays promulgated by the consumtarian tabloids rather than being aired and maintained in netocratic networks. This confirms that humanism is historically finished, and that its supporters, the bourgeoisie, are a busted flush. The last argument in defence of humanism, when its lack of intellectual rigour is starting to become abundantly clear, is therefore merely about its innate goodness. Let us pretend to be good, because goodness is such a delightful quality to demonstrate to our acquaintances, and let us at all costs keep quiet about the fact that Goodness and its counterpart, Evil, do not exist. This may serve to reinforce the last vestiges of enthusiasm in its few remaining supporters, but cannot possibly interest a netocracy which has rejected the whole moralistic conceptual apparatus in favour of the ethics of interactivity.

The third and final phase is affirmative nihilism. The nihilistic subject only reaches this point when fully aware of the consequences of maintaining the moralistic worldview in power. Only then is it possible to abandon moralism without any trace of loss or sorrow. In fact, this farewell is more of a necessary liberation, and releases feelings of euphoria. It is no longer necessary to put on an act.

The affirmative nihilistic subject realises that precisely what makes it a subject is the capacity and possibility to create its own subjective values. The role of the subject is no longer to manifest the metaphysical constant – in other words, to pretend, in true Cartesian spirit, to provide a home for the substance of society – but instead to be a productive and pleasure-taking component of the Net, the constantly changing, collective process that forms the metaphysical constant of informationalism. With this, the journey of the metaphysical constant is complete: from its home in the Pantheon above the clouds and below the earth in hell, via the soul that is presumed to be enclosed within the human body, the constant is journeying out into the virtual and global electronic network.

It is at this point that the ethics of interactivity enter the historical arena. The task of ethics is to explain to the affirmative nihilistic subject what its freedom looks like, and offer analyses and recommendations regarding the values that the subject can and ought to identify with. We are talking about affirmative nihilism because the subject affirms itself to itself through its identification with the capacity to produce the chosen values. And in the monistic worldview that is developing and replacing the old dualism – with its division between body and soul – there is no longer any room for a distinction between body and soul or between the subject and its values. Everything is body, everything is the world. How could it be otherwise?

The body precedes and encompasses the subject. I am one with my body, but I am also one with my values. Identification with both the body and the values that the subject encompasses is complete. And this is also how the subject is perceived by the world around it. The subject is thus partly bound to its values in a way that was previously unthinkable, at the same time as the subject and its values are changeable in a way that was also previously unthinkable. The subject has been pushed to the periphery of existence and become a producer and mobilise rather than fixed and manifesting.

Human beings think because they are forced to think, because they have been forced to develop a complex survival strategy during periods of extreme hardship. I exist not because I think, but rather I think in order to exist. Human beings think because they have access to language, abstract symbols for functional communication with the world around them, which they can also use internally to develop theoretical arguments. And these abstract symbols have access to human beings, which means that they can prompt precisely this sort of communicative and template-forming process. Who is to be regarded as the agent in these processes, the subject or the symbols, depends largely on which perspective you choose.

The capacity to think is not, therefore, as religion and humanism claim, a question of choice or of some gift from above that needs to be looked after for the good of some other subject. Thinking has no higher meaning nor any noble purpose – as though there were some greatest and highest thought that is presumed to lie in hiding somewhere waiting to be thought, which would round the story off nicely – but rather is concerned with the pure management of paradoxes, a prominently reactive mechanism that only exists because it has become over the course of history part of human beings' advantage in survival terms. And even if our human thinking is more advanced than anyone else's, we are far from being alone in thinking. Simple forms of symbol management and self-awareness can be observed in other intelligent animal species like the apes, whales and elephants. Thinking is thus not a unique, isolated talent, but a phenomenon that occurs on a sliding scale. This also applies, of course, to human thought. It is an ability that is distributed extremely unevenly between different people.

One basic reason for the development of thought is that life is fundamentally paradoxical. Life is both eternalistic and mobilistic at one and the same time. Because the eternalistic worldview and the mobilistic worldview cannot be combined, at first glance life always appears chaotic and incomprehensible. At the same time, this incomprehensibility is both the root of and the driving force behind thought. Because the subject is a direct product of and a precondition for thought, the subject itself is paradoxical: according to the eternalistic worldview, body and subject are strictly separate entities. In contrast, according to the mobilistic worldview, body and subject are synonymous with one another. We are simply living in the middle of an ongoing dialectic between eternalism and mobilism, and that is precisely why we think the way that we think. As far as we know, this isn't a problem for whales and elephants.

If we take this argument to its conclusion, we can say that, according to eternalism, the subject is the centre of existence, its purpose and meaning, its beginning and end, whereas mobilism does not believe that the subject exists at all, and that it is in any case completely irrelevant. The paradoxical subject is the subject which is conscious of this fundamental contradiction and constructs its worldview out of this awareness. In this way, and from that perspective, the paradoxical subject is precisely the subject that affirmatively identifies itself with affirmative nihilism. Moralism is not merely a stage that has passed: it has also been vanquished. And this is where the ethics of interactivity come in.

When we write that the subject, according to eternalism, is the purpose and meaning of life, its alpha and omega, it is important to be clear about exactly what this means: that the eternalist subject only exists because there has to be a subject in order for existence to be comprehensible at all. The eternalist subject is therefore no empirical phenomenon that can be found by scientists after an arduous search of the human brain or the body of society. Rather, it is a purely linguistic phenomenon, a necessity in order for language, thought, logic, and social and symbolic order to appear as remotely coherent. From a mobilistic perspective, both subject and free will are completely illusory. The paradoxical interplay between these two convictions is the arena in which the paradoxical subject both arises and is active.

The eternalistic subject is thus something entirely different to the Cartesian subject of rationalism. Descartes and the other Enlightenment philosophers sought a morally responsible subject that took pleasure in duty, which could be subordinate to God and State. They therefore imagined the subject as a sort of quasi-physiological substance with a specific spatial location, hidden somewhere within the human brain. The dualistic Enlightenment philosophers did not do this because they had found a separate subject of this sort in some scientific investigation, but because a distinction between body and soul was essential to save their beloved moralism. Historically, the Cartesian subject goes under the name of the Individual ('indivisible' in Latin). Humanism is thus synonymous with individualism. So that the eternalist subject is not confused with the Cartesian subject, we identify that instead as the Dividual ('divisible'), a concept which correctly reflects its schizoid character, its paradoxical and thus pluralistic core.

The reason why the rationalist Enlightenment philosophers and their humanist successors took the individualistic axiom as their starting point is their intense desire for the subject (the soul) and the rest of the person (the body) to remain clearly separate. Because it is only through this radical separation that the Individual can be held publically responsible for its actions: as a result of the dualistic division between soul and body, the Soul can be held to answer in moralistic courtrooms and the Body can be dealt with by an authoritarian care apparatus as soon as its actions transgress the norms of the governing power structure.

Body and Soul have to be kept apart if God and Creation, and even the State and the Individual, are later to be kept separate. Cartesianism is thus driven, as Nietzsche points out, not by some whole-hearted search for the Truth, but by the need to invent a new right of existence for Moralism once religion's articles of faith have become historically obsolete. Social cohesion and subordination are more important than the Truth. This nihilism is either naive or cynical, but it is not yet affirmative. The need of a truth that appeals to power is greater than the desire to use reason to discover a higher truth that is logically coherent.

We can clarify this logic by turning the argument around: if the Soul cannot be held responsible for the mistakes of the Body, and the Body cannot be charged with the deviant opinions of the Soul, because Soul and Body are really one and the same thing, then there is no longer any object for the apparatus of power to hold responsible or deal with. All that remains is a body directly driven and identified by its urges and desires. A monistic view of humanity like this would be a fatal blow to the moralistic power structure. What would we need a moral court for when there is no longer anything for it to do? As a result, ongoing developments are unthinkable for the Enlightenment philosophers, unmentionable for the romantics, and a tragedy for the postmodernists. It threatens their positions of power. It undermines their enjoyment of their social identities.

At the same time, the unveiling of the moralistic agenda of the rationalists and humanists is paving the way for a deeper understanding of our existential conditions. Neither the eternalistic nor the mobilistic perspective, and thus not the dialectic between them either, permits any space for the existence of a soul independent of the body. Instead, the eternalist subject turns out not to have any requirement of some pseudo-physiological substance, but can exist perfectly well as merely the precondition for perception, a rarefied product of its own thinking. As a result, the Subject no longer needs to be kept separate from the Body, but is, rather, synonymous with it. The eternalist subject can be described as the ambassador of the body in the world of thought and language; and, like all good ambassadors, the subject identifies entirely with the body it represents.

The eternalist subject is the prime eternalisation of the chaos of existence, from which perception goes on to organise all other ensuing eternalisations, as it rapidly invents and continually modifies the worldview necessary for survival. Perception may well always take note of the world around it first, because there has to be a backdrop against which the subject and its worldview can perform, which is why mobilism takes precedence over eternalism. But it is only when perception is forced to distinguish between the external and internal states of chaos that the need for a primary eternalisation arises. Eternalisation takes precedence over the subject itself.

In order for existence itself to be seen as the primary object, the subject must first be invented, quite simply: be borrowed into the equation from nowhere. It is their attitudes to this necessary loan that divide eternalistic and mobilistic logic. Eternalistically, the subject is the centre of existence, whereas mobilistically, the subject is and will remain an invalid and irrelevant illusion. Or, to put it in schizoanalytical terms: our existential experience of being a subject – an 'I' or a 'we' – is nothing more than the habitual and socially ingrained management of the fundamental trauma of our considerably deeper and subconscious experience of ourselves as nothing more than a loan from nowhere, an existential vacuum. We experience the subject as something that must be added to memory, something that must be added to the fantasy of ourselves as historical phenomena. At the same time, we understand mobilistically that there is nothing beyond memory itself.

We cannot actually make any meaningful pronouncements of any sort without first presupposing that a subject exists, a subject that makes this pronouncement, as well as an object to which this pronouncement relates. But this illusion is far from sufficient. Because we need at least one more subject, a subject to which the pronouncement in question can be directed. Within schizoanalysis this subject is known as The Other. So, the eternalist subject only exists in its capacity as a necessary linguistic construction, a social convention, and is also therefore inevitably a schizoid entity. No other evidence of the existence of the subject is necessary, because the subject is eternalistic and not mobilistic, and is thus of no interest outside self-reflective philosophical logic.

The eternalist subject's identification with the Body and its functions has far-reaching consequences for the production of values. The transition from moralism to ethics is complete. Identification with the Body means that the subject's ambition is redirected to create initially the largest possible arena for this body's urges and desires. The body is transformed into a compact and selfish machine that is governed precisely by urges and desires. This relationship is, however, complicated by the fact that human beings are pack animals. Not even the lofty hermit spending years sitting on top of a pillar actually intends to leave humanity for good. Like all other pack animals, human beings are born and raised within a social system. The Other is constantly present as a reference point. The existing network can be swapped for another, but at least one network is always present, maintaining the metaphysical role of the Net in the governing worldview.

Group belonging is genetically conditioned, the form is preprogrammed in the subconscious even before the primary externalisation process consisting of subject-object-subject starts to act. This means that The Other, the necessary second subject in the primary perception formula, is far more than an eternalistic and linguistic necessity. The Other takes the form of a facade, and is projected right from the start onto a tangible face. The clearest example of what we might call this facadisation is the relationship between parent and child: because the odds of survival are directly related to the degree of emotional connection, the projection of The Other on your counterpart's face is an obvious survival strategy. The Other is synonymous with me outside my own body, an extension of myself in space-time. The narcissistic impulse is running at top speed when the subject in this way experiences itself as greater and more extensive than its own mortal body.

For the same reason, the dividuals in a network are programmed to perceive The Other in each other. But The Other is also projected onto the counterpart in power-relationships: the Master perceives the Slave as The Other, just as the Slave does the Master. Social identity only starts to be produced when the projections of master and slave respectively are in place. Because abstract thought is a product of language, The Other also arises internally within the subject itself: the other within me, with whom I imagine I am communicating when I think, takes the form of The Other within me. Or, to return to how the creation of identity is the management of facades: The Other is precisely that in my own face which, in my own self-facadisation, remains alien to me when I look in the mirror. 'Je est un autre', as Arthur Rimbaud wrote.

For pack animals like human beings, The Other is thus the subject's optimal object, an immense opportunity but also a fatal threat, and always endlessly fascinating in the role of the only possible emotional escape from the threat of being locked into the hyper-narcissistic bubble of psychopathy. Regardless of whether The Other assumes the role of beloved saint or despised demon, it is the strength of emotion itself which prevents the psyche from shutting itself away in an isolation that is so dangerous for pack animals. Indifference towards The Other is the beginning and end of narcissism.

Because thought is based on language, and language is produced socially – we do not invent our own vocabularies, but take them from our surroundings – the pack animal moves into us and constitutes the primary identity, even for the dividual to himself. The subject regards itself right from the start as a pack or a network consisting of at least two primary components: the observer (the superego, or the subject as subject to itself) and the actor (the subego, or the subject as object to itself). The actor is The Other for the observer, and the observer is The Other for the actor. Thinking cannot in fact be thought of as pure thinking, which would only appear as an unbearable, isolated and endless loop of always the same self-referential information. So thinking can only be imagined by itself precisely as a network dynamic, a conversation between at least two parties, even if the conversation remains limited to one single specific physical body.

Because the network is thus of primary rather than secondary significance for the subject's understanding of itself, eternalistic theory's of the subject must be subordinated to the laws of network dynamics, and according to these laws we can never deal with a number smaller than two (a network always has at least two nodes). The child's relationships to its parent and to itself function in this way right from the start. The child perceives relationships as completely interchangeable with one another because it hasn't yet learned to evaluate and place the various subjects in a hierarchy. It projects its own identity onto its parent and internalises the parent as a component within its own identity. The human psyche exhibits an astonishing capacity to switch between different positions within and between different subject-object relations. During an analytical process the transfers occur in all directions through the relation of the story, and thus within the production of identity.

One result of this is the collapse of the classical psychoanalytical idea that the subject is whatever it experiences itself to be, or rather that the subject is and remains at the coordinates fixed by the authoritarian analyst. Role play and transference are a central and unavoidable function of identity. Being conscious of this condition means that the psychoanalytical axiom – which has its basis in Cartesian dualism – has to be replaced by a schizoanalytical understanding of the human psyche as a pure, network phenomenon. This doesn't mean that the paradoxical subject needs to be reinstated as a healthy ideal, but rather that the paradoxical subject is necessary for orientation in a society suffused with interactivity and network dynamics, a society that rests on a worldview characterised by an awareness of the dialectic between eternalism and mobilism.

The fundamental role of the network dynamic in the production of the subject has two interesting consequences for the ethics of interactivity: the first is that all processes of subjectification are analogous with each other. Whether we are talking of a dividual subject in a single person, or a universal subject for the whole of humanity, the subjectification process proceeds according to the same pattern. The theory of the subject can be applied to all types of subject with the same precision. This means that there are universally applicable ethical coordinates to be garnered from network dynamics, empirically proven experiences which both organisations and single dividuals can make use of. This continually adjusted empiricism constitutes the core of the ethics of interactivity.

The second consequence is the appearance of the network dynamic that indicates our need for the ethics of interactivity. If existence is primarily made up of networks, then the secondary relationships must be relationships between networks. So it is at the nodes, the points where the networks and therefore also the interests of the networks meet, that we most of all need functional ethics. Because it is precisely these conflicts of interest that arise between different subjects at the nodes that the various parties gain by having prepared themselves for. The task for the ethics of interactivity is to prepare the way for non-zero-sum games that are as comprehensive and mutually beneficial as possible between the involved subjects, subject components and subject clusters. The most important thing is to take account of which underlying urges and desires the various subjects have, and then to explore whether or not these are compatible or possibly even mutually enhancing.

The schizoid character of the subject means that it is simultaneously striving towards a solid entity (the hermit urge) and the expanding plurality directed towards existential dissolution (the symbiosis urge). The paradoxical subject arises precisely because it is existentially necessary to maintain a functional balance between the hermit urge and the symbiosis urge. Only through this balancing act can the subject hold itself together. If the hermit urge becomes too strong, this triggers a neurosis, and if the symbiosis urge becomes too strong, this triggers a psychosis. All functioning subjects are, in other words, paradoxical eternalisations which both arise and are maintained in order to cover over a fundamental contradiction, a mobilistic illusion, which in turn constitutes both the origins of the subject, and its driving force. Neuroses and psychoses can thus be social as well as dividual phenomena. How many wars and conflicts throughout history have not been started as an internal neurotic paranoia within a particular collective subject?

The concept of enjoyment-plus means that we as pack animals get more enjoyment from being the focus of the other pack members' enjoyment than from our own enjoyment. There is a sociobiological reason why enjoyment-plus is greater than enjoyment: enjoyment-plus has been necessary in a Darwinian sense in order to satisfy individual pack members' interests and to ensure the survival of the pack as a pack. Altruism is basically the same as a sophisticated group act of egotism, and moralism always presupposes a naive suppression of this fact. It does not even recognise it as the necessary starting point for enjoyment-plus as a phenomenon. Instead of a complicated process of weighing up the interests of dividual and collective, constructive and destructive intentions, short-term and long-term ambitions, Moralism always leaps at the one-dimensional but false division between good and evil. Instead of ethics' complex but necessary balance between different interests, all decisions are subordinated to the presumed interest of one single power: The Big Other, the overriding Other behind all other Others: in other words, the metaphysical constant itself.

The moralistic logic only hangs together as long as it denies the moralist's comprehensive enjoyment-plus in transferring his own enjoyment to the illusory judge of moralism. It is precisely this denial which inevitably results in moralism's bizarre infatuation with the victim mentality, which is the exact opposite of enjoyment-plus. Ethics, on the other hand, only becomes possible once the enjoyment-plus principle has been revealed. The conditions of the lives of pack animals are then known, and humanity's bestiality is no longer regarded – after, for instance, Charles Darwin's scientific, Friedrich Nietzsche's philosophical and Sigmund Freud's analytical breakthroughs in the 1800s – as a problem, but rather as a liberating fact. From this point, ethics and moralism go their separate ways through history.

Once ethics has broken through, it is clear why egotism and altruism do not need to be each other's opposites. They look more like two sides of the same coin, two connected aspects of the pack animals' existential conditions. Consciousness of the enjoyment-plus principle means that sound egotism is also sound altruism, and vice versa. The incitement to conceal this fact disappears when transparency has been established: it is not just me who is aware of the enjoyment-plus phenomenon, and the same applies to my fellows in the social game. So all players discount enjoyment-plus in all its complexity. No-one stands to gain anything any longer by moralising. Ethical altruism therefore contains a credible recognition of the selfish motives behind the actions in question. The ethical altruist realises that he must acknowledge that he is carrying out an altruistic act primarily for the sake of his own increased and long-term pleasure.

The logic of network dynamics is this: I enjoy being the cause of your enjoyment. You experience enjoyment if and when you perceive yourself to be the object of my enjoyment. Consciousness of the conditions and possibilities for enjoyment-plus gives us an opportunity to cultivate a collective non-zero-sum game of enjoyment. Suddenly the desire to be the object of someone else's enjoyment looks like a constructive act. We are, quite simply, stimulating collective enjoyment by continually facilitating the production of even more enjoyment-plus. We are shamelessly making ourselves the objects of other people's enjoyment. Thus we ultimately also enjoy the existential experience of our relationship. This would not be possible if we did not first see the Net, the metaphysical constant of network society, as the cohesive factor.

Where moralism promoted the single dividual at the expense of the pack – God is, of course, the ideal of moralism, and God clearly lacks any sense of pack mentality after the onset of monotheism – the ethics of interactivity build instead upon the socioeconomic foundations of human enjoyment. We are not only dependent on each other for the survival of the pack, but we also enjoy this mutual dependency. This is, then, a question of an enjoyment which ought to be stimulated still further with an increased awareness of its preconditions.

Discounted knowledge is itself always beneficial to civilisation. The ethics of interactivity therefore build upon a socioexistentialist foundation, where the metaphysical starting point is the primary relationship of network dynamics, the Net, rather than the obsolete individual of moralism. The difference between the ethical and moralistic worldviews could hardly be greater.

In contrast to moralism, ethics has no predetermined laws or rules. Because there is no supreme judge, there are no objectively valid values to take account of. Instead, all values are revealed to be strictly subjective, and applicable only to the contingent processes within the network of communicating actors in question. Whether or not affection arises among the bodies involved is largely a matter of random chemical reactions. No-one can be held responsible for a specific reaction occurring, so no-one can be held responsible if a desired affection is not reciprocated or does not even exist.

The distinction between morals and ethics is fundamental for the schizoanalytical method. The goal of the analysis is to liberate human beings from the faulty thinking that is an unavoidable consequence of the moralistic worldview, and instead get them to see the world in accordance with the ethics of interactivity. This leads to a worldview where hierarchies of values have collapsed, a world liberated from the belief in objective values, where values are merely subjective and contingent, linked to the affections of the subconscious and the pragmatic calculations of the conscious mind. When nothing has an objective value any more, everything has the same objective value, in other words, the value zero. Because $0 = 0$, this means that everything and everyone is objectively, radically equal. In so far as we can actually talk of any form of ranking within ethics, this is always contingent, transitory, strictly subjective, emotional, aesthetic, and, above all, of only marginal significance.

Ethics takes no account of any external forces, but only analyses the chains of cause and effect that are presumed to exist within the current communicative process. Whereas morality judges the degree of good and evil in human behaviour – which means that morals have to exclude such otherwise obvious factors as coincidence and unforeseen events; for understandable reasons, moralists have always had a tendency to look shamelessly and feverishly for scapegoats, whilst simultaneously fleeing any complexity – ethics is only concerned with maximising the opportunities for the constructive aspects of the intentions which precede events, and minimising the risks for the destructive aspects.

Here the axiomatic transferability of subject theory plays a central role. Ethics arises, of course, from the fact that all actors, given the same set of circumstances, will act in the same way in similar situations. It is thus not the actors themselves, but only the consequences of the action, taking coincidence and unforeseen events into account, which are ultimately judged. The ethical subject is de-personified, universal, contingent and neutral. All that remains is an intention, which in turn is dependent on a history of urges, desires, and those conditions which are connected to the situation in question. The subjects are completely interchangeable with one another. I am whoever I happen to be, and, because the subject is empty, anyone would behave in exactly the same way as me if they were in my position. Affection is strictly linked to contingent urges and desires which govern me, rather than me imagining that I could govern them. I am no longer my morality, as moralists claim, but instead identify myself directly with my fate, with my urges, desires and circumstances.

Classical ethics were formulated long before the dark origins and dynamics of Moralism had been revealed. Since Moralism ruled more or less uninhibited, ethics had to be transformed into pseudo-ethics and incorporated as an element in the overall moralistic perception. Otherwise it would, as memetics teaches us, never have been able to establish any credibility or achieve any level of dissemination. The odds were simply too poor. One illuminating example is how Jesus advised his disciples to treat other people as they themselves would wish to be treated. Immanuel Kant followed the same principle when in the 1700s he formulated his moralistic imperative of desirable equality in order to achieve the best of all possible worlds.

The stress on the equal value of all human beings makes this a question of ethical behaviour. But we are still dealing with pseudo-ethics. Classical ethics does not fall back on a process of cause, effect and coincidence. Nor is there any understanding of the subconscious or the schizoid division of the subject between observer and actor. It is still a matter of determining the value of actions and results in relation to a frozen background, rather than an evaluation of intentions against a backdrop of uncertain randomness. Consequently, classical ethics eventually became yet another in the long line of moral imperatives. We ought to treat others as we would like to be treated because it pleases the constantly present Judge, and only for that reason. Correct behaviour makes the Judge regard us with longed-for goodwill, and grants us generous treatment on Judgement Day.

Pseudo-ethical principles are thus mixed up in general moralism. They simply have to be formulated and preached as moralistic orders from the Judge himself in order to function. This fact that this is the case is revealed by human beings not only lacking the radical equality of interactive ethics, but above all that they have been granted a positive and substantial value. This is a value which is obviously never specified – because quantification would reveal that there is really no objective value. The point of classical ethics is thus first and foremost to protect Morals. The paradigm shift from a moralistic to an ethical worldview therefore requires that even classical ethics are buried.

The ethics of interactivity and its radical equality is something entirely different to classical ethics and its moralistic imperatives. Equality is no longer a general piece of advice or a high-minded maxim for life, but just a fact coldly accepted in advance. We treat other people as we would like to be treated, and therefore treat ourselves as we treat other people. We do this subconsciously, whether or not we are aware of wanting to do it or not. Because in network society my self-image is also my worldview, and my worldview is reflected directly in my self-image, and thus also determines my view of my fellow human beings. Every valuation of another person is simultaneously an equivalent valuation of myself, even if the valuation of my fellow human being becomes part of my consciousness while the valuation of myself is locked into my subconscious.

The subject is always completely transferable. If we take the theory of the subject to its extreme, all that is left is a single subject, no matter whether dividual or collective: the metasubject which is the precondition for the process of subjectification itself. Genetic inheritance, environment and circumstances differentiate us, but the illusory substance of the subject, the vacuum which cannot be defined other than with a symbolic name, is universal and common to all of us. The 'I' is a 'you', the 'we' is also a 'you', and vice versa. The poetic facade of every object is, deep down, an ambassador for the universal subject.

All those lovely words of wisdom, from Jesus to Kant, are largely one-dimensional platitudes when compared to the ethics of interactivity and its radical equality. Because we have no need to struggle to follow these men's moralistic imperatives: we are already doing so before we are aware of it, whether we believe that we want to do so or not. The ethics of interactivity only arise once this has happened. The subject's transfer of itself to other subjects is already in full flow.

The first imperative of ethics is to fight moralism ethically rather than moralistically, in order credibly to grant ethics its historically justified place as the field of values for the global empire. The collective transition from cynical to affirmative nihilism means a paradigm shift of immense proportions: becoming conscious of this process implies an ethical responsibility to spread and support ethics in all its forms. What could be more enjoyable in terms of the creation of identity, and thus more meaningful, than precisely this work? And this work starts with our immediate surroundings.

The fact that the concepts of morals and ethics are still connected and confused in today's increasingly ethical society reveals that moralists, consciously or unconsciously, imagine that they can see advantages in hiding their moralistic intentions behind supposedly ethical ambitions. Schizoanalysis aims to uncover this attempt, and as a result to facilitate liberation from moralism. Because Moralism aims to produce and preserve an external, universal authority, the battle against moralism in all its forms is ultimately a collective work of liberation. When Moralism is replaced by the ethics of interactivity, social relationships can be built upon genuine equality between both the parties involved as well as their surroundings. But this is impossible as long as any remnants of Moralism are exonerated and preserved from examination, and thus given the opportunity to cling on within the system. Schizoanalysis will therefore not finish its work until Moralism has been entirely eradicated and replaced by the ethics of interactivity.

Even if we have left moralism's banal opposition between good and evil behind us and have begun to grapple with the complicated everyday evaluations within the pragmatic world of ethics, we will never escape the subject's primary need for a universal reference point. The Big Other is always there in our subconscious, and in network society it assumes the form of the new metaphysical constant, the Net. The ethics of interactivity have a higher and greater purpose beyond concrete evaluations of conflicts of interest at the nodes between networks.

In order for our decisions to have genuine existential value for us, the Net itself must benefit from the decisions we make. The cosmos in abstract form, the Net in concrete form, is the furthest horizon against which we can make our decisions and build our dividual and collective identities under informationalism. We can call this spontaneous metaphysics a form of empirical pantheism, religious atheism, secular religion, or merely refer to the phenomenon as network worship. But we will never get away from the central role of metaphysics when we look at network society as its own paradigm, standing on its own legs, genuinely independent of its predecessors, capitalism and industrialism. But the metaphysics are already securely embedded in our subconscious, regardless of whether we have got this clear for ourselves and given it a name.

11.

THE THEORY OF SCHIZOANALYSIS

HUMAN THOUGHT HAS ALWAYS been strangely attracted to oppositional pairs, like soul / body and form / materia, and to the eternal discussion of how one takes precedence over the other. This is how we perceive and orientate ourselves in reality. This applies particularly to human thought about human thought itself. Ever since antiquity and the very earliest philosophy, the human psyche has been contested territory, a central front in the historical battle between materialism and idealism.

The divided figure of thought itself is easy to comprehend. Aristotle described form as 'that which makes something what it is', whereas materia is 'that which is potentially but not actually an individual object'. In other words, this is about two different dimensions of one and the same occurrence. The organism in general and the human being specifically is defined by its form, its innermost being, which in turn is another word for the soul. Bodily matters are therefore something completely separate from those of the soul; each is described with its own vocabulary, and treated with its own methodology. We might argue about whether one takes precedence over the other, and which perspective should be decisive, but the dichotomy itself is, for most people, undeniable and beyond all discussion.

The academic production of knowledge in our own age is no exception. Either/or is what counts. You either choose the natural sciences and stick to a strictly materialistic explanatory model where the psyche that is the object of study is a piece of stable bodily tissue, a brain whose functionality varies according to what hormones and other exotic chemicals are flowing through it at that moment. Or you choose an idealistic-analytical investigation of the psyche and stick to an appropriate explanatory model where the object of study is an endless and difficult to comprehend chain of fantastical constructions of a hypothetical complex of connected instances such as the superego, the subego, consciousness, subconsciousness, urges and desires. Representatives of the different fields of research imagine that they have very little to say to one another seeing as they are talking about such different things and use such different conceptual apparatus.

You might imagine that we choose to presume that there are fundamental obstacles of an ontological sort which make it by definition impossible to unite the psychological way of seeing things with the psychoanalytical. Or you could think that we choose to presume that recent explanatory models are so complicated that not even the most brilliant experts could hope to master and move between these two areas of research to any meaningful degree. But regardless of what your starting point is, the discourse itself does not permit any comparisons between – still less any partial combination of – these two areas of knowledge. Psychology finds itself in the less than glamorous role of a science with no philosophical ambitions, while psychoanalysis, after a long series of clinical setbacks, has been downgraded to the status of applied philosophy with no scientific credibility. This means that if you want to understand yourself and your psyche better, you have to choose between either a therapist or an analyst. You can't have them both at the same time. The fear of once again ending up in the nineteenth century's war of attrition between materialism and idealism has a solid hold over public discourse.

The price of the current ceasefire is that the underlying conflict remains unaddressed. A ceasefire, of course, should not be confused with the end of hostilities: oppositional positions are made permanent by being swept under the carpet. Consequently the psychological establishment regularly rejects all analytical explanatory models of the mechanisms of the psyche as nonsense and speculation with no foundation, while schools of psychoanalysis reject psychology's pretensions to universal applicability as naive and arrogant. One illustrative example of the latter is how Slavoj Zizek, one of the most renowned practitioners of contemporary psychoanalysis, has named one of his books after 'the universal exception'. As a result, the Hegelian Zizek elevates the irritating little remnant that has never been caught by any scientific explanatory model – such as when psychology vainly attempts to offer a universal understanding of the human psyche – as the very raison d'être of psychoanalysis itself.

But if we choose to ignore academic disciplines for the time being, and instead look at the human psyche from an independent, third starting point, it turns out that a synthesis between psychology and psychoanalysis is entirely possible. In the same way as the conflict between materialism and idealism has reached a solution in other areas within philosophy, it is entirely possible to solve it even where the human psyche itself is concerned. In contradiction to the insistent claims of idealists, the psyche has no ontological or axiomatic special status. Ironically, we cannot achieve the sought-after synthesis by attacking or rejecting the advances of either psychology or psychoanalysis, but by employing exactly the opposite manoeuvre. By regarding psychology and psychoanalysis alike as principally complete disciplines, we can get past the artificial historical antagonism between them, and, in a philosophical sense, speculate our way towards a schizoanalytical rather than a psychological or psychoanalytical view of the human psyche.

It is abundantly clear that psychology and psychoanalysis use widely divergent conceptual apparatus. But are they actually talking about different things? Is not instead the case that the differences in their narratives are only a case of two different traditions, in the same way as a printer and a literary critic express themselves in different but equally valid ways about one and the same book? Because once souls hidden in glands and invisible spiritual ears and other supernatural nonsense have been swept aside, and when the most pretentious excesses have been removed from the conversation, we can see that each of them is trying, in an almost poetic way, to describe exactly the same causal processes.

We can express this synthetically by stating that a specific thought gives rise to a particular electrochemical pattern in the brain, which in turn causes a new thought, which gives rise to new electrochemical patterns, and so on, ad infinitum. Or we can turn the argument round and state that a particular electrochemical arrangement of patterns gives rise to a particular phantasm, which in turn nurtures an electrochemical modification in the brain, which nurtures a further modified phantasm, and so on. It makes no difference how we shuffle the pack, there is still no contradiction between the two. So, the human psyche is basically a question of the continual interaction between mental and electrochemical processes which take place in the human brain, which is interacting with the rest of the body and the world around it the whole time. Nothing precedes anything else in this endlessly complicated but nonetheless uniform process. One can be translated into the other, and vice versa.

But can it really be this simple? Yes, but the simplicity of this synthesis is also its difficulty, in the same way as the genial simplicity of Spinoza's seventeenth-century monism became the difficult trauma that western thought had to wrestle with for 400 years before the issue was disentangled by the post-structuralism of the late-twentieth century. When Spinoza kills the Soul and gives life to the Body, as constituting the Human Being in its totality, he is already encompassing the modernism that followed, with its focus on philosophical rationality and rationalist science as the superior opponents of, rather than the defenders of, superstitious religion with its collapsing power structure. In Spinoza's writings we can actually find the eternalistic view of the human psyche; all we have to do is project his 400-year-old monism onto the psychological and psychoanalytical processes, and we will soon see how they reinforce and clarify each other, rather than being contradictory. Spinoza beat all of his Enlightenment rivals. Whether we are aware of it or not, we are all Spinozists today (rather than Cartesians). We are living in a Spinozist age, and all we have to do is find a common language for the disciplines.

The important thing is to understand that the pertaining dualism between psychology and psychoanalysis – like all other forms of dualism between materialism and idealism – does not, in contrast to accepted wisdom, have its roots in human fascination with the mysteries of existence. This is not, then, some sort of guessing game that arose around the primitivist campfire, as we have been encouraged to believe, in true historical romantic spirit. Instead this dualism, like all other ideologies, has its roots in the battle for power and survival. Organised religion's fascination with the mysteries of life is of considerably more recent vintage than the appearance of this dualism, and has in any case always been of secondary importance compared to the primary human occupation with power and survival.

The fact that this dualism became the ruling supra-ideological pattern of thought does not, therefore, mean that the nature of life is divided in two in any interesting sense. The reason is quite simply that dualism fulfilled its memetic Darwinian function by offering an adequate ideological frame for feudal society. Dualism was born at the same moment that nomadic, short-term-thinking hunters and gatherers needed to be tamed and re-educated as settled, long-term-thinking farmers. The established and necessary oppositional pair of good and evil needed to be complemented by a metaphysical explanatory model if it was to remain credible. It was in this context that the division between soul and body, between The Written and The Spoken, and thus between God and the World, showed itself to be the perfect meme. Naturally, this encompassed a dramatic narrative with the nobility on the side of good with God, the Soul and Writing, and the slaves on the side of evil, with the World, the Body and the Speech.

Because we have long since left feudal society behind, we need have no qualms about sweeping away the rotten remnants of the dualistic worldview and instead constructing a monistic synthesis between psychology and psychoanalysis which will be more credible and functional in today's informationalist society. One problem with which we are confronted is what terminology to use when the established concepts are so closely associated to either one or other of the two traditional disciplines which regard each other with mutual suspicion and hostility.

The Spinozist philosophers Gilles Deleuze and Felix Guattari started to grapple with this question in the 1970s, when they began to develop a new synthetic model for the human psyche. They rejected both the psychological and psychoanalytical perspective – in a direct response aimed squarely at Sigmund Freud and his successor Jacques Lacan, the called their first joint work Anti-Oedipus (1972), in which they presented the thesis that the fundamental flaw of both systems is that they ultimately produce a reductive and domesticated idea of Humankind. The two disciplines could not see the necessity of the whole.

Deleuze and Guattari's solution was a new discipline, beyond the classical dualistic categories, a field of knowledge which, in true anarchistic spirit, they termed schizoanalysis. They claimed that if the fulfilment of capitalism had finally crushed the Cartesian ideal of an integrated individual as the centre of existence, then it made sense to declare both paternalistic psycholanalysis and naive and uncritical psychology dead, in order to start experimenting with a more comprehensive schizoanalytical model. Modern research into the brain ought not to be left out of the analysis, but instead placed at its very centre, steadily illuminated by critical analysis. Deleuze and Guattari thus replace the Cartesian idea, the Individual, with a schizoid and, in all senses, pluralistic being, which they call the Dividual. Schizoanalysis is the new arena in which psychology and psychoanalysis meet and combine, and where, thanks to the new dividualistic ideal, they can both be set aside. A hypothesis is no longer reinforced simply because both psychology and psychoanalysis nod their approval. In a globalised and multicultural society which communicates in all directions, more than this is required. We are living in a new paradigm which observes and understands Humankind in an entirely new way.

Let us look back through history for a moment: psychoanalysis is created by Freud and his disciples in the years around the turn of the last century. Freud's groundbreaking discovery is that the human psyche ought to be compared to an iceberg: consciousness makes up just the tiny proportion of the psyche that is clearly visible above the surface. Beneath the level of consciousness there are considerably larger and more important parts of the psyche, a turbulent whirlpool of desires and urges that govern our thoughts and ultimately even our actions. Freud calls this invisible and powerful combustion engine of the psyche The Unconscious.

Within schizoanalysis we use the more flexible term The Subconscious instead. The basic idea comes from Freud, but the concept of The Subconscious better illustrates how this great complex functions in relation to the small and marginal Conscious than Freud managed to illustrate. The relationship between the Conscious and what Freud tries to characterise as The Unconscious is of course not the pure dualism that he, typically for his age, presumes; instead, the Conscious and The Subconscious overlap and echo each other in the most sophisticated and intricate way. There is absolutely no clear boundary or dualism at all. Nonetheless, of course Freud's theories were groundbreaking, possibly even more revolutionary than he himself realised, and he was not a man overly afflicted by modesty. In other words: a lot of the explosive power of psychoanalysis has its roots in The Unconscious. Or rather: in The Subconscious.

It is in the nature of the beast that The Subconscious is not immediately visible to the investigative gaze of consciousness. But it constantly leaves subtle impressions in what we say and do, in expressions and behaviour that were not planned and which often surprise the person speaking or acting. And it speaks to us through dreams, where our secret desires find expression. Slavoj Zizek points out that Freud's dream analysis has interesting similarities with Karl Marx's analysis of commodity. Just as commodity reveals an underlying truth about the brutal dynamics of capitalism on closer inspection, so dreams often reveal – for someone with the necessary skill to conduct a proper interpretation – uncomfortable and shocking truths about the conflicts raging beneath the surface of consciousness.

It is important to remember that Freud's theories were seriously influenced by, and in practical terms a result of, the society and power structures that constituted the frame of his life and work. The Europe of the late-nineteenth century was as the zenith of industrialisation. The power, self-absorption and self-satisfaction of the urban bourgeiosie has never been as high as it was in Vienna at the turn of the last century. The patriarchal power-structure was regarded as an axiomatic, obvious fact of nature; there was great fascination for the apparently highly effective Napoleonic hierarchy as an organisational model. All important organisations – factories, schools, hospitals, bureaucracies and armies – were constructed with this hierarchical model in mind. The worldview rested upon an idea of a venerable, almost mystical, patriarchy at the top of a totalistic pyramid. The nation state was the basis for the production of social identity – citizens were genuinely prepared to die for their country – and its Napoleonic armies of universally conscripted soldiers marching in rigid formation, adorned with a strict hierarchy of officers, was seen as the guarantor of society's survival. The destructive efficiency of the burgeoning industrialism meant that the Factory replaced the old Palace as the social phallus: the signifier of the governing power structure around which the rest of society's activity was presumed to revolve.

It is hardly surprising that the Factory was also the ideal in Freud's ambitions for psychoanalysis: the Cartesian subject is the psyche's very own phallus, under which the other components of the psyche have to be organised in an effective hierarchical pyramid in order for balance and harmony to be achieved and maintained. The goal must be for the person under analysis to find their predetermined place in society, like an effective factory worker in a rapidly growing cosmopolitan city. Obviously the relationship of the person in question to the Father-figure must also be central to their understanding of themselves. The son is jealous of the Father and wishes to defeat and replace him. The Daughter wants most of all to please the Father because she is envious of him and other men for their possession of actual phalluses. The fact that men, in a corresponding fashion, are entirely capable of envying women their breasts and wombs is a thought that never seriously occurred to Freud. He believed that with this foundation in place, psychoanalysis had at its disposal all the necessary tools to maintain the natural power structure in its place. This was equally true within the psyche itself.

What made Freud an international megastar and spread his admittedly controversial theories across the whole of the western world was the way that they chimed with the fundamental values of the capitalist era. Psychoanalytical societies – often run like fanatical sects whose leaders were regarded as enlightened oracles – sprang up in major cities across the whole of the industrialised world. The most important explanation of the success of psychoanalysis was that it was launched as a powerful alternative to the religious institutions of the crumbling aristocracy. While the aristocrats were still confessing their sins to the local priest, the urban bourgeoisie was instead queuing enthusiastically for the couch of Freudian analysis. Analysts obeyed the same confidentiality as priests, of course; they were soon regarded as the confessors of secularised society.

Now the bourgeoisie was no longer obliged to pay any kind of lip service to a god it no longer believed in. You need not pray for forgiveness for sins for which you no longer felt any guilt. Instead your own personality, your Ego, was the centre of attention. This suited the individualistic bourgeoisie much better. No more talk about the keys to heaven and the blessedness of eternal life. On the analyst's couch, the narrative instead was all about personal development and a burning desire to achieve concrete progress, here and now, for your own benefit. With the onset of capitalism, faith in constant Progress had replaced the belief in an elusive Eternity as the metaphysical engine of society, a fact which was extremely beneficial to psychoanalysis. Analysts were richly rewarded, and soon comprised an acclaimed and well-integrated part of the very bourgeoisie that psychoanalysis originally set out to unmask. Psychoanalysis had thus been transformed into one more profit-maximising factory among many others in capitalist society. Soon Freud's disciples could boast of bulging bank accounts and social status.

Freud may have been regarded as unsettling and offensive by contemporary society, with his constant talk of sexuality and cultural unhappiness. Both his theories and his methods were regularly questioned by the medical and philosophical establishments. But his provocations were entirely in line with the way the age saw itself, and therefore never gave rise to any more serious reaction than a reflex gesture of annoyance. Even Freud himself moved in time to, and was a loyal servant of the system of which he was a part. No matter how much he might talk about the sordid and hidden underbelly of the bourgeoisie, the eventual result was, more than anything, a sophisticated form of entertainment for the moneyed classes. Like a talented ringmaster Freud tickled the bourgeoisie with metafantasies, fantasies about their own fantasies, to help the class in power to find itself as interesting as possible. Freud therefore did not permit any deviation from the fundamental requirement of the governing paradigm: the cultivation and maintenance of the patriarchal, Napoleonic hierarchy. Freudianism itself has no place outside the phallocentric worldview.

If the nineteenth century was the golden age of the bourgeoisie and Cartesianis, the twentieth century was a time of transition. Both world wars revealed the brutal underside of the hierarchical Factory as an idea, and the dream of the homogenous nation state as a secure home on earth. The concentration camps and the gulag archipelago showed that the Factory, not least when led by dysfunctional father figures like Adolf Hitler and Josef Stalin, was better suited to creating a hell rather than a heaven on earth. The multiculturalism of American culture beckoned, giving rise to new ideals. The democratic and open society, built on solid judicial institutions, accessible to all, with all citizens equal in the eyes of the law, became the new universal norm. Factory workers won influence and the right to participate in decisions. Women made their concerted entry into the workplace. The colonies in Africa, Asia and South America freed themselves from the rapidly shrinking European empires. Ethnic and sexual minorities demanded and were granted more space and influence.

As a consequence, Freud's explanatory model for the functioning of the psyche looked increasingly tired. It was patched up and repaired feverishly within psychoanalytic sects. Conflicts between various groups were bitter and had brutal consequences, not entirely unlike the old European wars of religion. When psychoanalysis's most spectacular thinker, Jacques Lacan, arrived on the scene in the 1950s as one of the leading figures within French structuralism, there was practically nothing left of Freudianism but its name. Lacan sought to reach beyond the messages of industrialism and post-industrialism, stuck as they were in their own time, and concentrate instead on the more enduring aspects of the psyche. The increasingly silly dream interpretations and other nonsense were chucked out, the factory metaphor abandoned; Lacan was instead inspired by Hegel and Nietzsche. He concentrates on the timeless structures of the psyche, which he presents as complex but strikingly apposite mathemes in a new borderland between philosophy and science. Lacan made such an impression on contemporary philosophers that he was soon regarded as one of the twentieth century's great thinkers, in spite of the fact that he turned down social invitations from the academic establishment and stuck to his psychiatric clinics and the couch he used for consultations in his apartment in Paris.

One consequence of Lacan's growing popularity and influence was that he became persona non grata in Freudian circles. American Freudians in particular raged against this new French way of thinking, which they preferred to regard as continental sophistry. Lacanians were therefore forced to found their own school, which soon grew to become at least as strong as, and, above all, more influential, than the Freudian school. The definitive break from the Freudian line only came, however, when Gilles Deleuze and Felix Guattari – two of the heroes of the French 1968 movement, the latter of whom had been one of Lacan's students – broke away from the whole concept of psychoanalysis in the 1970s. Instead of trying to patch up and repair the old Freudian model that was no longer functional, they unapologetically announced the birth of schizoanalysis, despite the fact they had not yet developed a complete model. According to Deleuze and Guattari, if the Cartesian subject has crashed to the ground in the turbulence of late-capitalism, there is no reason whatsoever to try to keep it alive on the analyst's couch.

Critical questions mounted up. Why retain the analyst's couch at all, when its main function had been to draw out the narcissistic perversions and desires of the increasingly marginalised bourgeoisie after expensive journeys down into the subconscious ? Lacan had amassed a small fortune from his sadistic analyst's sessions, still with the analyst in the role of axiomatic and infallible Patriarch, and lord of the masochistic client. Was it not the case that the analyst's couch itself, rather than the analysis, had become the focus of events, precisely because it was the analyst's couch that generated the capital and the status that the increasingly naive, lazy and corrupt psychoanalysts had come to desire? Didn't this new development demand a complete break, an entirely new school of analysis, a school that included a critical attitude to the current power structure? Wasn't it high time to get rid of the theoretical naivety and radicalise analysis in this crass and complex age?

Deleuze and Guattari believe that the new, increasingly interactive and multicultural society also needs a more radical explanatory model for the most basic functions of the psyche. A new self-image for humankind in an entirely new situation. The hypercapitalist state of globalised society no longer has anything in common with the Europe in which René Descartes formulated his individualistic philosophy in the 1600s, or with the Vienna where Freud sat and interpreted the bourgeoisie's dreams through the eyes of the patriarch in the late-nineteenth and early-twentieth century. Deleuze and Guattari are adamant that Oedipus has abdicated. As early as the 1950s, Lacan was talking about the retreat of the patriarchy from the social arena. As the dominance of the bourgeois nuclear family has declined, Oedipus has become less relevant. Deleuze and Guattari believe that they are completing the project that their mentor, Lacan, began, and they are doing so not by questioning Lacan's theories, but rather by placing analysis in a larger social context which had earlier been overshadowed.

This means that other forms of rebellion and the complexes connected to it are becoming relevant. As a result, Deleuze and Guattari are even attacking the very starting point of the capitalist worldview: the Cartesian subject. The permanent Ego as the centre of existence is an ideal that was created and nurtured in order to maximise the advance of capitalism, and ultimately in order to legitimise its claims to power. Capitalism produced the Cartesian subject, rather than the reverse. However the concept lacked both a scientific basis and, above all, relevance for the new interactive age, which instead finds itself in desperate need of a new, more creative and flexible subject. Lacan shows that the Cartesian subject is both empty and divided (and, precisely because of this, dearly cherished); Deleuze and Guattari want to go further and, taking Spinoza as their inspiration, construct an analysis from foundations other than the Ego. In tense expectation of a functional form of schizoanalysis, Deleuze and Guattari see a world coloured by rapidly escalating neuroses and paranoid psychoses. There is absolutely no shortage of work for new schizoanalysts.

The historical transition from late-capitalism's highly effective, electronic one-way communications to informationalism's complex, digital interactivity as the dominant force of power- and identity-producing communication technology also means, ironically, that the new ideal for the psyche that is developing is the radical opposite of Freud's ideal. Metaphysical Progress is gone, as represented by the solid, cohesive Ego. In its place is the metaphysical Event, represented by the schizoid Dividual as the new ideal.

This dividual seeks out intensity and longs for abstract events. The Event is therefore replacing Progress as the metaphysical engine. For the interactive netocrat, this means that the more numerous, and the more exciting personalities which can be contained within one and the same nominal psyche, the stronger the identity and greater the creativity that the dividual – for good and ill – will be able to produce, experience, and represent in interactive society. The Dividual is thus striving to become an event itself; not a permanent event (like the Individual), but many different events in the plural, continually new intensities which come and go through the Dividual, a fluid self-image in a constantly changing world.

Like all the other patriarchal hierarchies of the capitalist era, psychoanalysis will not manage to survive the transition to informationalist society. The dark analyst's couch in a dusty study – with its obsolete connections to patriarchal oversight, libidinal submission and military metaphors – belong to an entirely different world than today's meritocratic and changeable network projects on the internet. The relationship between the fundamentally sadistic and moralising psychoanalyst and the masochistic patient is therefore undergoing a transformation. In its place, an ethical, equal relationship is gradually emerging between the analyst and patient, with the Event rather than Progress as the metaphysical horizon, and where Society is a common problem that both can and should be criticised, but which must nonetheless be dealt with. By proclaiming the arrival of schizoanalysis, Deleuze and Guattari are declaring psychoanalysis dead and buried. As its replacement, they are launching a new philosophy for both the creative and critical understanding of the human psyche in the age of interactivity.

If the idea of a solid, permanent and substantial subject is dead, if the Ego has lost its soul and been reduced to an empty, linguistic convention, and if interactive society both facilitates and enforces the production of a torrent of other social identities in its place, we are forced to address the question of whether there is any cohesive ideal for all these personalities which have to be nurtured simultaneously? The subject is formed and maintained by the ongoing construction of a narrative about itself and its context. But how should the new dividual which is replacing the old individual compose itself? How much is possible? And what, of everything that is possible, is reasonable and functional?

We will find the answer by studying the boundary between the specific conditions of the new age and the constant conditions for our existence that are independent of forms of communication, in other words: the unavoidable genetic preconditions which arose in the bestial, pre-human state, and were later clarified during the primitivist era, where spoken language was the only form of language, and the nomadic tribe humankind's only social network. It turns out that informationalism has one important characteristic in common with the primitivist era, in the interactive nature of the dominant form of communication. Deleuze and Guattari therefore refer to the thinking of the new age as nomadic philosophy. Once again, it is movement rather than stability that is idealised in civilisation. Nietzsche's materialist revolt against Plato's dualism and the prioritising of the world of ideas are being fulfilled.

Whereas feudalism's written language and capitalism's printing presses and electronic mass media gave rise to vast concentrations of power around the institutions that produced, unquestioned, the pertaining truths, the onset of digital interactivity is facilitating an actual return to the multi-directional communication that was characteristic of primitivism, but on an entirely different scale. This explains why contemporary sociologists talk about a technological primitivism as one of the signifiers of the age of interactivity. New internet sociology is observing the rise and growth of virtual tribes, internet-based subcultures or global proportions, with immense powers of attraction, not least because of the their role as the centre of informationalism's production of identity. New interactive technologies are thus fulfilling an old utopian dream: the original and mythical tribe can be reinstated through new technology. But it is no longer gathered round a geographically specific campfire as it once was: instead its members are seeking out and finding one another in the virtual jungles and savannahs of informationalism.

The phallus and the production of identity always go hand in hand. Capitalism's social identities and ideals were consequently constructed from the factory floor, the academic titles of universities and the bureaucratic corridors of the nation state. Informationalism's identities are, in contrast, constructed out of the social roles of the virtual networks. The phallus of our age is therefore the Net, the metaphysical abstraction that our subconscious is constantly preparing itself for examination by. The Other is the playful identities that our own dividual identities communicate with. The Big Other is nothing more than the metaphysical abstraction itself, the Net.

By studying technological primitivism and the powerful elements of nomadic tribal life that we find on the internet, we can identify a new, functional norm for the human psyche for informationalism. It is hardly surprising that there turns out to be a recurrent universal formula with primitivistic origins. It is important to clarify here that we are not talking about a formula that is objectively true or applicable forever, in the scientific way that Freud liked to regard his psychoanalytical hypotheses. This is more a matter of a formula that is productive and functional for us in our time, a pragmatic starting point for the dividual ideals of schizoanalysis. This formula is known as the 12+1 model, and we shall be returning to that in the next chapter.

One dramatic consequence of the collapse of the modern project during the twentieth century was that the human psyche lost its presumed substance. Lacan's psychoanalytical theories denied the psyche its substance on the analytical plane: the Lacanian subject is a subject whose illusory quality, its fundamental emptiness, is also the very foundation of its existence. This is a question of a paradoxical subject which gains its substance precisely from its actual lack of substance. The recurrent attempt to give the Lacanian subject a substance is in itself its only substance. Thus, for Lacan, the Cartesian subject has fulfilled the development from the naive phase, through the cynical phase, to affirmative nihilism. The death of the subject is nothing to either shout about or to lament, naively or hypocritically, but rather a fundamental precondition for the creation of identity. This is in contrast to many of the postmodern theories that followed, with their misdirected criticism of the subject's Hegelian necessity in Lacan's theoretical construction.

Modern research into the brain has in a corresponding way eliminated the substance of the psyche not only on the analytical plane, but also the psychological: the psyche is reduced to processes of cause, effect and a minimal amount of coincidence, where the transition from one electrochemical complex to another encourages a psychic reaction that can largely be predicted in advance. Feelings that are linked in this way to other feelings create predictable patterns. It is in theory entirely possible to reduce the entire activity and expression of the psyche to complete chains of electrochemical-hormonal complexes, where complete determinism is avoided only because we have to take account of the unpredictability that is always present on the quantum physical level.

It is worth noting that it is the Cartesian subject that is dead and buried. Hegel's purely metaphysical subject from the nineteenth century is, on the other hand, still thriving within Lacanian analysis – because this subject requires neither dualism nor the pineal gland. The point is that the Ego's experience of itself as an ego does not disappear, however strong the sense of the ego's illusory character actually is. The reverse is in fact the case: the Hegelian subject, which thinks itself into being as its own self-reflecting necessity, and nothing more, and which only sees itself as a loop of thought without material foundation, is actually strengthened by the ultra-materialistic explanations of its existence.

The philosophers Slavoj Zizek and Judith Butler have thus correctly identified the link between the Lacanian revolution and Hegel: Lacan completes the Hegelian revolution which was started in the nineteenth century, and places Hegel deservedly in the role of one of modernism's most prophetic thinkers. The door is actually open for a renaissance of romantic idealism: if we delve deep enough into consequential materialism, materia itself begins to dissolve into abstract patterns, a mysterious dance of particles in the great void. It is, then, important to remember that acceptance of the monistic worldview is not so much a question of materialism's victory over idealism, but rather merely of monism's victory over dualism, or, in other words: existence is merely one single substance, and we have the freedom to give this single substance whatever attributes we want, as long as we allow it to remain one and the same substance.

Admittedly, it is true that the chemical status of the brain at any given moment governs the experiences of the psyche, but it is equally true that these experiences in turn govern the chemical processes. We are talking about two sides of the same coin, two sides which it is as pointless as it is in principal impossible to separate or set in opposition to one another. All attempts at this have failed, like all attempts to erase the particular characteristics of the different sides and enforce an artificial uniformity. In the light of affirmative nihilism, the human psyche appears to be extremely paradoxical, but it is not a paradox that needs to be dealt with until it ceases to exist, either in the short or long term. Instead, it is the paradox that we recognise as the very foundation for our understanding of who we are and how we think and understand anything at all.

12.

THE PRACTICE OF SCHIZOANALYSIS

☐

THE WEAKEST POINT OF Freudian psychoanalysis is not the fact that it insists on proclaiming the idealistic Hegelian position in the face of psychology's dogmatic materialism. Pure idealism is perfectly exchangeable with pure materialism. No, the really weak point is the Kantian premise for this reasoning: the isolated and unified subject. No matter how we look at the problem, this is an untenable position in need of comprehensive upgrading. The cohesive subject is a shattered illusion; the subject is fundamentally and definitively split. It is, to express it in Nietzschean terms, never fewer than two. It was Jacques Lacan who opened the door to the historic necessity of the pluralisation of the subject, albeit without ever quite leaving the hierarchical abode of Freudian psychoanalysis.

It was only after Lacan – in, for instance, Gilles Deleuze and Felix Guattari's critique of Lacan in the 1970s – that psychoanalysis's mathemes and putatively scientific stories were abandoned as merely another expression of totalistic ambitions and of western, patriarchal fantasies of once and for all identifying a universally valid, detailed description of how the human psyche functions. According to Deleuze and Guattari, the starting point for any understanding of the psyche ought instead to be, for good and ill, its fundamental schizoid quality, its division into and absorption by the surrounding culture. And in light of these insights we find it particularly worthwhile to conduct a credible analysis of the human psyche in our globalised and virtualised age.

Classical psychoanalysis has deep and obvious roots in the Judeo-Christian worldview. It is therefore constructed with the metaphysical Patriarch as its starting point. This organisation happens symbolically, since all of the analysand's other relationships – including his or her relationship to him or herself – is presumed to be organised according to the fundamental relationship to the metaphysical Father (clearly exemplified by the famous Oedipus Complex). The relationship to the Father is therefore primary: the theory presupposes that all other relationships are governed according to the structural pattern set by this relationship at the top of the hierarchy. When it comes down to it, identity is always inextricably linked to the relationship to the Father, or the relationship to the 'name of the Father', as Lacan cryptically prefers to express it. The alpha and omega of analysis is to map and then shift this primary relationship in the desired direction.

Like other doubting, naive nihilists, Sigmund Freud insists on his method being implemented and reinforced with the help of dramaturgy. Nothing must be left to chance. Freud therefore positions the Patriarch quite literally at the centre of physical space: it is absolutely no coincidence that the analyst, like a substitute father, is expected to sit and work in a chair as an active subject, whereas the subordinate analysand has to lie prostrate on a couch, as a passive, non-working object. The roles in this play are strengthened rather than weakened by the central role that is given to the auditory experience: Freud clearly takes it for granted, for instance, that it is necessary for the analysand to have their back to the analyst, their eyes either closed or facing a neutral wall.

Note the biblical aspect of the proffered strategy. Like the Jewish god in his encounters with the metaphysical Prophet in the Old Testament, the analyst can only be heard, and must never be seen by the analysand during the analytical process. The most important tool of Mother and Woman throughout history has been the Image – which explains why cultures which take care to oppress their women render them invisible, by for instance excluding them from public places or forcing them to hide under thick layers of fabric – while Father and Man have governed most effectively with the help of the Voice (the king on his throne, the preacher on the mountain top, the dogmatic speaker at his lectern, the general commanding troops before a big battle, the muezzin in his minaret, and so on). Not to mention the fact that the most brutal genocides of the twentieth century were organised with the help of the constantly present but invisible, fatherly radio voice: Hitler's Germany, Stalin's Russia, Pol Pot's Cambodia, Mao Zedong's China, Saddam Hussein's Iraq, the Rwandan genocide in the 1990s. There are therefore good reasons to consider radio, rather than newspapers or television, as the dictator's best friend during the late-capitalist period.

But if we have torn down the western patriarchal fantasies about the psyche, why should we cling on to the Freudian analyst's study with all its associations to the traditional confession? What do the classical analyst's couch and its surroundings have to offer today's divided, schizoid analysand? How can this model be of any use at all for analytical work when we are now living in an increasingly interactive, transparent, globalised and meritocratic society? Isn't there a more credible and constructive way of organising the analytical process? The answer, surprisingly, is to be found in the work of the thinker that we have earlier tried, at least in part, to turn away from: Lacan himself. The answer is the metaphysical component known as the Signifier.

The fictives that are in constant motion in the Lacanian analytical arena actually have their credibility strengthened rather than weakened in the transition to interactive society. The human Game with symbols can no longer be regarded as a banal and childish activity, but must instead be understood as the practice through which informationalism's netocrats understand and describe the world in depth, a paradigm shift that the American philosopher Mark Pesce convincingly advocates in his book The Playful World (2000).

It is, then, no longer assumed that the analytical arena describes the world as it is – in an objective and timeless sense. Instead, the arena gains its value as a temporarily useful tool for someone trying to understand how the psyche might be thought to see itself. The point is that it is only through this metaphysical game that we can reach a deeper understanding of the mechanisms of the mind. Fictives offer the playfulness that is necessary for schizoid analysis to achieve its goals. As soon as we have defined the fictives in question and playfully given them their name – we are focusing, then, on the name itself rather than the virtual father figure behind 'the name of the Father', Lacan's term for the primary signifier – we have also acquired the most important and functional tools of schizoanalytical work.

The phenomenological process needs certain fundamental building blocks to be in place in order that the separate fictives can be organised and positioned in relation to one another. Categories like time and space, motion and stability, chaos and order, and so on, have to function if the production of fictives is to be possible. But we can let phenomenology take care of this; we are more interested instead in how the fictives relate to each other, or, in other words: what happens when the categories are in place? Which fictives are primary and which are secondary for the psyche, when it spontaneously organises the world and evaluates its components?

When the schizoanalyst has managed to identify the fictive around which all the other fictives revolve in the worldview of the analysand in question – in other words: the actual signifier – he or she has actually found an almost embarrassingly simple way of removing the analysand's actual worldview from the game at the right time. When the new, more functional worldview has been prepared, and is ready to take over and furnish the psyche in question, the old fantasy can quickly be removed and disarmed through a refined technique known as psychopuncturing.

The technique of psychopuncturing is based upon the idea that the signifiers are not just metaphysical abstractions: if this were the case, they would never have gained the control over the psyche that they actually have. No, instead the signifiers, like other types of iceberg, have a small but important aspect that is visible above the line between consciousness and the subconscious. This visible aspect takes the form of a verbal symbol.

The point here is the exploitation of the fact that the psyche is organised around language. The analyst must find a phrase – often just a single word – which acts as a verbal substitute for the signifier in question within the analysand's psyche. When this symbolic substitute is mentioned in passing, it causes an unconsciously irritated response in the analysand, which the experienced schizoanalyst learns to recognise, register and remember. This verbal symbol might at first seem completely arbitrary, but as the analyst gets to know the analysand's life story – and particularly the subconscious part of it – the historical and often tangible explanation of this phrase will be revealed.

Psychopuncturing can either be carried out by the symbolic substitute phrase being spoken clearly and forcefully in a direct confrontation with the analysand, or by the phrase being repeated consciously time after time in subtle but important discussion (the discussion might well concern something trivial, in order to act as a distraction, but the analyst ought not to be interrupted). But when the technique is conducted correctly, however this is done, the signifier will collapse. The outward behaviour of the analysand will suddenly change, subtly or dramatically, but certainly in a noticeable way. It is as if a new personality has woken up and taken over the analysand's body (which is in practice precisely what has happened).

Before psychopuncturing takes place, it is vital that a new, credible ficitive has already been constructed and is ready to take over the role of signifier in the analysand's psyche. Otherwise the technique risks unleashing a psychotic reaction in an otherwise healthy and balanced analysand, because the signifier really does play a critical role in the psyche. This risk is avoided if the analyst, together with the unsuspecting analysand, carefully constructs a new signifier during the course of the analysis that is more relevant to the life circumstances in question, which can nurture a more credible and congruent self-image and worldview than the old signifier was able to do. Consequently psychopuncturing facilitates an exchange of signifiers which radically changes and enhances the analysand's experience of life in a way which neither psychotherapy nor classical psychoanalysis is capable of, seeing as these methods are condemned to circle endlessly around the signifier and never reach the depths of the subconscious where it is actually located.

It is important to point out here that even if traditional metaphysical figures like the Father and Mother have functioned in a meaningful way within classical psychoanalysis, this is not because of any inbuilt objective truth or universal validity in the figures in question. The explanation of this is that the psyche is constantly producing and using fictives – like Plato's ideal forms or Immanuel Kant's categories – to sort and manage all the chaotic impressions or the world around us, and then collate these into an internally comprehensible and coherent worldview.

The traditional focus of psychoanalysis on the Father and Mother has a perfectly understandable explanation. Industrial society was organised around the idea of the nuclear family, relocated from the socially stagnant agrarian countryside to the dynamic industrial city, with the father as provider and the mother raising children. It was therefore thought necessary to train children to understand the value of father and mother for their own physical and psychic survival. This means that instead of classical psychoanalysis tracing the central roles of the Father and Mother in the psyche's construction of the world anthropologically, the pack is shuffled: the norms of industrialism are so strong as to govern the science behind the work of analysis. Because it was seen as desirable that the child raised in the Judeo-Christian or humanist tradition venerated its parents in order for the industrial city and its requisite power-structures to hold together and function, it was also presumed, more or less uncritically, that the parents played the objectively decisive role in the child's view of itself and the world. Everything else was subordinated to the relationship of parent-child, and the Oedipus complex remained a particularly successful meme as long as capitalism structured the worldview and society's values.

But there is a logical explanation for the supposed pre-eminence of parents within classical psychoanalysis, even beyond the capitalist idealisation of the nuclear family that was so typical of its time. The mother's body is presumably the very first thing that the child experiences in life. Even if the embryo in the womb has no consciousness, its emotional life is formed during pregnancy. And psychoanalysis hits the nail on the head when it identifies what kick-starts the psychic process at birth: the moment of birth, when the child leaves the safe and warm womb and is ejected to cope with the world on its own is The Great Trauma above all others in life. The moment of birth is the metaphysical experience around which every following emotional experience in life is organised and takes its meaning.

This does not depend on the fact that the moment of birth precedes all other experiences, but because The Great Trauma is so much more powerful, so much more traumatic, than every experience that follows it. It takes place, after all, against an entirely blank canvass, and cannot be relativised, but is instead the experience against which every other emotional experience in life is relativised. This is also the explanation of why the experience cannot be recalled with the help of memory. The terror of the moment of birth is so great that it is suppressed to the very deepest level of the subconscious. It is in fact the impenetrable foundation upon which the subconscious, and thus also the psyche as a whole, is constructed. It is the pathological complex caused by The Great Trauma which kick-starts the whole of the existential experience. It is the tangible and desperate loneliness of this bewildering experience which is the beginning of the Ego, even if the Ego is only materialised much later with the arrival of language and the castration experience when Mother and Child are separated.

The Great Trauma is so powerful that it is entirely reasonable to presume that the literal deathwish – in other words, the urge to stop existing as a separate entity and return to the womb in order to be 'absorbed by the cosmos' – is strong enough to be the driving force in life. Because we usually experience the desire to live and survive as our strongest and deepest desire, this means that all the desires and urges we experience are fundamentally pathological: we really want to die, we want to cease to exist as independent entities separated from the rest of the world, we long to return to the womb right from the moment we leave it. The only way to handle this literal deathwish is therefore to convince ourselves that the very reverse is the case. It is this relationship we mean when we say that the nature of the psyche is dialectic.

For easily understandable Darwinian reasons, the psyche has to suppress the deathwish and therefore turns it inside out. The brain is – as we have shown earlier – a master of self-deception. We believe that we want to live because it makes our survival easier, and our survival is necessary for obvious, Darwinian reasons. The desire for life that is so tangible to us is thus formally merely a meta-desire: a desire to desire to live, nothing more nor less. So we believe in our consciousness that it is our utmost desire to live and go on living – an idea which is reinforced by the fact that our fellows and thus the whole of our culture are constructed upon this understanding, condemning all thoughts of self-destruction – while The Subconscious is instead organised around the literal deathwish, and therefore reacts dialectically to all wishes and values that are consciously organised in the name of the desire for life.

This contradictory attitude to the deepest truth of our urges and desires explains why we deep down experience The Subconscious as 'more genuine' and 'truer' than consciousness, even if this is only intermittently apparent. The explosive insight about the psyche's fundamental dialectic and the central role of the deathwish is the greatest cultural achievement of psychoanalysis. We have been absolutely fascinated with the dialectical performance of The Subconscious ever since Freud discovered and proved its existence. No other intellectual achievement has influenced our self-image and worldview to the same extent either during or after modernity.

The Lacanian theory of The Great Trauma gives the Mother's body a central role in relation to the birth of the worldview. It is only through modern psychology that we have begun to understand that the newborn child does not comprehend any mother that is separated from itself. But even Lacan realised that the experience of separation of Mother and Child takes place long afterwards, and constitutes a new, second trauma, which Lacan defines as the Birth of Ego. We have no proof, however, that this experienced separation of Mother and Child is universally constitutive in any way.

Of course this seems a reasonable explanatory model for the birth of the Ego in, for instance, a home in a western suburb in the twentieth century, where the Mother spends her days at home and is alone in caring for the young child. But an environment like this is, from a historical and anthropological perspective, a negligible exception rather than the norm in any real sense. So the child's natural production of a worldview is seldom dependent on its parents as any sort of objectively valid categories. Freud overestimates the roles of Father and Mother, and Lacan was not prepared to distance himself sufficiently from Freud's patriarchal theories. Both commit the mistake of interpreting culturally specific truths as objectively valid for all societies and ages in history.

But if the role of the Mother has only been dismantled in our time, how could the Father logically have had any central role at all? Was the Father not a physical absence in most environments surrounding a child in capitalist society, from the maternity room to the playroom and classroom? Surely almost any other adult has more influence on the child's construction of a worldview? Classical psychoanalysis solves this logical dilemma by giving the Father an entirely new role, as the mystical coordinator of symbolic organisation. What is this mystical object which exerts an even greater power of attraction on the mother than the narcissistic child itself? Surely this eminently attractive object must have such immense power that it is superior to everything else in t he world? And surely it must be something that the child both fears and is simultaneously attracted by, even more so that the cherished mother figure?

In this way classical psychoanalyst gives the Father the most significant role in society itself. This was a role that seemed extremely credible, and, above all, one which appealed to all the powerful men who needed to be attracted by the psychoanalytical theory in order for it to be accepted and disseminated through industrialised society with its universal worship of the patriarch.

This mutation of the psychoanalytical meme meant that it was better suited for survival and reproduction. Not least, this theory appealed to gentlemen like Freud and Lacan themselves. The envy directed to their gender and social standing had to be endowed with an objective and eternally valid explanation and status.

The theory of the Father as The Big Other, the idea of the Father as the mystical and constitutive centre around which everything else in the child's universe revolved, was far too suitable for the men in power under capitalism for it to be exposed to any genuinely sharp criticism. Who would willingly turn down status and power? Who wouldn't want to be the most important figure in other people's lives, particularly if this importance is actually strengthened rather than weakened by actual physical absence and a lack of concrete engagement? This is the perfect example of an attractive meme. What we should be asking ourselves today is whether the Oedipal son is really tormented by jealousy of his father's primary role in his mother's emotional life – as Freud supposed when he constructed his patriarchal phantasm – or if the reverse is not actually the case (which would mean that Freud's theory won its popularity as a necessary dialectical lie rather than as a profound truth about the father-son relationship in the capitalist nuclear family)?

Beyond the patriarchal order of capitalist society we discover that the objective truths of classical psychoanalysis do not hold water. Neither anthropological studies of nomadic societies outside the western cultural sphere, nor today's postmodern society where children have a wealth of relationships with various adults (and of course other children), provides a suitable projection screen for these Freudian fantasies. The basic fictives in the child's worldview have to be considerably vaguer and more abstract that the Father and Mother if they are to be credible as universally recurrent phenomena. We have to get beyond culturally specific characteristics and instead find forms which can be presumed to be valid at least for the societies we know today. We have to free ourselves from arrogant navel-gazing.

Schizoanalysis is therefore built upon three considerably more abstract fictives: 1) the world as an assumed whole, as the backdrop onto which all other fictives are positioned. 2) The child itself as ego-experience, as existentially conscious. And 3) the mystical Other, the other human being who seems to hide behind every other face in the child's surroundings and which exhibits traces of an emotional life just as rich as the child's own, but without the frustrated child ever being able to experience these feelings for itself.

Eventually, of course, these fictives slip in and out of each other: the Ego is part of the World, the World makes its presence felt in all manner of ways within the Ego. The same applies to The Other's relationship with the World and vice versa. But the child soon develops an awareness that the Ego itself is divided, that there is an Other inside the Ego itself which forces the Ego to remain open to its surroundings, and even uncomprehending and mysterious to itself. But the three basic components are in place, and the child can start to construct a worldview which can then be constantly renovated and expanded.

Here we see the most important difference between schizoanalysis and classical psychoanalysis. Whereas Freud gave the Father the central role as Signifier, the most primary of all fictives, the fictive from which all other fictives are organised, Lacan suggested that the Signifier is mobile and not at all tied to any particular person or object. Lacan realised that the Signifier plays its role best by being constantly evasive, something the child never manages to grasp. The surest way for a fictive to avoid being pinned down in a particular position in the arena, to remain constantly evasive, is to be a pure idea with no physical equivalent: in other words, an illusion. This means that the Signifier can hide behind a mass of other illusions, such as God, the Ego, Society, or The Big Other. But the most important characteristic of the Signifier is that it is empty and does not in itself have any substance – substance must be projected onto a blank surface in order to stick – and the Signifier plays that role best when it is in constant motion, with its presumed specific identity switched at regular intervals.

Language plays a decisive role in this process. Even if human beings, like several other intelligent animals (such as chimpanzees, dolphins and elephants) have an innate ability to experience individuality – for instance by understanding that the being looking back at us in the mirror is not a foreign body but actually the person looking in the mirror – there is no real consciousness outside of language. The verbalisation of the existential experience is a condition of becoming conscious. Memories and ambitions become memories and ambitions by being verbalised and thereby made concrete. Verbalisation is also the entrance to symbolic order. Only by inheriting and taking language from other people can the child's ambitions be matched to those of its fellows, and thus assume relevance in the social arena. This process is known within socioanalysis as 'domestication', and as 'castration' within psychoanalysis, and it is of decisive significance for the production of identity.

The price of language is a distancing between the speaking, thinking human being and the 'nature' around and within him or her. The castration process undoubtedly carries with it a tangible sense of turbulent loss. This mysterious 'loss' is experienced both as creative – not least in the form of enjoyable fantasies and nostalgic daydreams – and threatening, because 'the natural, 'the wild', 'the bestial' and 'the unpredictable' both within a human being and in their surroundings is at constant risk of returning and thus ruining the rewards that castration brings with it. This distance caused by castration, this unexpected and dramatic by-product of language, provides excellent fertile ground for signifiers. Precisely because of its emotional tangibility and mysterious nature, the distance in our existential experience is the perfect raw material for signifiers. Freud's error is to identify the Father as the universally valid signifier, when the Signifier can actually appear anywhere within the unavoidable distance which pertains between Language and Nature.

The Big Other needs neither God not Father, but can take the form of any figure in the surrounding society, in the world of fantasy, or in the wilderness of nature. The important thing for the psyche is that there is always a Big Other, a primary fictive around which all other fictives can dance. Otherwise the psyche would collapse in a psychosis. It is worth noting that a psychosis is analytically defined as a state where all experienced objects become signifiers, whereas a neurosis, in contrast, is a state in which the Signifier has got stuck on a single fictive, and the Signifier and Object has become confused with each other. A socially functional psyche balances, for understandable reasons, between psychosis and neurosis. The significance of the Signifier is tangible and directly experienced, but never ultimately defined or fixed forever. It does not absorb its surroundings in the way that happens when the world around the subject is sucked into a psychotic breakdown. The delicate distance between subject and its surroundings remains untouched.

Because schizoanalysis understands the importance of the Signifier – without tying it to any temporal or culturally specific point such as for instance God or the Father – it can play with potential signifiers in order to achieve its goal. A suitable way is to find a universally recurrent form of this game. In other words: not tying yourself to a form which is presumed to be universally valid and objectively true in any way, but rather to choose pragmatically a form which often recurs anthropologically and can thus be presumed to mirror the conditions for survival well enough for the human flock within most cultures and ages.

The most common and effective model for games involving signifiers and identities within current schizoanalysis is the 12+1 model. The form is both magnificently simple and, from a creative point of view, extremely multi-layered. It also has the accuracy of Lacanian mathemes without being burdened by their weight and complexity. The mathematics are simple: 12 symbolises the perfect form, the geometric circle. The best way to divide time (a clock-face) or to cut a cake is to divide the circle into twelve identical sections. So the number 12 illustrates the desire for the perfect form, for all-encompassing knowledge, the cohesive cosmos, the perfect person, absolute power.

However, of course, every totalistic fantasy is afflicted sooner or later by disturbances of various sorts: a new piece of knowledge appears from nowhere, the cosmos turns out to have a hidden dimension of which we were not previously aware, people make constant mistakes, we are confronted with hitherto unknown islands of resistance, places and environments which the governing power does not control, and so on. So we add a little +1 to the formula. This does not result in the number 13, because the +1 is a free-standing number whose only purpose is to keep the system open, to make us unsure, receptive, but also critically alert towards threats from our surroundings. It is the inclusion of +1 in the formula which stops the psyche collapsing in either psychosis or neurosis. Totality therefore remains by definition impossible. The world remains Nietzschean rather than Hegelian.

The massive impact of the 12+1 formula is best demonstrated through illustration. First we draw an outer circle as a symbol of perfection; the world as a whole must always be regarded as all-encompassing if it is to be understood as the World. This circle is then divided, like the hours on a clock-face, into twelve exactly equal sections. But we leave a smaller circle empty in the middle of the larger circle. This smaller circle symbolises the +1, the transcendental dimension: the part of ourselves that we are unaware of, that we don't understand, the part which makes us change and forces us in new directions, but which also threatens to devour and destroy us, the unknown within us. This vacuum is, in short, our blind spot. The other twelve sections are there, on the other hand, to be filled with identity. During the schizoanalytical process this happens when the analysand is given the task of allocating a specific dividual identity to each of the twelve sections. These identities should be both playful and at the same time faithful to the analysand's reality. A balance of six cherished dreams and six directly experienced dividities is often a productive mix. That holds the analysis to the realms of what is pragmatically credible, and enhances the utopian dimension of identity production.

This 12+1 formula recurs throughout culture. Jesus and the disciples is one good example within western culture. There are twelve disciples, and together they symbolise humankind as a complete unit. But Jesus is not one of them, even if he belongs intimately among them. Without Jesus the disciples would be nothing, and similarly he would be nothing without them. Jesus is simultaneously the disciples' lord (he stands above them) and the servant who washes their feet (he stands below them). He is also the channel through which the disciples are said to be able to communicate with each other (the holy spirit). This is typical for a +1 in relation to the 12. The shortest way between the twelve zones of the divided circle is of course through the smaller circle at the centre of the larger circle: in other words, the +1!

Another striking example is the classic pack of cards. The pack consists of four different categories, but each of the categories has twelve separate members organised in a hierarchy going up from 2, through 10, jack, queen, to king. However, there is a 13th card, the ace. The value of the ace is, interestingly, both lower than 2 and simultaneously higher than the king, depending on the context in which the ace appears and is used. This means that while the hierarchy remains as definitive and eternal between the twelve cards on their own, the potential presence of the ace is always felt as the 13th card, which regularly disrupts the calm in the agreed hierarchy. The existence of the ace reminds the player that the hierarchy within the pack is illusory and arbitrary. There is no objectively true hierarchy. On the back all the cards look exactly the same, which reveals the truth of this supposed hierarchy. The ace is not the 13th card in a hierarchical sequence, but rather the card that stands outside the ordinary hierarchy. The ace is the +1 of the pack!

The reason why so many models that use the 12+1 formula actually work from a memetic Darwinian perspective is of course that this formula mirrors the experience of existence so well. The formula recurs constantly in the models that make it possible for us to orientate ourselves and deal with the world around us. So if we no longer believe in any predetermined objectively true formula for the psyche, but realise instead that the psyche still has to be organised around the Signifier – even if this is merely a metaphysical abstraction without any substance of its own – why not try playing with a formula that constantly recurs, and which has already proved itself useful for games with existence and the conditions for existence, time after time?

This is the greatest achievement of nascent schizoanalysis in relation to declining classical psychoanalysis: schizoanalysis not only understands how signifiers are produced and used, it contributes an excellent tool for accessing and treating a psyche where the production of identity, for one reason or another, no longer works satisfactorily. Schizoanalysis rejects classical psychoanalysis's rigid faith in analysis as a quasi-industrial process with predetermined timings. Instead, the work of creating or revealing dividual identities through the 12+1 model is given the time it requires, depending on the desire and ability of the analysand to play with identity.

The important thing is that the inner +1 circle is kept clinically clean. It must not be burdened with any other identity apart from the abstract, distanced and mysterious name +1. The work of analysis is complete only when the up to twelve identities around the +1 circle have simultaneously attained sufficient pragmatic tenability and utopian attraction for the analysand, so that the old, previously defined individual identity loses its credibility and attraction. Note that the number of identities is in no way obliged to reach exactly twelve. In fact, twelve is actually the maximum number of identities. It is perfectly acceptable to have as many as twelve identities to fill with content during the analytical work.

We have reached a decisive bifurcation, the emergence of the new identity. It is time for the schizoanalyst to apply the psychopuncturing technique: with the help of language, to erode the old identity by attacking its signifier directly and without compromise, in order to facilitate the desired shift to a new and more effective, more truthful and creative signifier. It is this mental change of snakeskin – this move from a shrinking ice-floe to another, expanding ice-floe – which constitutes the functional change of identity. In the new dividuality, identity is tied to the new signifier, the empty +1 circle. +1 is The New Ego, which is never in itself defined, but remains the undefined Signifier in the centre of the creative game where all definable aspects of the dividual identity from now on dance round the +1.

It is worth noting that it is extremely important that psychopuncturing is not embarked upon too early in the analytical process. At best, that would only result in the premature psychopuncturing failing completely, and the analysand not noticing any change at all. But in the worst cases this premature psychopuncturing instigates a psychotic breakdown. If the old signifier is dissolved without a new signifier already in place, the psyche responds by releasing a psychosis. The great risk is that the prematurely instigated psychopuncturing will create an even greater attraction to the old, 'secure' identity and thus force the analytical process back to its starting point, although with an even stronger fixation on the old signifier.

When psychopuncturing is timed correctly, it ought to proceed the way that you teach a child to ride a bicycle. The moment the child angrily turns round to accuse its supportive and instructing parent of breaking the agreement to hold on to the bicycle at all times – by sneakily releasing the bicycle early – and then suddenly discovers, either on his or her own or because the parent points it out, that he or she has actually managed to cycle a considerable distance entirely without help, is when the work is done. The process is completed partly with the child's sudden realisation that, astonishingly, he or she can cycle without help, and partly through the child's mental distancing from the parent: because the parent is no longer the only one of the two who can ride a bicycle, who possesses this attractive and powerful knowledge, who has something to teach, the parent consequently loses his or her superior position in the hierarchy. The parent's role has been stripped of drama. He or she is no longer 'the one who knows', and thus no longer the person to whom the child aims its pathos.

Schizoanalysis concludes in the same way: the analyst separates from the analysand in a state of radical equality, with a shared insight that the project is complete and that the hierarchy that existed between them has now been dismantled. The two people involved no longer have a project that ties them together, and they can and ought to separate, and from now on consider each other passing acquaintances in the never-ending maelstrom of history. For maximum effect they ought to agree not even to acknowledge one another if they happen to meet again. With that coolness, with that control over emotional impulses, constructive enjoyment of life can be achieved and maximised in strict accordance with the Spinozan ethics of schizoanalysis. The meaning of life is never any more profound than this. But, once again: it really is fine, just as it is.

+1.

(A Sort of Afterword)

THE ATTENTIVE READER WOULD be justified in feeling pretty surprised at this point, possibly even suspicious. The fact that this book contains not only twelve regular chapters, but an additional one, and that this is absolutely not the thirteenth chapter, but bears the title it does – +1 – is entirely in order. We have explained the function and point of +1. But in that case, if we were going to be the slightest bit consistent, these final pages ought to be completely white – a blank surface for the projection of the reader's own thoughts now that he or she has made it through all the ideas contained in the book.

Certainly, that would have been an abrupt but consequential conclusion both to the account of the practice of schizoanalysis in the twelfth chapter, and to the book as a whole. But there is also a risk that it would be frustrating. Huh? Wasn't there more to it than that? A bit of wordplay and mucking about with identities instead of profound and eternal truths about life. Are these authors really serious?

Well, yes, we really are serious. This is it, there's nothing more to say. There are, quite simply, no soulful depths to be plumbed, there is no consciousness with its roots in anything other than the interaction between our neurones and their surroundings, and there is no difference at all between our subjective experiences and the physical processes in our brains. Nor is there any free will in the metaphysical sense, as we would like to believe: instead, the actions of the body machine are the result of specific conditions and preceding events acting upon impossibly complex systems. And, above all, there is no difference between what you do and what you are. So go out into the world and play with your identities, while at the same time taking care of your loyalties. The ideas in this book are now part of the existential equation, of course. New information is on the table! Be creative! Think new thoughts!

But consistency is not all that matters in this world. And the truly attentive reader will long since have realised that complete consistency would be complete inconsistency on our part. What unites the books in what we have chosen to call the Futurica trilogy – in which Netocracy is about how technology is changing the very foundations of society, The Global Empire about the political consequences of these changes from a philosophical perspective, and The Body Machines about humanity itself – is the idea of humanity as something fundamentally fallible. We all belong to the species homo pathologicus, which means that we are extremely inconsistent by nature. Our lives are ultimately paradoxical: consciousness itself consists of an endless number of contradictions. And we can be proud of the fact that we are unique in possessing brains that are constantly misleading us and persuading us to believe that we know far more than we actually do.

It is in the nature of human beings to stage and inhabit a never-ending stream of self-deceptions, and it is also entirely natural for us to grow up to be Cartesian dualists. This has been quite functional, and if we are to navigate our way out of the dead-end, we need to really start thinking, in most cases counterintuitively.

Psychologist Paul Bloom has demonstrated that even nine-month-old babies have a solidly dualistic worldview. The actions of young children indicate that they believe objects in their surroundings have an innate essence, or, if you prefer, a soul. This essentialism occurs in all cultures, even if it assumes different expression in later life in the form of different religions. Someone and something is always also, and fundamentally, something else, invisible and intangible, but nonetheless very real.

This idea of essences is, from what we can tell, unique to human beings. Other animals work entirely according to external characteristics: for them there is no reality beyond sensory impressions. And our essentialism/dualism has probably been advantageous for us in the eternal knock-out competition of natural selection; to a large extent we disregard surface and appearance, and instead intuit our way towards intentions, which is beneficial in a world that is both mysterious and threatening in terms of survival and reproduction. It is better to imagine hostile intent ten or a hundred times where it does not exist rather than risk missing the one occasion when it is real. In this sense, it is better to be wrong all the time than to be right most of the time: better to presume guilt than innocence.

This tendency to see intent everywhere leads us to presume the presence of actors where, on closer inspection, there actually aren't any. But this supposed intent presupposes someone who owns it, and who has the potential to execute it. For many people it is the most natural thing in the world that everything in creation presupposes a creator who has an agenda of some sort. Nothing more really needs to be said about the appearance of religion, and it really is as simple as this to find the reason why resistance to the theory of evolution has been so fierce. It is hard work, and seldom advantageous, to think outside the narrow but reassuring frame of intuition.

The whole of this systematic projection of intent and actors onto surroundings to which we only have indirect access is also directed internally, towards our own activity. What actually happens is that the various modules in the subconscious produce a steady stream of instructions which the body machine translates into actions. And in a parallel process the brain produces a mass of thoughts and ideas about these instructions and actions. The need for intent creates ideas about the causal link between thought and action. And the need for an identifiable actor as the instigator of intent gives rise to ideas about the ego, a very useful construction which makes it possible to describe all the actions and pronouncements of the body. We have no choice but to structure and make all the information the brain has to handle comprehensible. If there is no clear explanation, we create one that works. Things get done and said: Who was it doing that? It must have been 'me'.

The problem, of course, is that we can conjure up ideas about everything: that Father Christmas actually exists, and that Sweden will win the next World Cup, for instance. But the fact that we have ideas about something, and that it would be very practical and generally rather lovely if a few of them were real, does not necessarily mean that this is actually the case. It might seem obvious when presented like this, but this is actually a completely bewildering realisation for most people. And this realisation is growing ever stronger thanks to the rapid advances in research into the brain and consciousness, so it will be increasingly difficult to ignore in the future. The days of the ego are numbered. Neural Darwinism is waiting in the wings.

So the almost unavoidable question: is this good or bad news? The attentive reader will be aware that we would do almost anything to avoid answering that sort of question. But it is possible to state that clarity of vision is generally preferable to wishful thinking. The ideas we have about ourselves and our interaction with the world around us is the basis for the whole of our thinking, and provides the frame that we use to determine what is real, what is true, and what it is possible to achieve. Clinging to old humanist ideas about the individual and everything connected to it is hardly an ideal strategy for deeper understanding of, or successful adaptation to, the new social, political and cultural paradigm that is following in the wake of the information technological revolution going on all around us.

Nor does the triumphant entry of the body machine necessarily mean that our world will become colder and harsher: quite the contrary. The solace and comfortable relief from responsibility that was once offered by the traditional religions, because they allowed human beings to hand over their fates to a higher power, can now be provided by science and analytical thinking. There is no longer any reason for the illusory ego to worry about difficult decisions: the responsibility can usefully be delegated directly to the mental modules of the subconscious.

Decisions will always be made, that much is certain. Our genes, our desires, our upbringing, and the situations we find ourselves in will make them for us. We can't stop this, no matter how much we might like to, and acceptance of this fact will mean that a great weight is lifted from us. Of course, we will still have to continually monitor decisions that have been made, and add this new information to future decision-making processes, but this too will largely take place below the horizon of consciousness.

By ceasing to waste our conscious attention on all the decisions that have already been made, we are freeing considerable amounts of energy for life-giving, enjoyable games. But even this decision – whether or not to make the most of this suggested redistribution of resources – has already been made, or will be made subliminally. We have said what we have to say.

Futurica Glossary

CONCEPTS COMMON IN THE PHILOSOPHICAL WORKS OF ALEXANDER BARD & JAN SÖDERQVIST

☐

☐

☐ABSOLUTE MOBILISM: A natural romantic utopianism, a dream of pure thought superior to all culturally conditioned categories, free-flow philosophy. Unfortunately impossible to practice and communicate, because the medium, language, requires an eternalisation of thought.

ATTENTIONALISM: The value system which is gradually replacing economism as the informationalist paradigm is becoming established. Attention is determined by the interplay between the awareness and the credibility a person or network succeeds in creating.

BIFURCATION: In geometry, the point where a line divides or branches into two lines. Launched in philosophy by Gilles Deleuze, since when it has been used in the wider context for conditions in which cohesive eternalisations burst, are mobilised and have to be eternalised once more in order to be made comprehensible.

CAPITALISM: The social paradigm which was introduced with the printing press and made its broad breakthrough thanks to effective one-way communication with a mass audience created by these new media. The concept is therefore much more than what is sometimes referred to as capitalism in everyday speech, in other words: the market economy, economism, et cetera.

CONSUMTARIAT: The underclass of information society, a proletariat of consumption which lacks the power and initiative to produce its own social identity, and which is therefore condemned passively to consume a pre-produced identity.

DEMONOLOGY: Society's production of enemies and threats in order to reinforce internal cohesion and define the collective identity.

DIVIDUAL: A human being perceived as divisible rather than indivisible (the individual). The dividual nurtures a multiplicity of identities, regarding none of these as more 'real' or 'original' than any other, and allows the different sides to dominate according to context, whereas the individual strives for an integrated personality.

ÉTATISM: The supreme political ideology of the capitalist paradigm, of which conservatism, liberalism and socialism are closely-related varieties. The whole of political thought stems from the idea of the nation state as the principle social institution and self-evident centre of power.

ETERNALISATION: A freezing of a chosen piece of absolute movement in the chaos of the world, necessary to make life comprehensible.

ETERNALISM: The philosophy which through eternalisations and meta-eternalisations produces stability in full awareness of the fallacy of stability, and in close interaction with the entirely different but nonetheless unavoidable mobilism.

ETHICS: Original meaning 'habits' in Greek. Since Baruch Spinoza's definition in the 1600s, used philosophically as synonymous with presumed subjective values based on a monistic and secularised worldview. Operative from the oppositional pair constructivity v. destructivity.

THE EVENT: The glittering goal of the networking collective. The Event arises when productivity in the network reaches maximal levels and lasts as long as this state can be maintained. It replaces the capitalist era's idea of Progress as the subject's desired reward for hard work.

EVENTOLOGY: The theory of the conditions and social functions of the Event.

FEUDALISM: The social paradigm linked to the information-technological revolution of written language c.3,000 BC, and which stretched until the next revolution, that of the printing press. Feudalism includes the feudal society of the European Middle Ages, but is also a wider concept.

FICTIVES: The instruments that thinking itself produces in the dialectic between eternalism and mobilism, when the first set of eternalisations are mobilised and thereby set in motion, meaning that they have to be eternalised again.

THE GLOBAL EMPIRE: The idea of a global order – political, cultural and economic. A vision which appears in many different forms and with many different focuses in the history of philosophy, all of them supporting the view that the global platform for the exercising of power is unequivocally superior to regional interests.

GLOBALISATION: A genuine globalisation comprises infinitely more than merely free trade: a truly global, cultural and political arena for common problem-solving and mutual enrichment in all possible areas.

GLOBALISM: The political ideology which follows eternalism, and the activist movement towards a global order. Identity: Humankind's primary social needs, more or less satisfied by the collective subject's production of identity.

INFORMATIONALISM: The social paradigm which is replacing capitalism in conjunction with the information-technological revolution of interactive media. Synonyms: Information society and Network society.

INTERACTIVITY: Two-way communication, media technologies for mutual information exchange where the roles of producer and consumer are constantly being swapped.

MATHEMES: Philosophical diagrams used to illustrate relationships between phenomena, for instance the relationship between credibility and awareness in the production of attention. Frequently used within Lacanian psychoanalysis to illustrate how consciousness regards itself in order to function.

MEMETICS: The theory of memes and their fight to survive and reproduce. Memes are the cultural equivalent of genes.

THE METAPHYSICS OF PARADOXISM: The idea of the never-ending dialectic between eternalism and mobilism as the single but entirely sufficient metaphysical basis for both thought and life itself.

MOBILISATION: The return of single eternalisations to a state of movement and new, meaning-creating relations to one another.

MOBILISM: The philosophy which sees through the fiction of eternalisation (and totalism's ambitions of totality), and returns thought from artificial order to the productive chaos of the next level, all the time in close interaction with the entirely different but nonetheless unavoidable eternalism.

MORALS: Original meaning 'habits' in Latin. Since Baruch Spinoza's definition in the 1600s, used philosophically as synonymous with presumed objective values based on a dualistic and theological worldview. Operative from the oppositional pair good v. evil.

NIHILISM: The understanding that life lacks both divine and natural meaning, as a result of which the search for meaning has always been and will always be a production of meaning. Eternalism differentiates between naive, cynical and affirmative nihilism.

THE NET: The metaphysical aspect of networking as an idea, and therefore something much broader and more abstract than any specific network or any specific technology.

NETOCRACY: The dominant class of informationalism, in other words: the elite which attains power and status through its unique capacity to create attentional value, and which produces and controls its own social identity, primarily through intensive networking.

NETWORK DYNAMICS: The branch of socioanalysis which studies how relations, hierarchies, transparencies, topographies, non-zero-sum games, zero-sum games and minus-sum games arise and function within different networks.

NON-ZERO-SUM GAME: A concept taken from game theory. A non-zero-sum game is characterised by mutual benefit from the production of increased value: every player has good reason to hope for advantage. The result is greater than the sum of the parts. In a zero-sum game, you can only win what someone else loses. The result is exactly the same as the sum of the parts. In a minus-sum game, the productivity is negative, the result is less than the sum of the parts, as a result of which all players risk net losses.

PARADOXISM: The dialectic aspect of eternalism.
The Paradox of Metaphysics: The never-ending and apparently insoluble conflict between eternalism (stability philosophy) and mobilism (movement philosophy). While the former stems from being, the latter is based upon becoming. The solution to this conflict suggested by Bard & Söderqvist proposes a metaphysics of paradoxism, in which the relationship between eternalism and mobilism forms a circular but simultaneously open dialectic which itself constitutes the metaphysical foundation.

PLURARCHY: A political state where majority decisions have lost all weight, as a result of which all subordination is based upon some form of voluntary submission.

REPLICATORS: Molecules or cultural concepts (genes or memes) with the capacity to produce exact copies of themselves. Occasionally these copies are not exact, which gives rise to mutations, which in turn facilitate evolution and natural selection.

SCHIZOANALYSIS: Psychoanalysis modified for the needs of the dividual, intended to liberate a large but still manageable multiplicity of personalities, and to counteract every tendency towards restrictive uniformity.

SOCIAL TECHNOLOGIES: Principles for social interaction, consciously or unconsciously applied as instruments with which to steer the collective in a certain direction.

SOCIOANALYSIS: Schizoanalysis transferred to the level of the collective subject. Informational society's politics are applied socioanalysis, as a result of which the voters of the capitalist era will be replaced by socioanalysis, whose relationship to politicians/analysts will be characterised by interactivity and the plurarchic form of voluntary subordination.

SOCIOMETRY: The endlessly complex measuring and comparison of social status on attentional terms. Constructed upon sociograms, diagrams of who knows and interacts with whom and in which ways in informational society.

TOTALISM: The tradition of thought which has dominated western philosophy since Plato's day, and which aims to develop a form of thought which encompasses all of existence as it actually is, which, from a mobilistic perspective, is absurd, given that the world of existence is by definition different to the conceptual world.

TRANSRATIONALISM: A modified and pragmatic rationalism which accepts and stems from the in-built limitations of rational thought. Transrationalism is interested in what is functional rather than in objective truths and possible correspondences between thought and existence.

VIRTUAL NOMADIC TRIBES: Netocratic collectives in the wider sense. They are virtual because they are primarily organised via interactive media technologies, nomadic because mobility is a virtue and geographical location uninteresting, and tribes because they tend to form according to primitivism's tribal structures.

THE WORLD STATE: The Global Empire translated into judicial and political practice, meaning global jurisdiction and a global monopoly of violence, which in turn means the final death-throes of the sovereignty of the nation state.